HULLO
MY NAME
iS ZiGGY

...WeLCOMe
TO MY WORLD !!

ENCORE! ENCORE!!

ENCORE! ENCORE!!

By Tom Wilson

Foreword by Cathy Guisewite

Andrews and McMeel, Inc.

A Universal Press Syndicate Company
Kansas City

For information write Andrews and McMeel, Inc., a Universal Press Syndicate Company, 6700 Squibb Road, Mission, Kansas 66202.

ISBN: 0-8362-1150-2 cloth
0-8362-1151-0 paperback
Library of Congress Catalog Number: 79-88692

for YOU
my ZIGGY FRIEND!

Foreword by Cathy Guisewite

My professional respect for Tom Wilson began in
1971 when he rejected 12 greeting card ideas my mother
forced me to send to him at American Greetings.

As if charged by failure, this event launched a 5-year
crusade by my parents to get Tom Wilson interested in
publishing something I wrote. **Anything** I wrote.

When my mother happened to be browsing through
my locked underwear drawer at college and came across
an extremely personal love letter to my current sweetheart,
she clutched it over her head and exclaimed, "Tom Wilson
could make this into a wall poster for millions of young
couples to enjoy!"

When I wrote a letter home explaining how my hair
had caught on fire during a sorority pledge ceremony, my
father rushed to his office and made copies . . . one for the
grandparents, and "One for Tom Wilson!"

When I wrote and illustrated a little book for my
mother for Mother's Day one year, you could practically see
the tears well up in my parents' eyes: "Tom Wilson," they
cried, "Wait till Tom Wilson sees this!"

When someone in my family finally realized that the
Tom Wilson they'd become pen pals with at American
Greetings was the same Tom Wilson responsible for
"Ziggy" in the comic pages, the household practically went
berserk.

"I knew that Tom Wilson was a good man," my father
beamed. My mother volunteered to adopt him.

I hid in the closet and wadded my Econ. 101 term paper into a sock, for fear they'd try to submit it to Tom Wilson as a comic strip idea. It was getting embarrassing.

With this in mind, it should come as no big surprise that when I eventually signed a contract to do "Cathy," it was with Universal Press Syndicate, the same company that represents Tom Wilson and Ziggy.

Completely oblivious to the grueling, competitive nature of the syndication business, and that it had been a monumental feat to get someone to even consider my work, my mother could only sigh when she heard the news, "See? I knew they would be nice people if they liked Mr. Wilson."

Tom Wilson is just the kind of guy who gives people hope. In spite of how annoying it became to hear his name mentioned every 45 seconds for 5 years, I love him for that.

It isn't everyone who can be successful at two careers at once, raise a sweet, loving family, inspire young writers and artists on to great things, and still be able to see the world as a giant window shade that keeps falling down and crushing his foot.

Tom Wilson gives people hope. He sends Ziggy to a guru to ask the meaning of life, and Ziggy gets sold a vacuum cleaner . . . Ziggy wears a new "Patriotic Raincoat," and somebody mails a letter in his mouth . . . Ziggy gets screamed at by the Friendly Finance Company . . . the "Open 24-hours-a-day, 7-days-a-week, 52-weeks-a-year" gas station is closed when Ziggy gets there . . . his plants talk back . . . the sun sticks out its tongue at him in the morning.

Ziggy does everything everyone else does, but when he does it, it doesn't work. Our hearts have to go out to him because he keeps coming back for more.

One reason I feel so close to Ziggy is because my life and much of my work have been based on the same kind of sick, naive optimism that forces us to believe that no matter how many times we've failed in the past, somehow, tomorrow, it's all going to be different.

Like "Cathy," Ziggy never loses faith and love, no matter how many times life hands him a salt shaker with no top on it.

He wishes on stars. He lets the turkeys go free on Thanksgiving. He takes his plants to the movies. And he keeps feeding his lunch to the birds, even though they go to the bathroom on his head.

Obviously, I have reasons to be grateful to Tom Wilson that many people don't. Without the encouragement he offered my parents, their obsession to have me be published in some form would never have reached the levels it did. I doubt that I would ever have become a cartoonist, or even considered that I could, if Tom Wilson hadn't done it first.

Now, on those days when I'm crumpled on my desk, with no ideas, no inspiration, no sense of humor, and 2,000 M&M's in my stomach, asking myself "Why, why, why??!", and cursing the day Tom Wilson wrote that first sweet note to Mom and Dad . . . even now, Tom Wilson is there for me.

I need only to open the newspaper or one of his books and see, like millions of others, that no matter how bad I feel, Ziggy feels worse. No matter how strongly I believe I should change my name and move to Ohio, Ziggy will have more reason to give up, and yet he won't.

Tom and Ziggy give us hope.

For this, all mothers and fathers everywhere, and all sons and daughters, should hug this loving, trusting, insecure, bumbling man, and give him a great big kiss right on his fat little nose.

All things considered, we ought to give Ziggy a kiss, too.

Cathy Guisewite

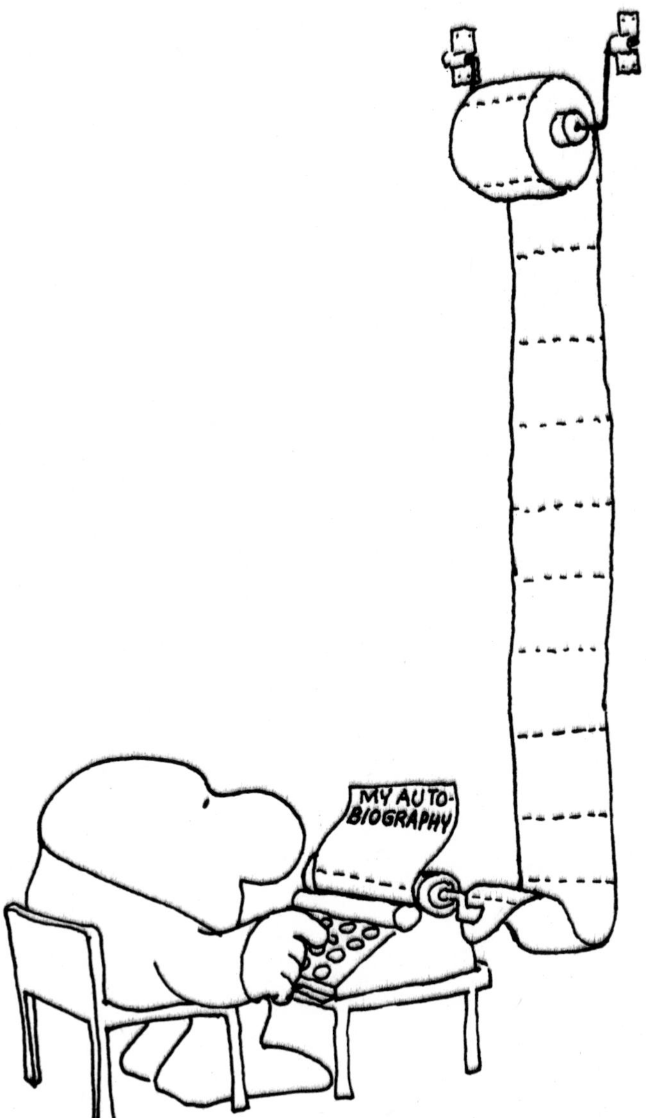
MY AUTO-
BIOGRAPHY

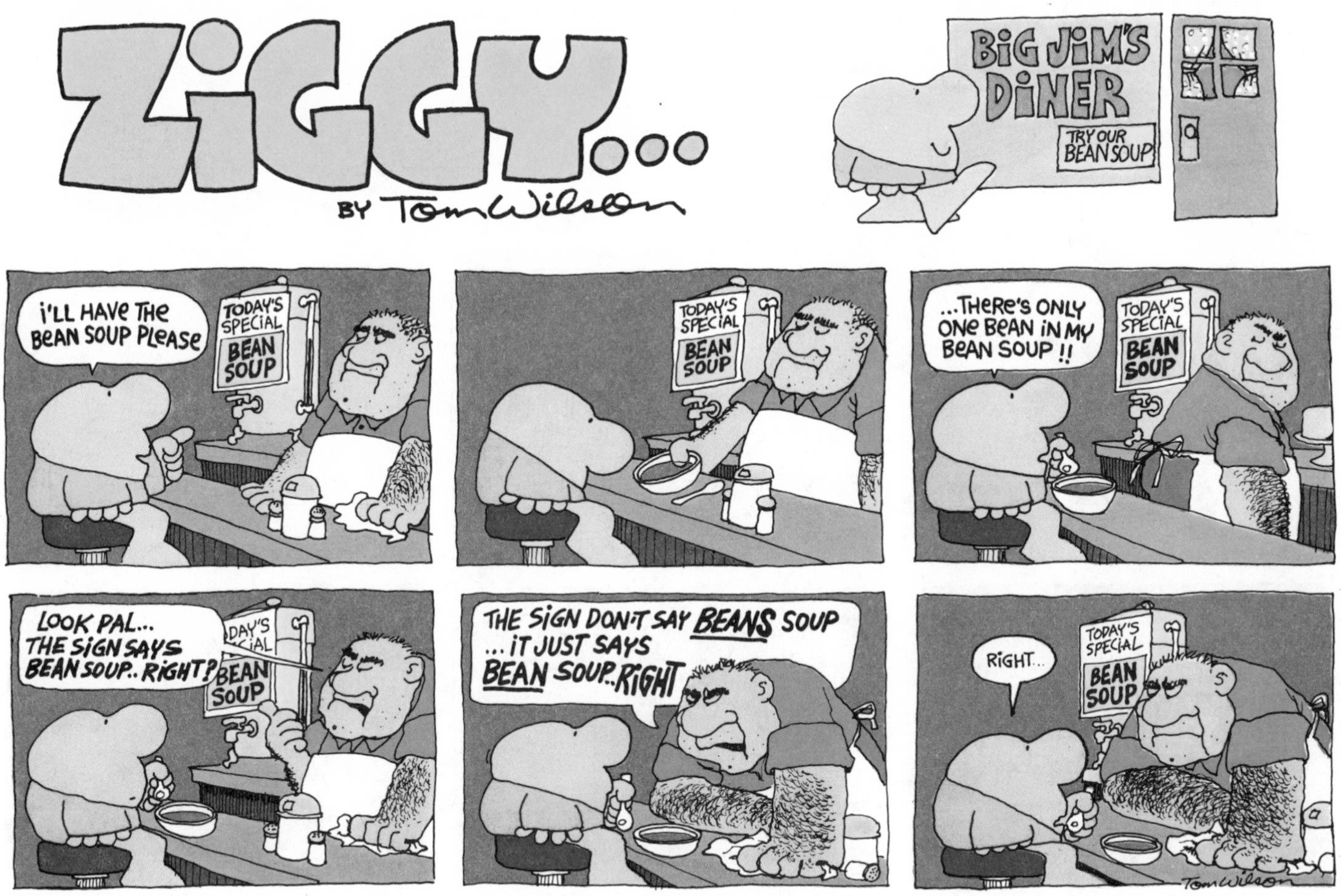
ZIGGY...
BY Tom Wilson
BIG JIM'S DINER
TRY OUR BEAN SOUP
I'LL HAVE THE BEAN SOUP PLEASE
TODAY'S SPECIAL BEAN SOUP
...THERE'S ONLY ONE BEAN IN MY BEAN SOUP !!
LOOK PAL... THE SIGN SAYS BEAN SOUP.. RIGHT?
THE SIGN DON'T SAY BEANS SOUP ... IT JUST SAYS BEAN SOUP.. RIGHT
RIGHT...
Tom Wilson

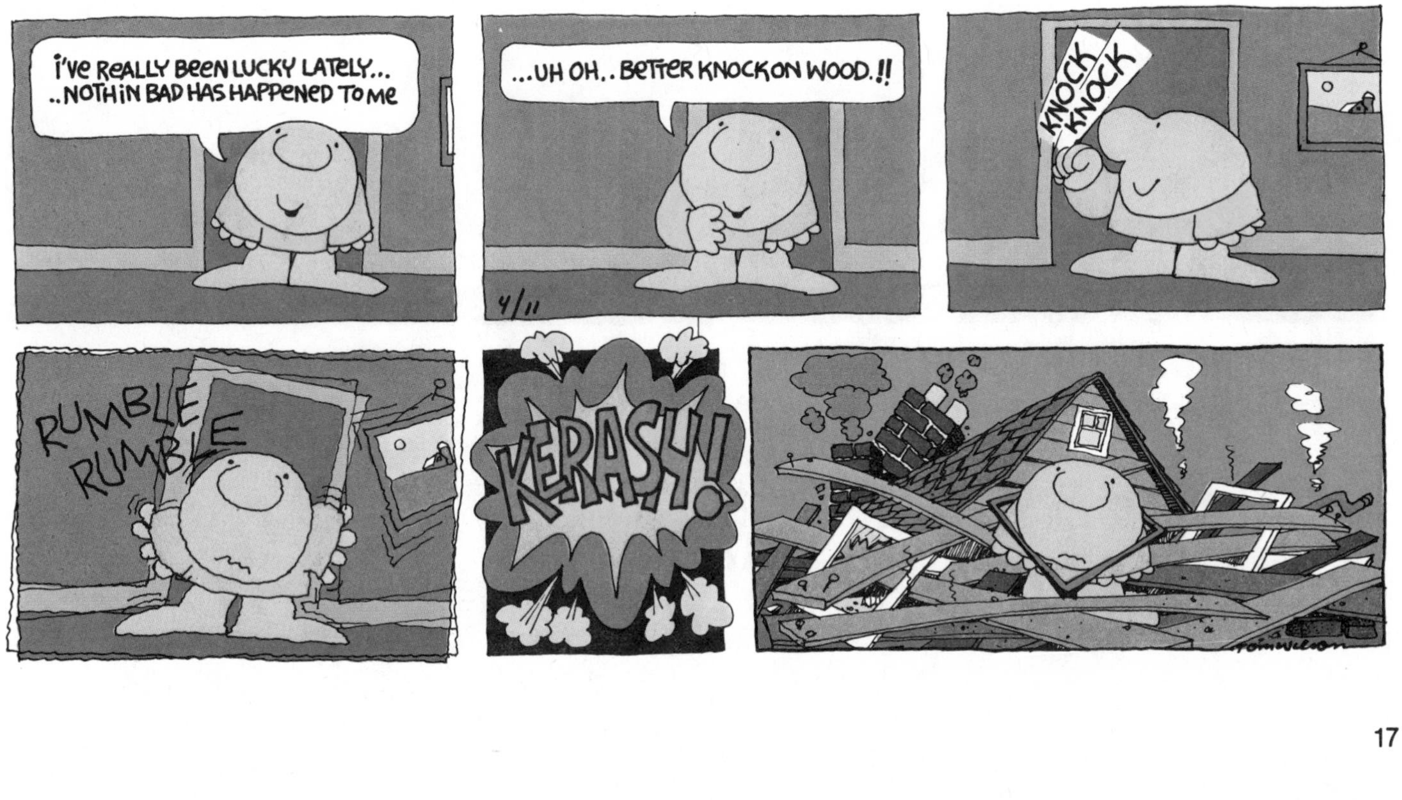
I'VE REALLY BEEN LUCKY LATELY... ..NOTHIN BAD HAS HAPPENED TO ME
...UH OH.. BETTER KNOCK ON WOOD.!!
4/11
KNOCK KNOCK
RUMBLE RUMBLE
KERASH!
Tom Wilson

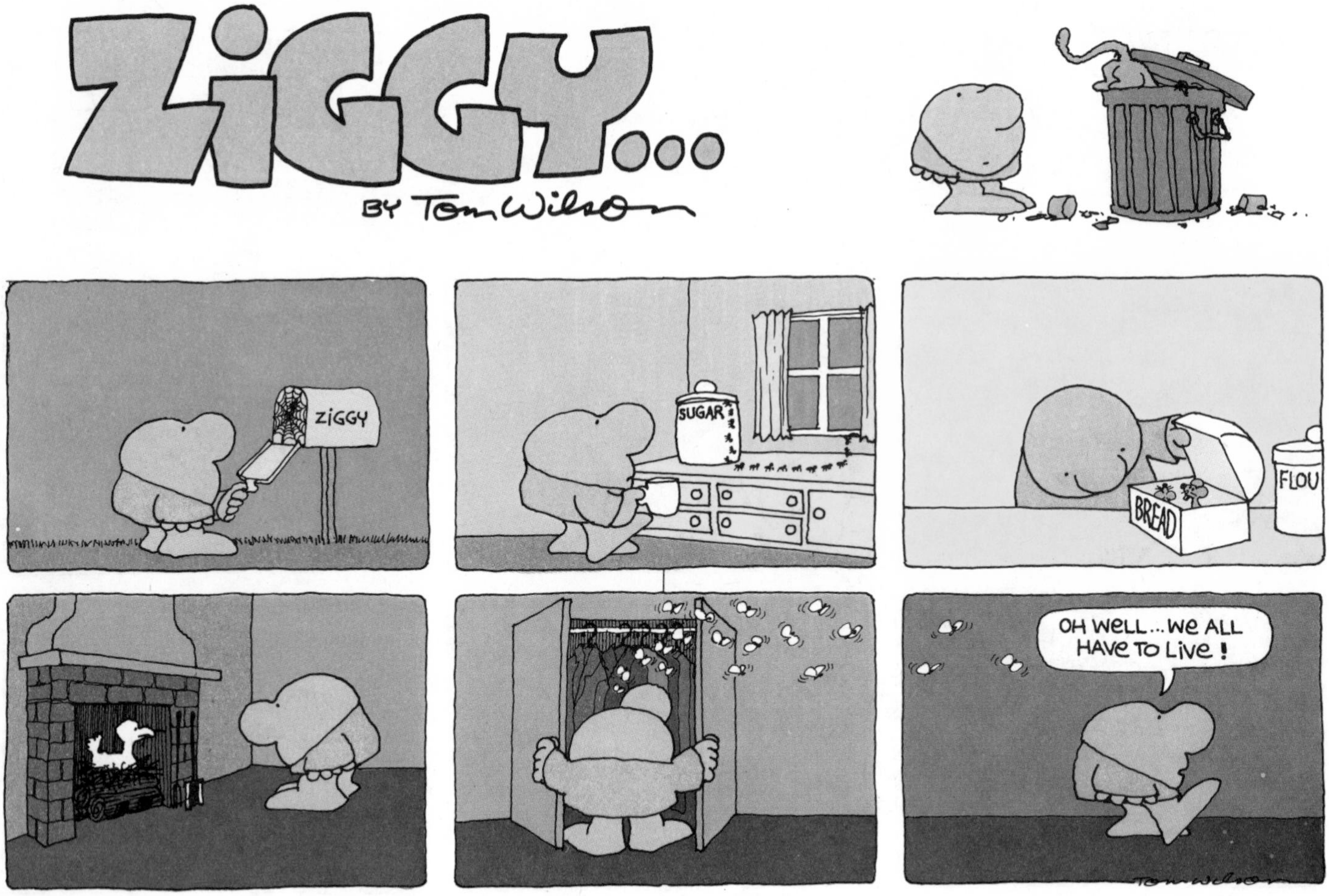
ZiGGY...
BY Tom Wilson
ZiGGY
SUGAR
BREAD
FLOU
OH WELL...WE ALL HAVE TO LiVE !

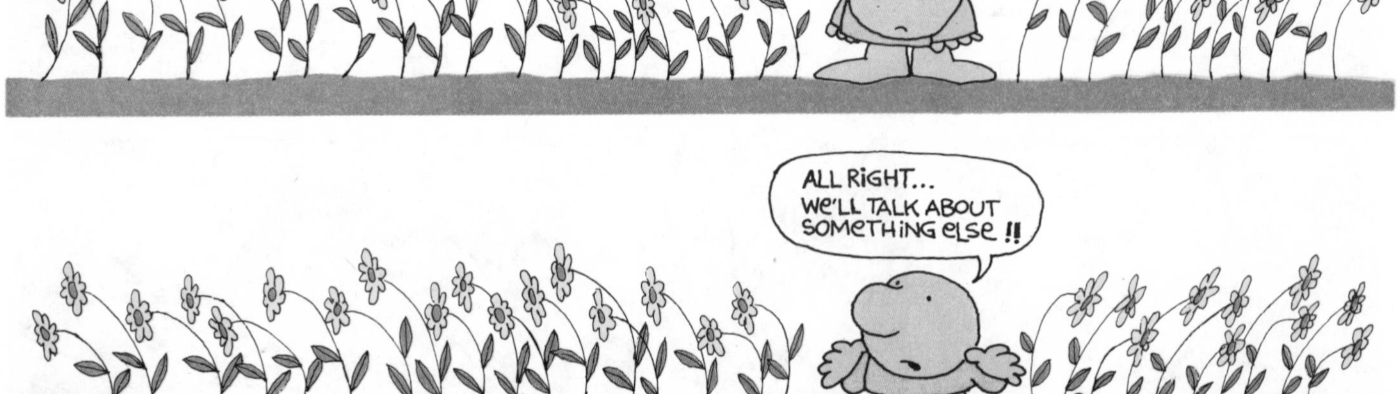
ALL RiGHT... WE'LL TALK ABOUT SOMETHiNG ELSE !!

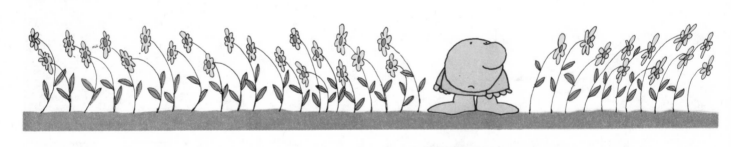

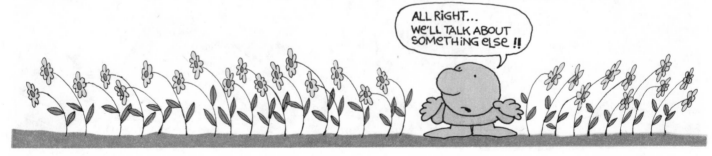

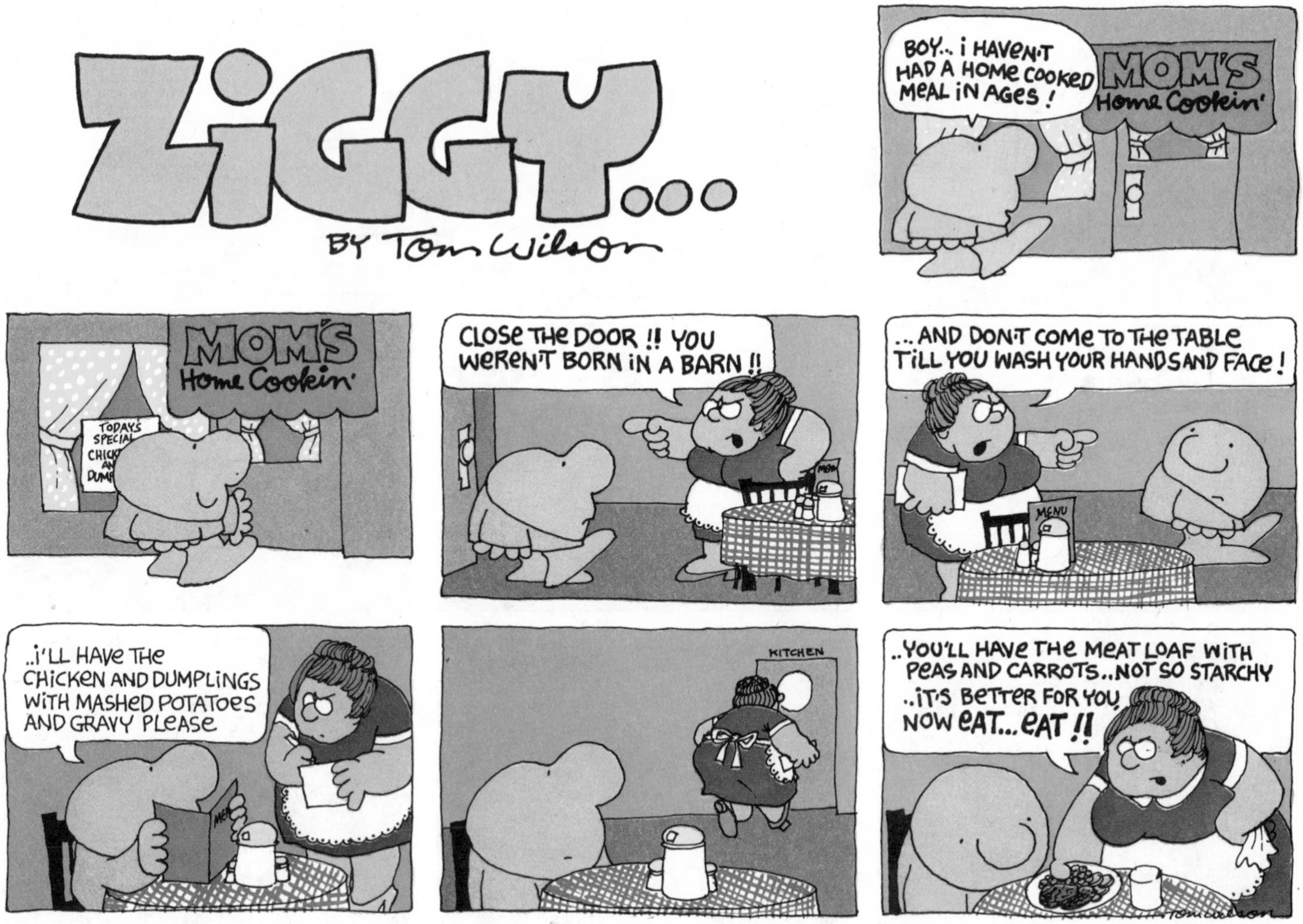
ZIGGY...
BY Tom Wilson
BOY.. i HAVEN'T HAD A HOME COOKED MEAL iN AGES !
MOM'S Home Cookin'
MOM'S Home Cookin'
TODAY'S SPECIAL
CLOSE THE DOOR !! YOU WEREN'T BORN iN A BARN !!
... AND DON'T COME TO THE TABLE TiLL YOU WASH YOUR HANDS AND FACE !
MENU
..i'LL HAVE THE CHiCKEN AND DUMPLiNGS WiTH MASHED POTATOES AND GRAVY PLEASE
KITCHEN
..YOU'LL HAVE THE MEAT LOAF WiTH PEAS AND CARROTS..NOT SO STARCHY ..iT'S BETTER FOR YOU NOW EAT... EAT !!
TOM WILSON

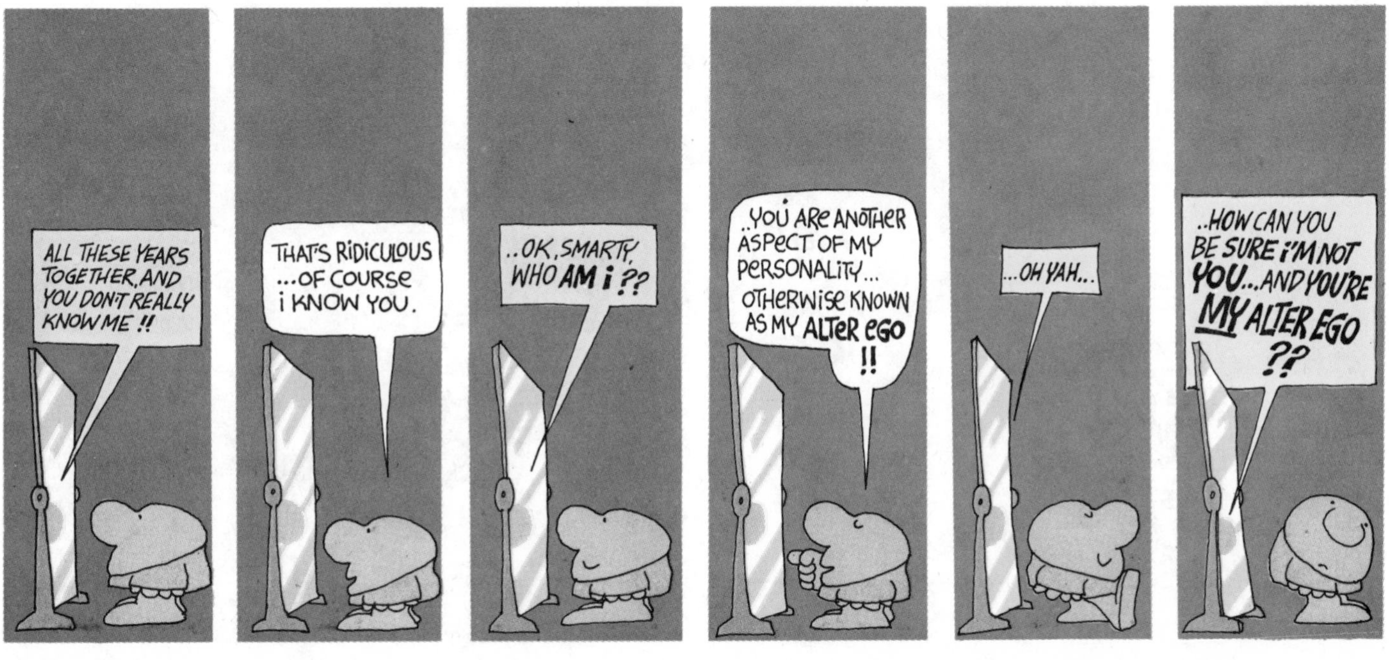
ALL THESE YEARS TOGETHER, AND YOU DON'T REALLY KNOW ME !!
THAT'S RiDiCULOUS ...OF COURSE i KNOW YOU.
..OK, SMARTY, WHO AM i ??
..YOU ARE ANOTHER ASPECT OF MY PERSONALiTY... OTHERWiSE KNOWN AS MY ALTER EGO !!
...OH YAH...
..HOW CAN YOU BE SURE i'M NOT YOU...AND YOU'RE MY ALTER EGO ??

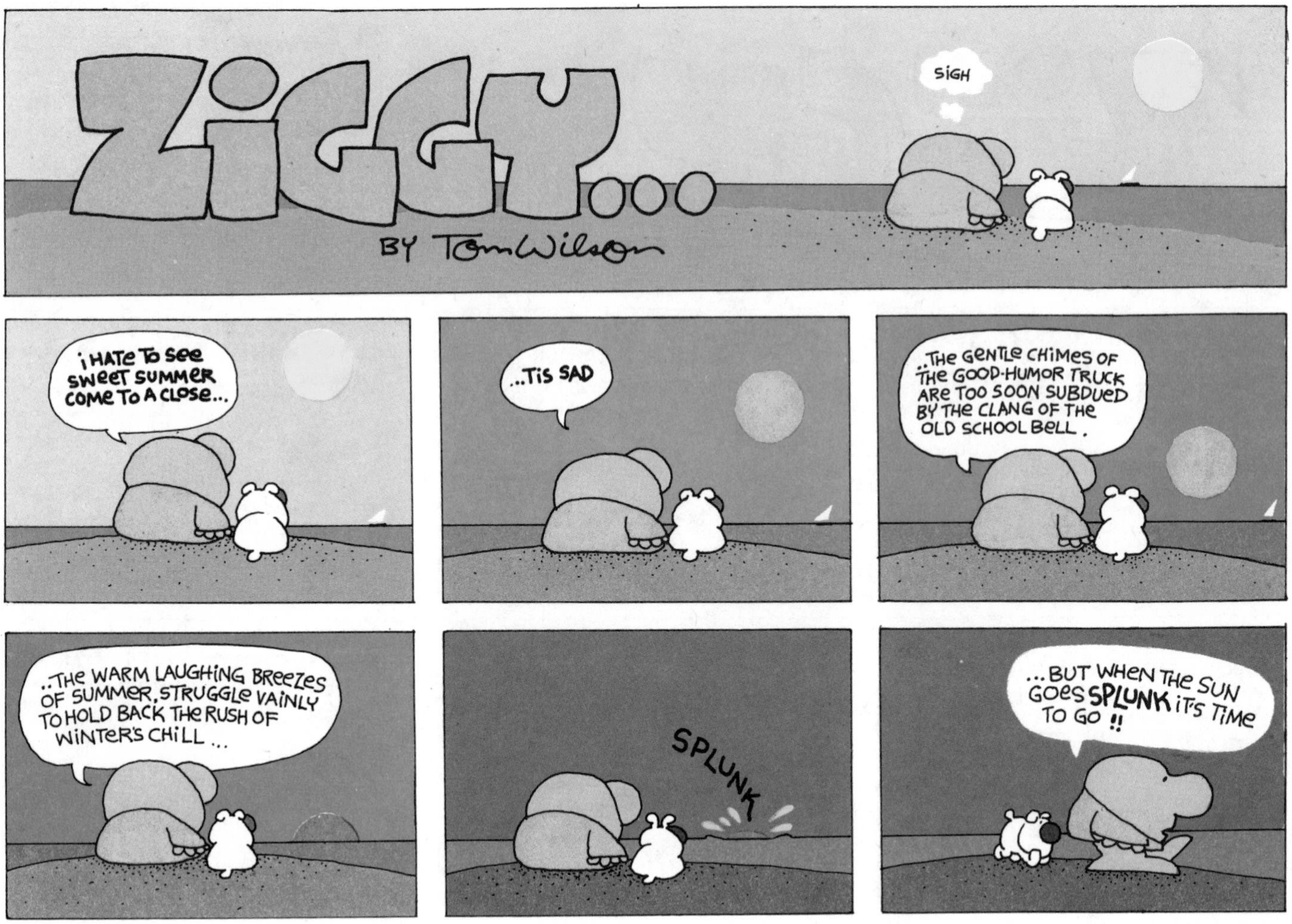
ZIGGY...
BY Tom Wilson
SIGH
i HATE To SEE SWEET SUMMER COME TO A CLOSE...
...TIS SAD
..THE GENTLE CHIMES OF THE GOOD-HUMOR TRUCK ARE TOO SOON SUBDUED BY THE CLANG OF THE OLD SCHOOL BELL.
..THE WARM LAUGHING BREEZES OF SUMMER, STRUGGLE VAINLY TO HOLD BACK THE RUSH OF WINTER'S CHILL...
SPLUNK
...BUT WHEN THE SUN GOES SPLUNK IT'S TIME TO GO !!

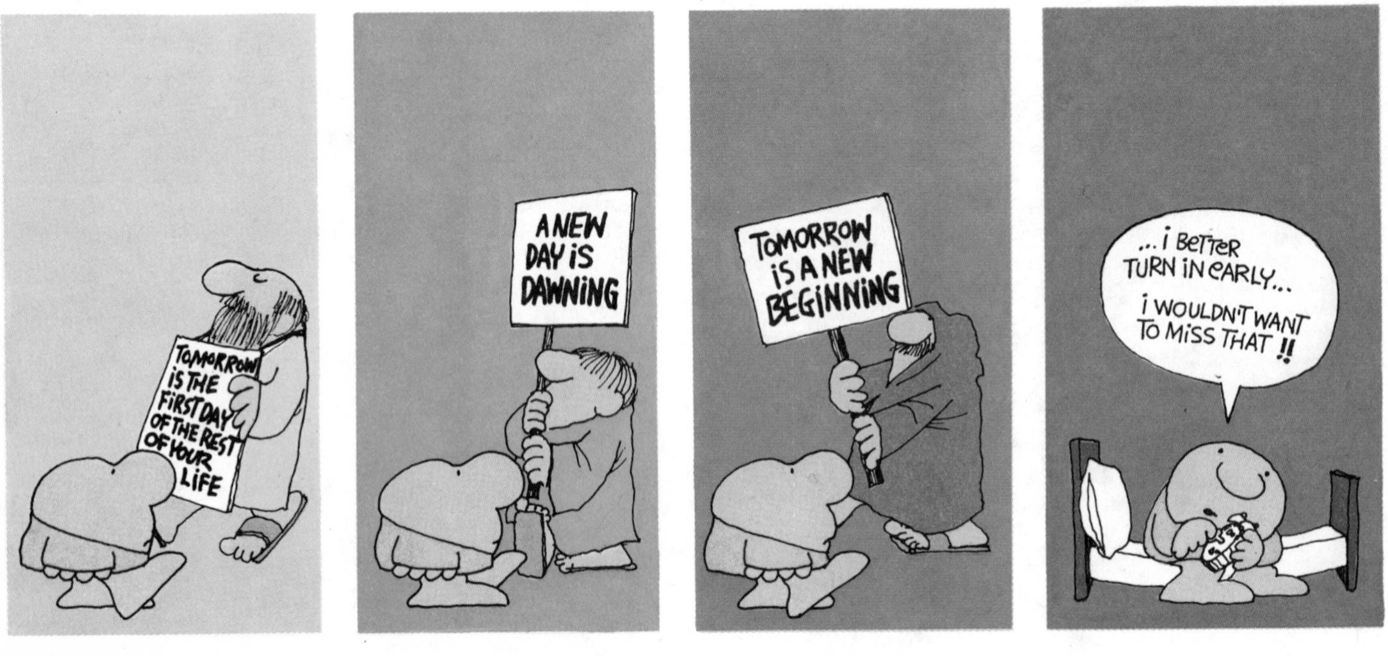
TOMORROW IS THE FIRST DAY OF THE REST OF YOUR LIFE
A NEW DAY IS DAWNING
TOMORROW IS A NEW BEGINNING
...i BETTER TURN iN EARLY... i WOULDN'T WANT TO MISS THAT !!

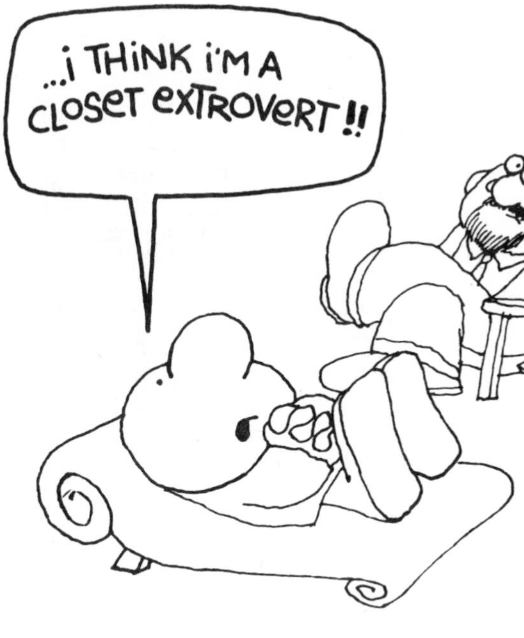
...i THINK i'M A CLOSET EXTROVERT !!

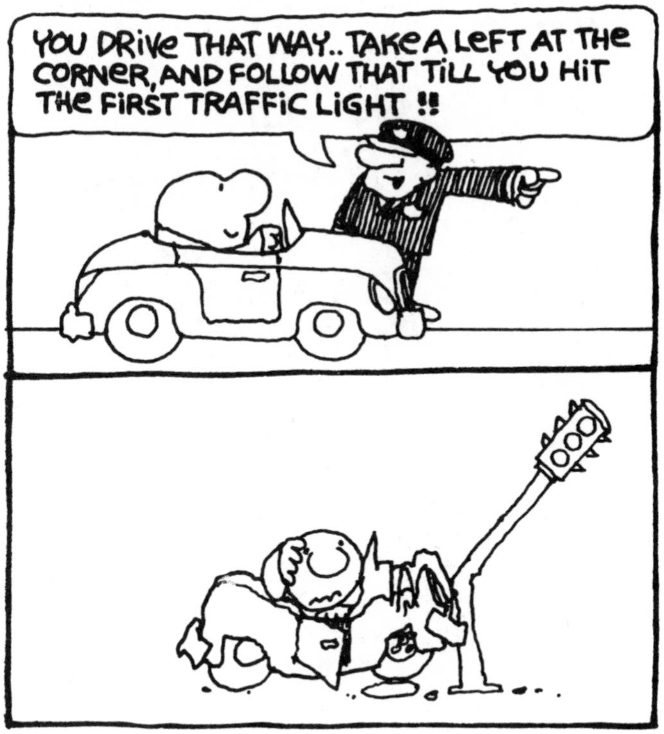
YOU DRIVE THAT WAY.. TAKE A LEFT AT THE CORNER, AND FOLLOW THAT TILL YOU HIT THE FIRST TRAFFIC LIGHT !!

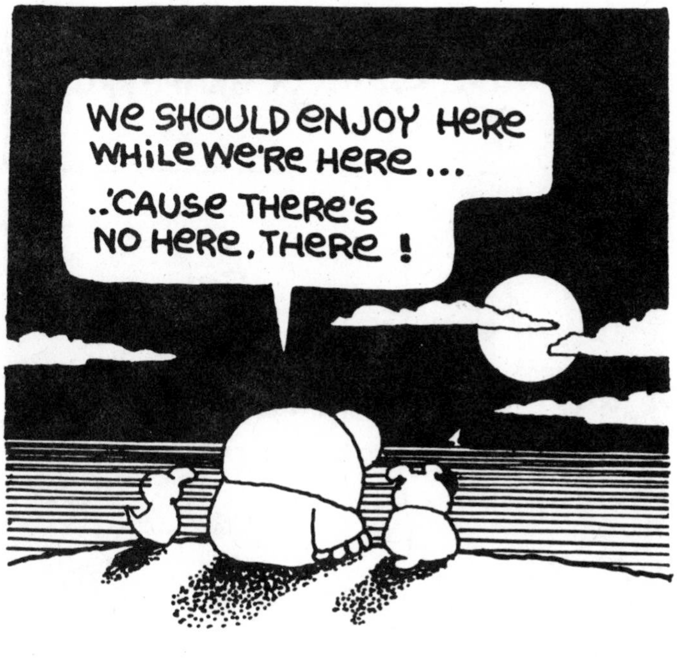
WE SHOULD ENJOY HERE WHILE WE'RE HERE ... ..'CAUSE THERE'S NO HERE, THERE !

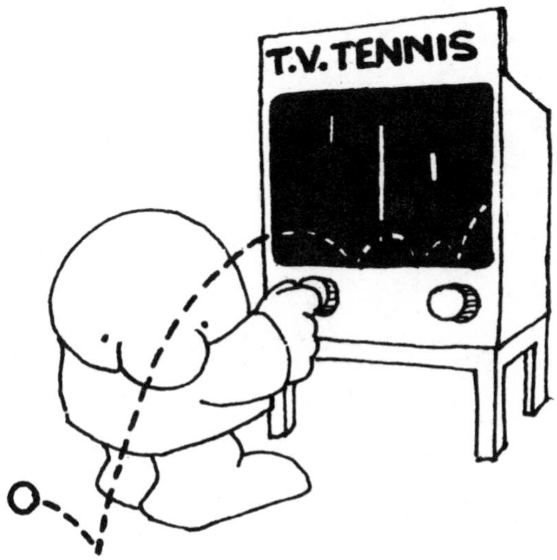
T.V. TENNIS

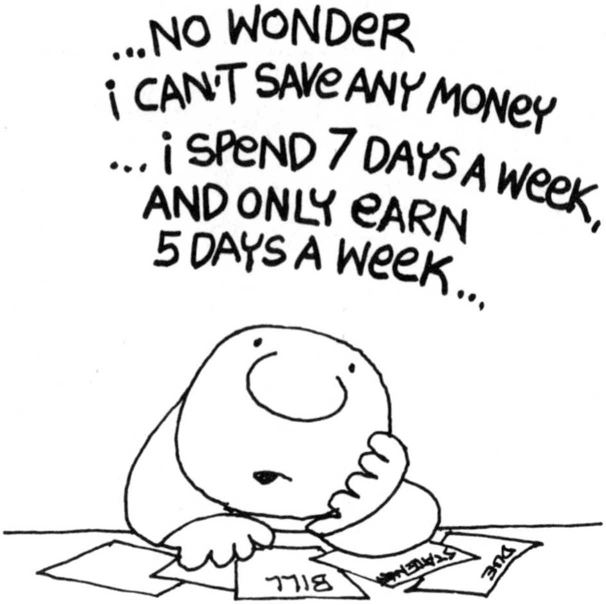
...NO WONDER
i CAN'T SAVE ANY MONEY
... i SPEND 7 DAYS A WEEK,
AND ONLY EARN
5 DAYS A WEEK...
BILL
STATEMENT
DUE

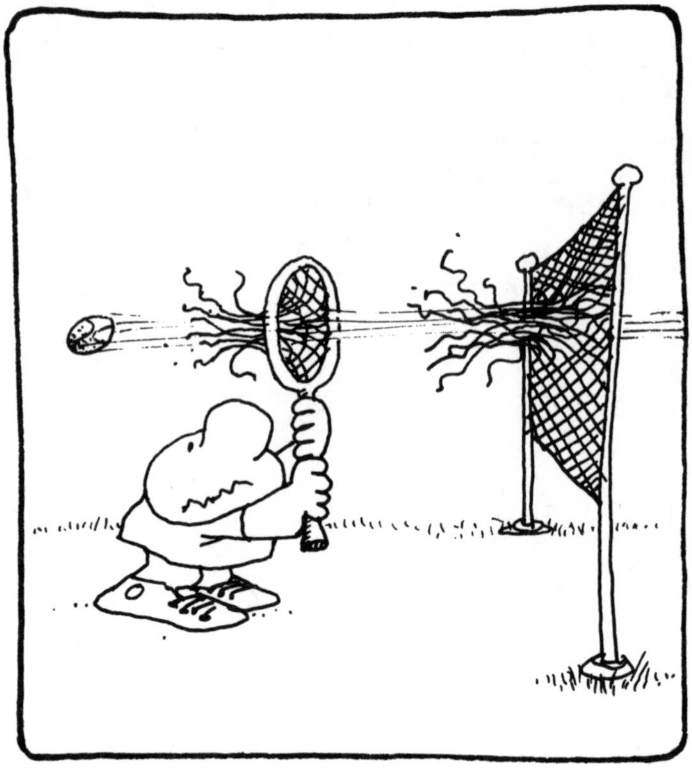

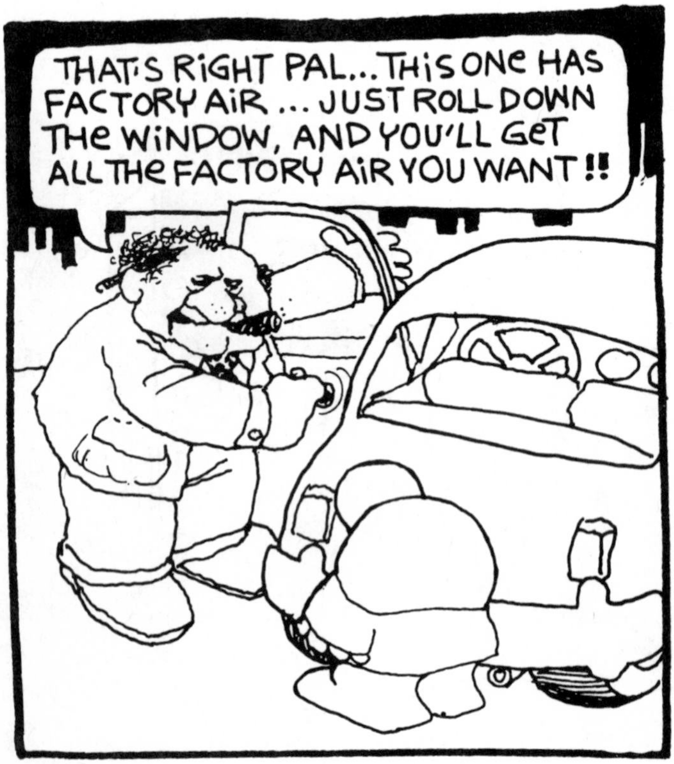
THAT'S RIGHT PAL... THIS ONE HAS FACTORY AIR ... JUST ROLL DOWN THE WINDOW, AND YOU'LL GET ALL THE FACTORY AIR YOU WANT !!

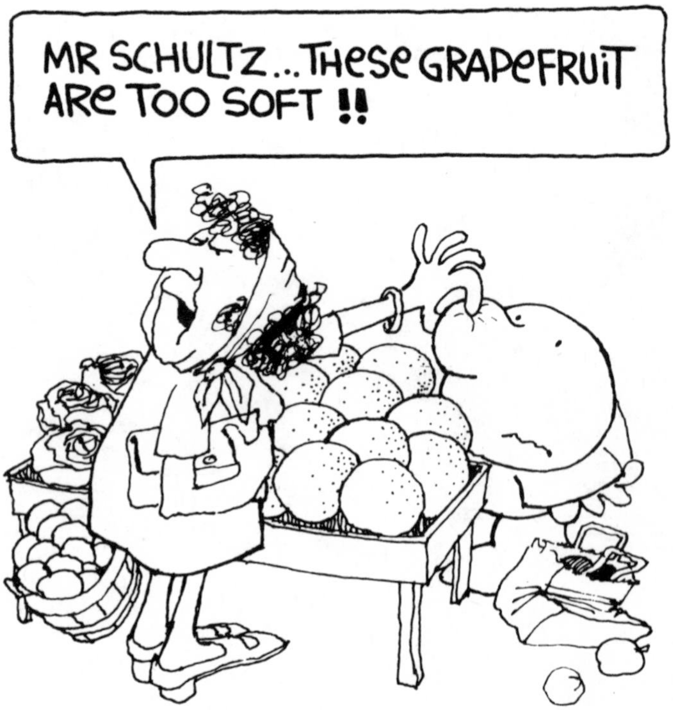
MR SCHULTZ... THESE GRAPEFRUIT ARE TOO SOFT !!

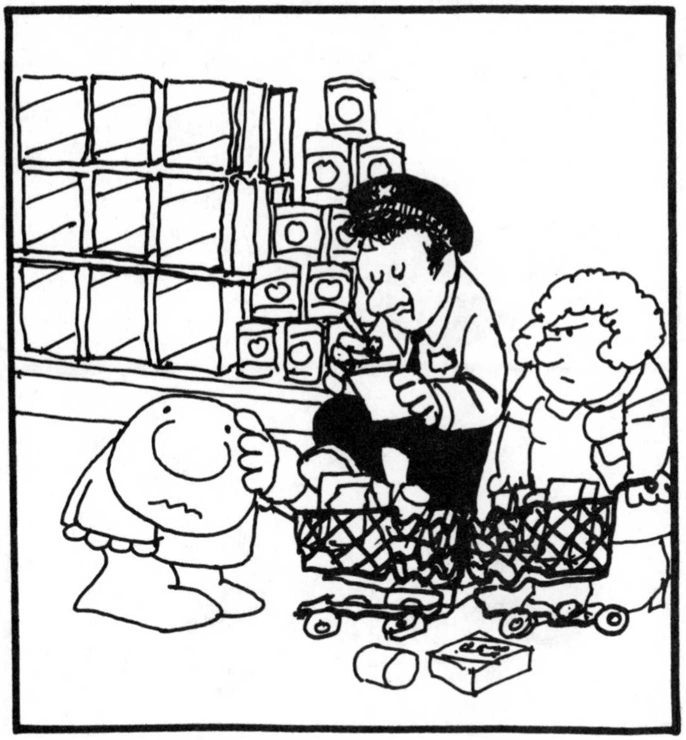

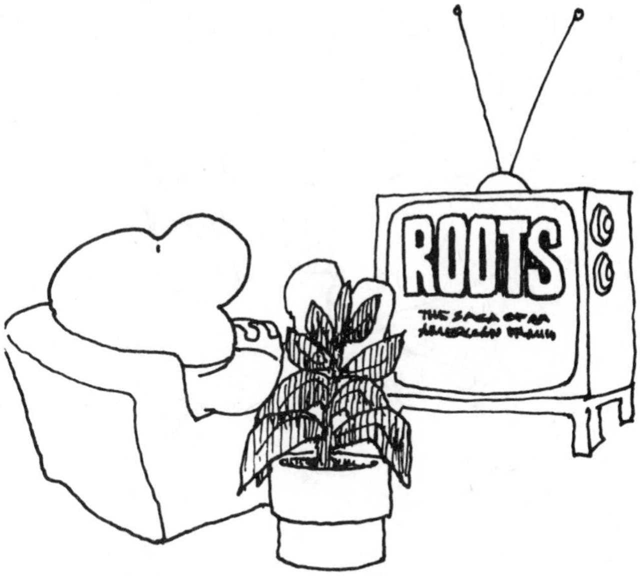
ROOTS

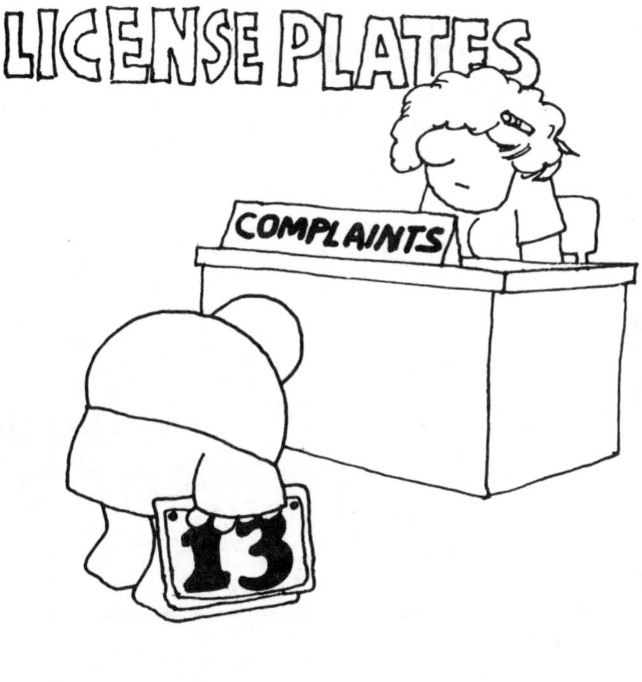
LICENSE PLATES
COMPLAINTS
13

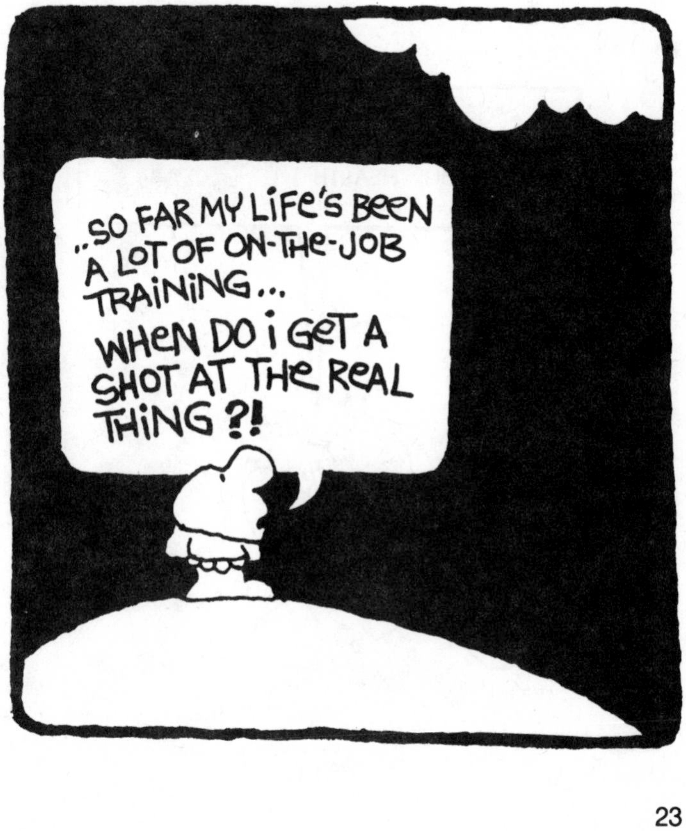
..SO FAR MY LIFE'S BEEN A LOT OF ON-THE-JOB TRAINING... WHEN DO I GET A SHOT AT THE REAL THING ?!

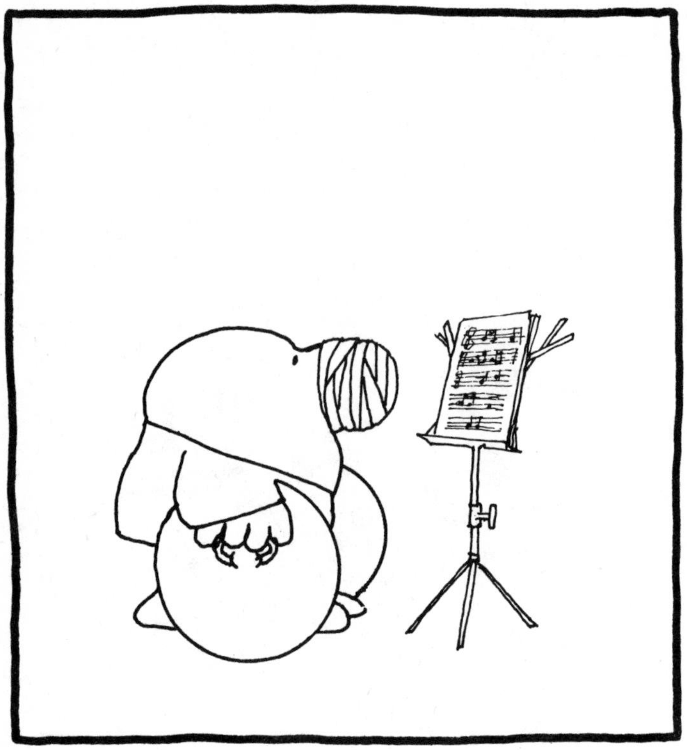

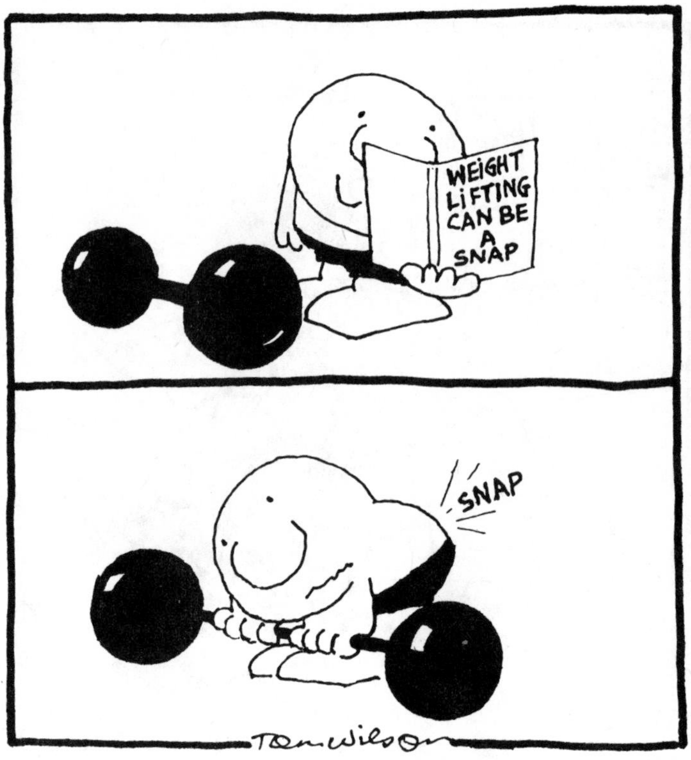
WEIGHT LIFTING CAN BE A SNAP
SNAP
Tom Wilson

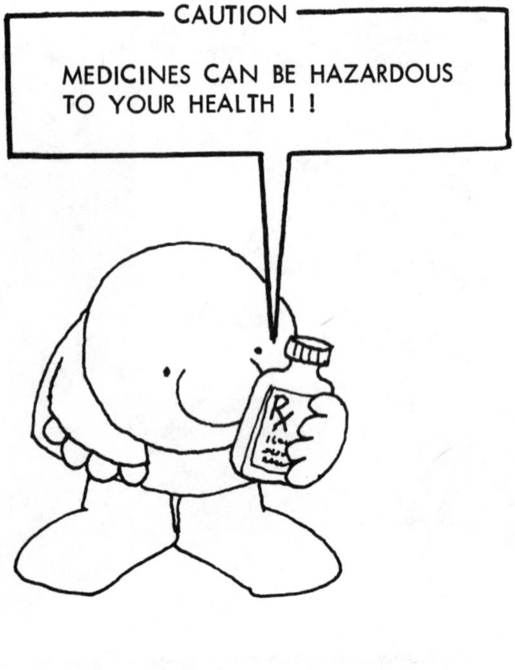
CAUTION
MEDICINES CAN BE HAZARDOUS TO YOUR HEALTH ! !
Rx

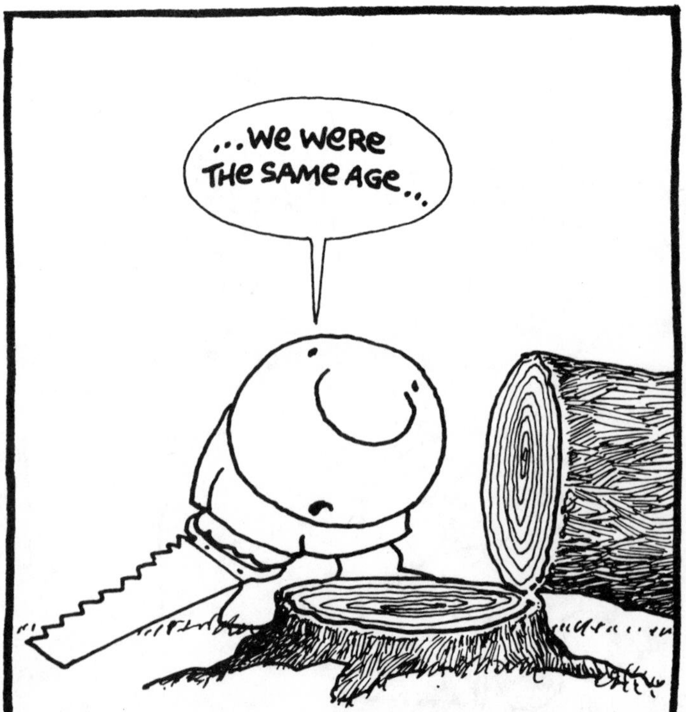
...we were the same age...

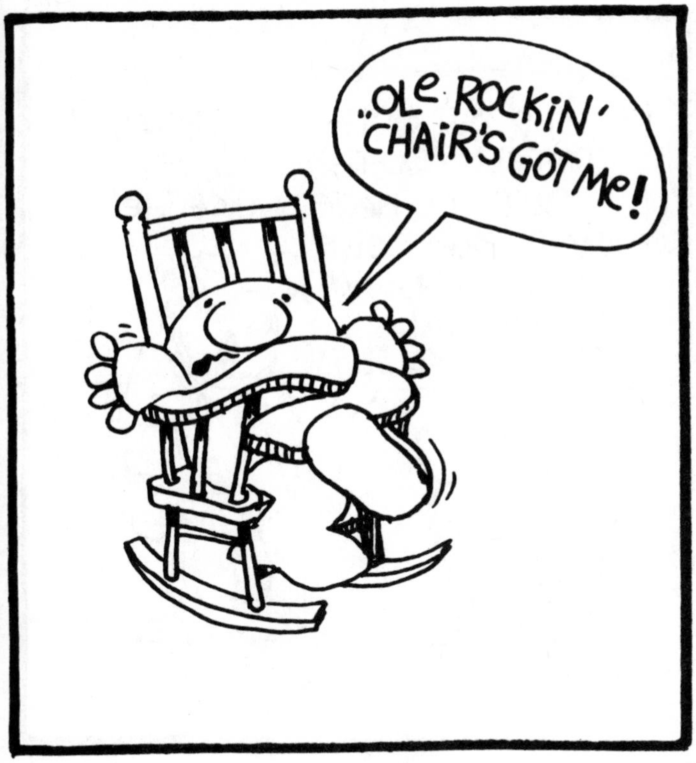
..OLE ROCKIN' CHAIR'S GOT ME!

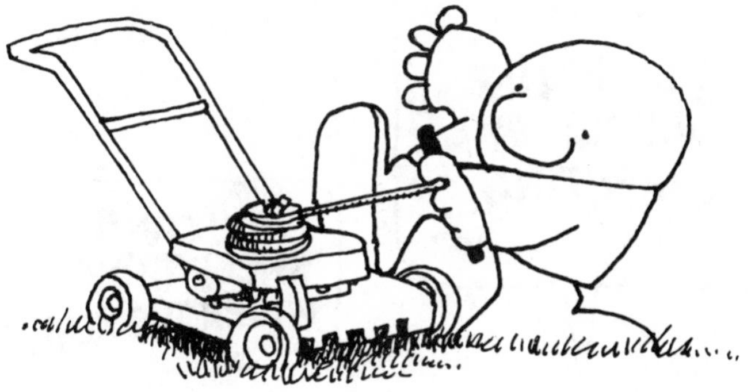

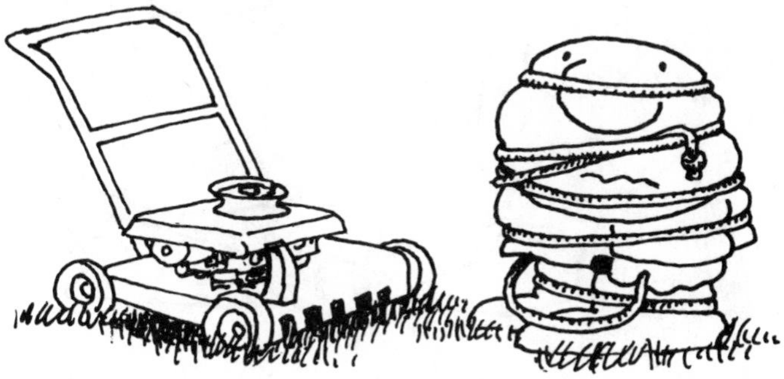

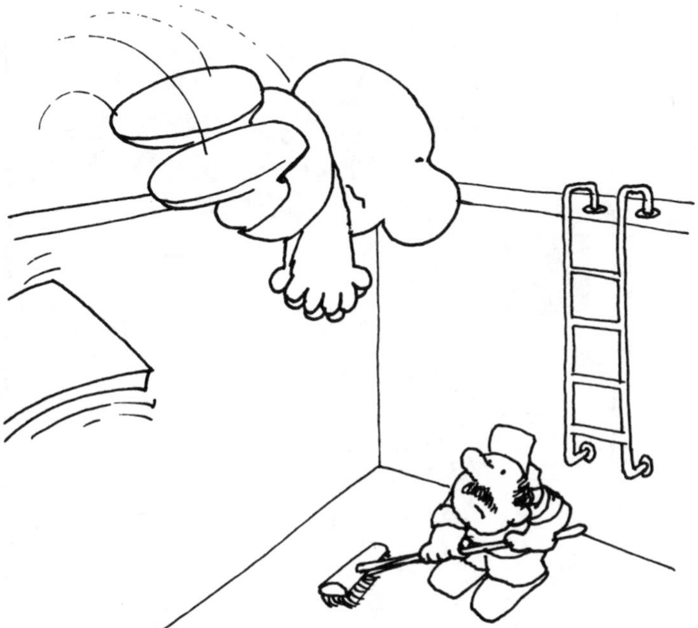

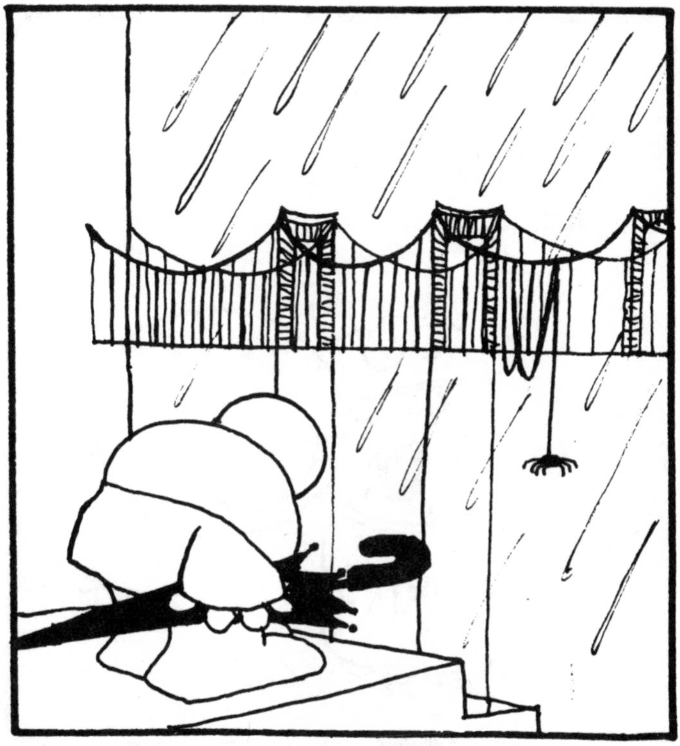

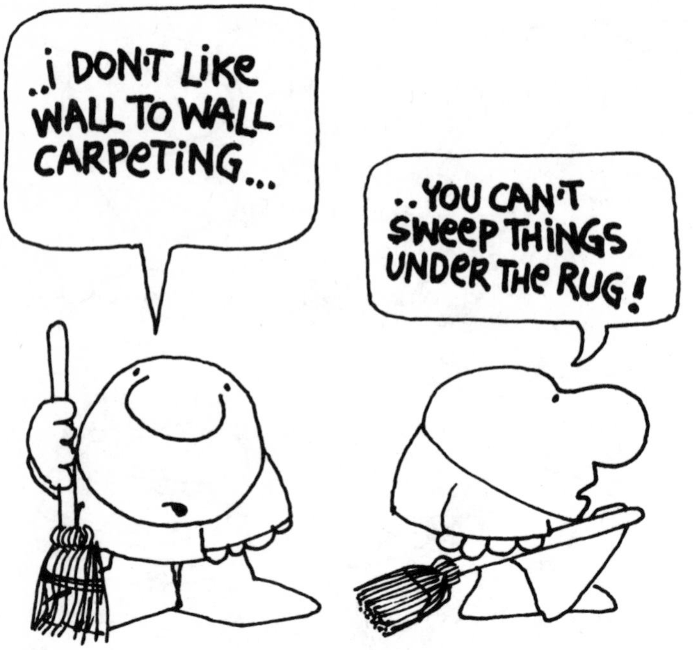
..i DON'T LiKe WALL TO WALL CARPeTiNG...
..YOU CAN'T SWeeP THiNGS UNDeR THe RUG!

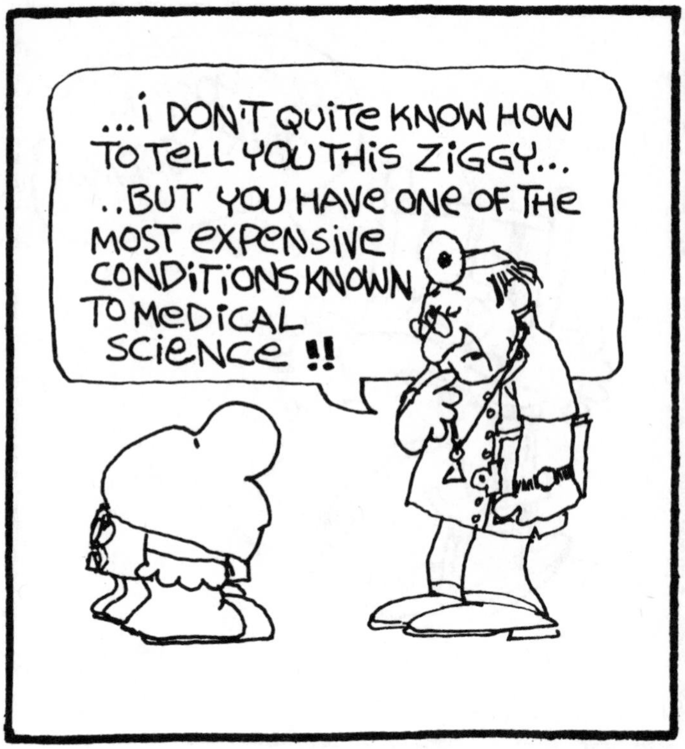
...i DON'T QUiTe KNOW HOW TO TeLL YOU THiS ZiGGY... ..BUT YOU HAVe ONe OF THe MOST eXPeNSiVe CONDiTiONS KNOWN TO MeDiCAL SCieNCe !!

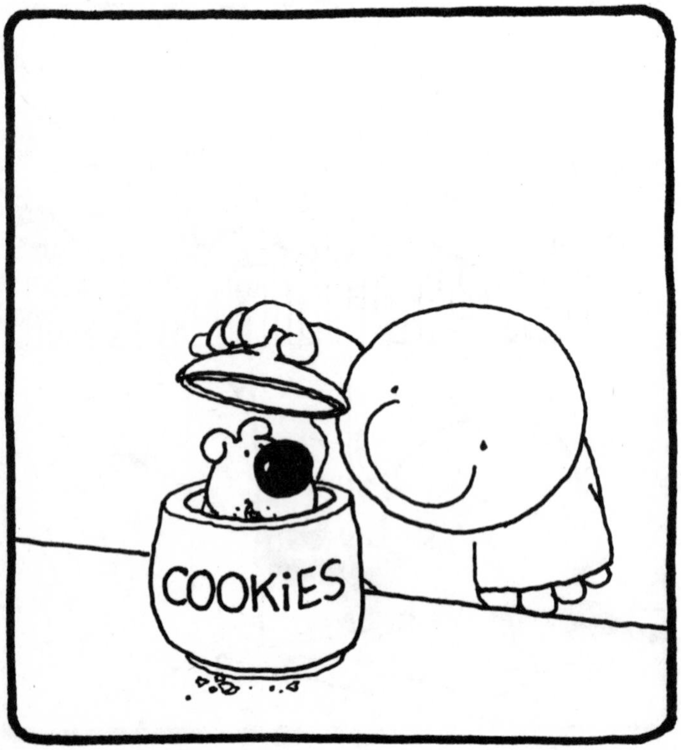
COOKiES

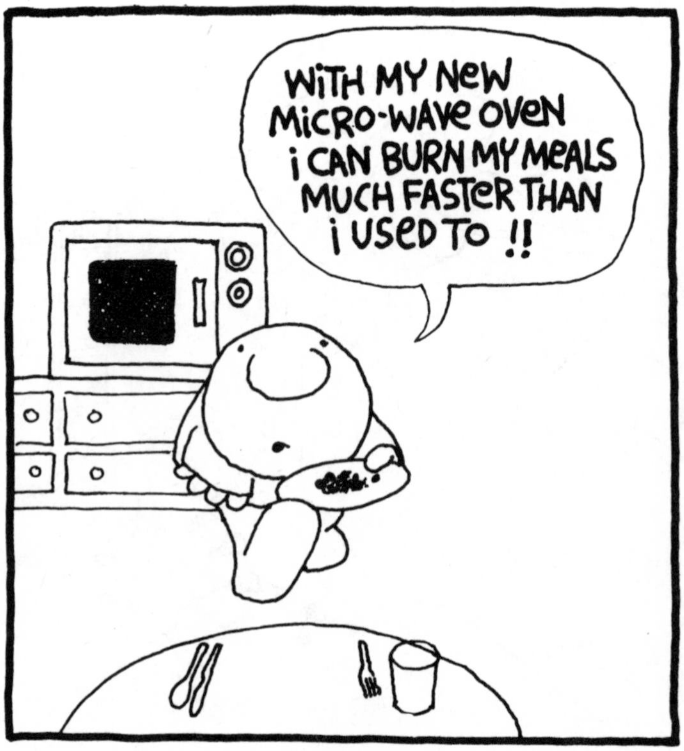
WiTH MY NeW MiCRO-WAVe OVeN i CAN BURN MY MeALS MUCH FASTeR THAN i USeD TO !!

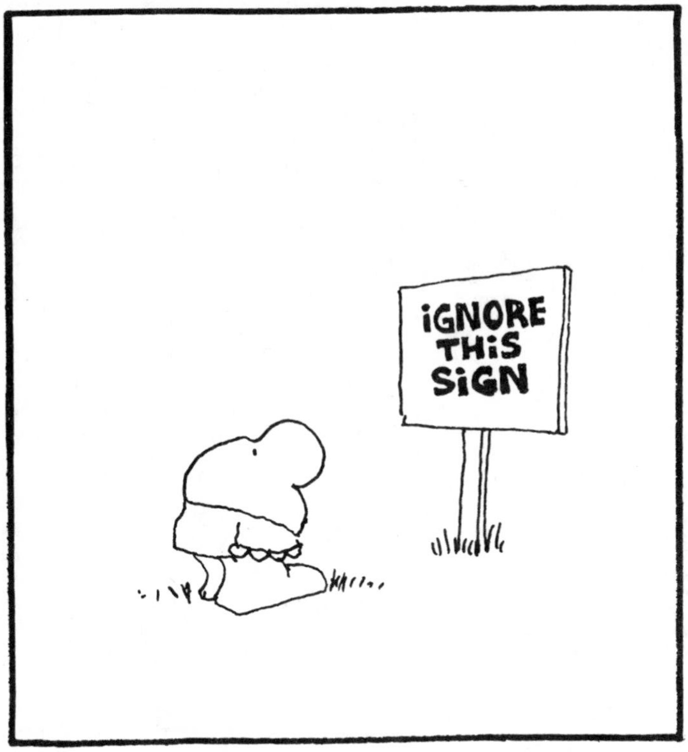
IGNORE THIS SIGN

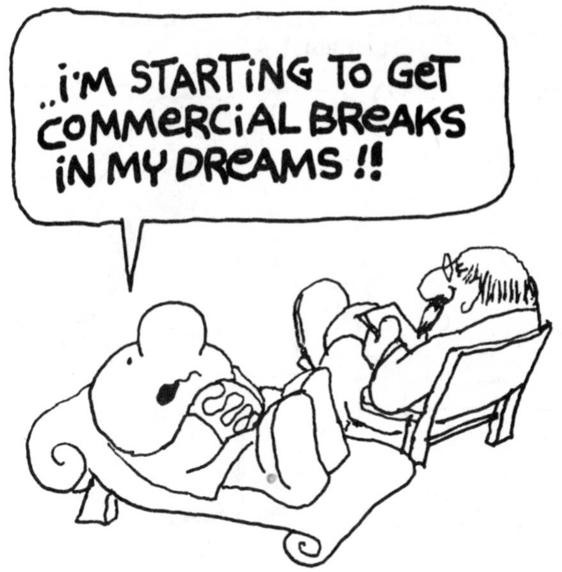
..I'M STARTING TO GET COMMERCIAL BREAKS IN MY DREAMS !!

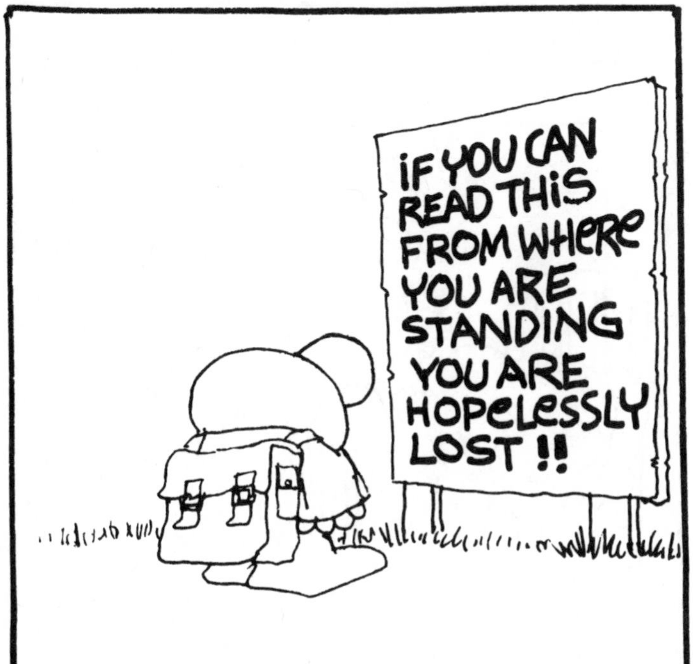
IF YOU CAN READ THIS FROM WHERE YOU ARE STANDING YOU ARE HOPELESSLY LOST !!

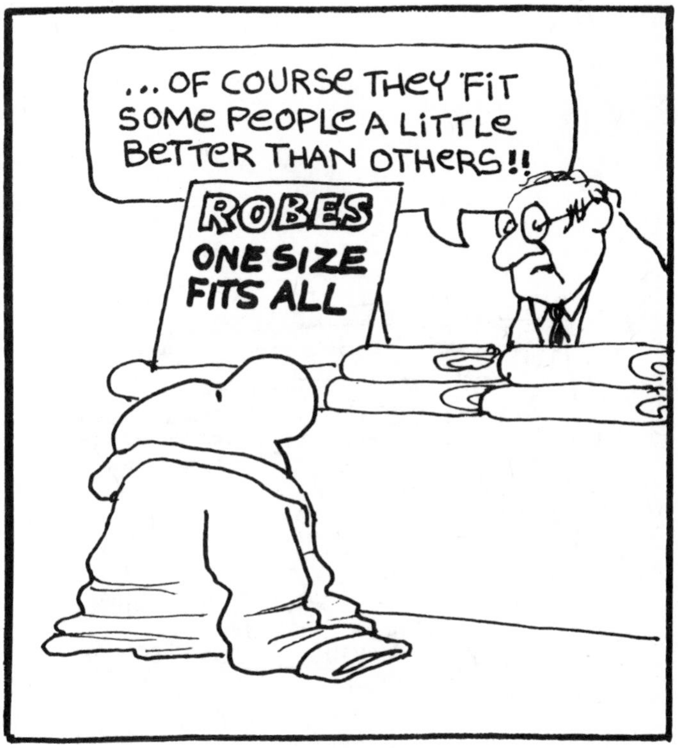
... OF COURSE THEY FIT SOME PEOPLE A LITTLE BETTER THAN OTHERS !!
ROBES
ONE SIZE FITS ALL

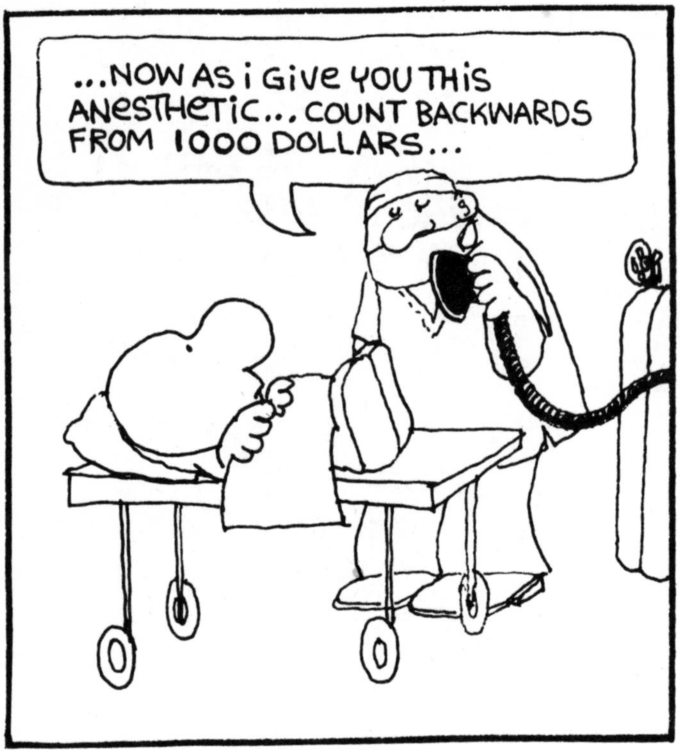
...NOW AS i GiVe YOU THiS ANeSTHeTiC... COUNT BACKWARDS FROM 1000 DOLLARS...

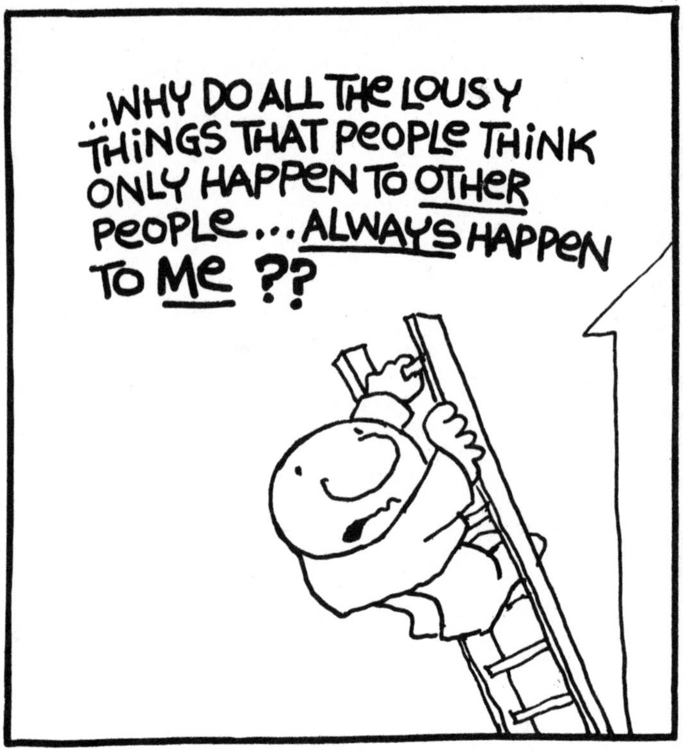
..WHY DO ALL THe LOUSY THiNGS THAT PeOPLe THiNK ONLY HAPPeN TO OTHeR PeOPLe... ALWAYS HAPPeN TO Me ??

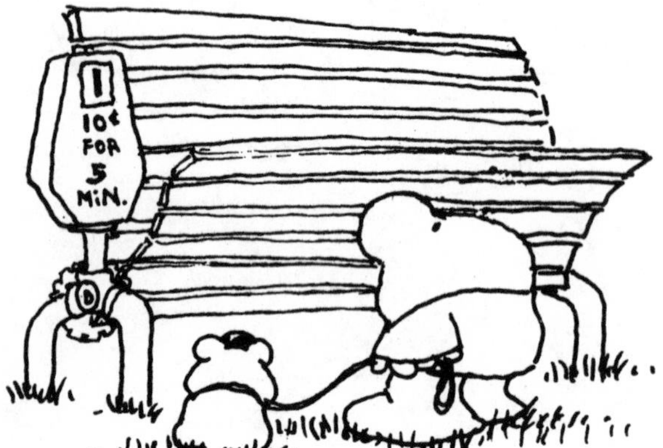
10¢ FOR 5 MiN.

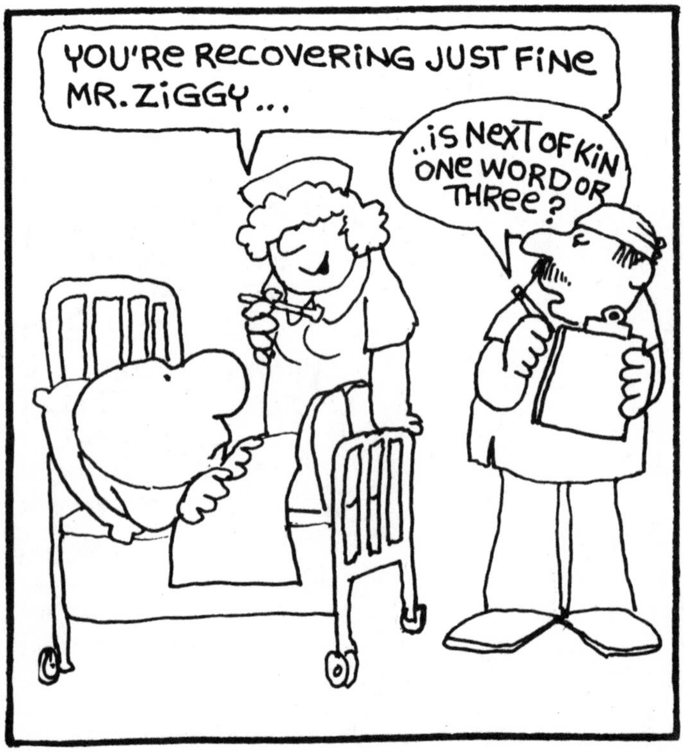
YOU'Re ReCOVeRiNG JUST FiNe MR. ZiGGY...
..iS NeXT OF KiN ONe WORD OR THRee ?

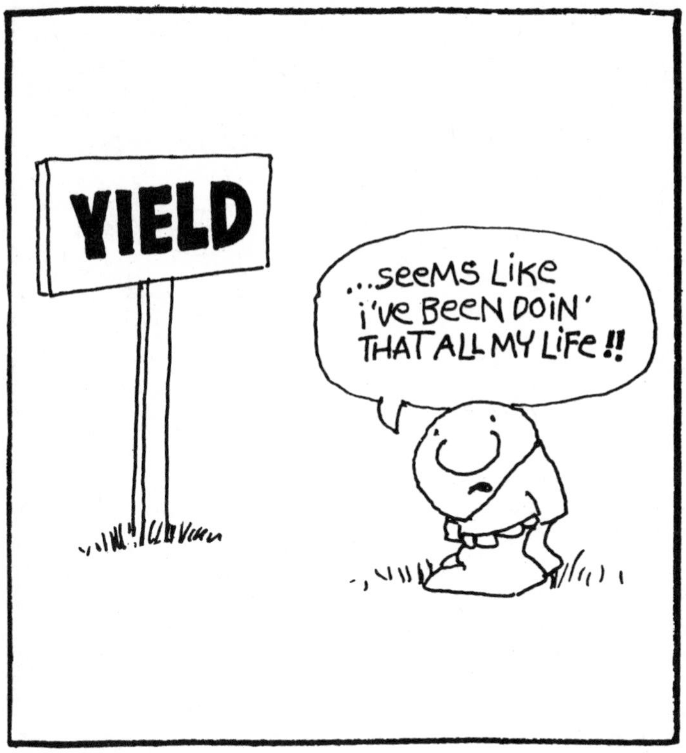
YIELD
...seems like i've been doin' that all my life !!

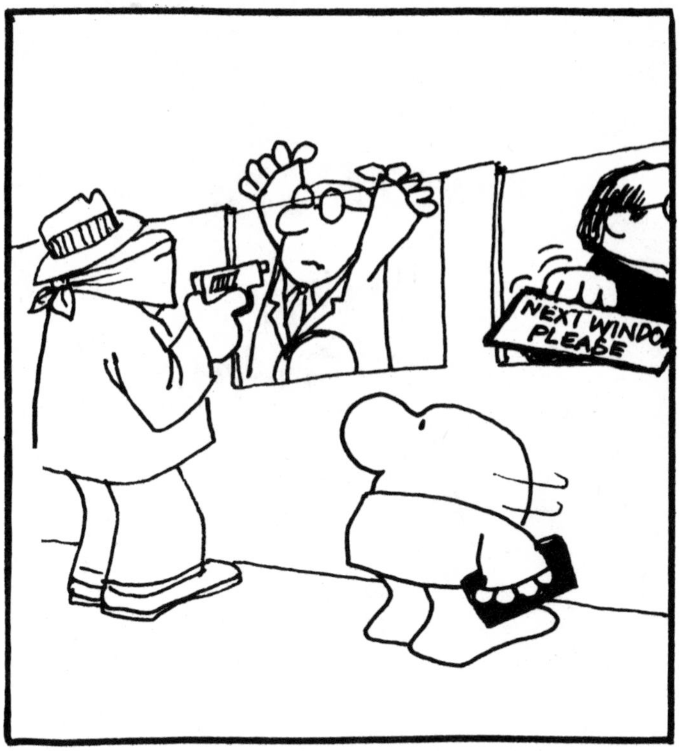
NEXT WINDO
PLEASE

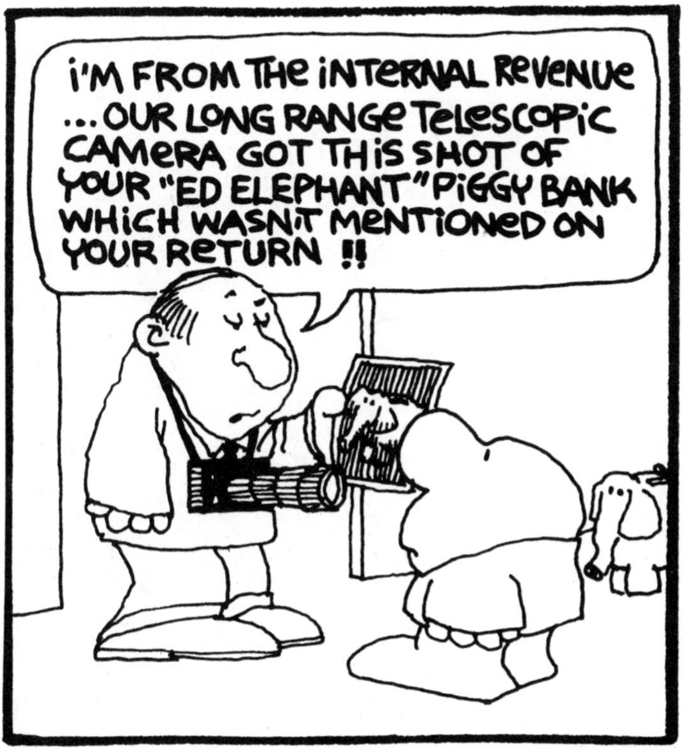
i'M FROM THE iNTERNAL REVENUE ...OUR LONG RANGE TELESCOPIC CAMERA GOT THIS SHOT OF YOUR "ED ELEPHANT" PiGGY BANK WHICH WASN'T MENTIONED ON YOUR RETURN !!

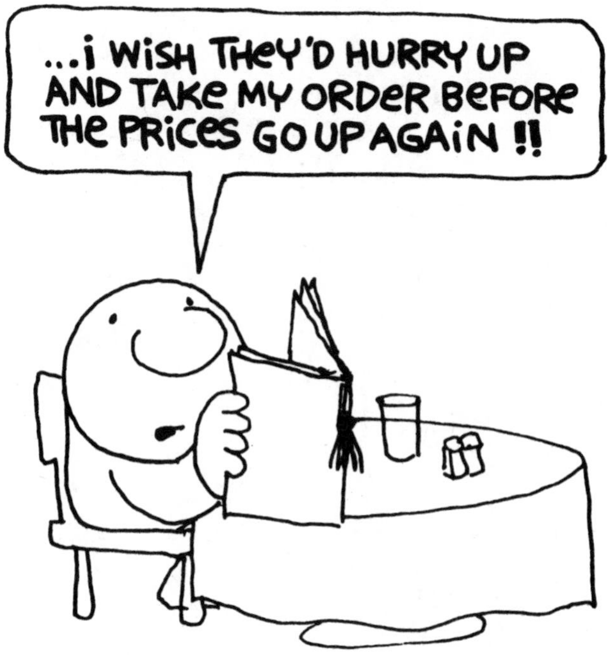
...i WiSH THEY'D HURRY UP AND TAKE MY ORDER BEFORE THE PRICES GO UP AGAIN !!

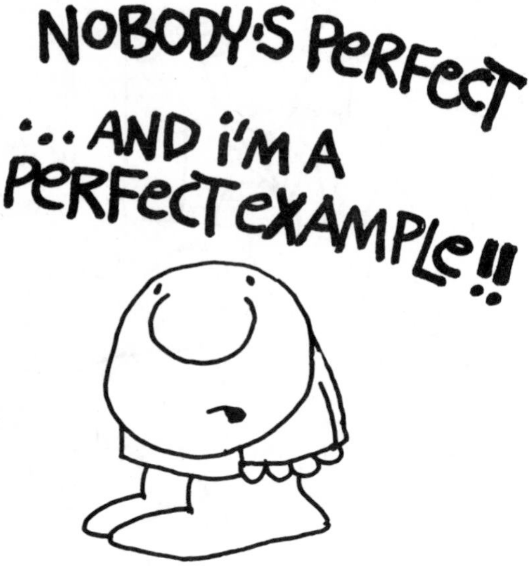
NOBODY'S PERFECT
...AND i'M A PERFECT EXAMPLE!!

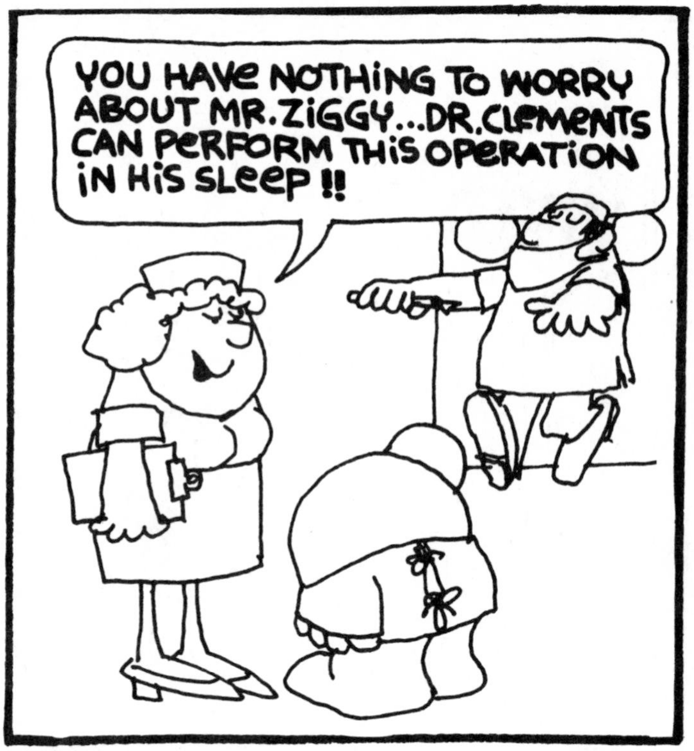
YOU HAVE NOTHING TO WORRY ABOUT MR. ZIGGY...DR. CLEMENTS CAN PERFORM THIS OPERATION IN HIS SLEEP!!

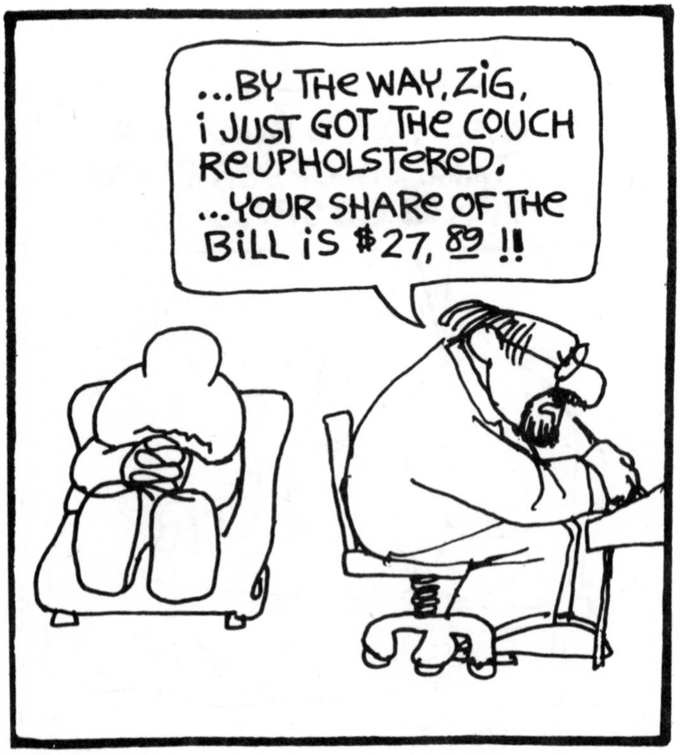
...BY THE WAY, ZIG, i JUST GOT THE COUCH REUPHOLSTERED. ...YOUR SHARE OF THE BILL iS $27,89 !!

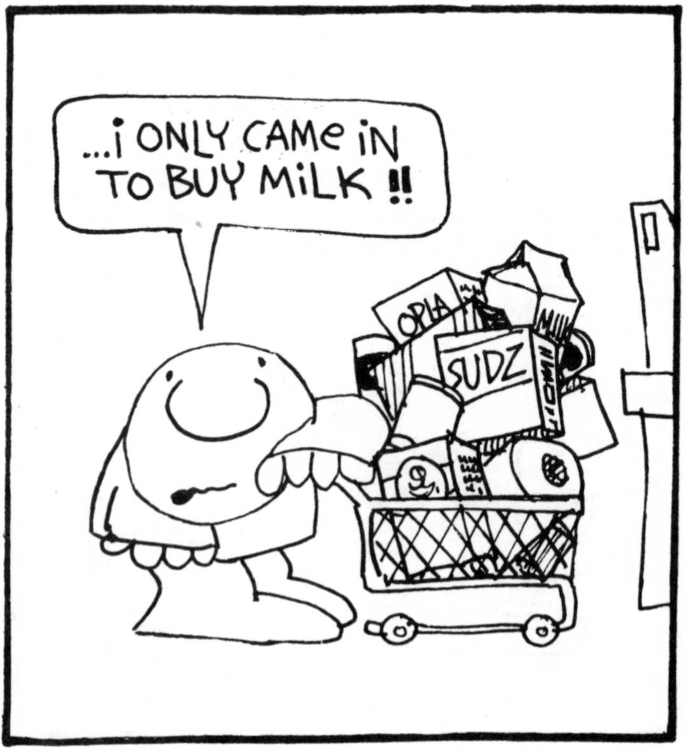
...i ONLY CAME iN TO BUY MiLK!!
OPLA
SUDZ

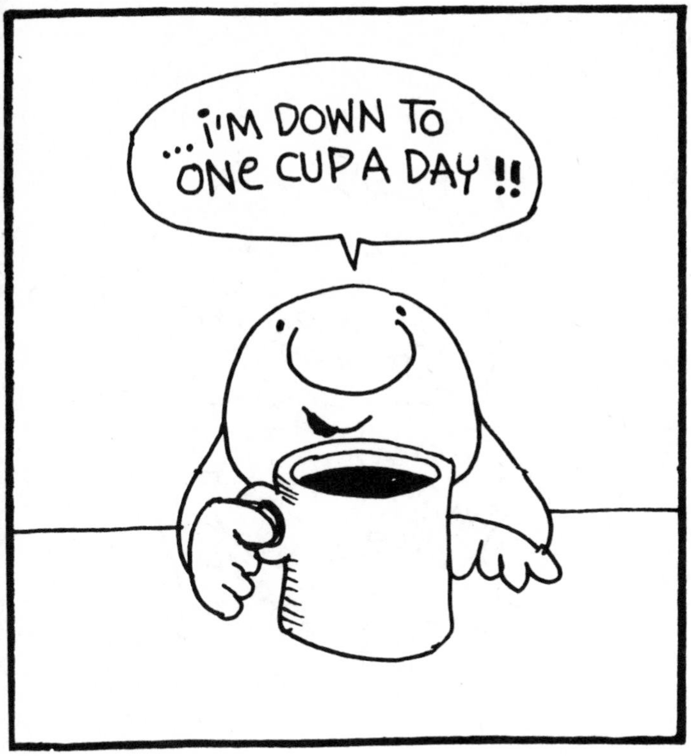
...i'M DOWN TO ONE CUP A DAY !!

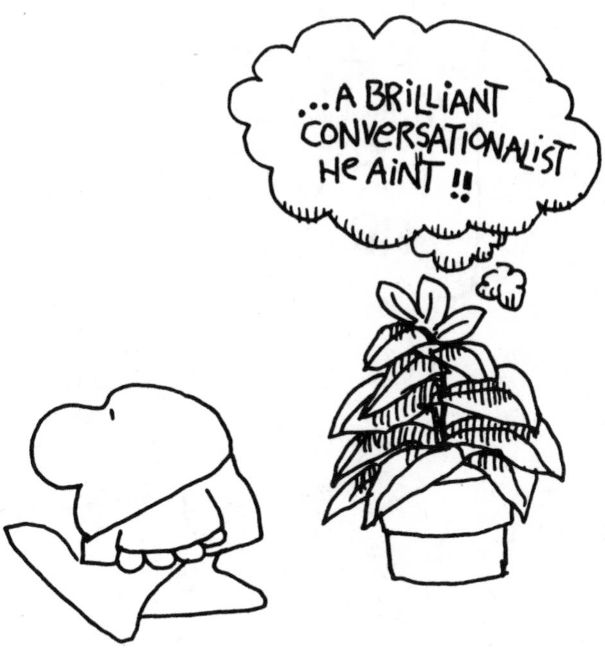
...A BRILLIANT CONVERSATIONALIST HE AINT !!

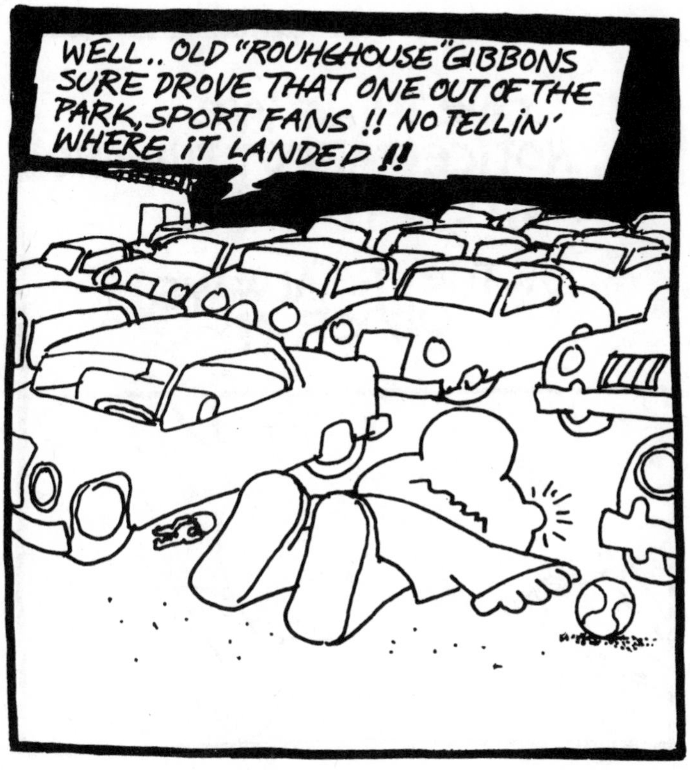
WELL.. OLD "ROUHGHOUSE" GIBBONS SURE DROVE THAT ONE OUT OF THE PARK, SPORT FANS !! NO TELLIN' WHERE IT LANDED !!

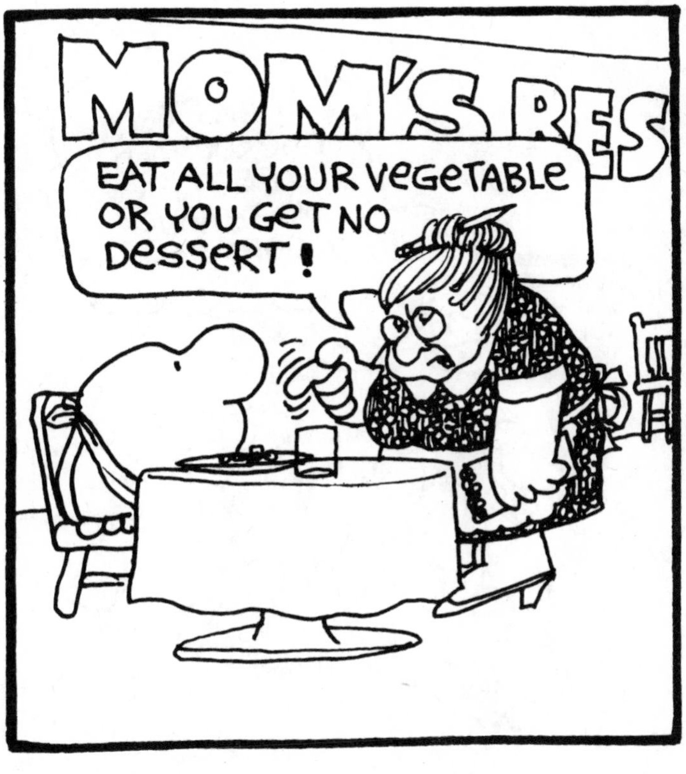
MOM'S RES
EAT ALL YOUR VEGETABLE OR YOU GET NO DESSERT !

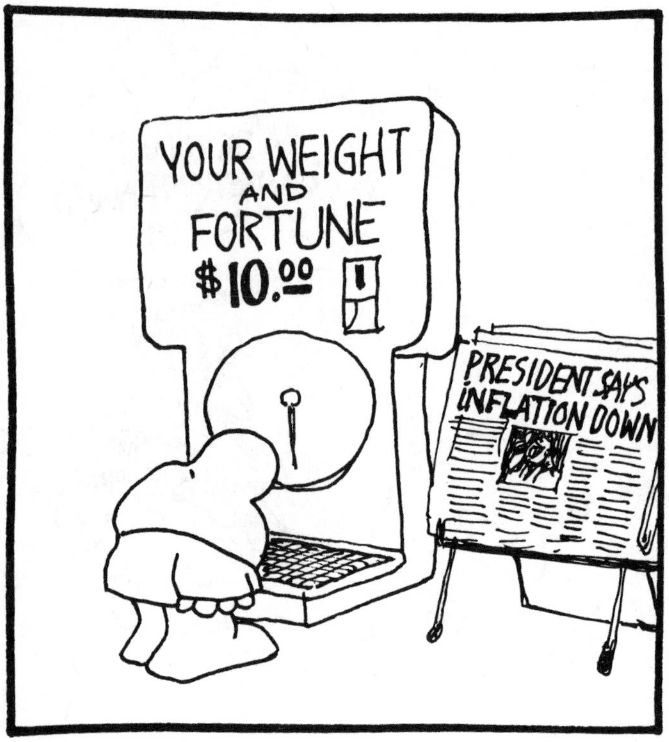
YOUR WEIGHT AND FORTUNE
$10.00
PRESIDENT SAYS INFLATION DOWN

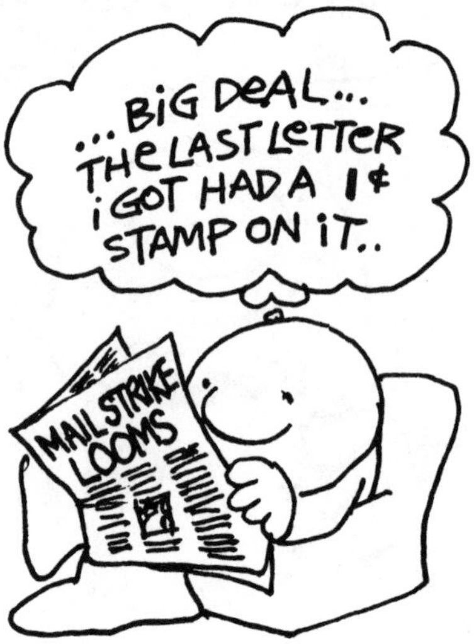
...BIG DEAL... THE LAST LETTER I GOT HAD A 1¢ STAMP ON IT..
MAIL STRIKE LOOMS

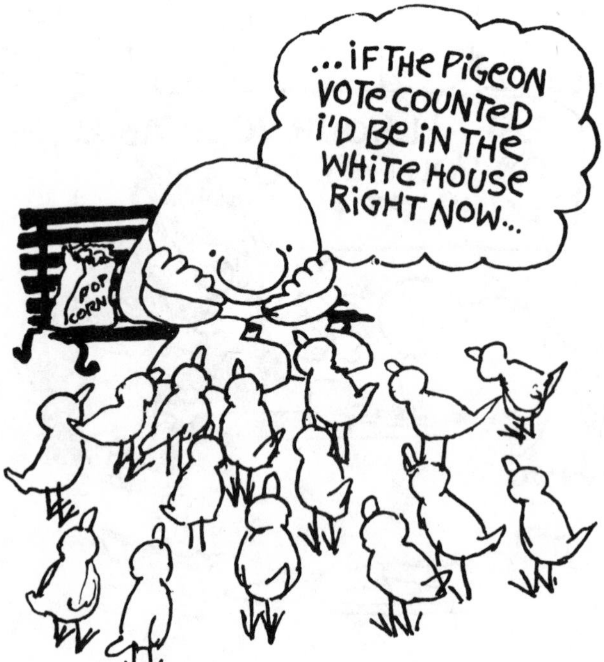
...IF THE PIGEON VOTE COUNTED I'D BE IN THE WHITE HOUSE RIGHT NOW...
POP CORN

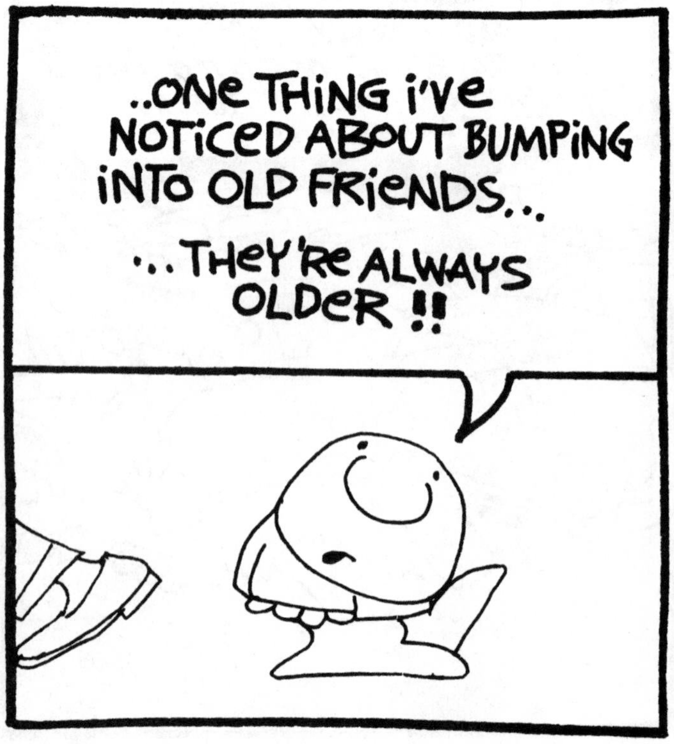
..ONE THING I'VE NOTICED ABOUT BUMPING INTO OLD FRIENDS...
...THEY'RE ALWAYS OLDER !!

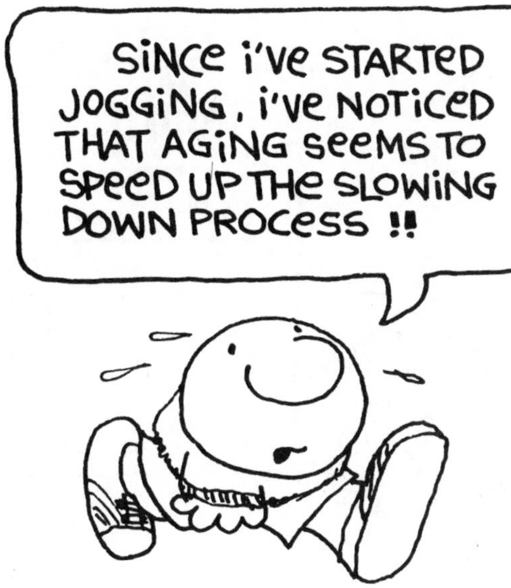
SINCE I'VE STARTED JOGGING, I'VE NOTICED THAT AGING SEEMS TO SPEED UP THE SLOWING DOWN PROCESS !!

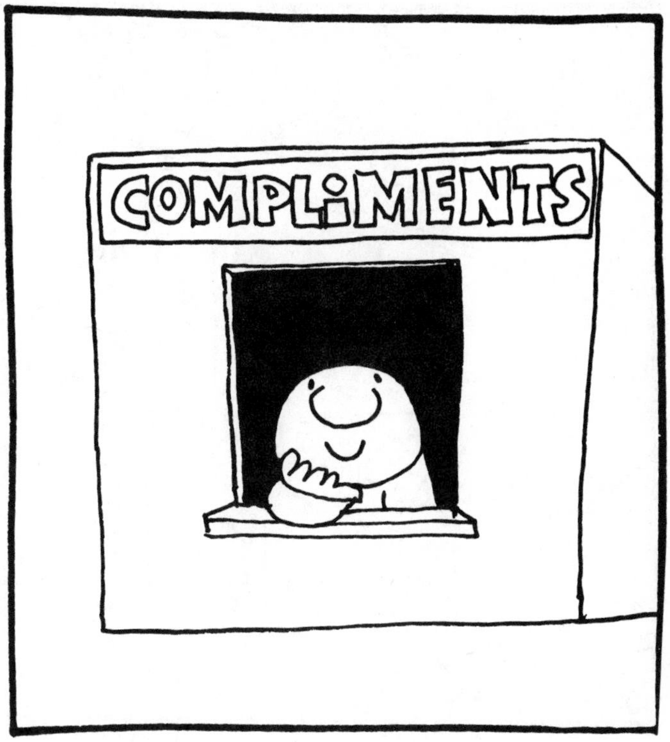
COMPLIMENTS

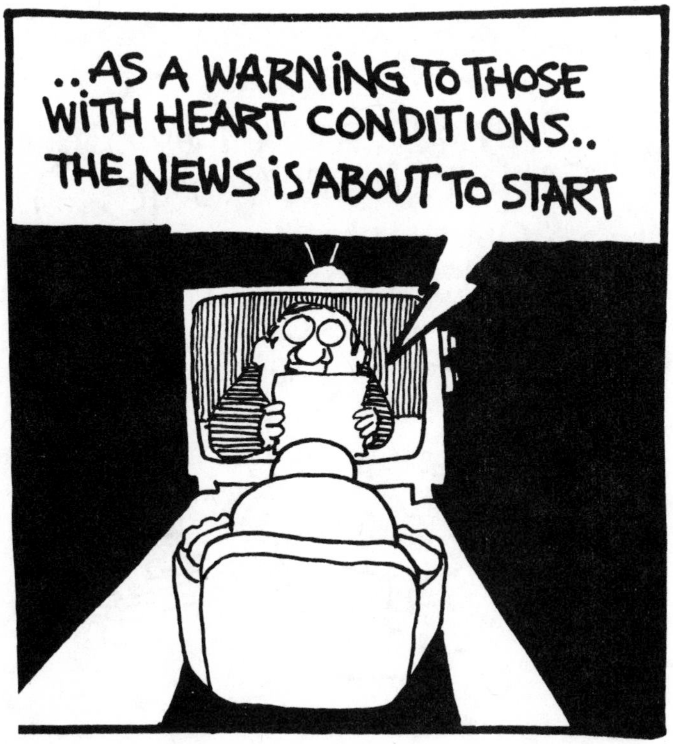
..AS A WARNING TO THOSE WITH HEART CONDITIONS.. THE NEWS IS ABOUT TO START

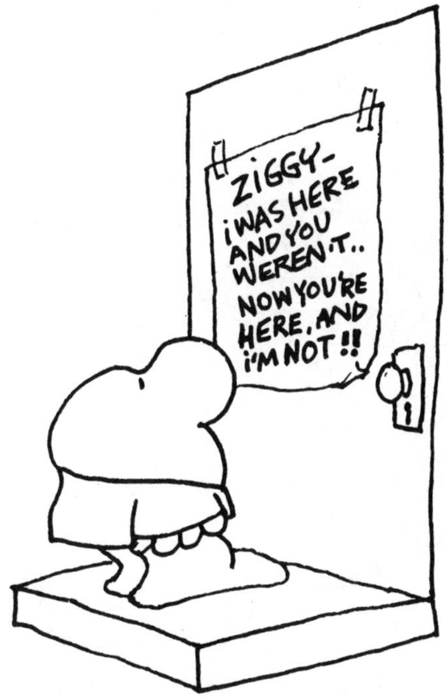
ZIGGY- I WAS HERE AND YOU WEREN'T.. NOW YOU'RE HERE, AND I'M NOT !!

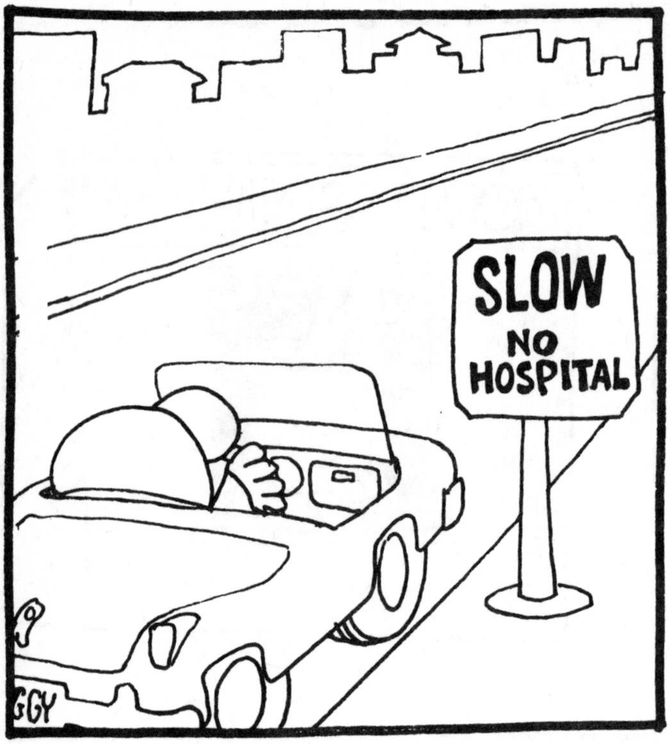
SLOW
NO
HOSPITAL

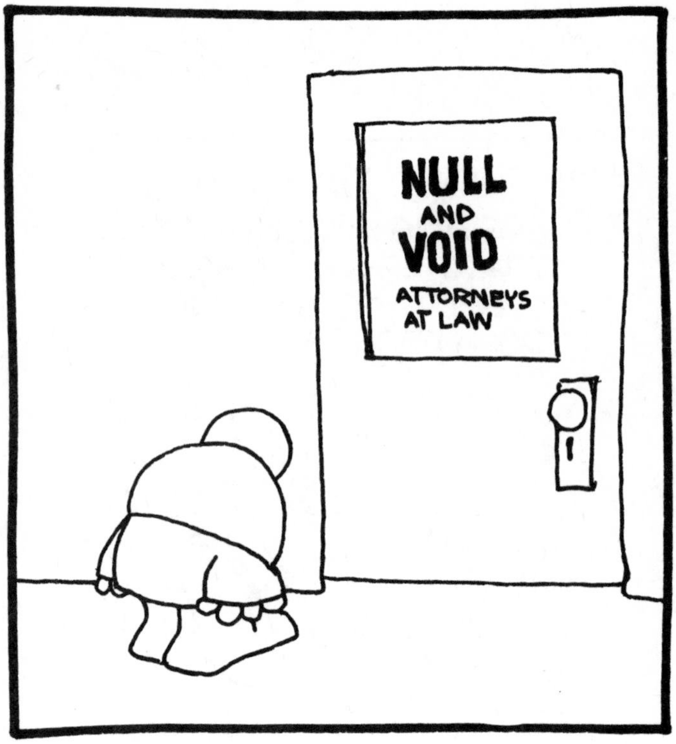
NULL
AND
VOID
ATTORNEYS
AT LAW

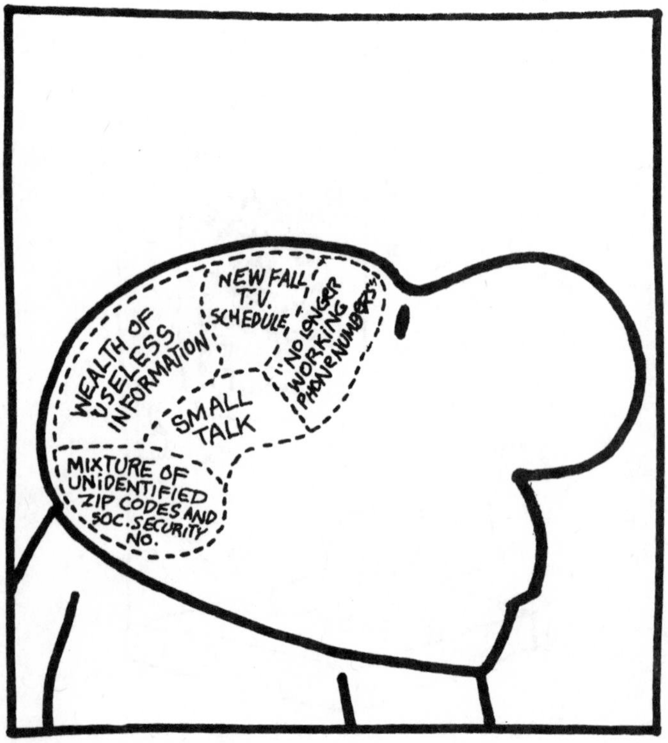
WEALTH OF USELESS INFORMATION
NEW FALL T.V. SCHEDULE,
"NO LONGER WORKING PHONE NUMBERS"
SMALL TALK
MIXTURE OF UNIDENTIFIED ZIP CODES AND SOC. SECURITY NO.

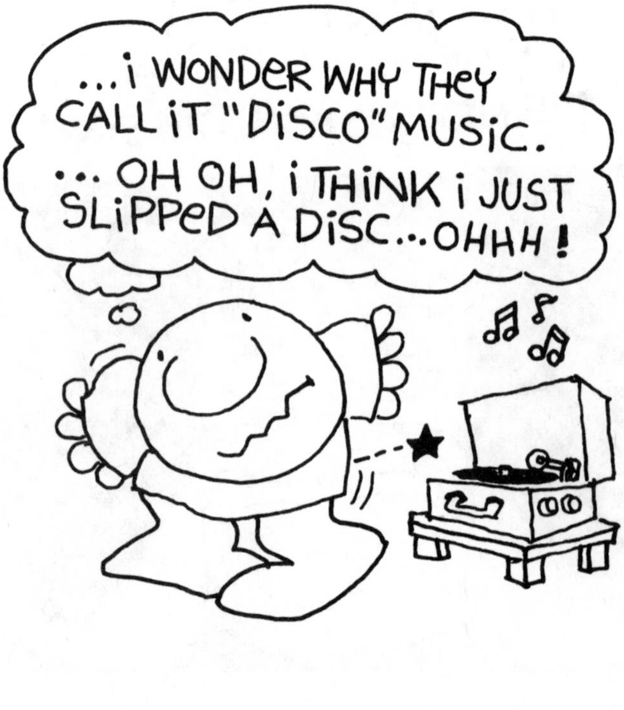
...i WONDER WHY THEY CALL iT "DiSCO" MUSiC. ... OH OH, i THiNK i JUST SLiPPED A DiSC...OHHH!

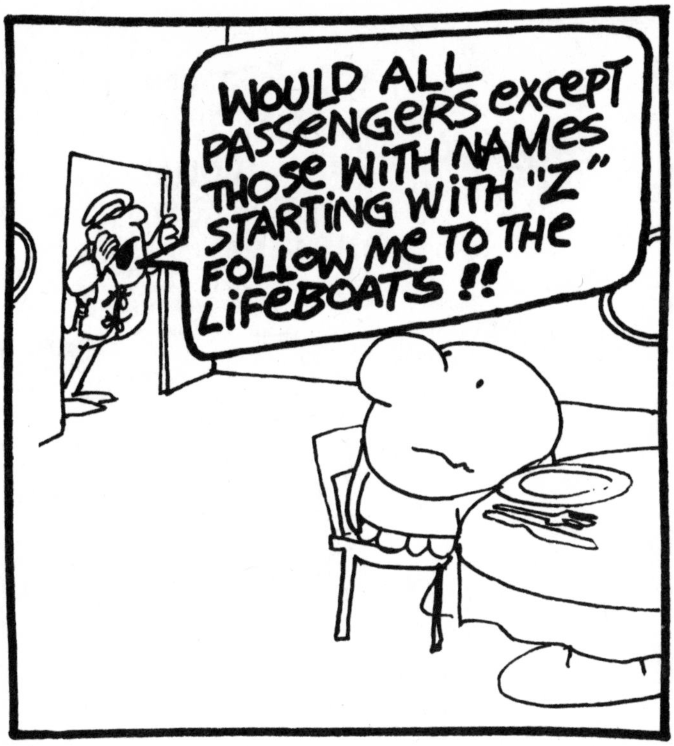
WOULD ALL PASSENGERS except THOSE WITH NAMES STARTING WITH "Z" FOLLOW ME TO THE LIFEBOATS !!

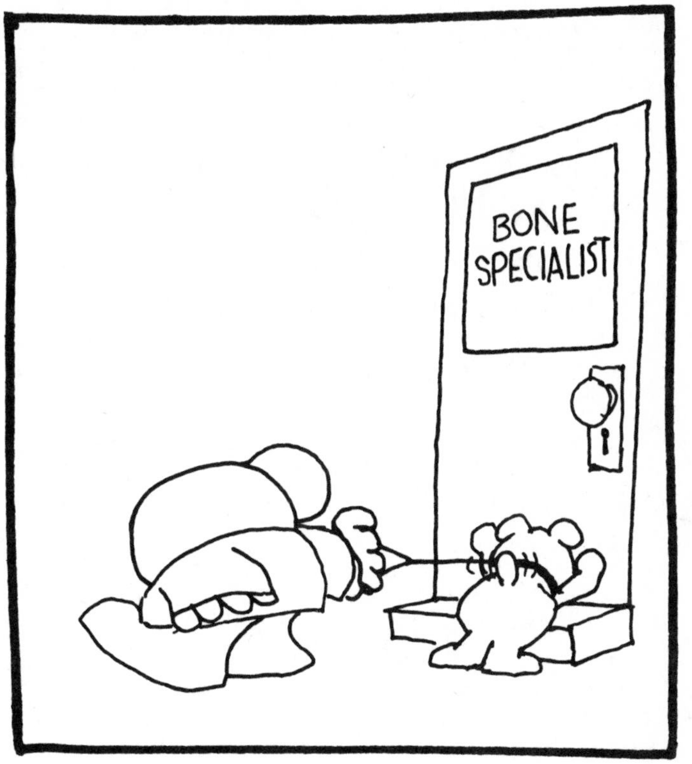
BONE SPECIALIST

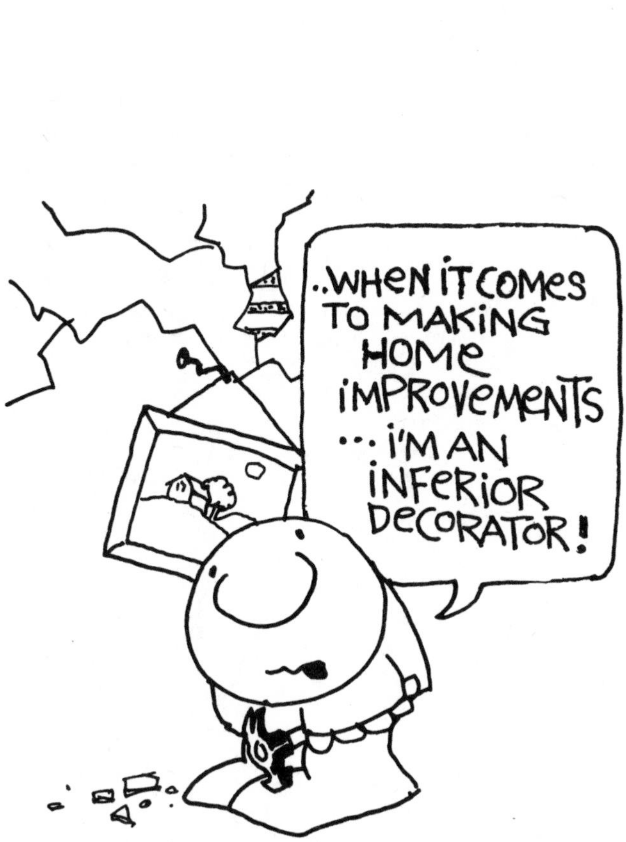
..WHEN IT COMES TO MAKING HOME IMPROVEMENTS ...I'M AN INFERIOR DECORATOR!

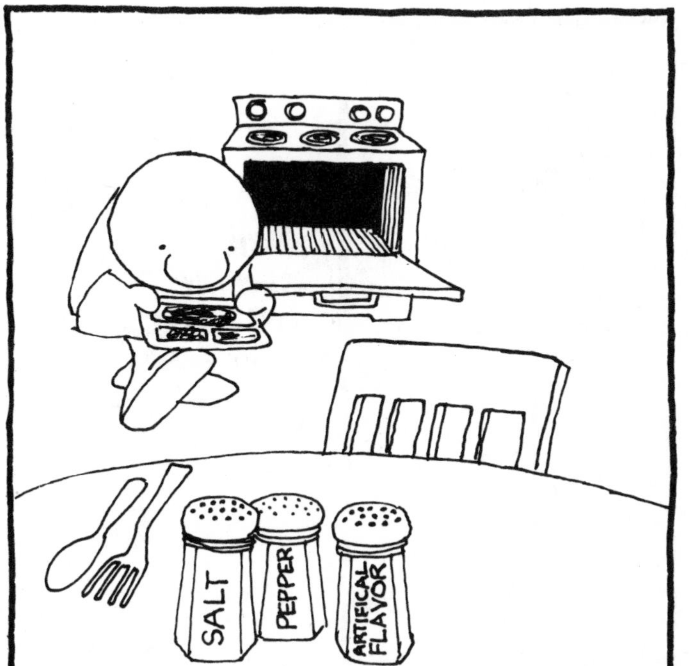
SALT
PEPPER
ARTIFICAL FLAVOR

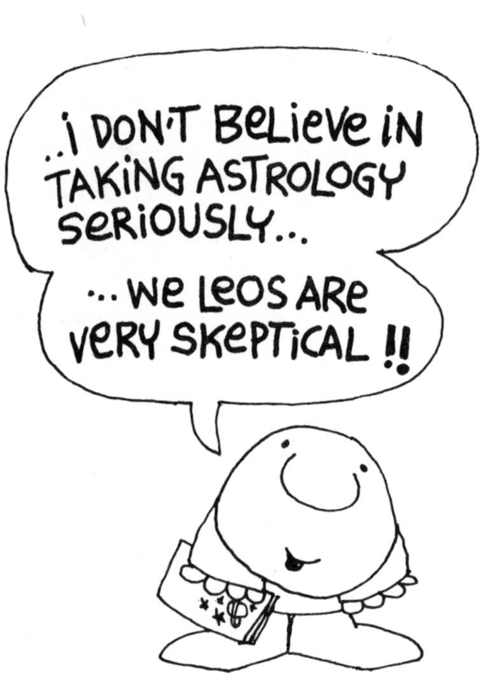
..i DON'T BeLieve iN TAKiNG ASTROLOGY SeRiOUSLY...
... We LeOS ARe VeRY SKePTiCAL !!

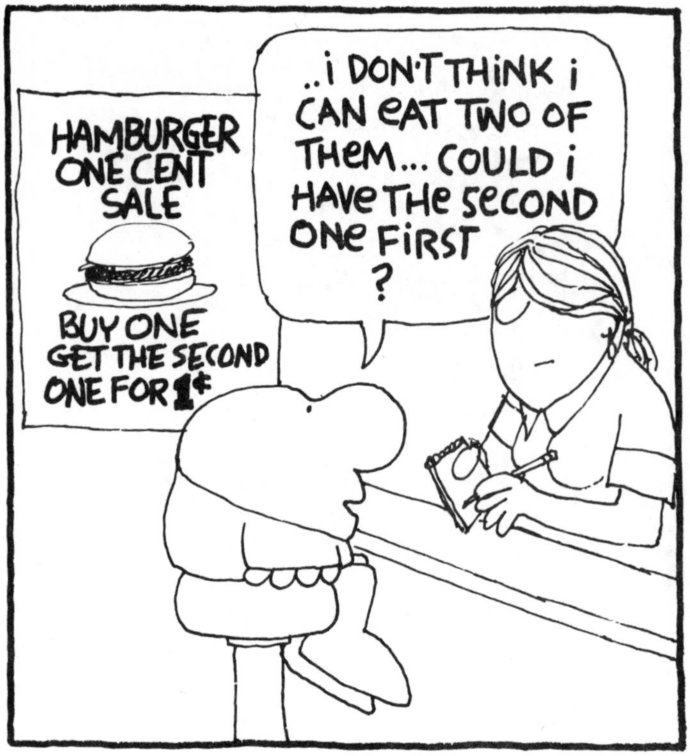
HAMBURGER ONE CENT SALE
BUY ONE GET THE SECOND ONE FOR 1¢
..i DON'T THiNK i CAN eAT TWO OF THeM... COULD i HAVe THe SeCOND ONe FiRST ?

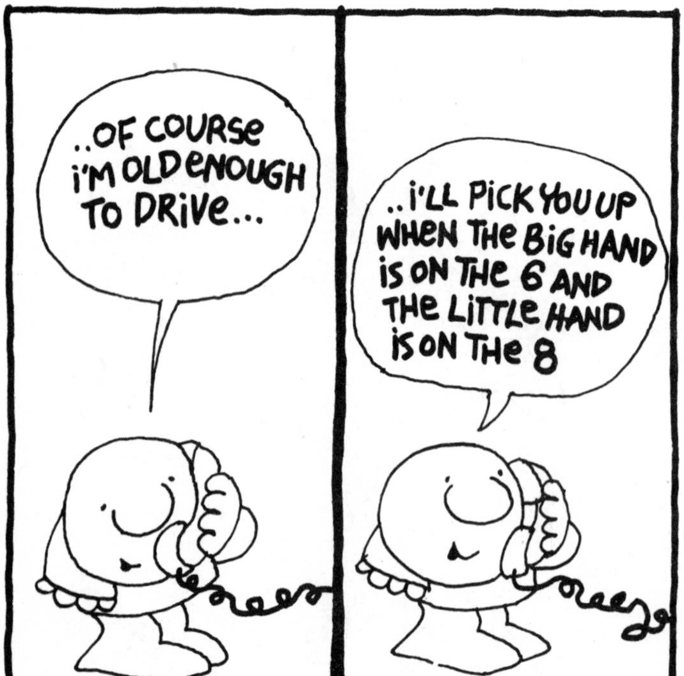
..OF COURSe i'M OLD eNOUGH TO DRiVe...
..i'LL PiCK YOU UP WHEN THe BiG HAND iS ON THe 6 AND THe LiTTLe HAND iS ON THe 8

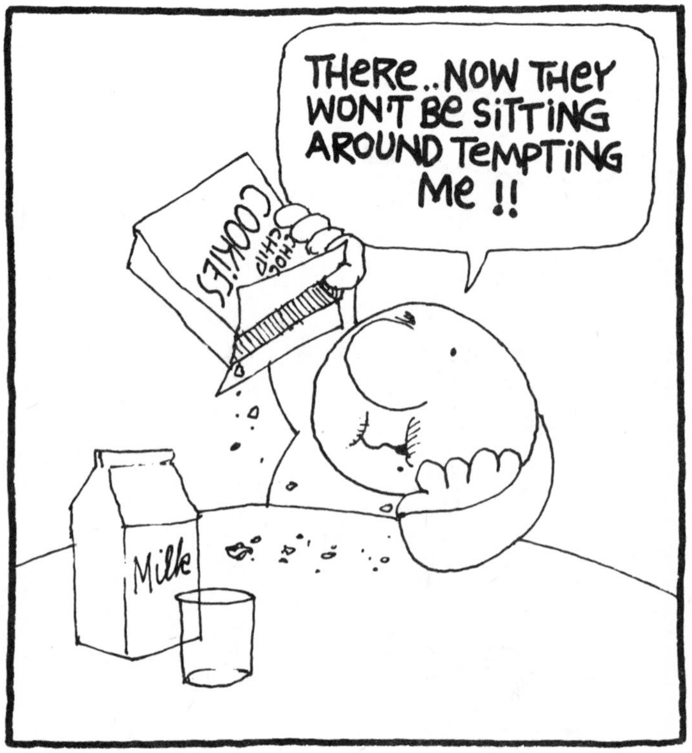
THeRe..NOW THeY WON'T Be SiTTiNG AROUND TeMPTiNG Me !!
Milk

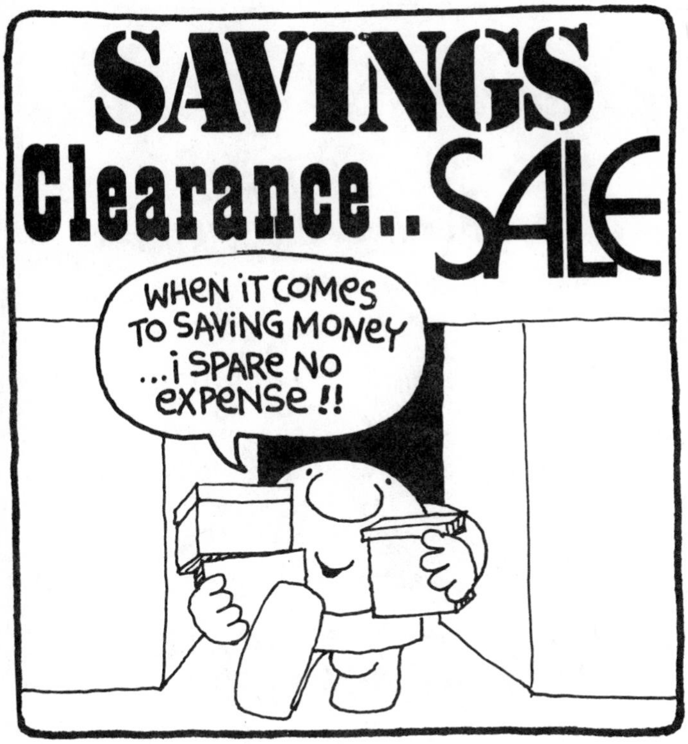
SAVINGS
Clearance.. SALE
WHEN IT COMES TO SAVING MONEY ...I SPARE NO EXPENSE !!

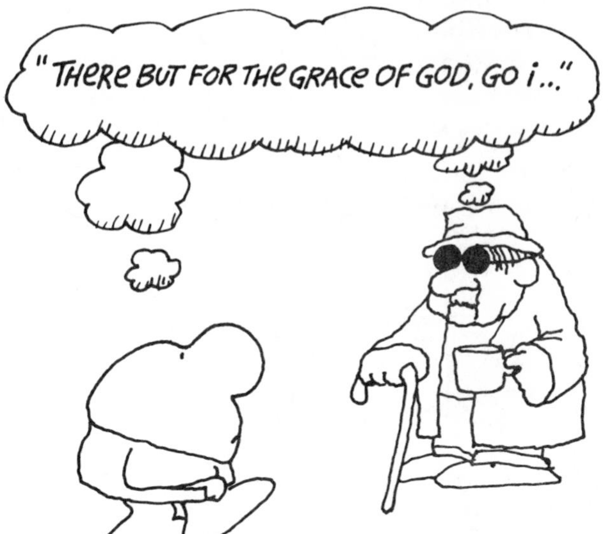
"THERE BUT FOR THE GRACE OF GOD, GO I.."

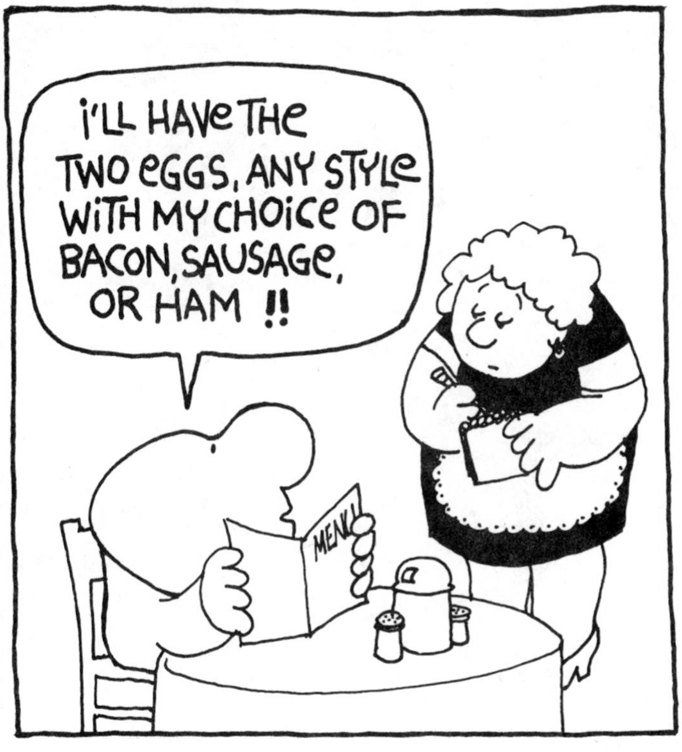
I'LL HAVE THE TWO EGGS, ANY STYLE WITH MY CHOICE OF BACON, SAUSAGE, OR HAM !!
MENU

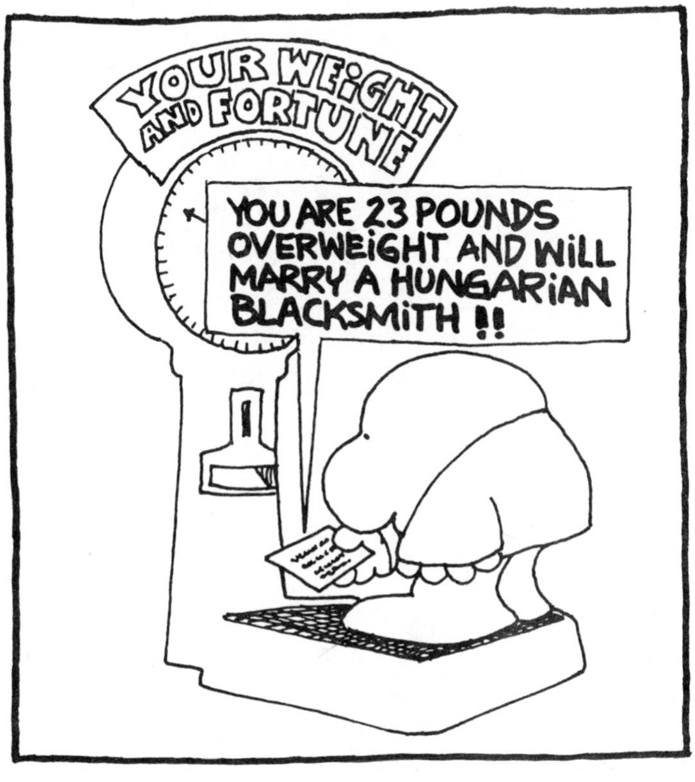
YOUR WEIGHT AND FORTUNE
YOU ARE 23 POUNDS OVERWEIGHT AND WILL MARRY A HUNGARIAN BLACKSMITH !!

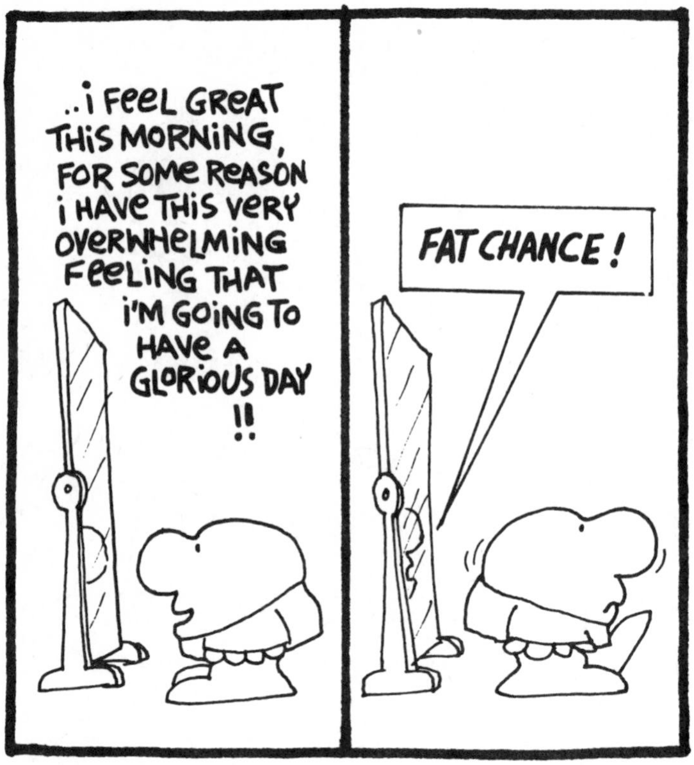
..i FeeL GREAT THIS MORNING, FOR SOME REASON i HAVE THIS VERY OVERWHELMING FEELING THAT i'M GOING TO HAVE A GLORIOUS DAY !!
FAT CHANCE !

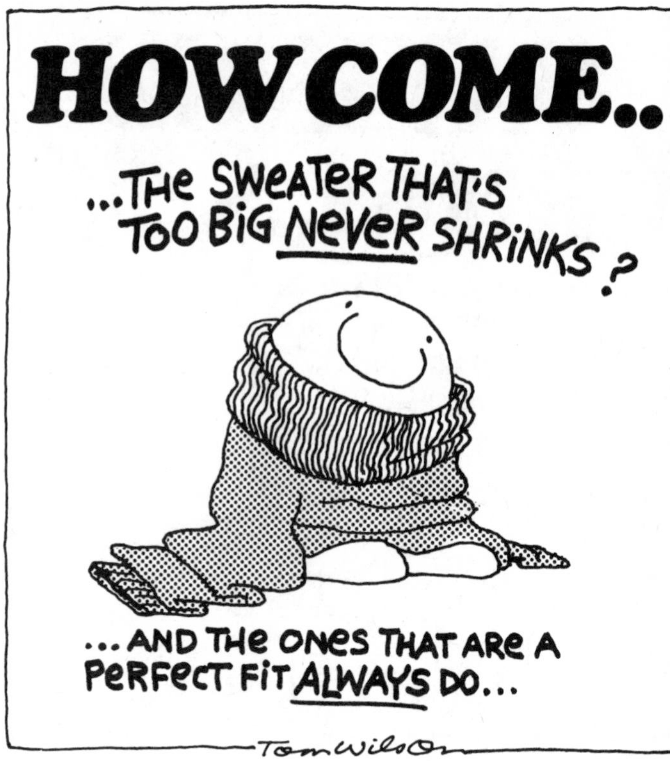
HOW COME..
...THE SWEATER THAT'S TOO BIG NEVER SHRINKS ?
...AND THE ONES THAT ARE A PERFECT FIT ALWAYS DO...
Tom Wilson

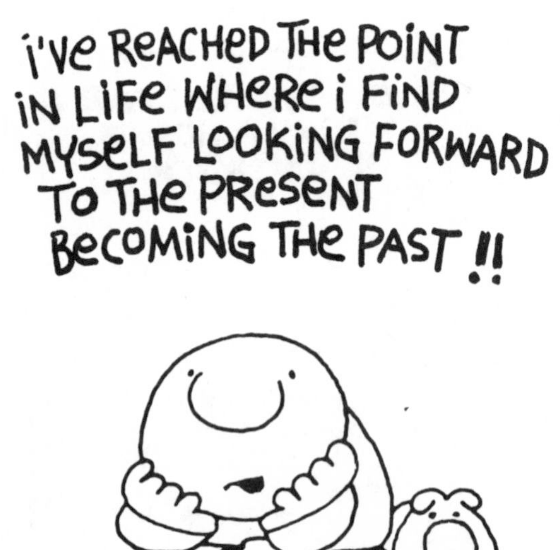
i'VE REACHED THE POINT IN LIFE WHERE i FIND MYSELF LOOKING FORWARD TO THE PRESENT BECOMING THE PAST !!

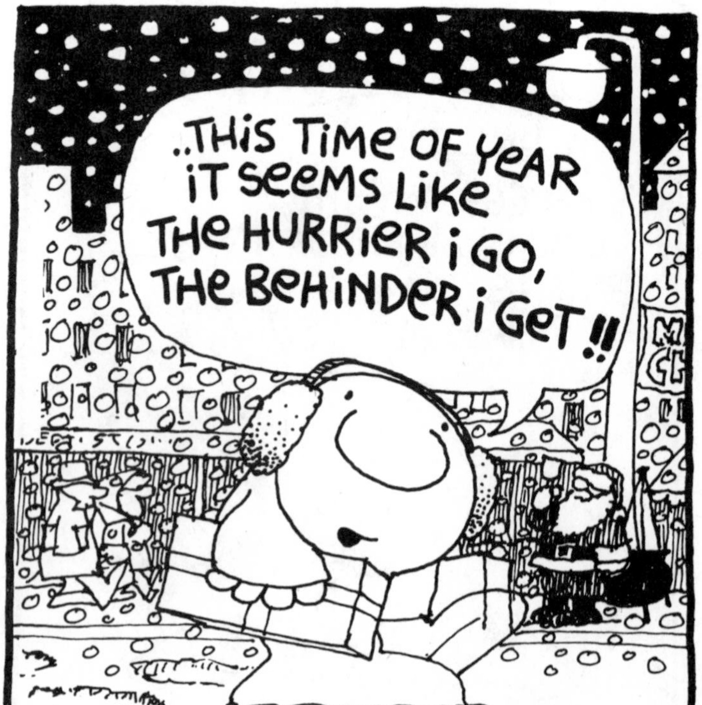
..THIS TIME OF YEAR iT SEEMS LIKE THE HURRIER i GO, THE BEHINDER i GET !!

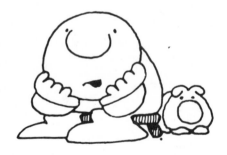

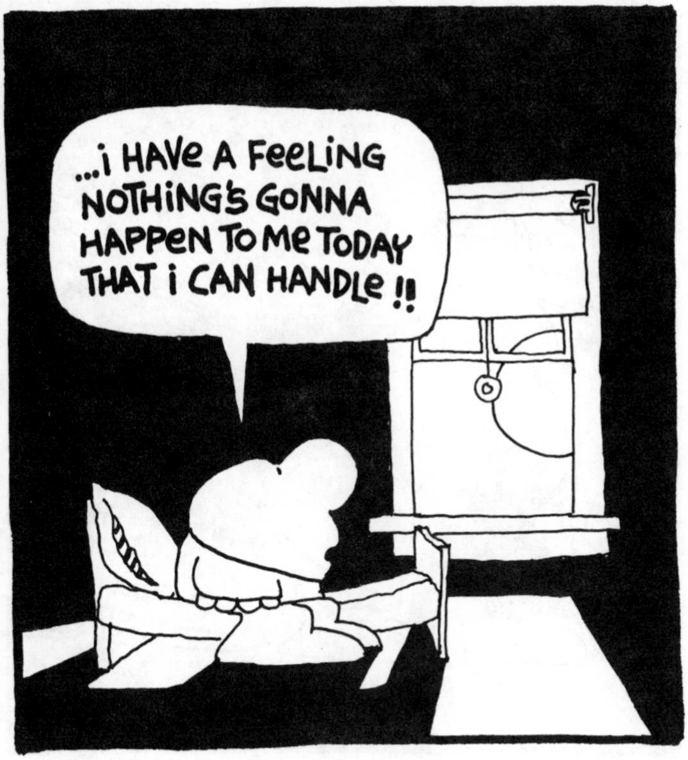
...I HAVE A FEELING NOTHING'S GONNA HAPPEN TO ME TODAY THAT I CAN HANDLE !!

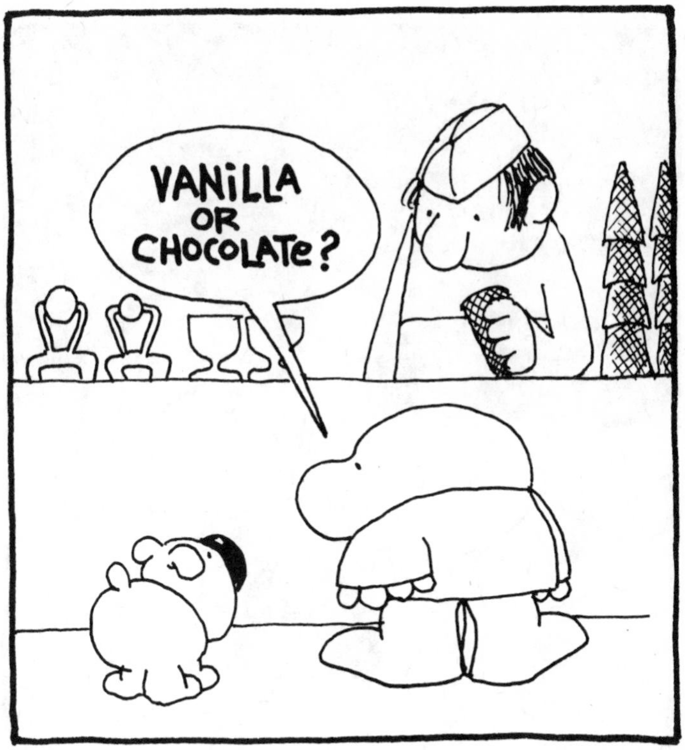
VANILLA OR CHOCOLATE?

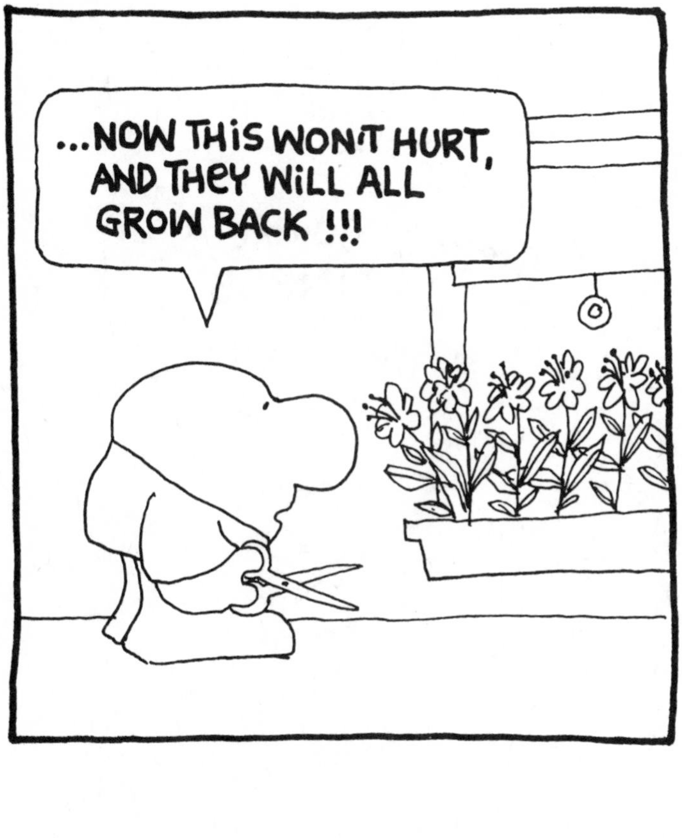
...NOW THIS WON'T HURT, AND THEY WILL ALL GROW BACK !!!

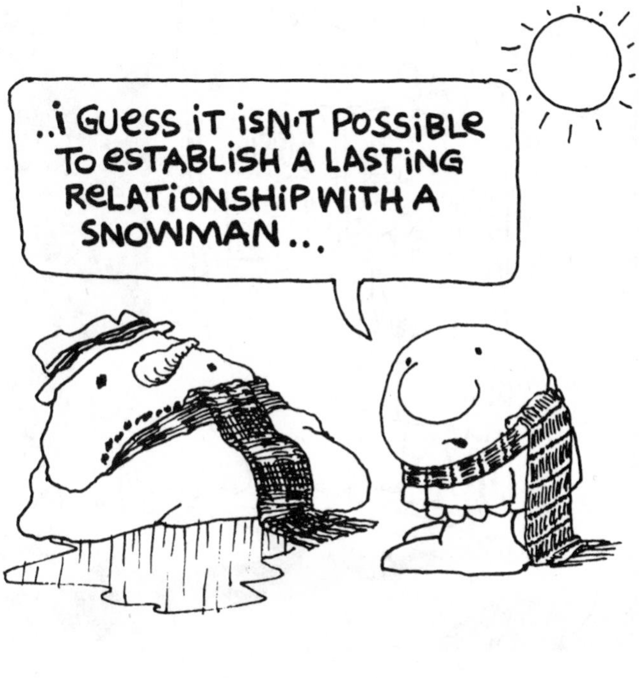
..I GUESS IT ISN'T POSSIBLE TO ESTABLISH A LASTING RELATIONSHIP WITH A SNOWMAN...

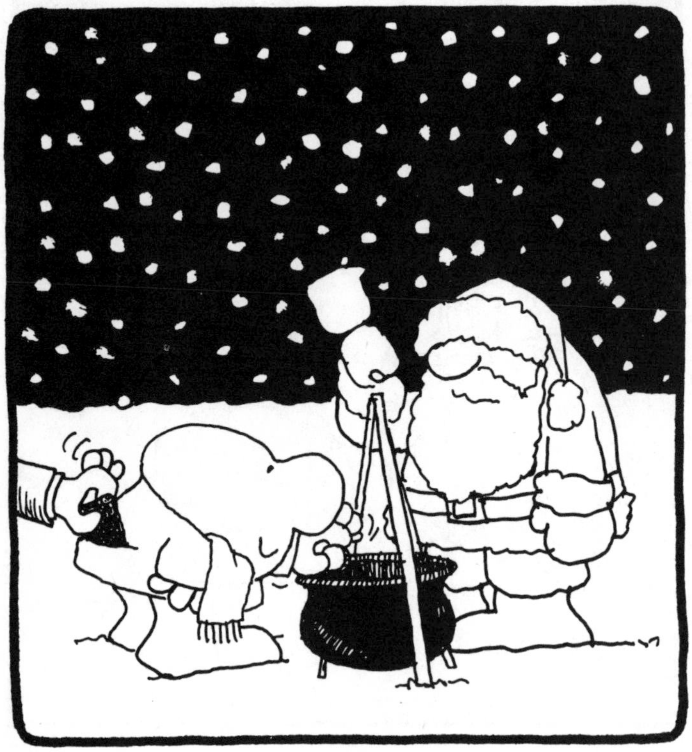

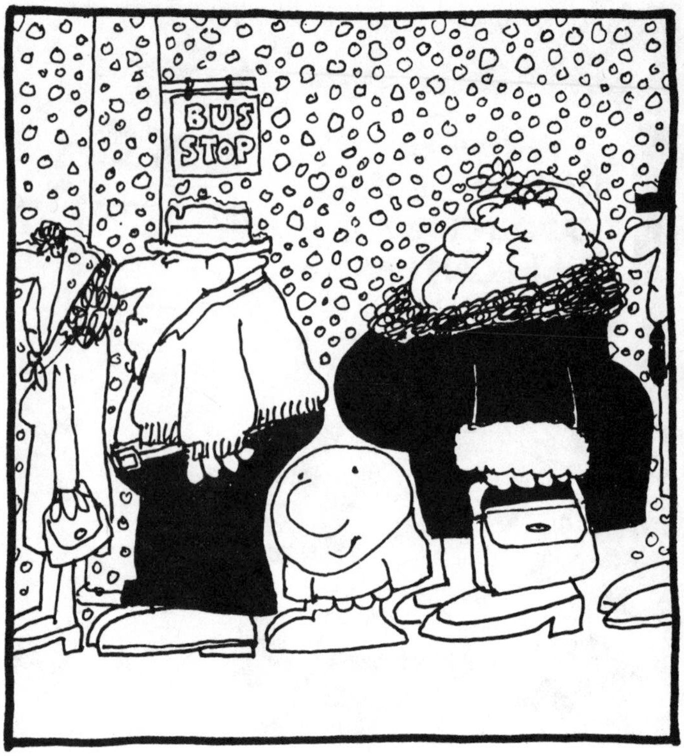
BUS STOP

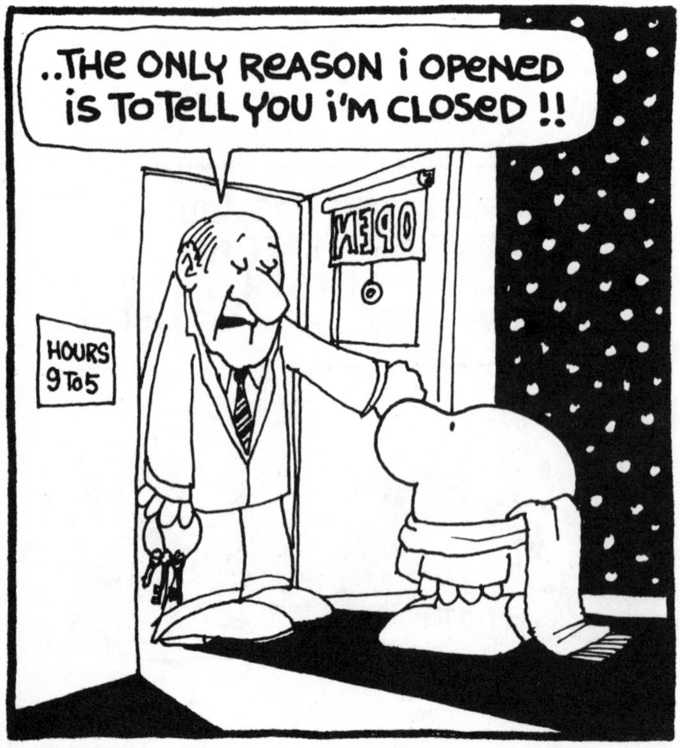
..THE ONLY REASON i OPENED is TO TELL YOU i'M CLOSED !!
HOURS 9 TO 5

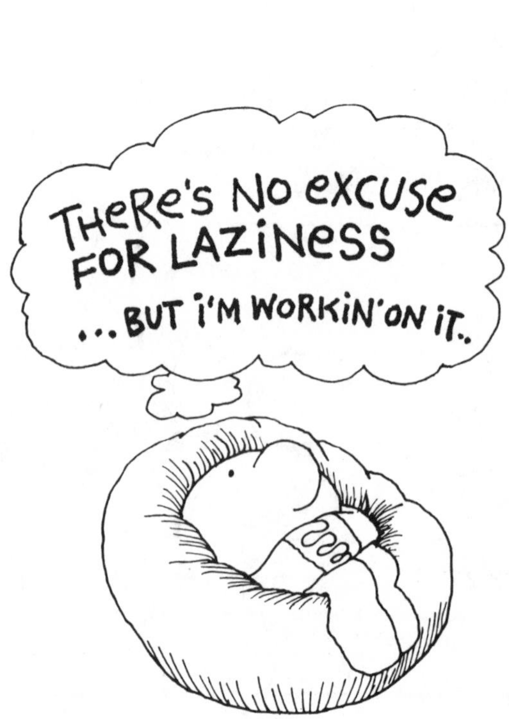
THERE'S NO EXCUSE FOR LAZINESS
... BUT i'M WORKiN' ON iT..

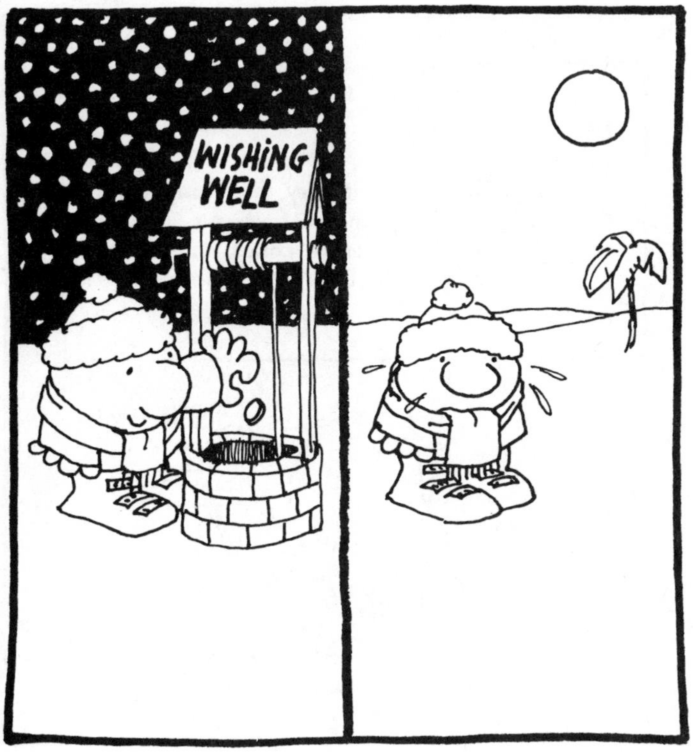
WISHING WELL

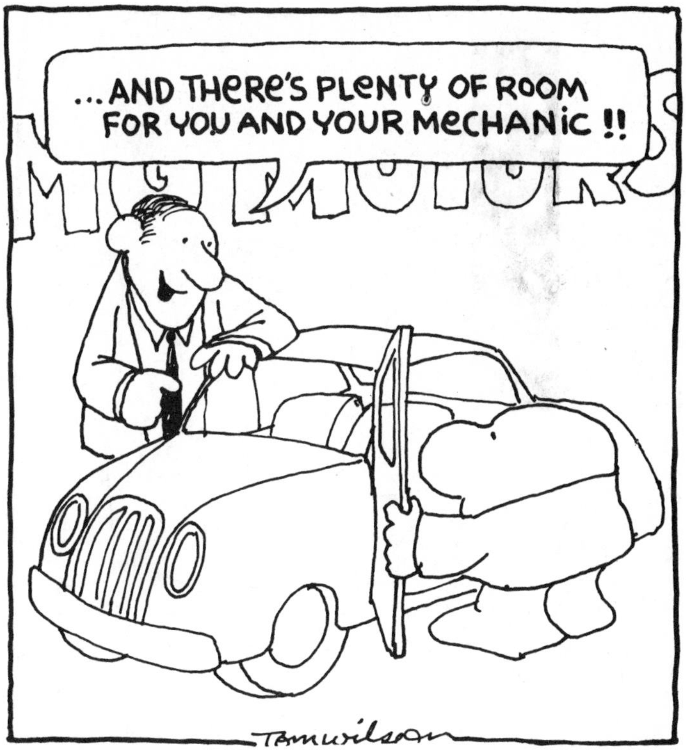
...AND THERE'S PLENTY OF ROOM FOR YOU AND YOUR MECHANIC !!

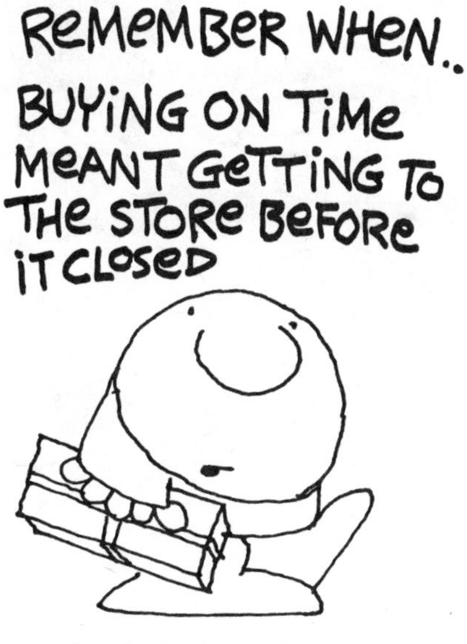
REMEMBER WHEN..
BUYING ON TIME MEANT GETTING TO THE STORE BEFORE IT CLOSED

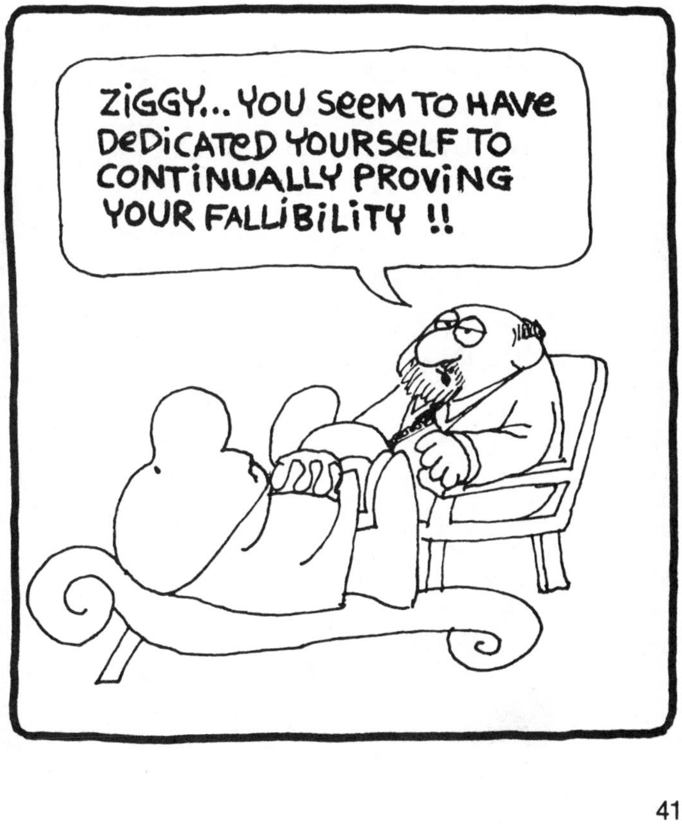
ZIGGY... YOU SEEM TO HAVE DEDICATED YOURSELF TO CONTINUALLY PROVING YOUR FALLIBILITY !!

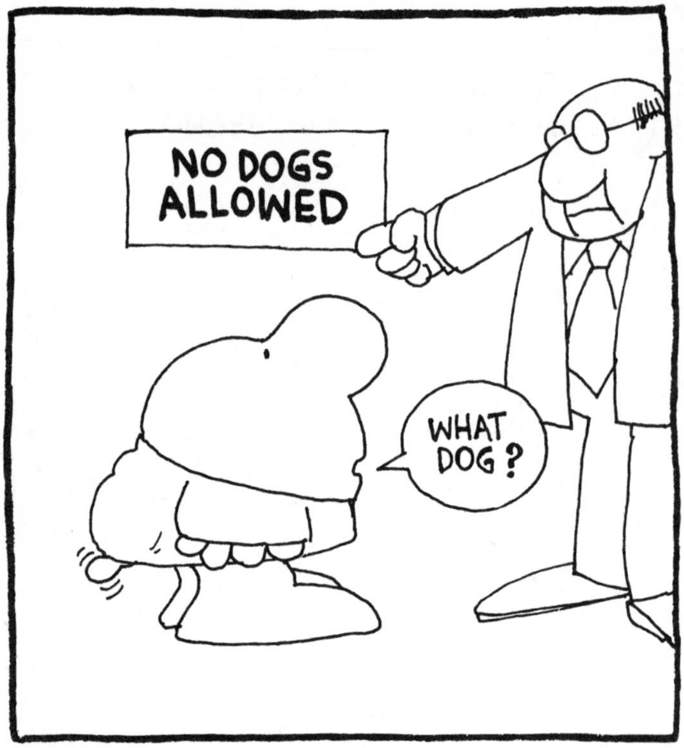
NO DOGS ALLOWED
WHAT DOG ?

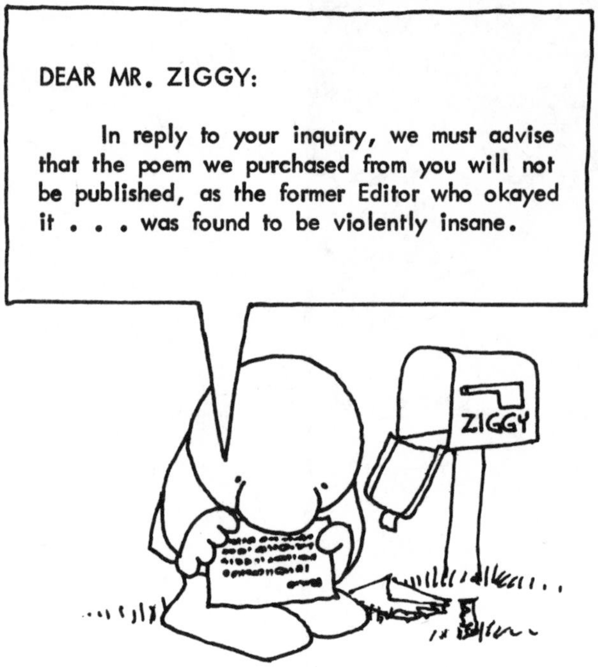
DEAR MR. ZIGGY:
In reply to your inquiry, we must advise that the poem we purchased from you will not be published, as the former Editor who okayed it . . . was found to be violently insane.
ZIGGY

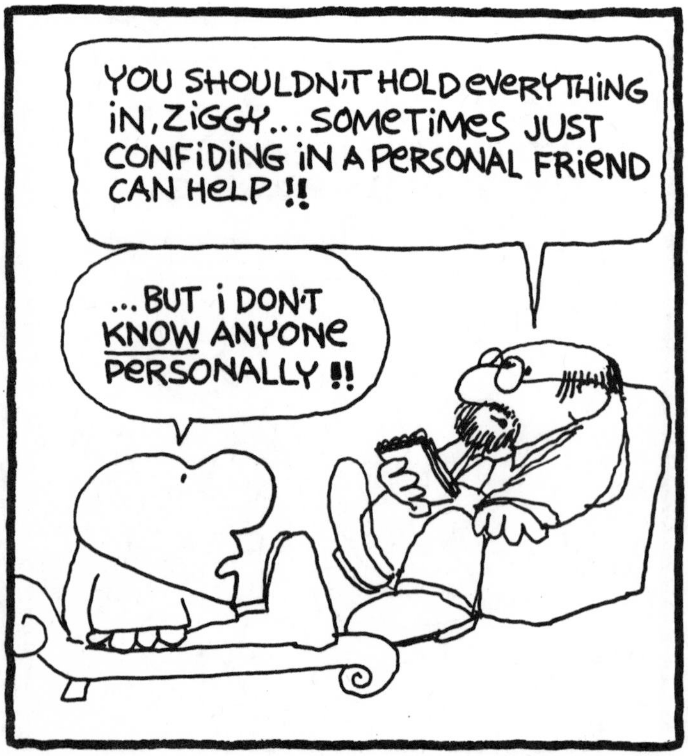
YOU SHOULDN'T HOLD EVERYTHING IN, ZIGGY... SOMETIMES JUST CONFIDING IN A PERSONAL FRIEND CAN HELP !!
...BUT I DON'T KNOW ANYONE PERSONALLY !!

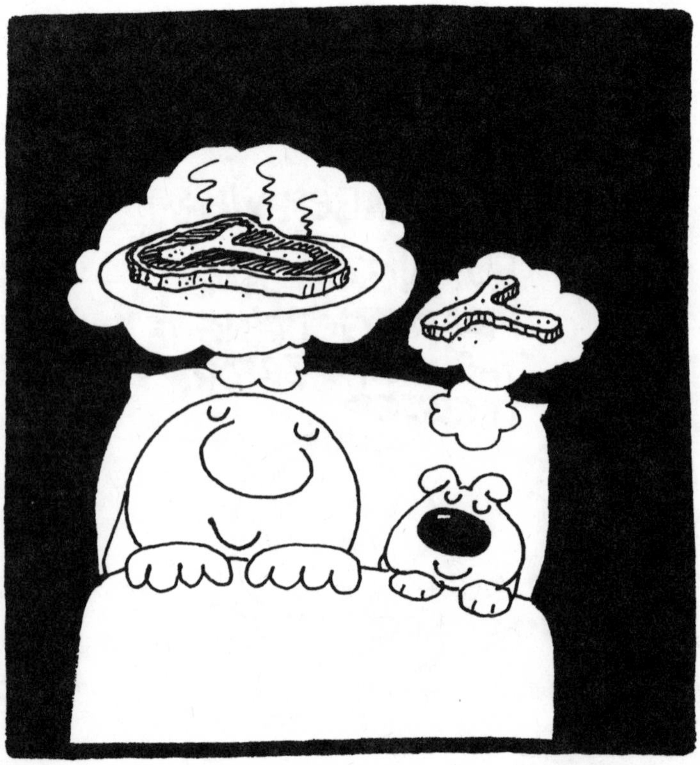

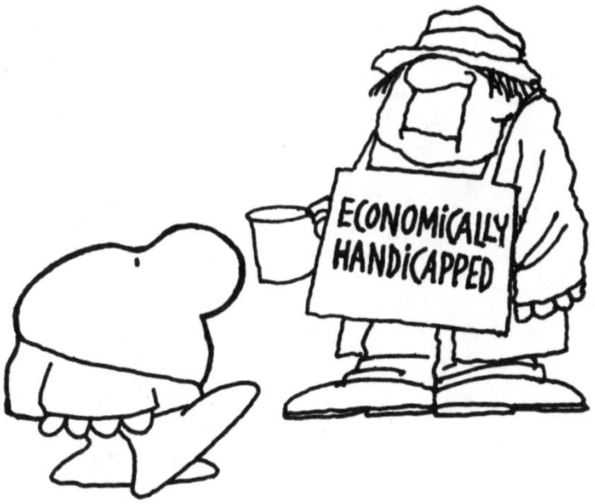
ECONOMICALLY HANDICAPPED

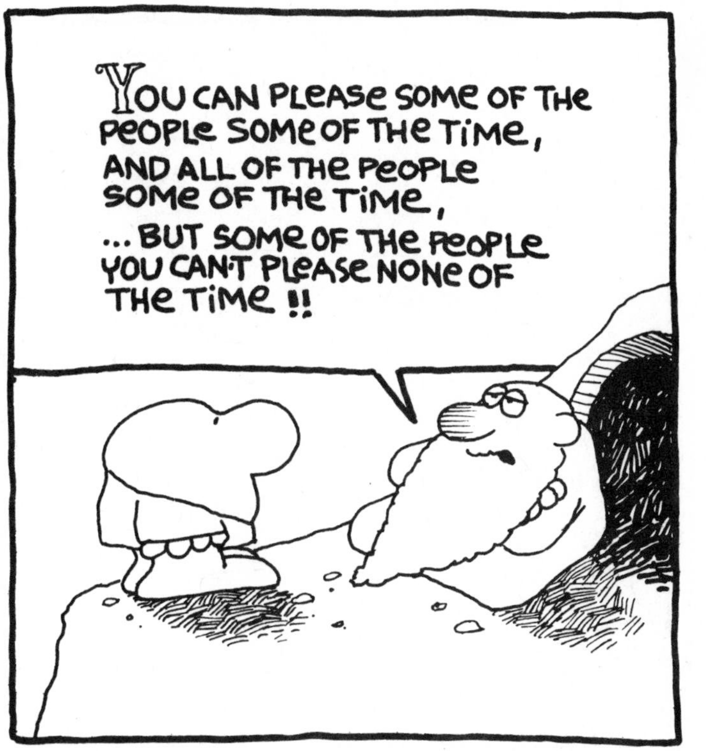
YOU CAN PLEASE SOME OF THE PEOPLE SOME OF THE TIME, AND ALL OF THE PEOPLE SOME OF THE TIME, ... BUT SOME OF THE PEOPLE YOU CAN'T PLEASE NONE OF THE TIME !!

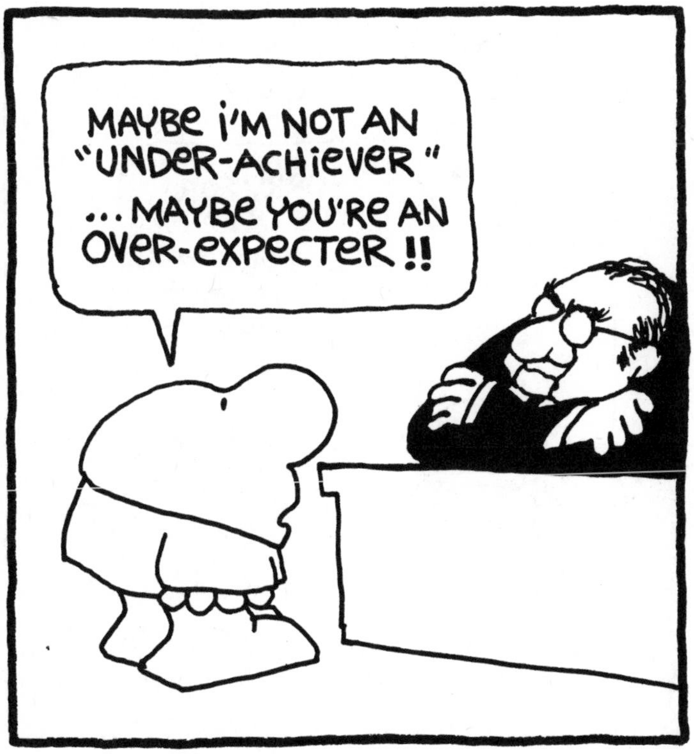
MAYBE I'M NOT AN "UNDER-ACHIEVER" ... MAYBE YOU'RE AN OVER-EXPECTER !!

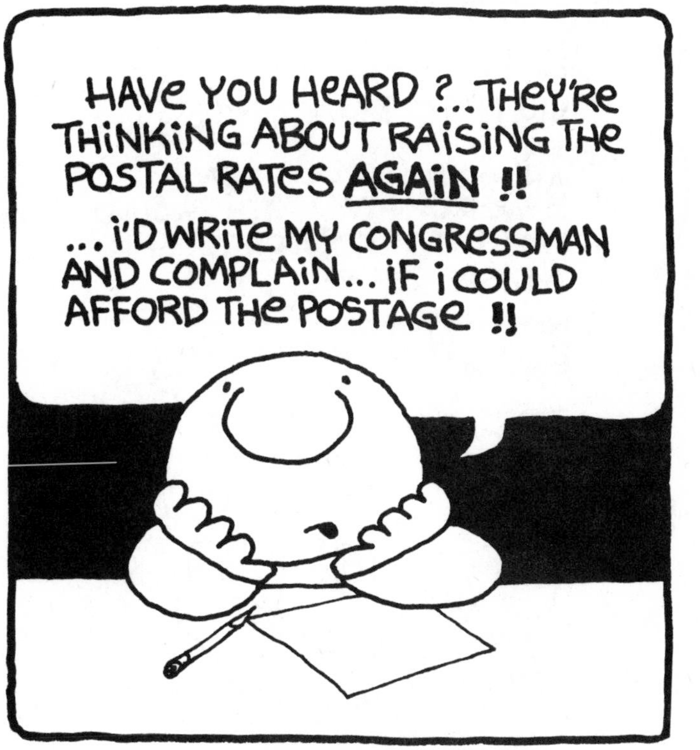
HAVE YOU HEARD ?.. THEY'RE THINKING ABOUT RAISING THE POSTAL RATES AGAIN !! ... I'D WRITE MY CONGRESSMAN AND COMPLAIN... IF I COULD AFFORD THE POSTAGE !!

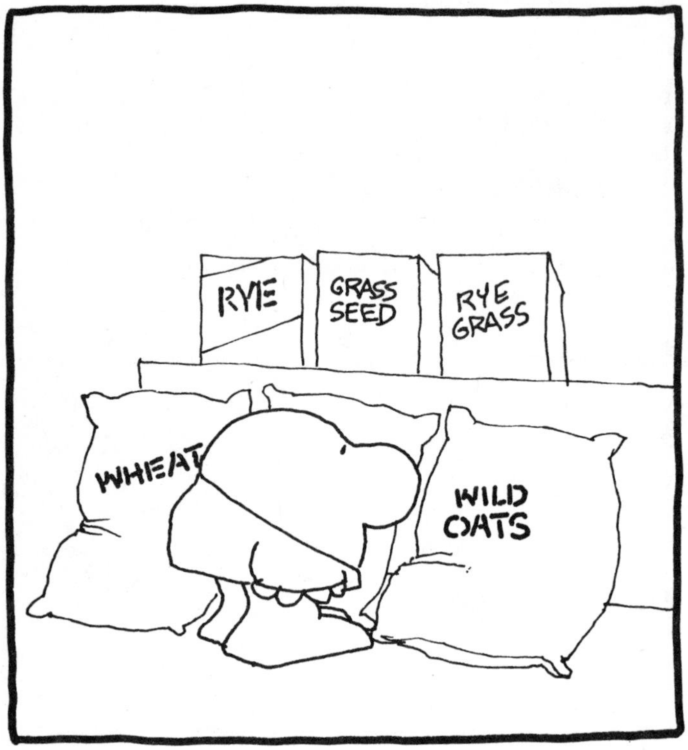
RYE
GRASS SEED
RYE GRASS
WHEAT
WILD OATS

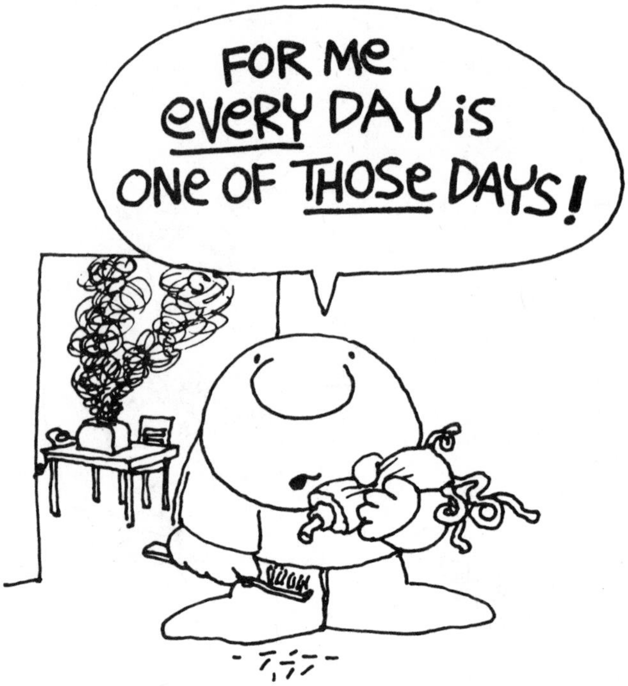
FOR ME EVERY DAY IS ONE OF THOSE DAYS!

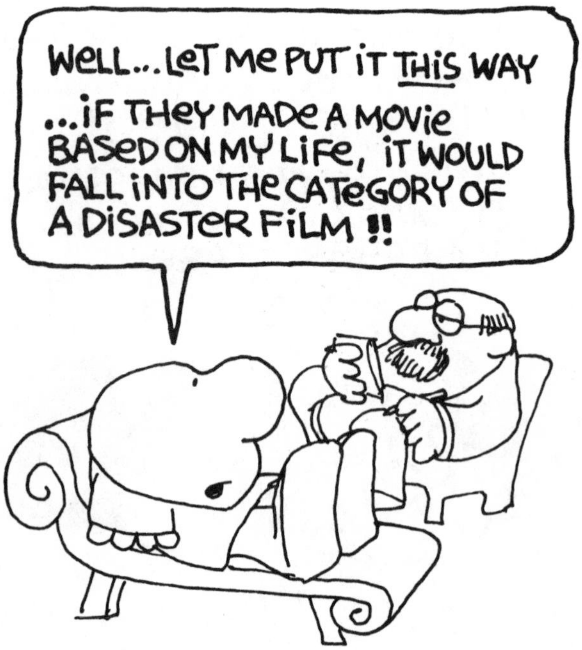
WELL...LET ME PUT IT THIS WAY ...IF THEY MADE A MOVIE BASED ON MY LIFE, IT WOULD FALL INTO THE CATEGORY OF A DISASTER FILM !!

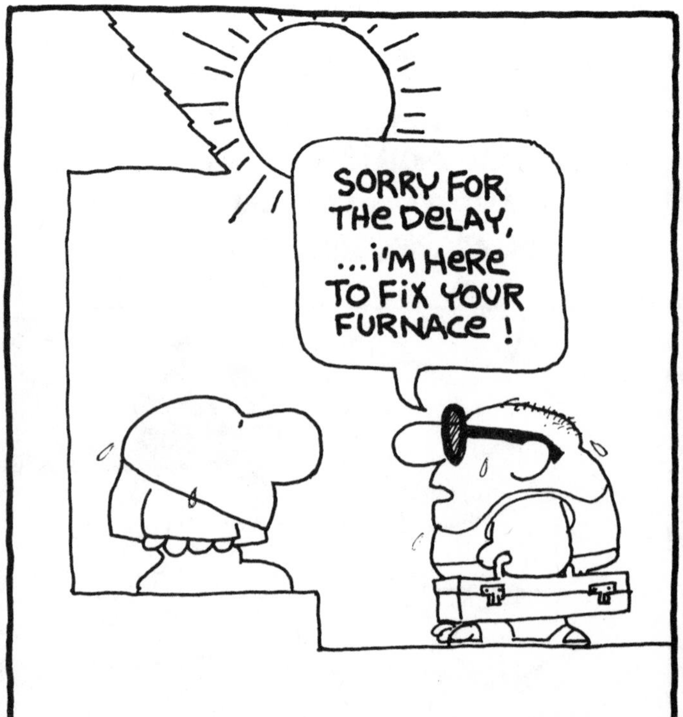
SORRY FOR THE DELAY, ...I'M HERE TO FIX YOUR FURNACE !

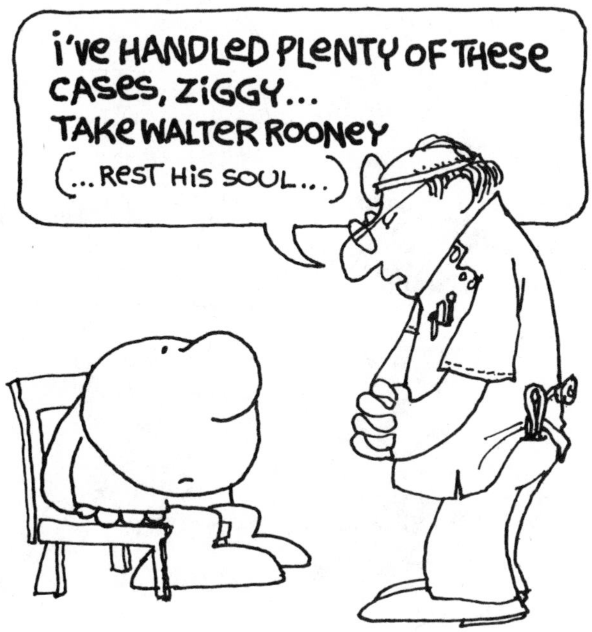
i've HANDLED PLENTY OF THESE CASES, ZIGGY... TAKE WALTER ROONEY
(...REST HIS SOUL...)

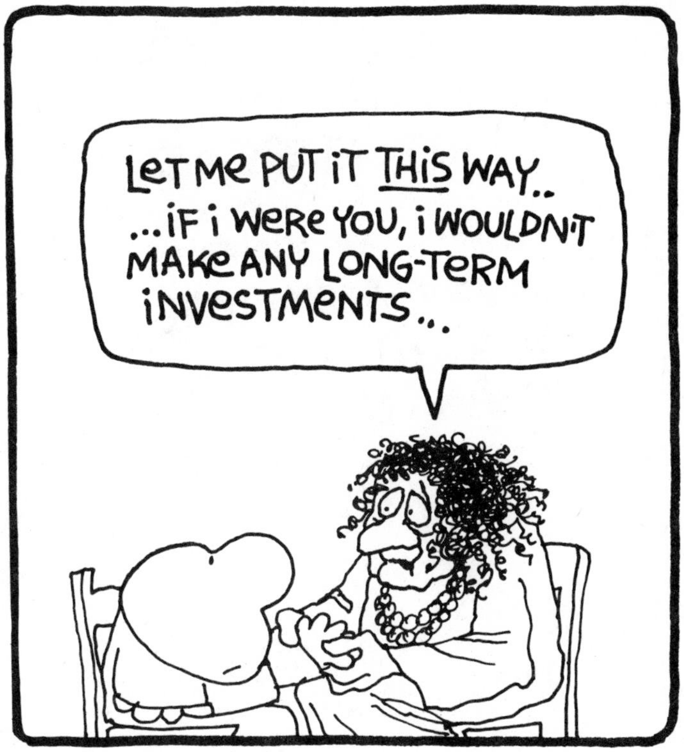
LET ME PUT IT THIS WAY.. ...IF i WERE YOU, i WOULDN'T MAKE ANY LONG-TERM iNVESTMENTS...

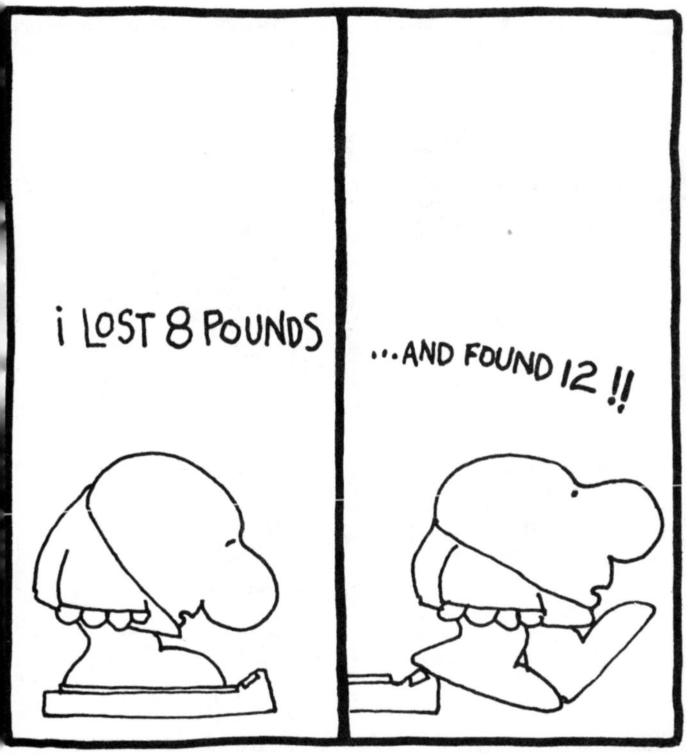
i LOST 8 POUNDS
...AND FOUND 12 !!

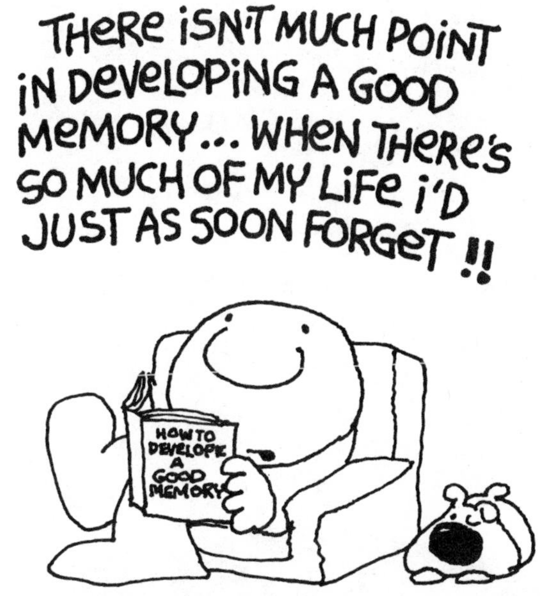
THERE iSN'T MUCH POINT iN DEVELOPiNG A GOOD MEMORY... WHEN THERE'S SO MUCH OF MY LIFE i'D JUST AS SOON FORGET !!
HOW TO DEVELOPE A GOOD MEMORY

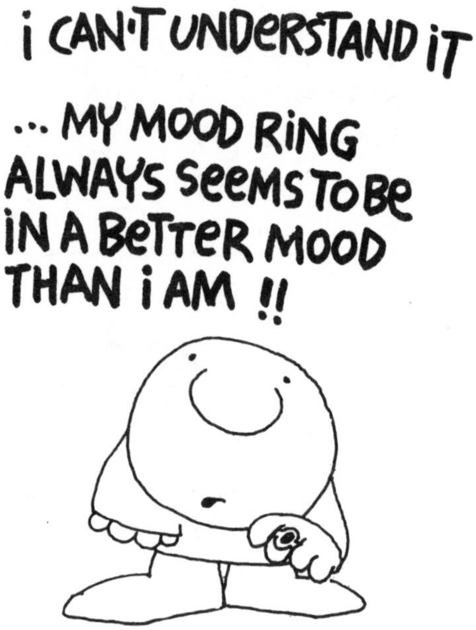
i CAN'T UNDERSTAND iT
... MY MOOD RiNG ALWAYS SeeMS TO Be iN A BeTTeR MOOD THAN i AM !!

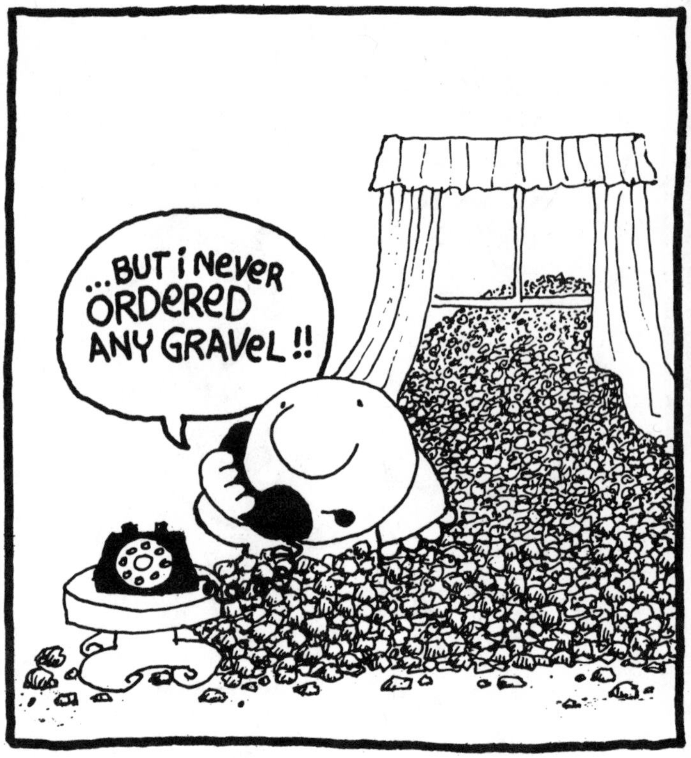
...BUT i NeVeR ORDeReD ANY GRAVeL !!

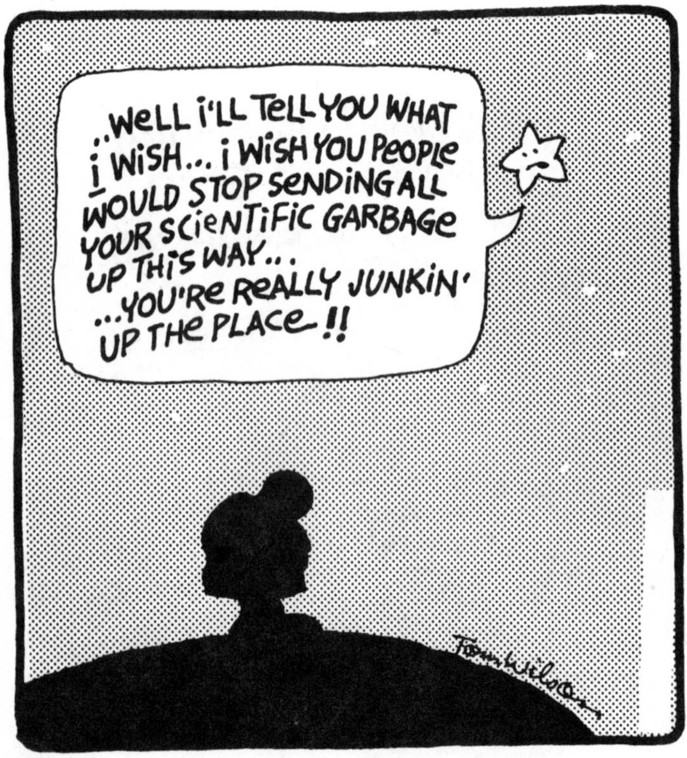
..WeLL i'LL TeLL YOU WHAT i WiSH... i WiSH YOU PeOPLe WOULD STOP SeNDiNG ALL YOUR SCieNTiFiC GARBAGe UP THiS WAY...
...YOU'Re ReALLY JUNKiN' UP THe PLACe !!

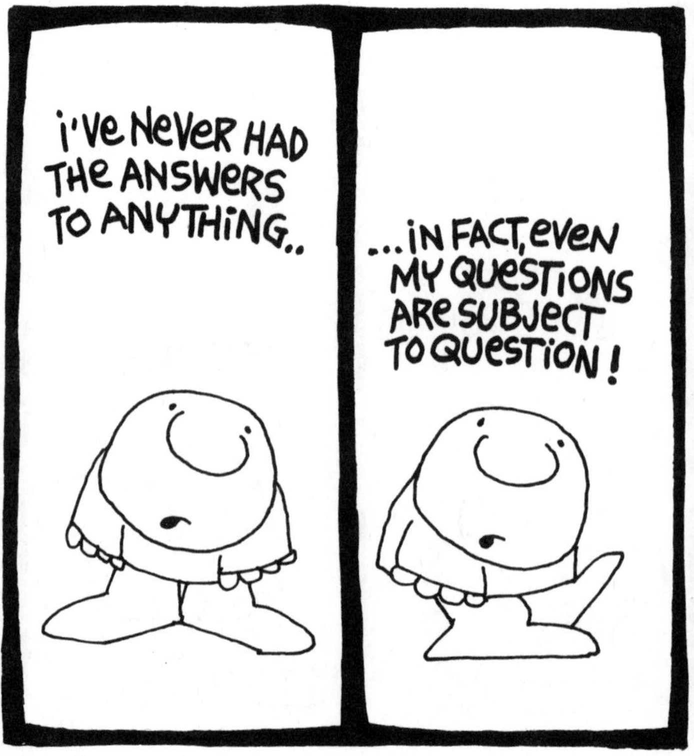
i'Ve NeVeR HAD THe ANSWeRS TO ANYTHiNG..
...iN FACT, eVeN MY QUeSTiONS ARe SUBJeCT TO QUeSTiON !

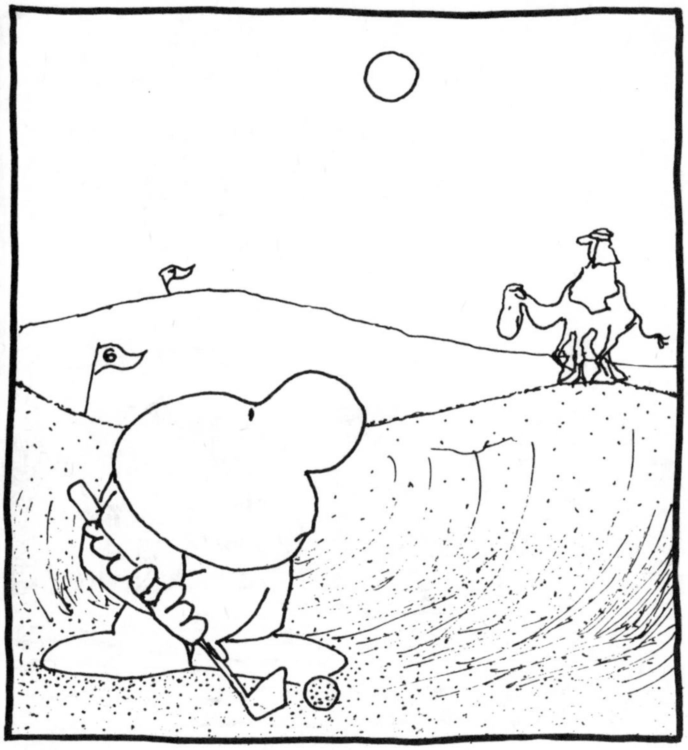

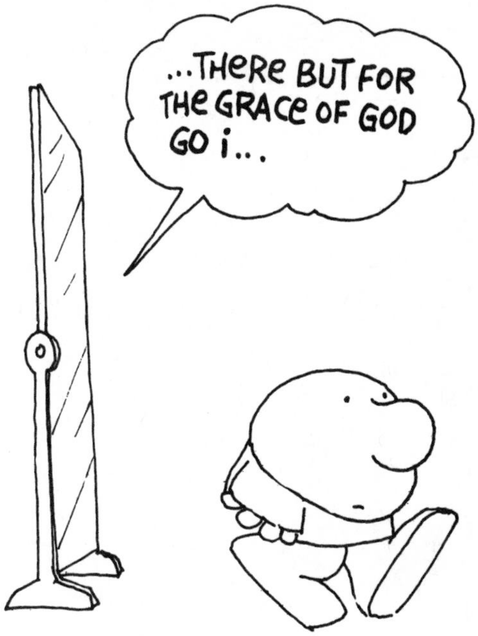
...THERE BUT FOR THE GRACE OF GOD GO i...

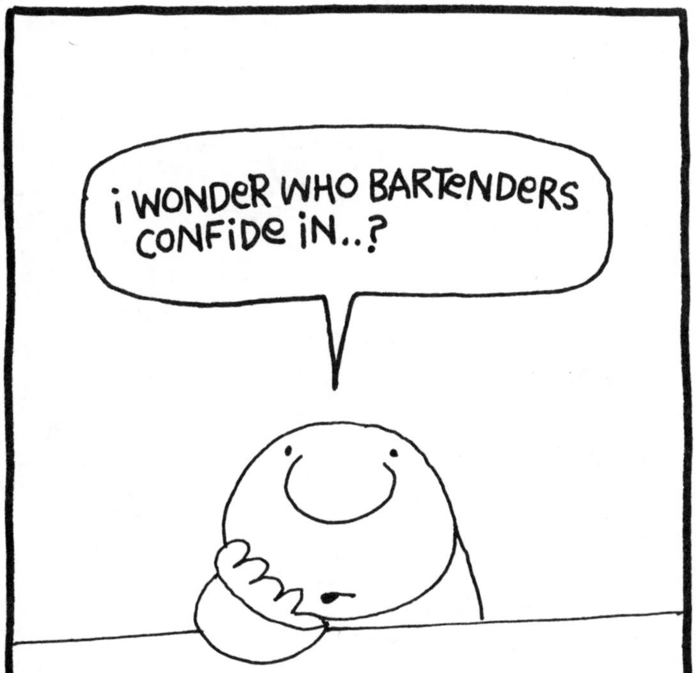
i WONDER WHO BARTENDERS CONFIDE IN..?

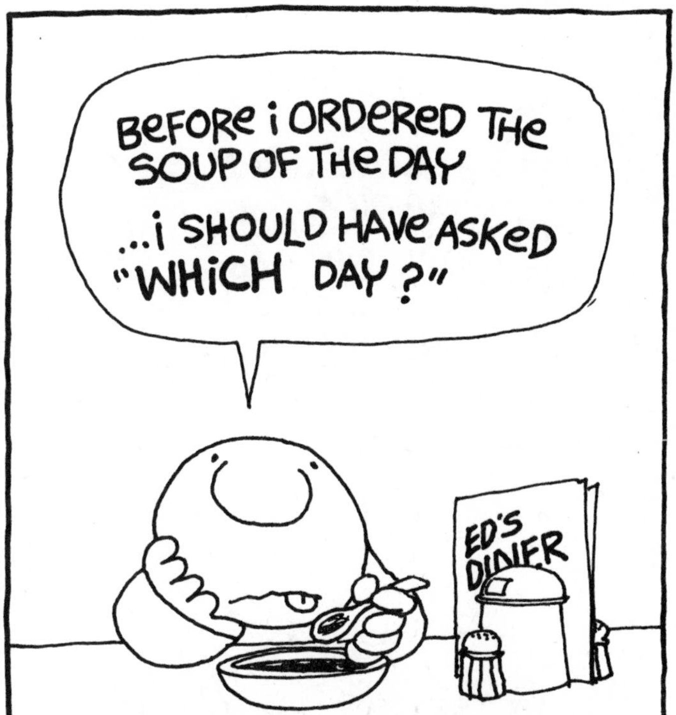
BEFORE i ORDERED THE SOUP OF THE DAY
...i SHOULD HAVE ASKED "WHICH DAY?"
ED'S DINER
TOM WILSON

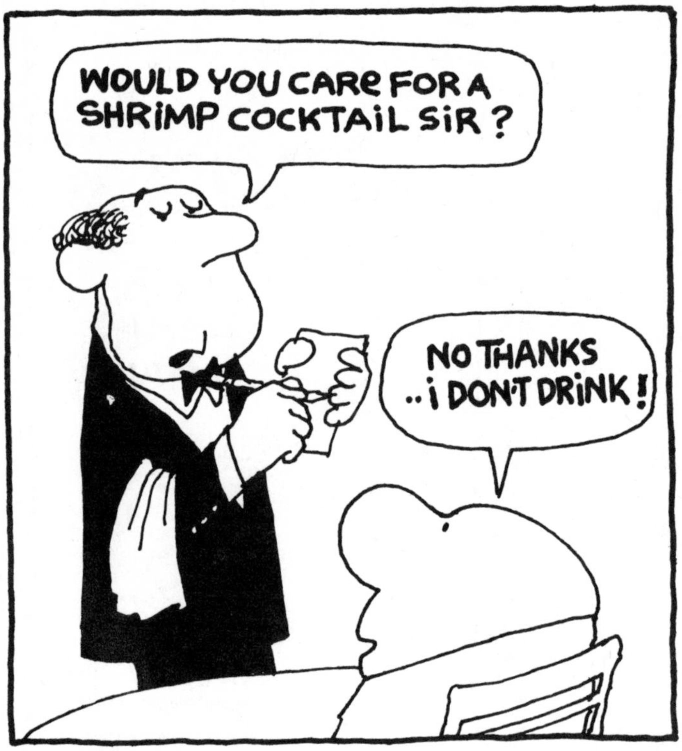
WOULD YOU CARE FOR A SHRIMP COCKTAIL SIR ?
NO THANKS ..i DON'T DRINK !

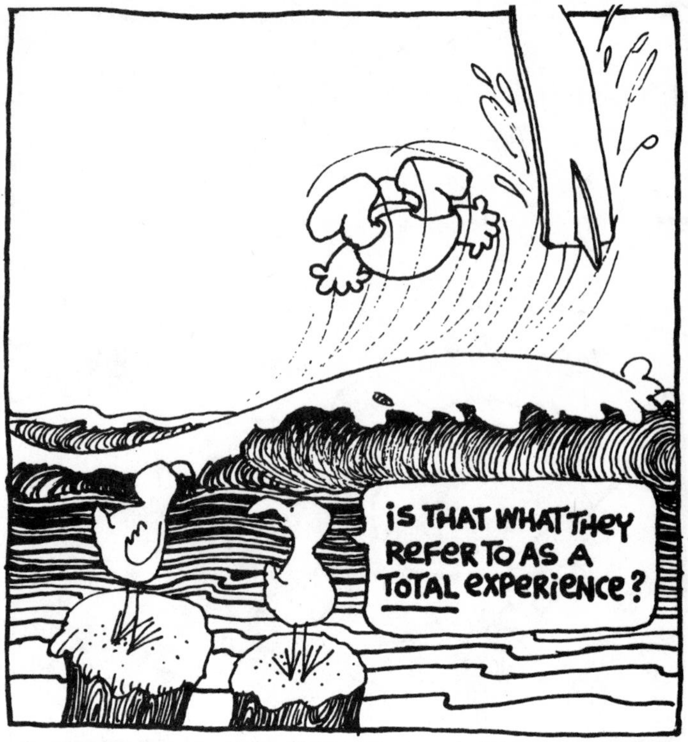
iS THAT WHAT THEY REFER TO AS A TOTAL experience ?

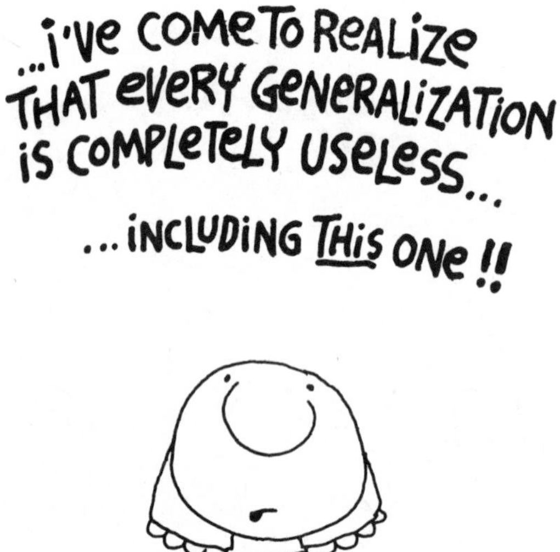
...i've COME TO REALIZE THAT every GENERALIZATION iS COMPLETELY USELESS...
...INCLUDING THIS ONE !!

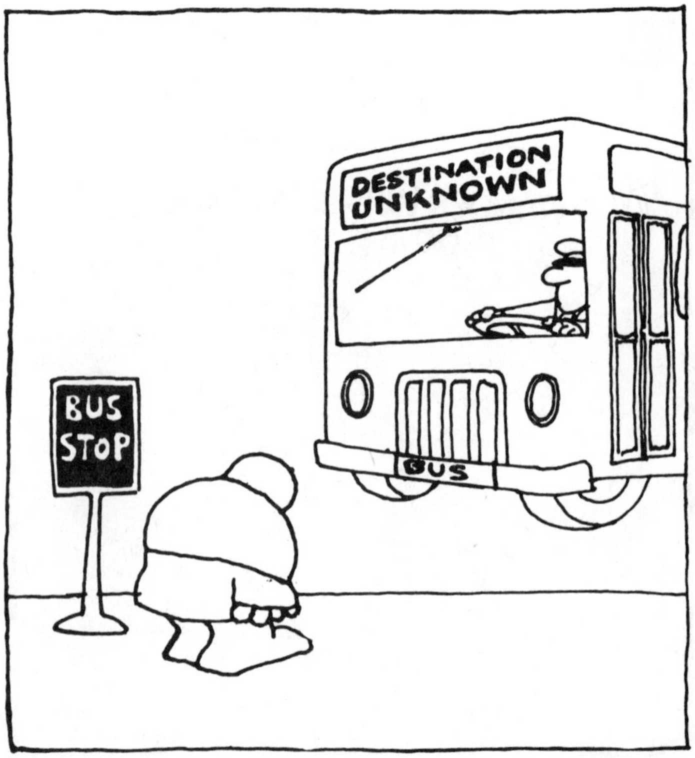
DESTINATION UNKNOWN
BUS STOP
BUS

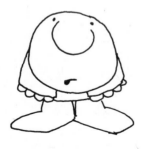

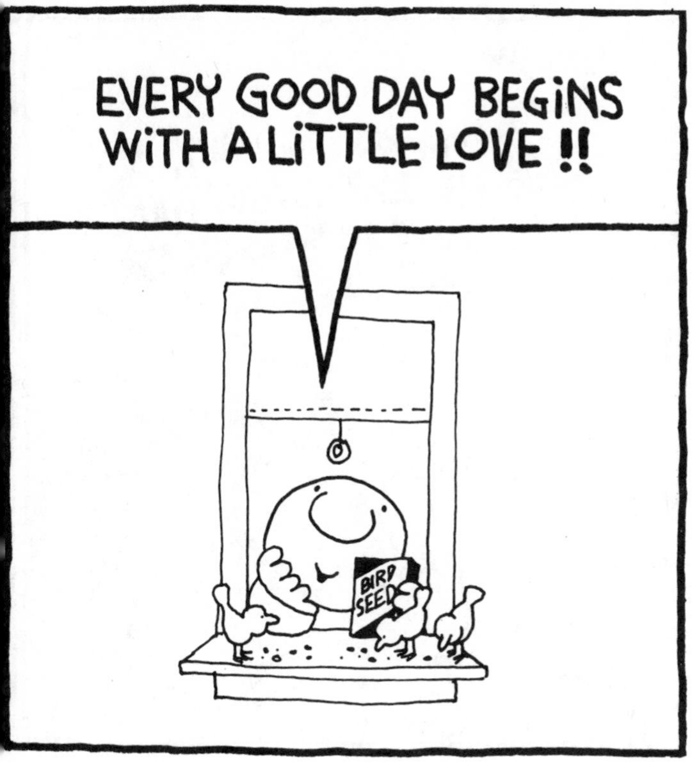
EVERY GOOD DAY BEGINS WITH A LITTLE LOVE !!
BIRD SEED

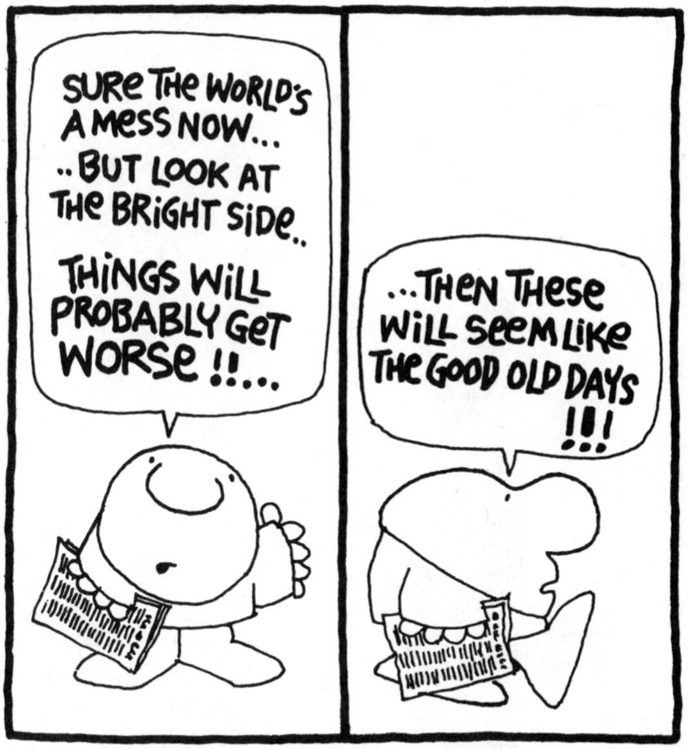
SURE THE WORLD'S A MESS NOW... ..BUT LOOK AT THE BRIGHT SIDE..
THINGS WILL PROBABLY GET WORSE !!...
...THEN THESE WILL SEEM LIKE THE GOOD OLD DAYS !!!

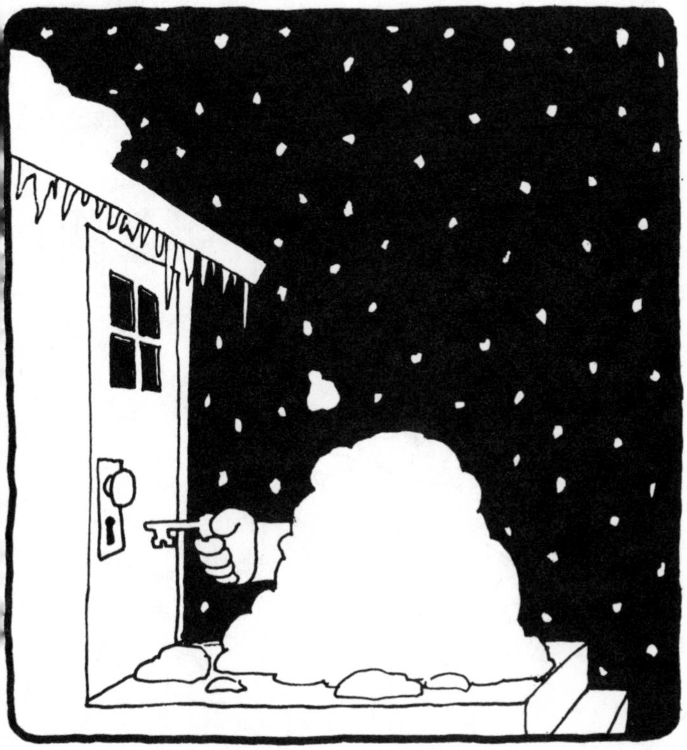

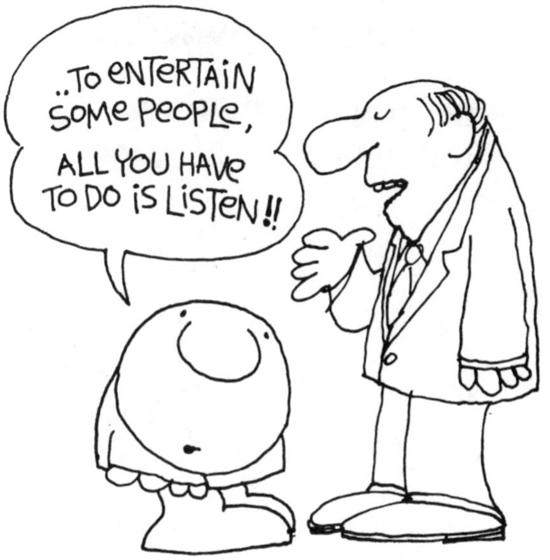
..TO ENTERTAIN SOME PEOPLE,
ALL YOU HAVE TO DO IS LISTEN !!

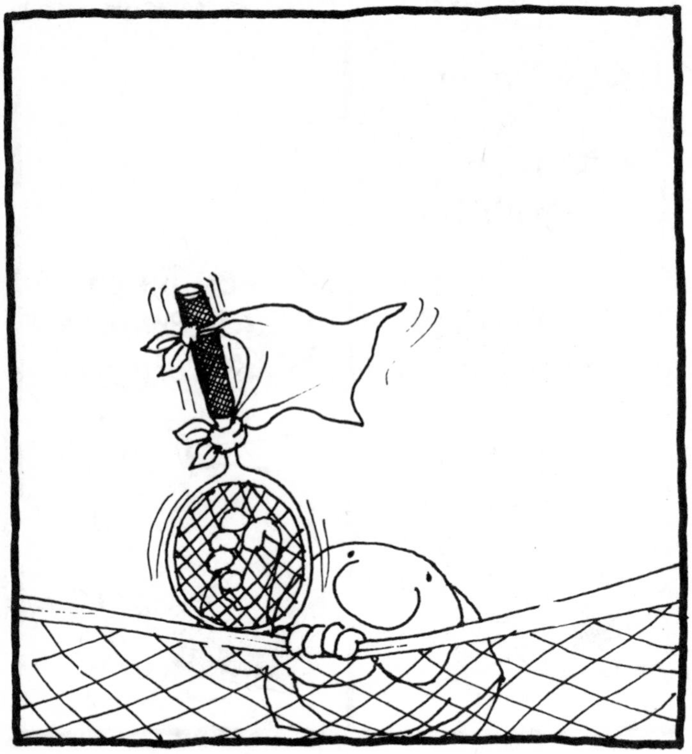

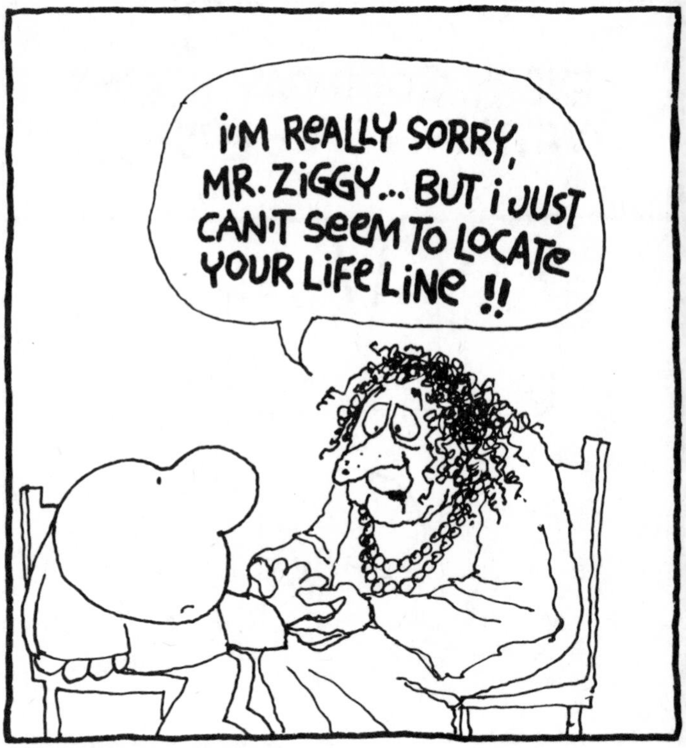
I'M REALLY SORRY, MR. ZIGGY... BUT I JUST CAN'T SEEM TO LOCATE YOUR LIFE LINE !!

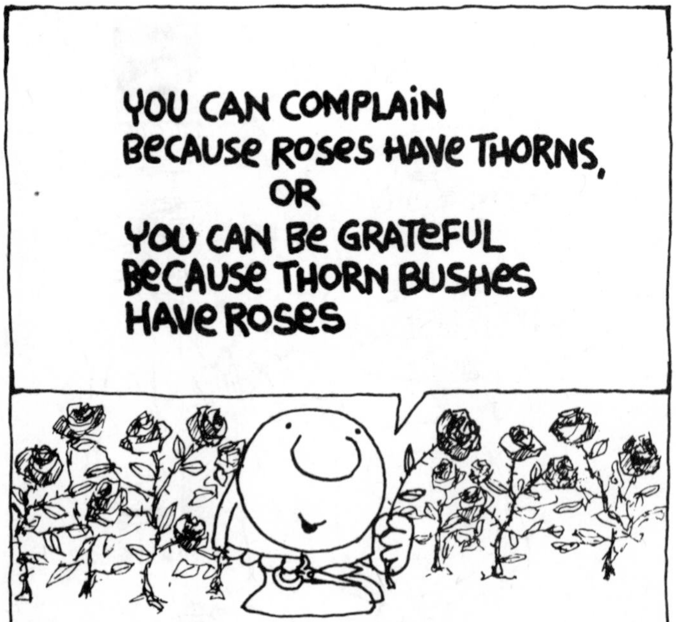
YOU CAN COMPLAIN
BECAUSE ROSES HAVE THORNS,
OR
YOU CAN BE GRATEFUL
BECAUSE THORN BUSHES
HAVE ROSES
tom wilson

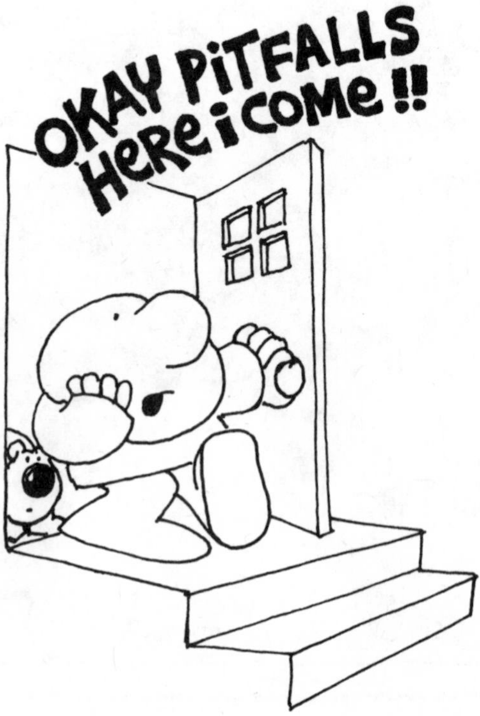
OKAY PITFALLS
HERE I COME !!

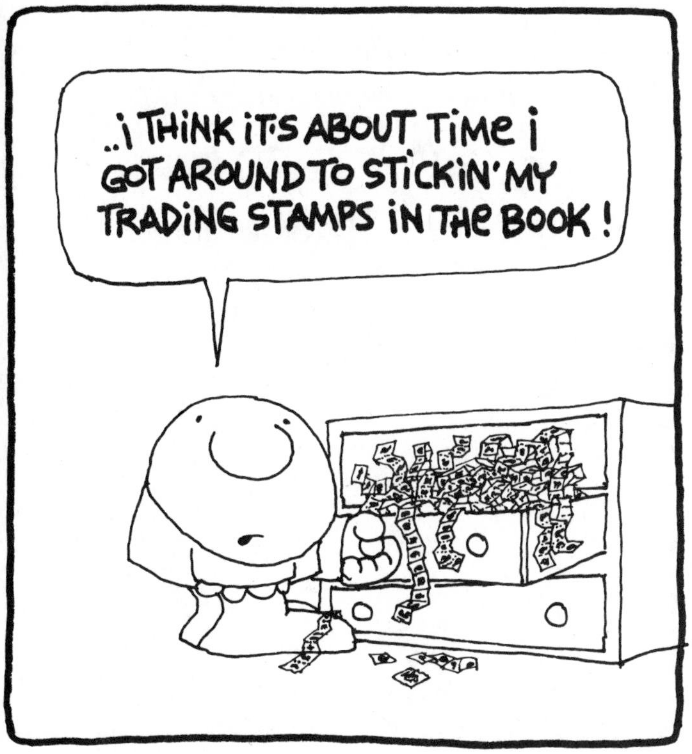
..i THINK iT'S ABOUT TiMe i GOT AROUND TO STiCKiN' MY TRADiNG STAMPS iN THe BOOK !

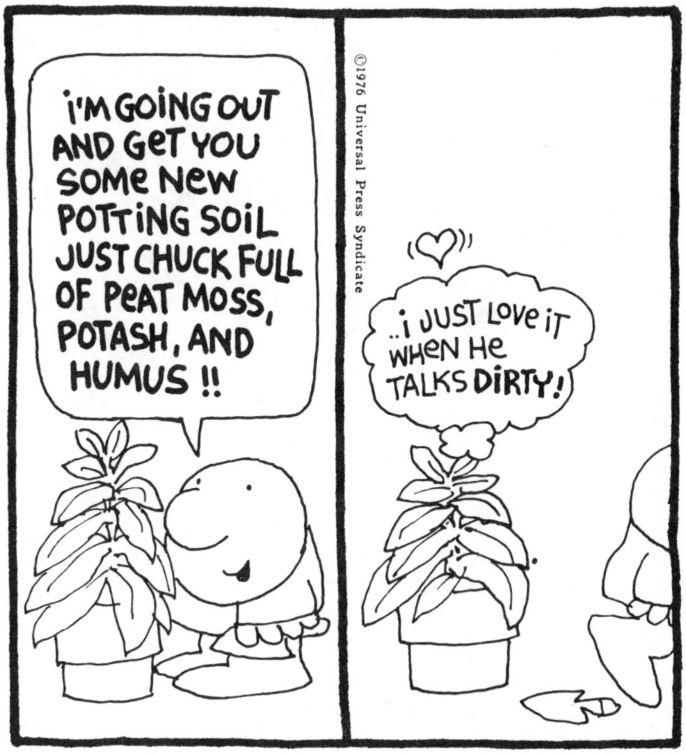
i'M GOiNG OUT AND GeT YOU SOMe NeW POTTiNG SOiL JUST CHUCK FULL OF PeAT MOSS, POTASH, AND HUMUS !!
©1976 Universal Press Syndicate
..i JUST LoVe iT WHeN He TALKS DiRTY!

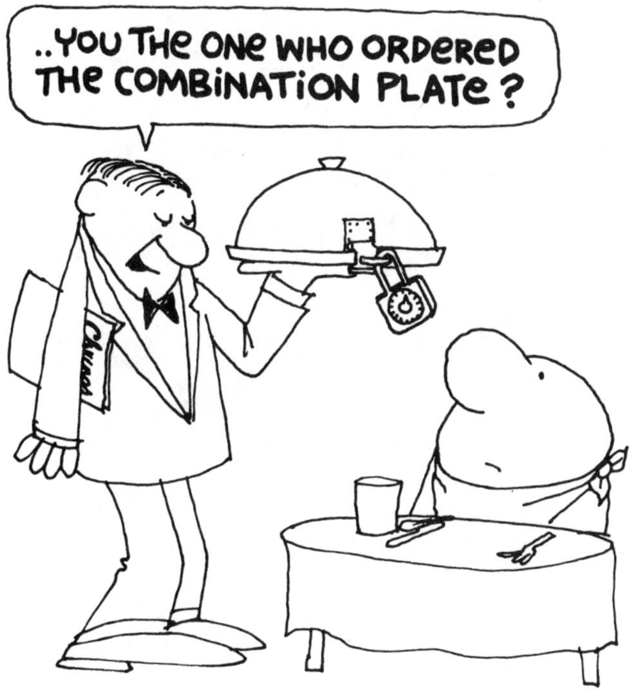
..YOU THe ONe WHO ORDeReD THe COMBiNATiON PLATe ?

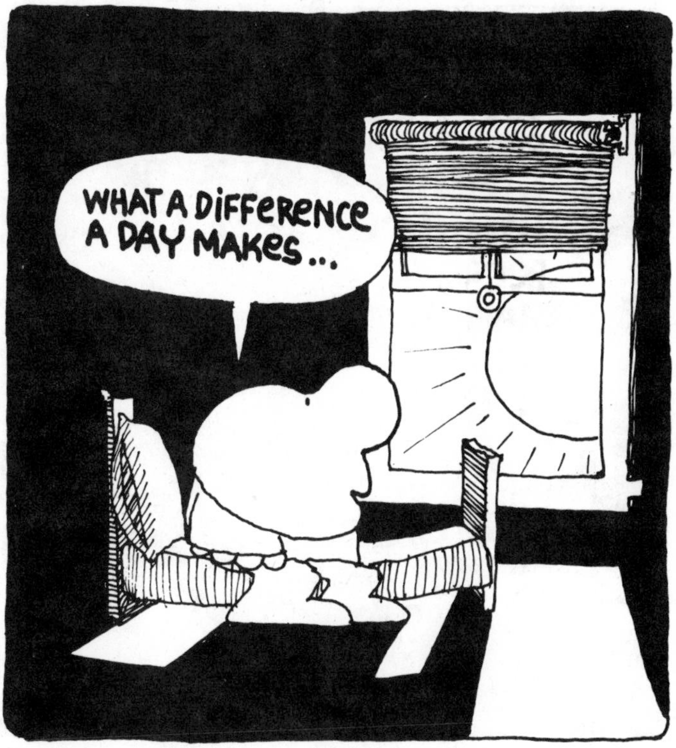
WHAT A DiFFeReNCe A DAY MAKeS...

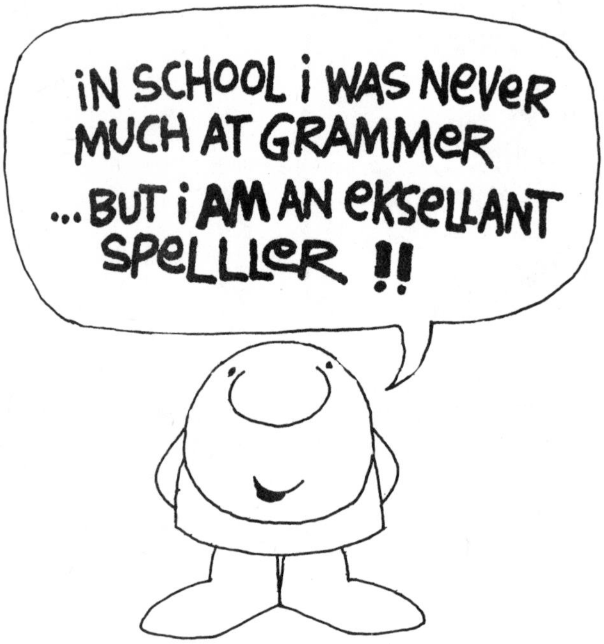
IN SCHOOL I WAS NEVER MUCH AT GRAMMER ...BUT I AM AN EKSELLANT SPELLLER !!

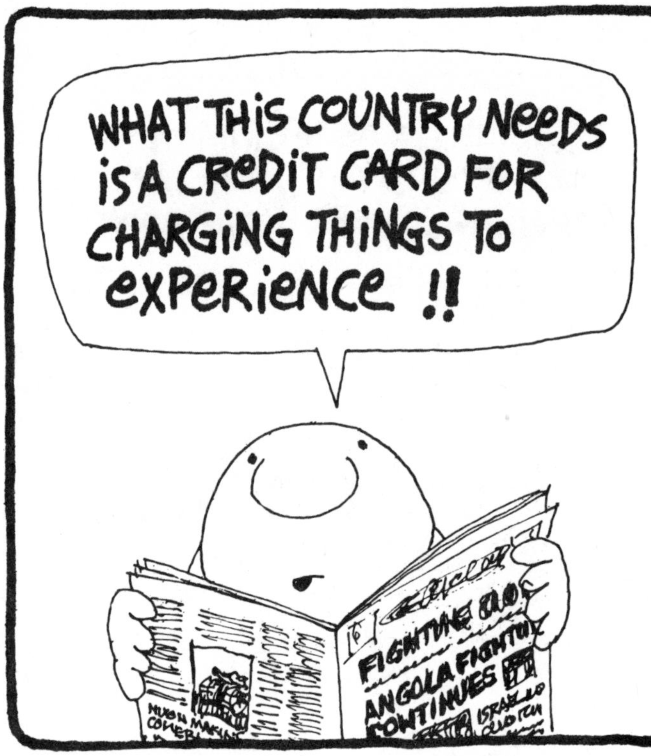
WHAT THIS COUNTRY NEEDS IS A CREDIT CARD FOR CHARGING THINGS TO EXPERIENCE !!

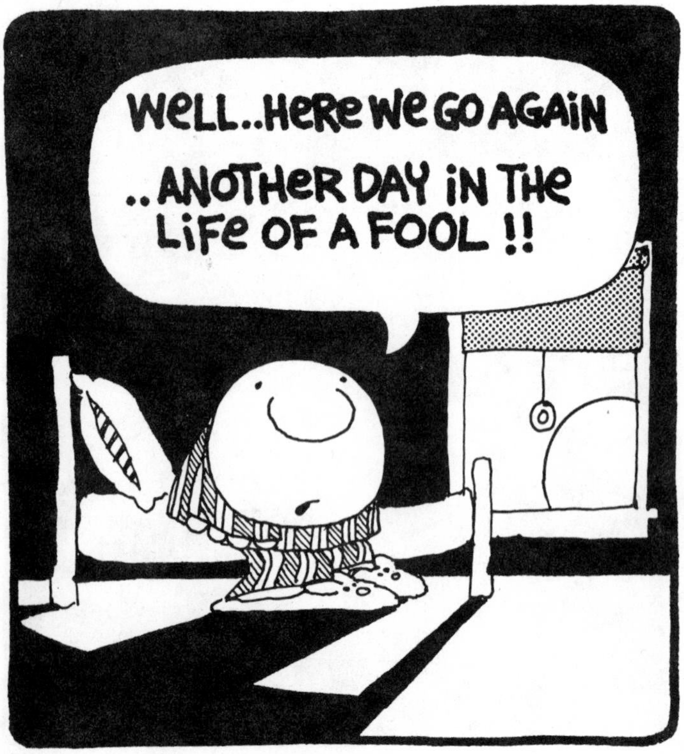
WELL..HERE WE GO AGAIN ..ANOTHER DAY IN THE LIFE OF A FOOL !!

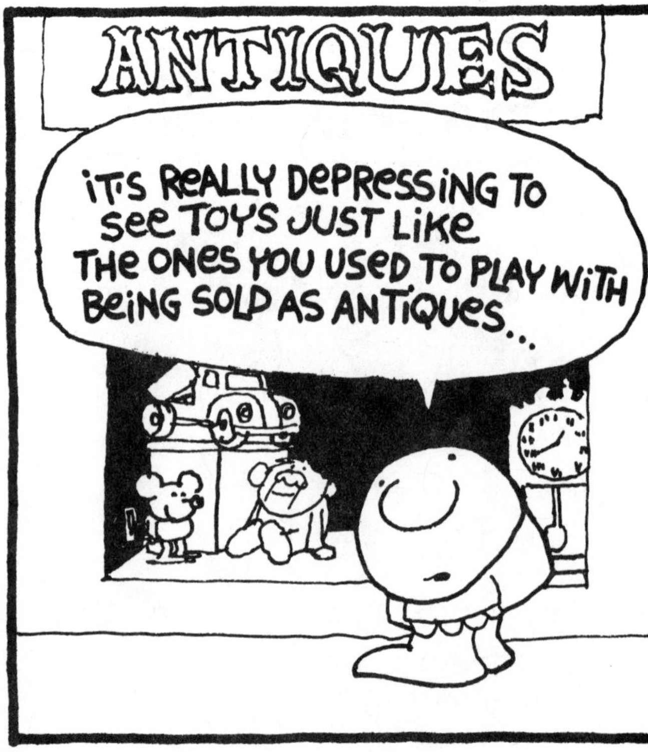
ANTIQUES
IT'S REALLY DEPRESSING TO SEE TOYS JUST LIKE THE ONES YOU USED TO PLAY WITH BEING SOLD AS ANTIQUES...

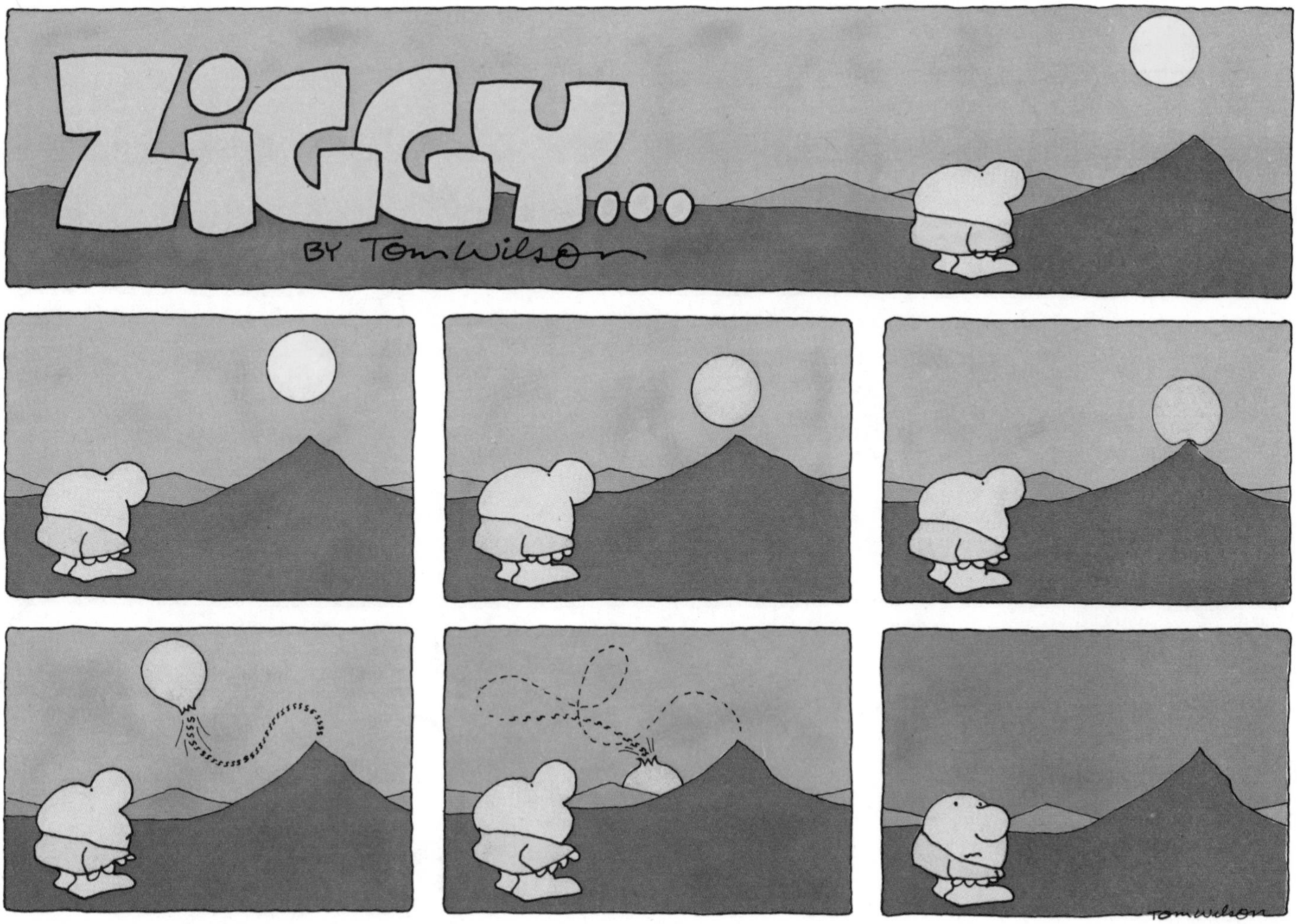
ZiGGY...
BY Tom Wilson
Tom Wilson

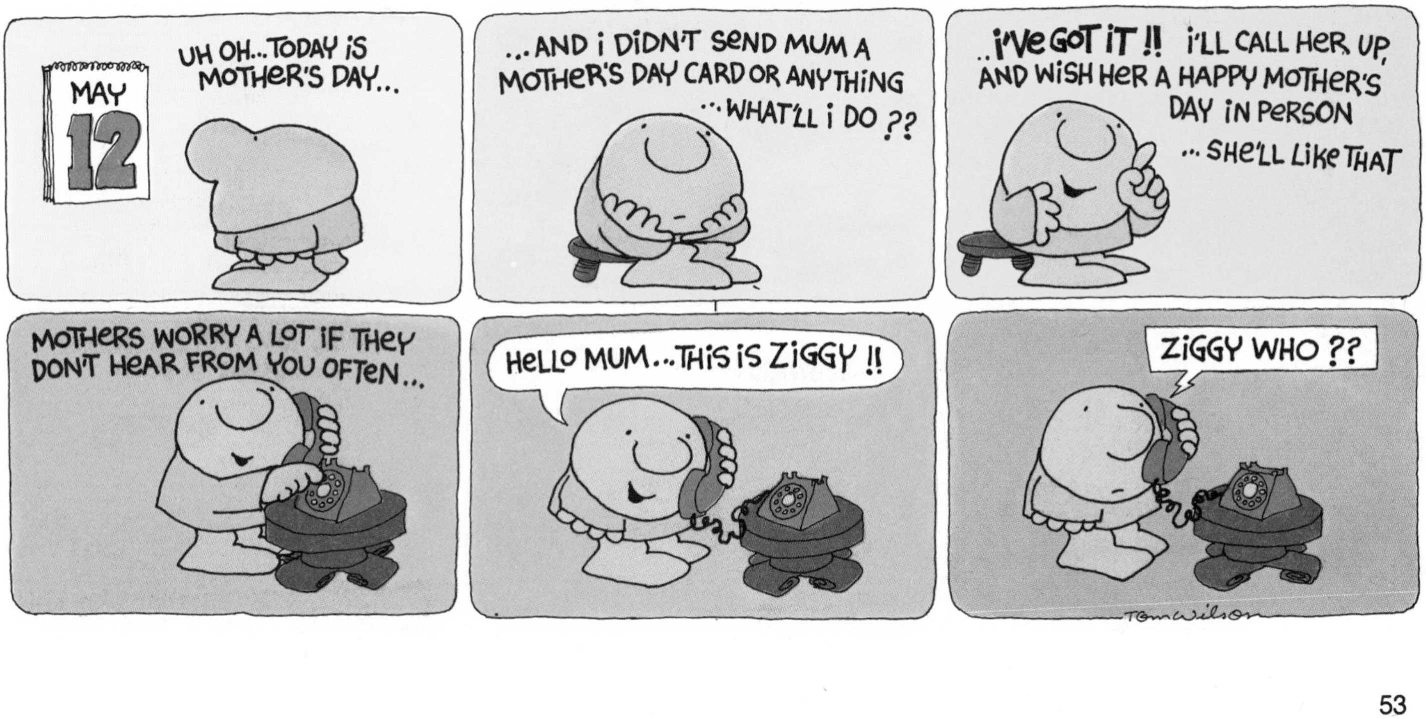
MAY
12
UH OH...TODAY iS MOTHER'S DAY...
...AND i DIDN'T SEND MUM A MOTHER'S DAY CARD OR ANYTHING
...WHAT'LL i DO ??
..i'VE GOT iT !! i'LL CALL HER UP, AND WiSH HER A HAPPY MOTHER'S DAY iN PERSON
... SHE'LL LiKE THAT
MOTHERS WORRY A LOT iF THEY DON'T HEAR FROM YOU OFTEN...
HELLO MUM...THiS iS ZiGGY !!
ZiGGY WHO ??
Tom Wilson

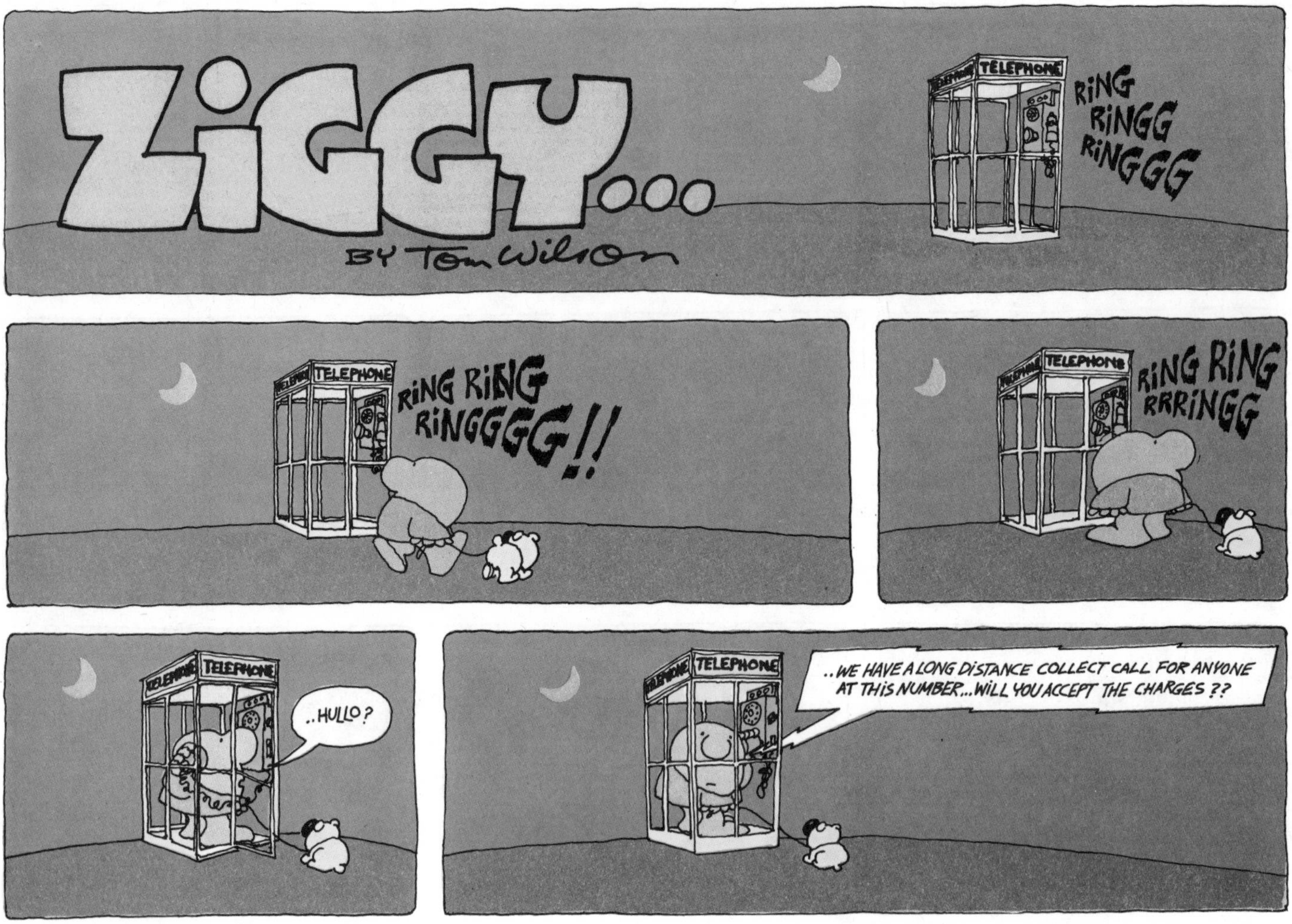
ZIGGY...
BY Tom Wilson
TELEPHONE
RING RINGG RINGGG
RING RING RINGGGG!!
RING RING RRRINGG
..HULLO?
..WE HAVE A LONG DISTANCE COLLECT CALL FOR ANYONE AT THIS NUMBER...WILL YOU ACCEPT THE CHARGES??

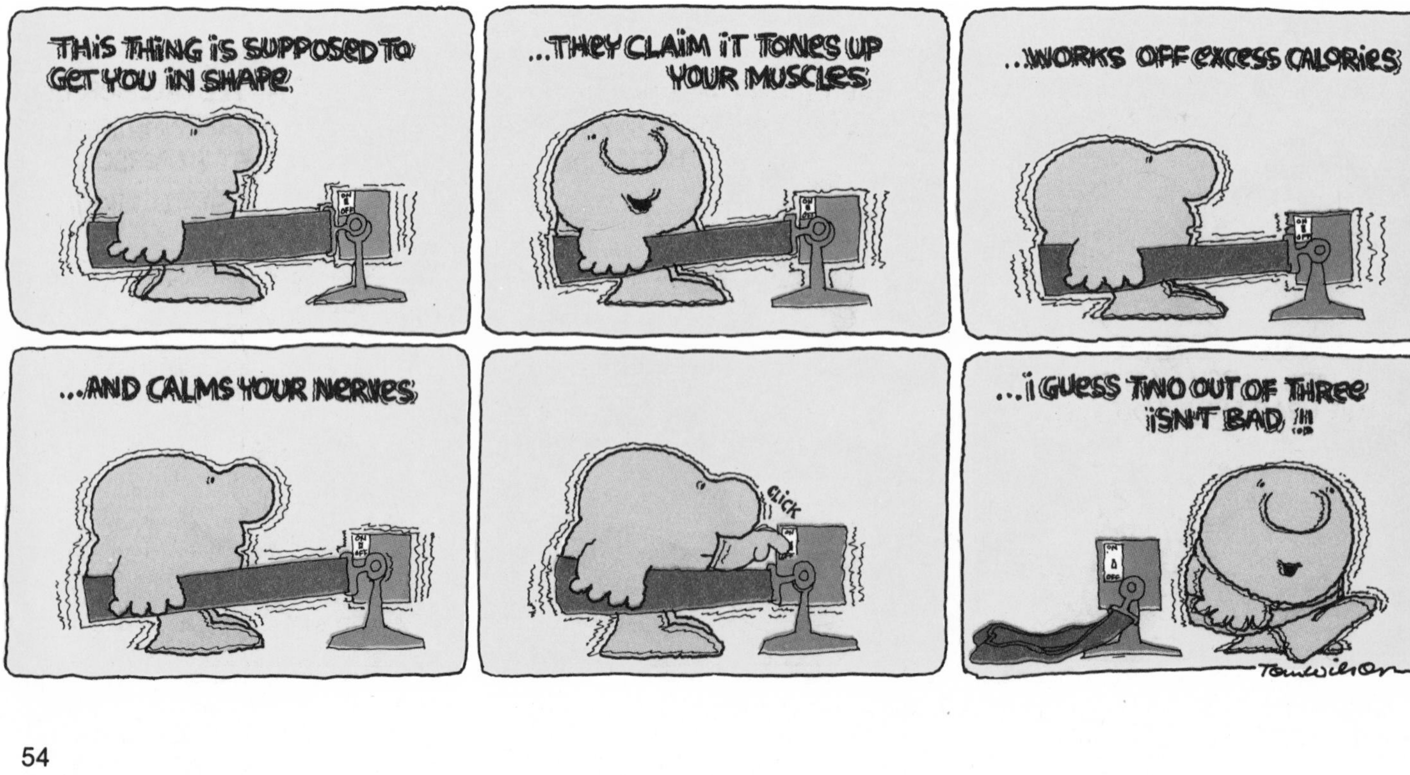
THIS THING IS SUPPOSED TO GET YOU IN SHAPE
...THEY CLAIM IT TONES UP YOUR MUSCLES
..WORKS OFF EXCESS CALORIES
...AND CALMS YOUR NERVES
CLICK
...I GUESS TWO OUT OF THREE ISN'T BAD!!
Tom Wilson

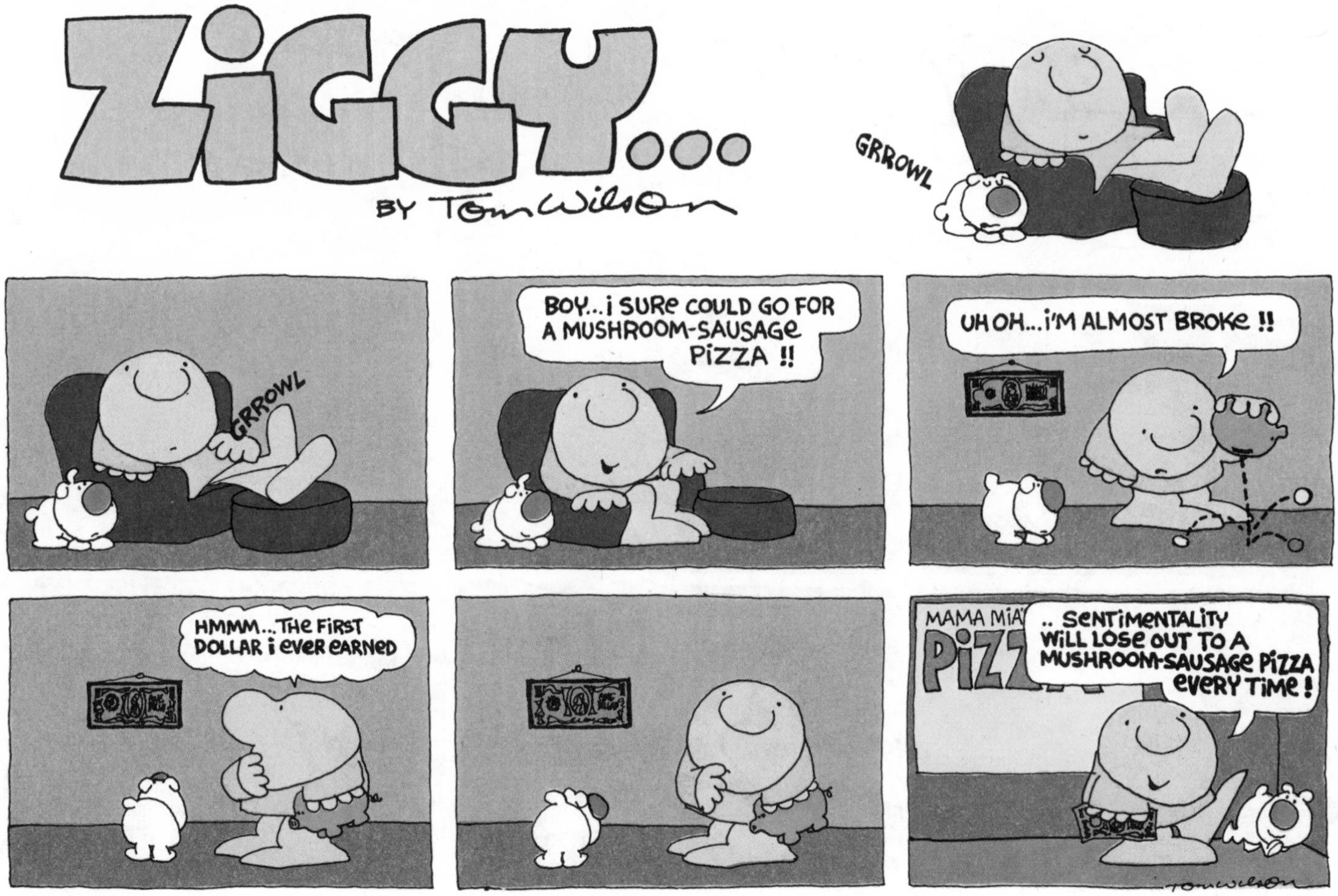
ZiGGY...
BY TOM WILSON
GRROWL
GRROWL
BOY...i SURE COULD GO FOR A MUSHROOM-SAUSAGE PIZZA !!
UH OH...i'M ALMOST BROKE !!
HMMM...THE FIRST DOLLAR i EVER EARNED
MAMA MIA'S
.. SENTIMENTALITY WILL LOSE OUT TO A MUSHROOM-SAUSAGE PIZZA EVERY TIME !
TOM WILSON

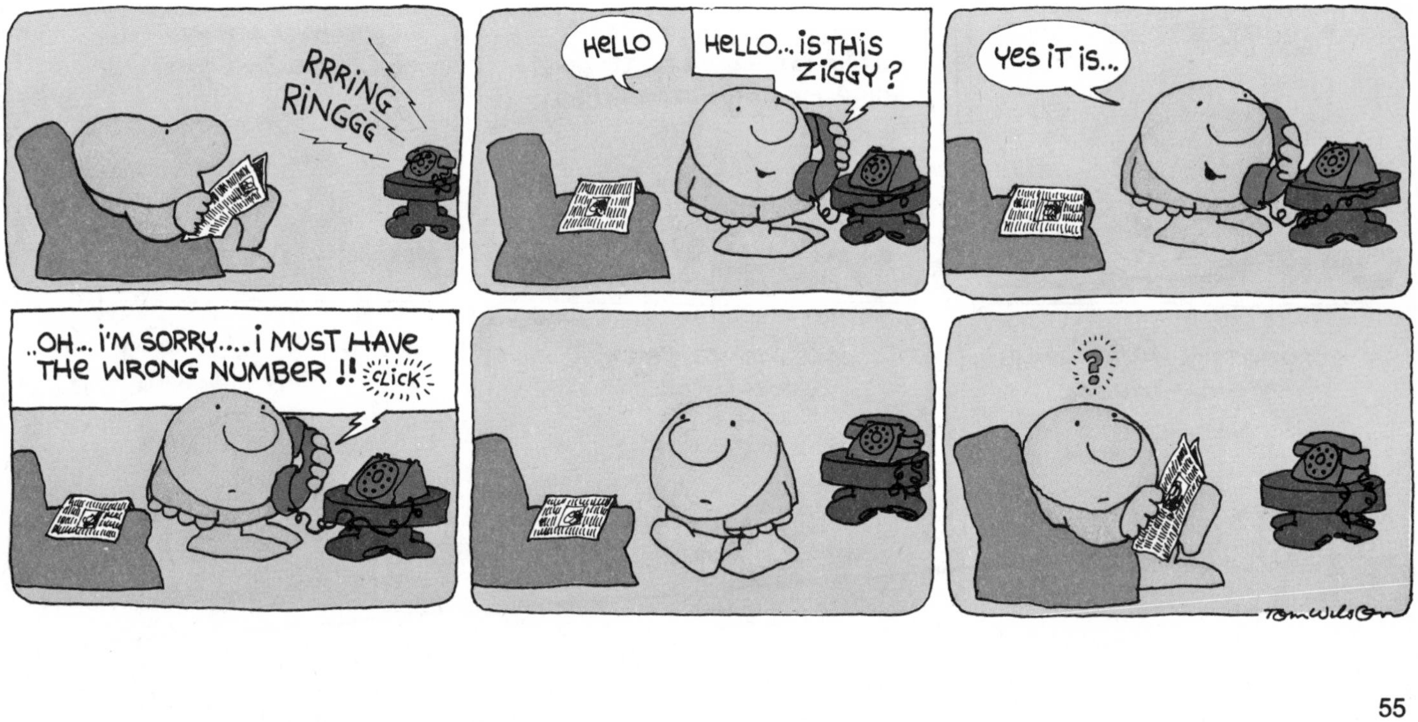
RRRING
RINGGG
HELLO
HELLO... IS THIS ZIGGY ?
YES IT IS...
..OH... i'M SORRY.... i MUST HAVE THE WRONG NUMBER !!
CLICK
?
TOM WILSON

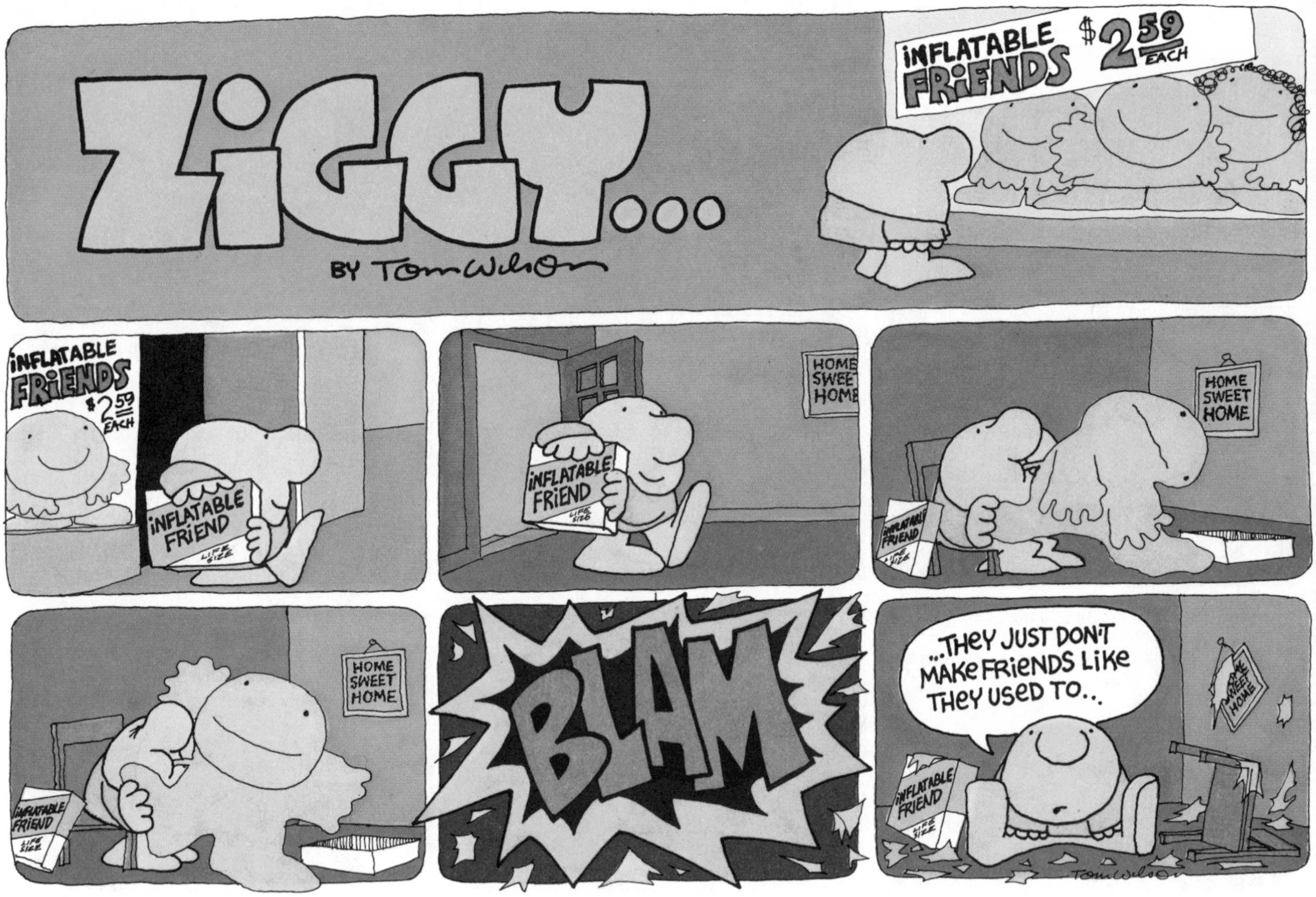
ZiGGY...
BY Tom Wilson
iNFLATABLE FRiENDS $2.59 EACH
iNFLATABLE FRiENDS $2.59 EACH
iNFLATABLE FRiEND LIFE SIZE
HOME SWEET HOME
BLAM
...THEY JUST DON'T MAKE FRiENDS LiKE THEY USED TO...
Tom Wilson

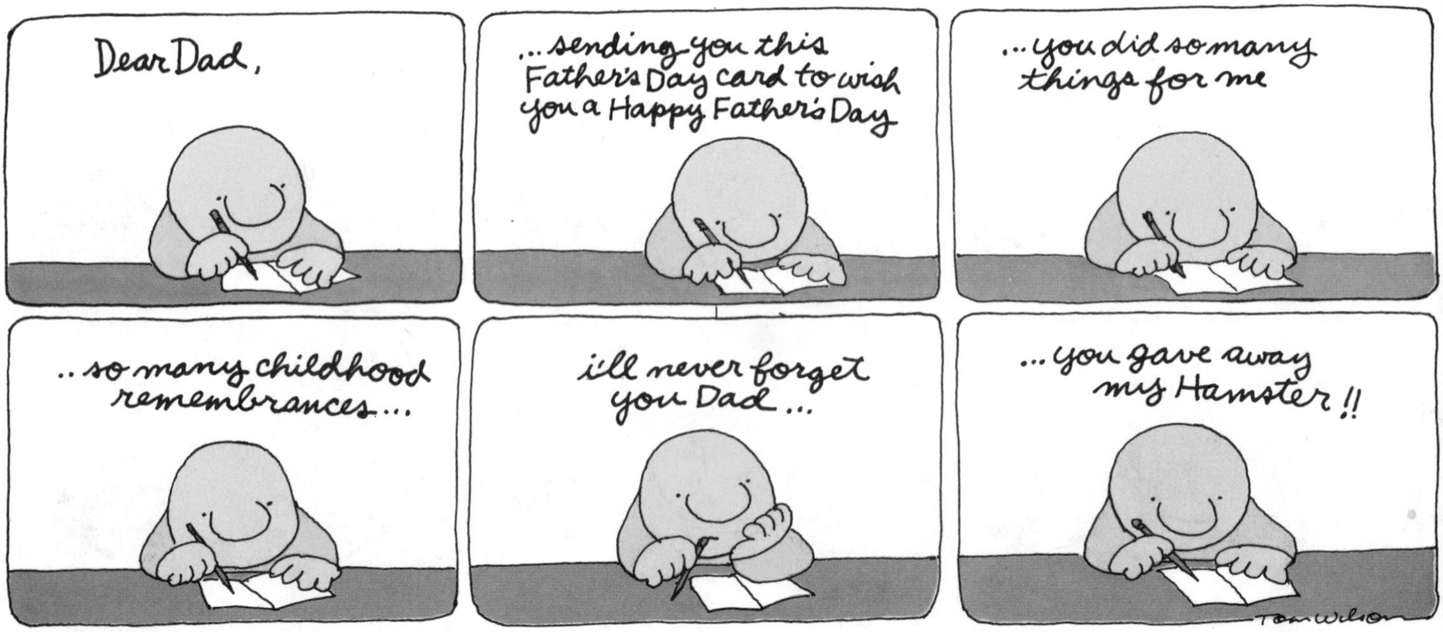
Dear Dad,
...sending you this Father's Day card to wish you a Happy Father's Day
...you did so many things for me
...so many childhood remembrances...
i'll never forget you Dad...
...you gave away my Hamster !!
Tom Wilson

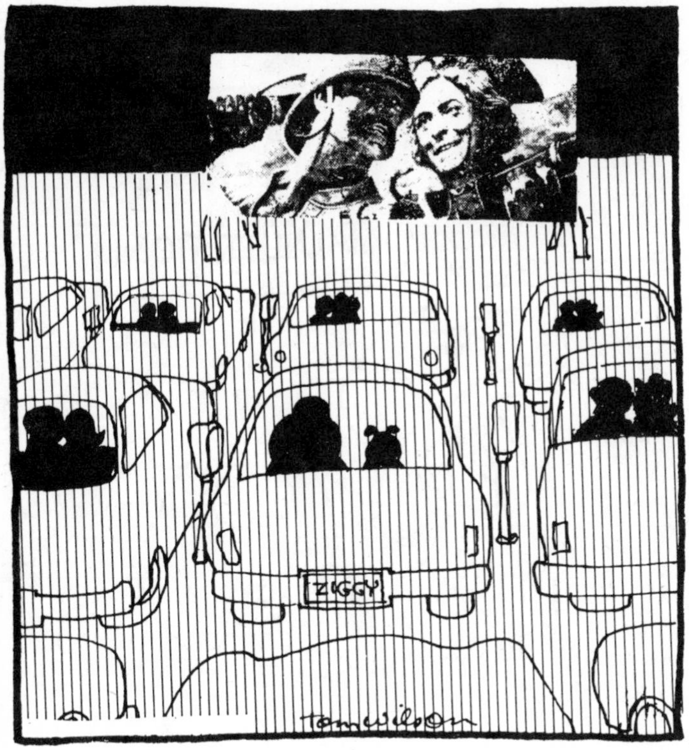
ZIGGY

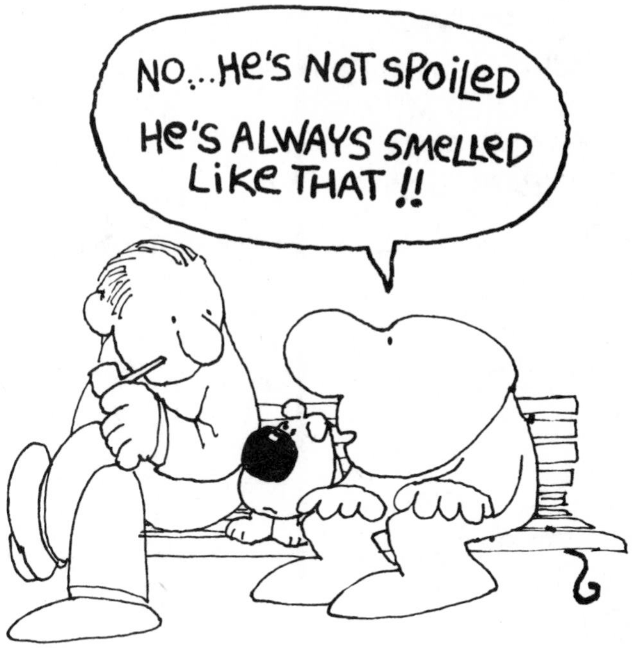
NO...HE'S NOT SPOILED
HE'S ALWAYS SMELLED LIKE THAT !!

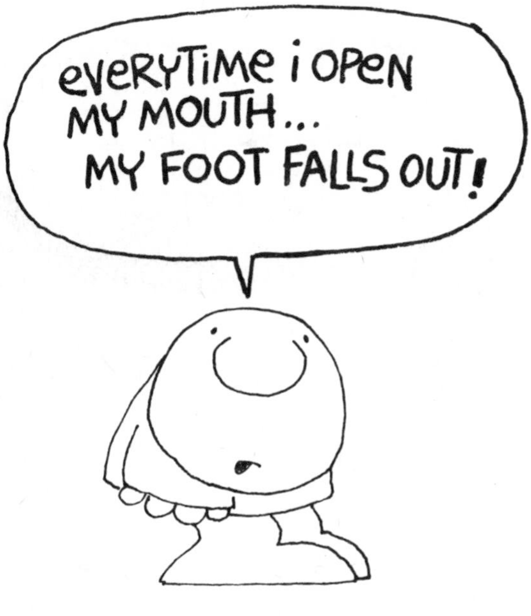
everyTime i OPEN MY MOUTH... MY FOOT FALLS OUT!

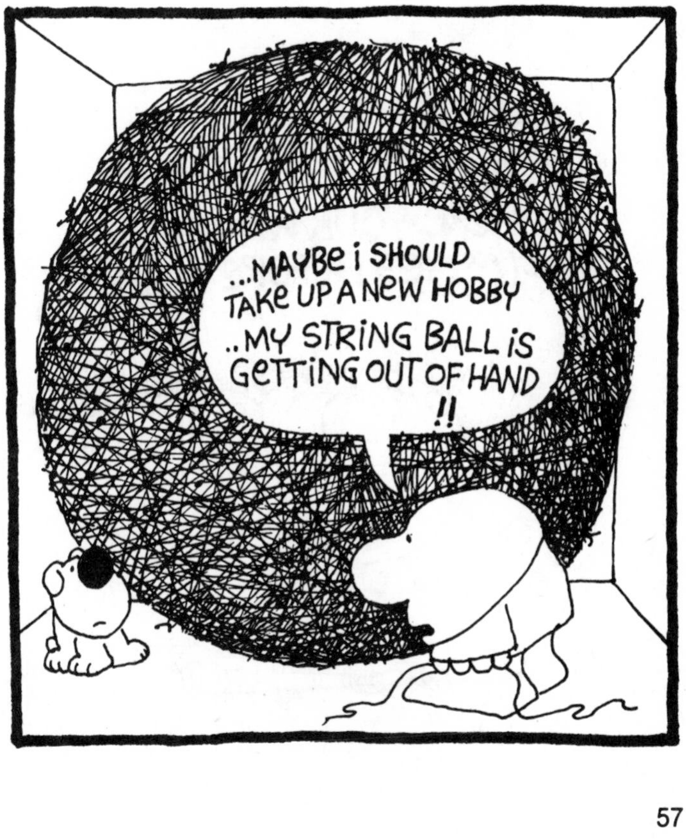
...MAYBE i SHOULD TAKE UP A NEW HOBBY ..MY STRING BALL IS GETTING OUT OF HAND !!

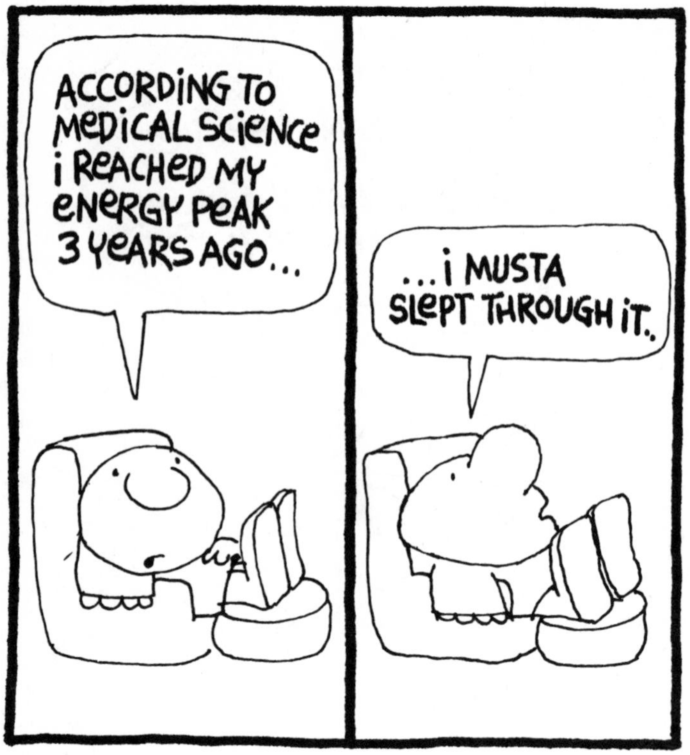
ACCORDING TO MEDICAL SCIENCE i REACHED MY ENERGY PEAK 3 YEARS AGO...
...i MUSTA SLEPT THROUGH iT..

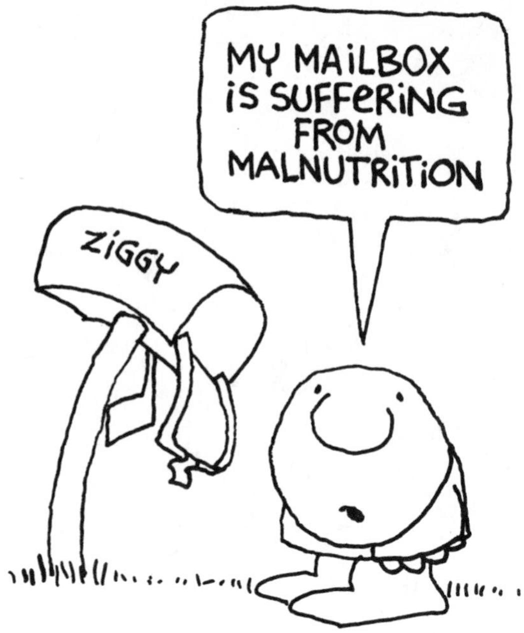
MY MAILBOX iS SUFFERiNG FROM MALNUTRITiON
ZiGGY

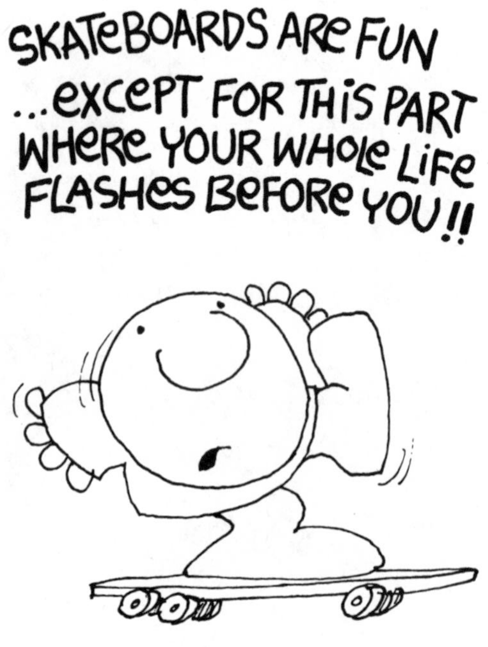
SKATEBOARDS ARE FUN ...EXCEPT FOR THiS PART WHERE YOUR WHOLE LiFE FLASHES BEFORE YOU!!

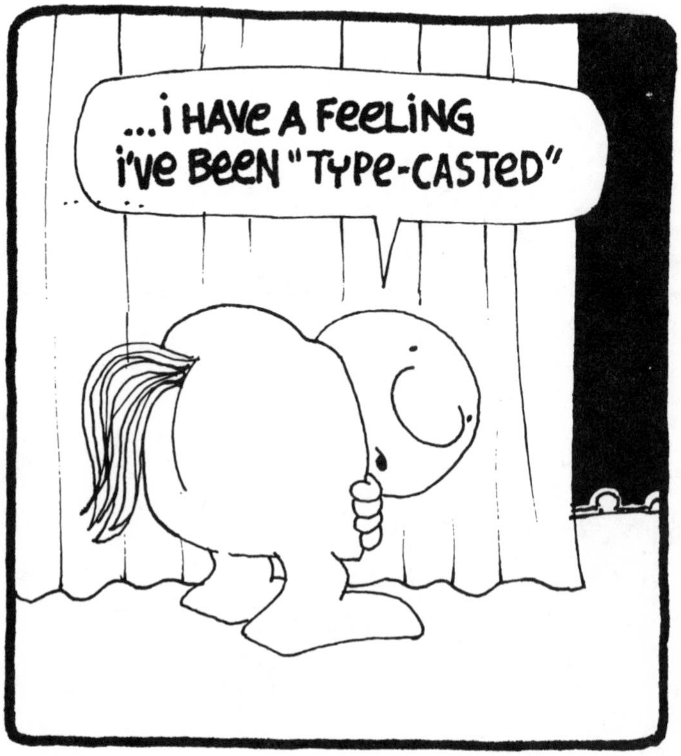
...i HAVE A FEELiNG i've BEEN "TYPE-CASTED"

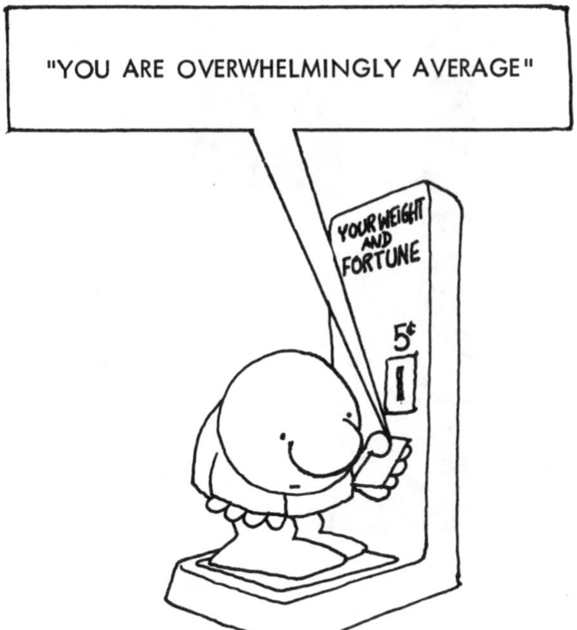
"YOU ARE OVERWHELMINGLY AVERAGE"
YOUR WEIGHT AND FORTUNE
5¢

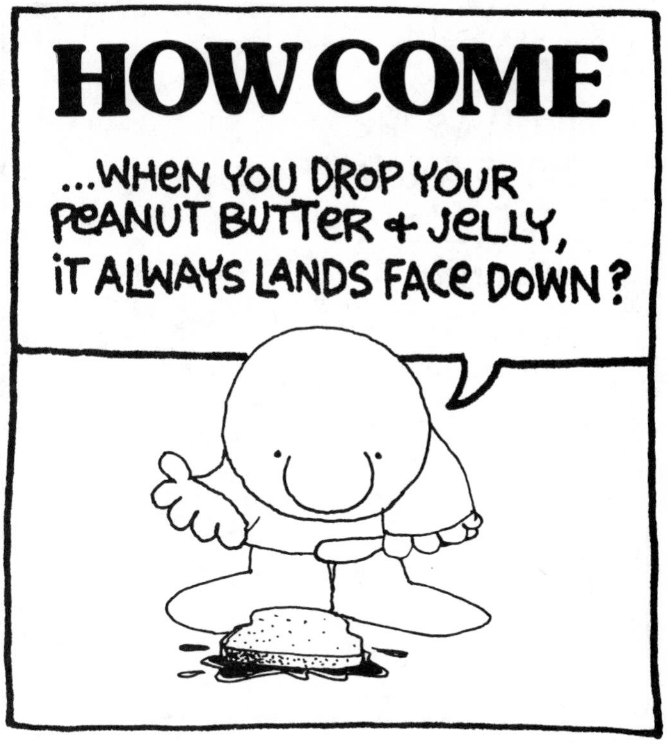
HOW COME
...WHEN YOU DROP YOUR PEANUT BUTTER + JELLY, IT ALWAYS LANDS FACE DOWN?

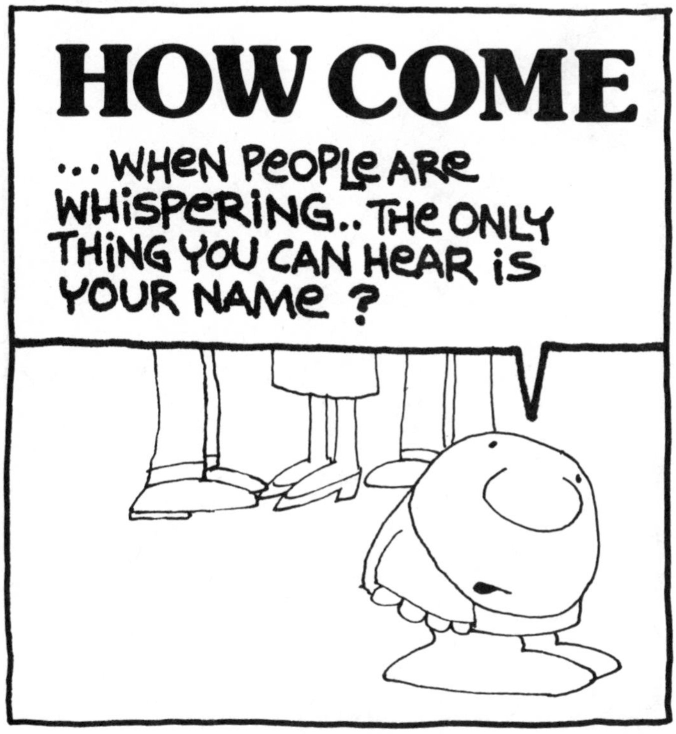
HOW COME
... WHEN PEOPLE ARE WHISPERING.. THE ONLY THING YOU CAN HEAR IS YOUR NAME ?

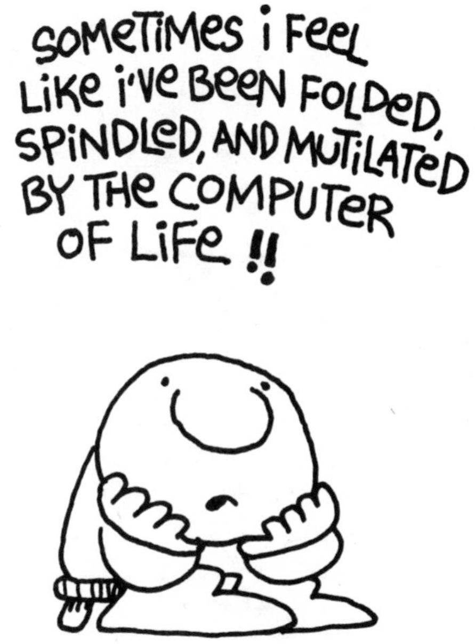
SOMETIMES I FEEL LIKE I'VE BEEN FOLDED, SPINDLED, AND MUTILATED BY THE COMPUTER OF LIFE !!

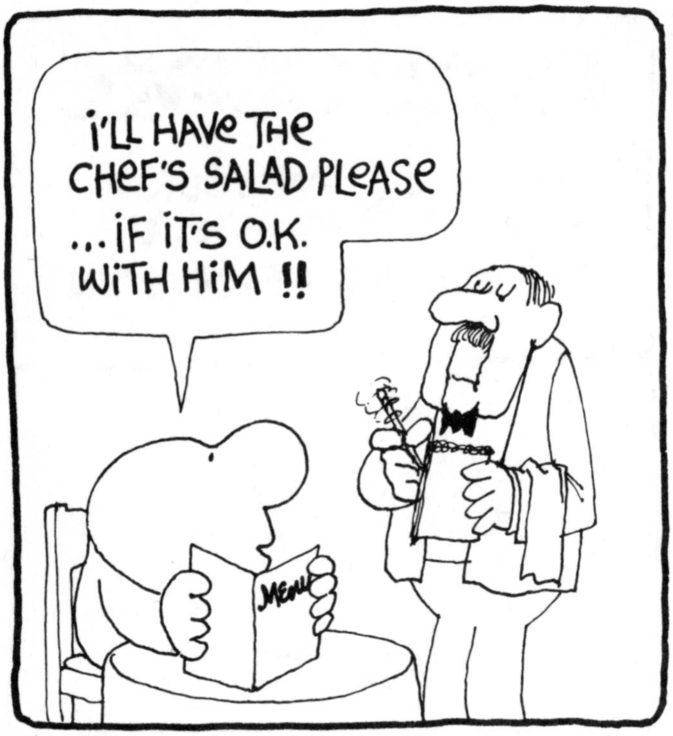
I'LL HAVE THE CHEF'S SALAD PLEASE ... IF IT'S O.K. WITH HIM !!

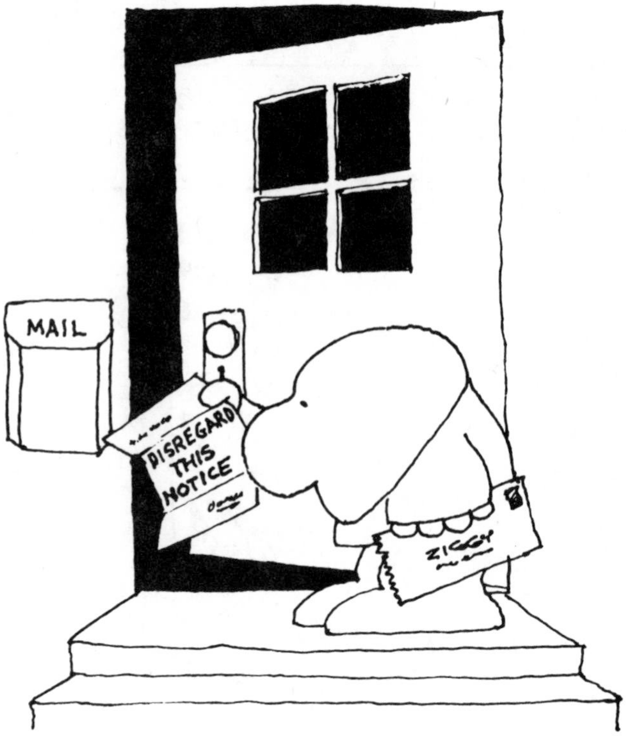
MAIL
DISREGARD THIS NOTICE
ZIGGY

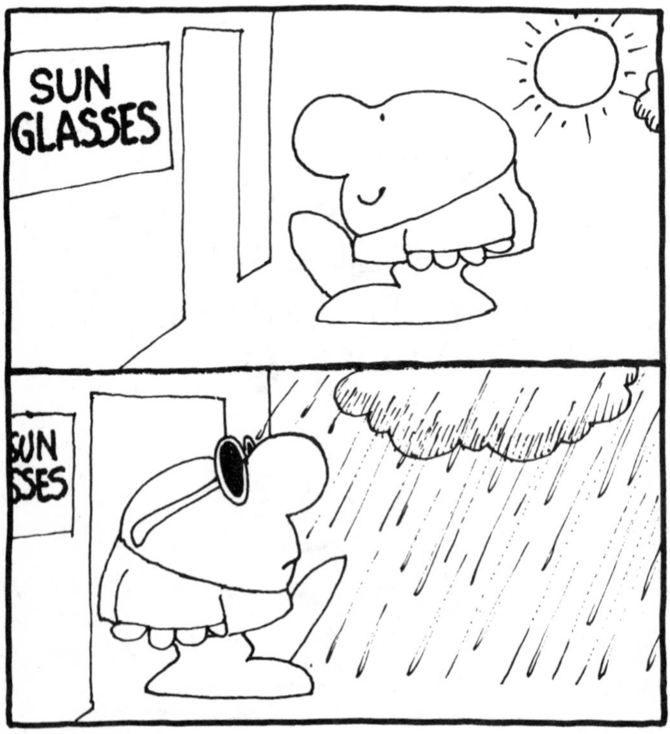
SUN GLASSES

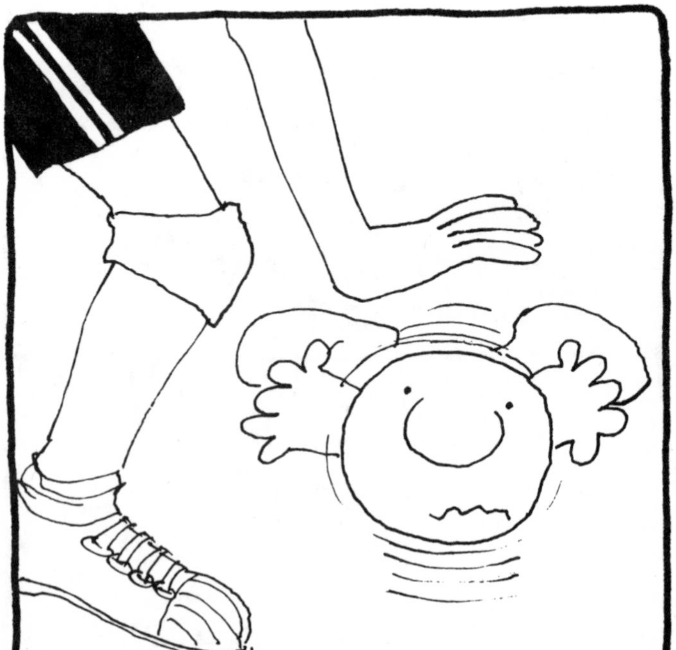

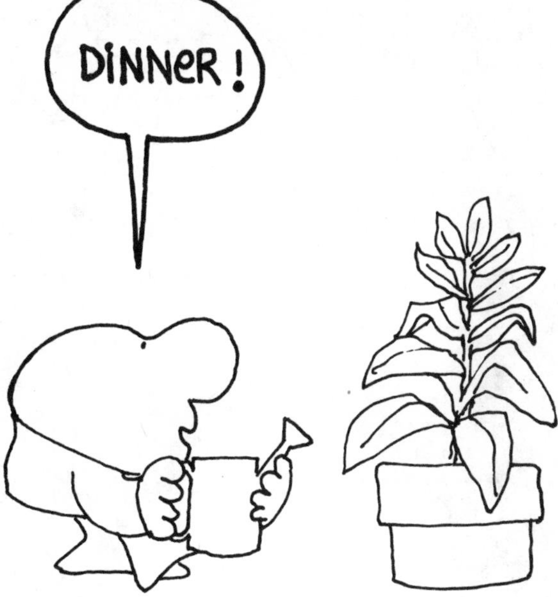
DINNER !

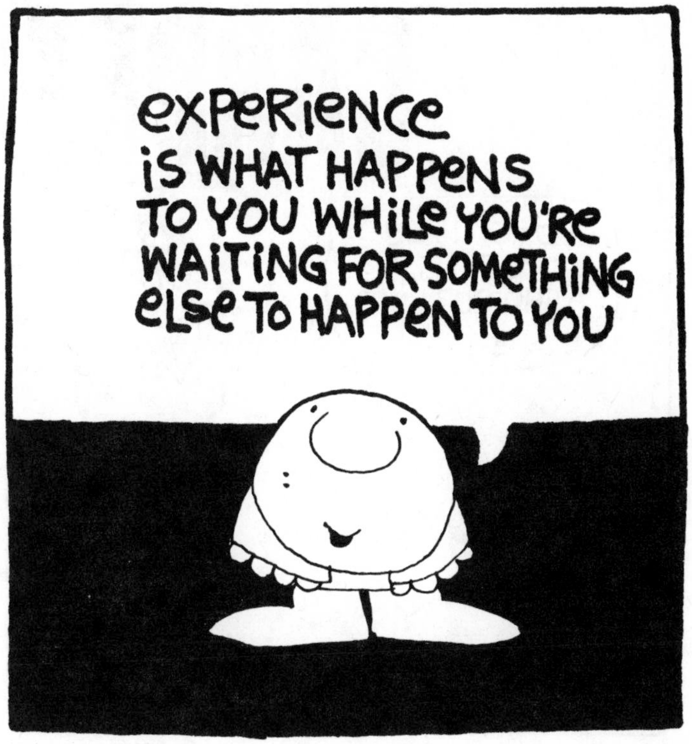
experience
is WHAT HAPPENS
TO YOU WHILE YOU'RE
WAITING FOR SOMETHING
ELSE TO HAPPEN TO YOU

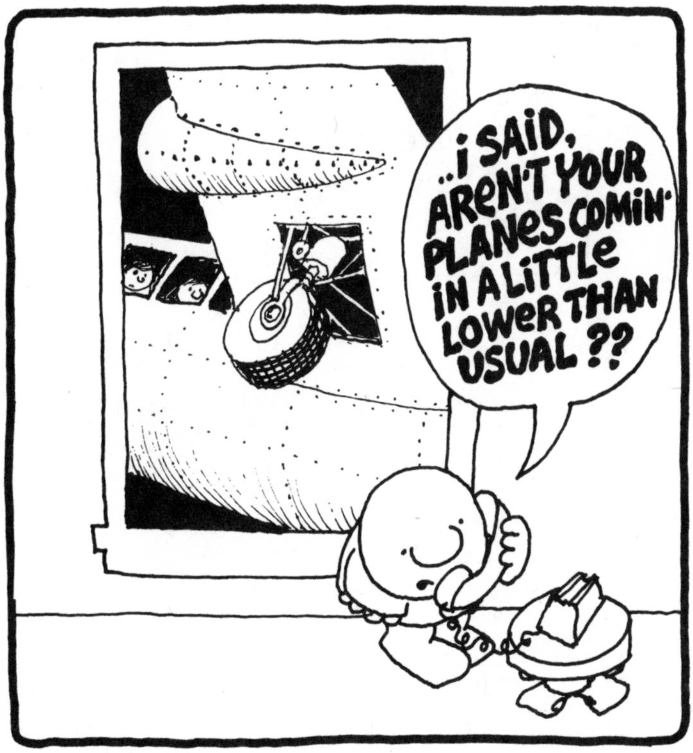
..i SAID, AREN'T YOUR PLANES COMIN' IN A LITTLE LOWER THAN USUAL ??

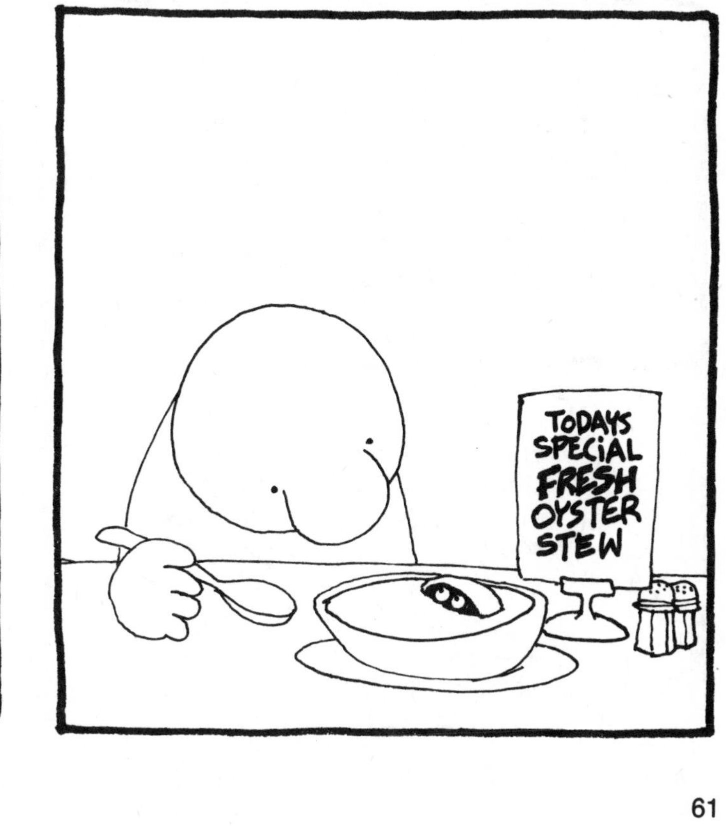
TODAYS SPECIAL FRESH OYSTER STEW

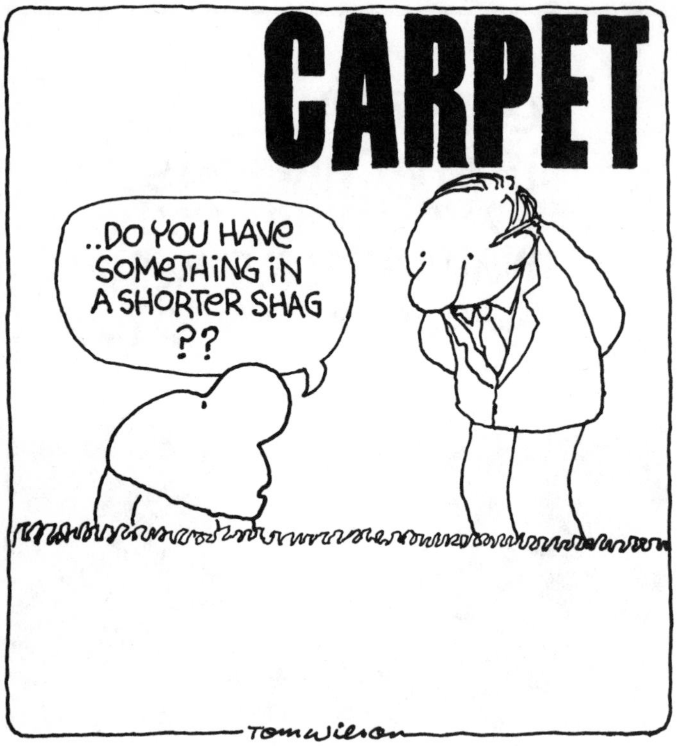
CARPET
..DO YOU HAVE SOMETHING IN A SHORTER SHAG ??
TOM WILSON

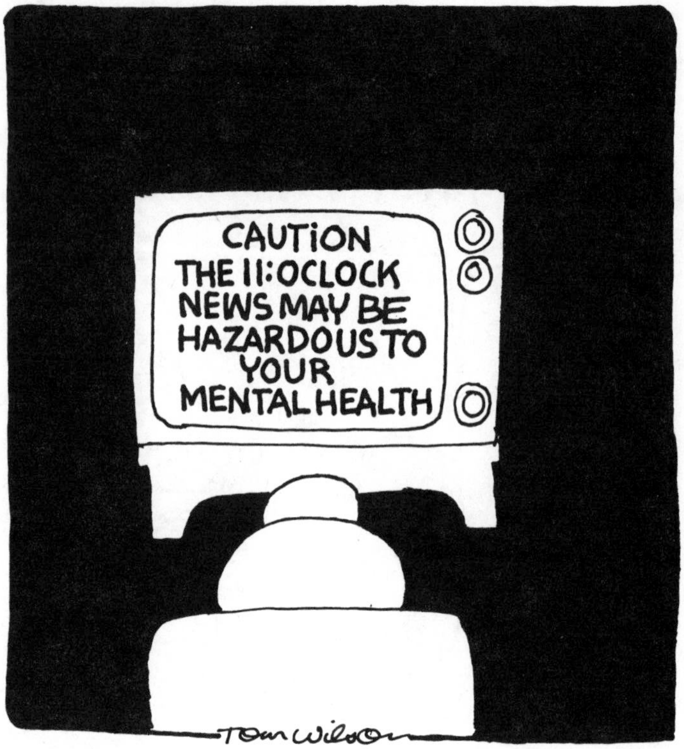
CAUTION THE 11:OCLOCK NEWS MAY BE HAZARDOUS TO YOUR MENTAL HEALTH
TOM WILSON

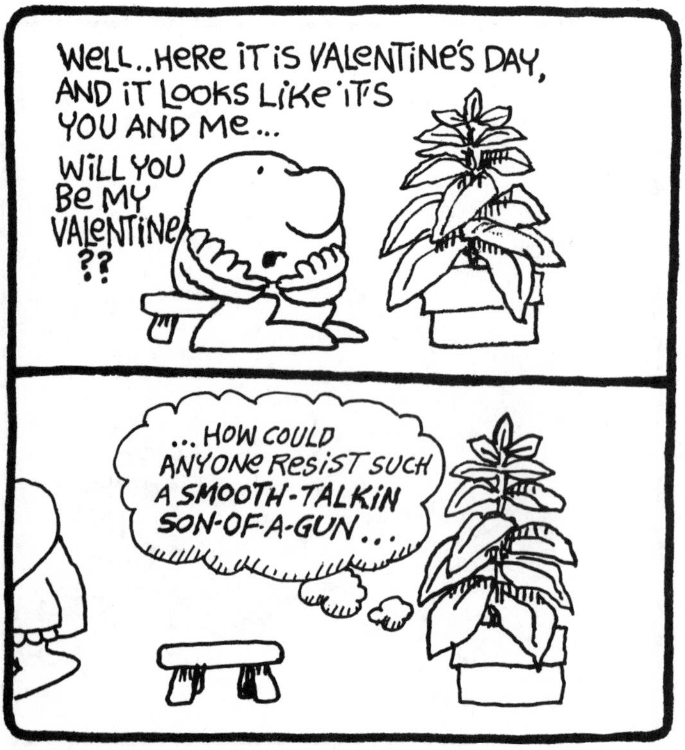
WELL..HERE IT IS VALENTINE'S DAY, AND IT LOOKS LIKE IT'S YOU AND ME...
WILL YOU BE MY VALENTINE ??
... HOW COULD ANYONE RESIST SUCH A SMOOTH-TALKIN SON-OF-A-GUN...

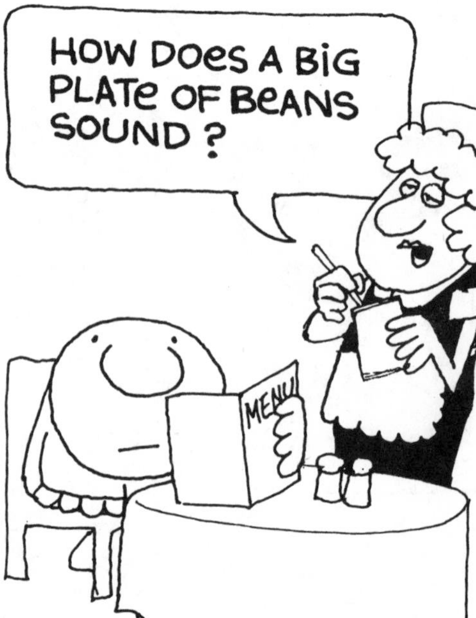
HOW DOES A BIG PLATE OF BEANS SOUND ?
MENU

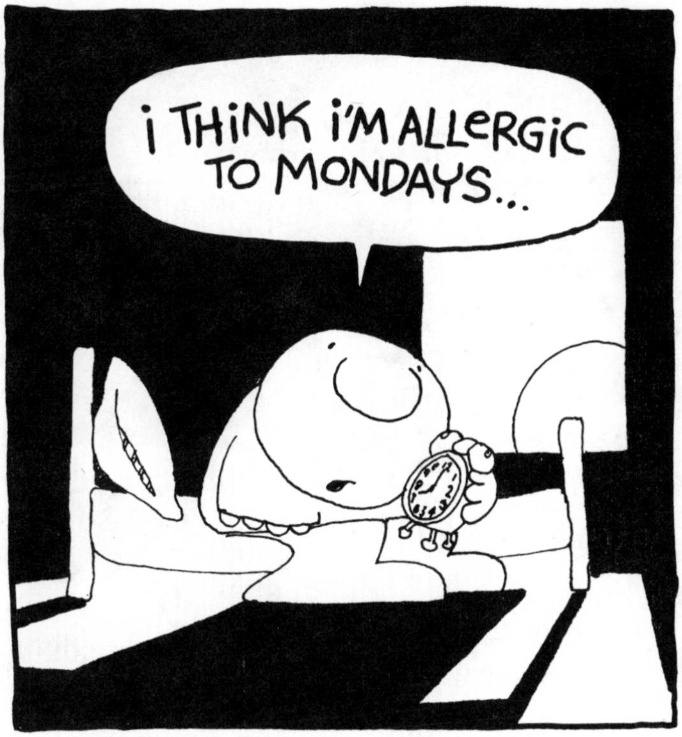
I THINK I'M ALLERGIC TO MONDAYS...

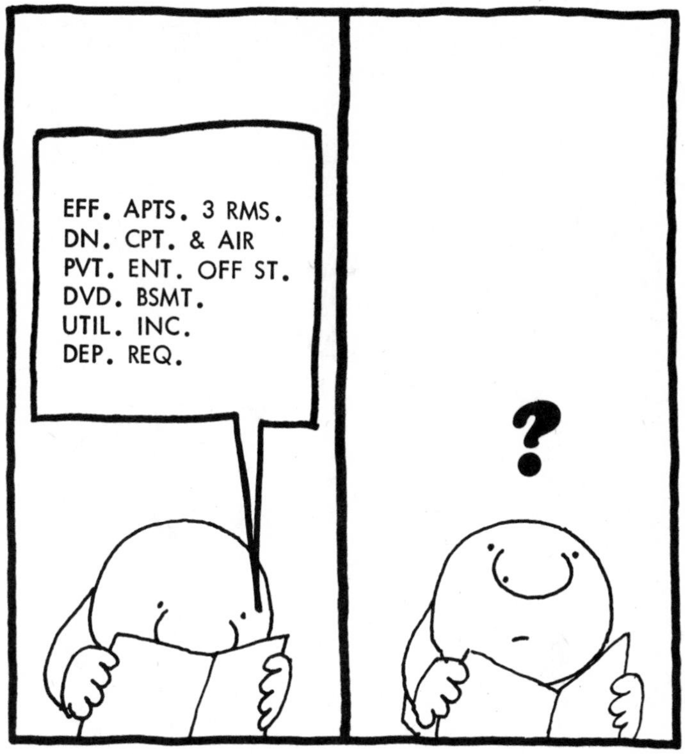
EFF. APTS. 3 RMS.
DN. CPT. & AIR
PVT. ENT. OFF ST.
DVD. BSMT.
UTIL. INC.
DEP. REQ.
?

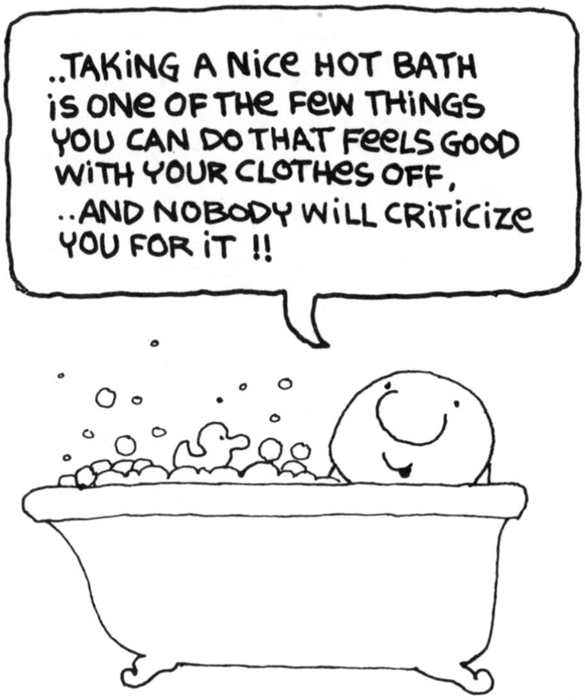
..TAKING A NICE HOT BATH IS ONE OF THE FEW THINGS YOU CAN DO THAT FEELS GOOD WITH YOUR CLOTHES OFF, ..AND NOBODY WILL CRITICIZE YOU FOR IT !!

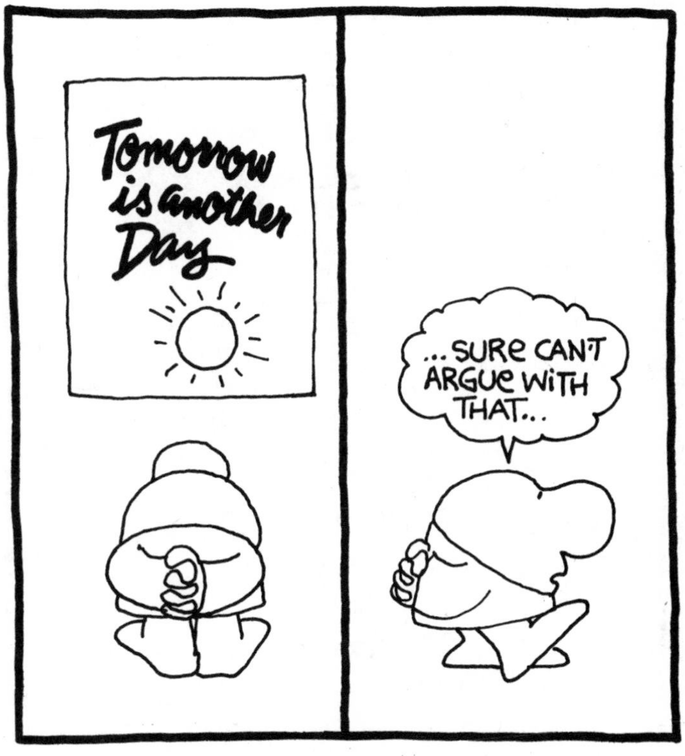
Tomorrow is another Day
...SURE CAN'T ARGUE WITH THAT...

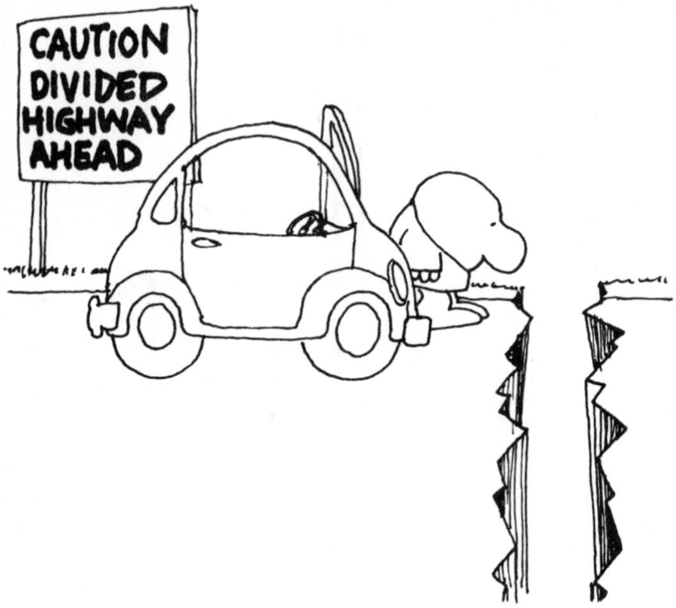
CAUTION
DIVIDED
HIGHWAY
AHEAD

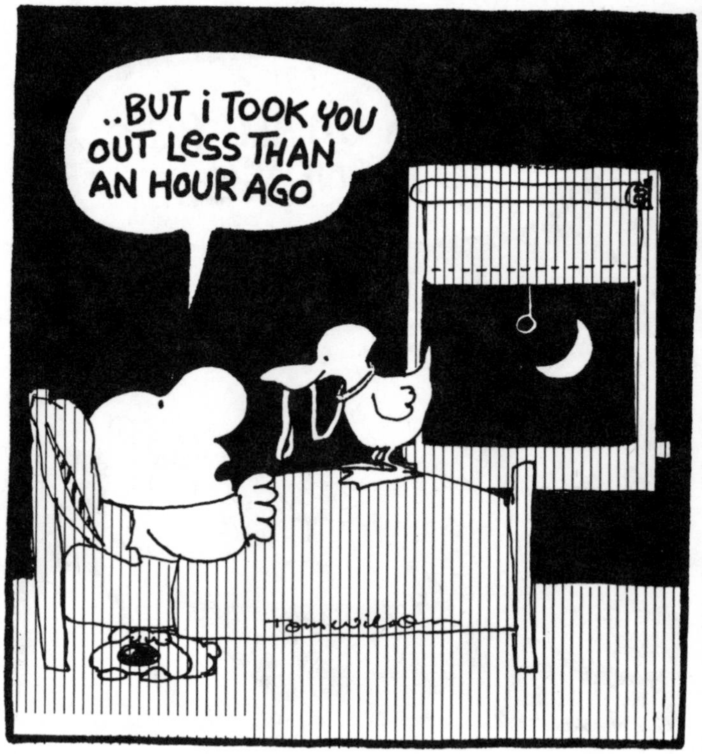
..BUT i TOOK YOU OUT LESS THAN AN HOUR AGO

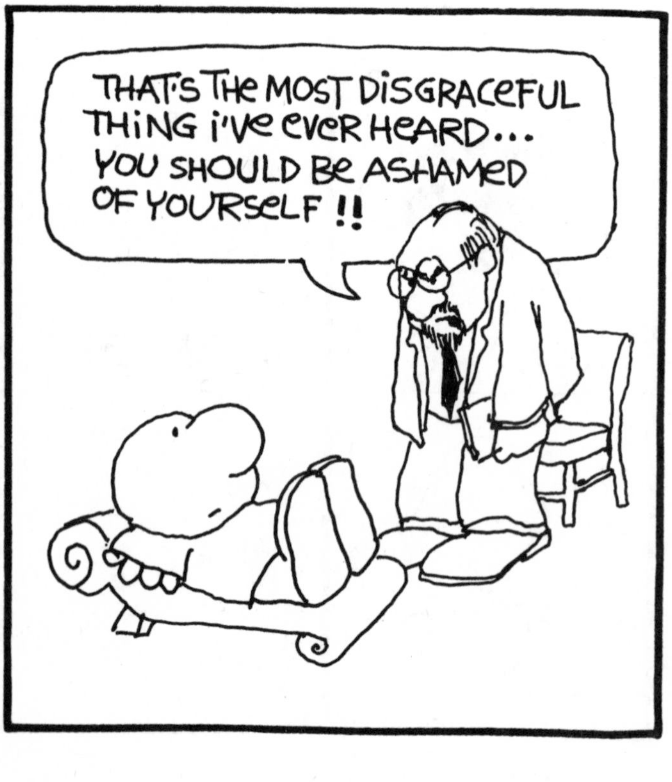
THAT'S THE MOST DiSGRACEFUL THiNG i'Ve eVeR HEARD... YOU SHOULD Be ASHAMeD OF YOURSeLF !!

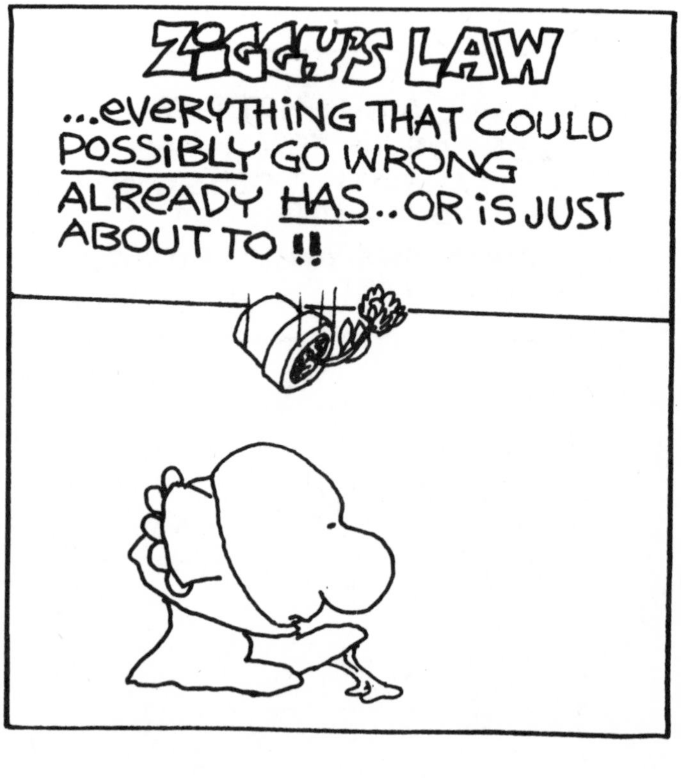
ZiGGY'S LAW
...eVERYTHiNG THAT COULD POSSiBLY GO WRONG ALReADY HAS..OR iS JUST ABOUT TO !!

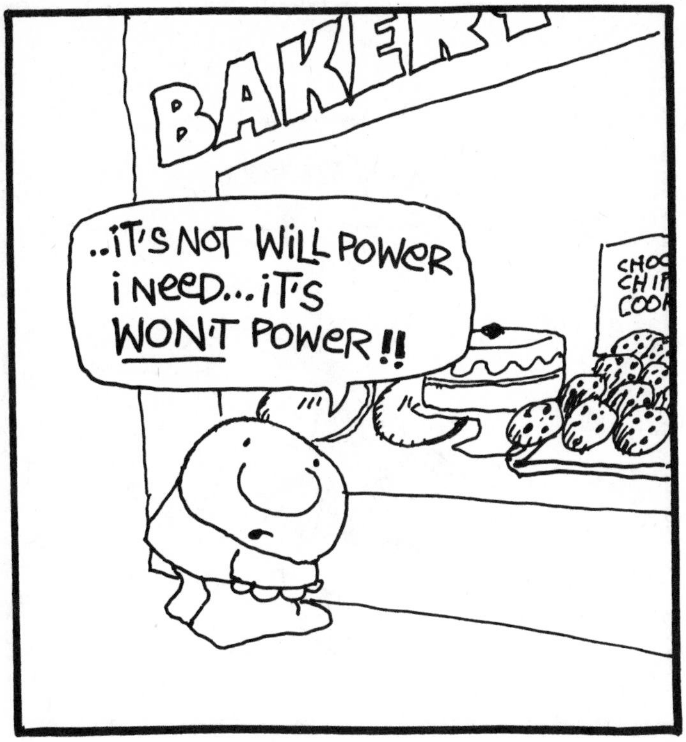
..IT'S NOT WILL POWER I NEED...IT'S WON'T POWER !!

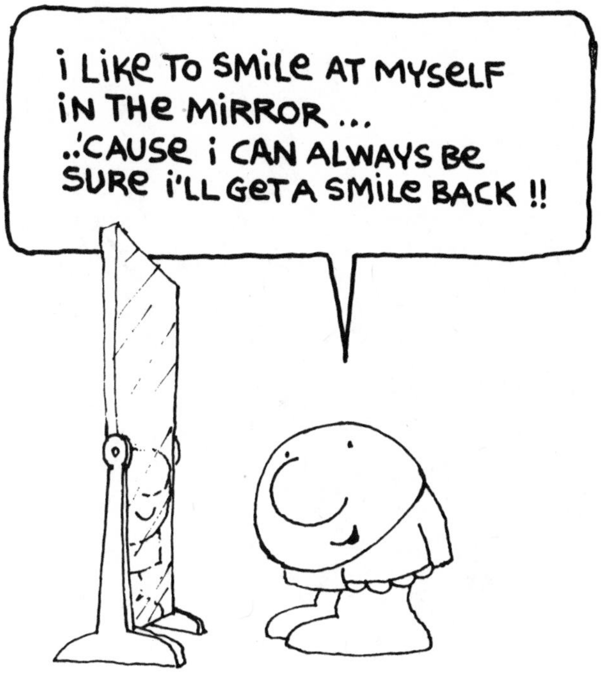
I LIKE TO SMILE AT MYSELF IN THE MIRROR ... ..'CAUSE I CAN ALWAYS BE SURE I'LL GET A SMILE BACK !!

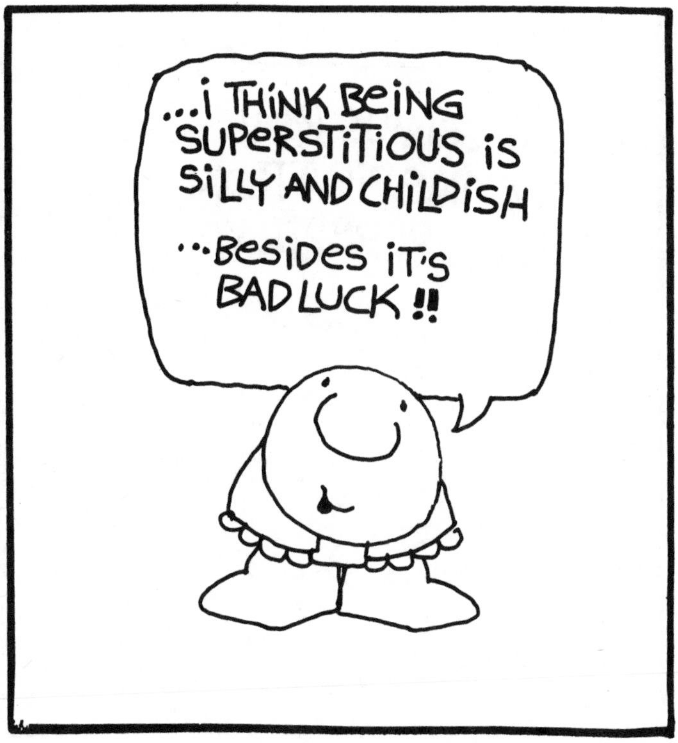
...I THINK BEING SUPERSTITIOUS IS SILLY AND CHILDISH ...BESIDES IT'S BAD LUCK !!

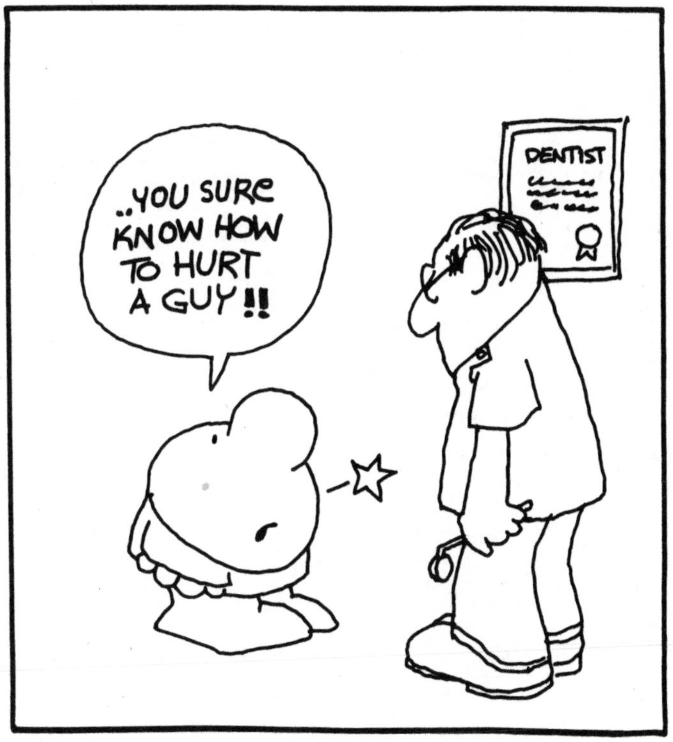
DENTIST
..YOU SURE KNOW HOW TO HURT A GUY !!

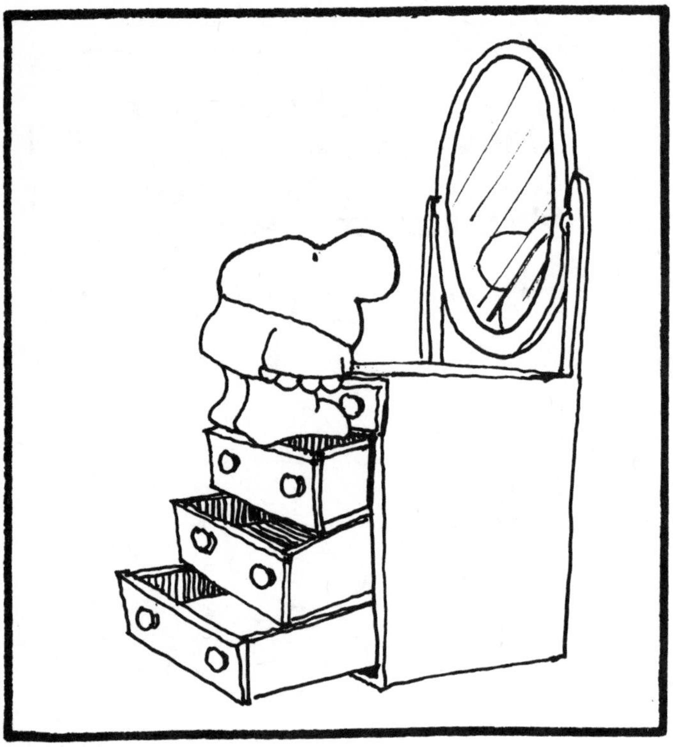

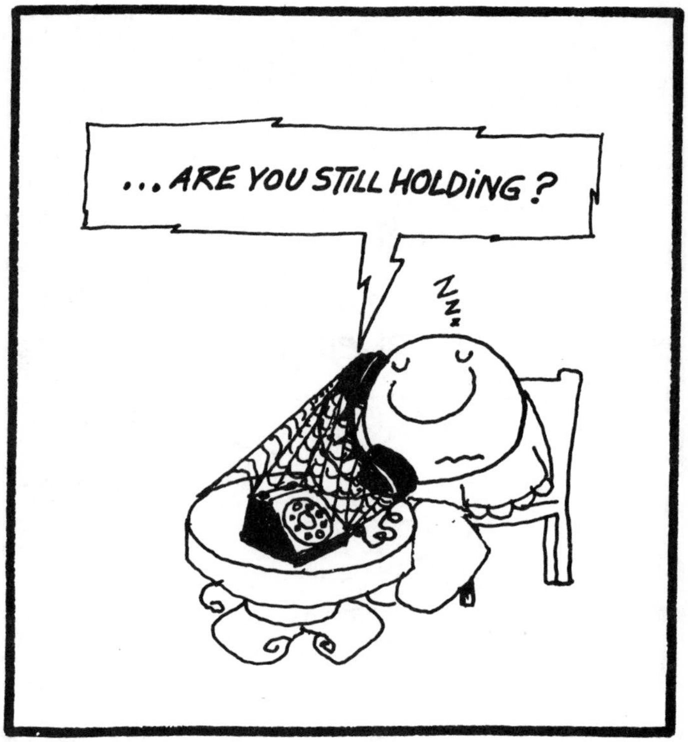

...ARE YOU STILL HOLDING?
ZZZ

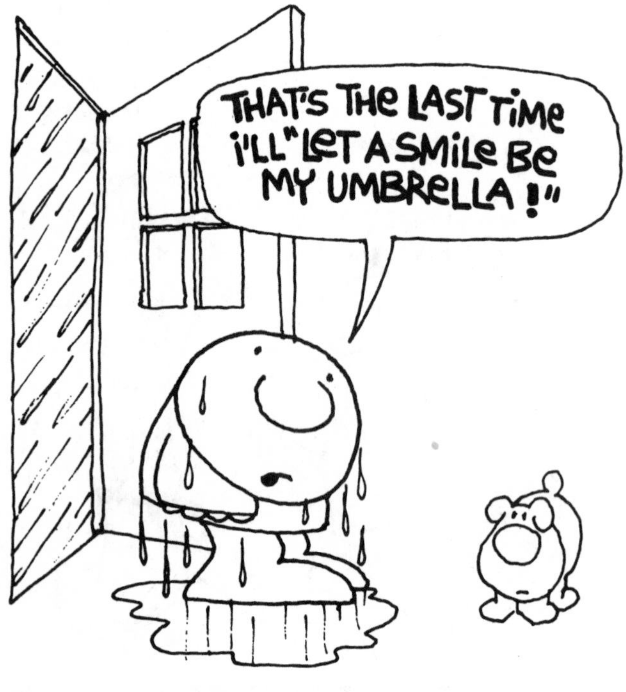

THAT'S THE LAST TIME I'LL "LET A SMILE BE MY UMBRELLA!"

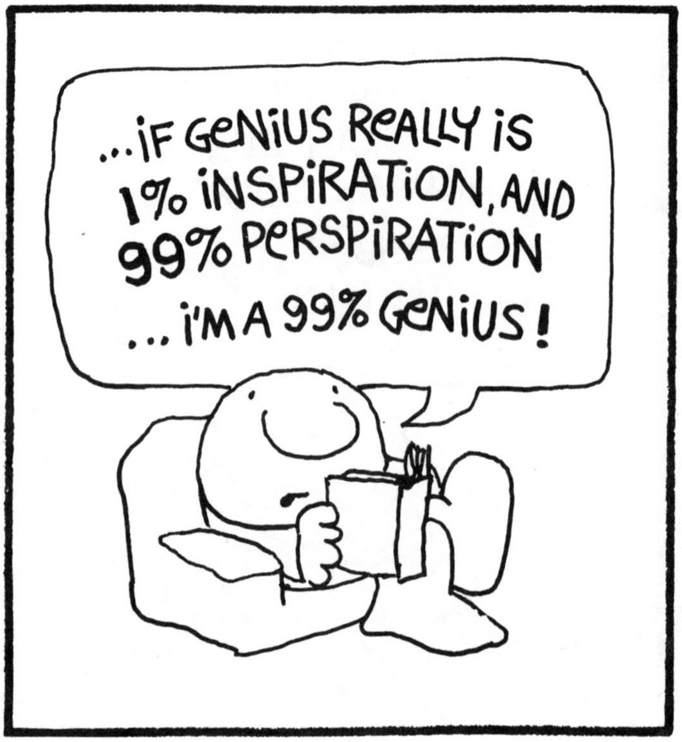

...IF GENIUS REALLY IS 1% INSPIRATION, AND 99% PERSPIRATION ...I'M A 99% GENIUS!

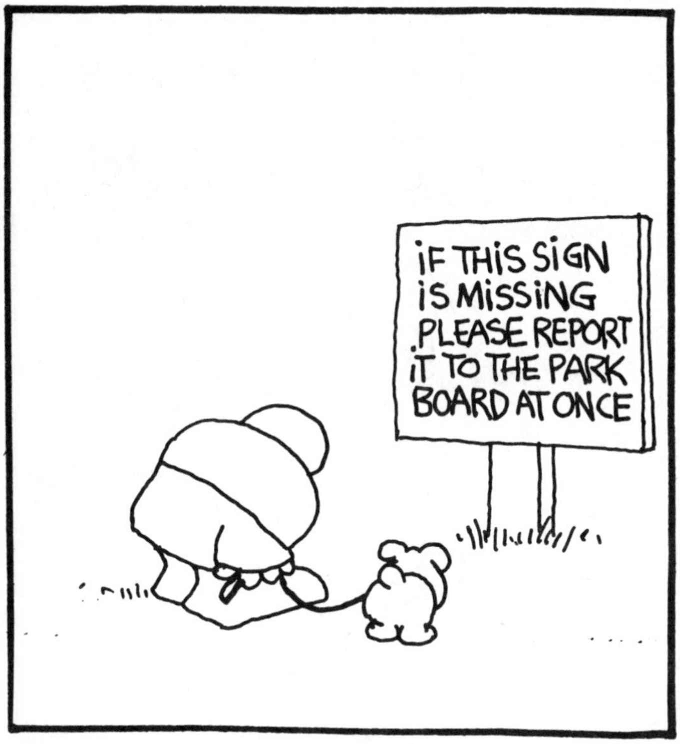
IF THIS SIGN IS MISSING PLEASE REPORT IT TO THE PARK BOARD AT ONCE

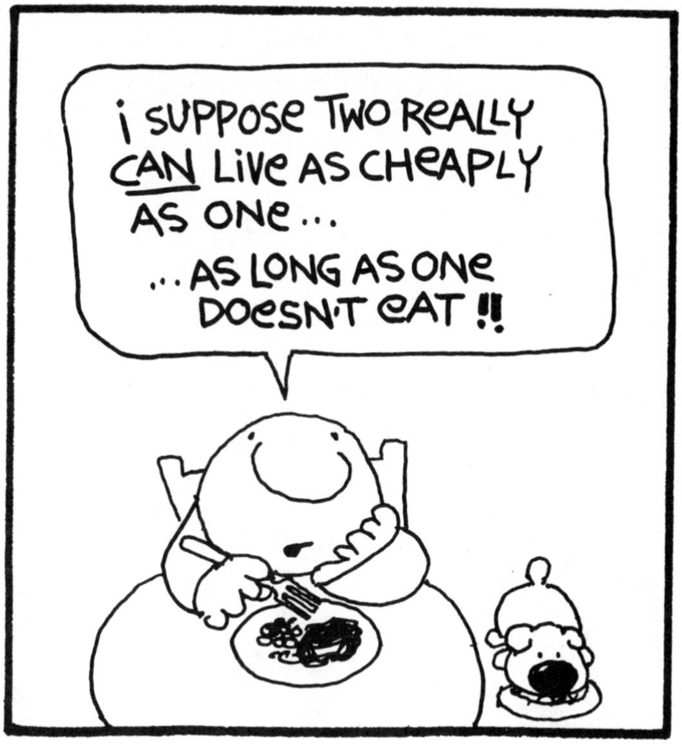
I SUPPOSE TWO REALLY CAN LIVE AS CHEAPLY AS ONE...
...AS LONG AS ONE DOESN'T EAT !!

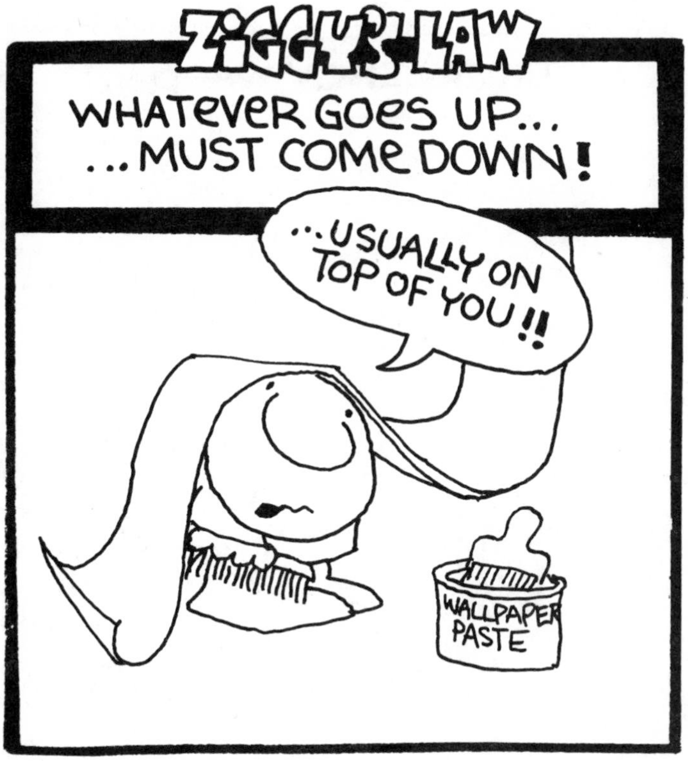
ZIGGY'S LAW
WHATEVER GOES UP... ...MUST COME DOWN!
...USUALLY ON TOP OF YOU !!
WALLPAPER PASTE

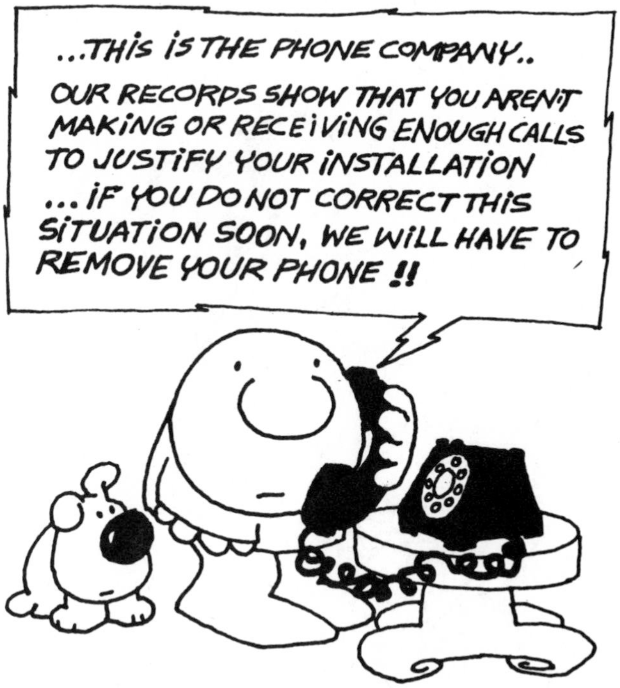
...THIS IS THE PHONE COMPANY.. OUR RECORDS SHOW THAT YOU AREN'T MAKING OR RECEIVING ENOUGH CALLS TO JUSTIFY YOUR INSTALLATION ... IF YOU DO NOT CORRECT THIS SITUATION SOON, WE WILL HAVE TO REMOVE YOUR PHONE !!

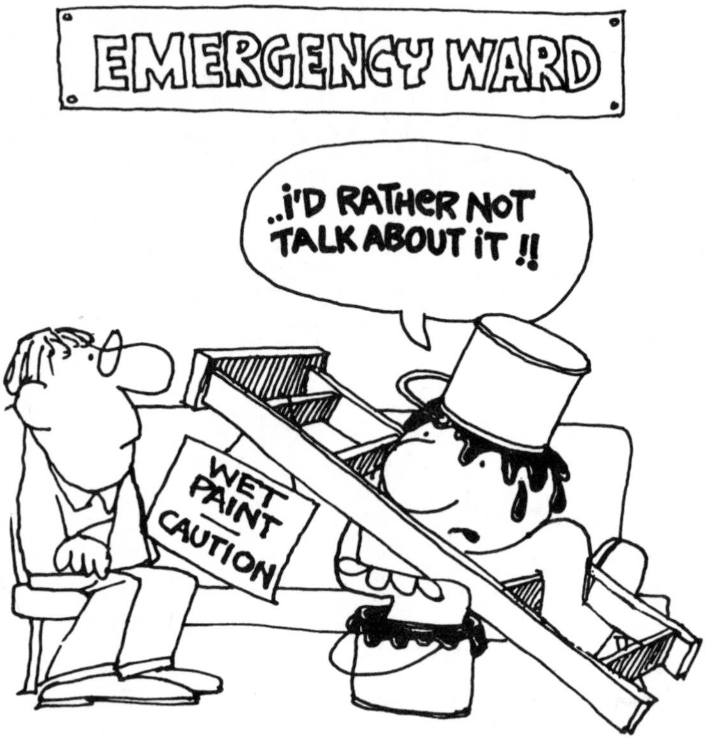
EMERGENCY WARD
..i'D RATHER NOT TALK ABOUT iT !!
WET PAINT CAUTION

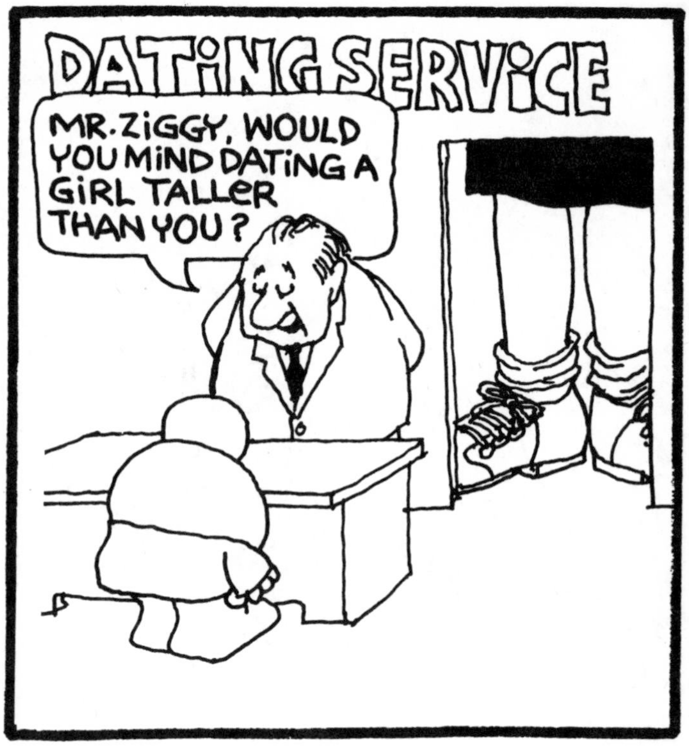
DATiNG SERViCE
MR. ZiGGY, WOULD YOU MiND DATiNG A GiRL TALLER THAN YOU ?

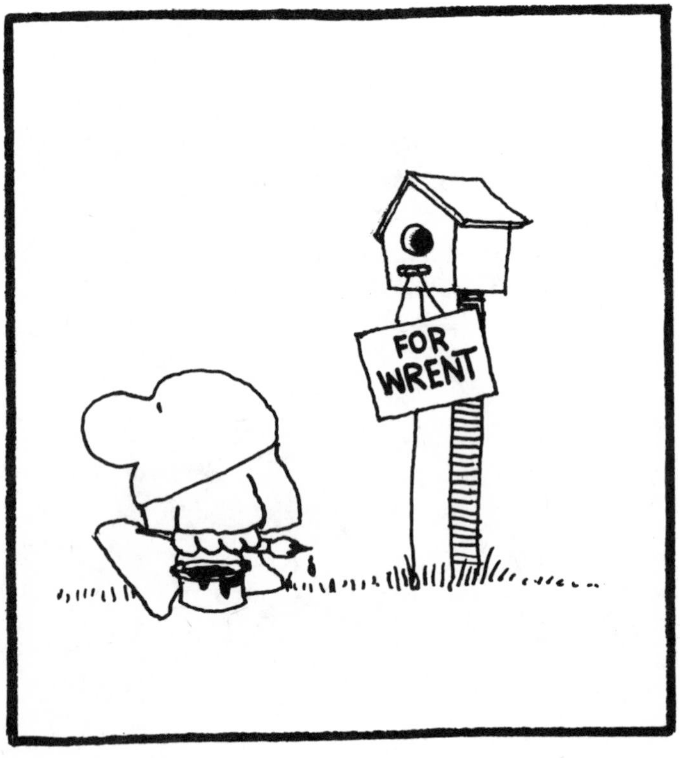
FOR WRENT

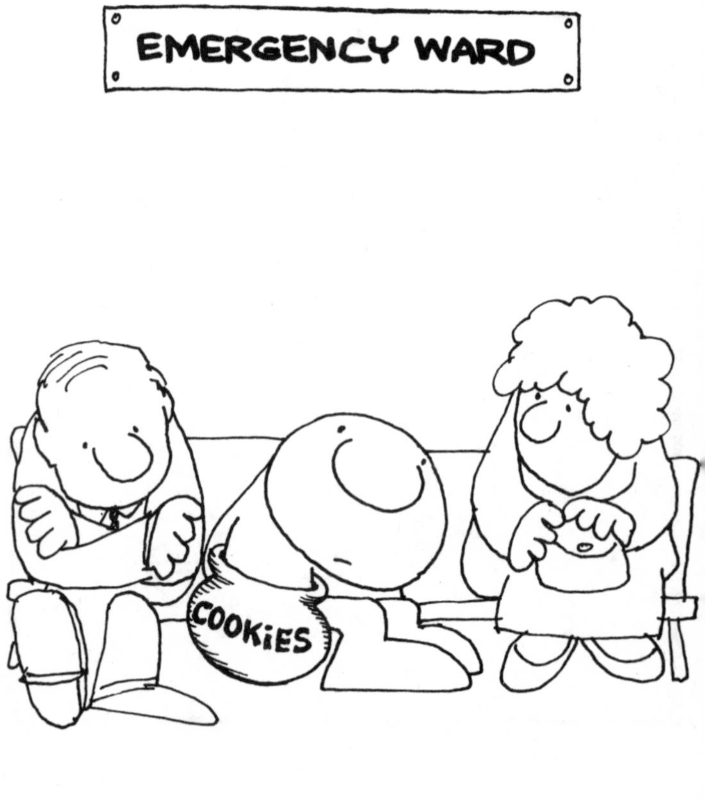
EMERGENCY WARD
COOKiES

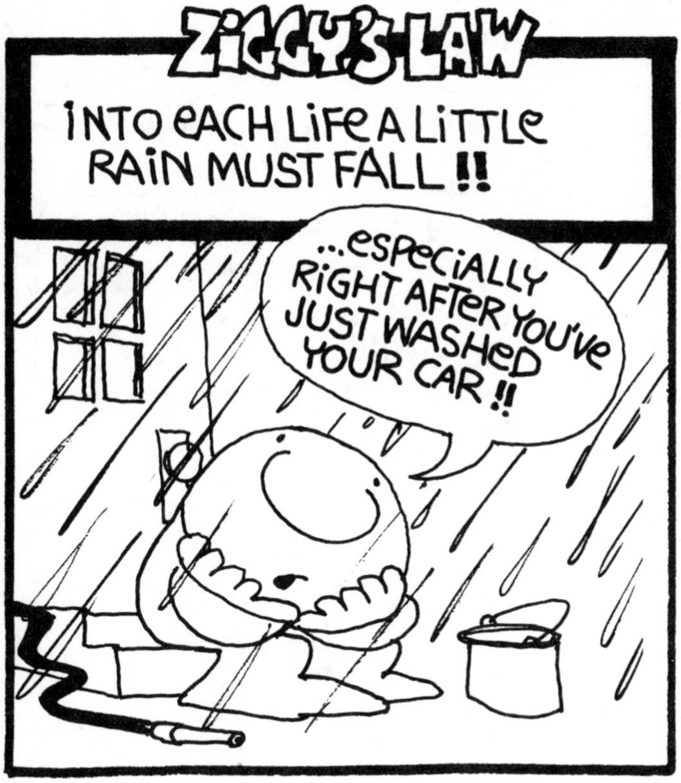
ZIGGY'S LAW
INTO EACH LIFE A LITTLE RAIN MUST FALL !!
...ESPECIALLY RIGHT AFTER YOU'VE JUST WASHED YOUR CAR !!

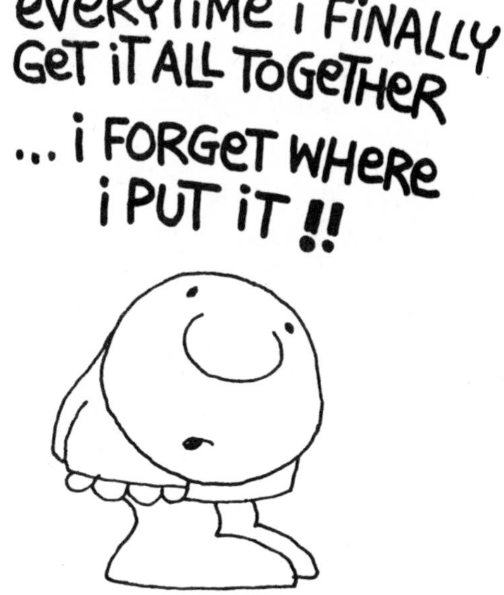
EVERYTIME I FINALLY GET IT ALL TOGETHER ...I FORGET WHERE I PUT IT !!

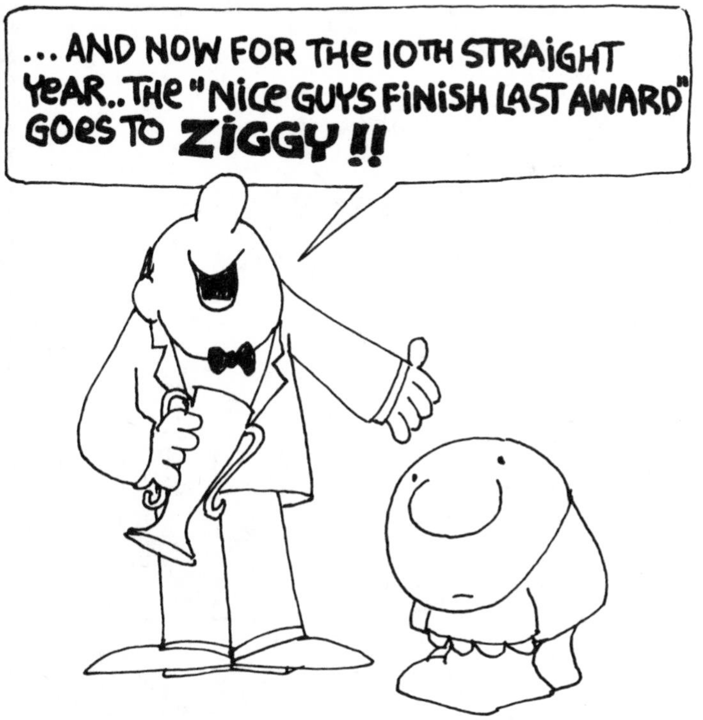
...AND NOW FOR THE 10TH STRAIGHT YEAR..THE "NICE GUYS FINISH LAST AWARD" GOES TO ZIGGY !!

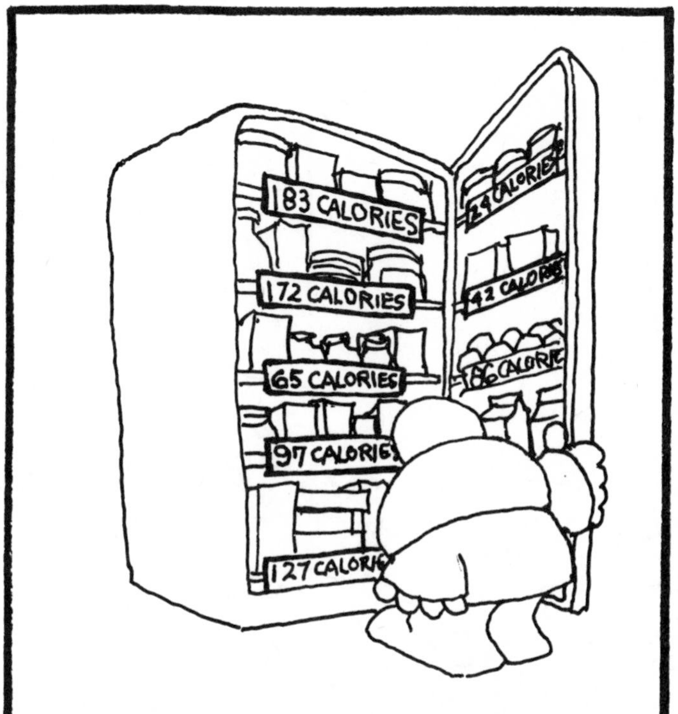
183 CALORIES
172 CALORIES
65 CALORIES
97 CALORIES
127 CALORIES

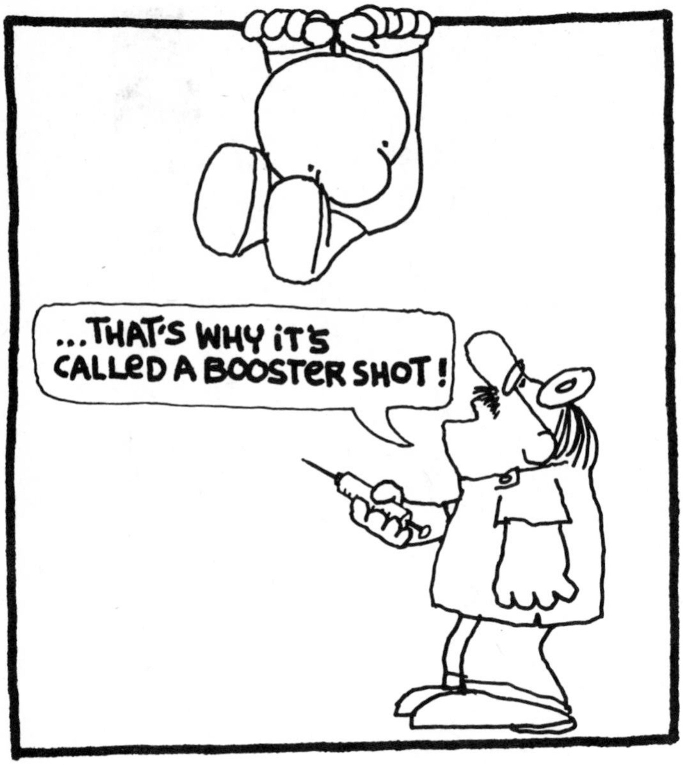
...THAT'S WHY IT'S CALLED A BOOSTER SHOT!

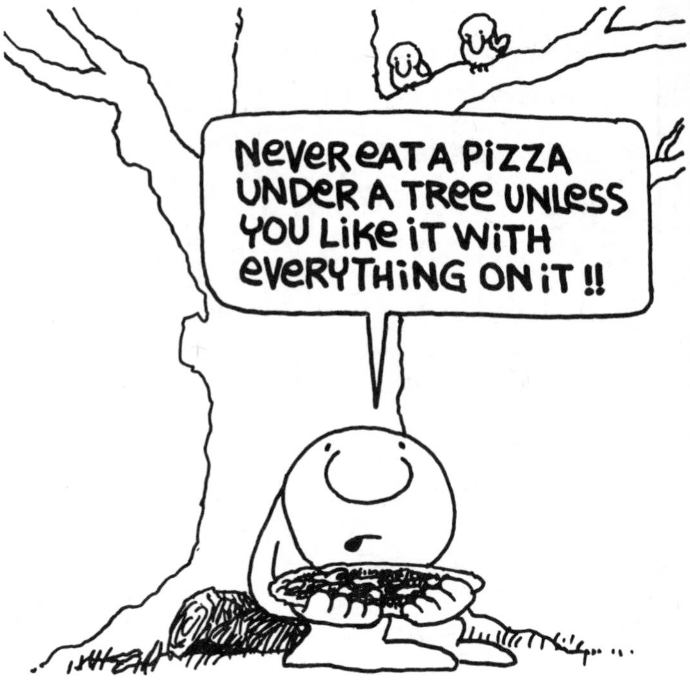
NEVER EAT A PIZZA UNDER A TREE UNLESS YOU LIKE IT WITH EVERYTHING ON IT!!

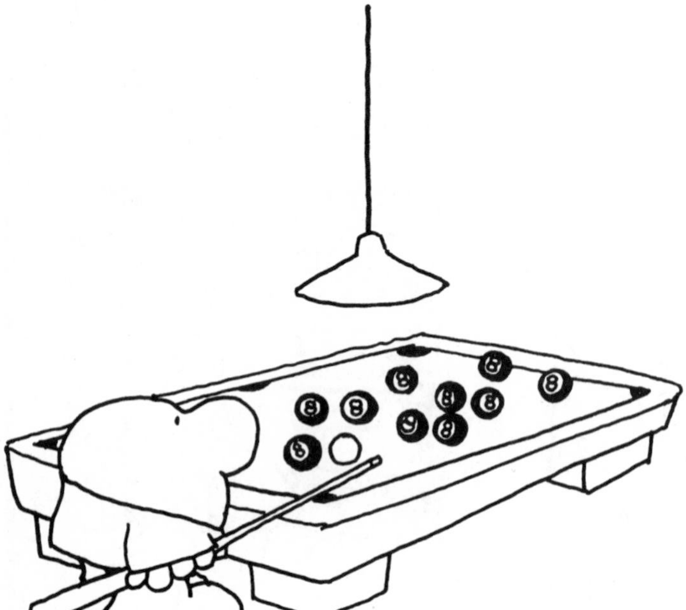

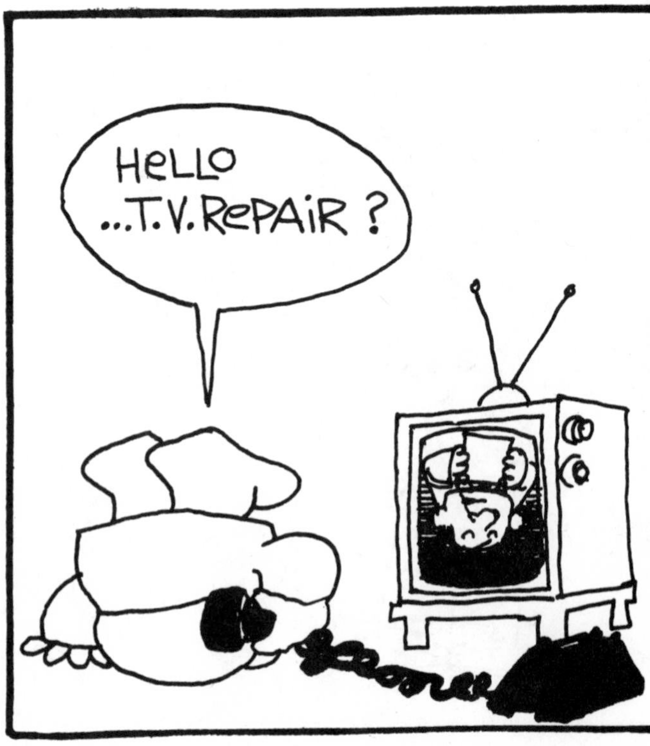
HELLO ...T.V. REPAIR?

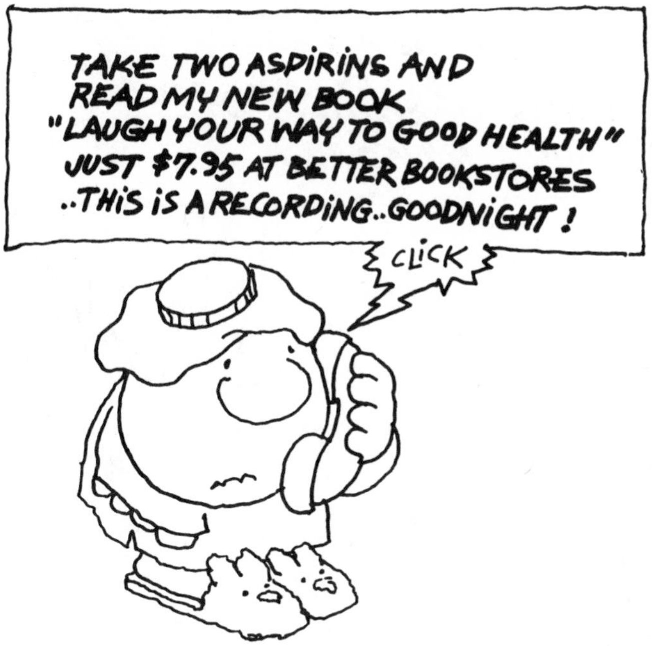
TAKE TWO ASPIRINS AND READ MY NEW BOOK "LAUGH YOUR WAY TO GOOD HEALTH" JUST $7.95 AT BETTER BOOKSTORES ..THIS IS A RECORDING..GOODNIGHT !
CLICK

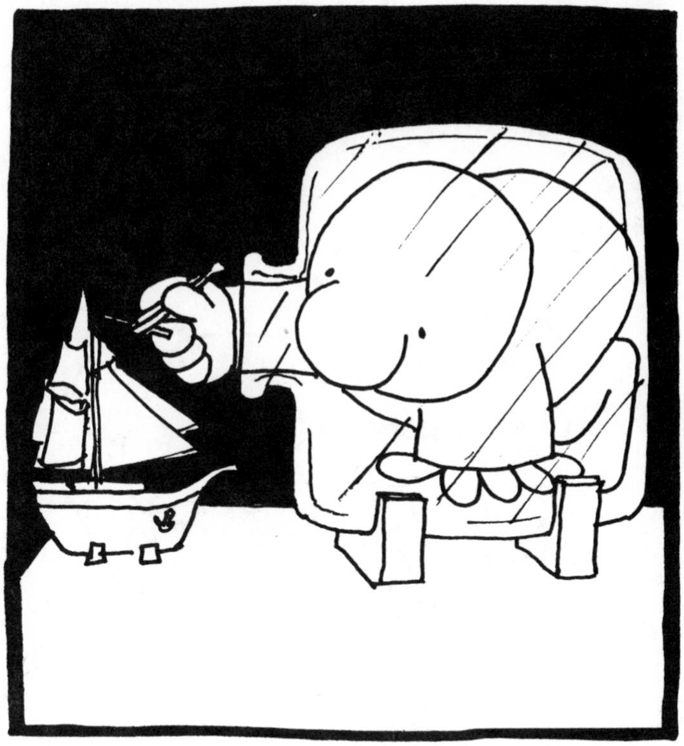

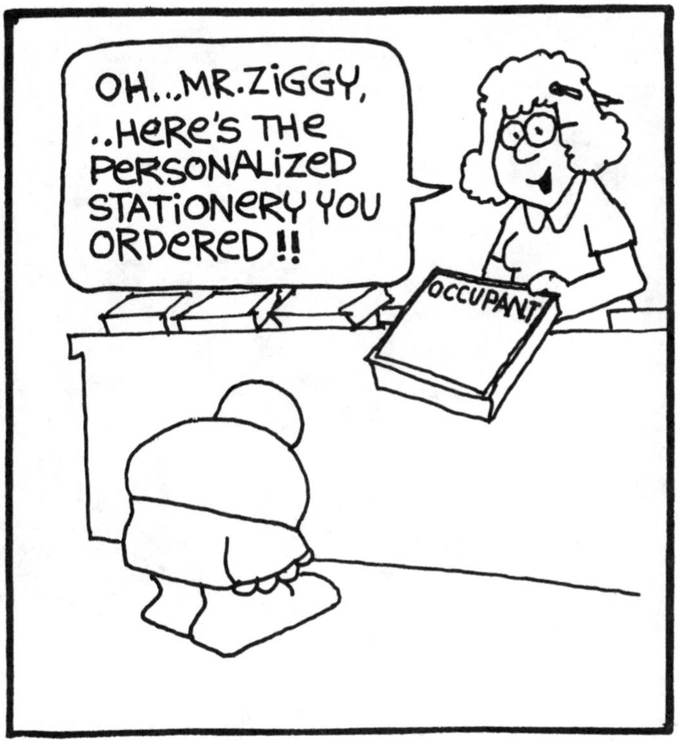
OH...MR.ZIGGY, ..HERE'S THE PERSONALIZED STATIONERY YOU ORDERED!!
OCCUPANT

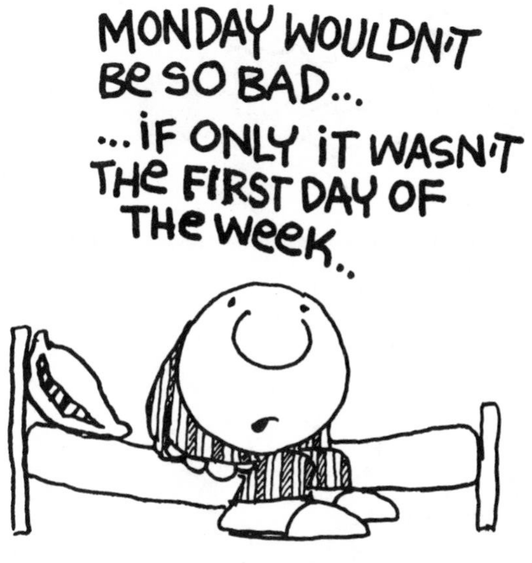
MONDAY WOULDN'T BE SO BAD...
...IF ONLY IT WASN'T THE FIRST DAY OF THE WEEK..

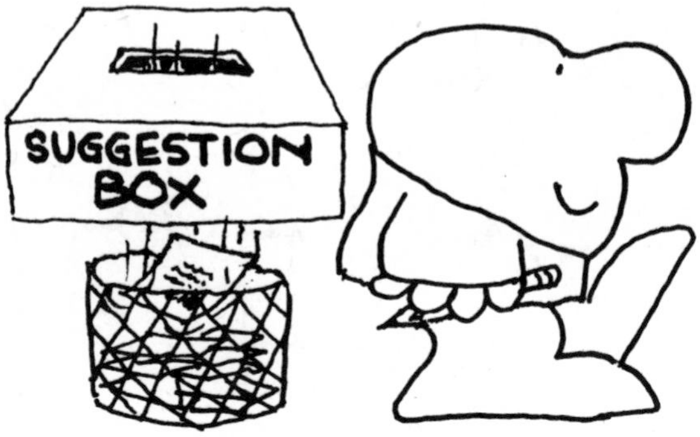
SUGGESTION BOX

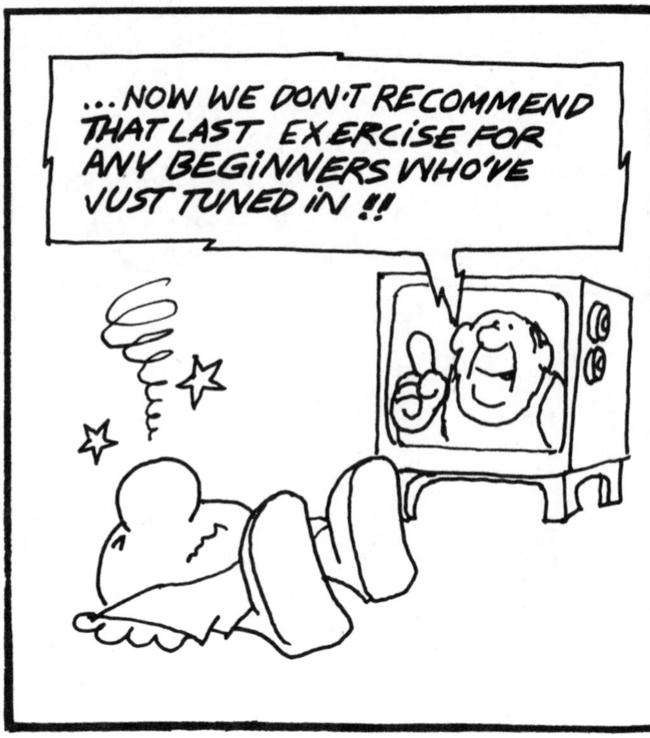
...NOW WE DON'T RECOMMEND THAT LAST EXERCISE FOR ANY BEGINNERS WHO'VE JUST TUNED IN !!

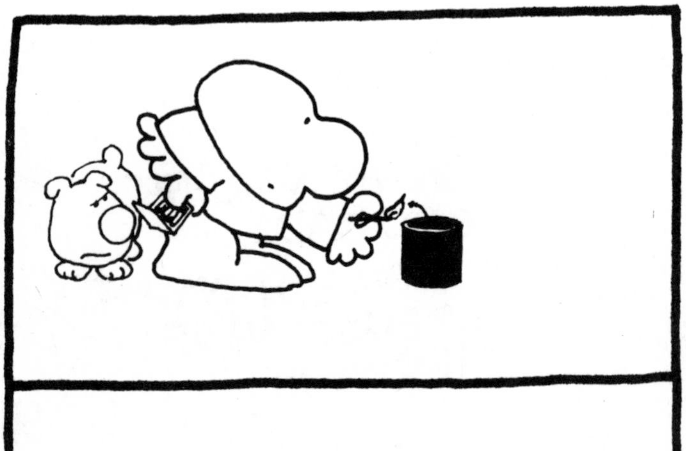

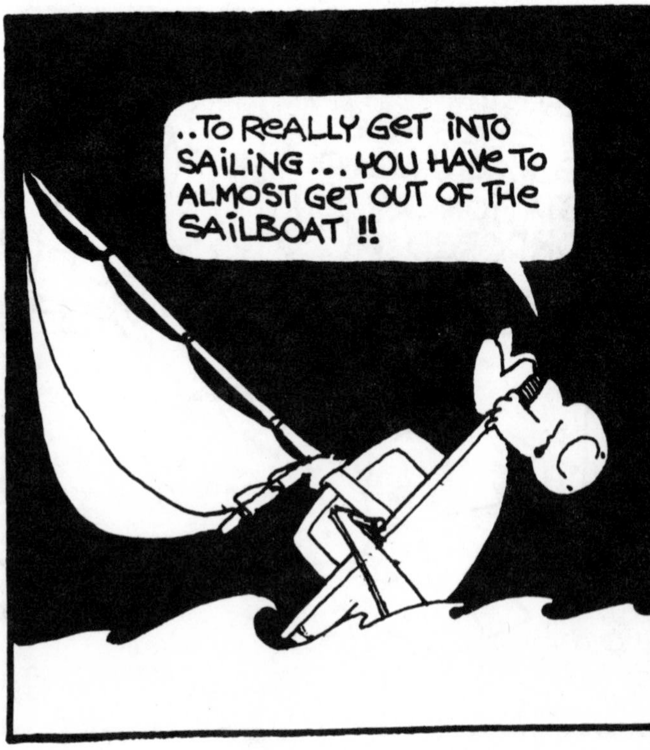
..TO REALLY GET INTO SAILING... YOU HAVE TO ALMOST GET OUT OF THE SAILBOAT !!

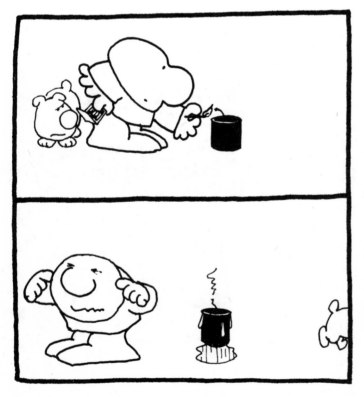

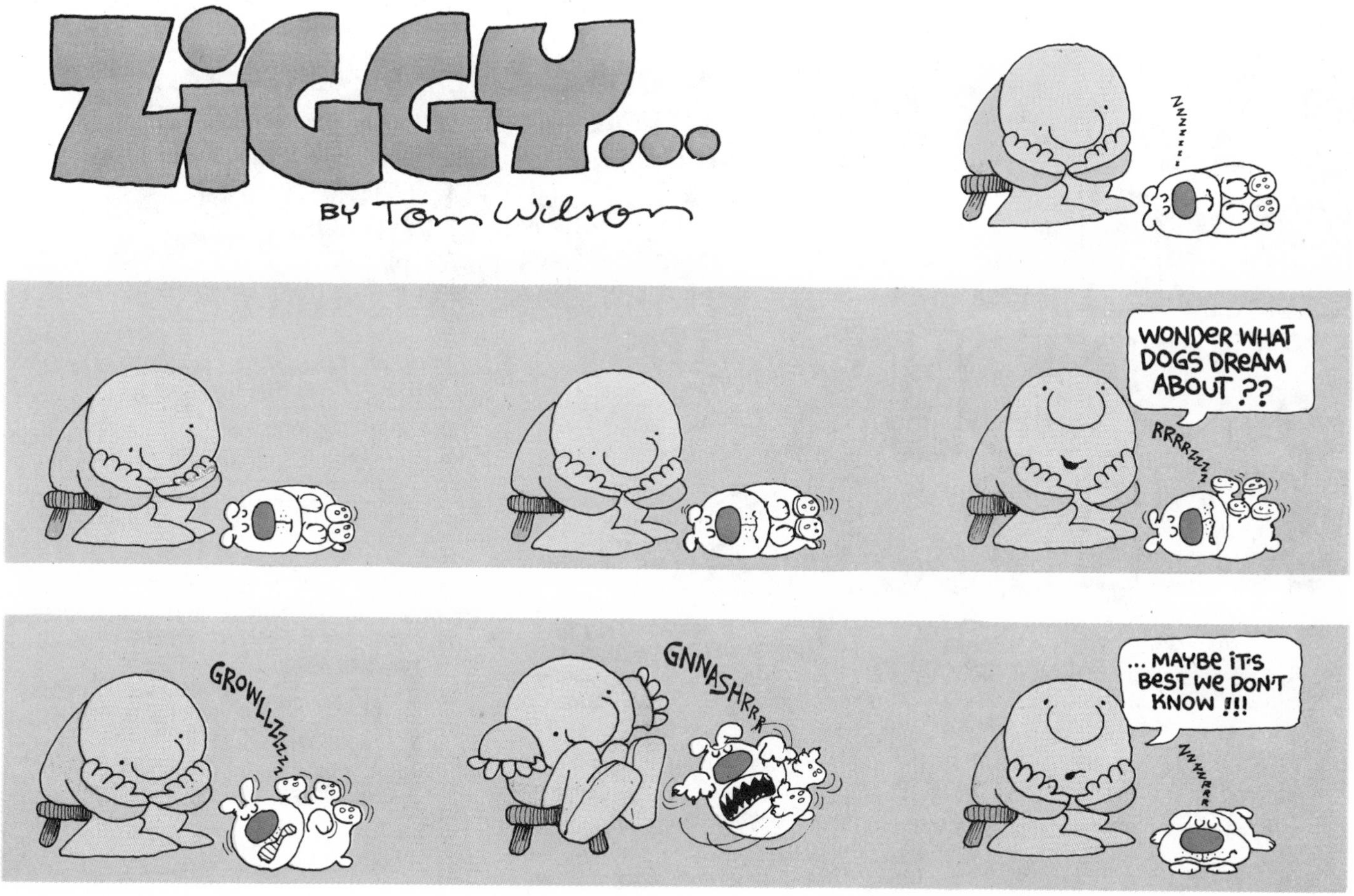
ZIGGY...
BY Tom Wilson
WONDER WHAT DOGS DREAM ABOUT ??
RRRRZZZZ
GROWLLZZZZZ
GNNASHRRRR
... MAYBE IT'S BEST WE DON'T KNOW !!!
ZZZZRRRR

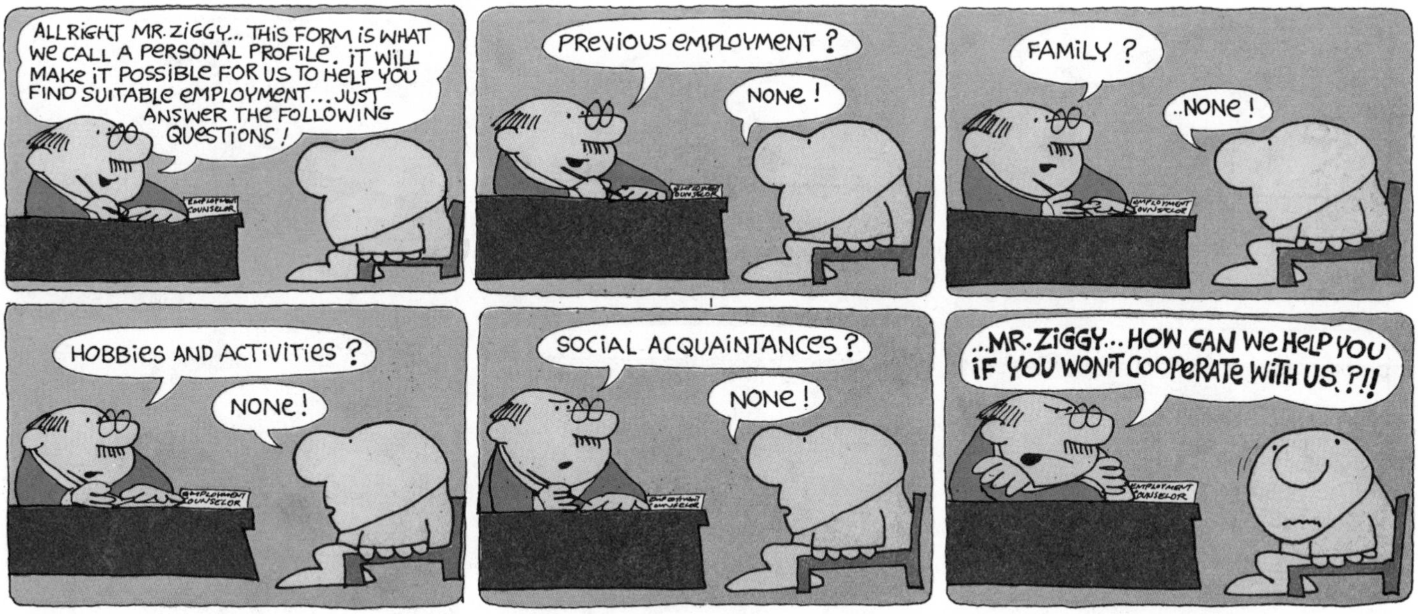
ALLRIGHT MR. ZIGGY... THIS FORM IS WHAT WE CALL A PERSONAL PROFILE. IT WILL MAKE IT POSSIBLE FOR US TO HELP YOU FIND SUITABLE EMPLOYMENT... JUST ANSWER THE FOLLOWING QUESTIONS!
EMPLOYMENT COUNSELOR
PREVIOUS EMPLOYMENT ?
NONE !
FAMILY ?
..NONE !
HOBBIES AND ACTIVITIES ?
NONE !
SOCIAL ACQUAINTANCES ?
NONE !
...MR. ZIGGY... HOW CAN WE HELP YOU IF YOU WON'T COOPERATE WITH US ?!!

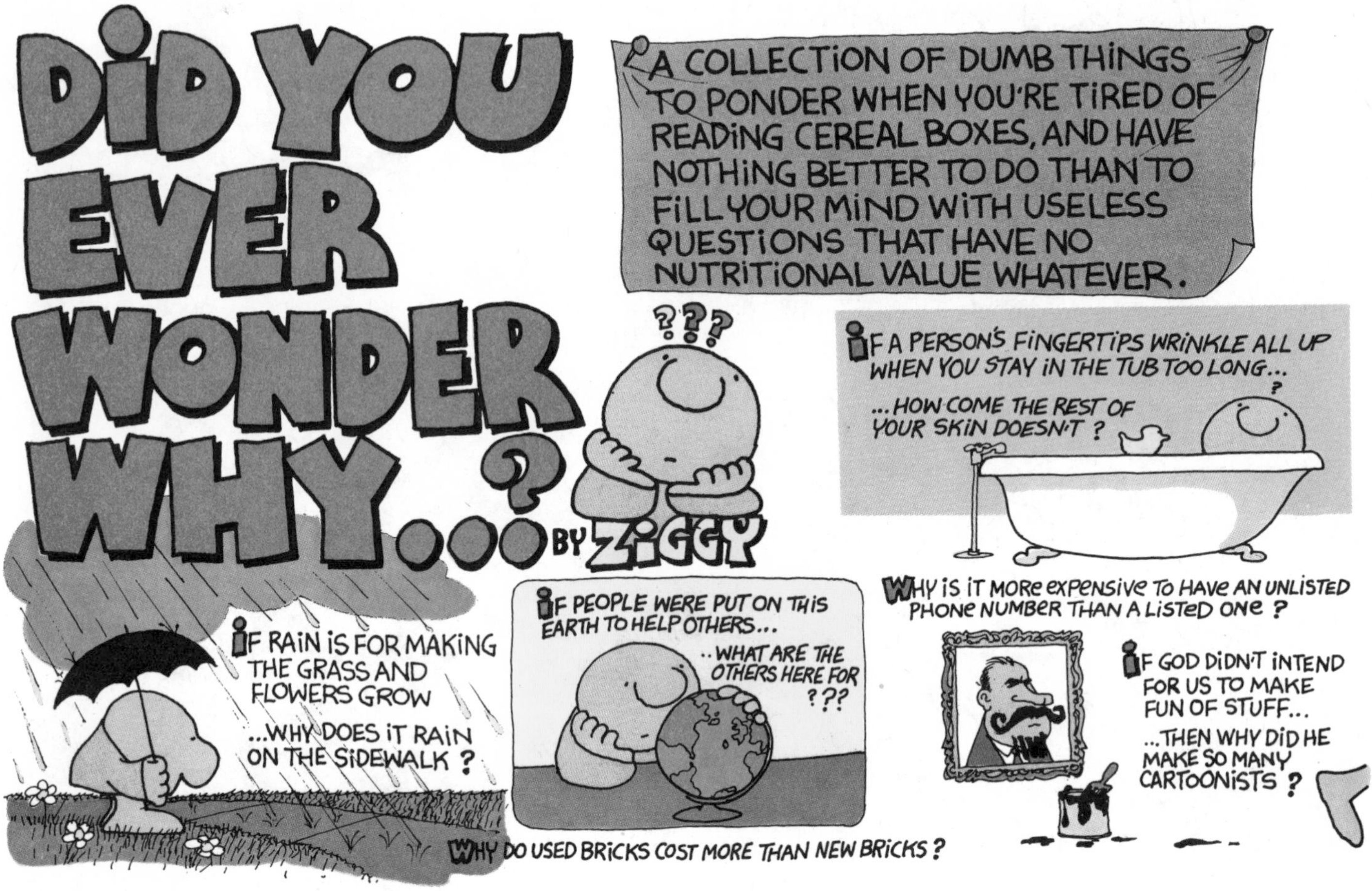
DID YOU EVER WONDER WHY...?
BY ZIGGY
A COLLECTION OF DUMB THINGS TO PONDER WHEN YOU'RE TIRED OF READING CEREAL BOXES, AND HAVE NOTHING BETTER TO DO THAN TO FILL YOUR MIND WITH USELESS QUESTIONS THAT HAVE NO NUTRITIONAL VALUE WHATEVER.
IF A PERSON'S FINGERTIPS WRINKLE ALL UP WHEN YOU STAY IN THE TUB TOO LONG...
...HOW COME THE REST OF YOUR SKIN DOESN'T ?
WHY IS IT MORE EXPENSIVE TO HAVE AN UNLISTED PHONE NUMBER THAN A LISTED ONE ?
IF RAIN IS FOR MAKING THE GRASS AND FLOWERS GROW
...WHY DOES IT RAIN ON THE SIDEWALK ?
IF PEOPLE WERE PUT ON THIS EARTH TO HELP OTHERS...
..WHAT ARE THE OTHERS HERE FOR ???
IF GOD DIDN'T INTEND FOR US TO MAKE FUN OF STUFF...
...THEN WHY DID HE MAKE SO MANY CARTOONISTS ?
WHY DO USED BRICKS COST MORE THAN NEW BRICKS ?

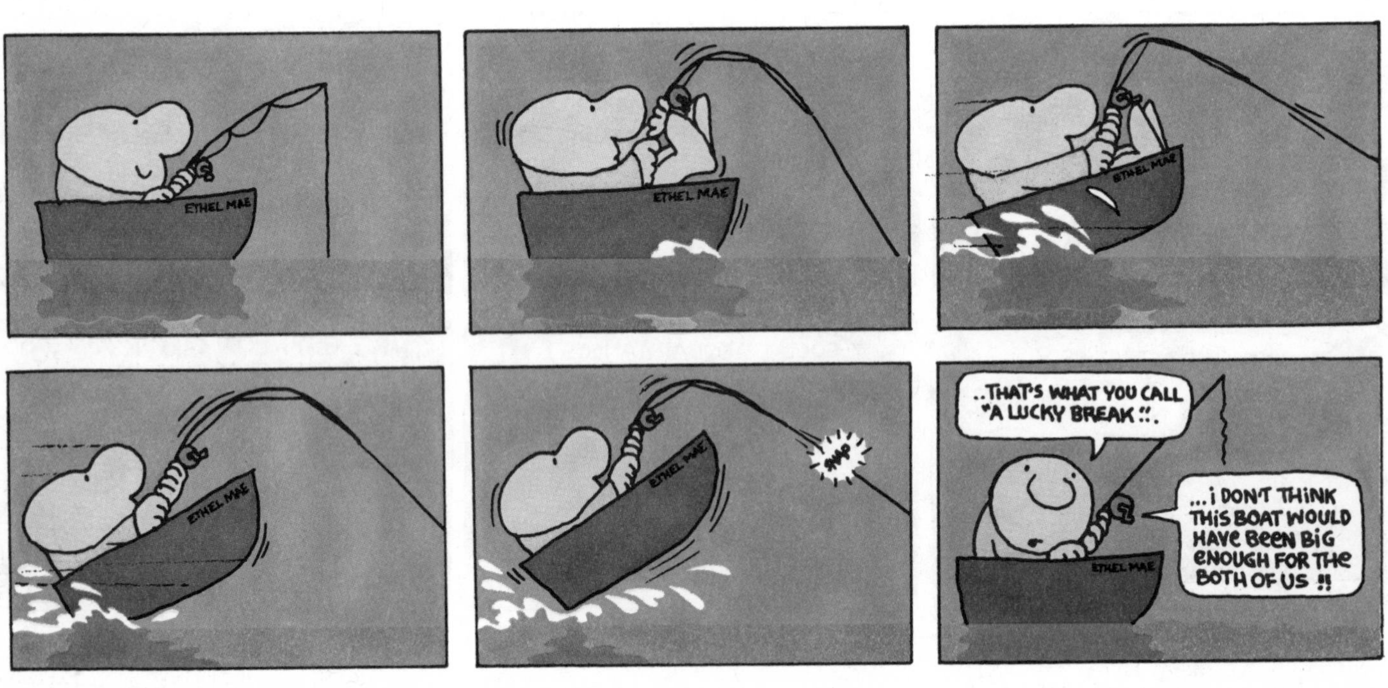
ETHEL MAE
SNAP
..THAT'S WHAT YOU CALL "A LUCKY BREAK"!.
...I DON'T THINK THIS BOAT WOULD HAVE BEEN BIG ENOUGH FOR THE BOTH OF US !!

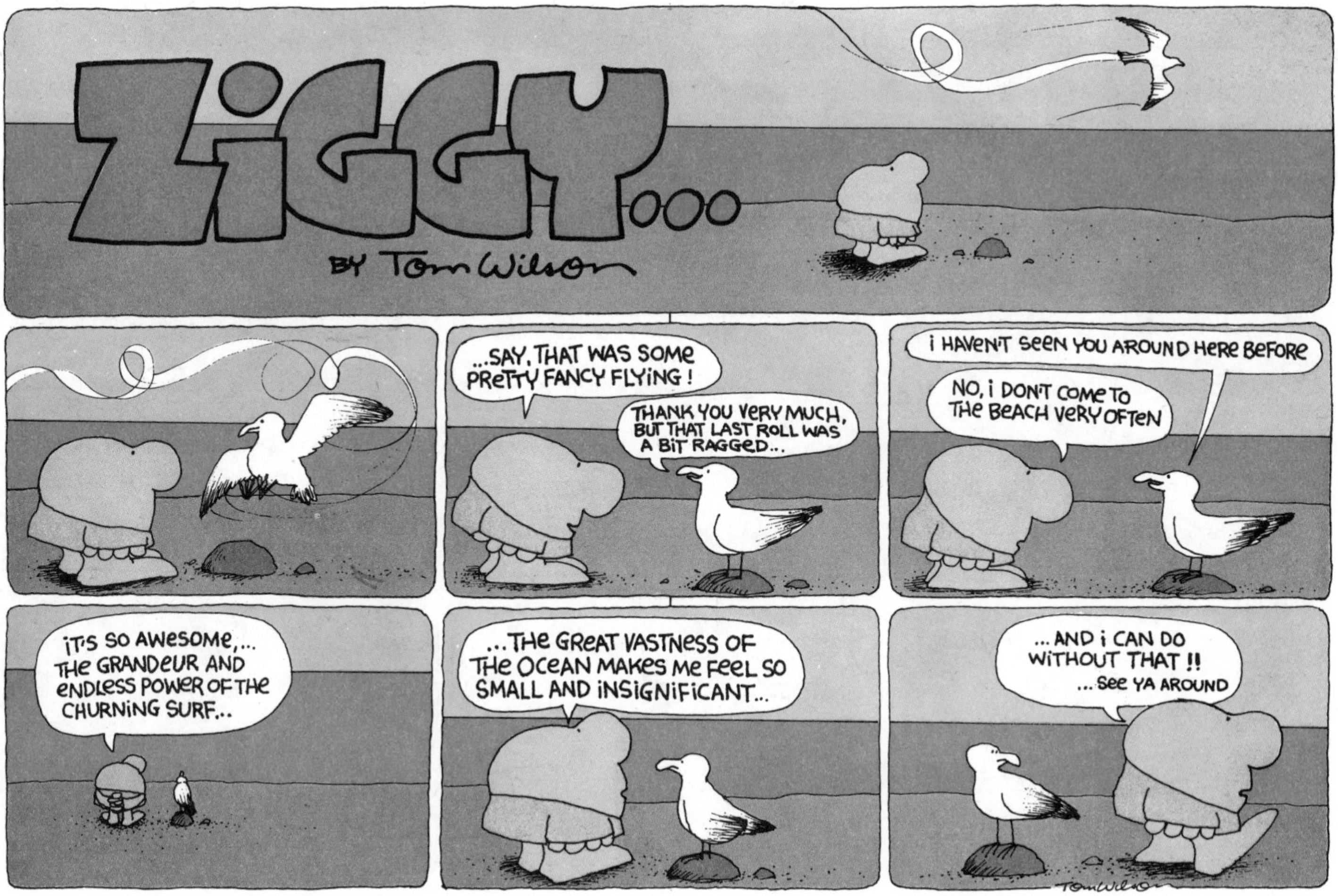
ZiGGY...
BY Tom Wilson
...SAY, THAT WAS SOME PRETTY FANCY FLYING!
THANK YOU VERY MUCH, BUT THAT LAST ROLL WAS A BIT RAGGED...
i HAVEN'T SEEN YOU AROUND HERE BEFORE
NO, i DON'T COME TO THE BEACH VERY OFTEN
iT'S SO AWESOME,... THE GRANDEUR AND ENDLESS POWER OF THE CHURNING SURF...
...THE GREAT VASTNESS OF THE OCEAN MAKES ME FEEL SO SMALL AND iNSIGNIFICANT...
...AND i CAN DO WITHOUT THAT !!
...SEE YA AROUND

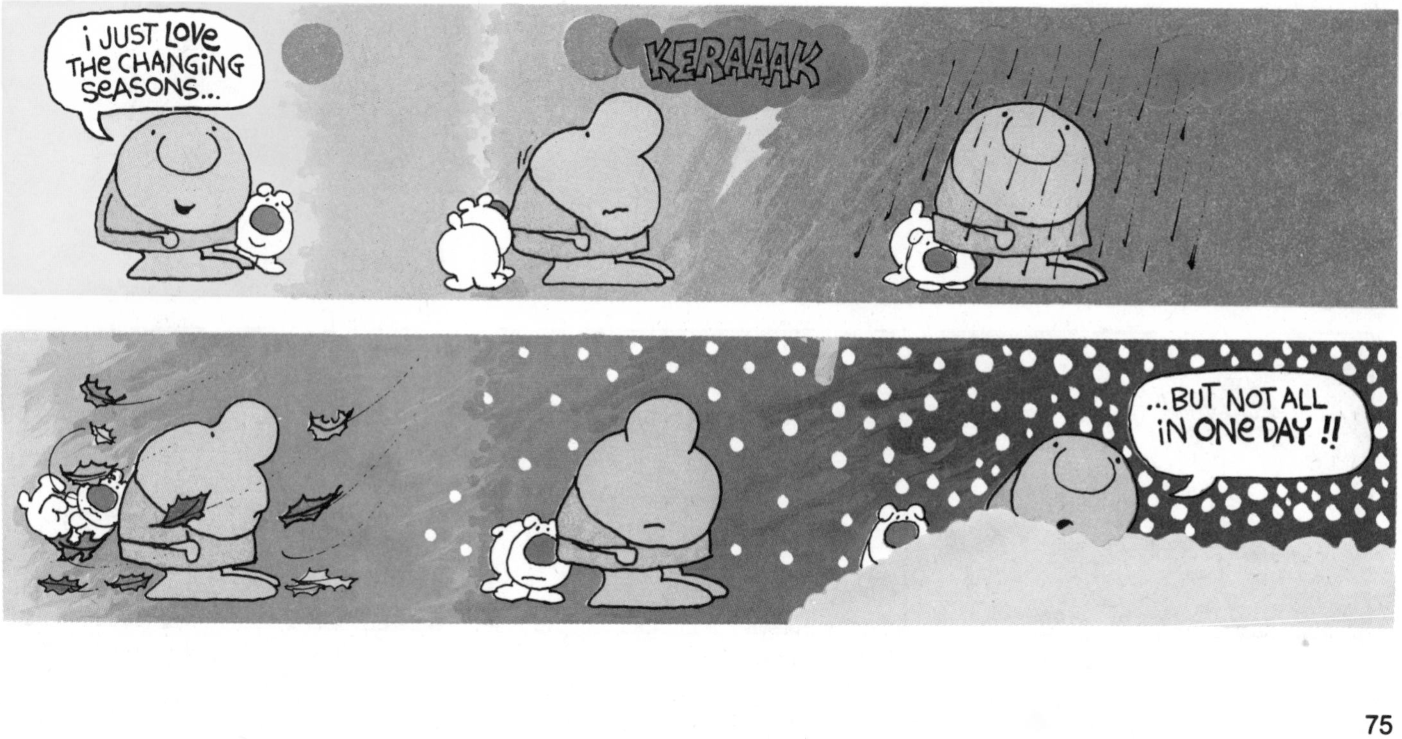
i JUST LOVE THE CHANGING SEASONS...
KERAAAK
...BUT NOT ALL iN ONE DAY !!

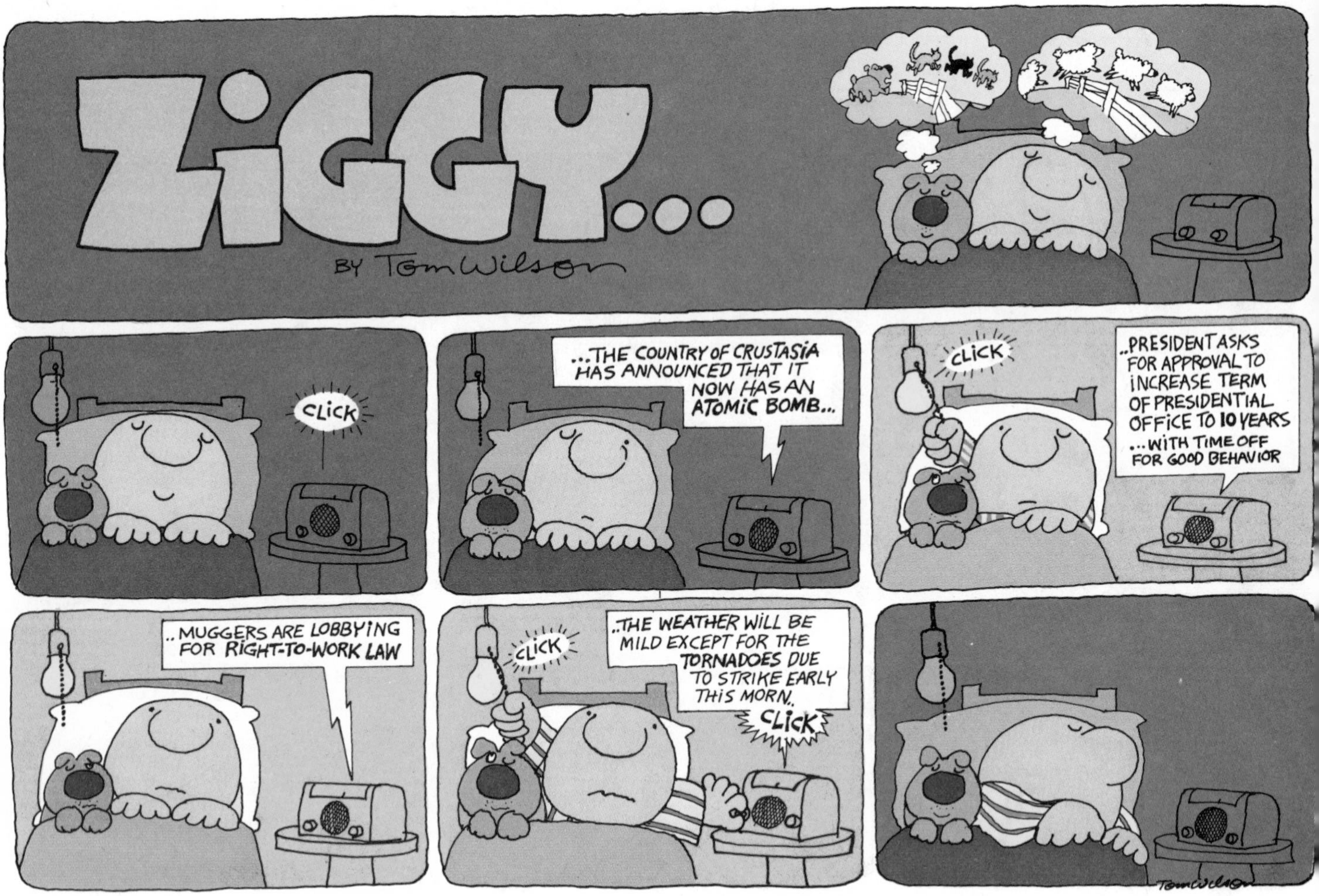
ZiGGY...
BY Tom Wilson
CLiCK
...THE COUNTRY OF CRUSTASiA HAS ANNOUNCED THAT IT NOW HAS AN ATOMiC BOMB...
CLiCK
..PRESIDENT ASKS FOR APPROVAL TO iNCREASE TERM OF PRESIDENTIAL OFFiCE TO 10 YEARS ...WITH TIME OFF FOR GOOD BEHAVIOR
..MUGGERS ARE LOBBYiNG FOR RiGHT-TO-WORK LAW
CLiCK
..THE WEATHER WiLL BE MILD EXCEPT FOR THE TORNADOES DUE TO STRIKE EARLY THIS MORN..
CLiCK
TOM WILSON

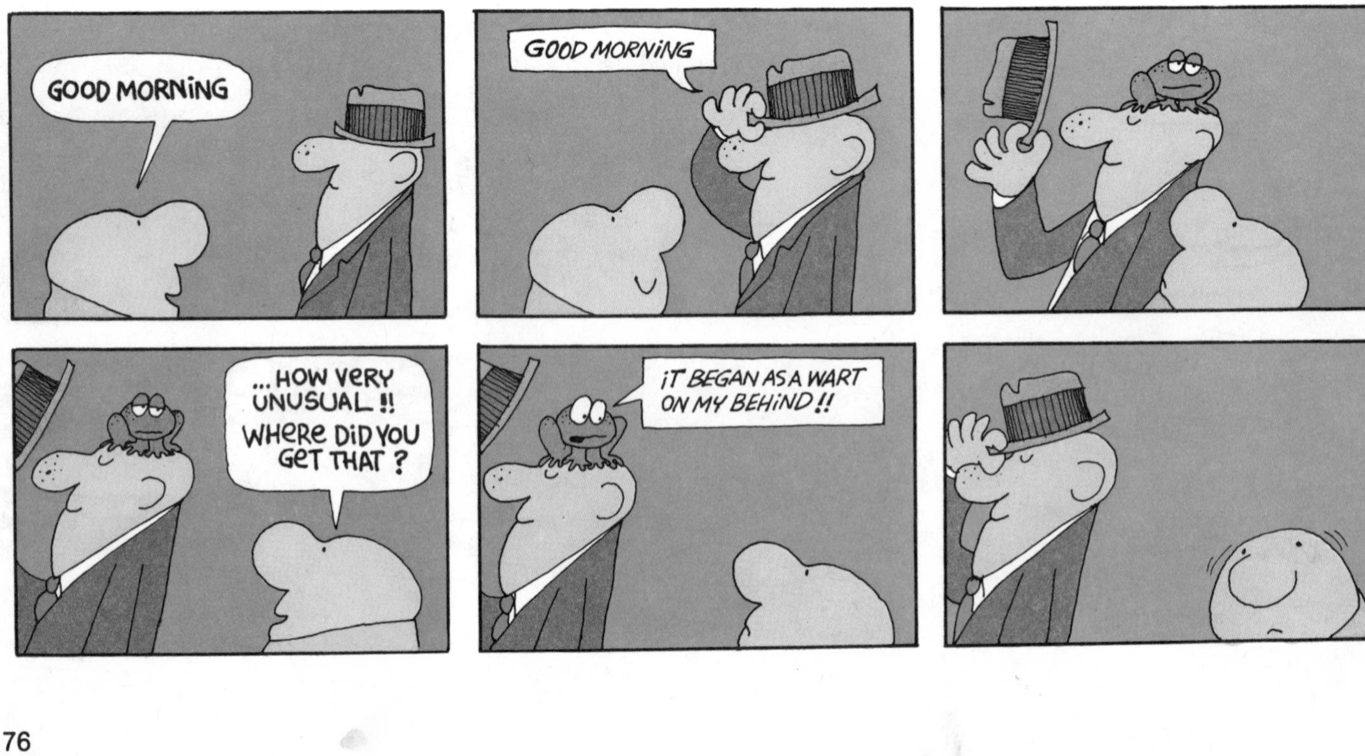
GOOD MORNiNG
GOOD MORNiNG
...HOW VeRY UNUSUAL !! WHeRe DiD YOU GeT THAT ?
iT BEGAN AS A WART ON MY BEHiND !!

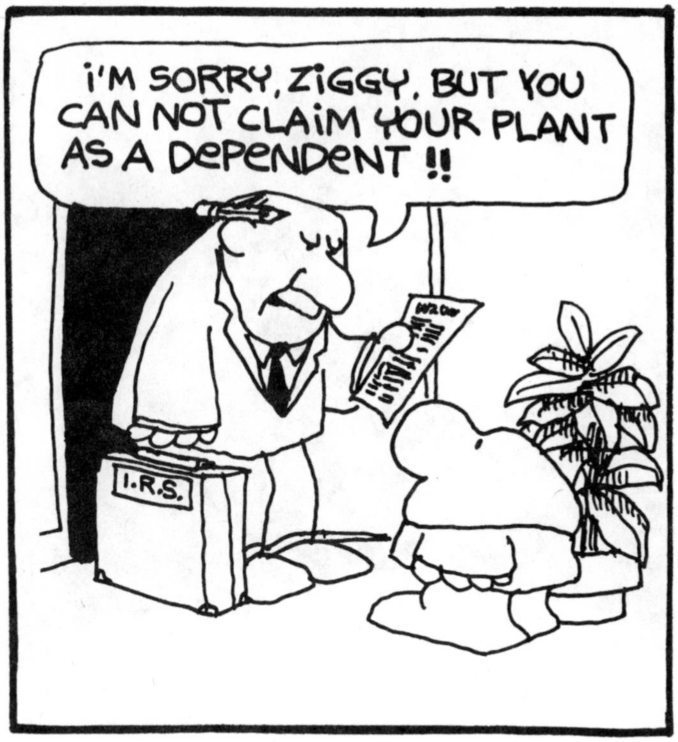
I'M SORRY, ZIGGY, BUT YOU CAN NOT CLAIM YOUR PLANT AS A DEPENDENT !!
I.R.S.

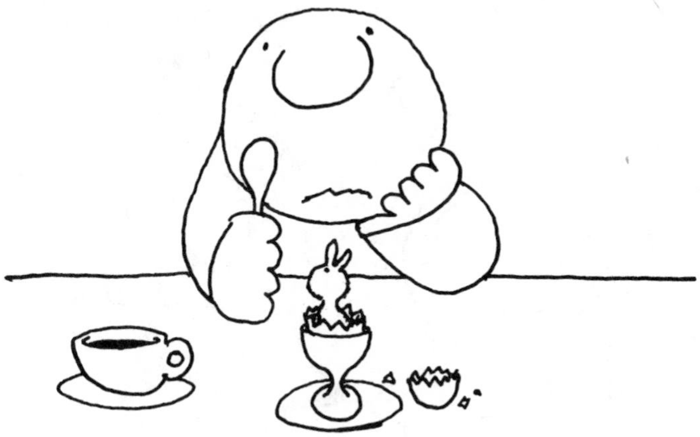

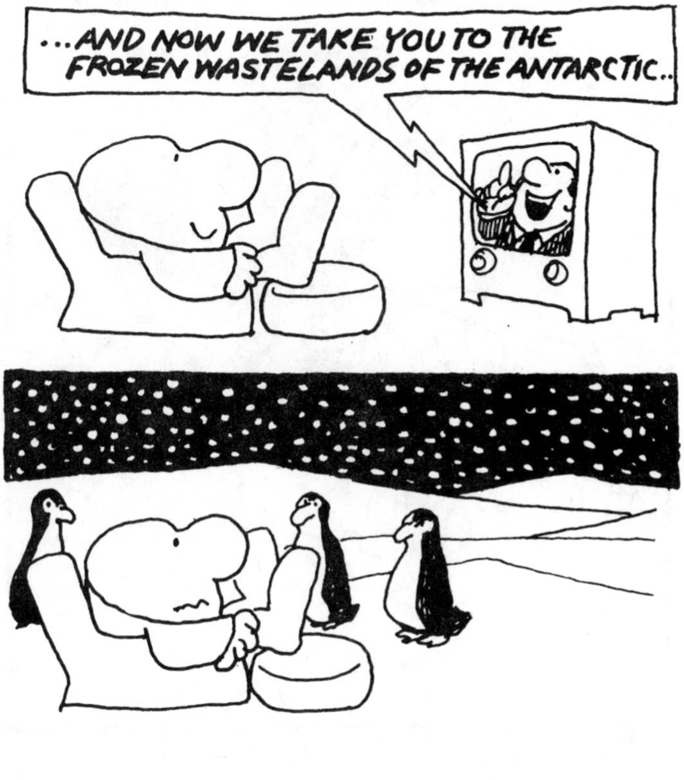
...AND NOW WE TAKE YOU TO THE FROZEN WASTELANDS OF THE ANTARCTIC..

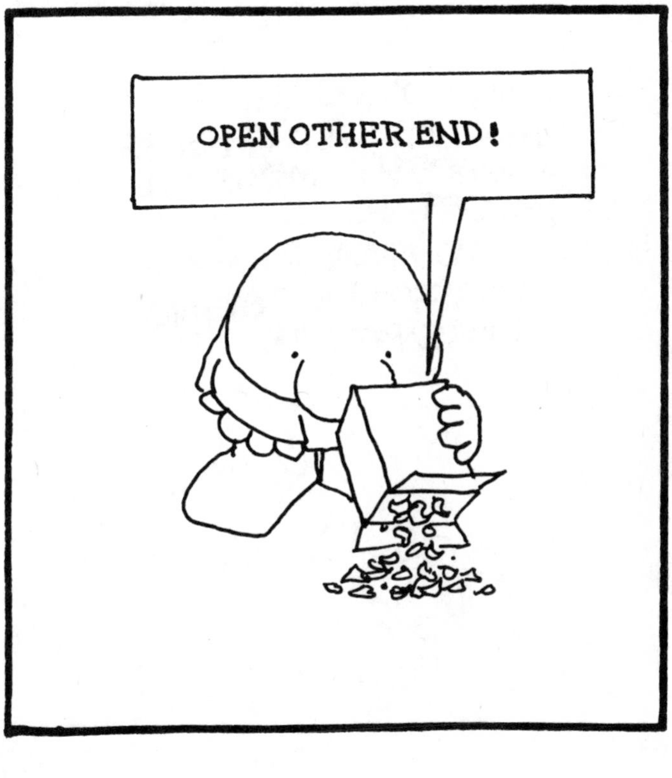
OPEN OTHER END !

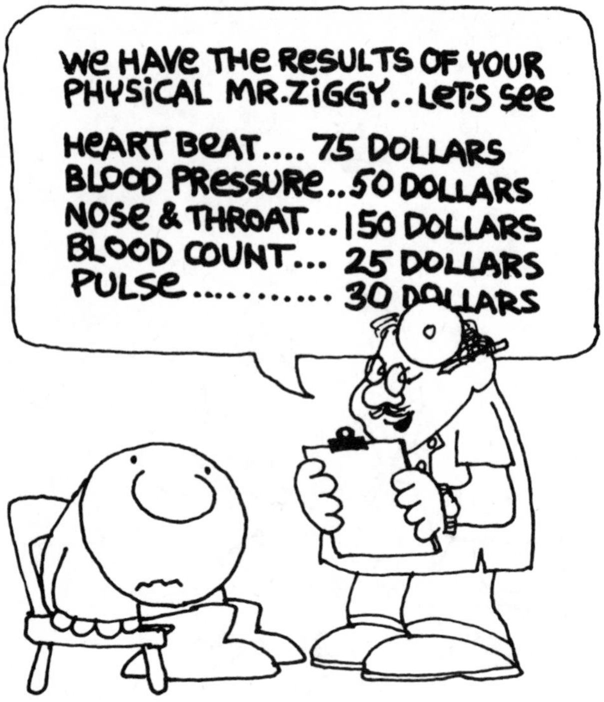
WE HAVE THE RESULTS OF YOUR PHYSICAL MR. ZIGGY.. LET'S SEE
HEART BEAT.... 75 DOLLARS
BLOOD PRESSURE..50 DOLLARS
NOSE & THROAT...150 DOLLARS
BLOOD COUNT... 25 DOLLARS
PULSE........... 30 DOLLARS

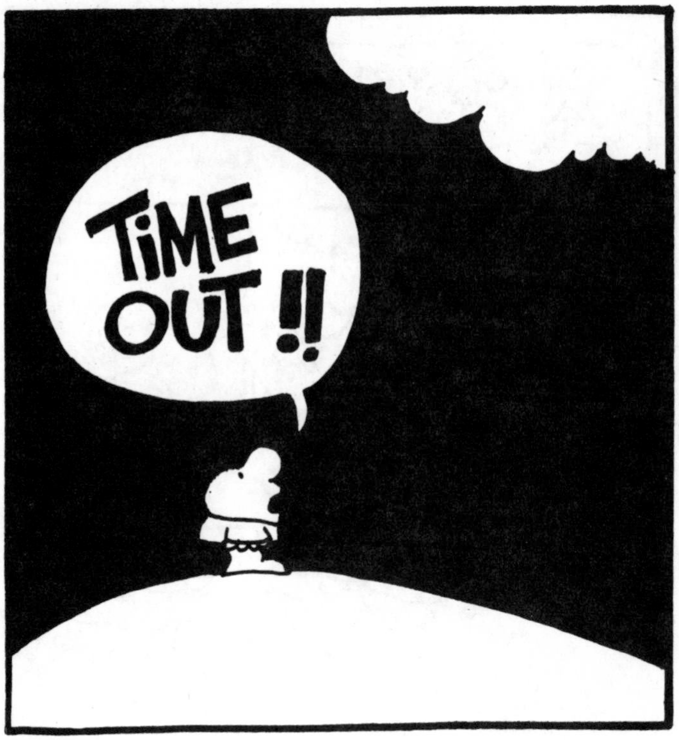
TIME OUT !!

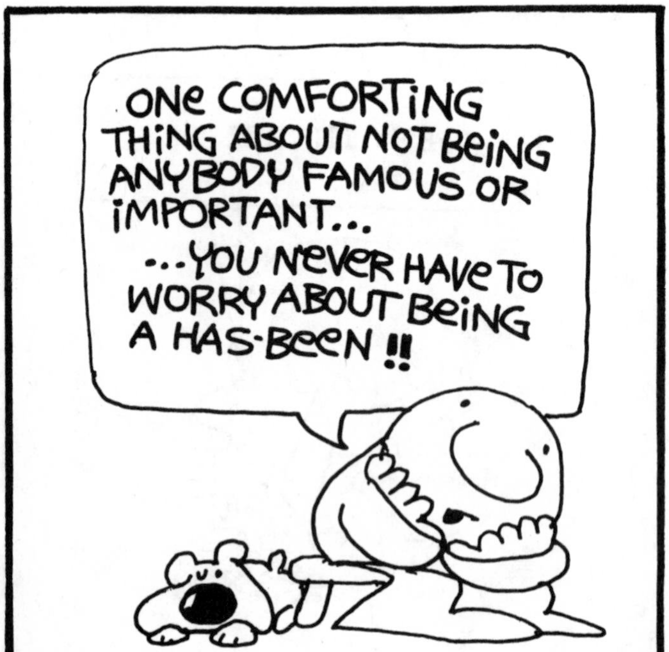
ONE COMFORTING THING ABOUT NOT BEING ANYBODY FAMOUS OR IMPORTANT...
...YOU NEVER HAVE TO WORRY ABOUT BEING A HAS-BEEN !!

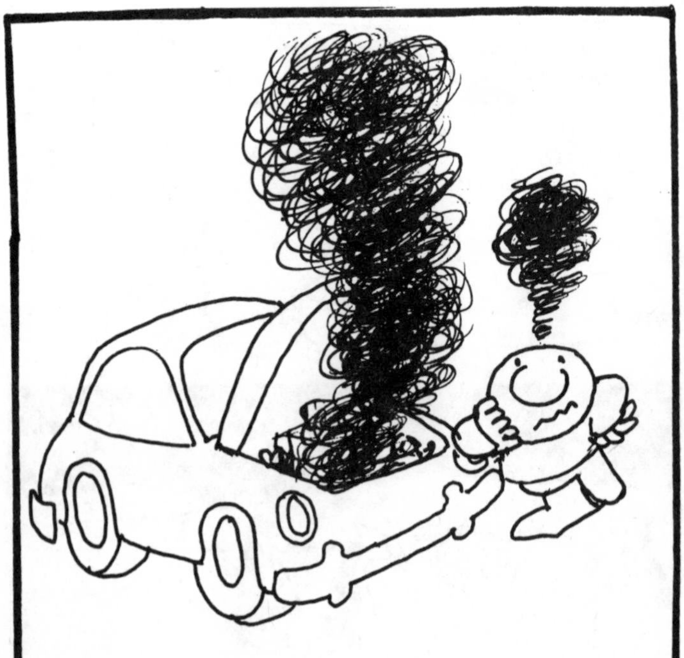

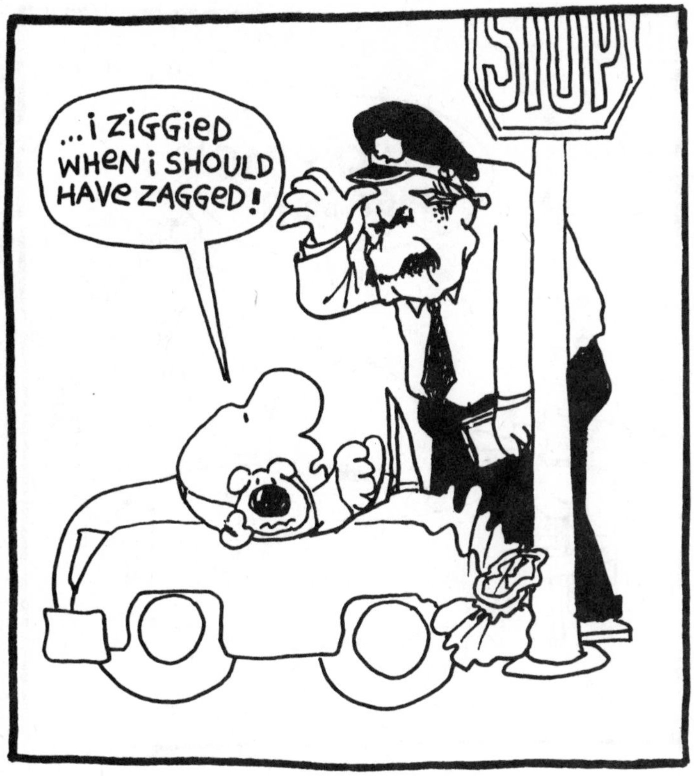
STOP
...i ZiGGied WHEN i SHOULD HAVE ZAGGED!

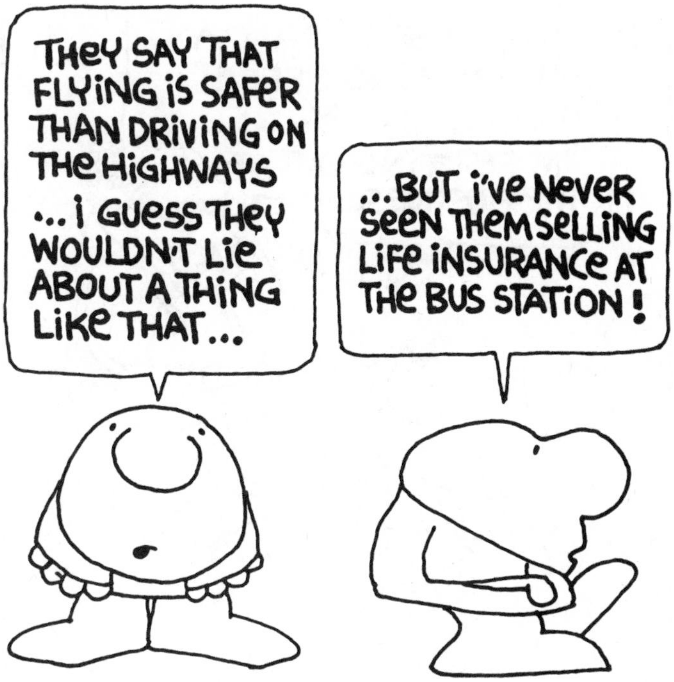
THEY SAY THAT FLYING IS SAFER THAN DRIVING ON THE HIGHWAYS ...i GUESS THEY WOULDN'T LIE ABOUT A THING LIKE THAT...
...BUT i've NEVER SEEN THEM SELLING LIFE INSURANCE AT THE BUS STATION!

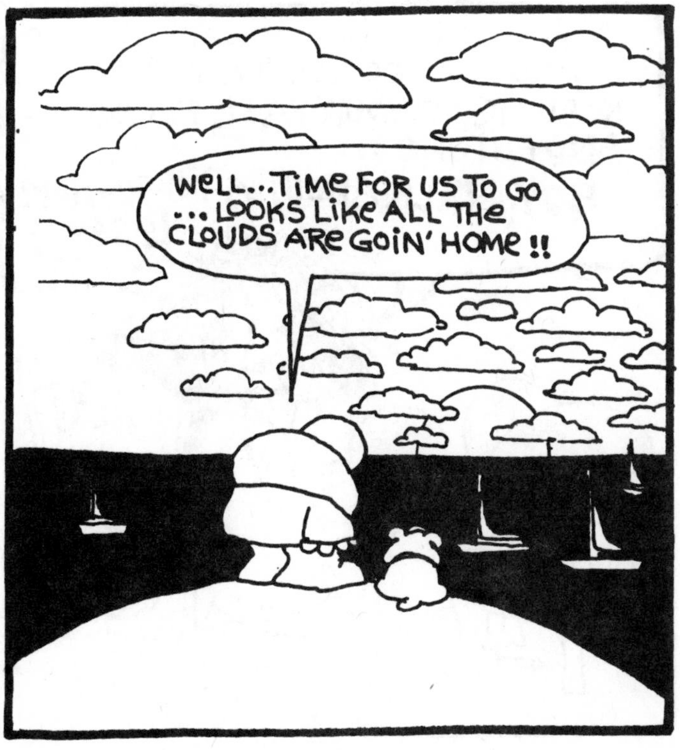
WELL...TIME FOR US TO GO ...LOOKS LIKE ALL THE CLOUDS ARE GOIN' HOME!!

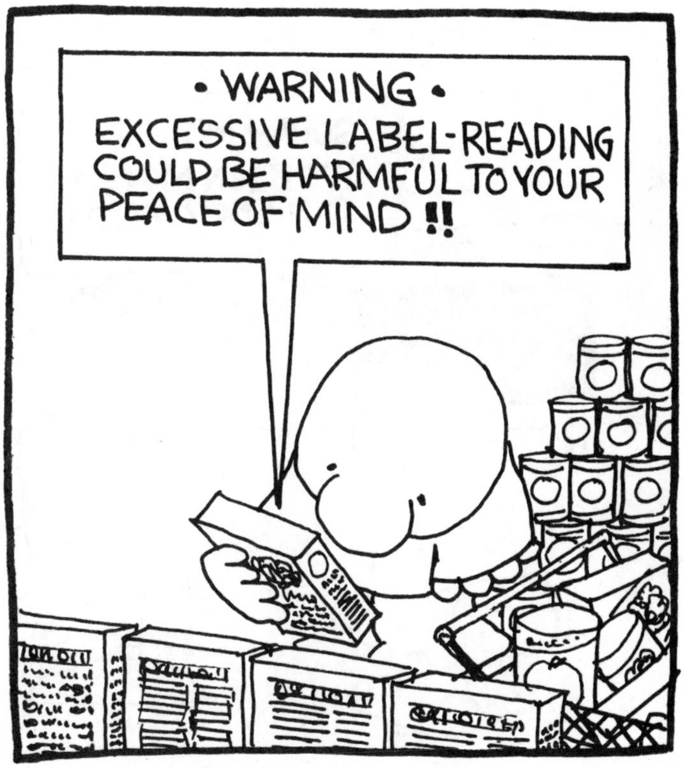
• WARNING •
EXCESSIVE LABEL-READING COULD BE HARMFUL TO YOUR PEACE OF MIND!!

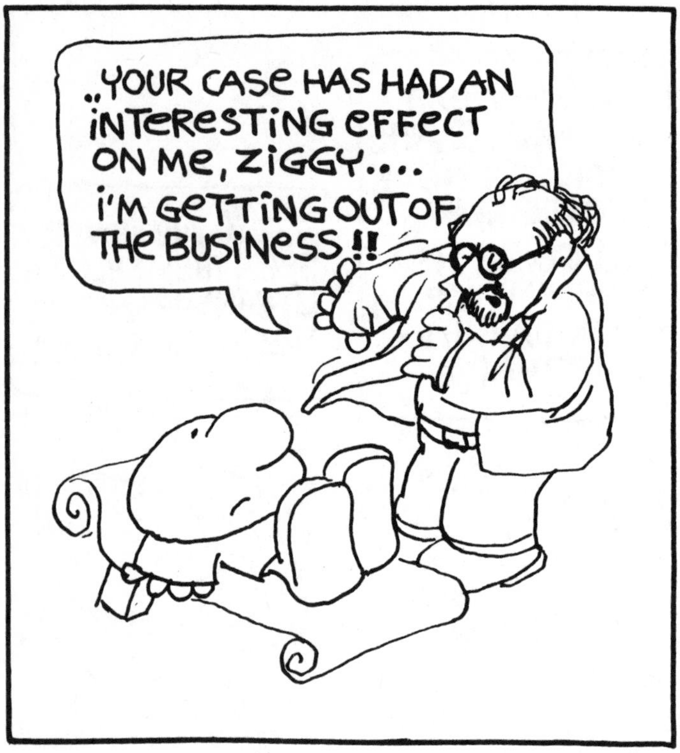
..YOUR CASE HAS HAD AN INTERESTING EFFECT ON ME, ZIGGY.... I'M GETTING OUT OF THE BUSINESS !!

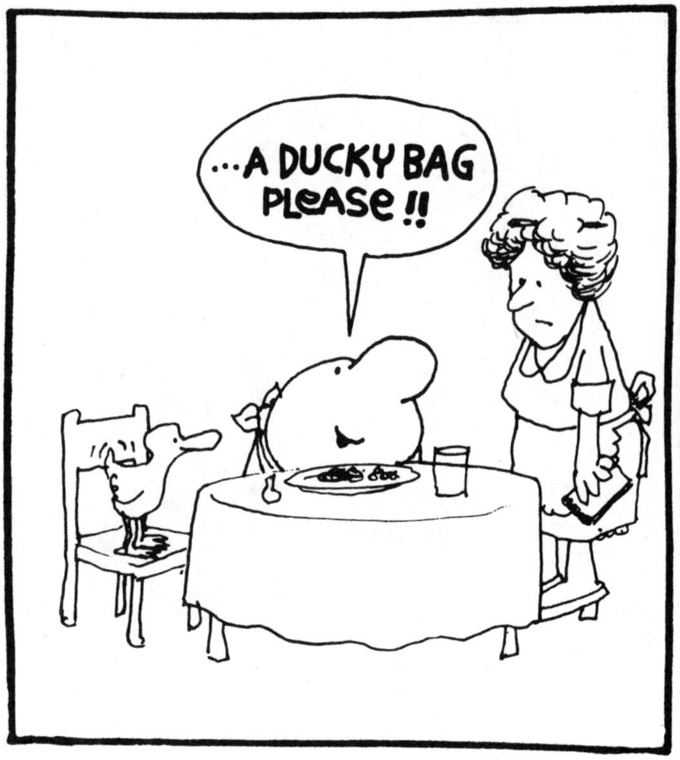
...A DUCKY BAG PLEASE !!

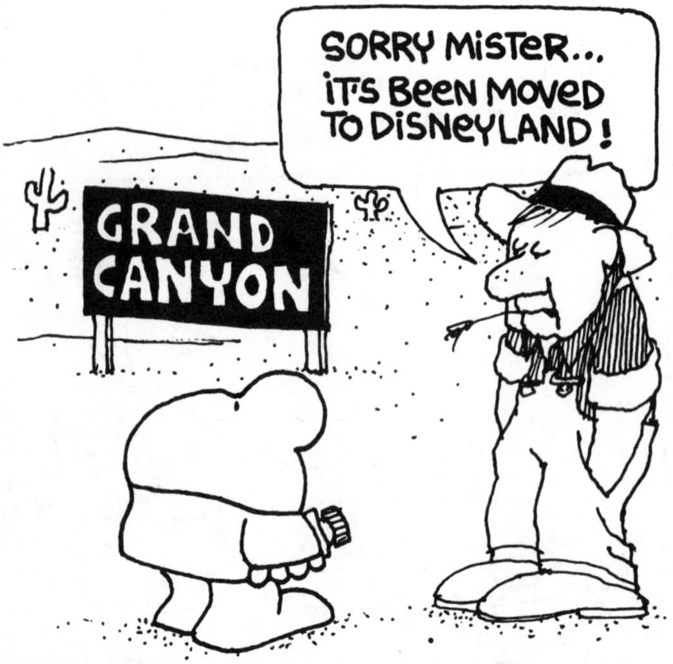
SORRY MISTER... IT'S BEEN MOVED TO DISNEYLAND !
GRAND CANYON

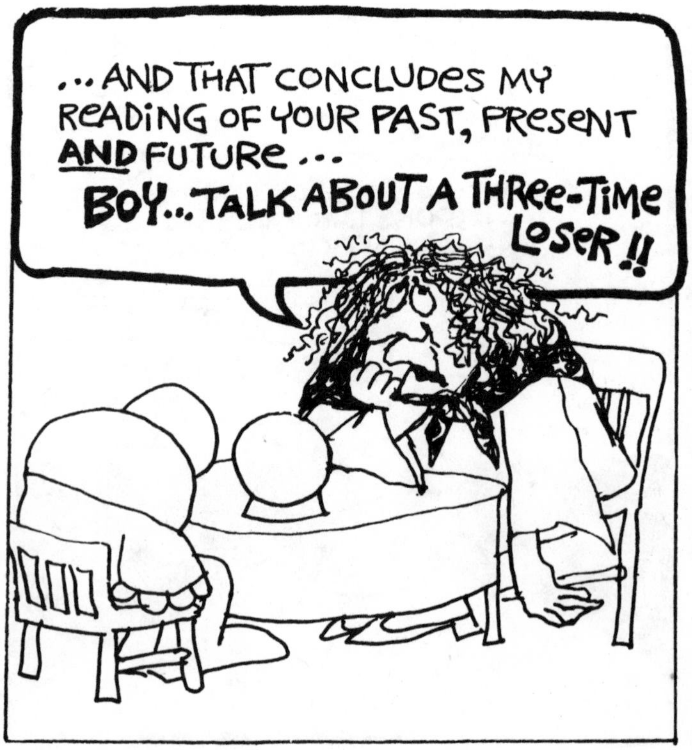
...AND THAT CONCLUDES MY READING OF YOUR PAST, PRESENT AND FUTURE ... BOY... TALK ABOUT A THREE-TIME LOSER !!

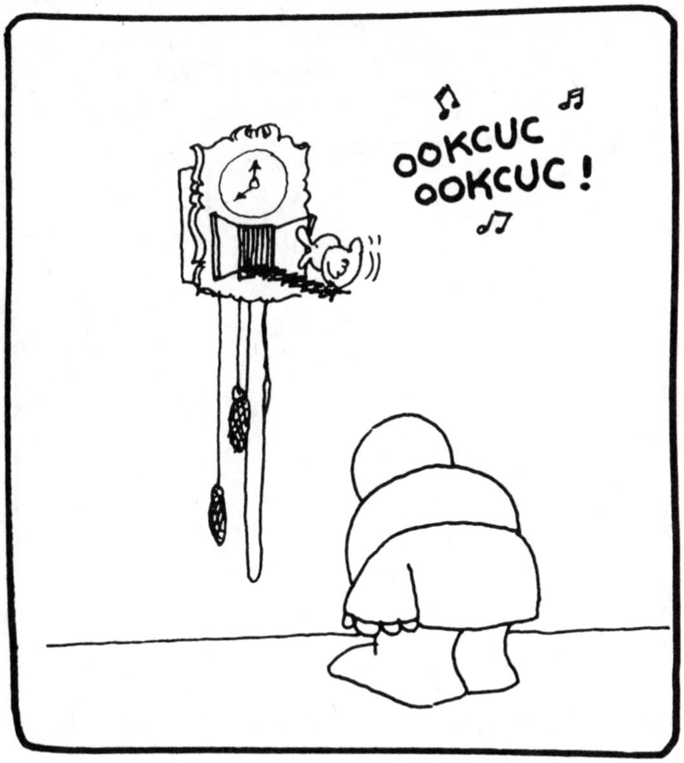
OOKCUC
OOKCUC!

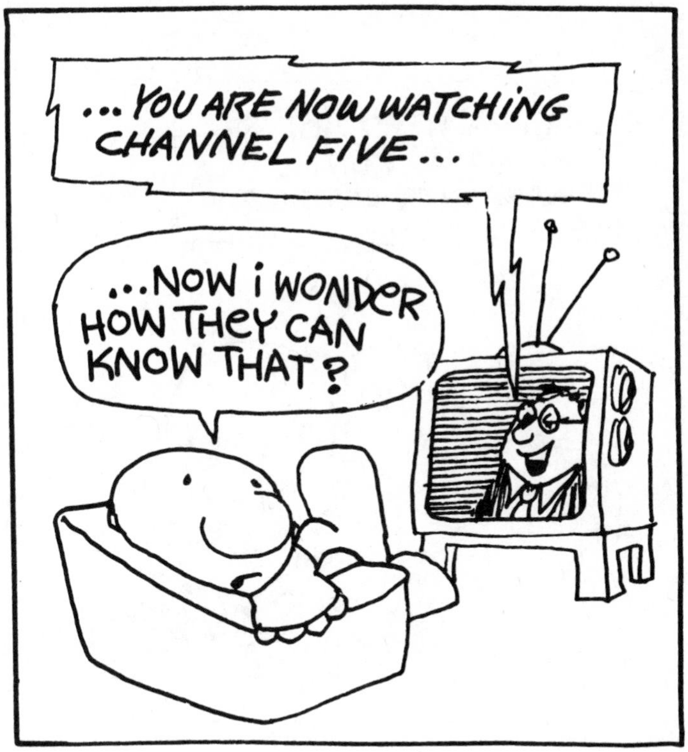
...YOU ARE NOW WATCHING CHANNEL FIVE...
...NOW I WONDER HOW THEY CAN KNOW THAT?

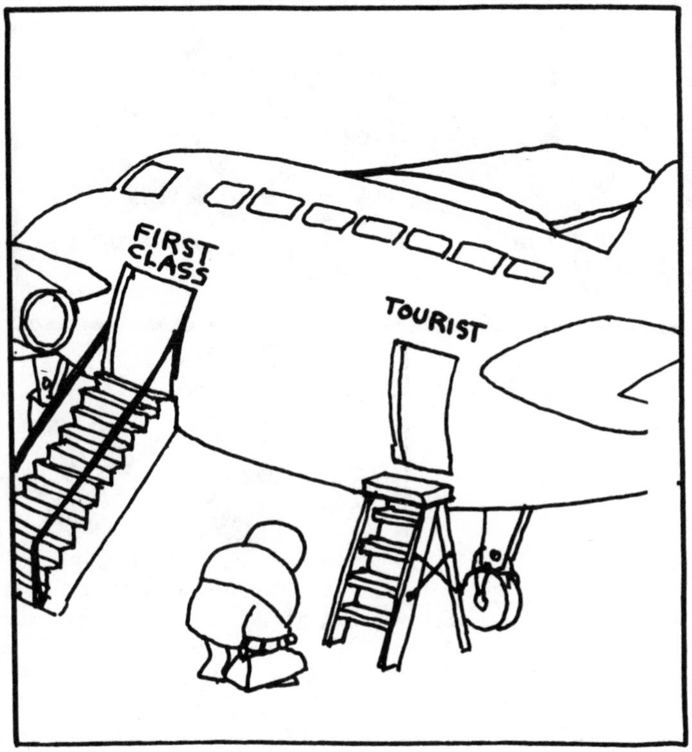
FIRST CLASS
TOURIST

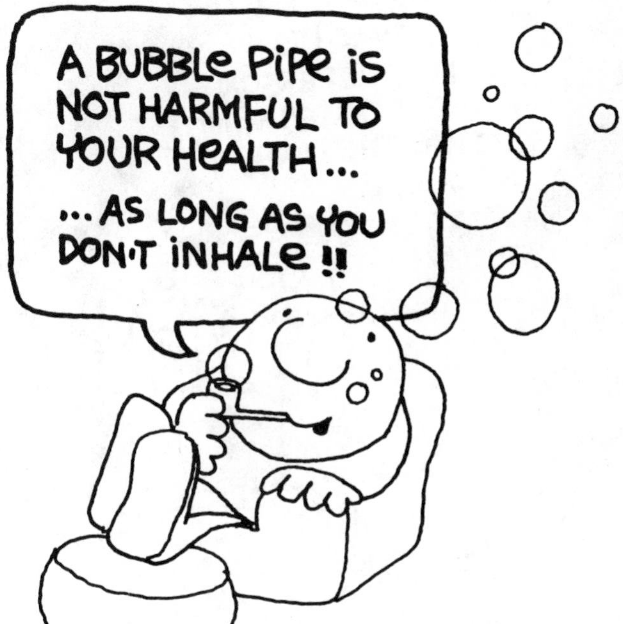
A BUBBLE PIPE IS NOT HARMFUL TO YOUR HEALTH...
...AS LONG AS YOU DON'T INHALE!!

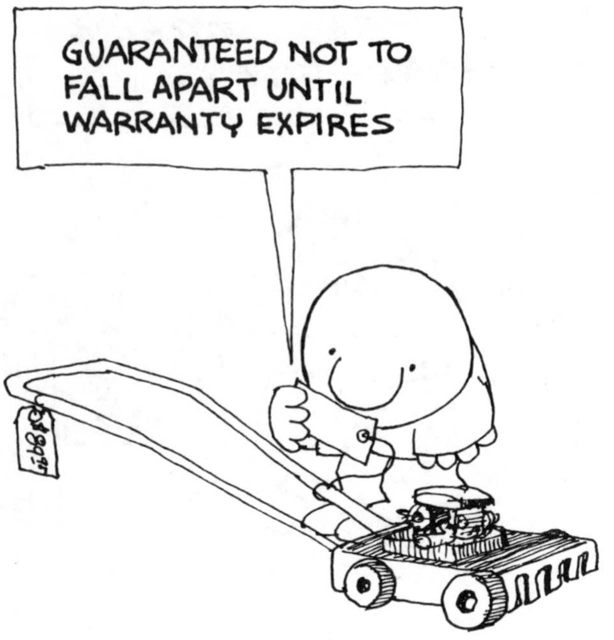
GUARANTEED NOT TO FALL APART UNTIL WARRANTY EXPIRES

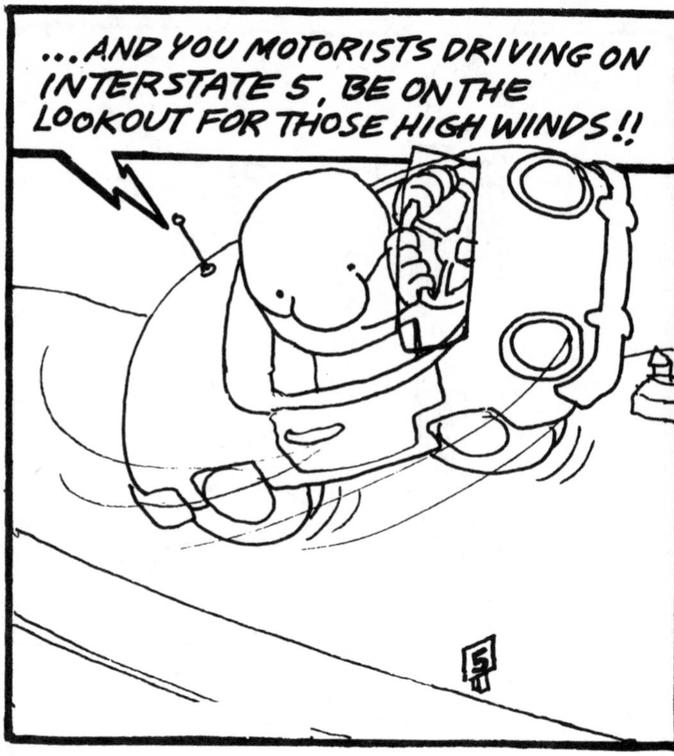
...AND YOU MOTORISTS DRIVING ON INTERSTATE 5, BE ON THE LOOKOUT FOR THOSE HIGH WINDS!!
5

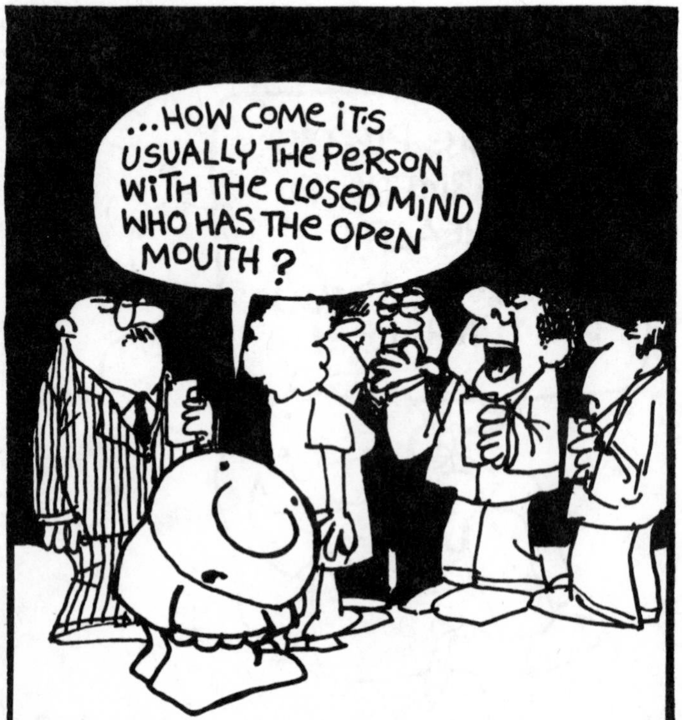
...HOW COME IT'S USUALLY THE PERSON WITH THE CLOSED MIND WHO HAS THE OPEN MOUTH?

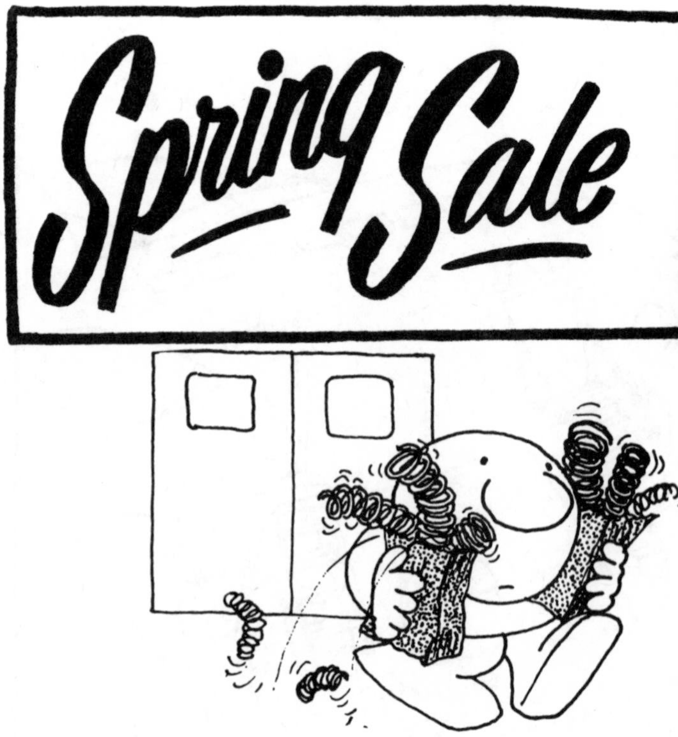
Spring Sale

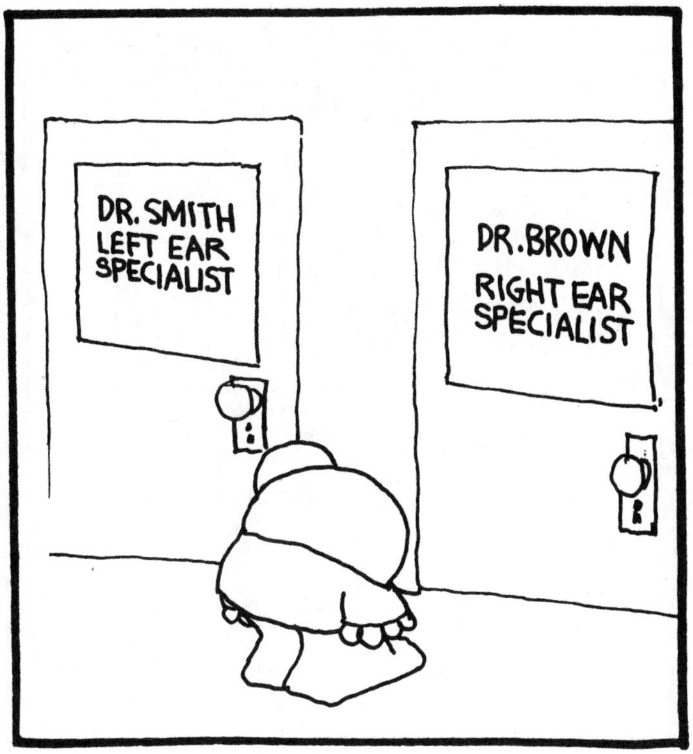
DR. SMITH
LEFT EAR
SPECIALIST
DR. BROWN
RIGHT EAR
SPECIALIST

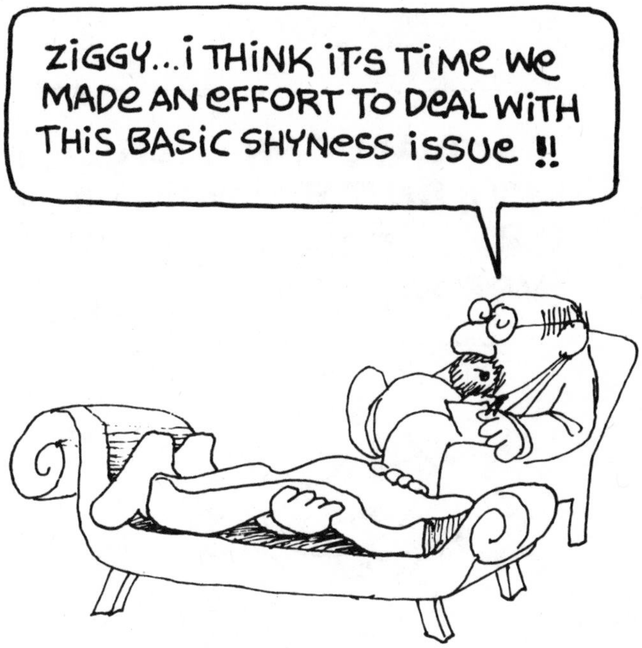
ZIGGY...I THINK IT'S TIME WE MADE AN EFFORT TO DEAL WITH THIS BASIC SHYNESS ISSUE !!

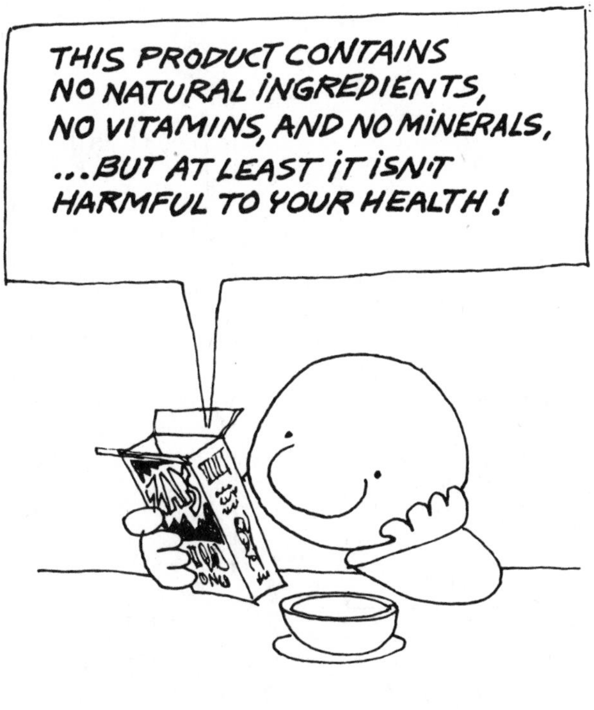
THIS PRODUCT CONTAINS NO NATURAL INGREDIENTS, NO VITAMINS, AND NO MINERALS, ...BUT AT LEAST IT ISN'T HARMFUL TO YOUR HEALTH !

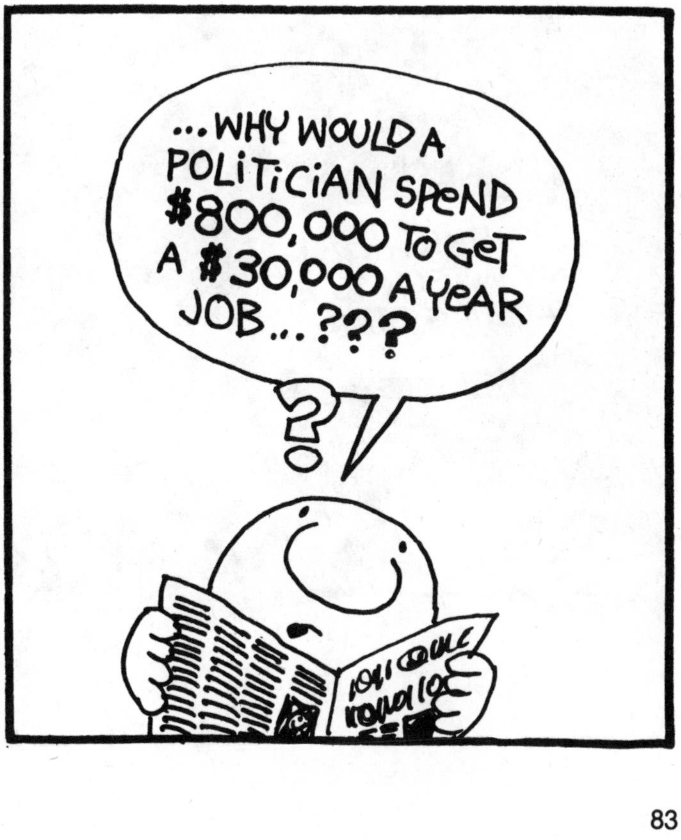
...WHY WOULD A POLITICIAN SPEND $800,000 TO GET A $30,000 A YEAR JOB...???

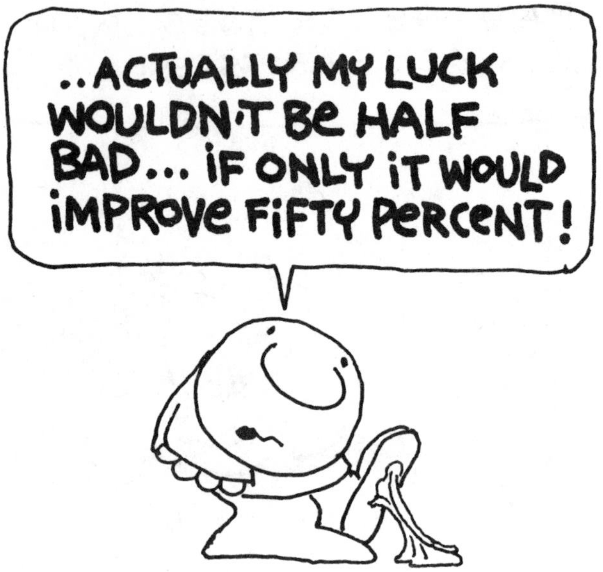
..ACTUALLY MY LUCK WOULDN'T BE HALF BAD... IF ONLY IT WOULD IMPROVE FIFTY PERCENT!

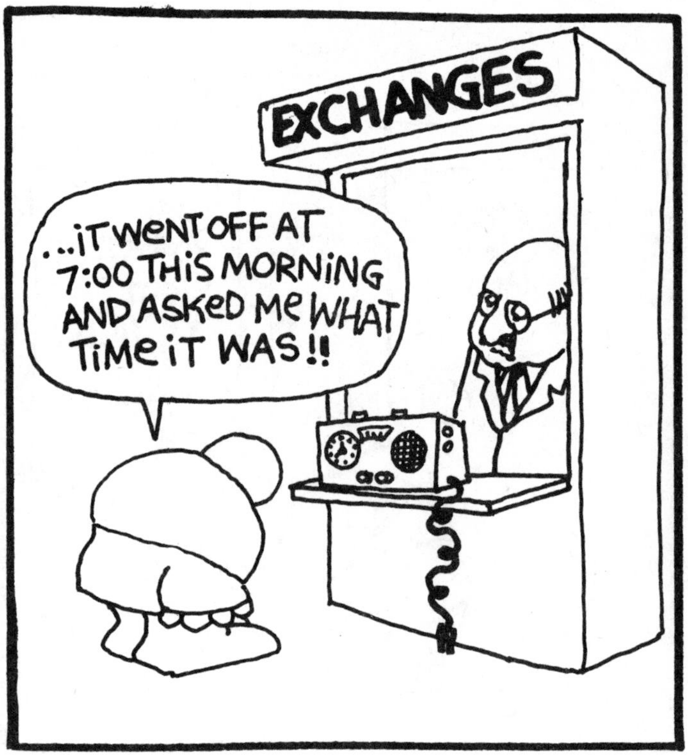
EXCHANGES
...IT WENT OFF AT 7:00 THIS MORNING AND ASKED ME WHAT TIME IT WAS!!

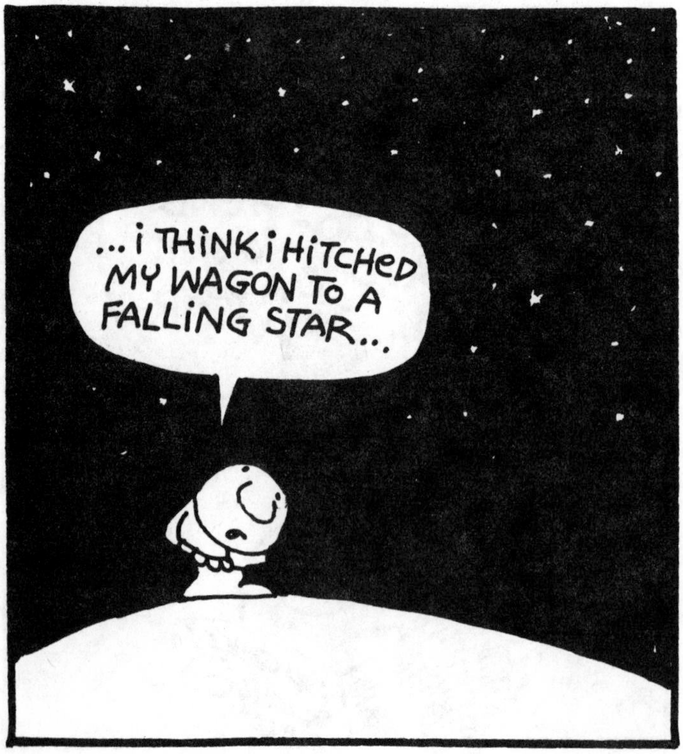
...I THINK I HITCHED MY WAGON TO A FALLING STAR...

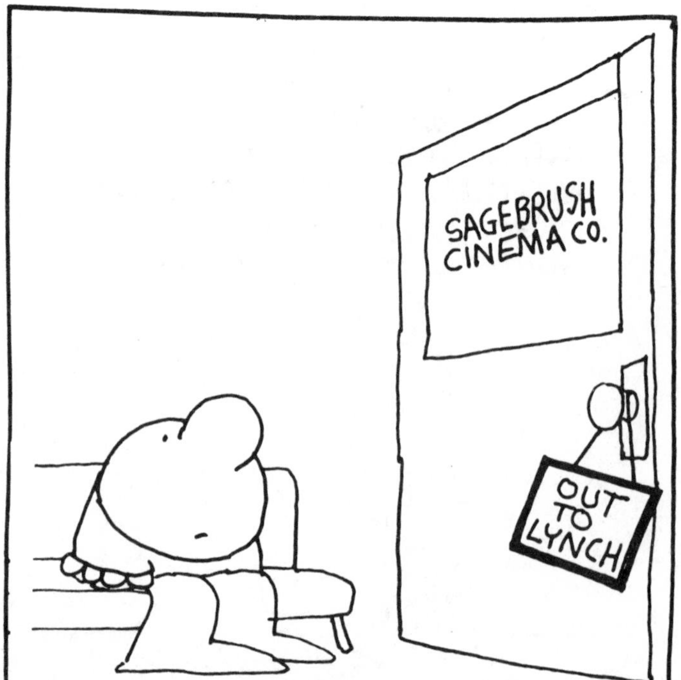
SAGEBRUSH CINEMA CO.
OUT TO LYNCH

..iF iGNORANCE WAS BLiSS...
i'D Be A LOT BeTTeR OFF THAN i AM !!

GOOD MORNiNG ZiGGY
GOOD MORNiNG ZiGGY

FiRST iT WAS "BREAD"... NOW "MeATLOAF"... PReTTY SOON YOU WON'T Be ABLe TO TeLL THe SiNGiNG GROUPS WiTHOUT A MeNU !!

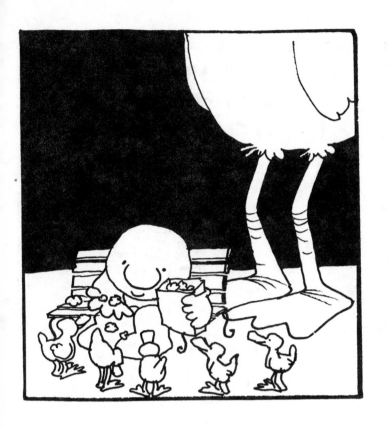

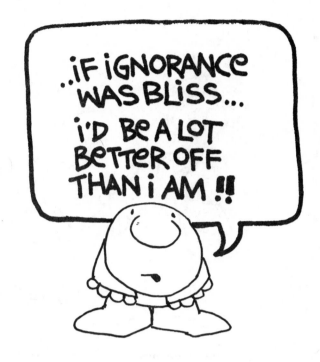

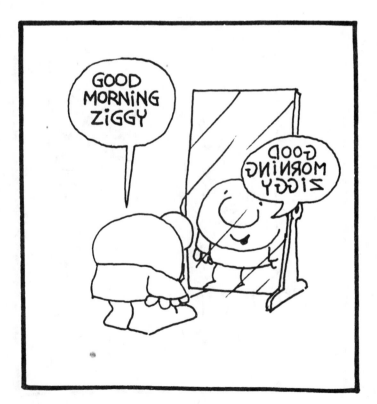

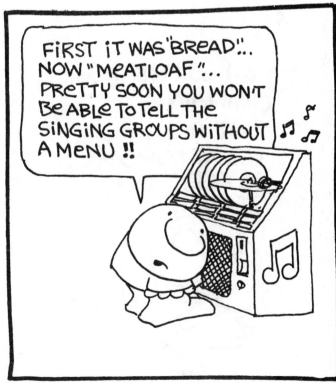

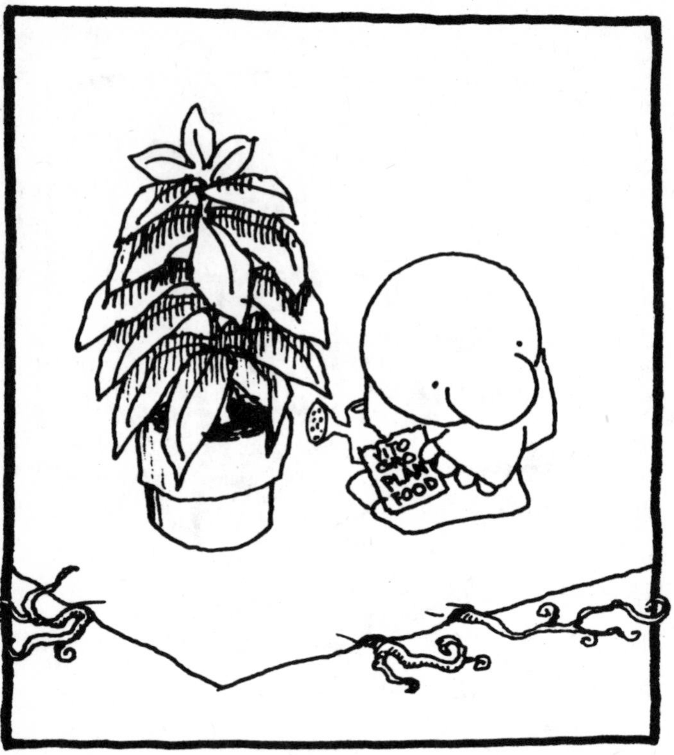

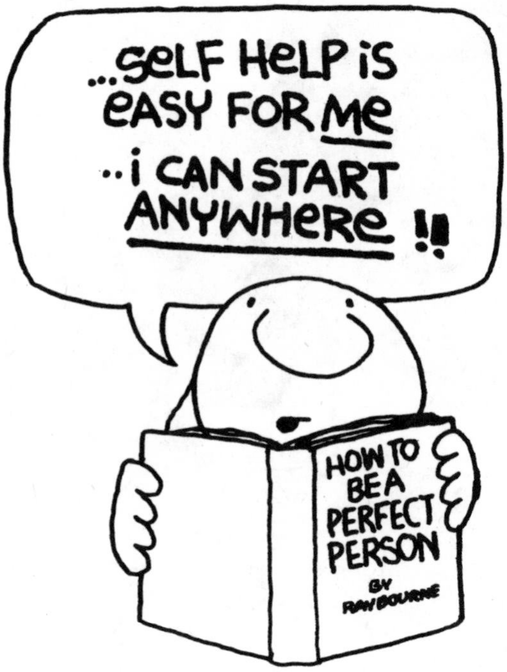
...SELF HELP IS EASY FOR ME
..I CAN START ANYWHERE !!
HOW TO BE A PERFECT PERSON

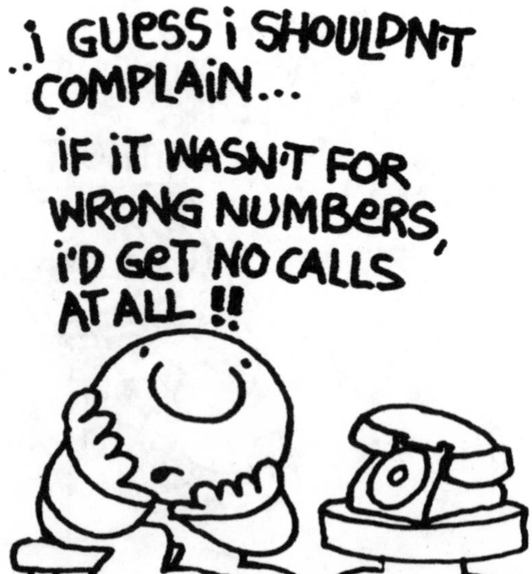
..I GUESS I SHOULDN'T COMPLAIN...
IF IT WASN'T FOR WRONG NUMBERS, I'D GET NO CALLS AT ALL !!

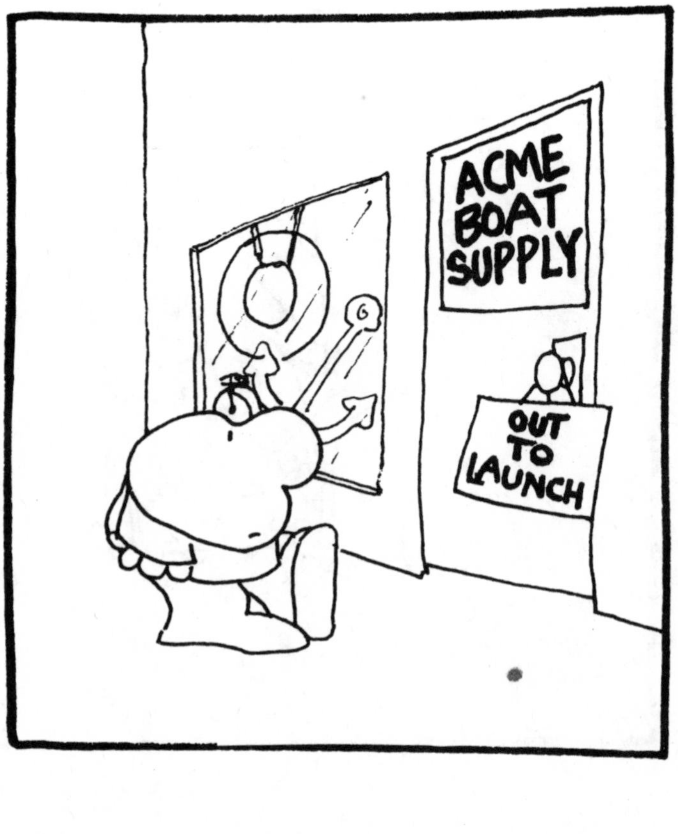
ACME BOAT SUPPLY
OUT TO LAUNCH

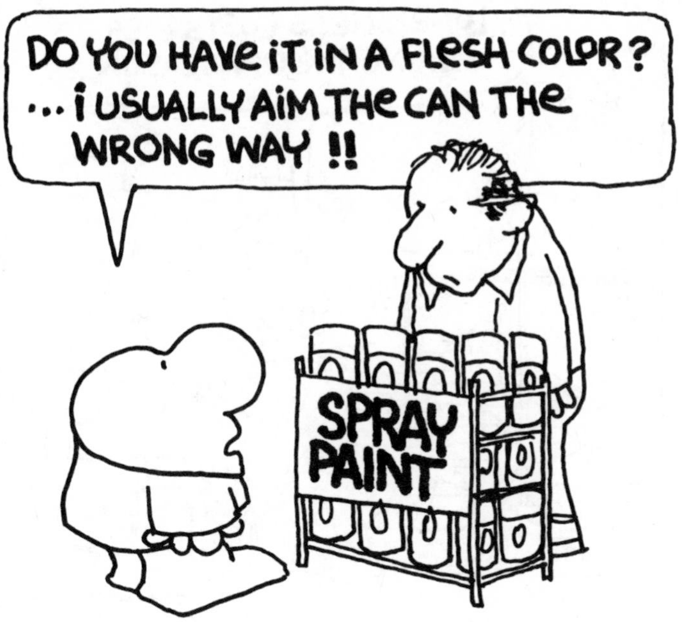
DO YOU HAVE IT IN A FLESH COLOR? ... I USUALLY AIM THE CAN THE WRONG WAY !!
SPRAY PAINT

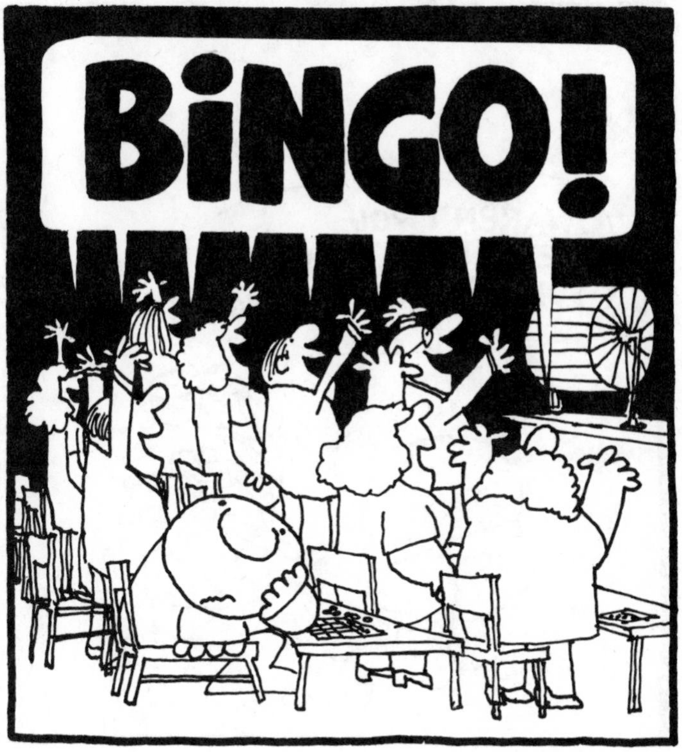
BINGO!

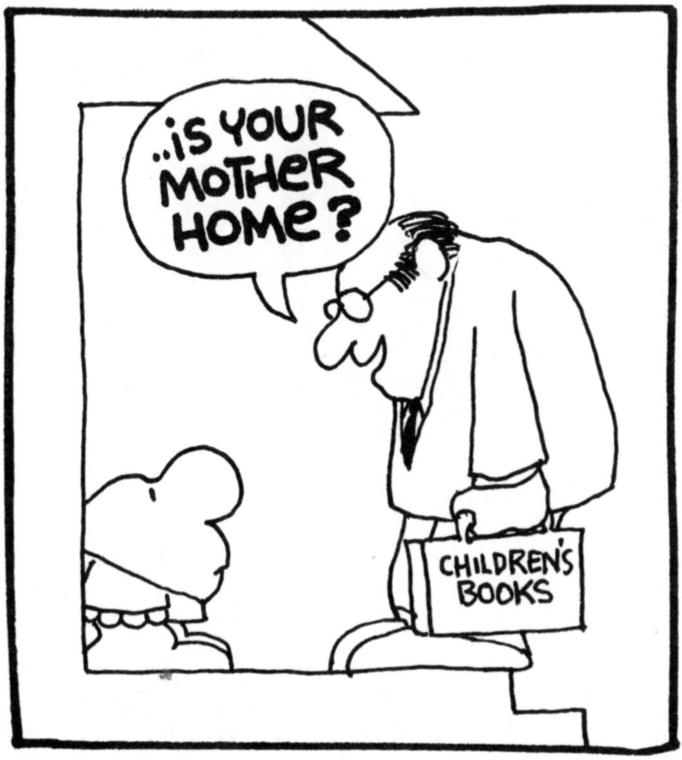
..IS YOUR MOTHER HOME?
CHILDREN'S BOOKS

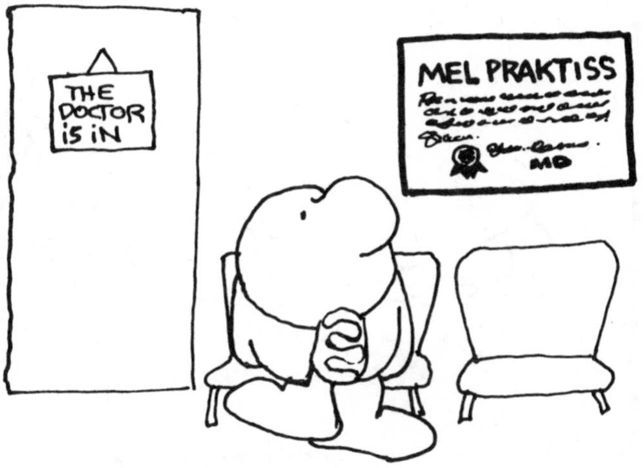
THE DOCTOR IS IN
MEL PRAKTISS
MD

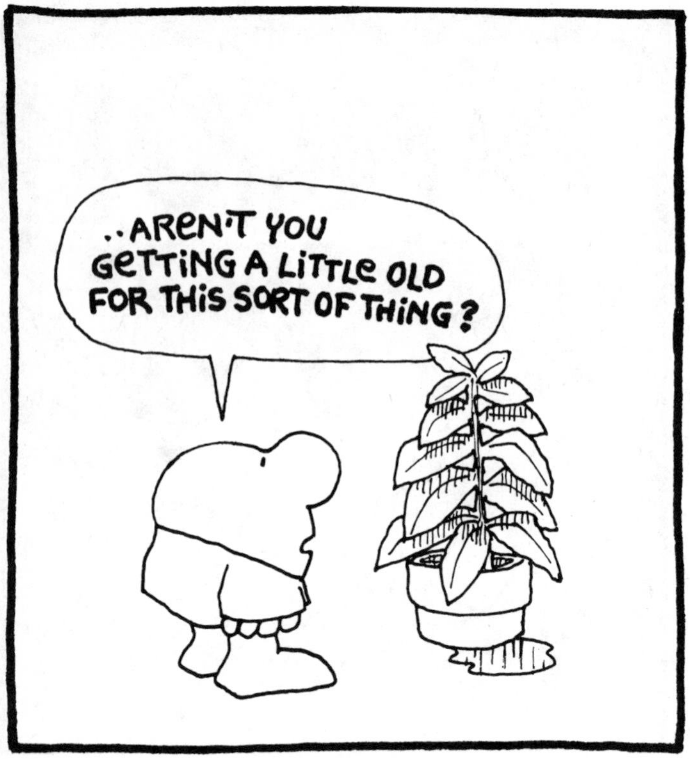
..AREN'T YOU GETTING A LITTLE OLD FOR THIS SORT OF THING?

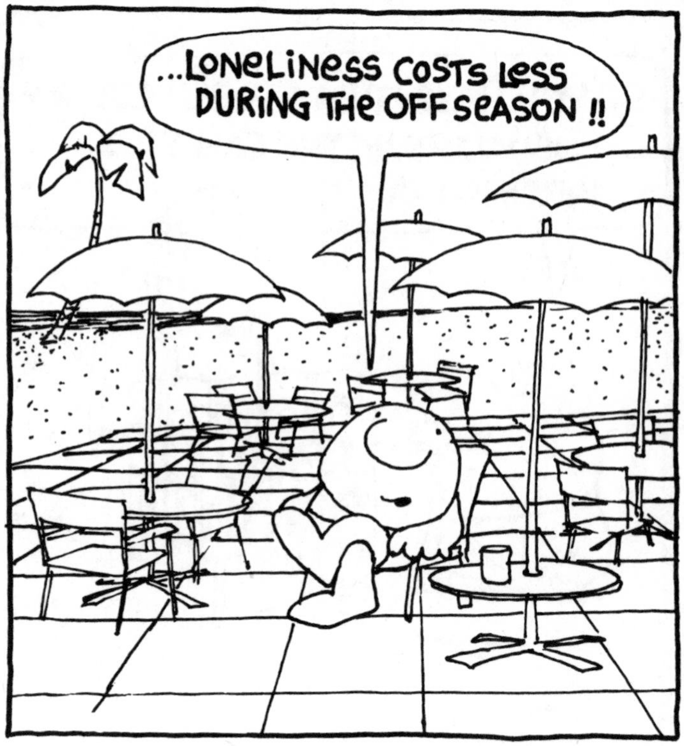
...LONELINESS COSTS LESS DURING THE OFF SEASON !!

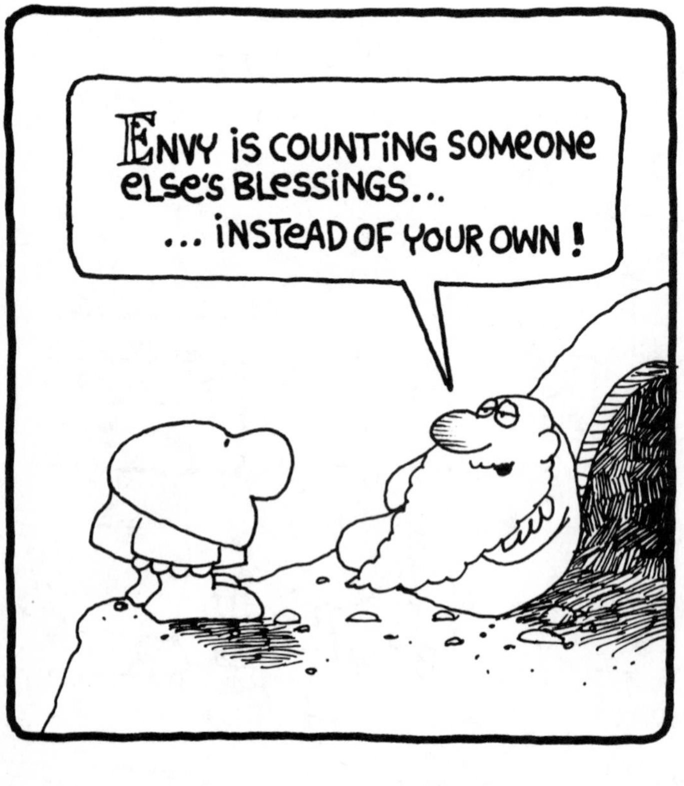
ENVY IS COUNTING SOMEONE ELSE'S BLESSINGS...
... INSTEAD OF YOUR OWN!

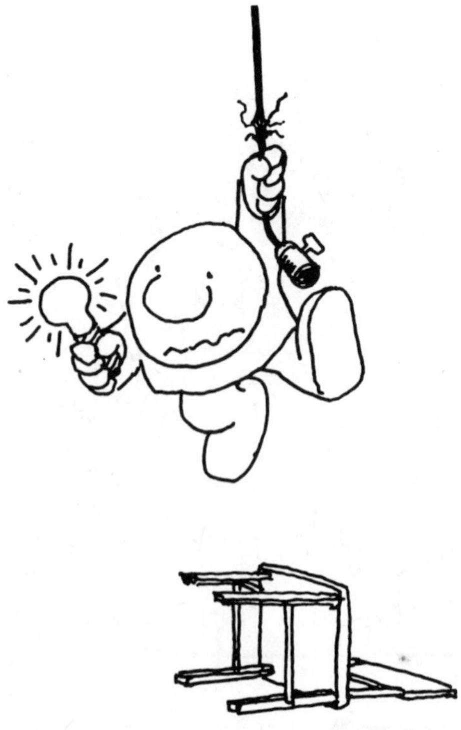

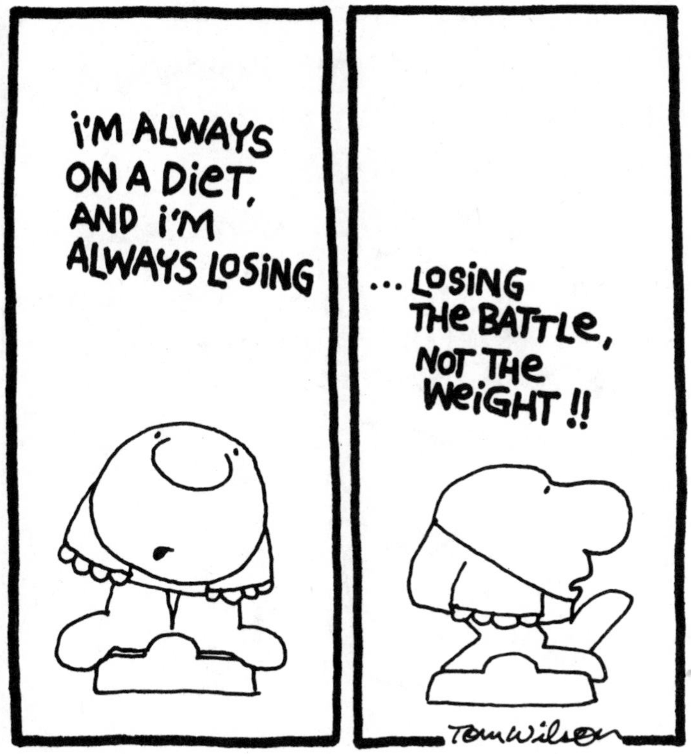
I'M ALWAYS ON A DIET, AND I'M ALWAYS LOSING
...LOSING THE BATTLE, NOT THE WEIGHT !!
Tom Wilson

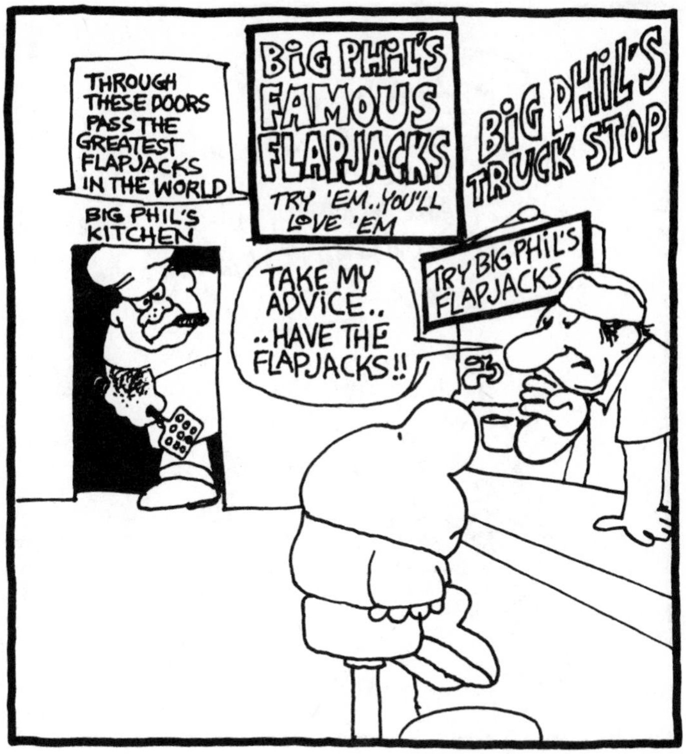
THROUGH THESE DOORS PASS THE GREATEST FLAPJACKS IN THE WORLD
BIG PHIL'S KITCHEN
BIG PHIL'S FAMOUS FLAPJACKS
TRY 'EM.. YOU'LL LOVE 'EM
BIG PHIL'S TRUCK STOP
TRY BIG PHIL'S FLAPJACKS
TAKE MY ADVICE.. ..HAVE THE FLAPJACKS!!

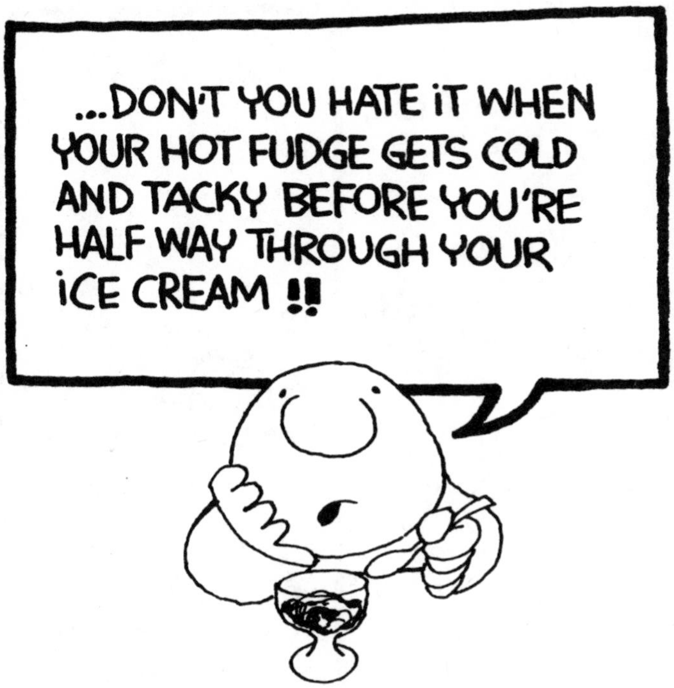
...DON'T YOU HATE IT WHEN YOUR HOT FUDGE GETS COLD AND TACKY BEFORE YOU'RE HALF WAY THROUGH YOUR ICE CREAM !!

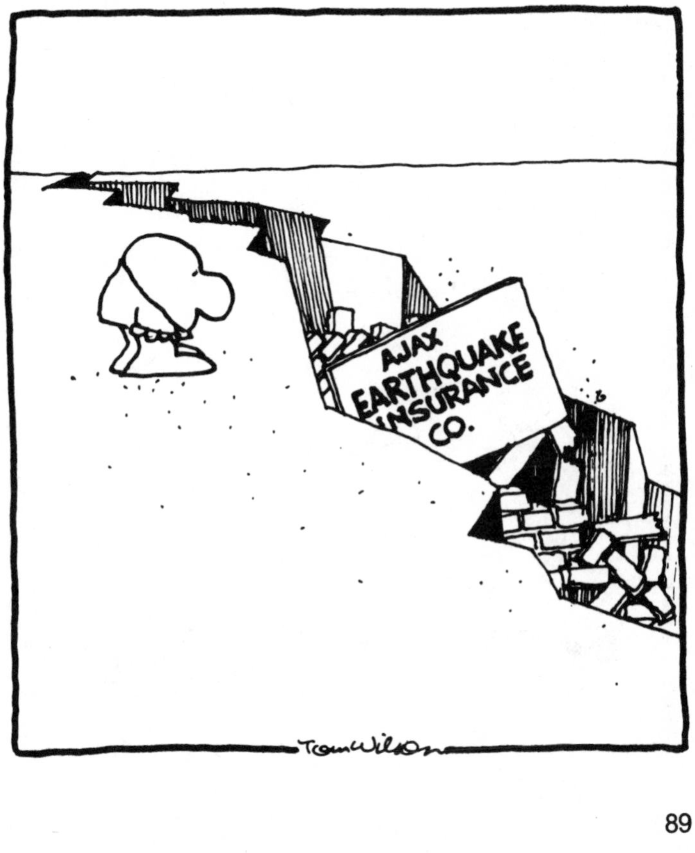
AJAX EARTHQUAKE INSURANCE CO.
Tom Wilson

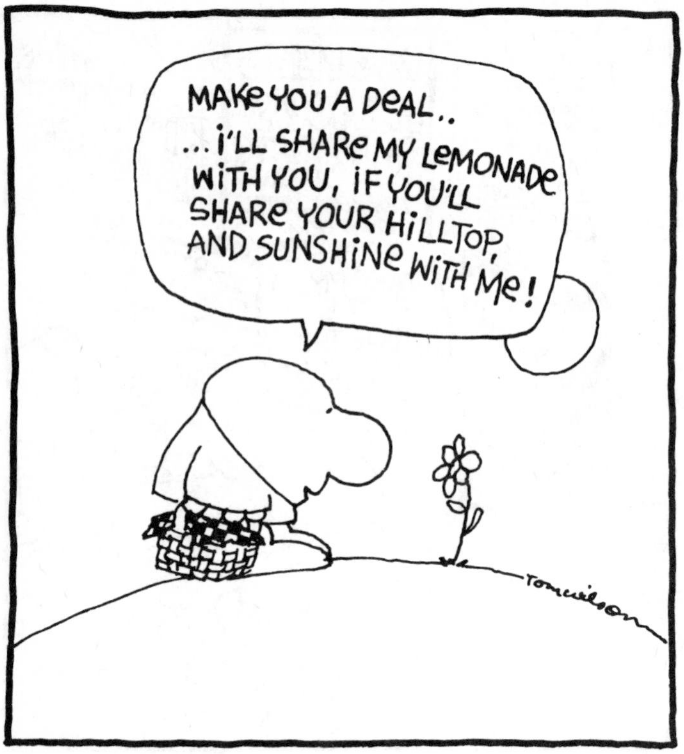
MAKE YOU A DEAL..
...I'LL SHARE MY LEMONADE WITH YOU, IF YOU'LL SHARE YOUR HILLTOP, AND SUNSHINE WITH ME!

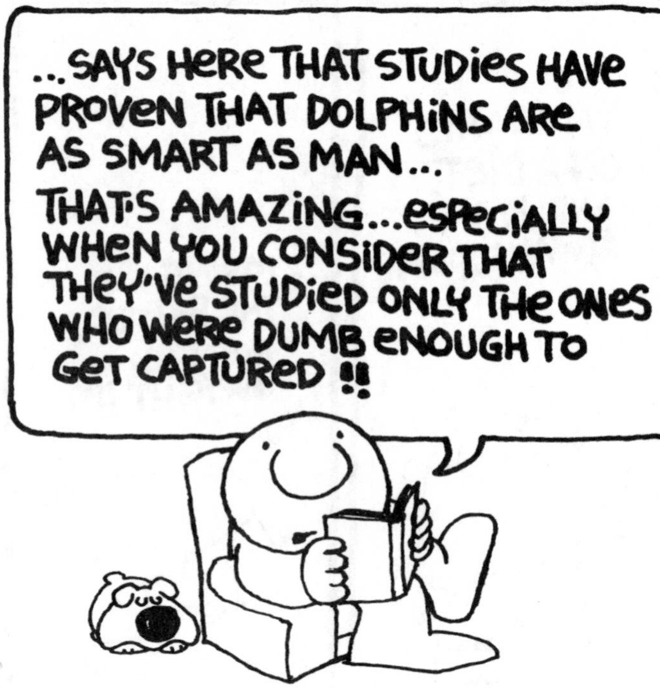
...SAYS HERE THAT STUDIES HAVE PROVEN THAT DOLPHINS ARE AS SMART AS MAN...
THAT'S AMAZING...ESPECIALLY WHEN YOU CONSIDER THAT THEY'VE STUDIED ONLY THE ONES WHO WERE DUMB ENOUGH TO GET CAPTURED!!

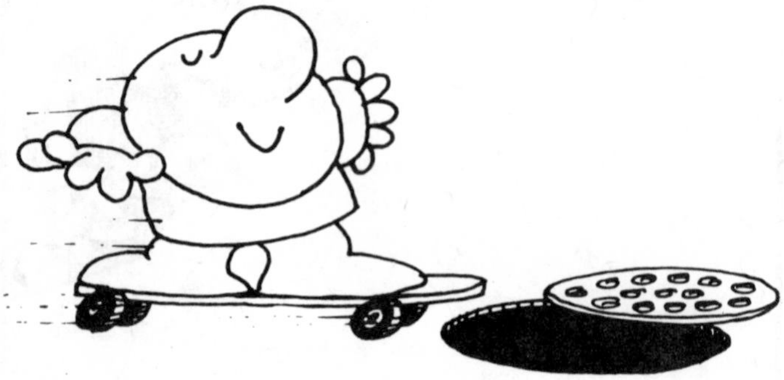

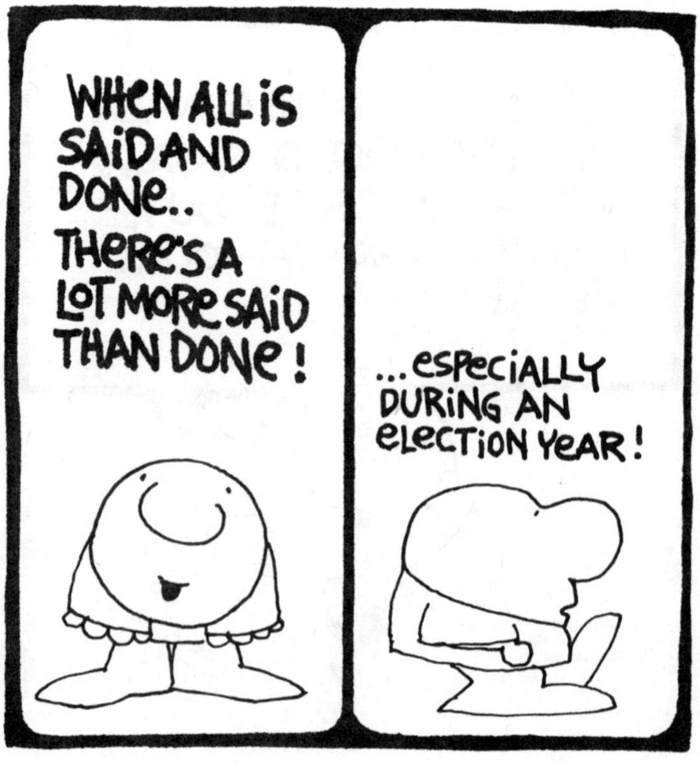
WHEN ALL IS SAID AND DONE..
THERE'S A LOT MORE SAID THAN DONE!
...ESPECIALLY DURING AN ELECTION YEAR!

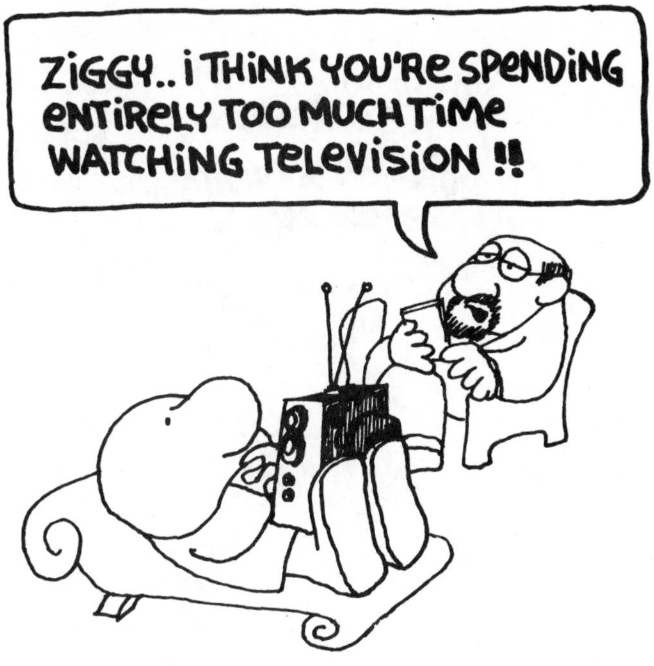
ZIGGY.. I THINK YOU'RE SPENDING ENTIRELY TOO MUCH TIME WATCHING TELEVISION !!

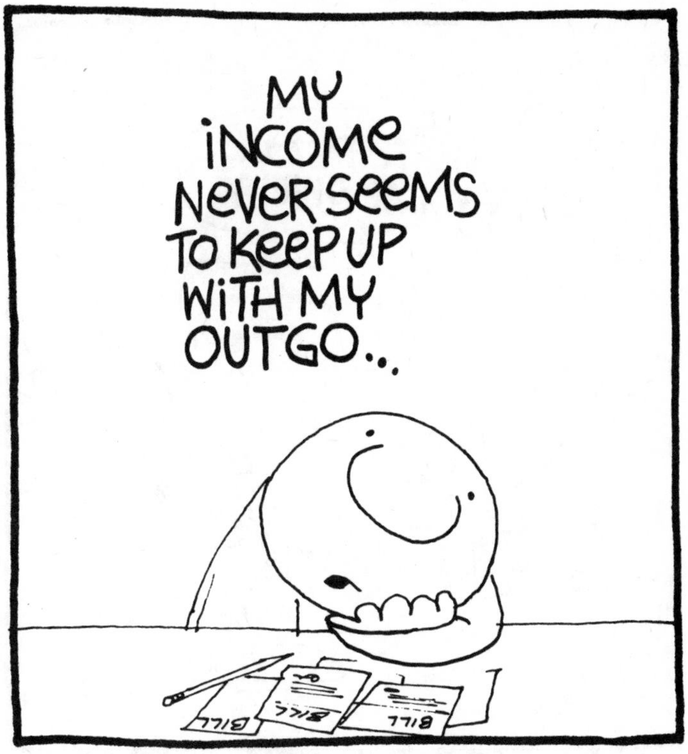
MY INCOME NEVER SEEMS TO KEEP UP WITH MY OUTGO...
BILL
BILL
BILL

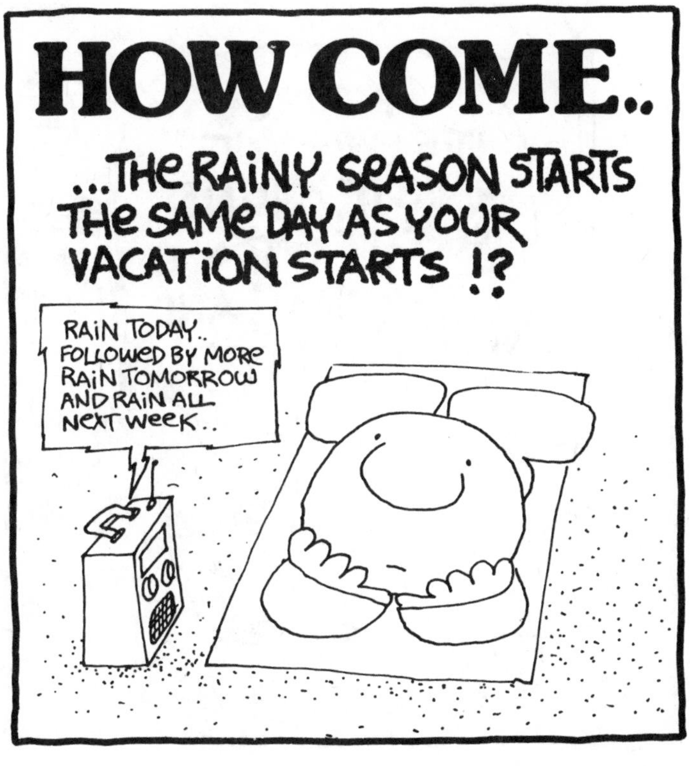
HOW COME..
...THE RAINY SEASON STARTS THE SAME DAY AS YOUR VACATION STARTS !?
RAIN TODAY.. FOLLOWED BY MORE RAIN TOMORROW AND RAIN ALL NEXT WEEK..

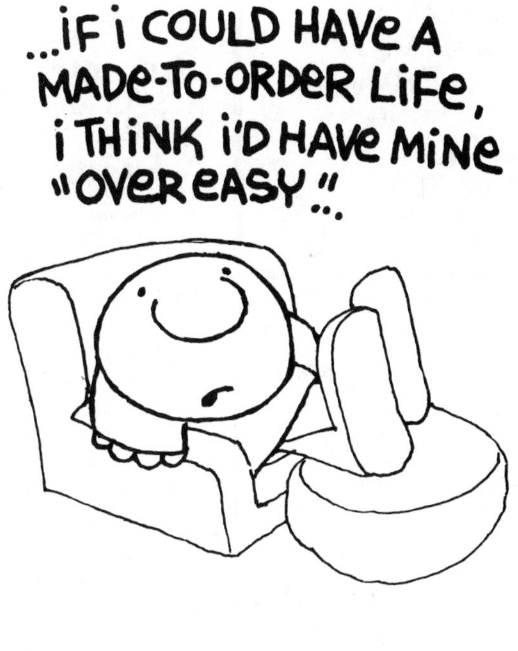
...IF I COULD HAVE A MADE-TO-ORDER LIFE, I THINK I'D HAVE MINE "OVER EASY"!..

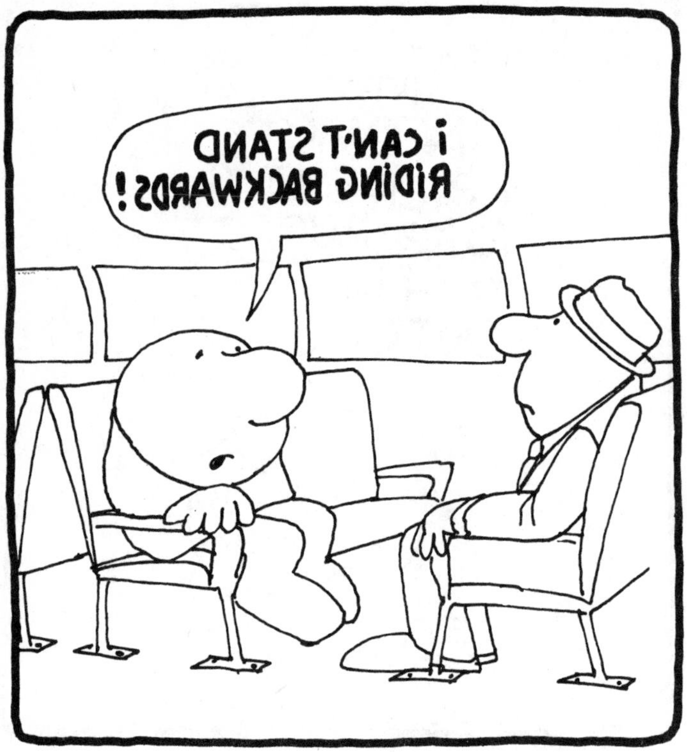
i CAN'T STAND RIDING BACKWARDS!

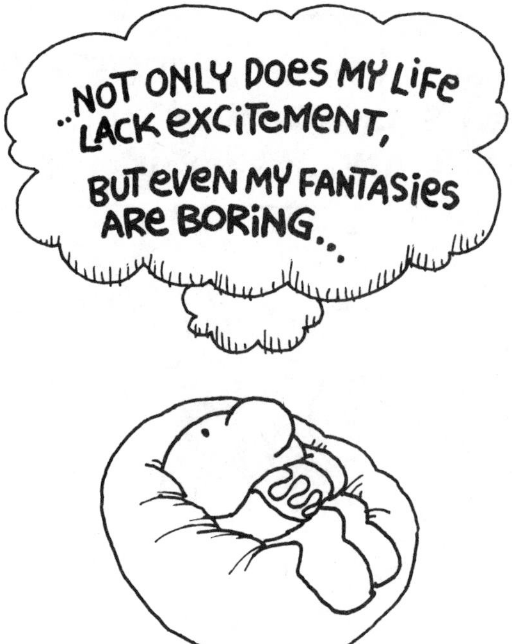
..NOT ONLY DOES MY LIFE LACK EXCITEMENT,
BUT EVEN MY FANTASIES ARE BORING...

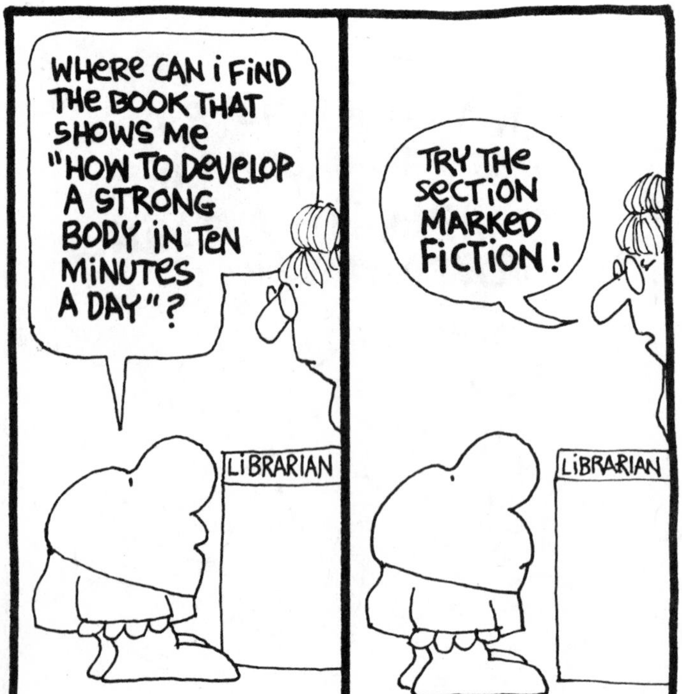
WHERE CAN i FIND THE BOOK THAT SHOWS ME "HOW TO DEVELOP A STRONG BODY IN TEN MINUTES A DAY"?
LIBRARIAN
TRY THE SECTION MARKED FICTION!
LIBRARIAN

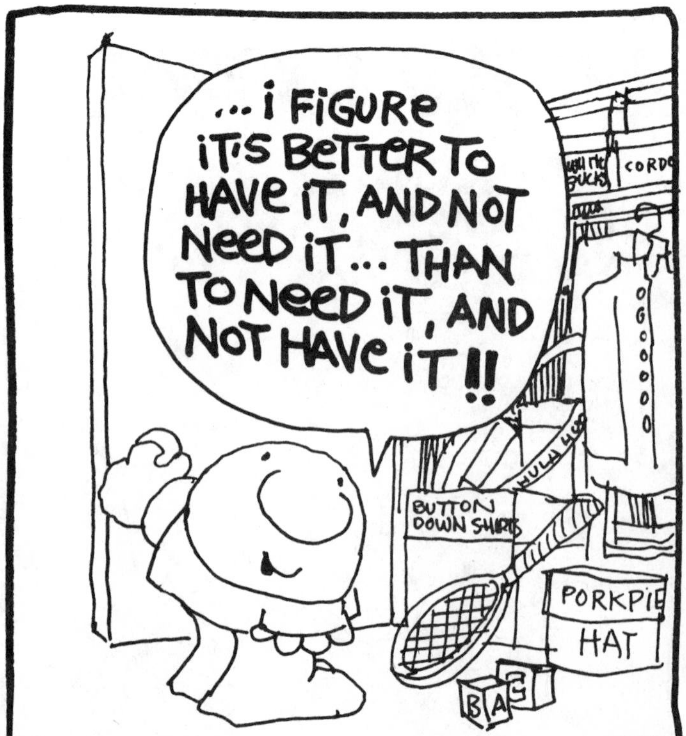
...i FIGURE IT'S BETTER TO HAVE IT, AND NOT NEED IT... THAN TO NEED IT, AND NOT HAVE IT!!
BUTTON DOWN SHIRTS
PORKPIE HAT
B A

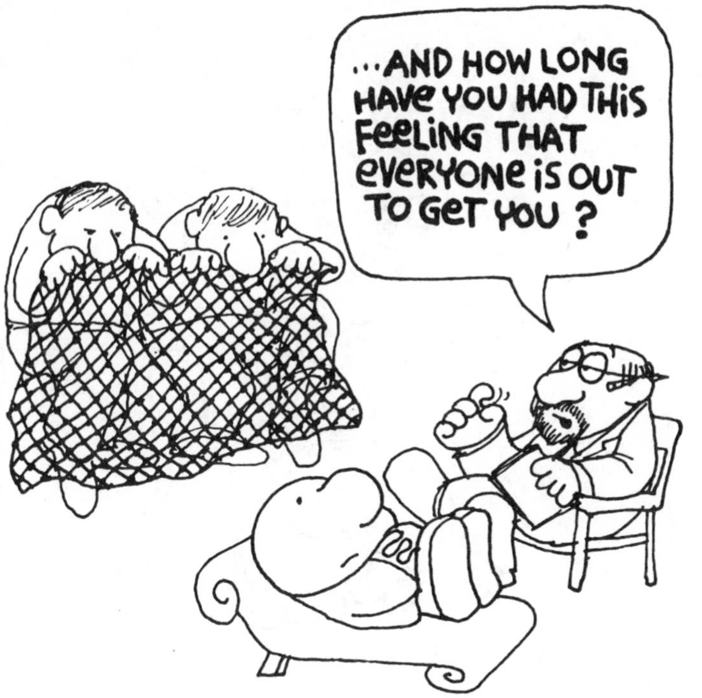
...AND HOW LONG HAVE YOU HAD THIS FEELING THAT EVERYONE IS OUT TO GET YOU ?

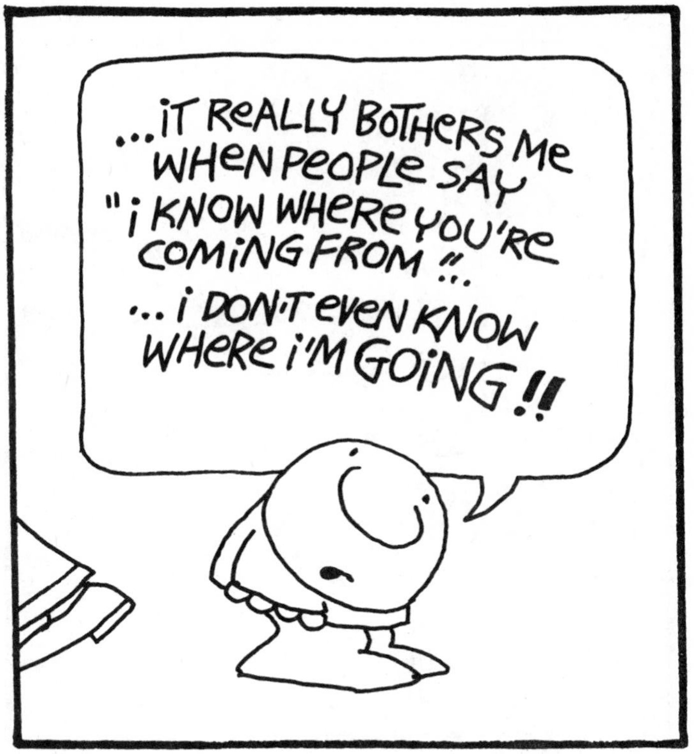
...IT REALLY BOTHERS ME WHEN PEOPLE SAY "I KNOW WHERE YOU'RE COMING FROM"... ...I DON'T EVEN KNOW WHERE I'M GOING!!

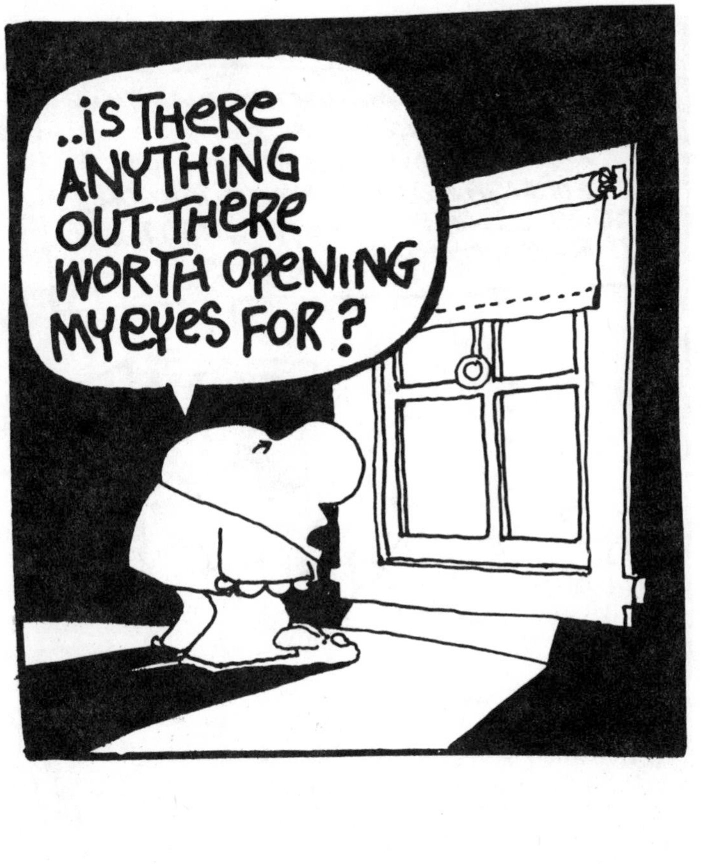
..IS THERE ANYTHING OUT THERE WORTH OPENING MY EYES FOR ?

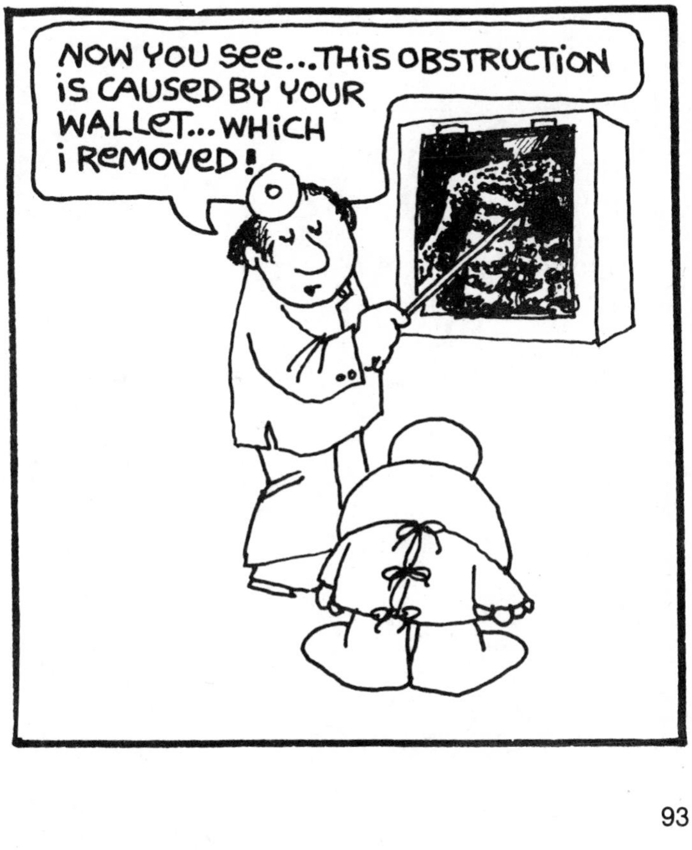
NOW YOU SEE...THIS OBSTRUCTION IS CAUSED BY YOUR WALLET...WHICH I REMOVED!

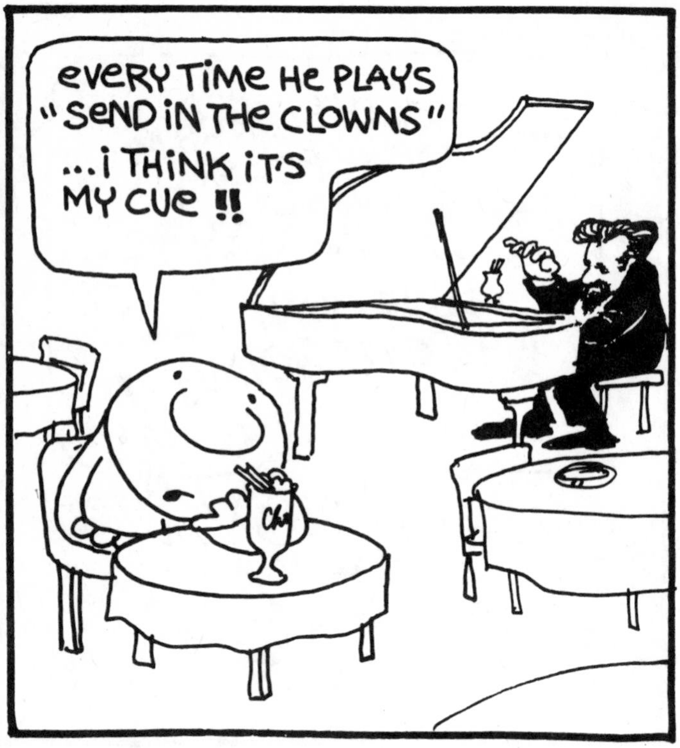
EVERY TIME HE PLAYS "SEND IN THE CLOWNS" ...I THINK IT'S MY CUE !!

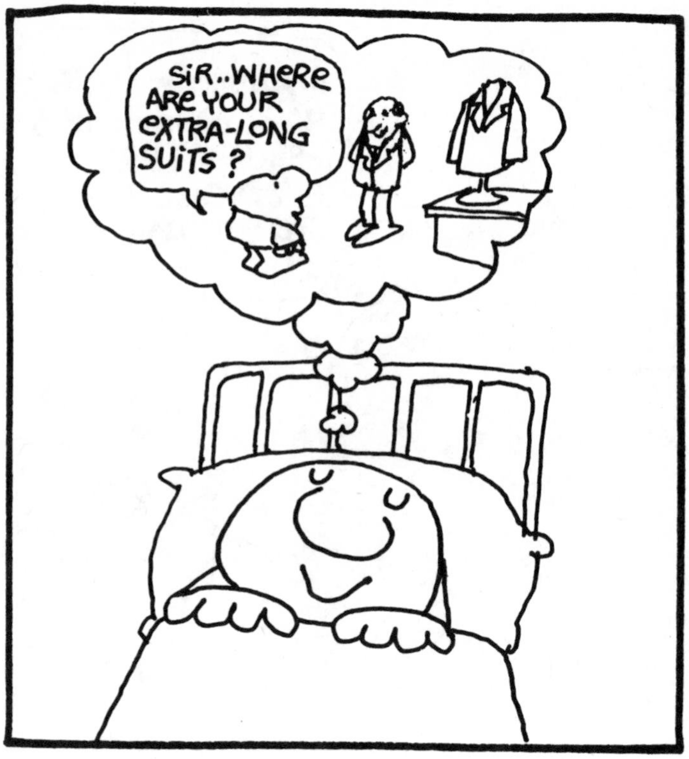
SIR..WHERE ARE YOUR EXTRA-LONG SUITS ?

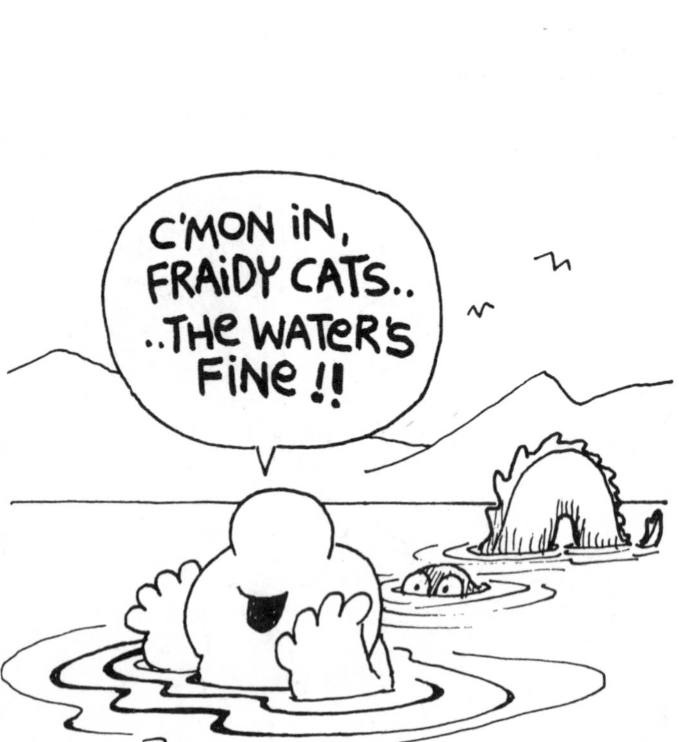
C'MON IN, FRAIDY CATS.. ..THE WATER'S FINE !!

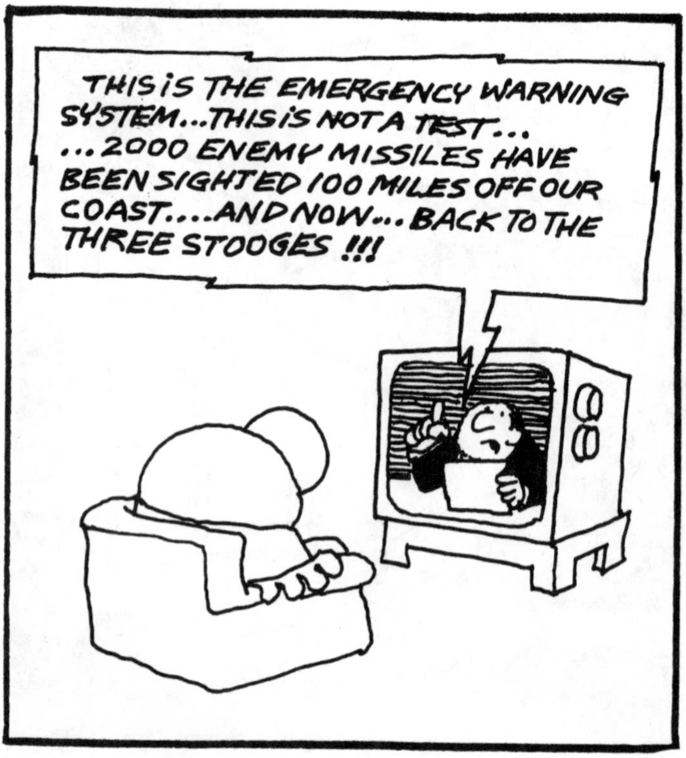
THIS IS THE EMERGENCY WARNING SYSTEM...THIS IS NOT A TEST... ...2000 ENEMY MISSILES HAVE BEEN SIGHTED 100 MILES OFF OUR COAST....AND NOW... BACK TO THE THREE STOOGES !!!

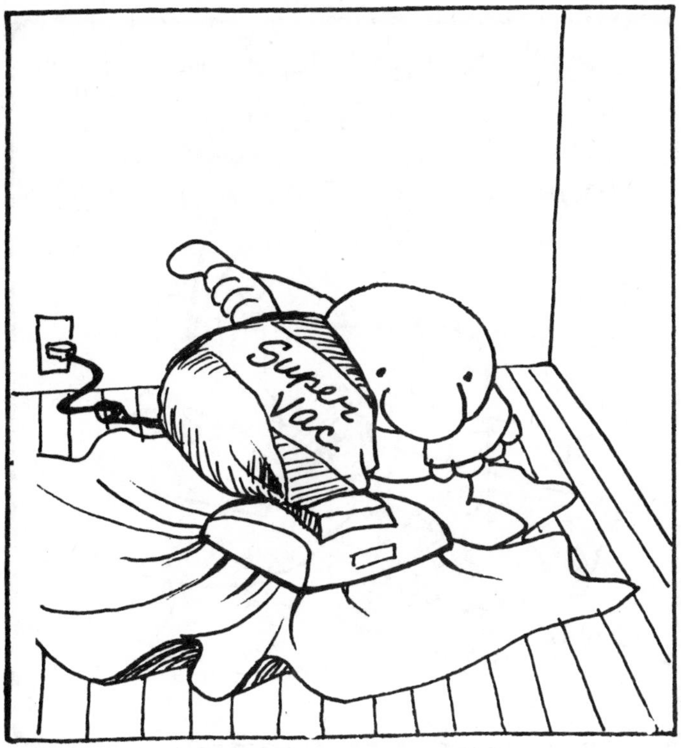
Super Vac

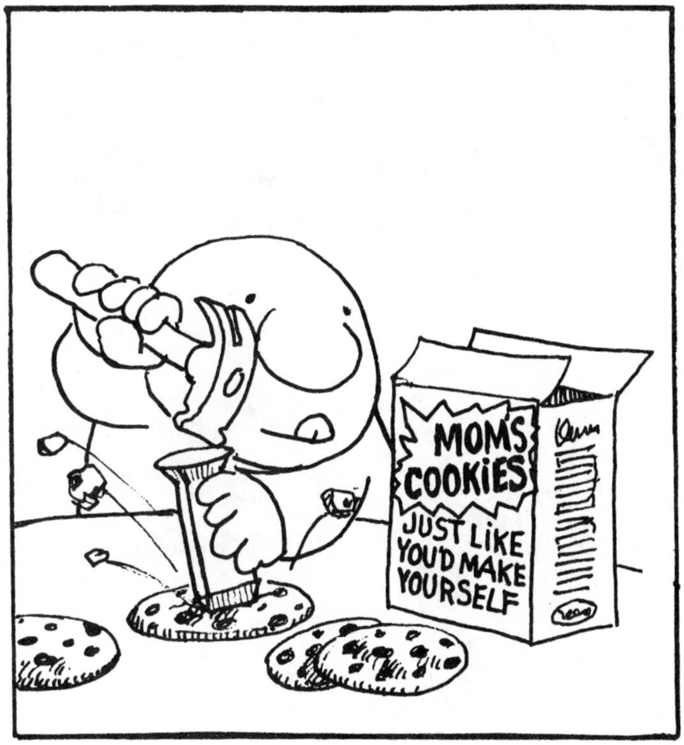
MOMS COOKIES
JUST LIKE YOU'D MAKE YOURSELF

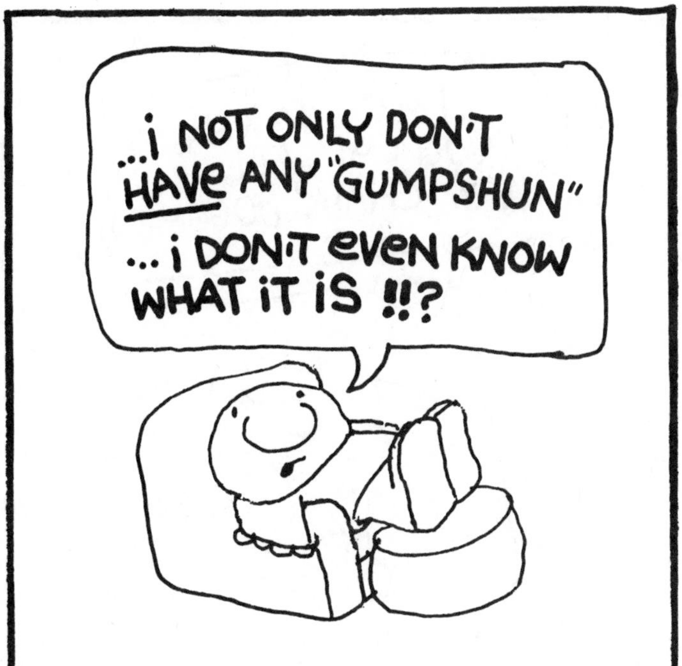
...i NOT ONLY DON'T HAVE ANY "GUMPSHUN" ...i DON'T even KNOW WHAT iT iS !!?

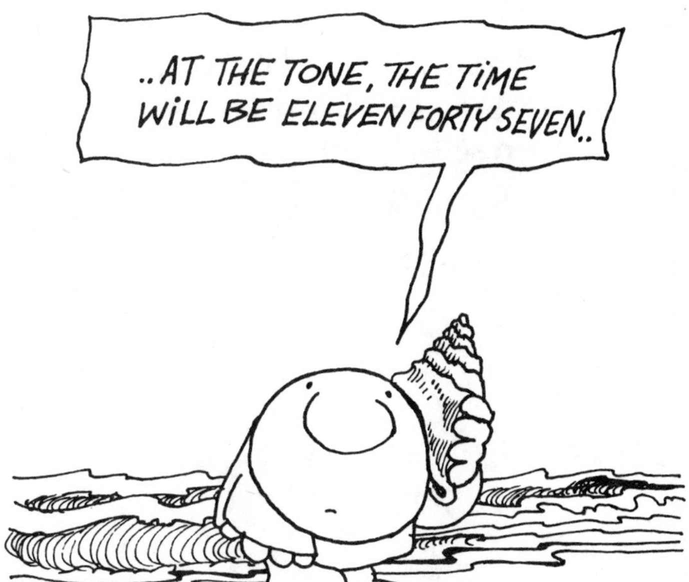
..AT THE TONE, THE TiME WiLL BE ELEVEN FORTY SEVEN..

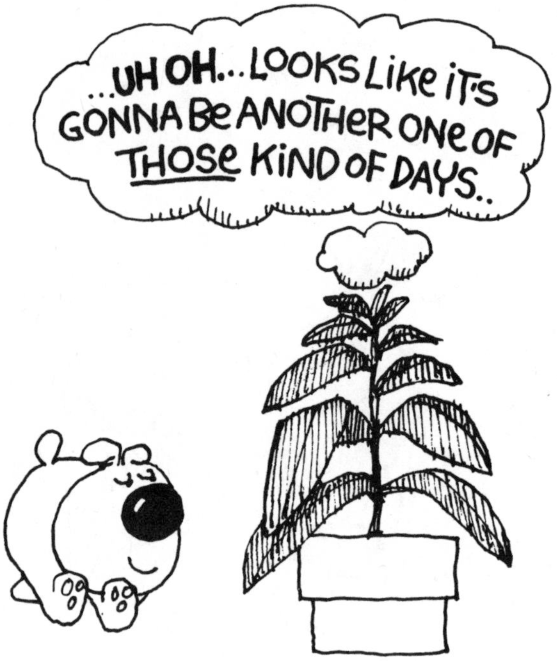
...UH OH... LOOKS LIKE IT'S GONNA BE ANOTHER ONE OF THOSE KIND OF DAYS..

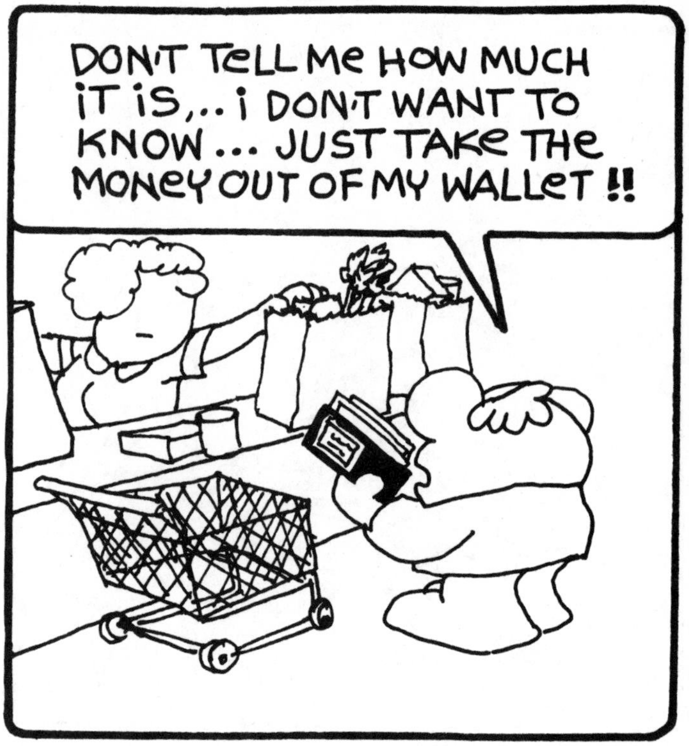
DON'T TELL ME HOW MUCH IT IS,.. I DON'T WANT TO KNOW ... JUST TAKE THE MONEY OUT OF MY WALLET !!

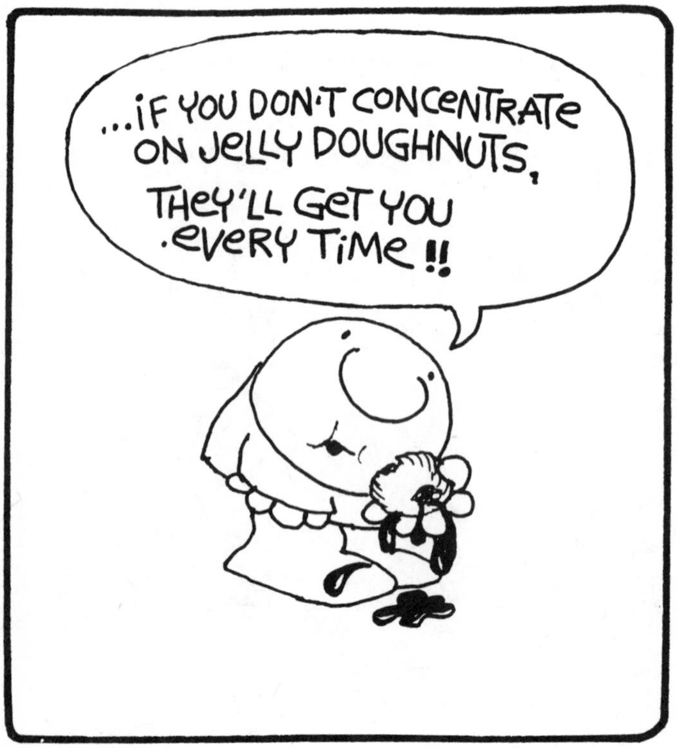
...IF YOU DON'T CONCENTRATE ON JELLY DOUGHNUTS, THEY'LL GET YOU .EVERY TIME !!

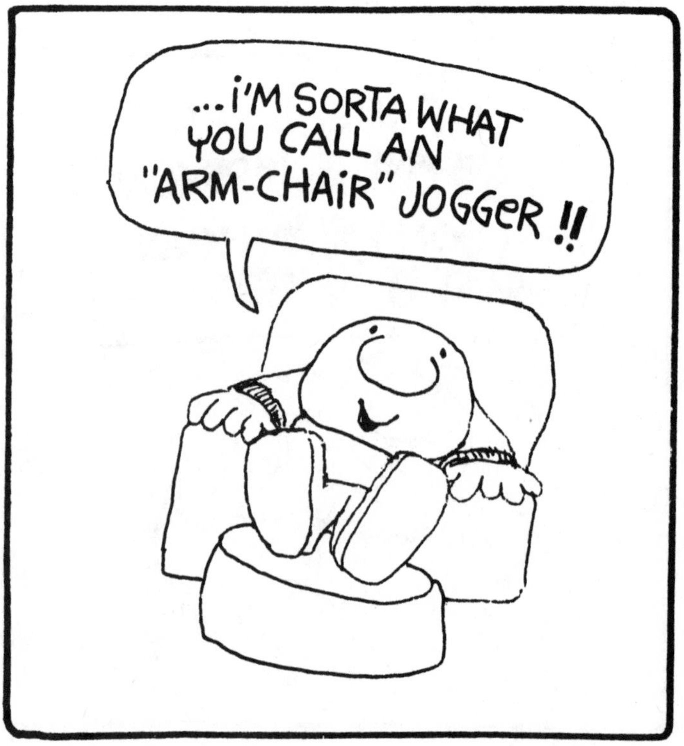
...I'M SORTA WHAT YOU CALL AN "ARM-CHAIR" JOGGER !!

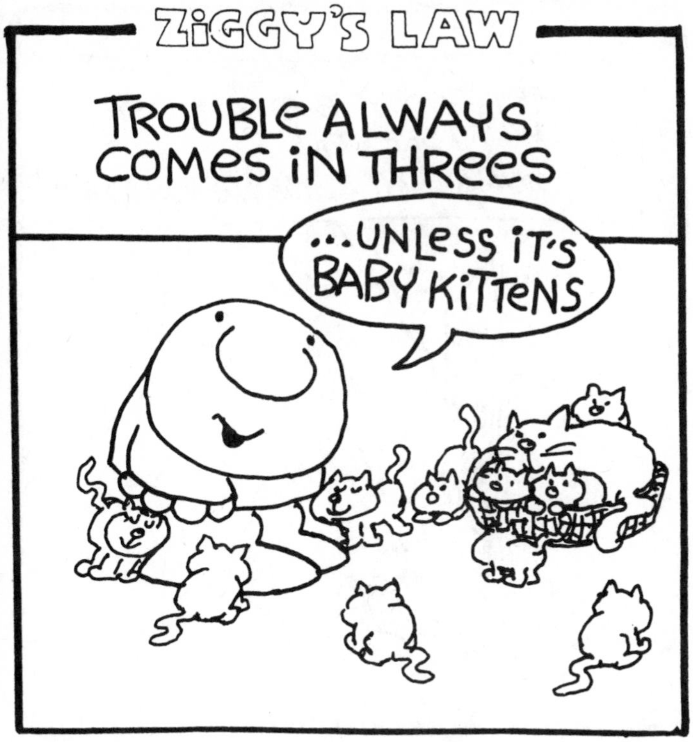
ZIGGY'S LAW
TROUBLE ALWAYS COMES IN THREES
...UNLESS IT'S BABY KITTENS

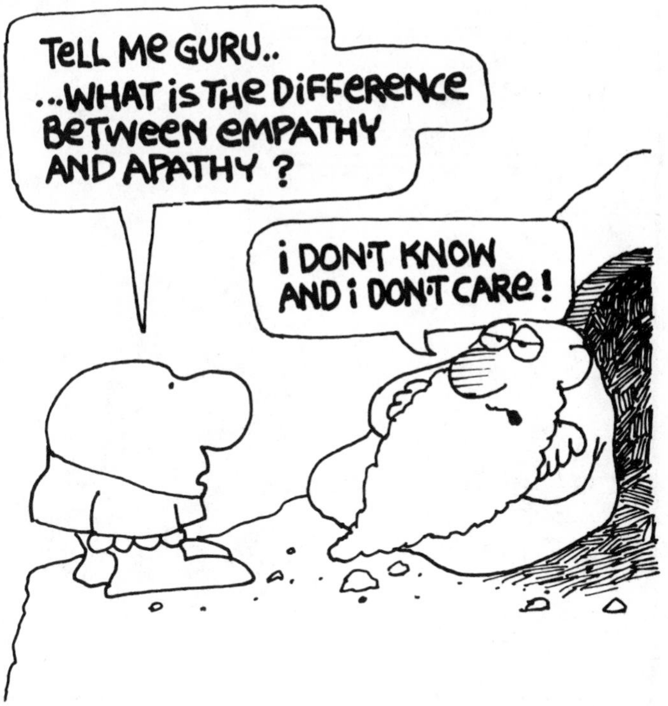
TELL ME GURU.. ...WHAT IS THE DIFFERENCE BETWEEN EMPATHY AND APATHY ?
I DON'T KNOW AND I DON'T CARE !

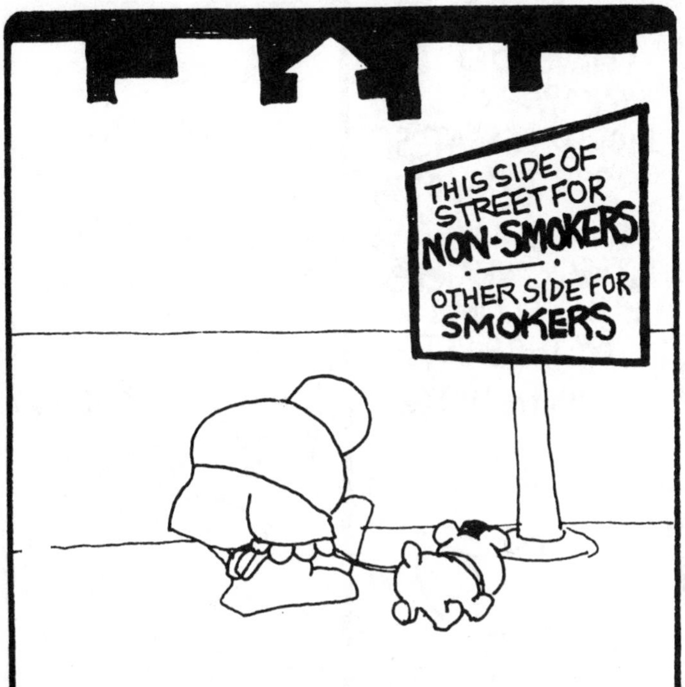
THIS SIDE OF STREET FOR NON-SMOKERS
OTHER SIDE FOR SMOKERS

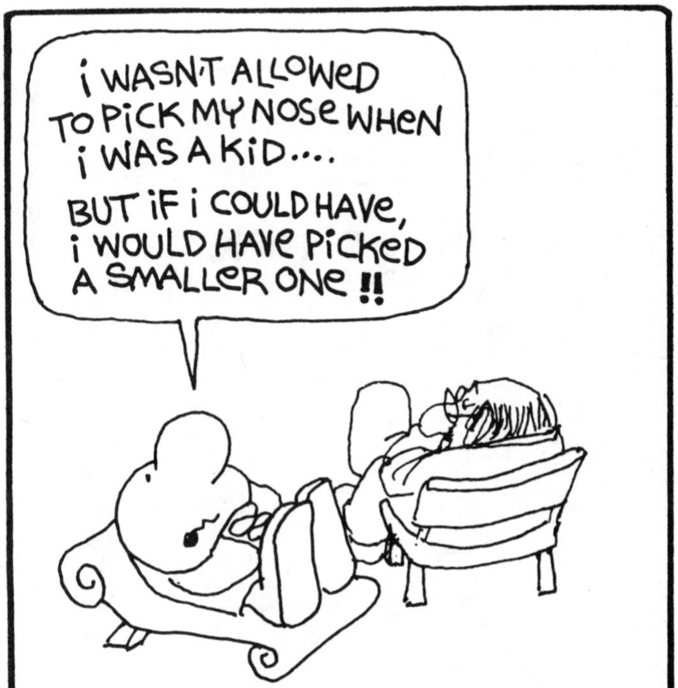
I WASN'T ALLOWED TO PICK MY NOSE WHEN I WAS A KID.... BUT IF I COULD HAVE, I WOULD HAVE PICKED A SMALLER ONE !!

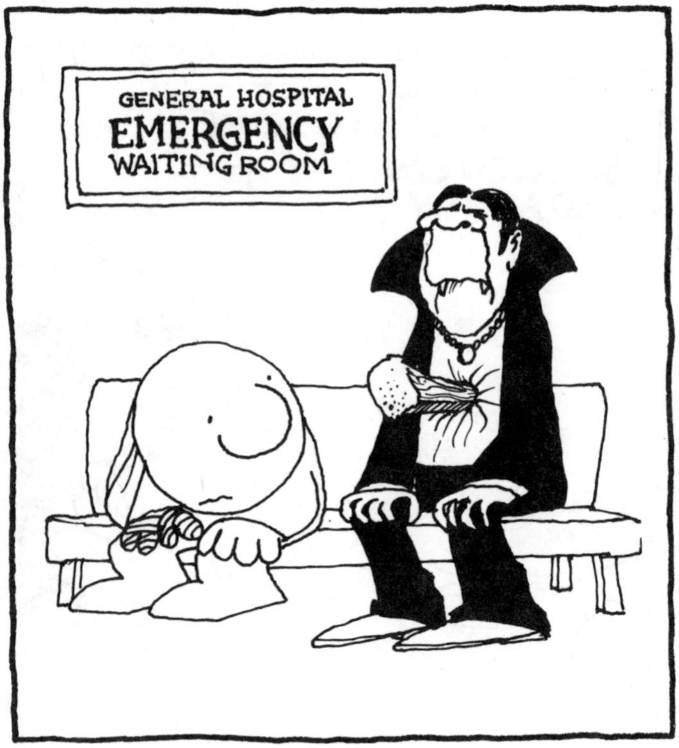
GENERAL HOSPITAL
EMERGENCY
WAITING ROOM

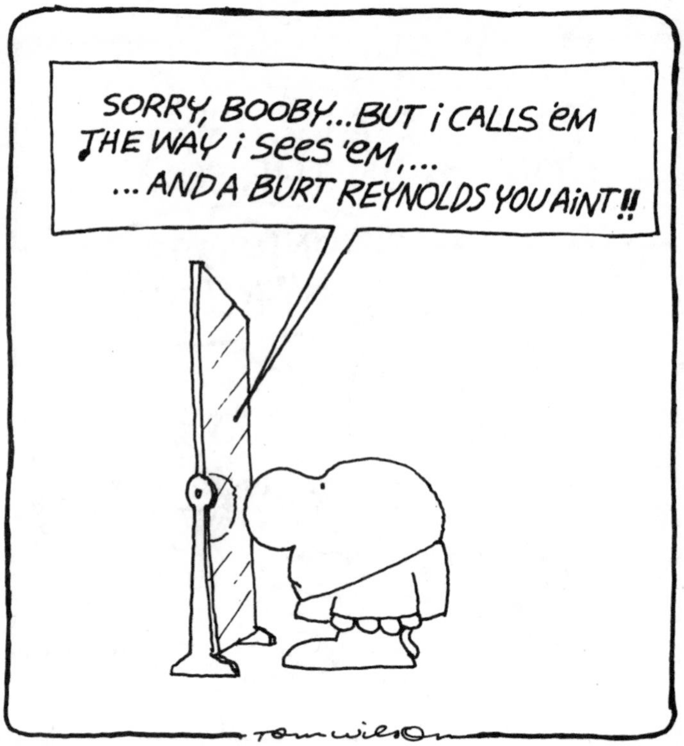
SORRY, BOOBY...BUT i CALLS 'EM THE WAY i SEES 'EM,... ...AND A BURT REYNOLDS YOU AINT!!

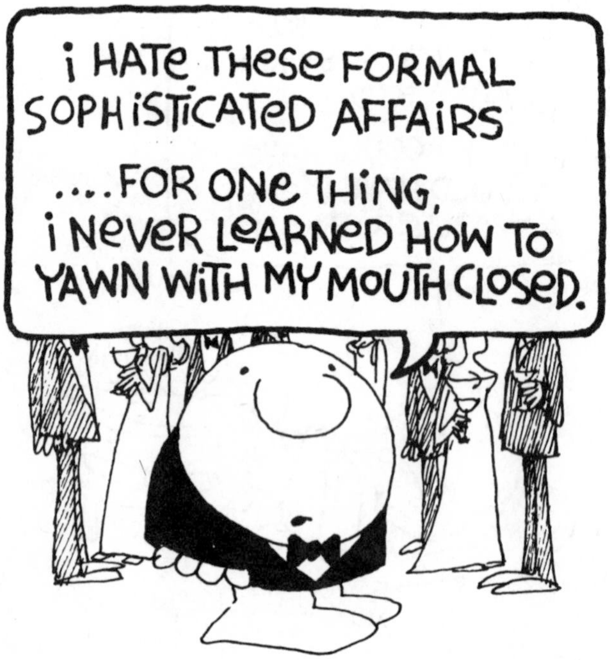
i HATE THESE FORMAL SOPHISTICATED AFFAIRS ....FOR ONE THING, i NEVER LEARNED HOW TO YAWN WITH MY MOUTH CLOSED.

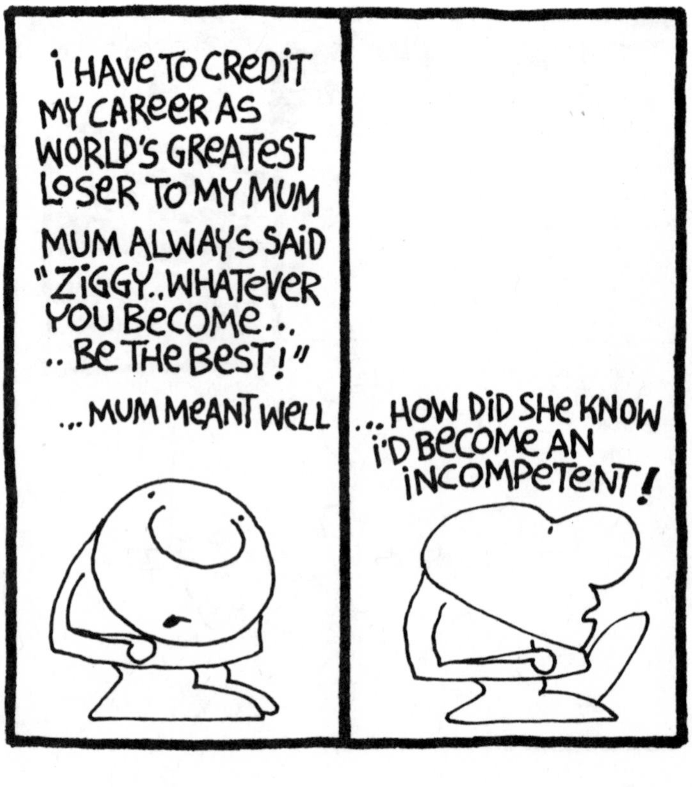
i HAVE TO CREDIT MY CAREER AS WORLD'S GREATEST LOSER TO MY MUM
MUM ALWAYS SAID "ZIGGY..WHATEVER YOU BECOME... ..BE THE BEST!"
...MUM MEANT WELL
...HOW DID SHE KNOW i'D BECOME AN iNCOMPETENT!

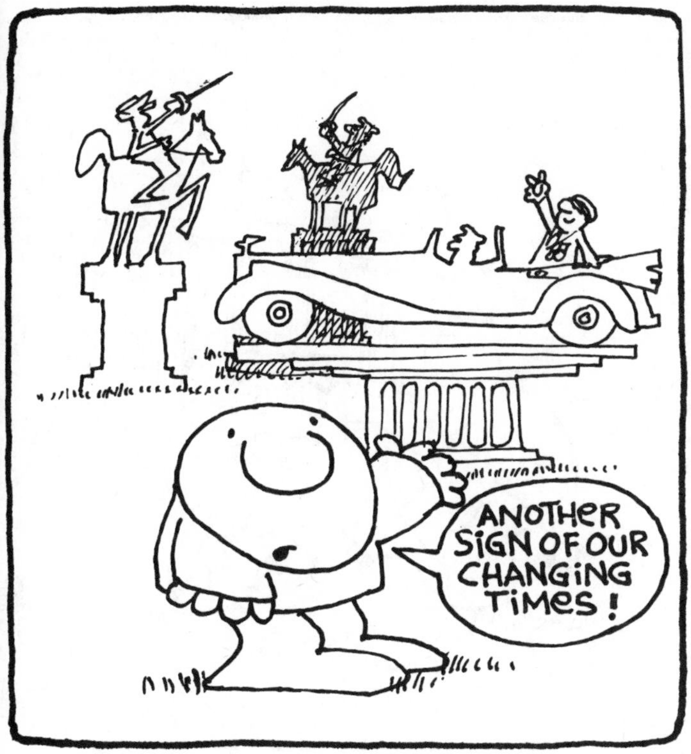
ANOTHER SIGN OF OUR CHANGING TIMES!

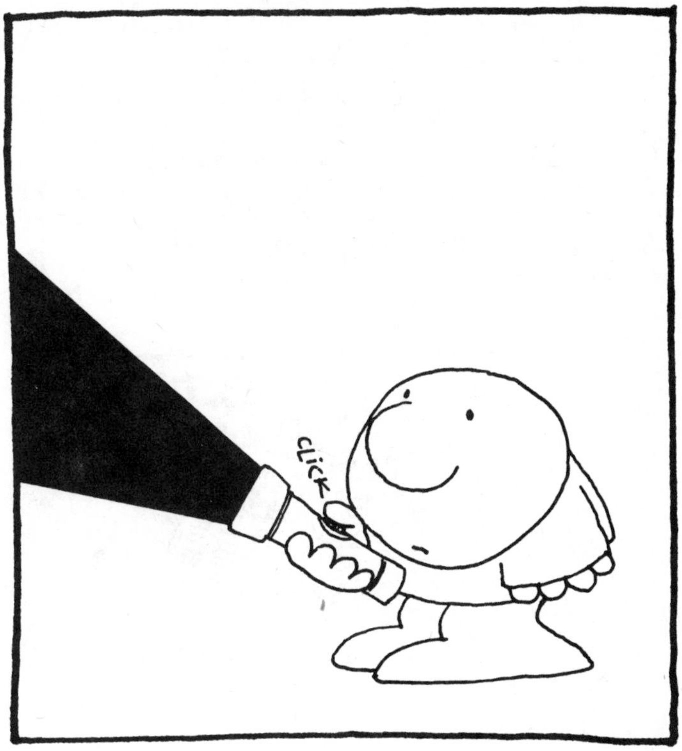
CLICK

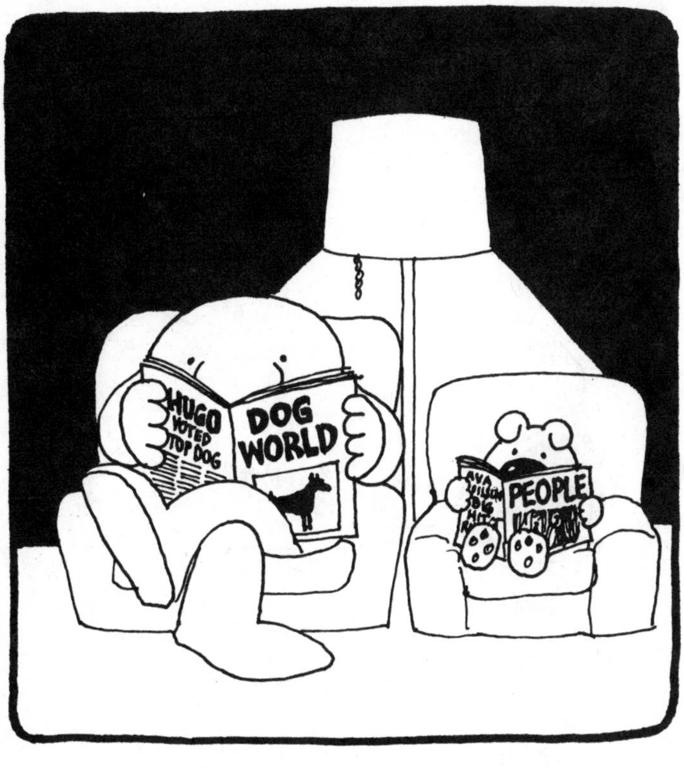
HUGO VOTED TOP DOG
DOG WORLD
PEOPLE

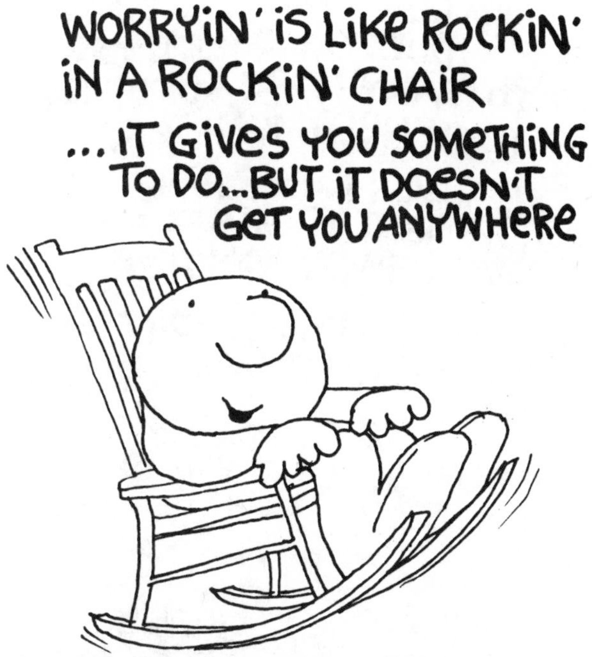
WORRYIN' IS LIKE ROCKIN' IN A ROCKIN' CHAIR
... IT GIVES YOU SOMETHING TO DO... BUT IT DOESN'T GET YOU ANYWHERE

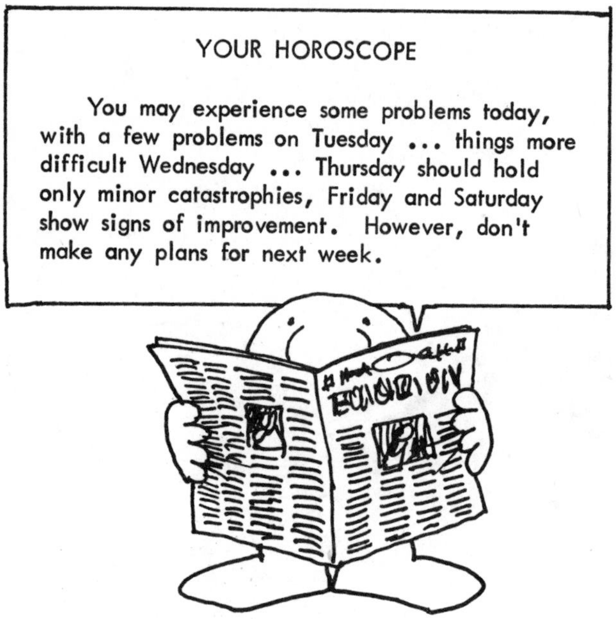
YOUR HOROSCOPE
You may experience some problems today, with a few problems on Tuesday ... things more difficult Wednesday ... Thursday should hold only minor catastrophies, Friday and Saturday show signs of improvement. However, don't make any plans for next week.

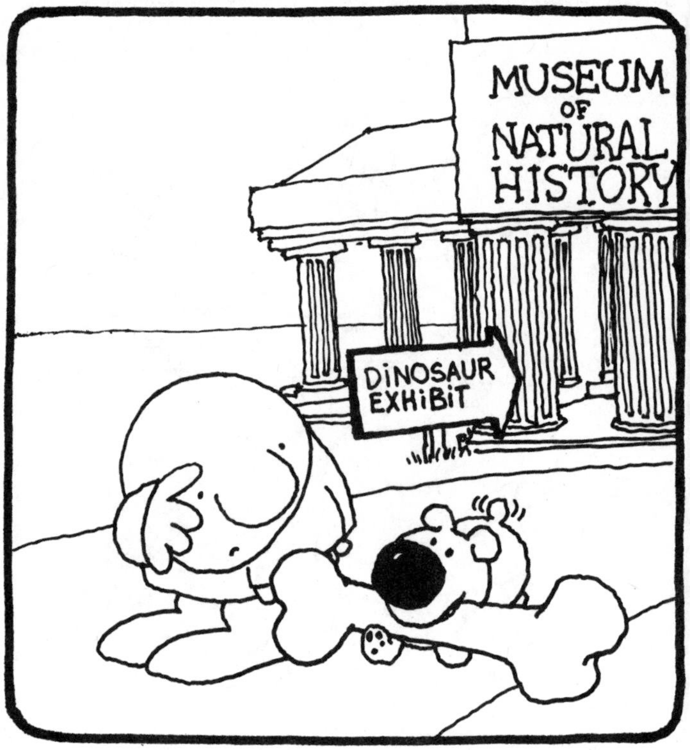
MUSEUM OF NATURAL HISTORY
DINOSAUR EXHIBIT

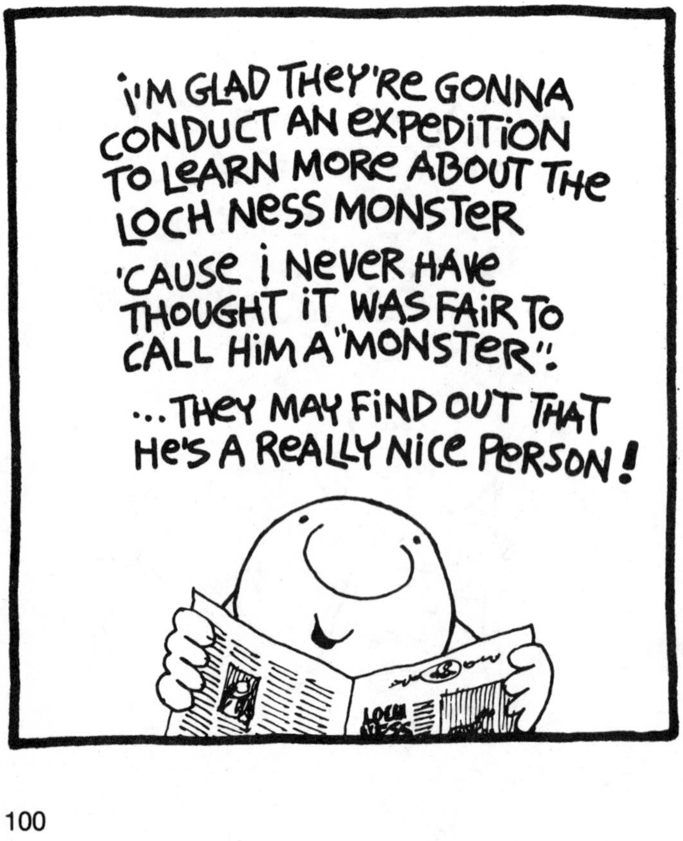
I'M GLAD THEY'RE GONNA CONDUCT AN EXPEDITION TO LEARN MORE ABOUT THE LOCH NESS MONSTER
'CAUSE I NEVER HAVE THOUGHT IT WAS FAIR TO CALL HIM A "MONSTER".
...THEY MAY FIND OUT THAT HE'S A REALLY NICE PERSON!

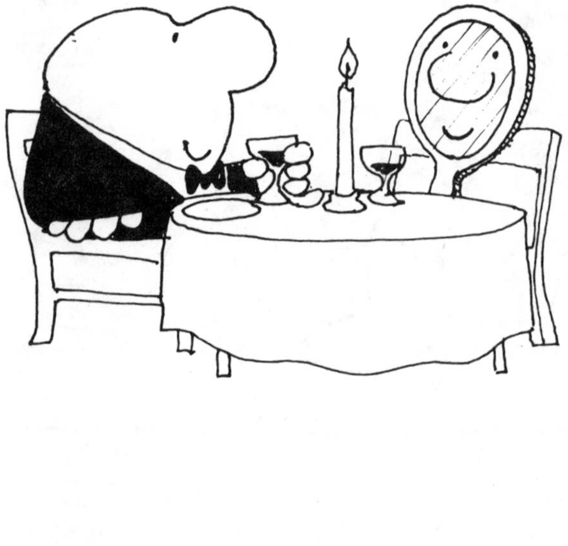

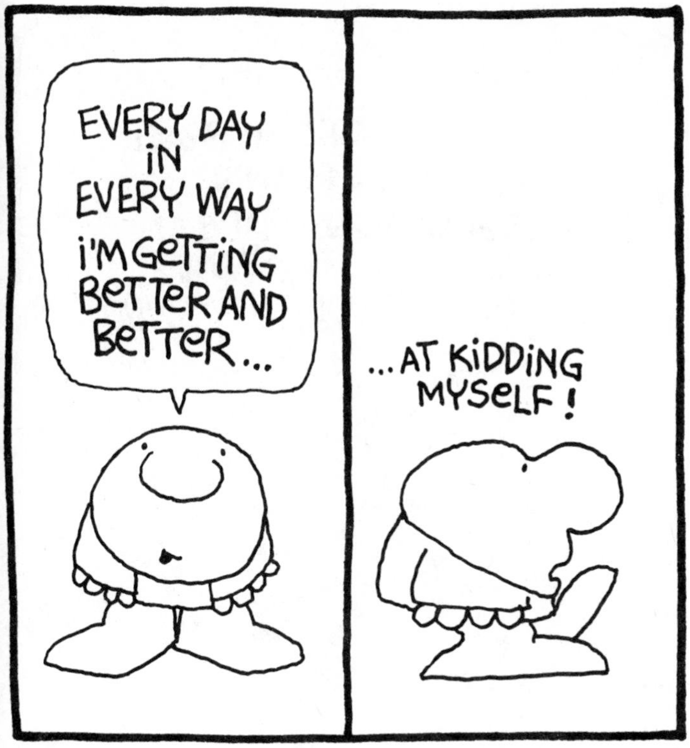
EVERY DAY IN EVERY WAY i'M GETTING BETTER AND BETTER...
...AT KIDDING MYSELF!

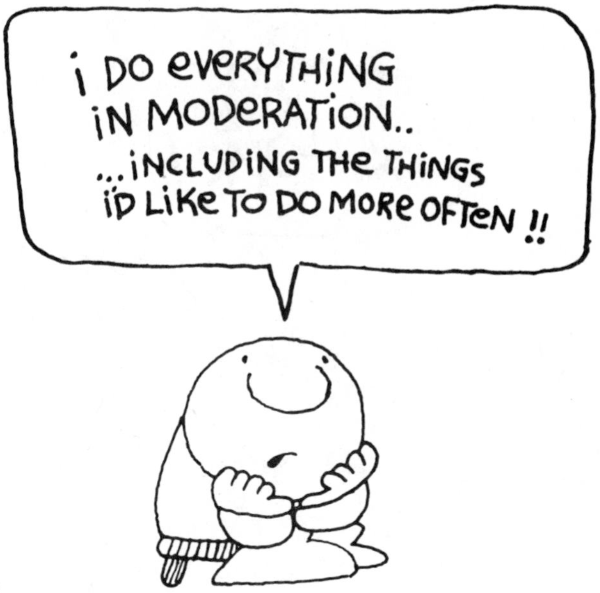
i DO EVERYTHING IN MODERATION.. ...INCLUDING THE THINGS iD LIKE TO DO MORE OFTEN!!

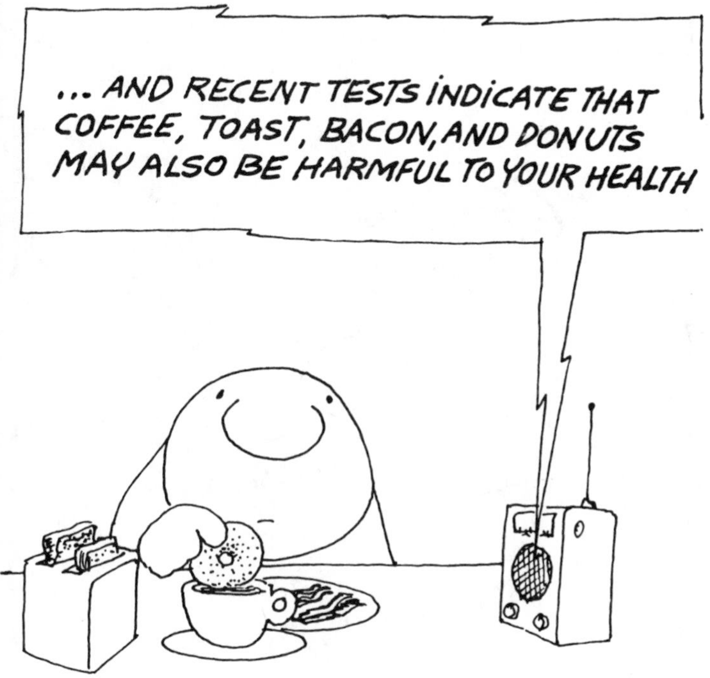
... AND RECENT TESTS INDICATE THAT COFFEE, TOAST, BACON, AND DONUTS MAY ALSO BE HARMFUL TO YOUR HEALTH

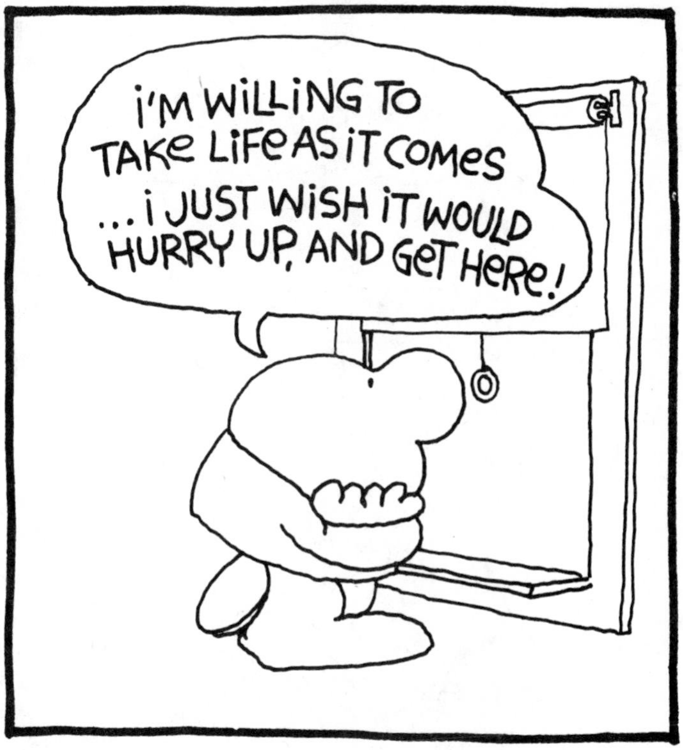
i'M WILLING TO TAKE LIFE AS IT COMES ...i JUST WISH IT WOULD HURRY UP, AND GET HERE!

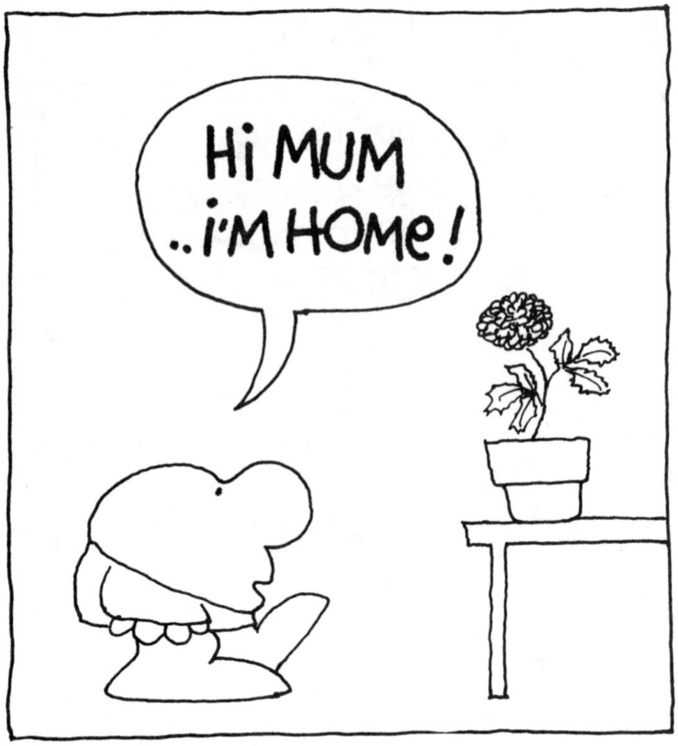
Hi MUM ..i'M HOME!

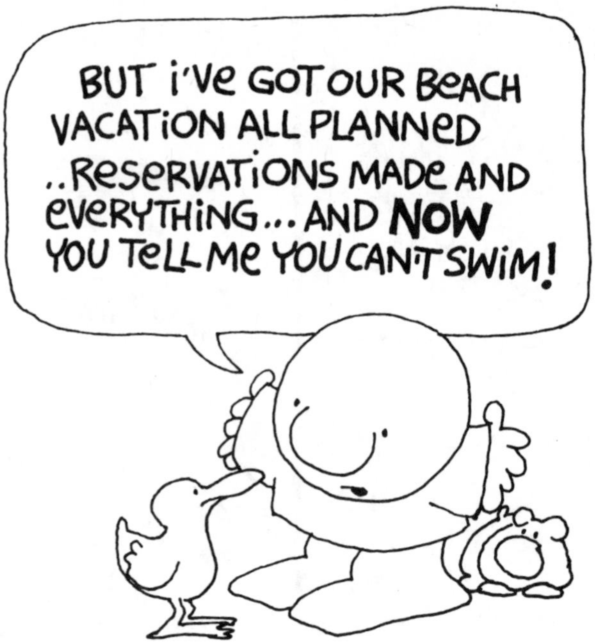
BUT i've GOT OUR BEACH VACATION ALL PLANNED ..RESERVATIONS MADE AND EVERYTHING... AND NOW YOU TELL ME YOU CAN'T SWIM!

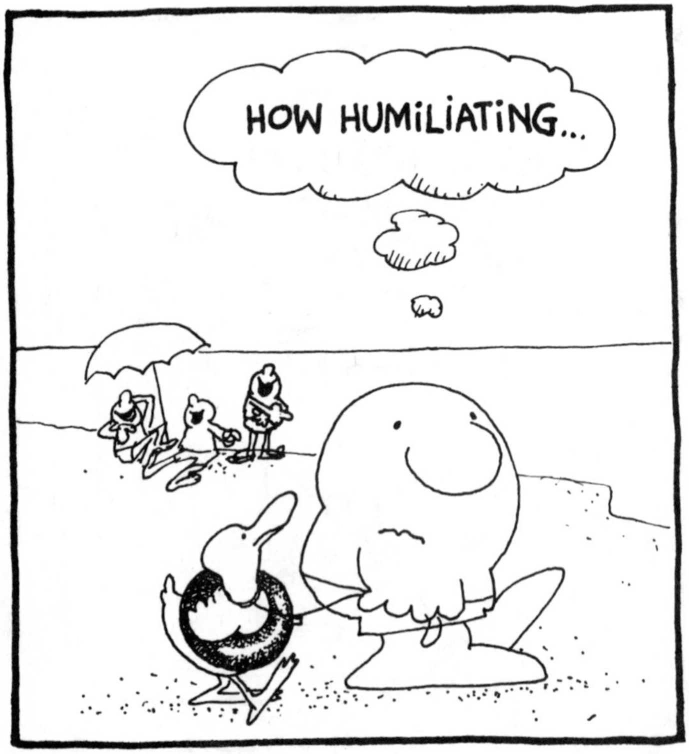
HOW HUMILIATING...

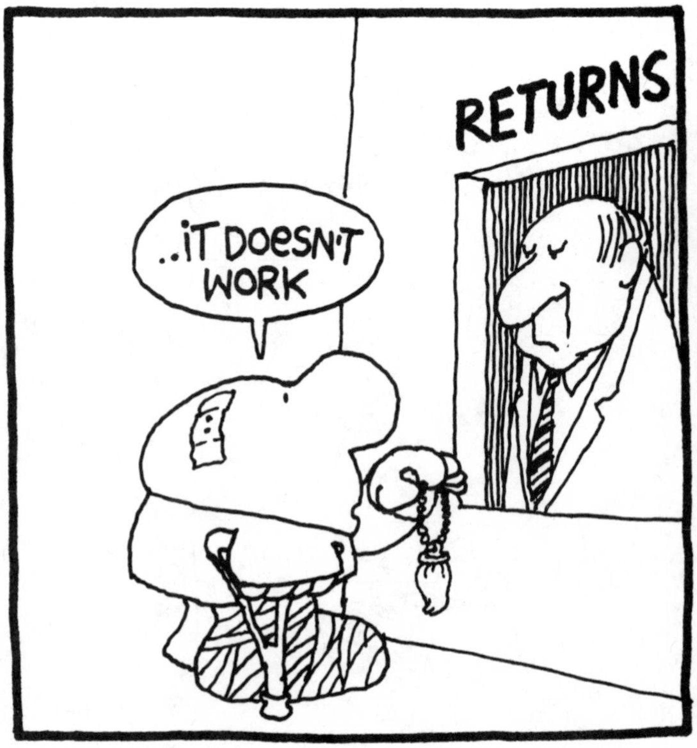
RETURNS
..IT DOESN'T WORK

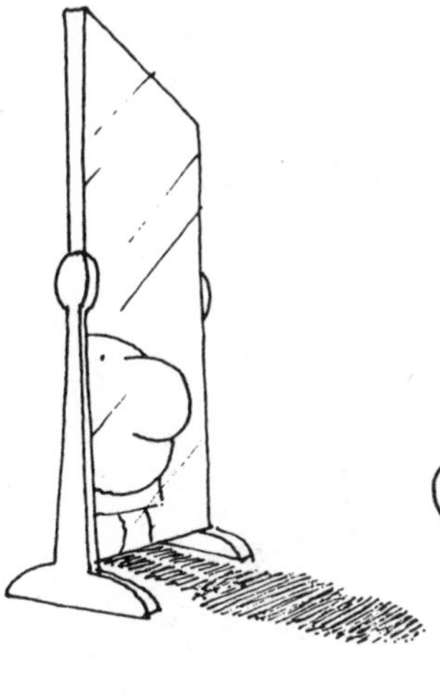

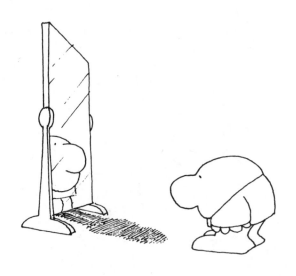

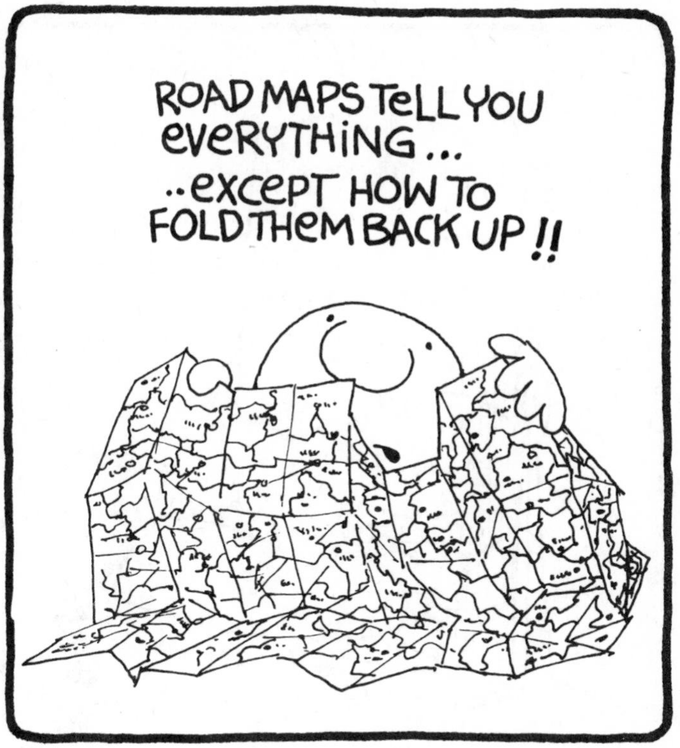
ROAD MAPS TELL YOU EVERYTHING...
..EXCEPT HOW TO FOLD THEM BACK UP !!

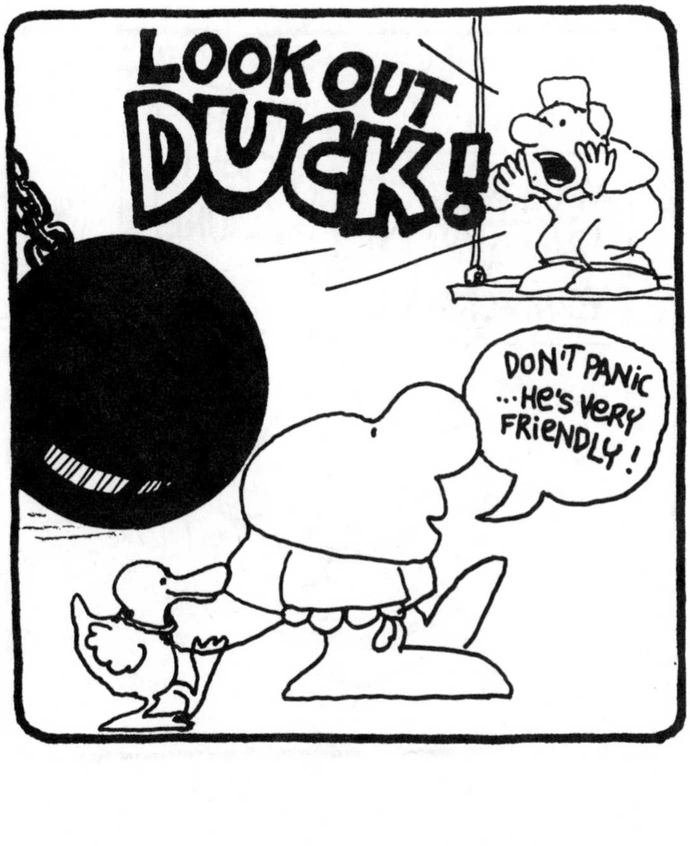
LOOK OUT DUCK!
DON'T PANIC ...HE'S VERY FRIENDLY!

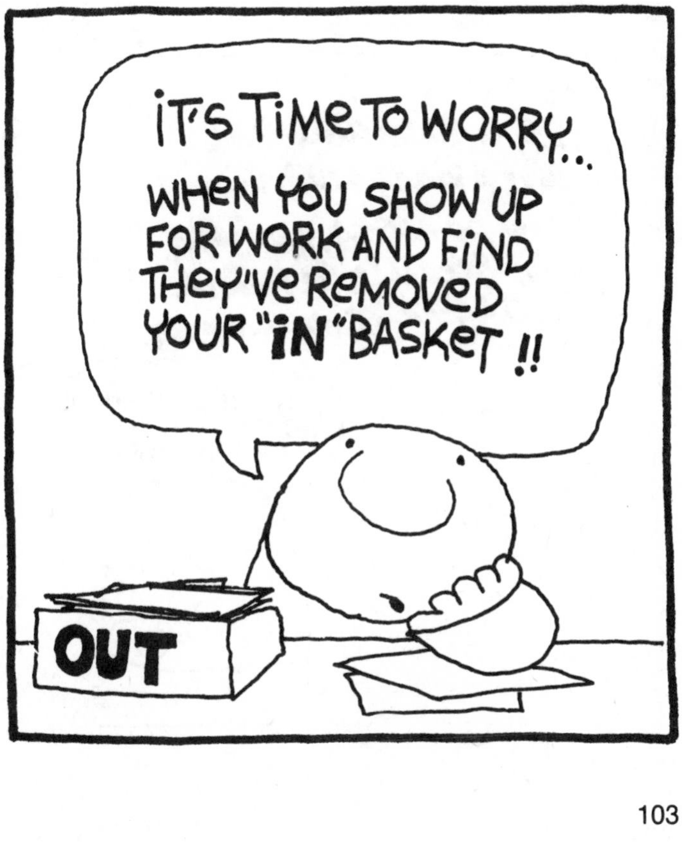
IT'S TIME TO WORRY...
WHEN YOU SHOW UP FOR WORK AND FIND THEY'VE REMOVED YOUR "IN" BASKET !!
OUT

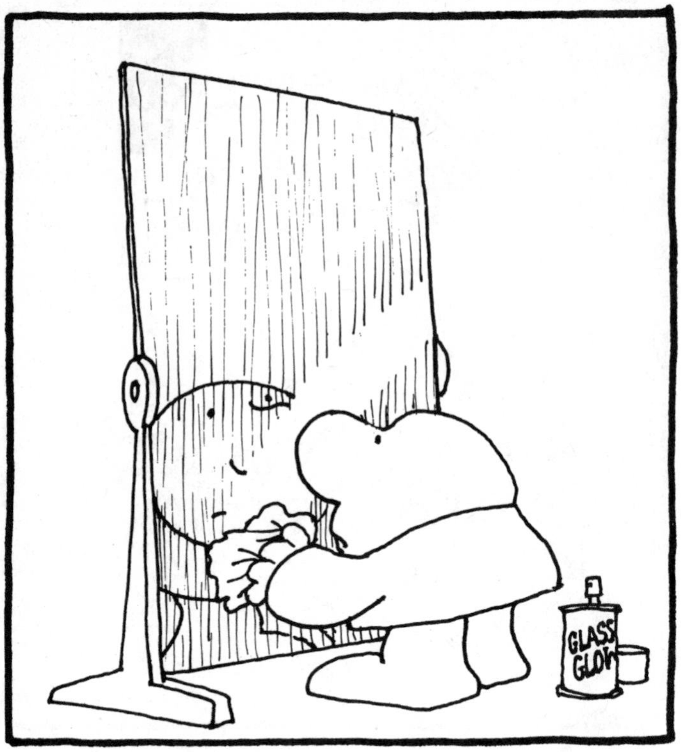
GLASS GLOW

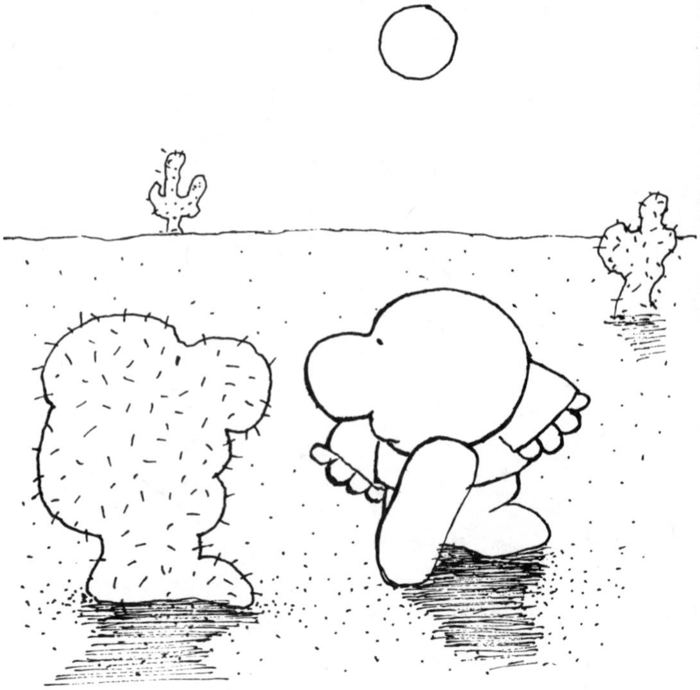

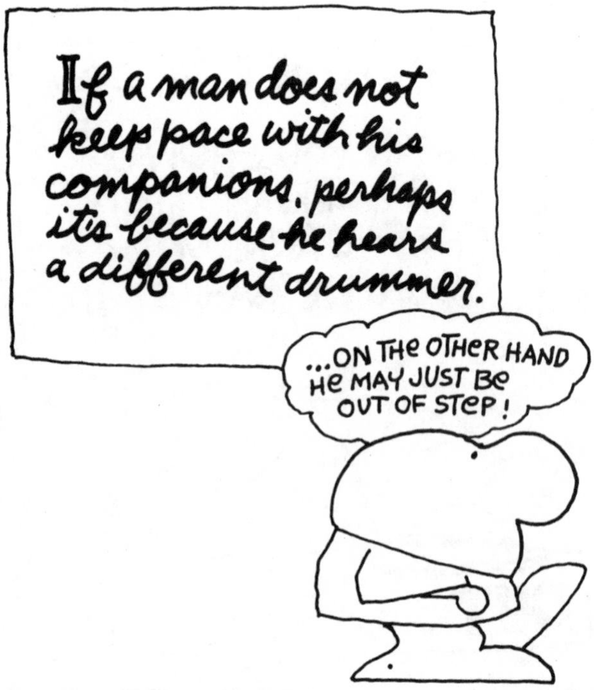
If a man does not keep pace with his companions, perhaps its because he hears a different drummer.
...ON THE OTHER HAND HE MAY JUST BE OUT OF STEP!

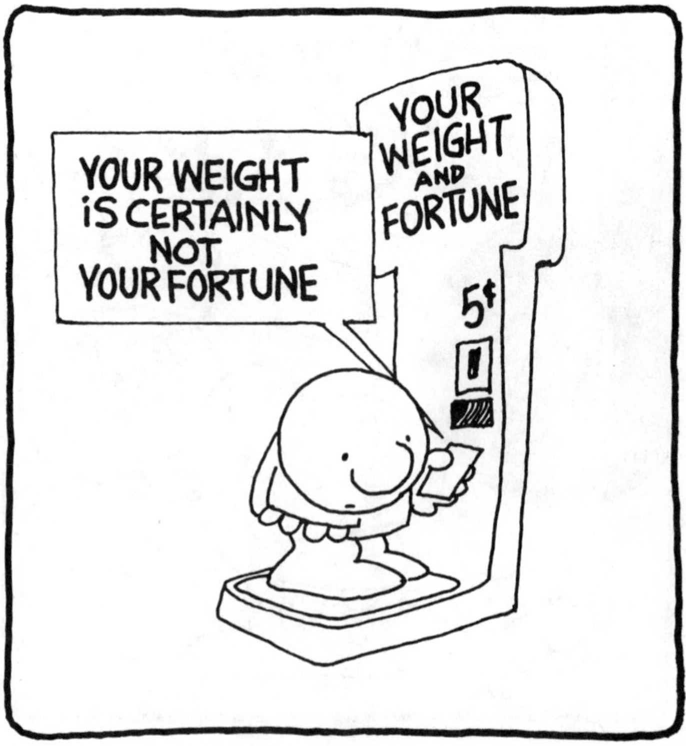
YOUR WEIGHT IS CERTAINLY NOT YOUR FORTUNE
YOUR WEIGHT AND FORTUNE
5¢

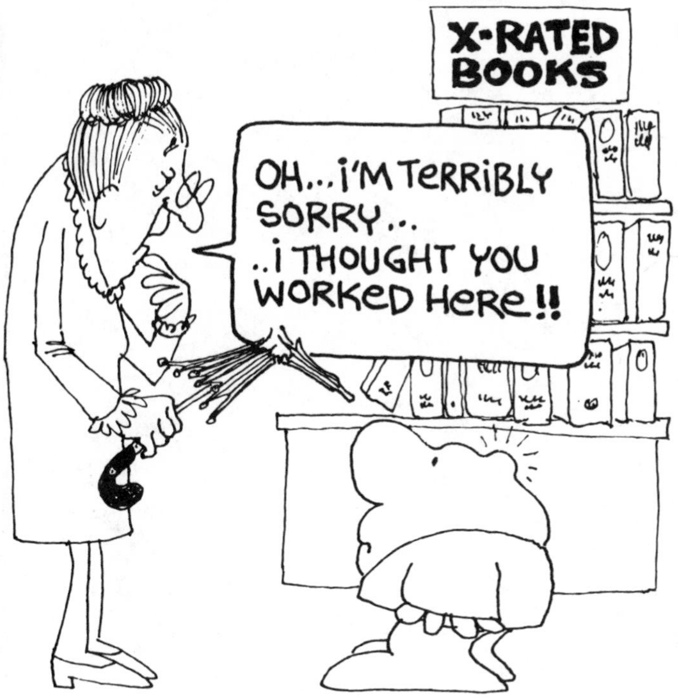
X-RATED BOOKS
OH...I'M TERRIBLY SORRY... ..I THOUGHT YOU WORKED HERE!!

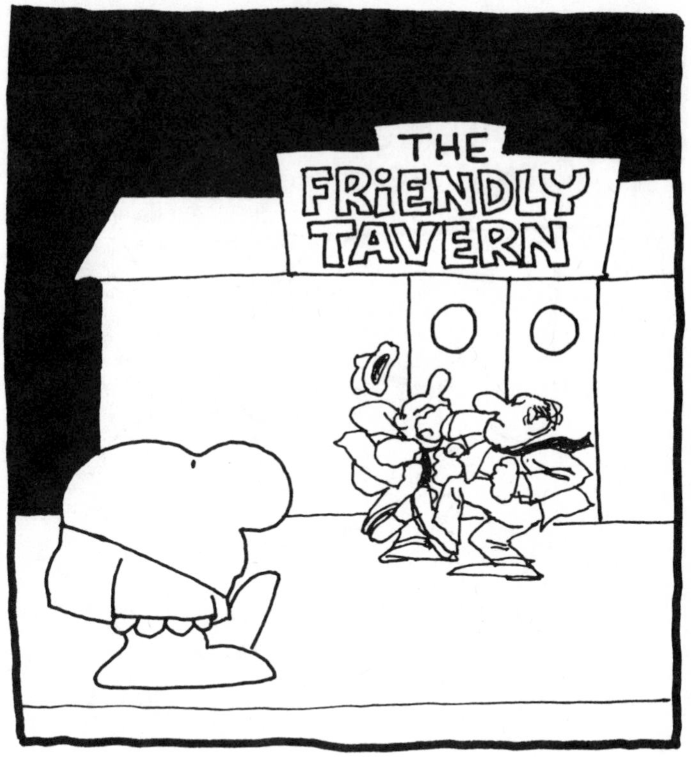
THE FRIENDLY TAVERN

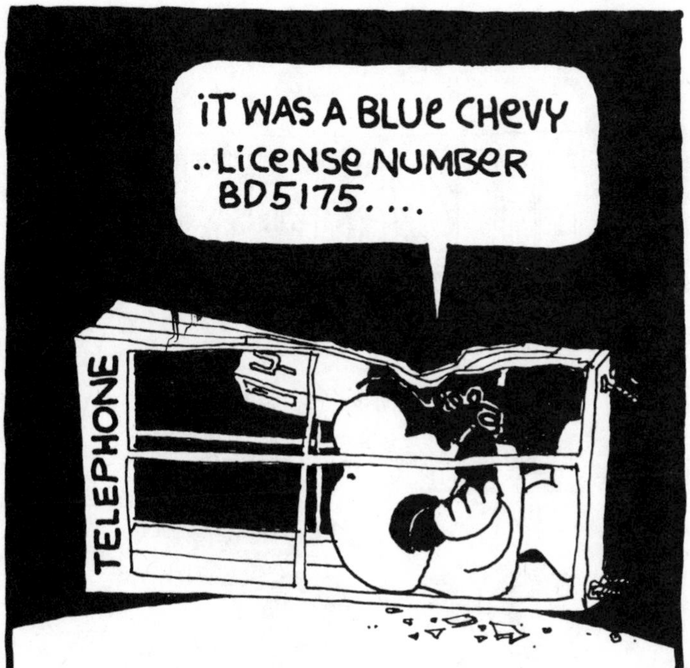
IT WAS A BLUE CHEVY ..LICENSE NUMBER BD5175....
TELEPHONE

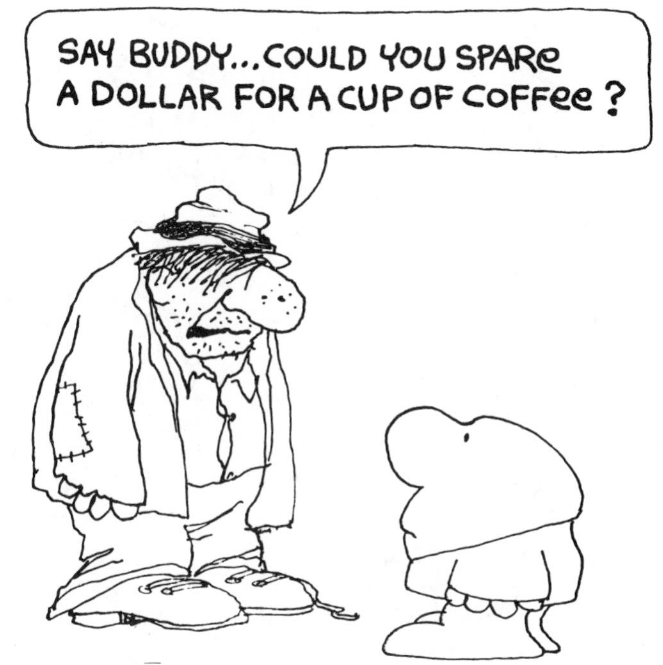
SAY BUDDY...COULD YOU SPARE A DOLLAR FOR A CUP OF COFFEE?

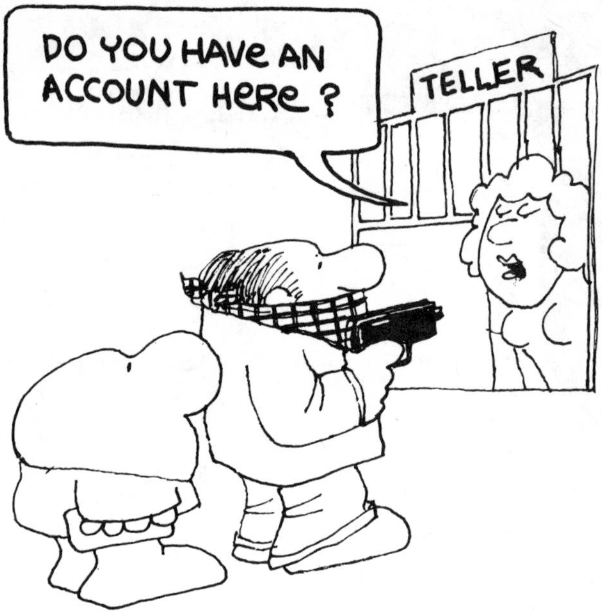
DO YOU HAVE AN ACCOUNT HERE ?
TELLER

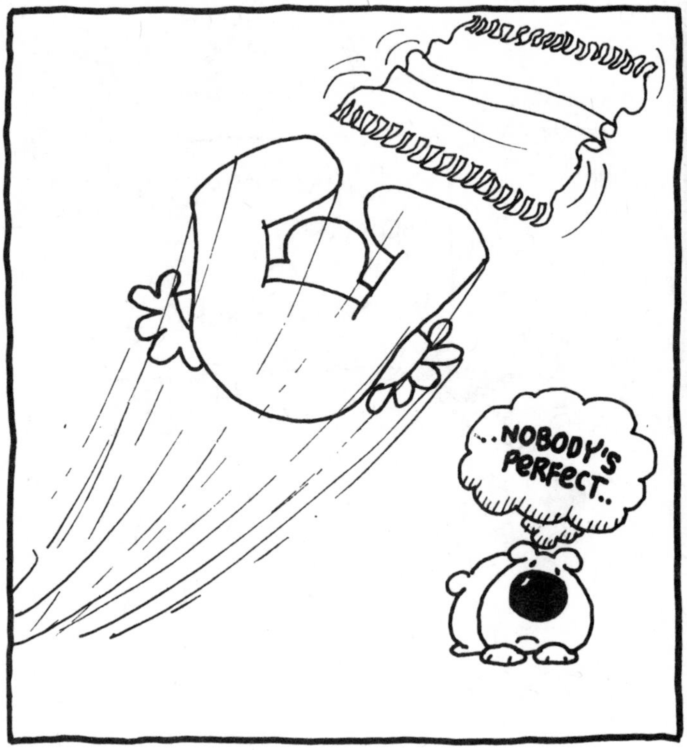
..NOBODY'S PERFECT..

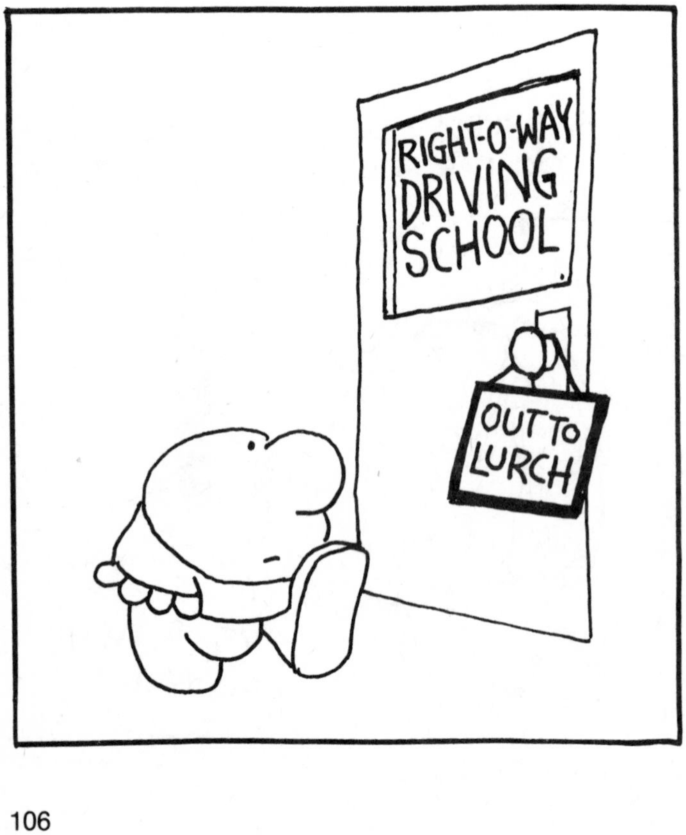
RIGHT-O-WAY DRIVING SCHOOL
OUT TO LURCH

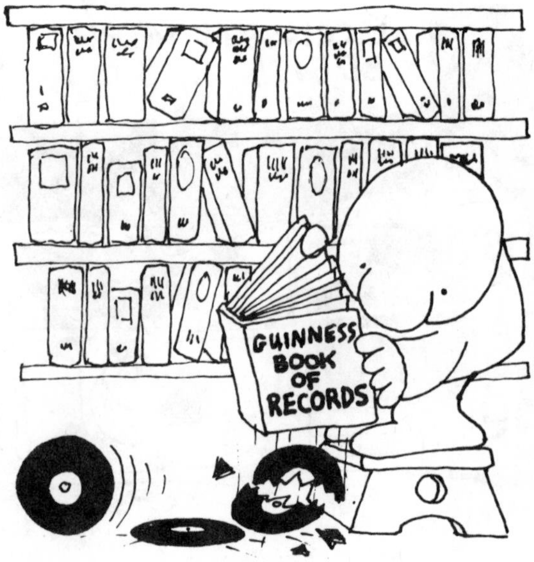
GUINNESS BOOK OF RECORDS

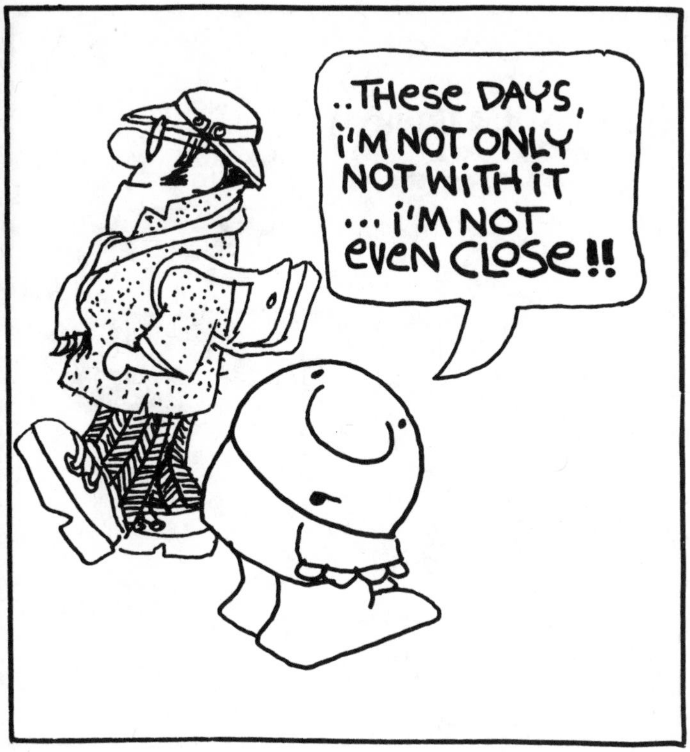
..THESE DAYS, I'M NOT ONLY NOT WITH IT ... I'M NOT EVEN CLOSE!!

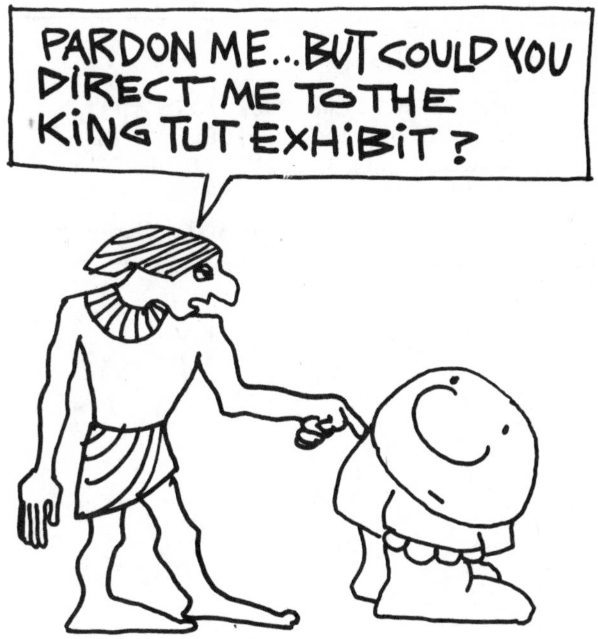
PARDON ME...BUT COULD YOU DIRECT ME TO THE KING TUT EXHIBIT?

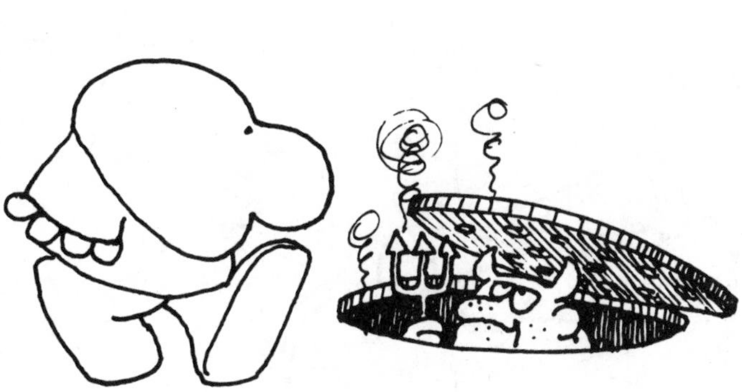

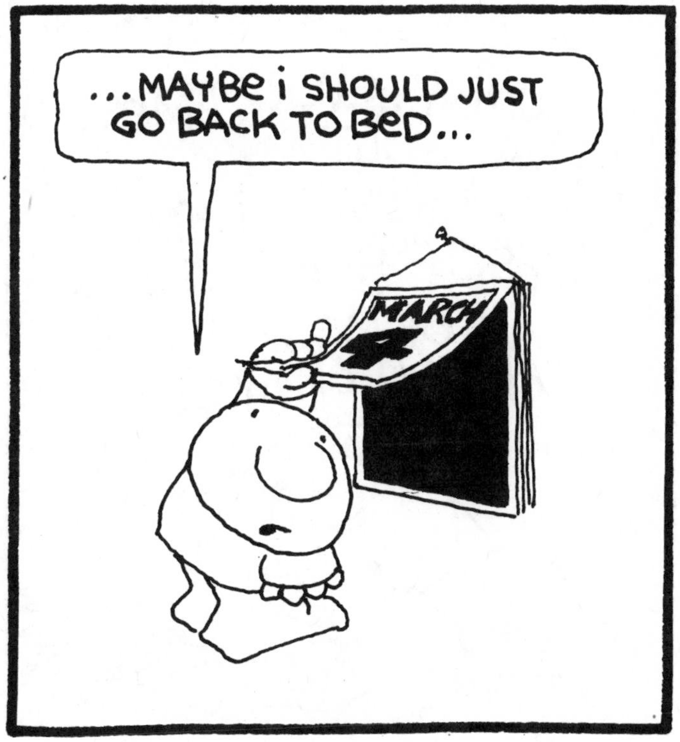
...MAYBE I SHOULD JUST GO BACK TO BED...
MARCH
4

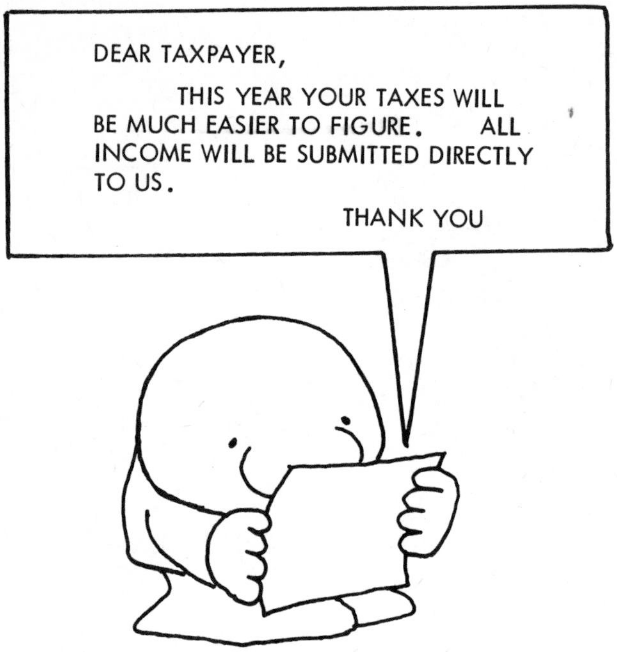
DEAR TAXPAYER,
THIS YEAR YOUR TAXES WILL BE MUCH EASIER TO FIGURE. ALL INCOME WILL BE SUBMITTED DIRECTLY TO US.
THANK YOU

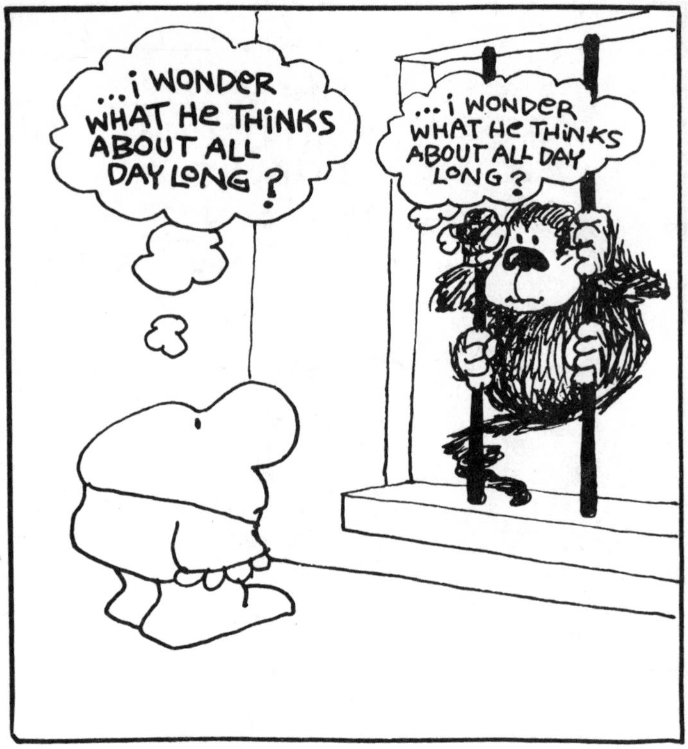
...i WONDER WHAT He THiNKS ABOUT ALL DAY LONG ?
...i WONDER WHAT He THiNKS ABOUT ALL DAY LONG ?

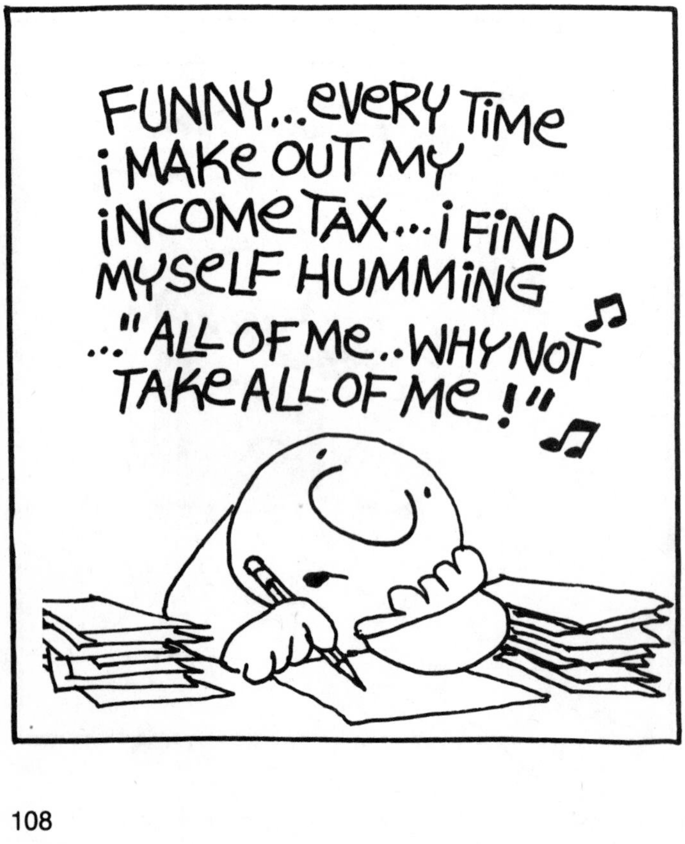
FUNNY...eVeRY TiMe i MAKe OUT MY iNCOMe TAX...i FiND MYSeLF HUMMiNG ..."ALL OF Me..WHY NOT TAKe ALL OF Me!"

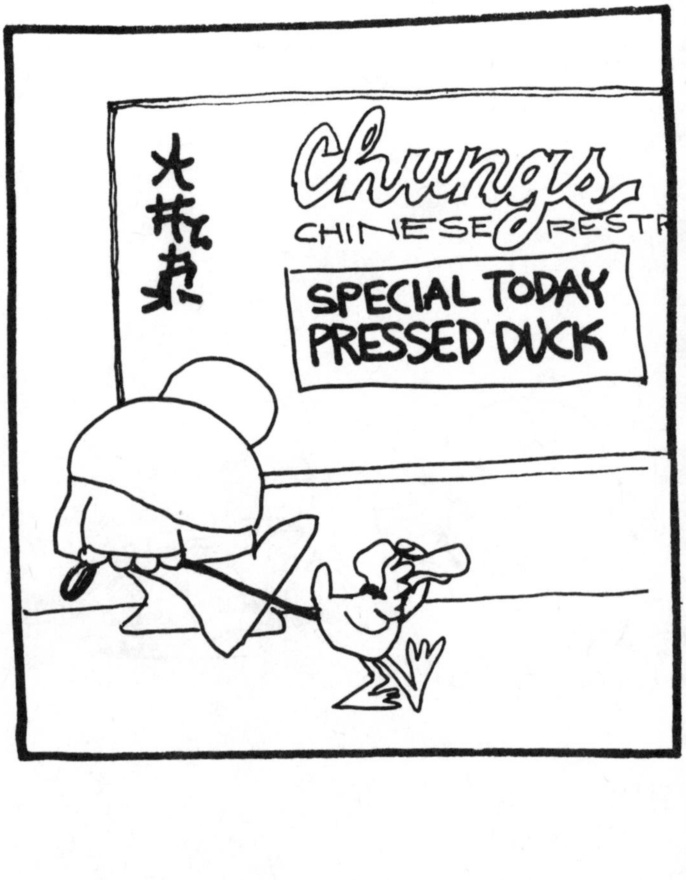
Chungs
CHINESE
SPECIAL TODAY
PRESSED DUCK

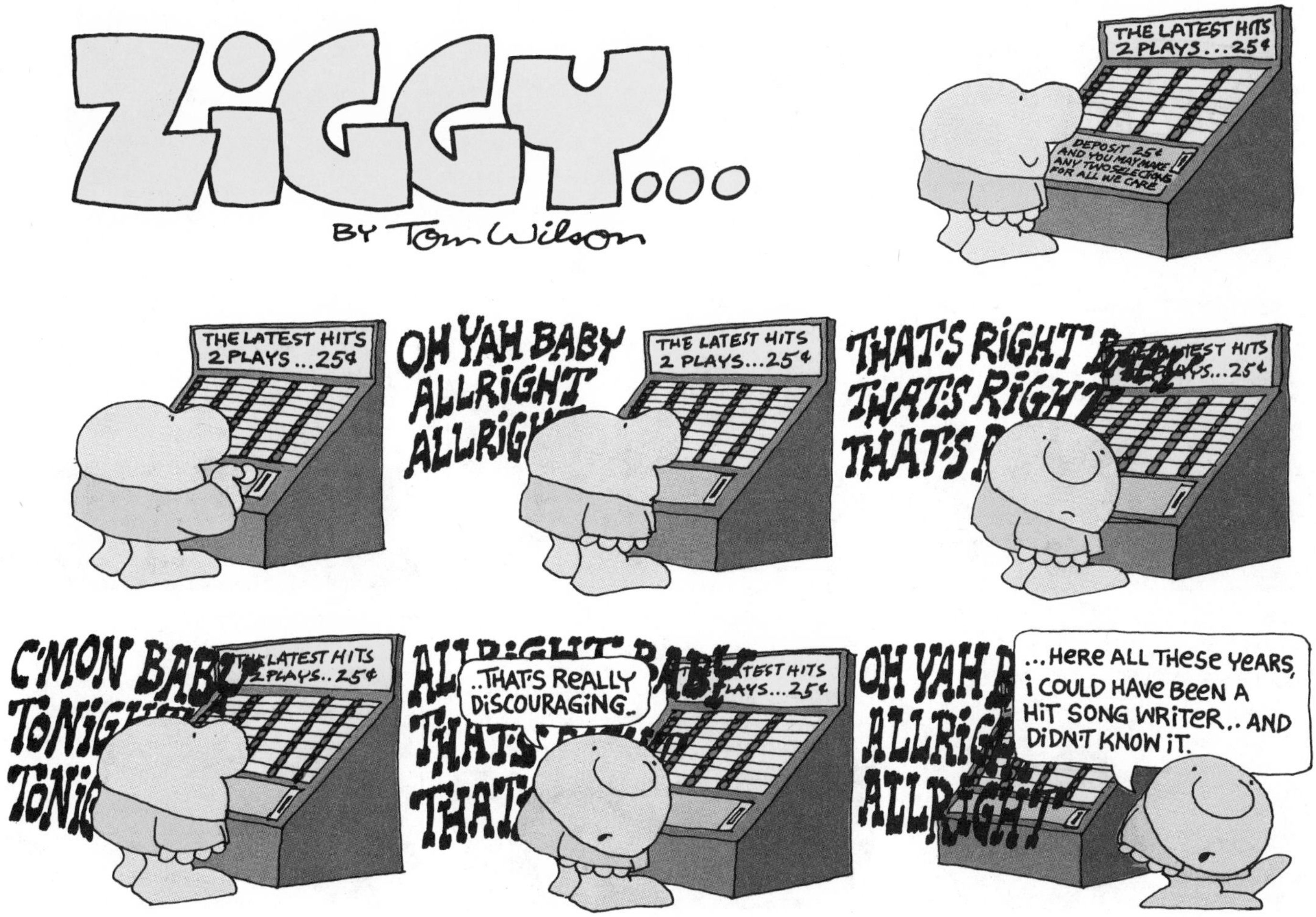
ZIGGY...
BY Tom Wilson
THE LATEST HITS 2 PLAYS...25¢
DEPOSIT 25¢ AND YOU MAY MAKE ANY TWO SELECTIONS FOR ALL WE CARE
OH YAH BABY
ALLRIGHT
THAT'S RIGHT
..THAT'S REALLY DISCOURAGING..
...HERE ALL THESE YEARS, I COULD HAVE BEEN A HIT SONG WRITER.. AND DIDN'T KNOW IT.

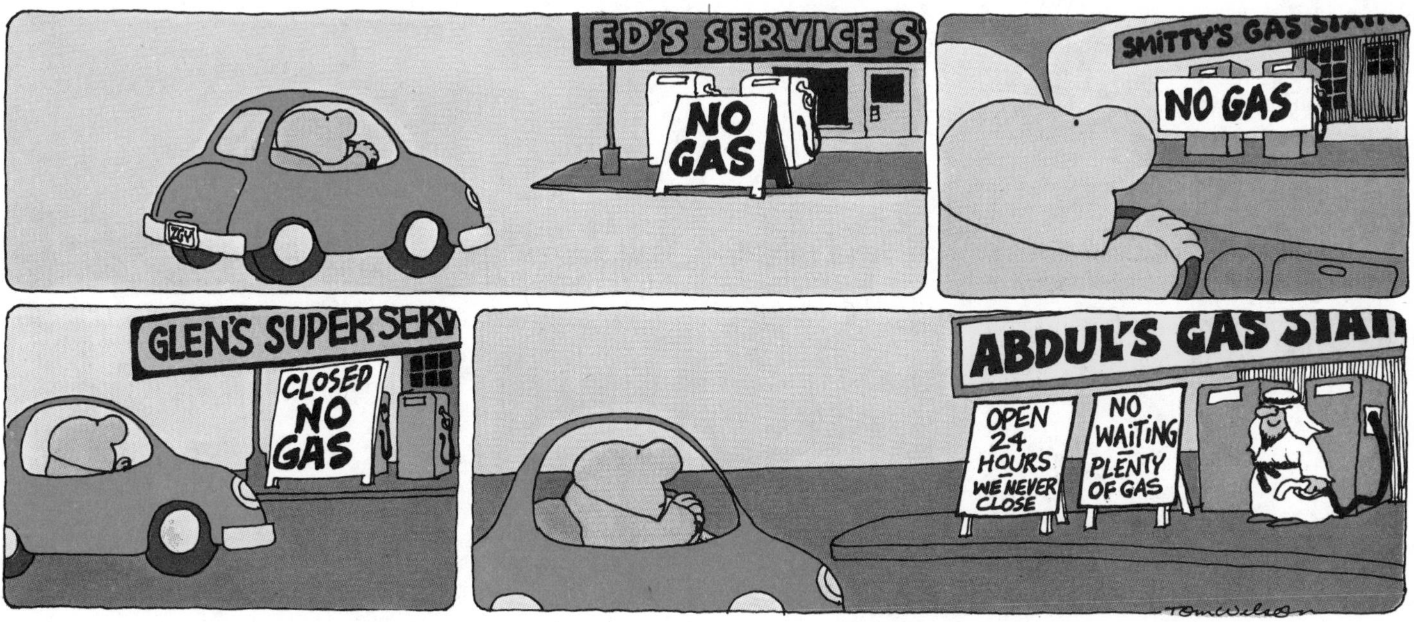
NO GAS
NO GAS
CLOSED NO GAS
OPEN 24 HOURS WE NEVER CLOSE
NO WAITING PLENTY OF GAS
Tom Wilson

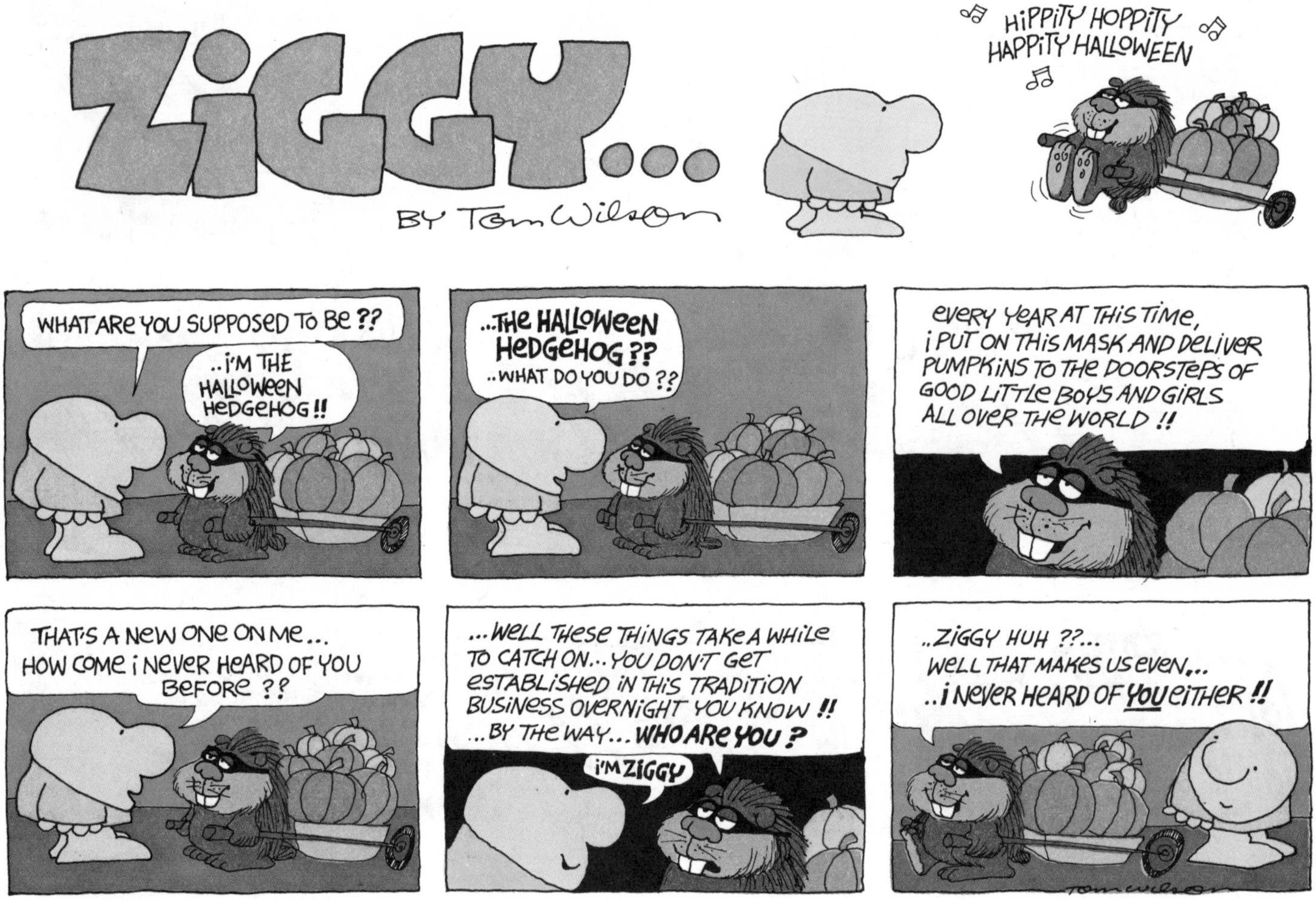
ZiGGY...
BY Tom Wilson
HiPPiTY HOPPiTY HAPPiTY HALLOWEEN
WHAT ARE YOU SUPPOSED TO BE ??
..i'M THE HALLOWEEN HEDGEHOG !!
...THE HALLOWEEN HEDGEHOG ?? ..WHAT DO YOU DO ??
EVERY YEAR AT THIS TIME, i PUT ON THIS MASK AND DELIVER PUMPKINS TO THE DOORSTEPS OF GOOD LITTLE BOYS AND GIRLS ALL OVER THE WORLD !!
THAT'S A NEW ONE ON ME... HOW COME i NEVER HEARD OF YOU BEFORE ??
...WELL THESE THINGS TAKE A WHILE TO CATCH ON...YOU DON'T GET ESTABLISHED IN THIS TRADITION BUSINESS OVERNIGHT YOU KNOW !! ...BY THE WAY... WHO ARE YOU ?
i'M ZIGGY
..ZIGGY HUH ??... WELL THAT MAKES US EVEN... ..i NEVER HEARD OF YOU EITHER !!

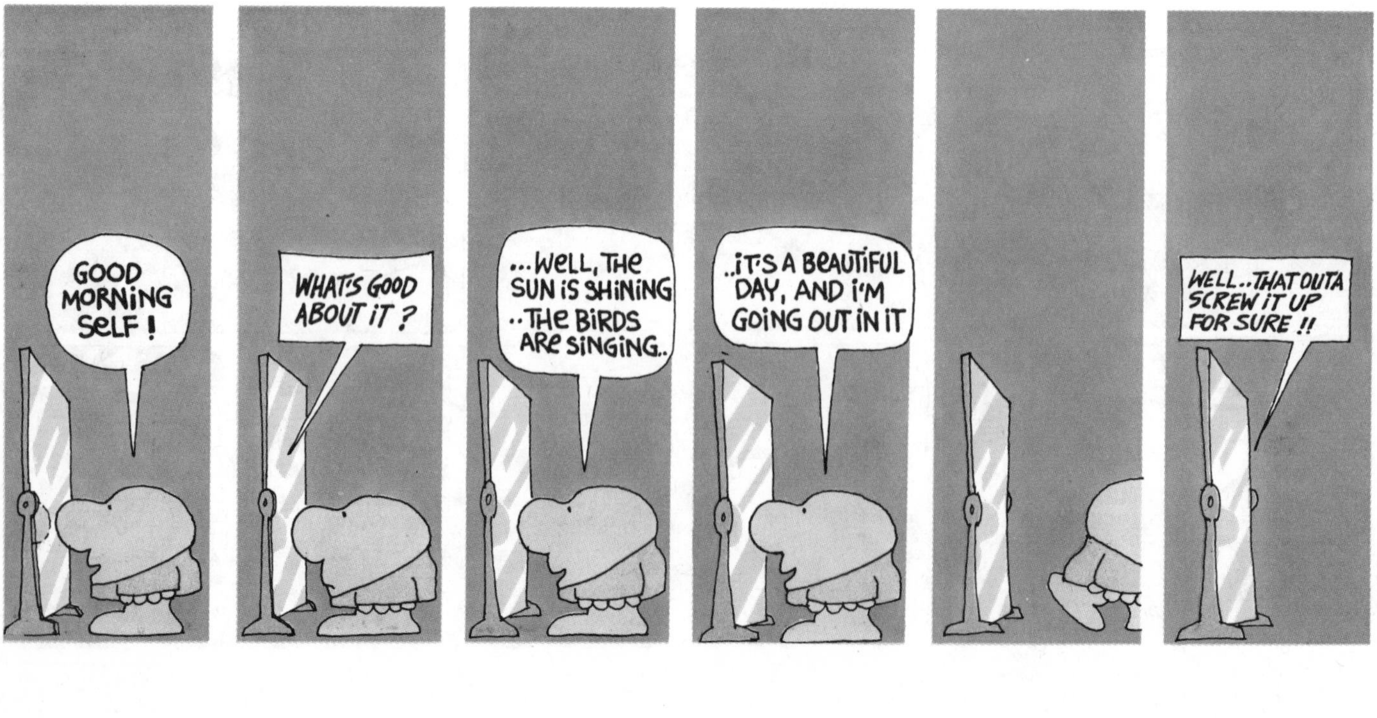
GOOD MORNING SELF !
WHAT'S GOOD ABOUT IT ?
...WELL, THE SUN IS SHINING ..THE BIRDS ARE SINGING..
..iT'S A BEAUTIFUL DAY, AND i'M GOING OUT IN IT
WELL..THAT OUTA SCREW IT UP FOR SURE !!

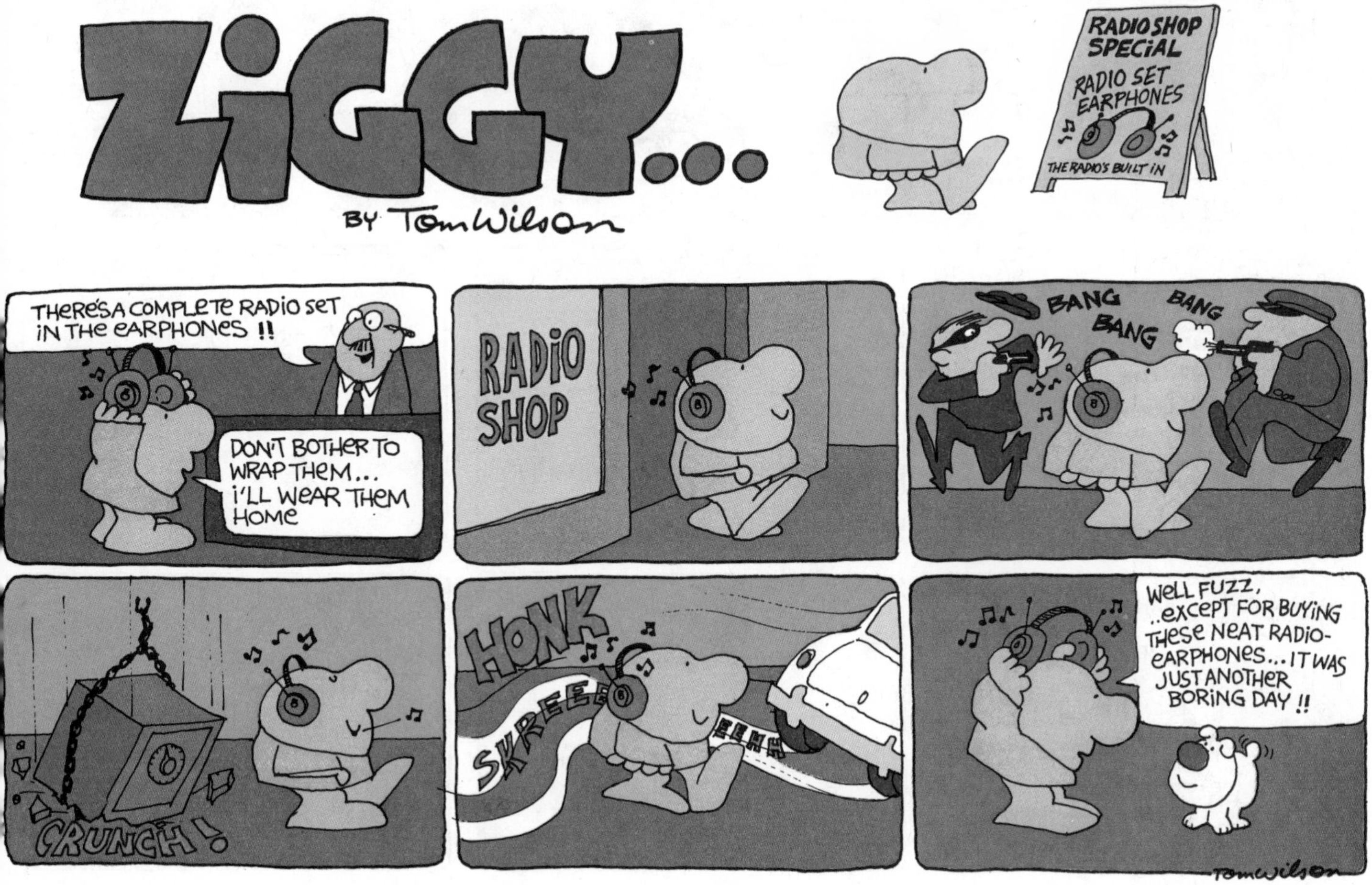
ZIGGY...
BY Tom Wilson
RADIO SHOP SPECIAL
RADIO SET EARPHONES
THE RADIO'S BUILT IN
THERE'S A COMPLETE RADIO SET IN THE EARPHONES !!
DON'T BOTHER TO WRAP THEM... I'LL WEAR THEM HOME
RADIO SHOP
BANG
BANG
BANG
CRUNCH!
HONK
SKREEE
WELL FUZZ, ..EXCEPT FOR BUYING THESE NEAT RADIO-EARPHONES... IT WAS JUST ANOTHER BORING DAY !!
Tom Wilson

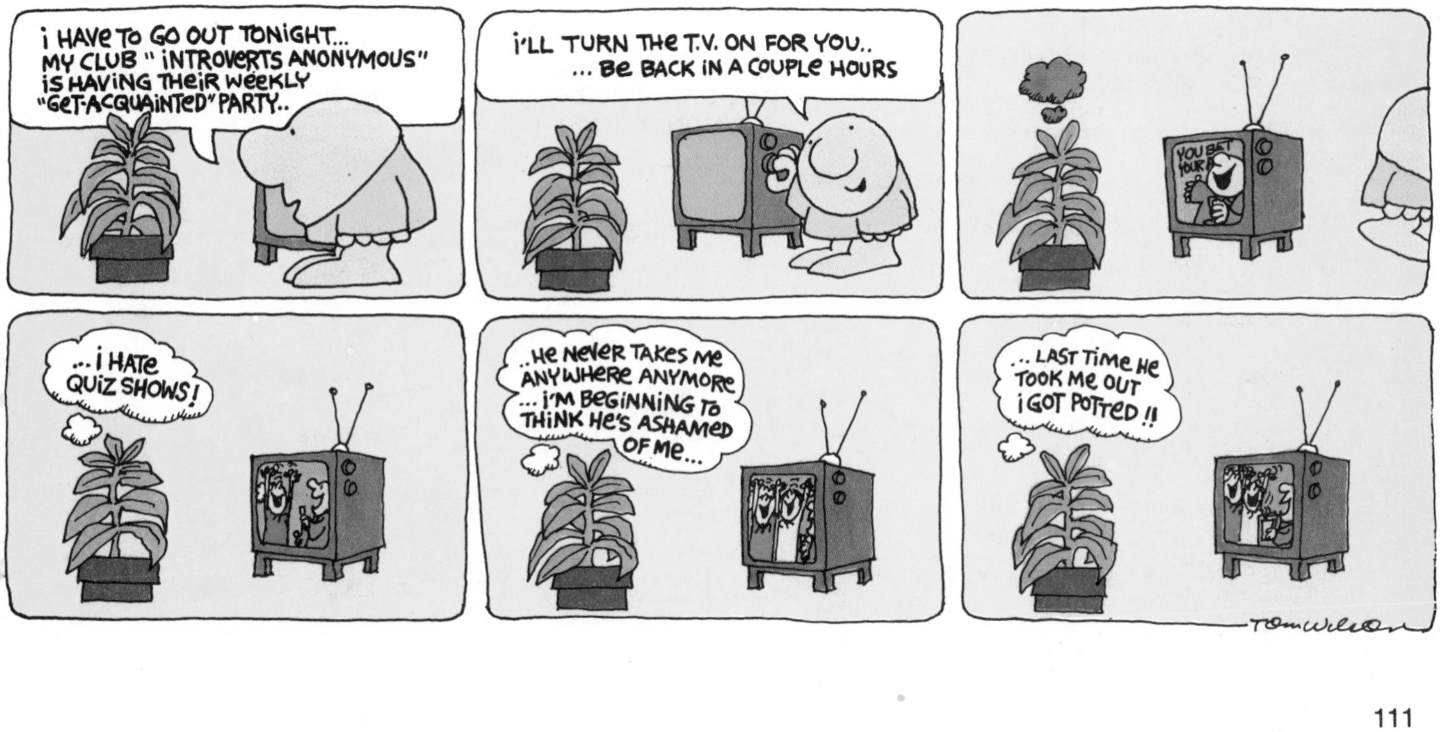
I HAVE TO GO OUT TONIGHT... MY CLUB "INTROVERTS ANONYMOUS" IS HAVING THEIR WEEKLY "GET-ACQUAINTED" PARTY..
I'LL TURN THE T.V. ON FOR YOU.. ... BE BACK IN A COUPLE HOURS
YOU BET YOUR
...I HATE QUIZ SHOWS!
..HE NEVER TAKES ME ANYWHERE ANYMORE ...I'M BEGINNING TO THINK HE'S ASHAMED OF ME...
...LAST TIME HE TOOK ME OUT I GOT POTTED !!
Tom Wilson

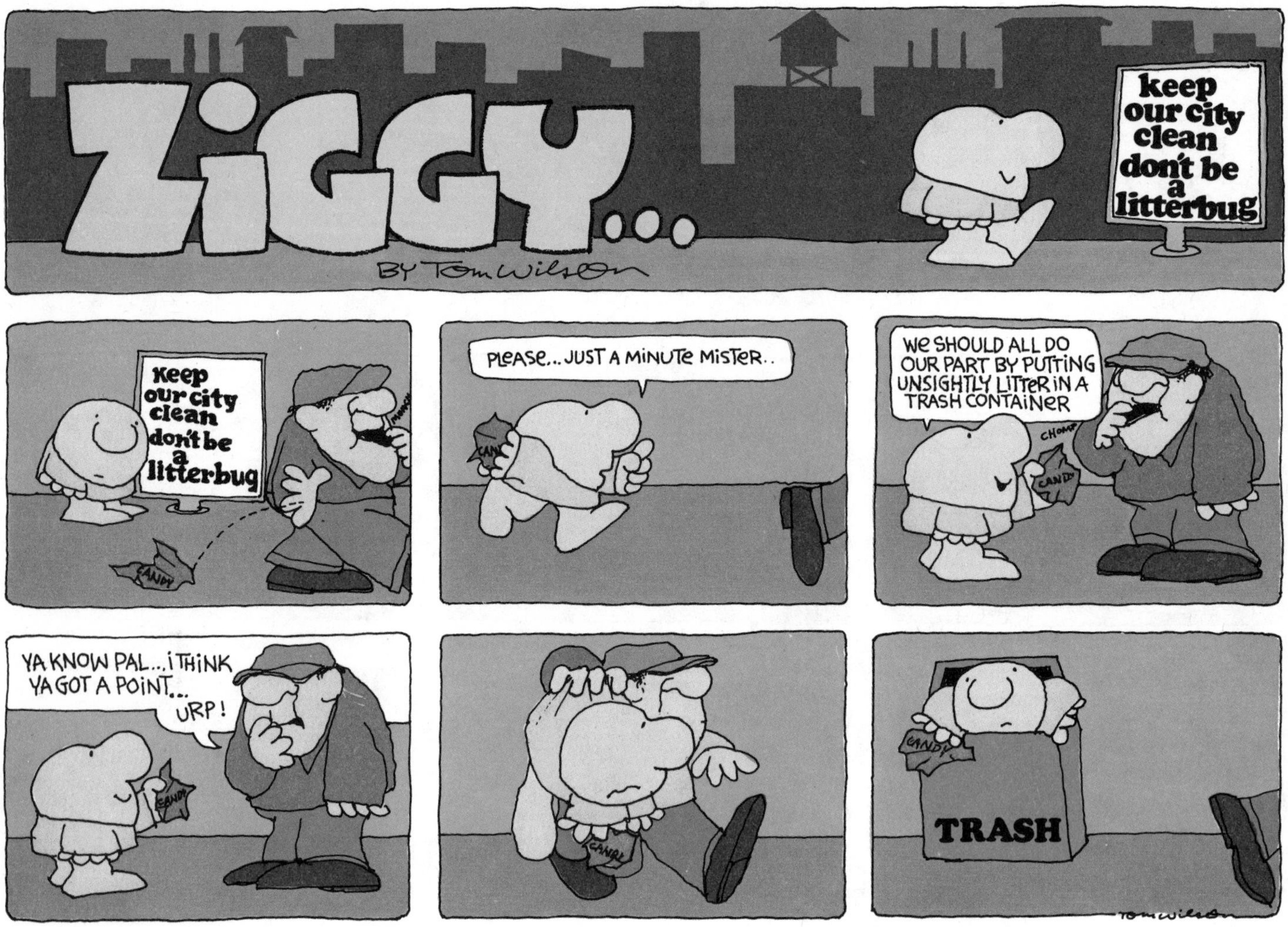
ZIGGY...
BY Tom Wilson
keep our city clean don't be a litterbug
keep our city clean don't be a litterbug
PLEASE.. JUST A MINUTE MISTER..
WE SHOULD ALL DO OUR PART BY PUTTING UNSIGHTLY LITTER IN A TRASH CONTAINER
CHOMP
YA KNOW PAL...I THINK YA GOT A POINT...
URP!
TRASH
Tom Wilson

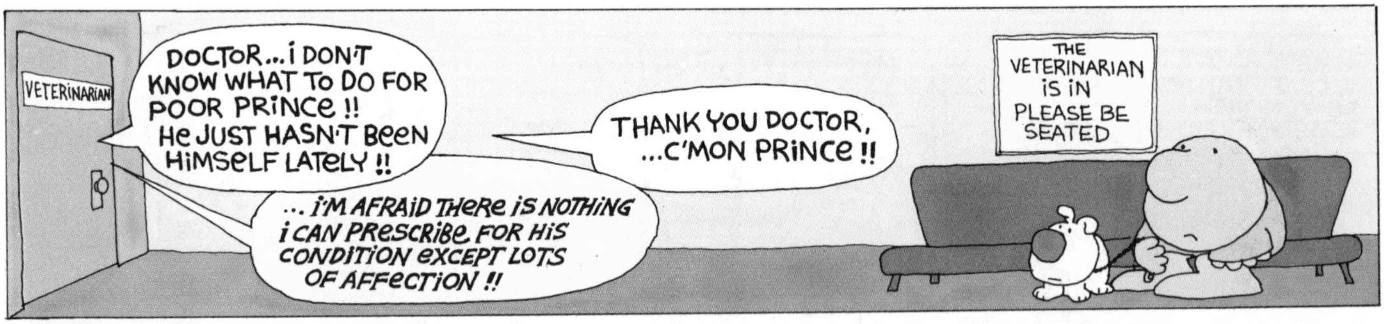
VETERINARIAN
DOCTOR...I DON'T KNOW WHAT TO DO FOR POOR PRINCE!! HE JUST HASN'T BEEN HIMSELF LATELY!!
...I'M AFRAID THERE IS NOTHING I CAN PRESCRIBE FOR HIS CONDITION EXCEPT LOTS OF AFFECTION!!
THANK YOU DOCTOR, ...C'MON PRINCE!!
THE VETERINARIAN IS IN PLEASE BE SEATED

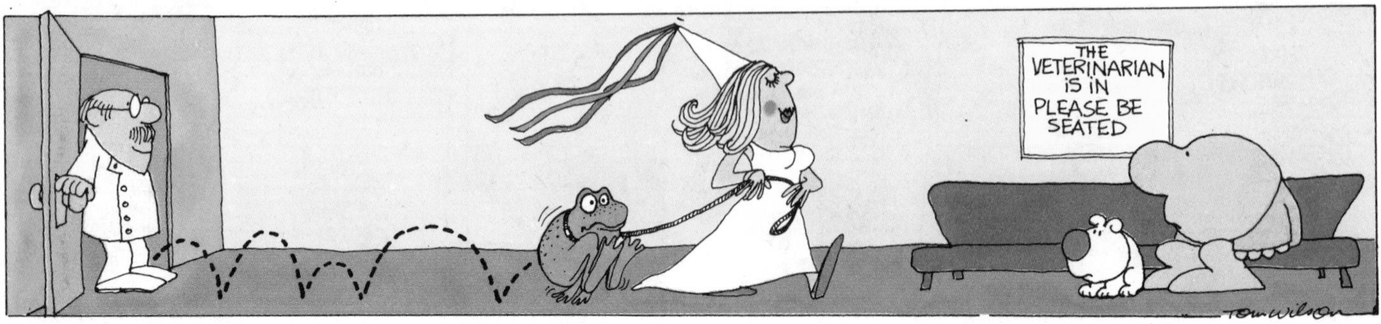
THE VETERINARIAN IS IN PLEASE BE SEATED
Tom Wilson

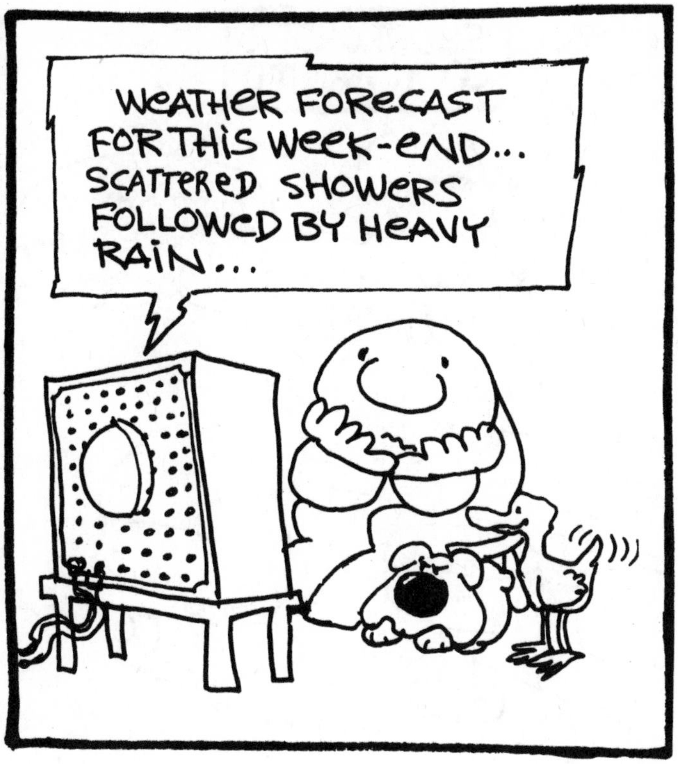
WEATHER FORECAST FOR THIS WEEK-END... SCATTERED SHOWERS FOLLOWED BY HEAVY RAIN...

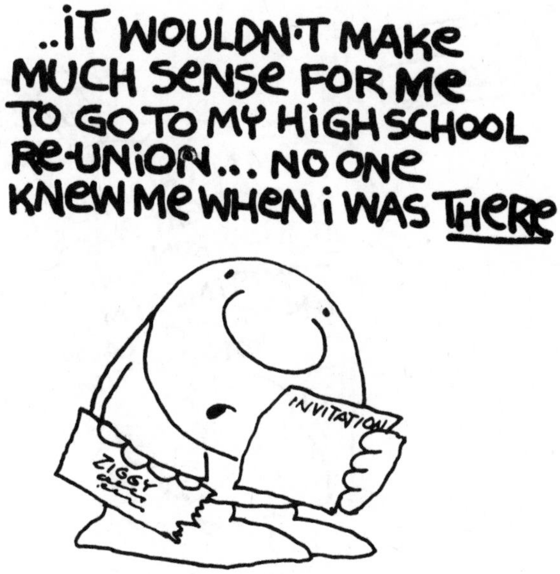
..IT WOULDN'T MAKE MUCH SENSE FOR ME TO GO TO MY HIGH SCHOOL RE-UNION... NO ONE KNEW ME WHEN I WAS THERE
INVITATION
ZIGGY

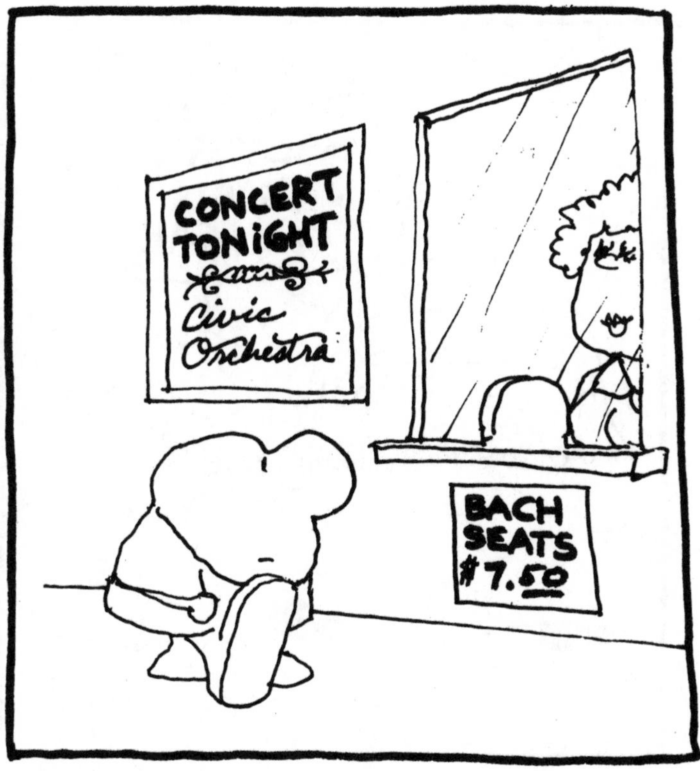
CONCERT TONIGHT
Civic Orchestra
BACH SEATS $7.50

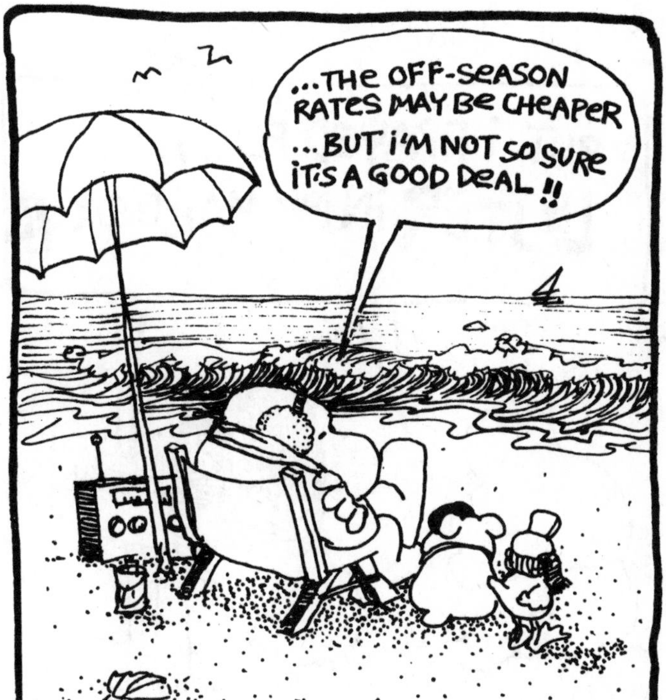
...THE OFF-SEASON RATES MAY BE CHEAPER ...BUT I'M NOT SO SURE IT'S A GOOD DEAL!!

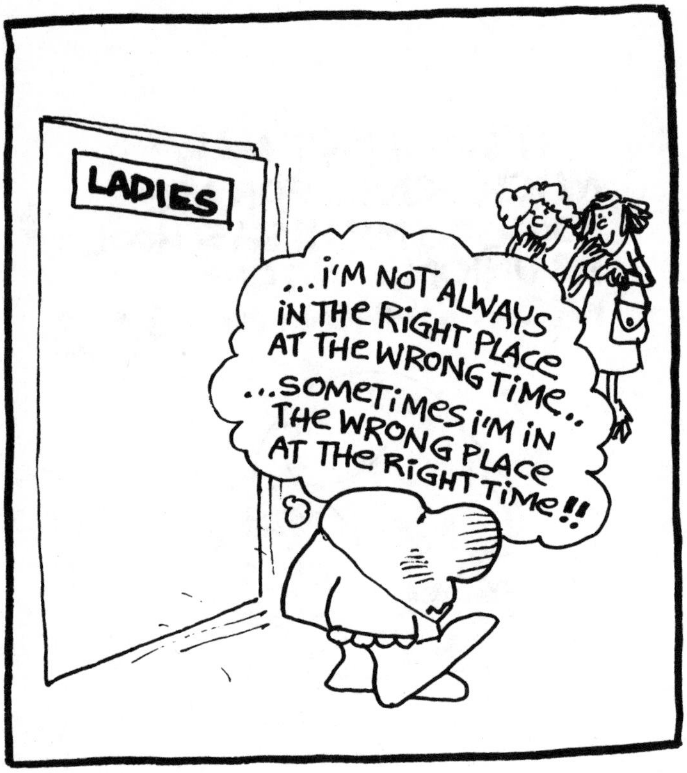
LADIES
...i'M NOT ALWAYS IN THE RiGHT PLACE AT THE WRONG TiME.. ...SOMETiMES i'M IN THE WRONG PLACE AT THE RiGHT TiME!!

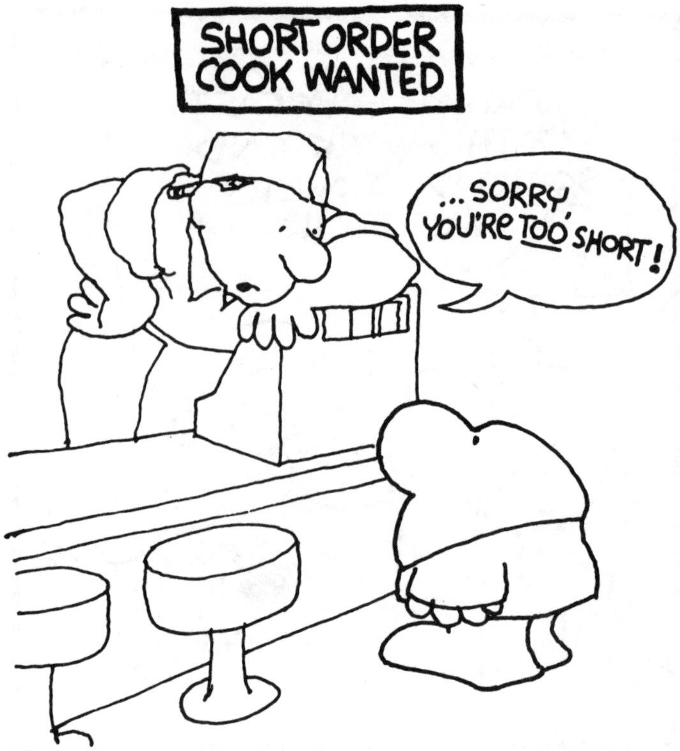
SHORT ORDER COOK WANTED
...SORRY, YOU'RE TOO SHORT!

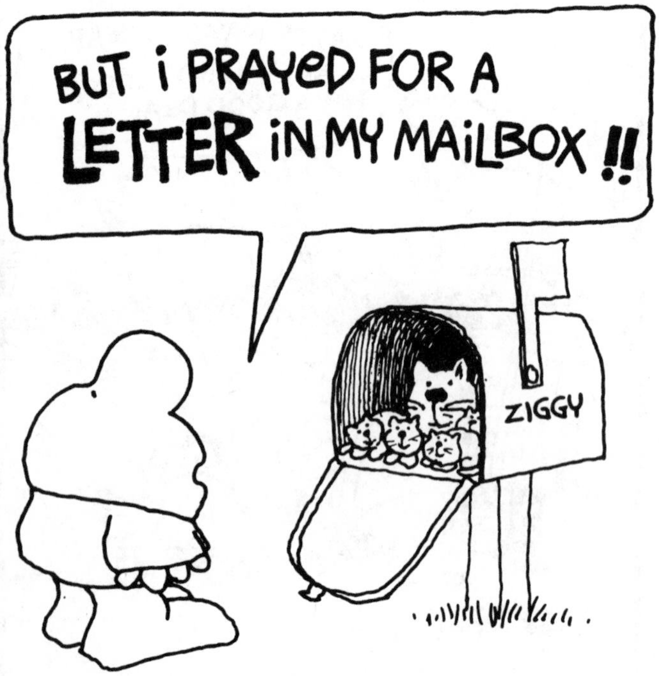
BUT i PRAYED FOR A LETTER iN MY MAiLBOX!!
ZIGGY

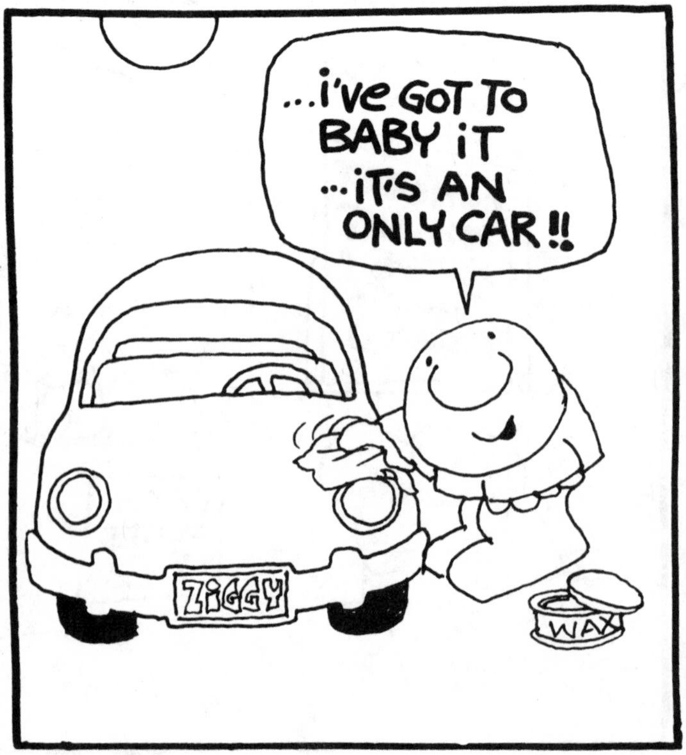
...i've GOT TO BABY iT ...iT'S AN ONLY CAR!!
ZiGGY
WAX

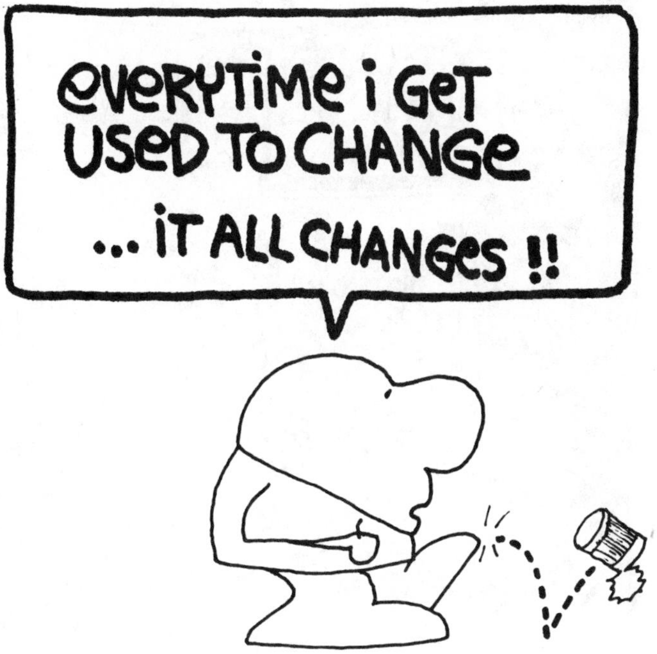
everytime i get used to change
... it all changes !!

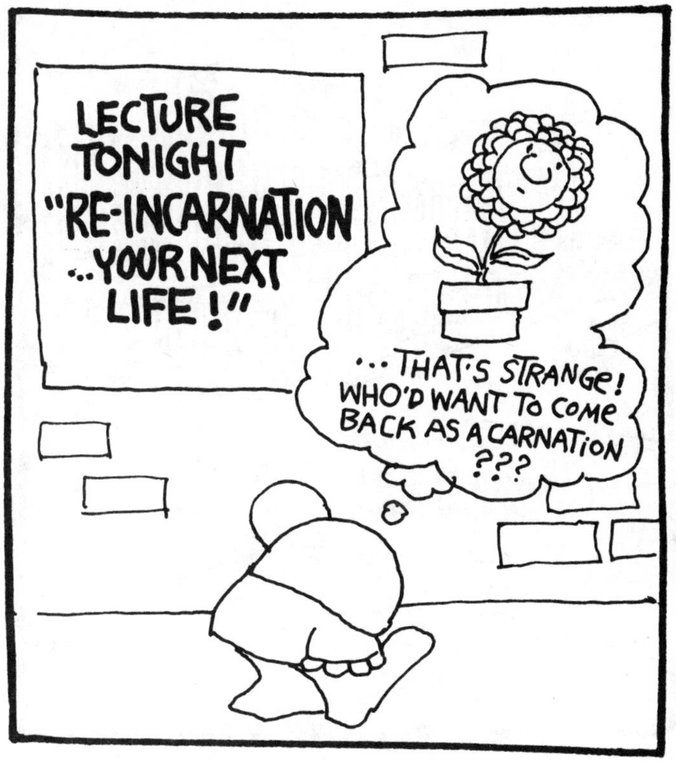
LECTURE TONIGHT "RE-INCARNATION ... YOUR NEXT LIFE!"
... THAT'S STRANGE! WHO'D WANT TO COME BACK AS A CARNATION ???

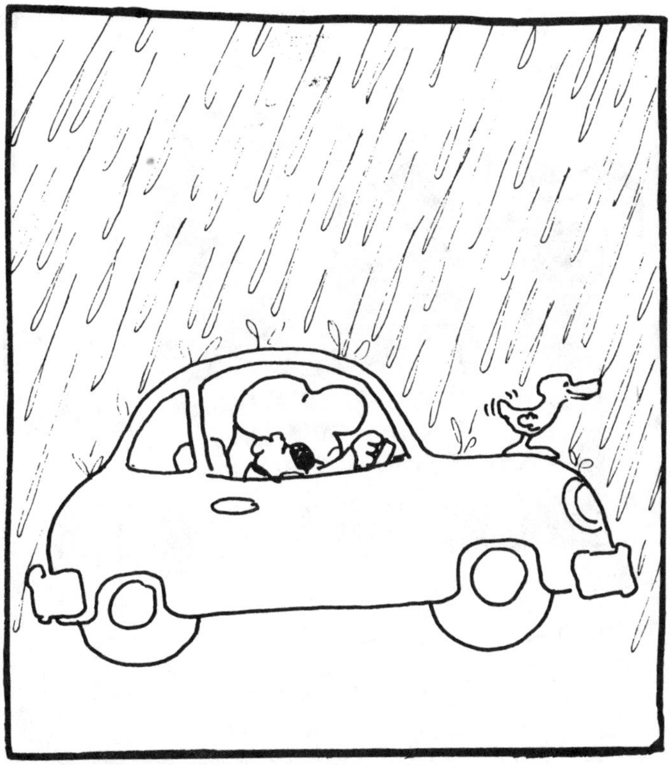

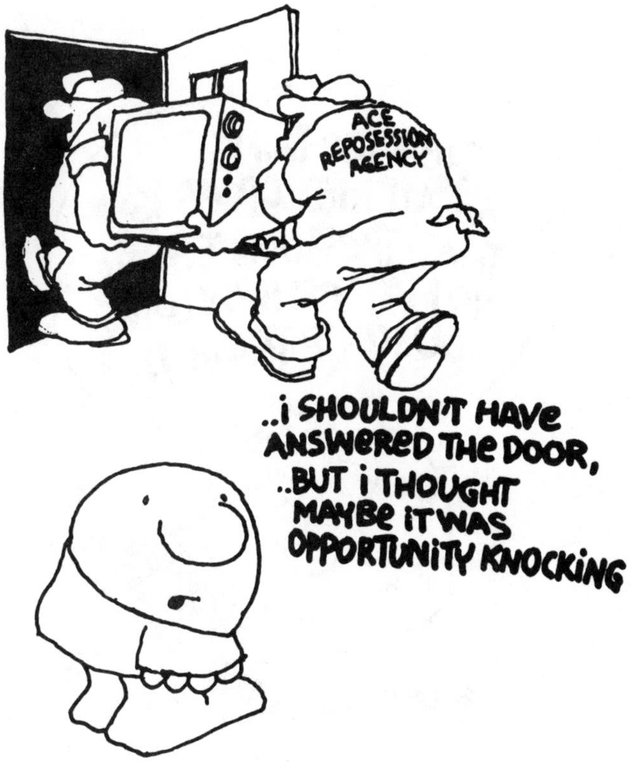
ACE REPOSESSION AGENCY
..i shouldn't have answered the door, ..but i thought maybe it was opportunity knocking

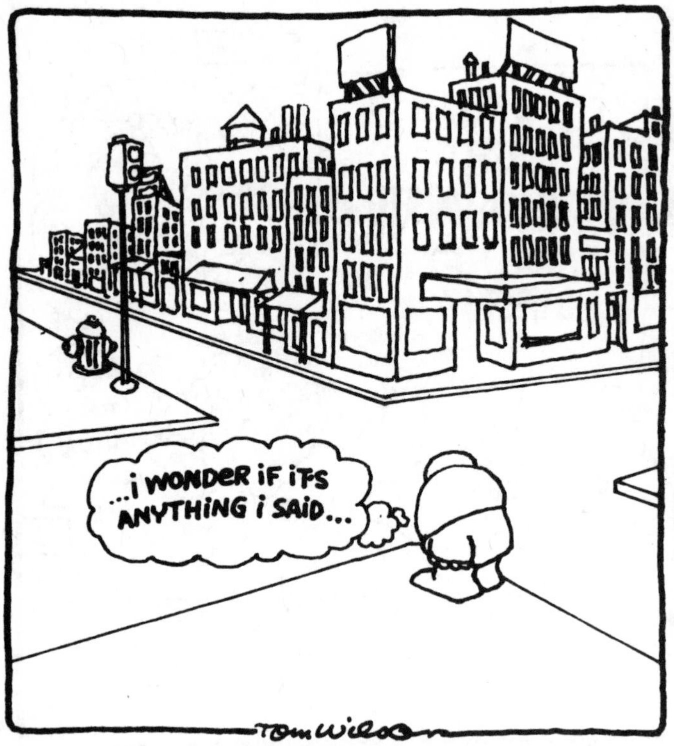
...i WONDER iF iT'S ANYTHiNG i SAiD...
TOM WILSON

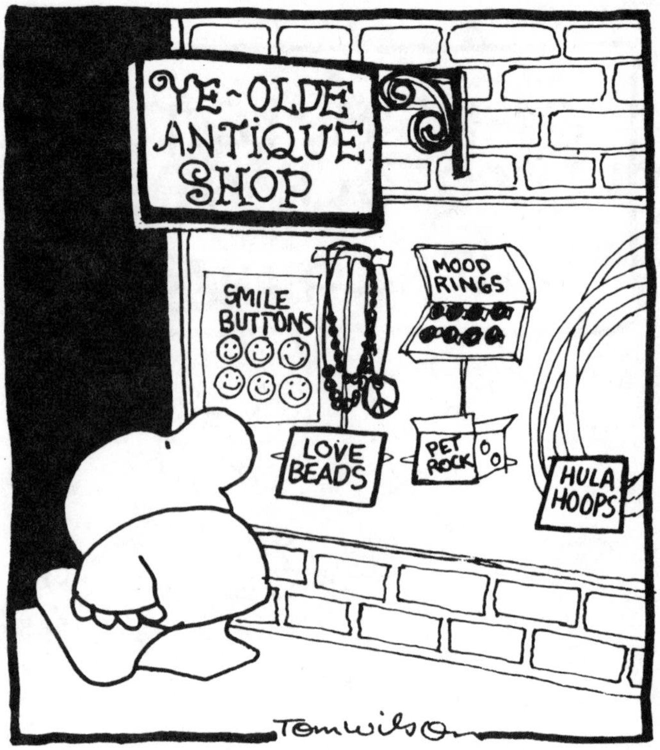
YE-OLDE ANTIQUE SHOP
SMILE BUTTONS
MOOD RINGS
LOVE BEADS
PET ROCK
HULA HOOPS
TOM WILSON

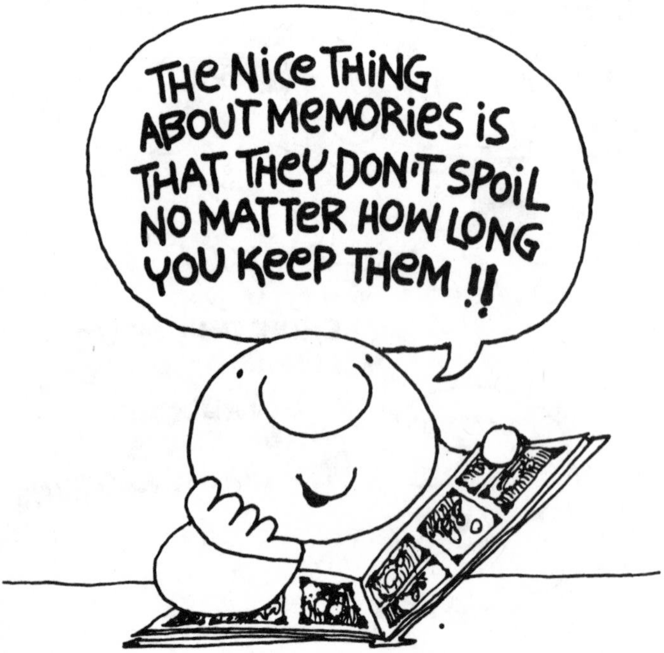
THE NiCE THiNG ABOUT MEMORiES iS THAT THEY DON'T SPOiL NO MATTER HOW LONG YOU KEEP THEM !!

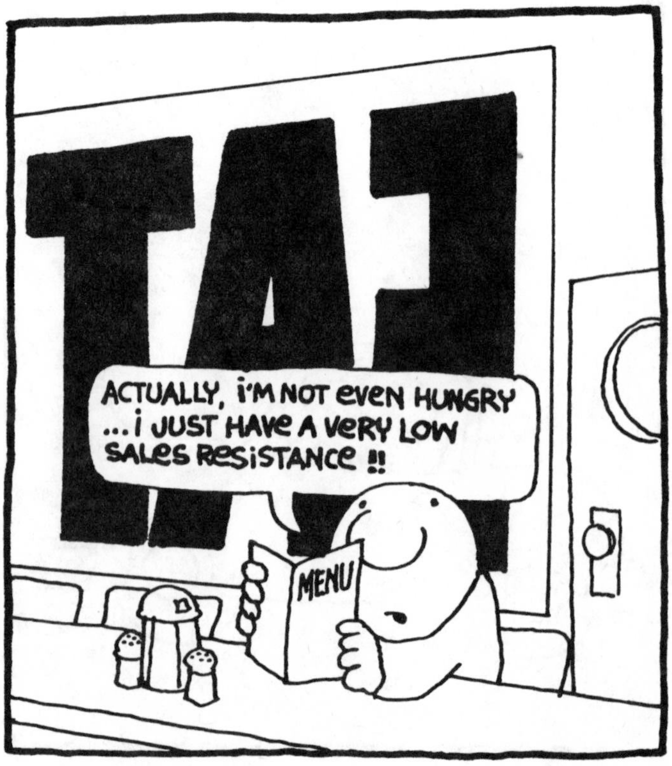
ACTUALLY, i'M NOT EVEN HUNGRY ...i JUST HAVE A VERY LOW SALES RESiSTANCE !!
MENU

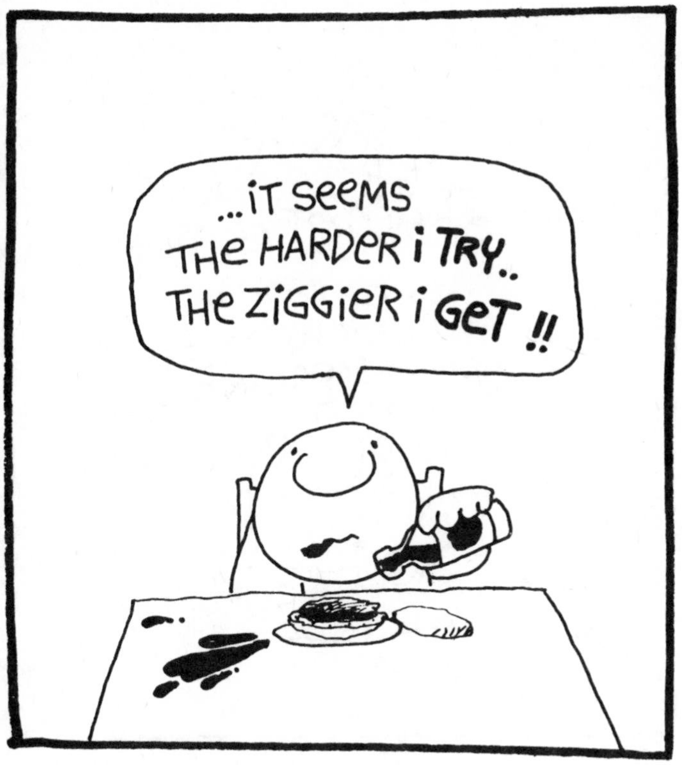
...IT SEEMS THE HARDER I TRY.. THE ZIGGIER I GET !!

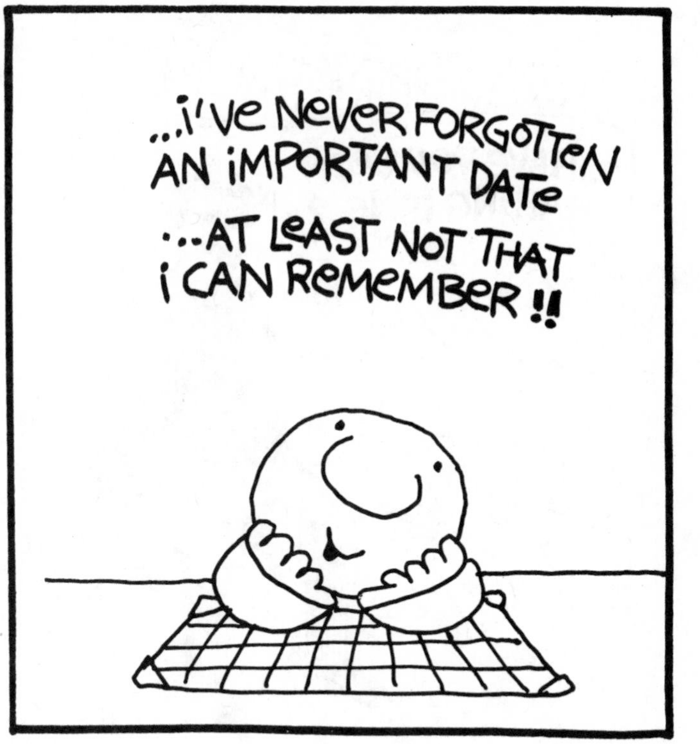
...I'VE NEVER FORGOTTEN AN IMPORTANT DATE
...AT LEAST NOT THAT I CAN REMEMBER !!

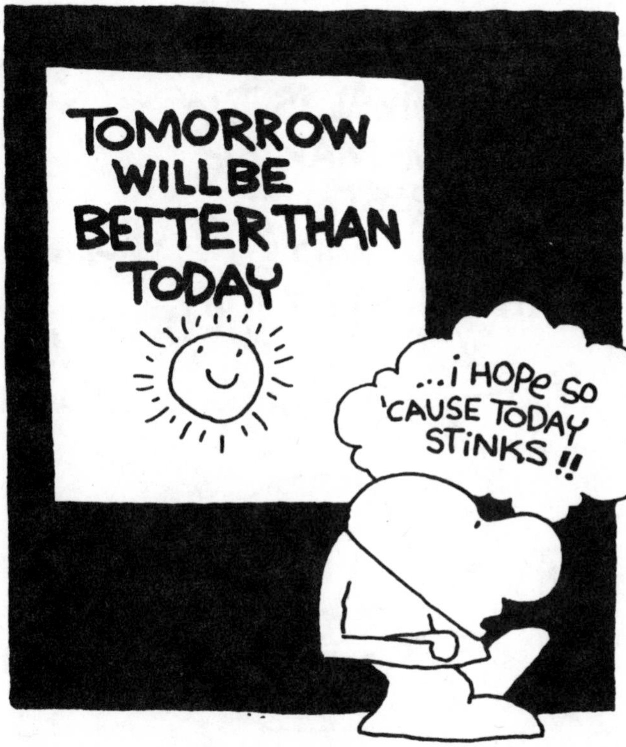
TOMORROW WILL BE BETTER THAN TODAY
...I HOPE SO 'CAUSE TODAY STINKS !!

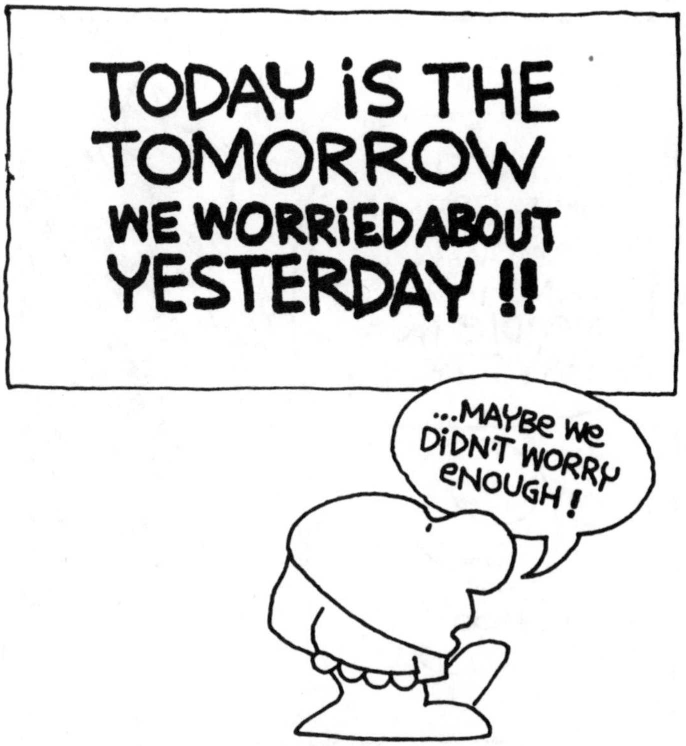
TODAY IS THE TOMORROW WE WORRIED ABOUT YESTERDAY !!
...MAYBE WE DIDN'T WORRY ENOUGH !

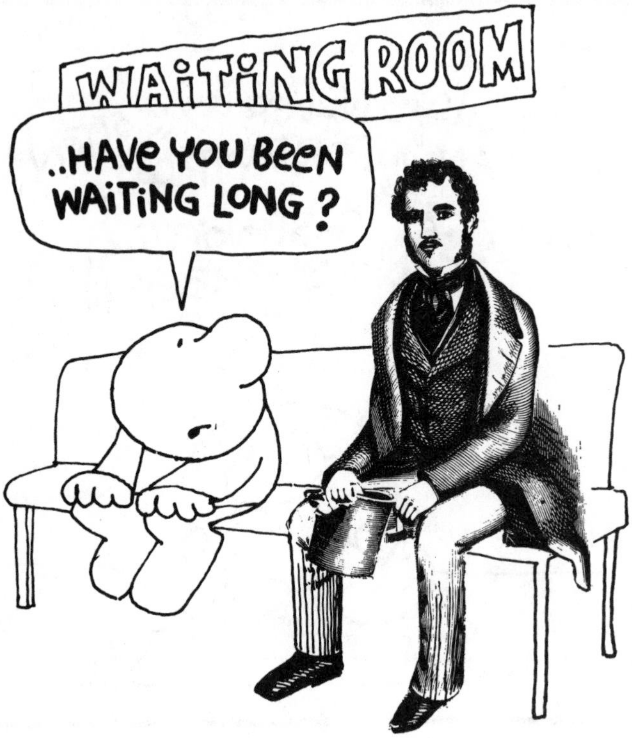
WAITING ROOM
..HAVE YOU BEEN WAITING LONG ?

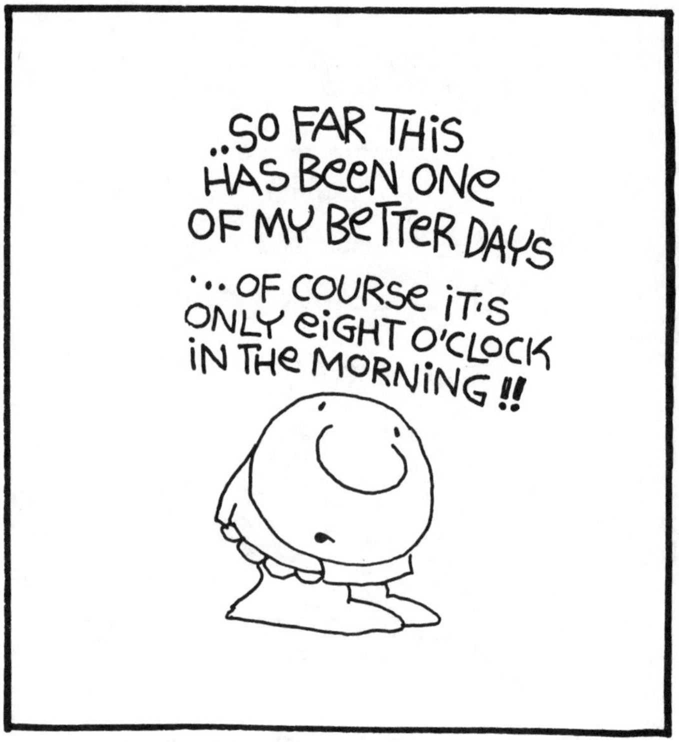
..SO FAR THIS HAS BEEN ONE OF MY BETTER DAYS
...OF COURSE IT'S ONLY EIGHT O'CLOCK IN THE MORNING !!

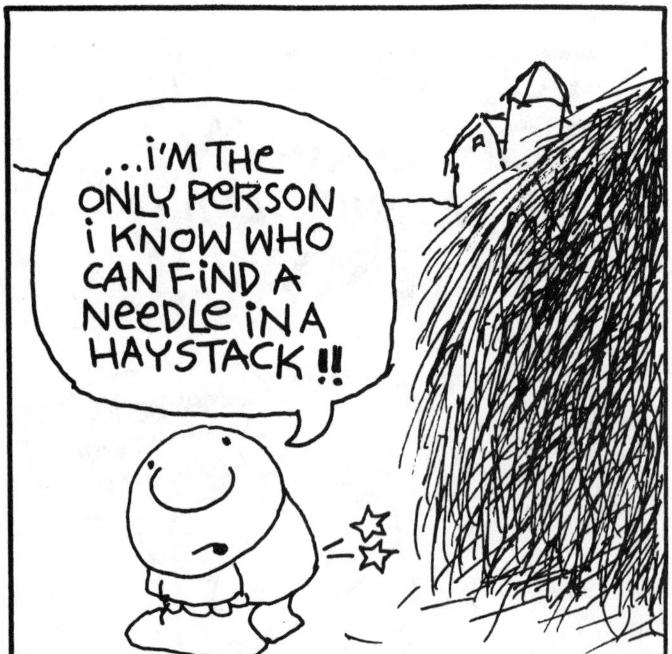
...I'M THE ONLY PERSON I KNOW WHO CAN FIND A NEEDLE IN A HAYSTACK !!

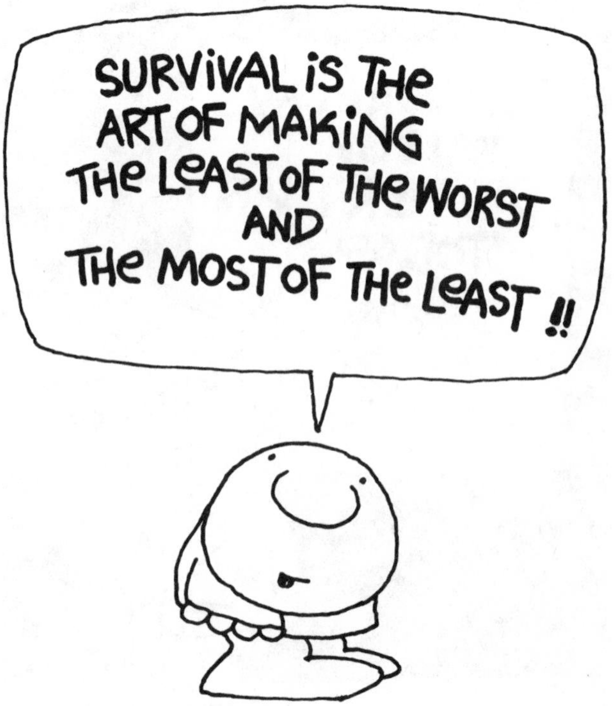
SURVIVAL IS THE ART OF MAKING THE LEAST OF THE WORST AND THE MOST OF THE LEAST !!

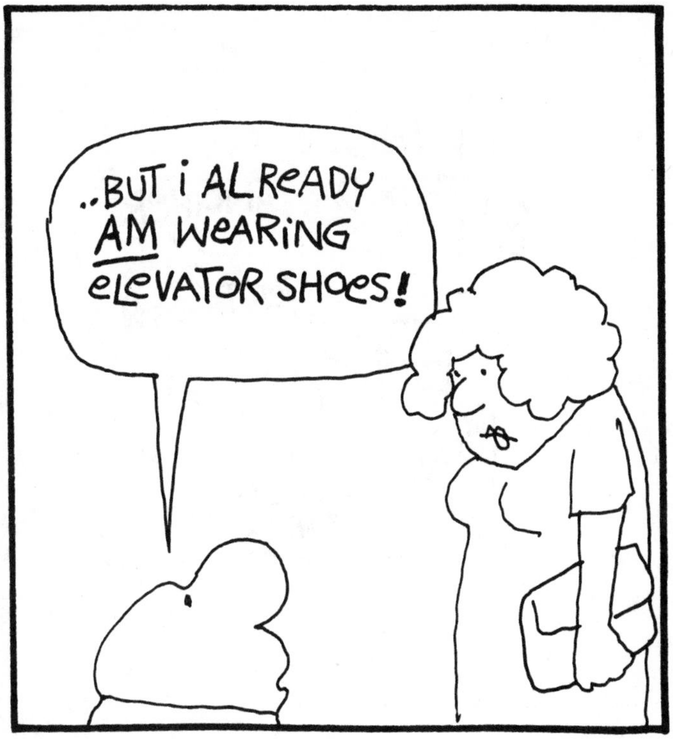
..BUT i ALREADY AM WEARING ELEVATOR SHOES!

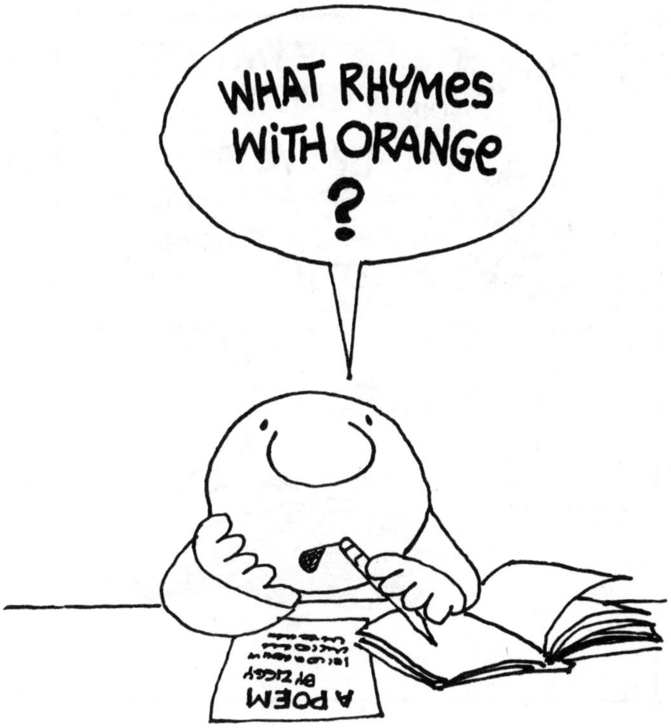
WHAT RHYMES WITH ORANGE ?
A POEM
BY ZIGGY

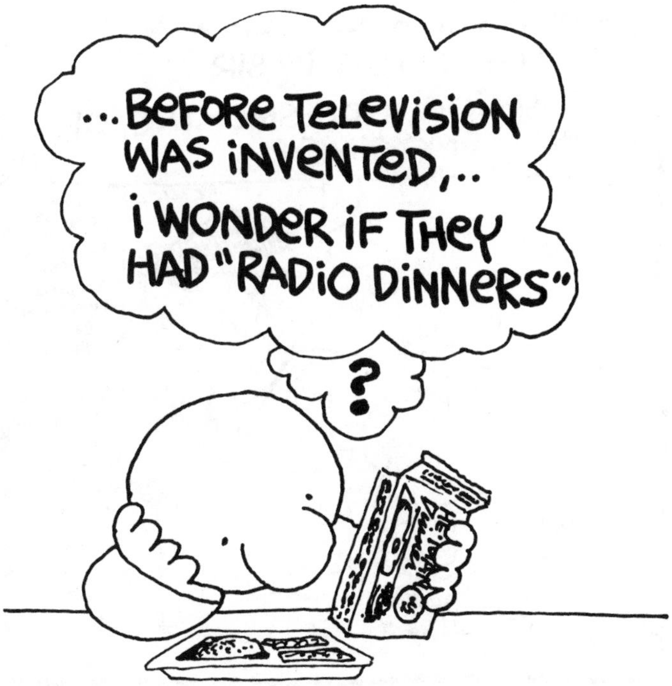
...BEFORE TELEVISION WAS INVENTED,.. i WONDER iF THEY HAD "RADIO DINNERS" ?

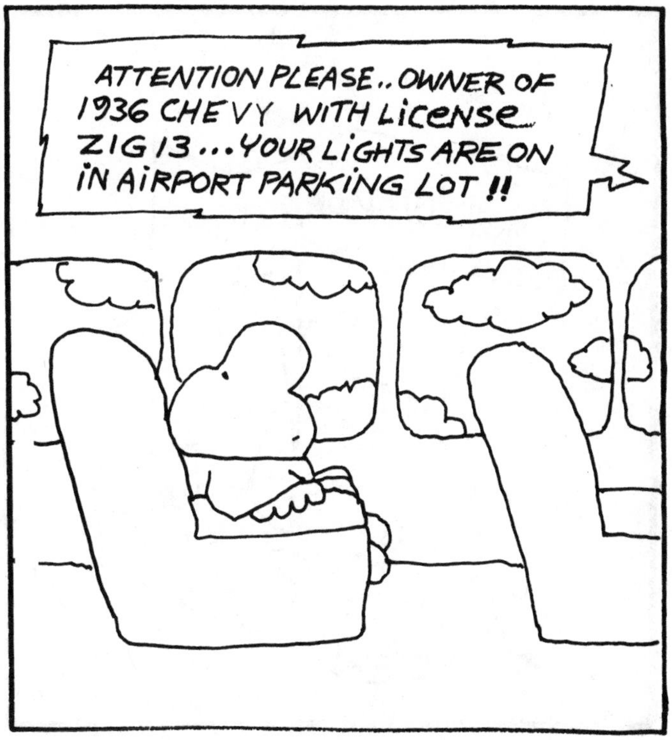
ATTENTION PLEASE.. OWNER OF 1936 CHEVY WITH LICENSE ZIG 13 ... YOUR LIGHTS ARE ON IN AIRPORT PARKING LOT !!

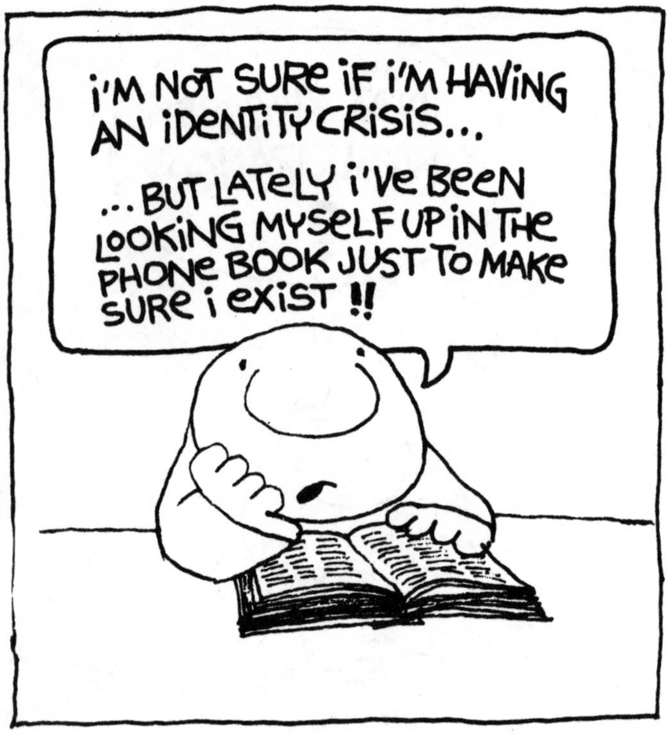
I'M NOT SURE IF I'M HAVING AN IDENTITY CRISIS...
...BUT LATELY I'VE BEEN LOOKING MYSELF UP IN THE PHONE BOOK JUST TO MAKE SURE I EXIST !!

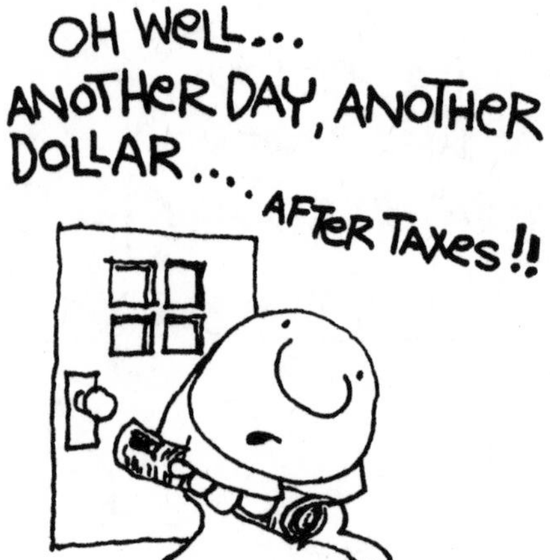
OH WELL...
ANOTHER DAY, ANOTHER DOLLAR.... AFTER TAXES !!

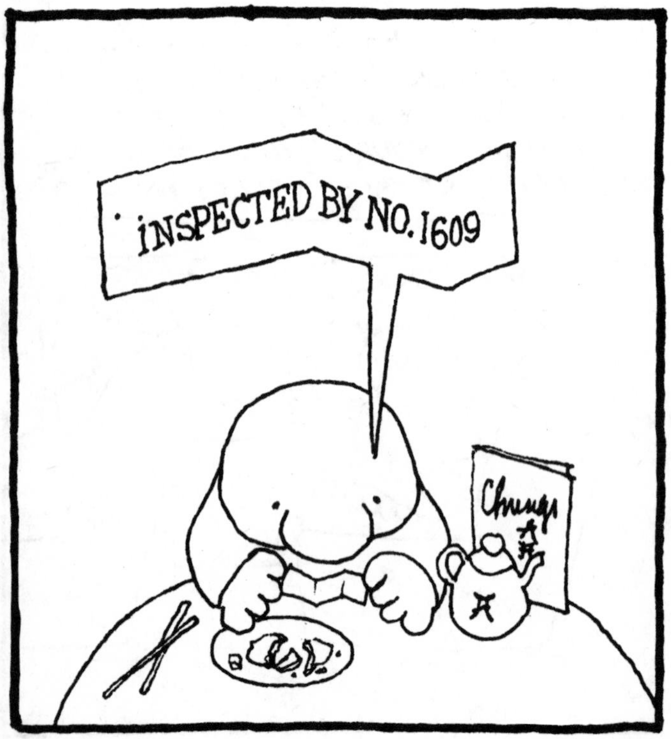
INSPECTED BY NO. 1609

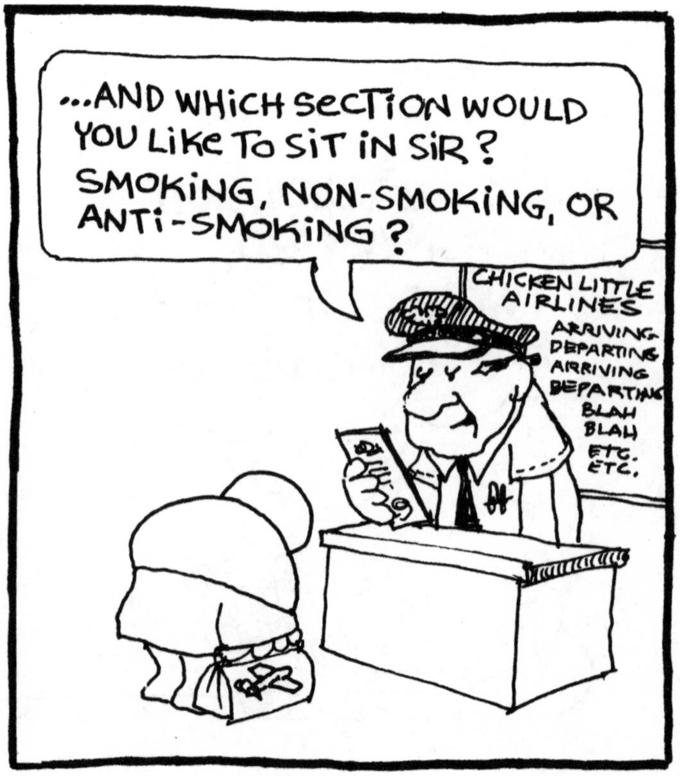
...AND WHICH SECTION WOULD YOU LIKE TO SIT IN SIR? SMOKING, NON-SMOKING, OR ANTI-SMOKING?
CHICKEN LITTLE AIRLINES
ARRIVING
DEPARTING
ARRIVING
DEPARTING
BLAH
BLAH
ETC.
ETC.

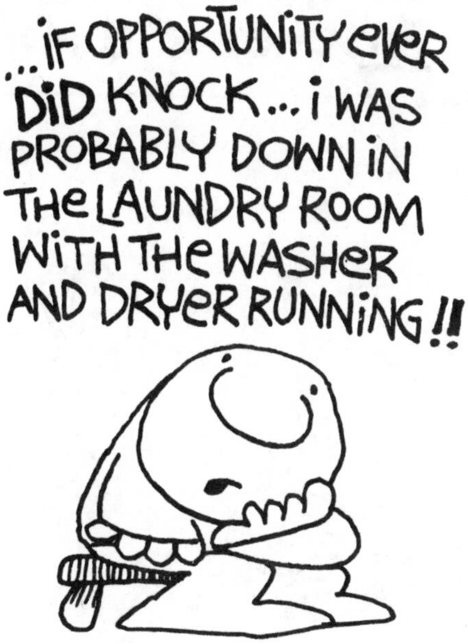
...IF OPPORTUNITY EVER DID KNOCK... I WAS PROBABLY DOWN IN THE LAUNDRY ROOM WITH THE WASHER AND DRYER RUNNING!!

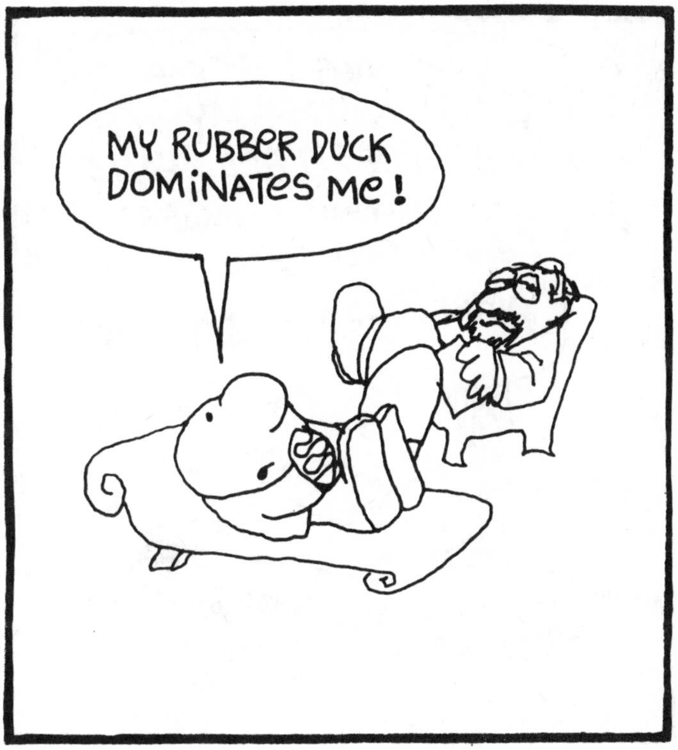
MY RUBBER DUCK DOMINATES ME!

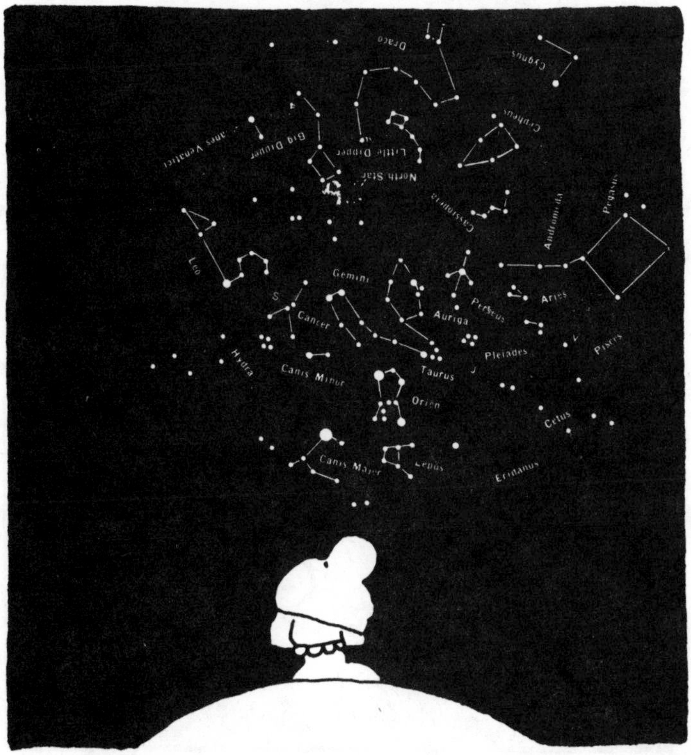
Gemini
Cancer
Auriga
Taurus
Pleiades
Canis Minor
Orion
Cetus
Canis Major
Eridanus

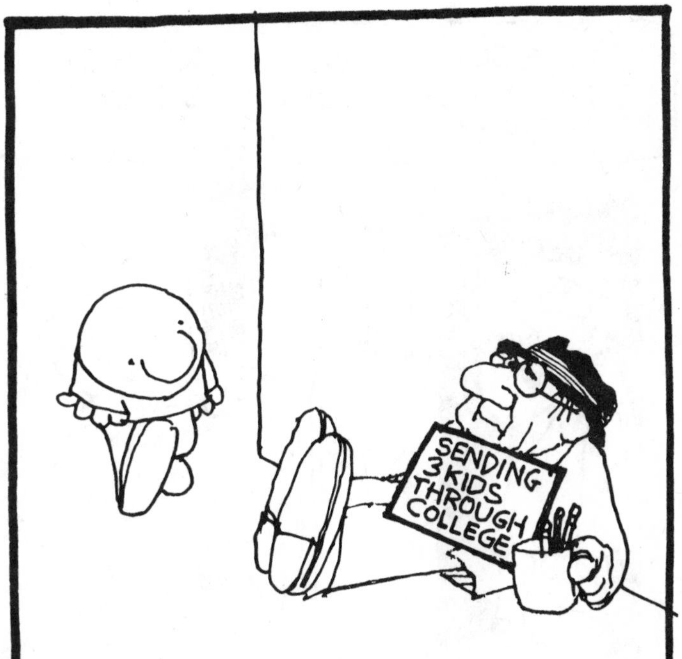
SENDING 3 KIDS THROUGH COLLEGE

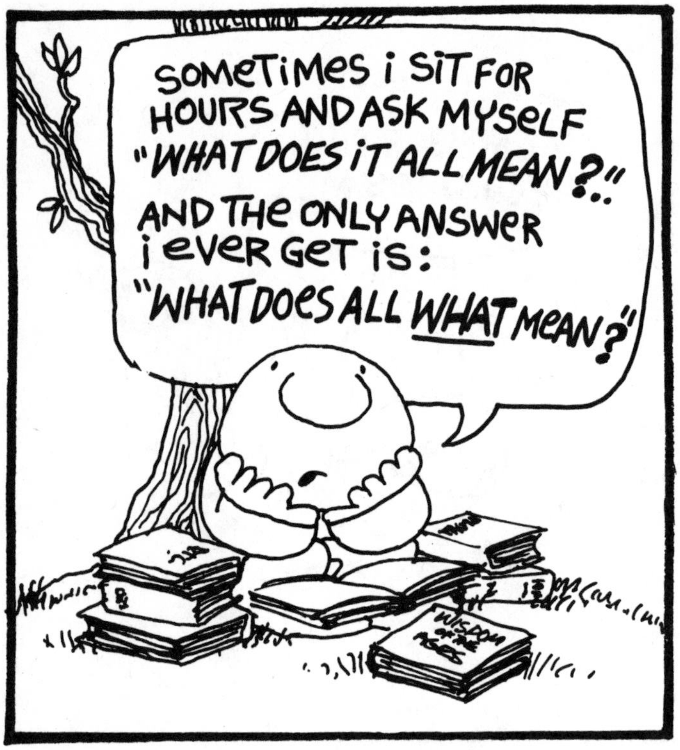
SOMETIMES i SIT FOR HOURS AND ASK MYSELF "WHAT DOES iT ALL MEAN ?.." AND THE ONLY ANSWER i EVER GET IS: "WHAT DOES ALL WHAT MEAN ?"
WISDOM OF THE AGES

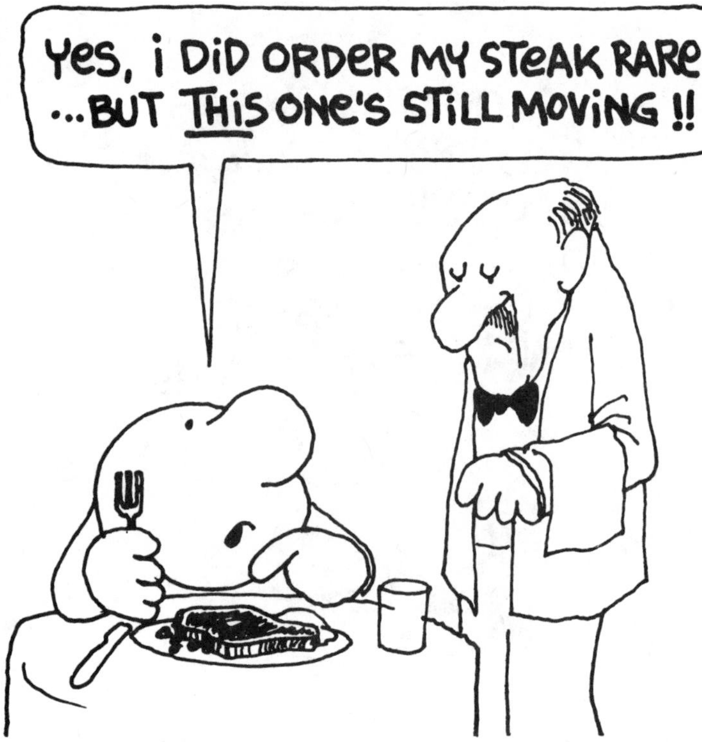
YES, i DID ORDER MY STEAK RARE ...BUT THIS ONE'S STILL MOVING !!

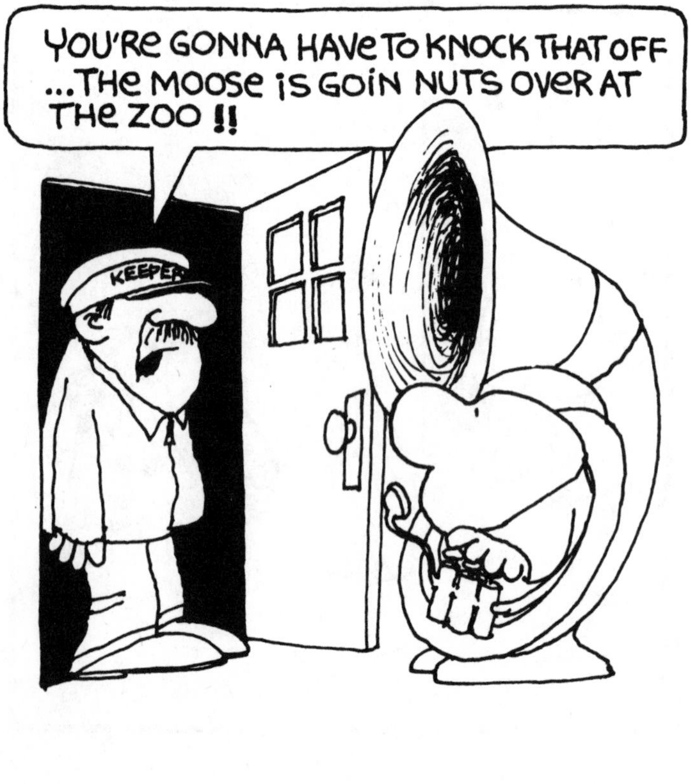
YOU'RE GONNA HAVE TO KNOCK THAT OFF ...THE MOOSE iS GOiN NUTS OVER AT THE ZOO !!
KEEPER

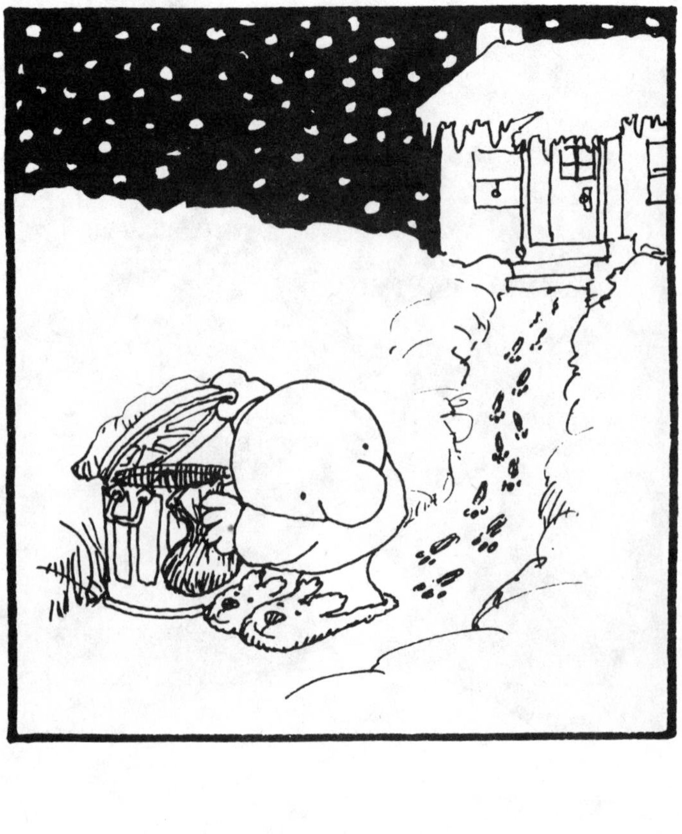

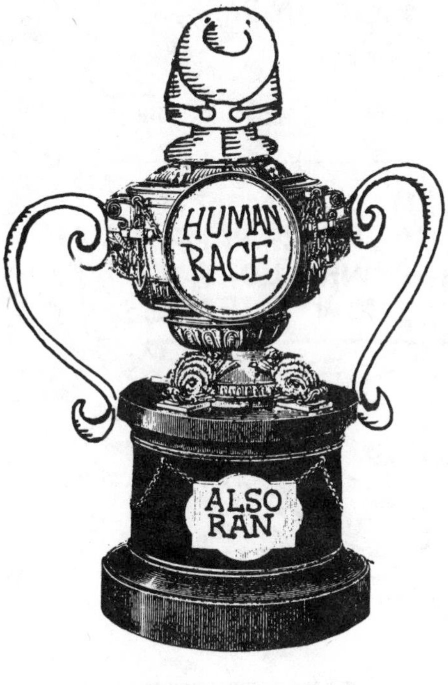
HUMAN RACE
ALSO RAN

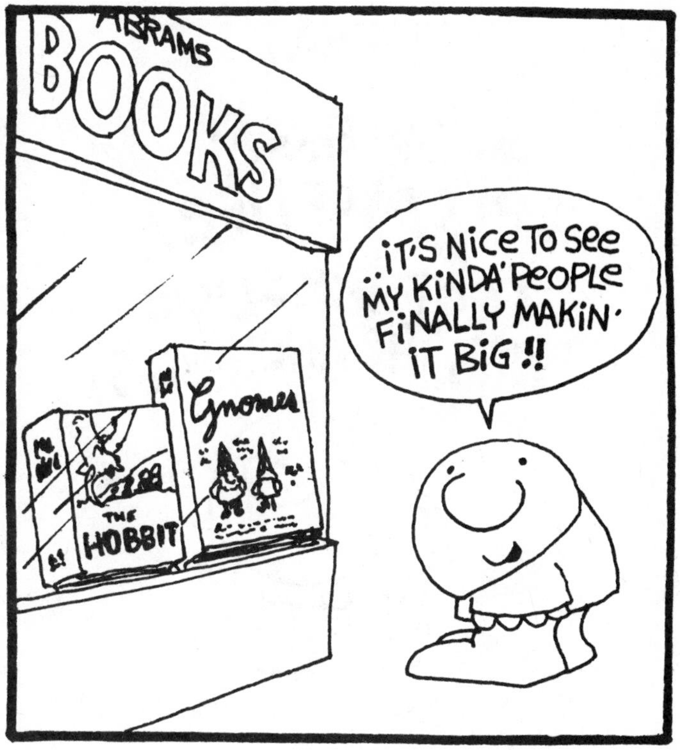
ABRAMS
BOOKS
THE HOBBIT
Gnomes
..IT'S NICE TO SEE MY KINDA' PEOPLE FINALLY MAKIN' IT BIG !!

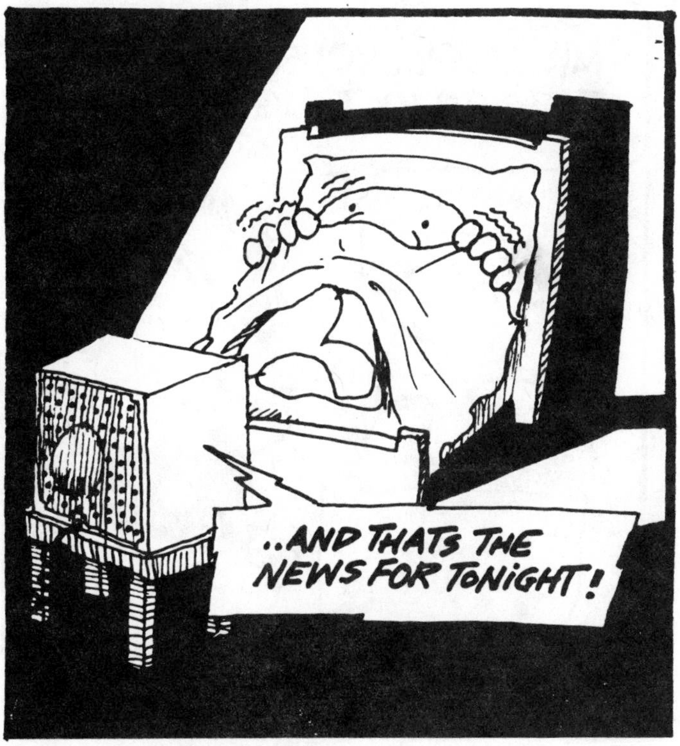
..AND THATS THE NEWS FOR TONIGHT !

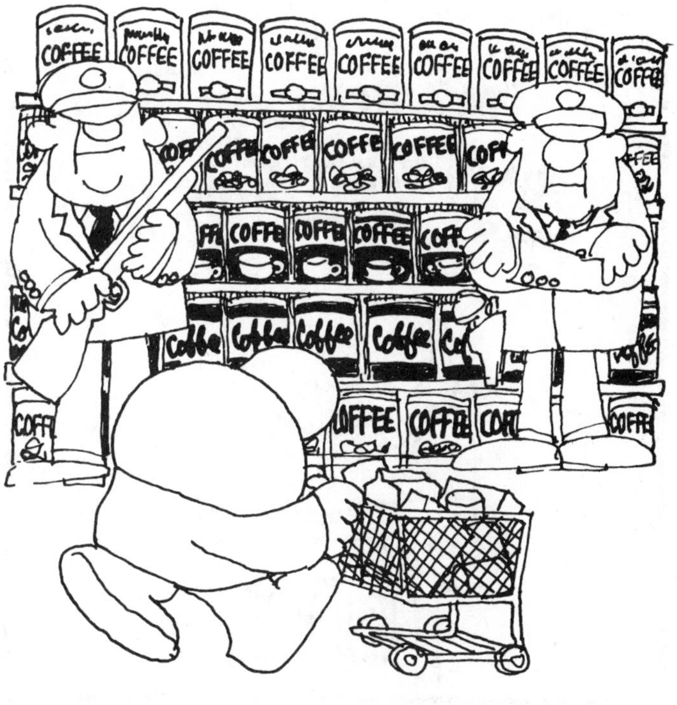
COFFEE

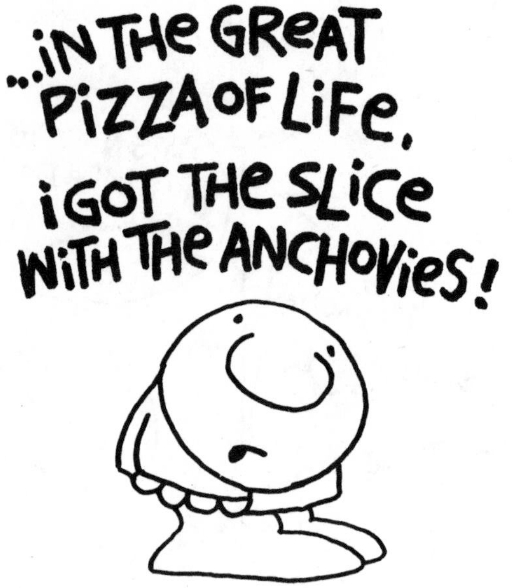
...iN THE GREAT PIZZA OF LiFE, i GOT THE SLiCE WiTH THE ANCHOViES!

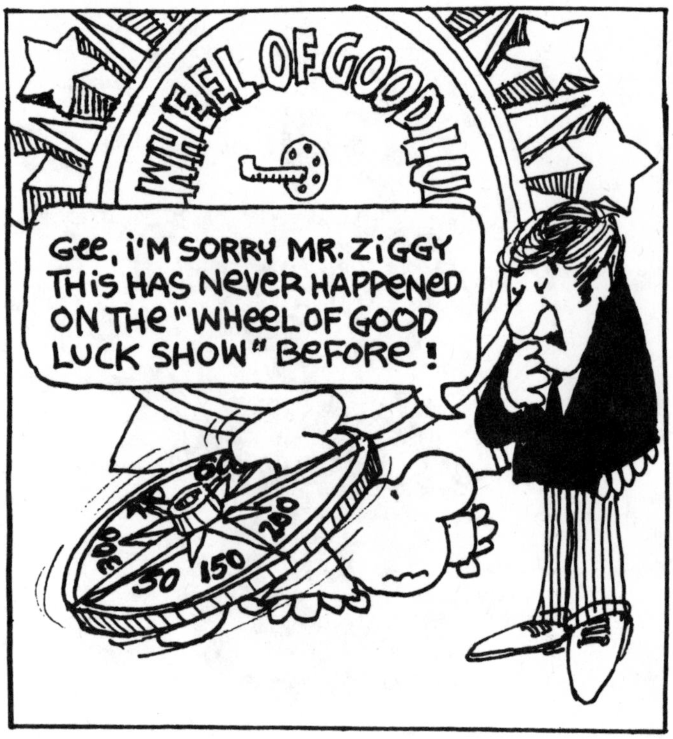
WHEEL OF GOOD LU
GEE, i'M SORRY MR. ZiGGY THiS HAS NEVER HAPPENED ON THE "WHEEL OF GOOD LUCK SHOW" BEFORE!
600
300
150
50
200

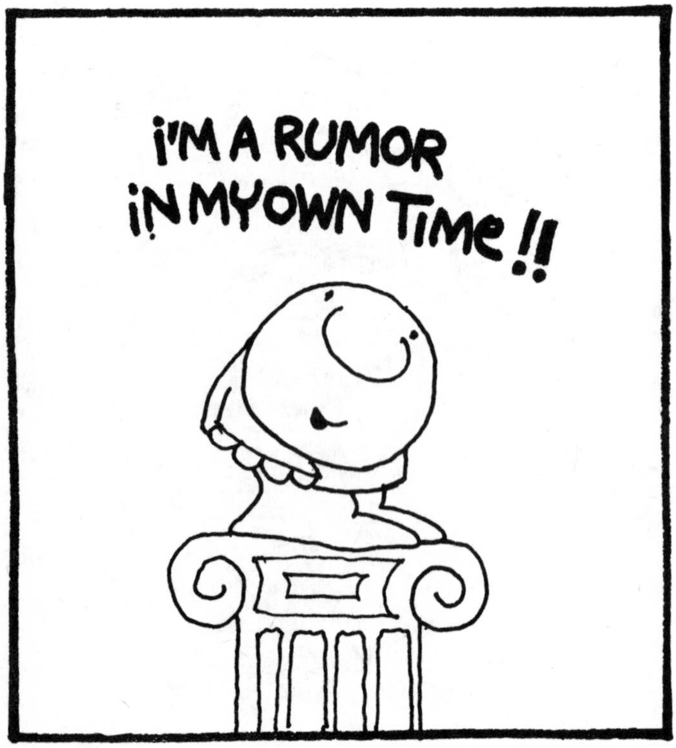
i'M A RUMOR iN MY OWN TiME!!

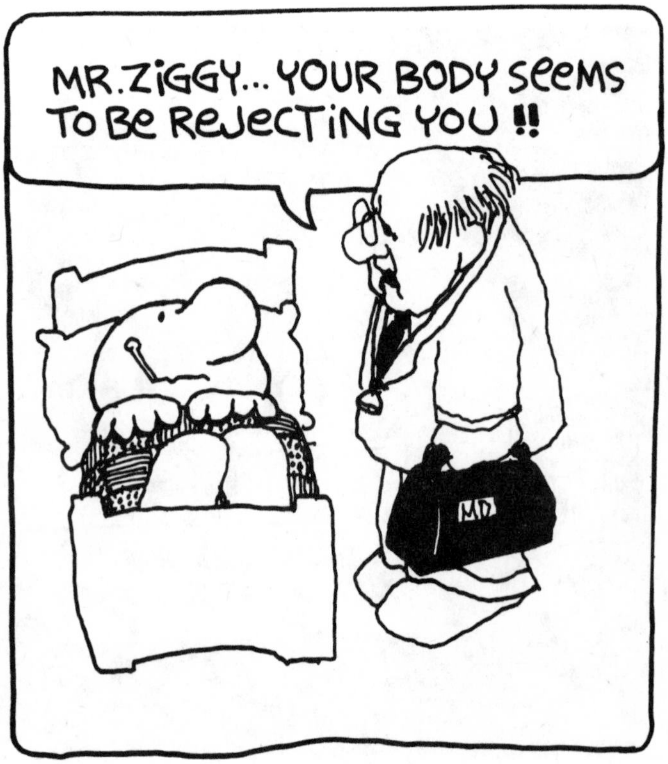
MR. ZiGGY... YOUR BODY SEEMS TO BE REJECTiNG YOU!!
MD

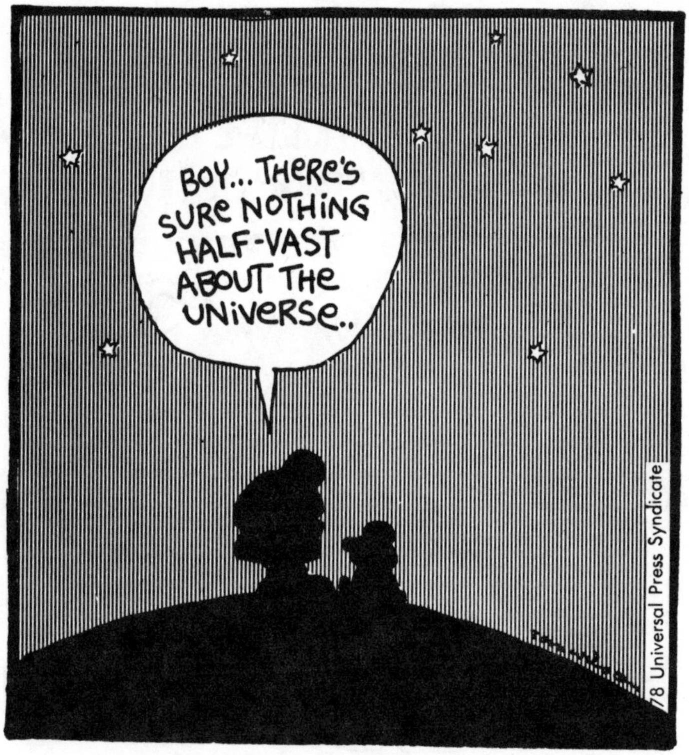
BOY... THERE'S SURE NOTHING HALF-VAST ABOUT THE UNIVERSE..
78 Universal Press Syndicate

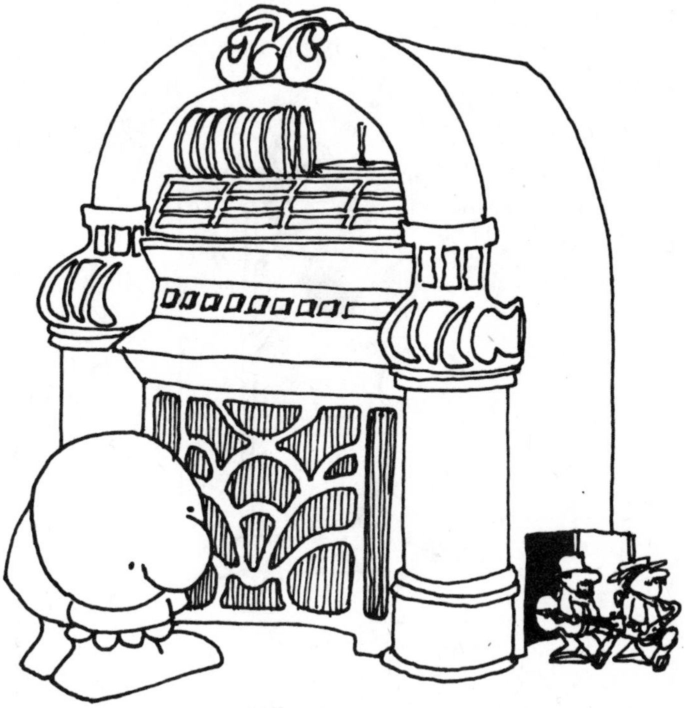

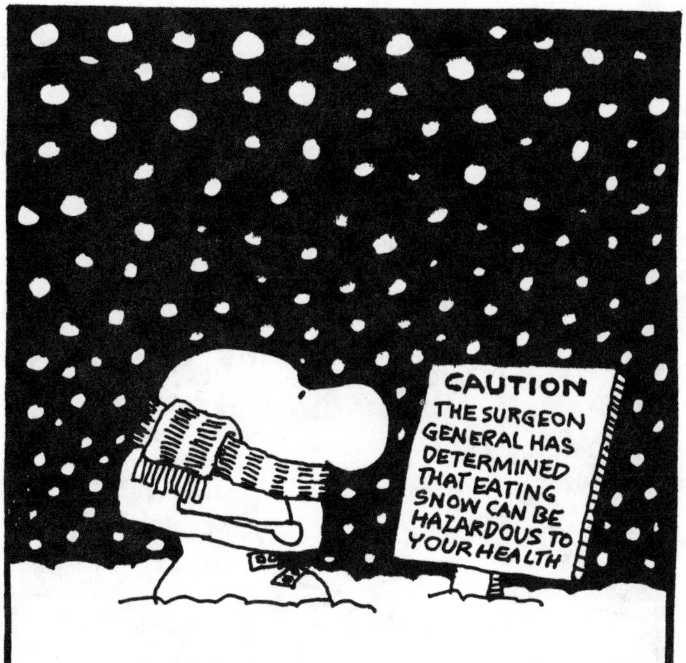
CAUTION
THE SURGEON GENERAL HAS DETERMINED THAT EATING SNOW CAN BE HAZARDOUS TO YOUR HEALTH

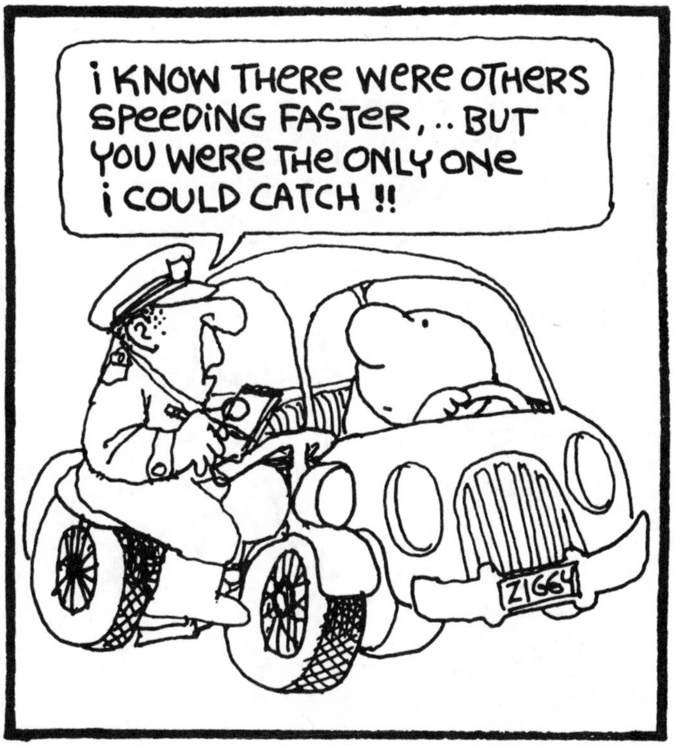
I KNOW THERE WERE OTHERS SPEEDING FASTER, .. BUT YOU WERE THE ONLY ONE I COULD CATCH !!

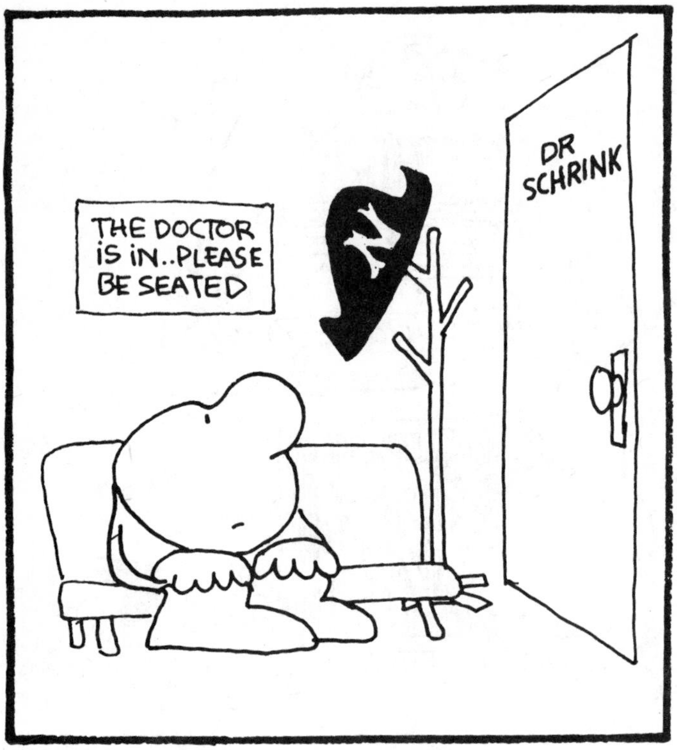
THE DOCTOR IS IN..PLEASE BE SEATED
DR SCHRINK

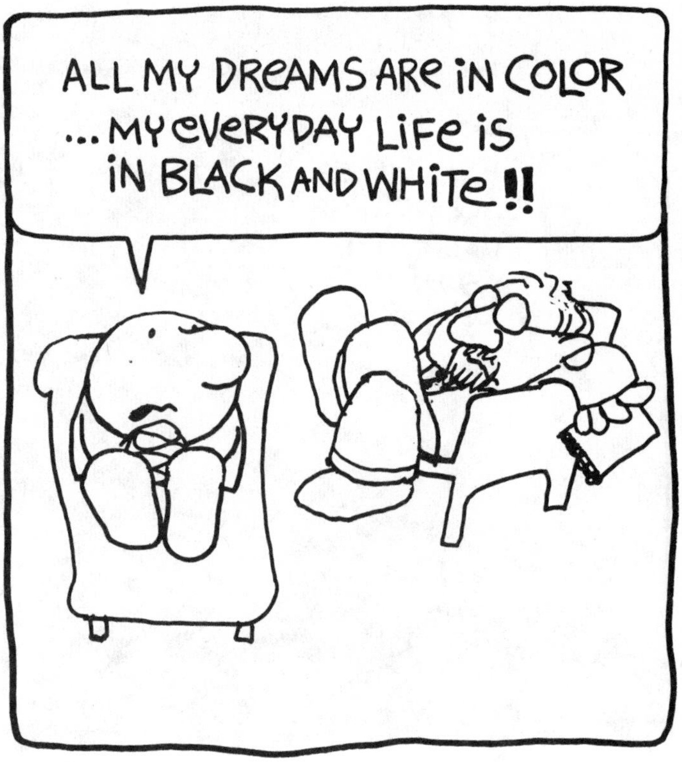
ALL MY DREAMS ARE IN COLOR ...MY EVERYDAY LIFE IS IN BLACK AND WHITE !!

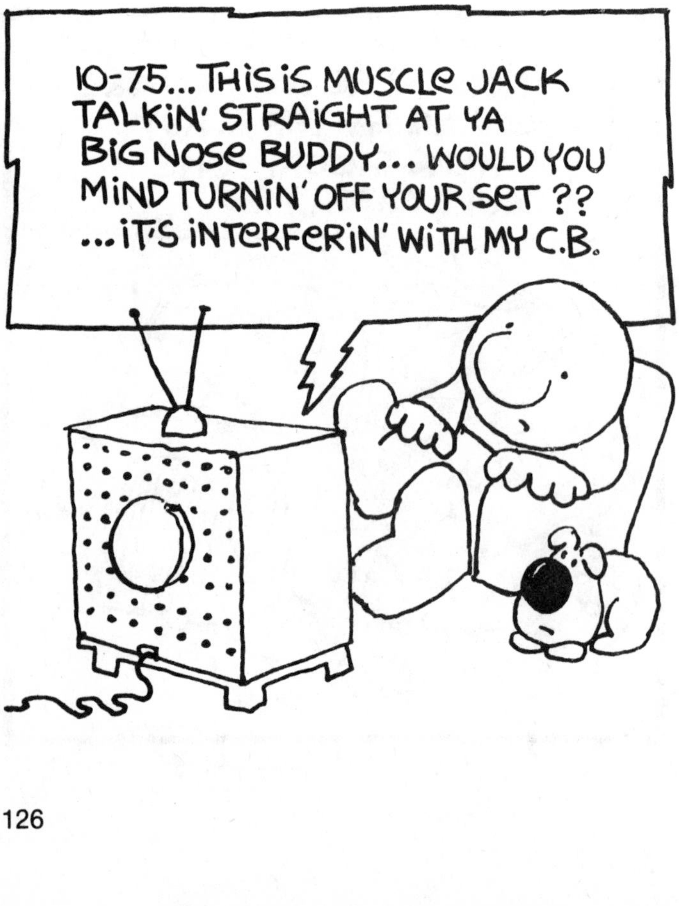
10-75...THIS IS MUSCLE JACK TALKIN' STRAIGHT AT YA BIG NOSE BUDDY... WOULD YOU MIND TURNIN' OFF YOUR SET ?? ...IT'S INTERFERIN' WITH MY C.B.

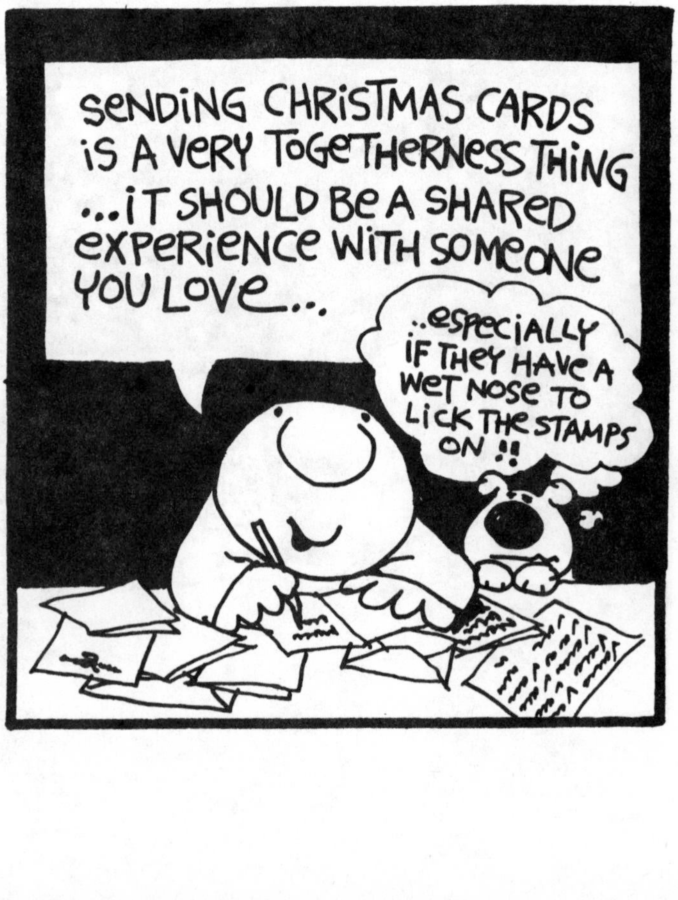
SENDING CHRISTMAS CARDS IS A VERY TOGETHERNESS THING ...IT SHOULD BE A SHARED EXPERIENCE WITH SOMEONE YOU LOVE...
..ESPECIALLY IF THEY HAVE A WET NOSE TO LICK THE STAMPS ON !!

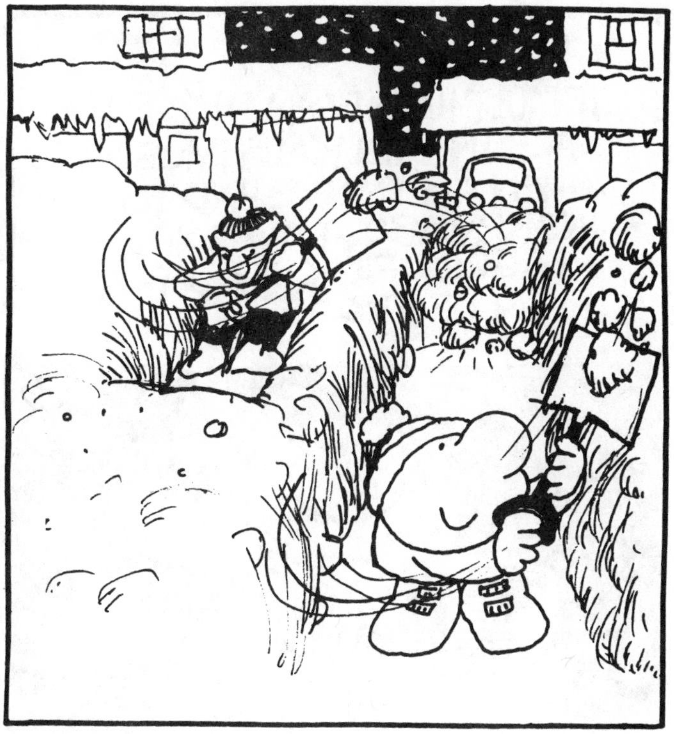
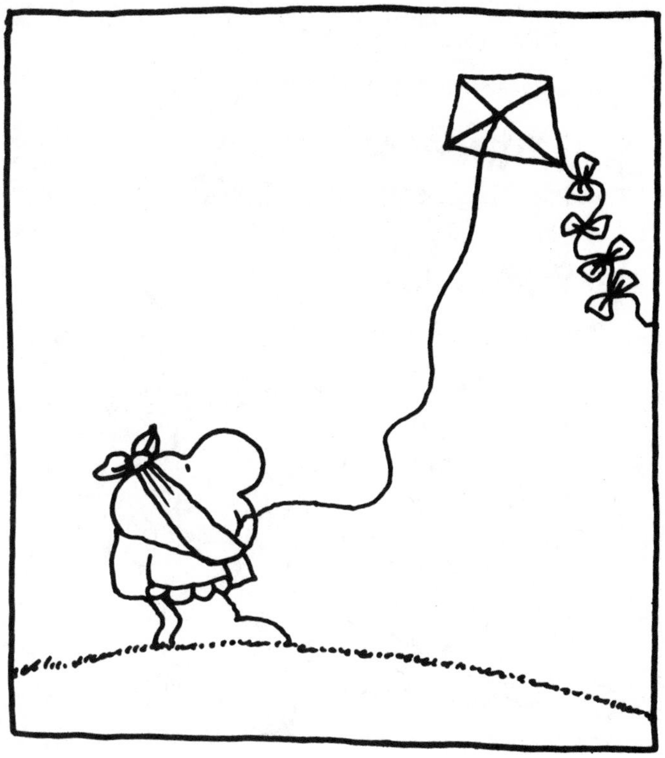
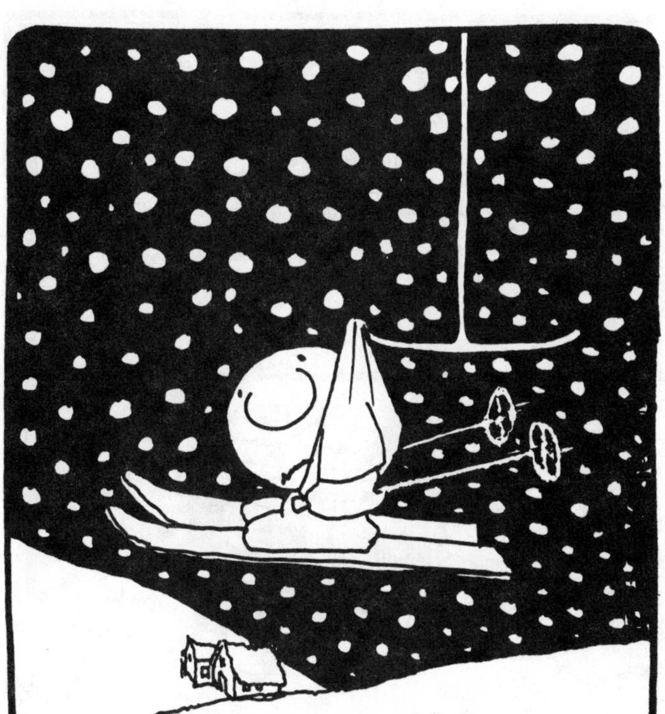
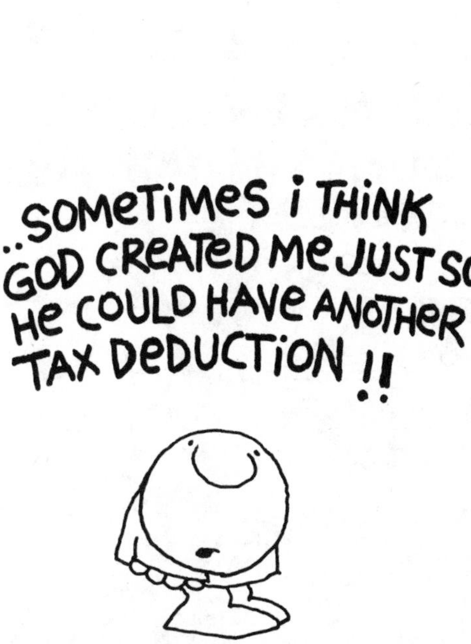
..SOMETIMES i THINK ..GOD CREATED ME JUST SO HE COULD HAVE ANOTHER TAX DEDUCTION !!

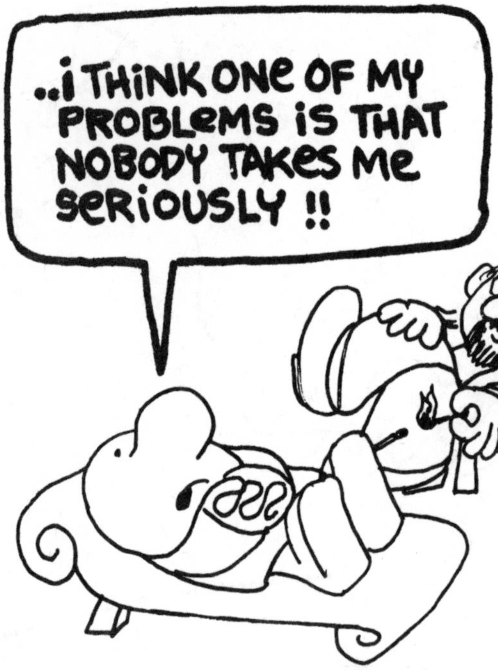
..i THINK ONE OF MY PROBLEMS iS THAT NOBODY TAKES ME SERIOUSLY !!

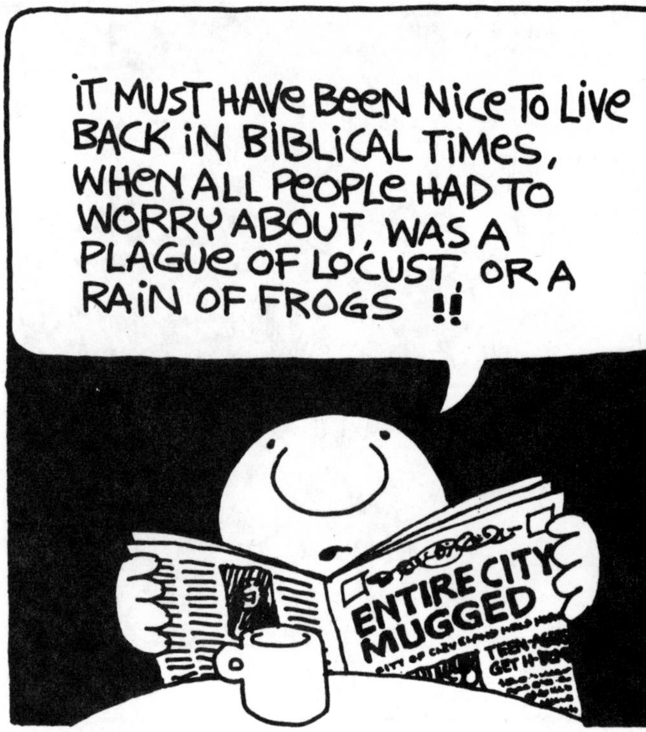
IT MUST HAVE BEEN NICE TO LIVE BACK IN BIBLICAL TIMES, WHEN ALL PEOPLE HAD TO WORRY ABOUT, WAS A PLAGUE OF LOCUST, OR A RAIN OF FROGS !!
ENTIRE CITY MUGGED

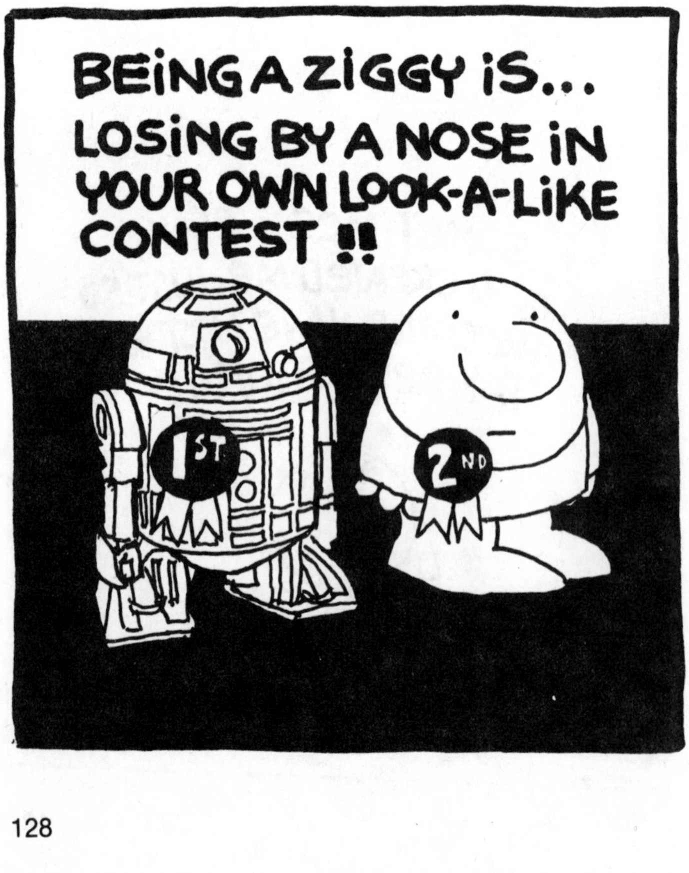
BEING A ZIGGY IS...
LOSING BY A NOSE IN YOUR OWN LOOK-A-LIKE CONTEST !!
1ST
2ND

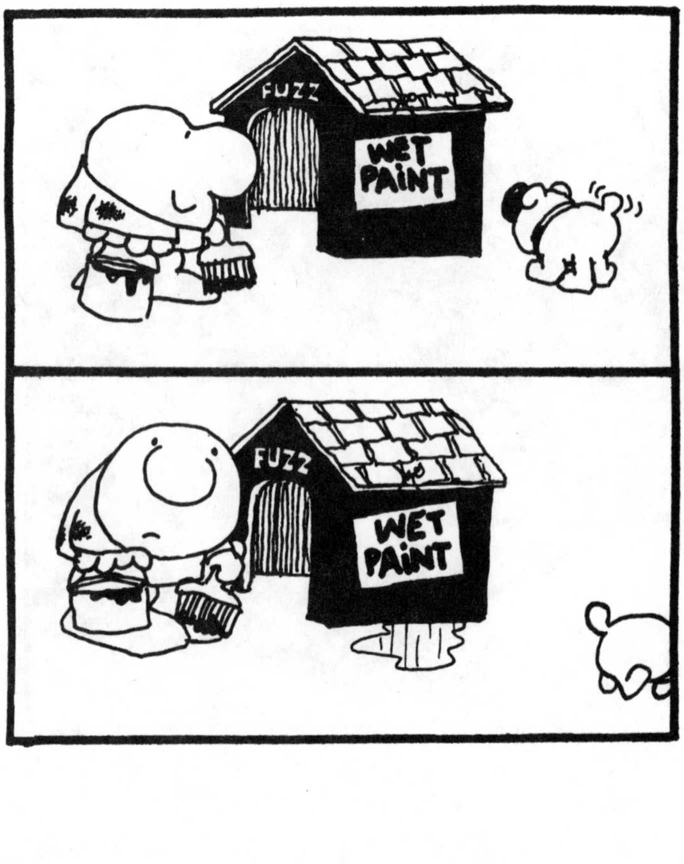
FUZZ
WET PAINT
FUZZ
WET PAINT

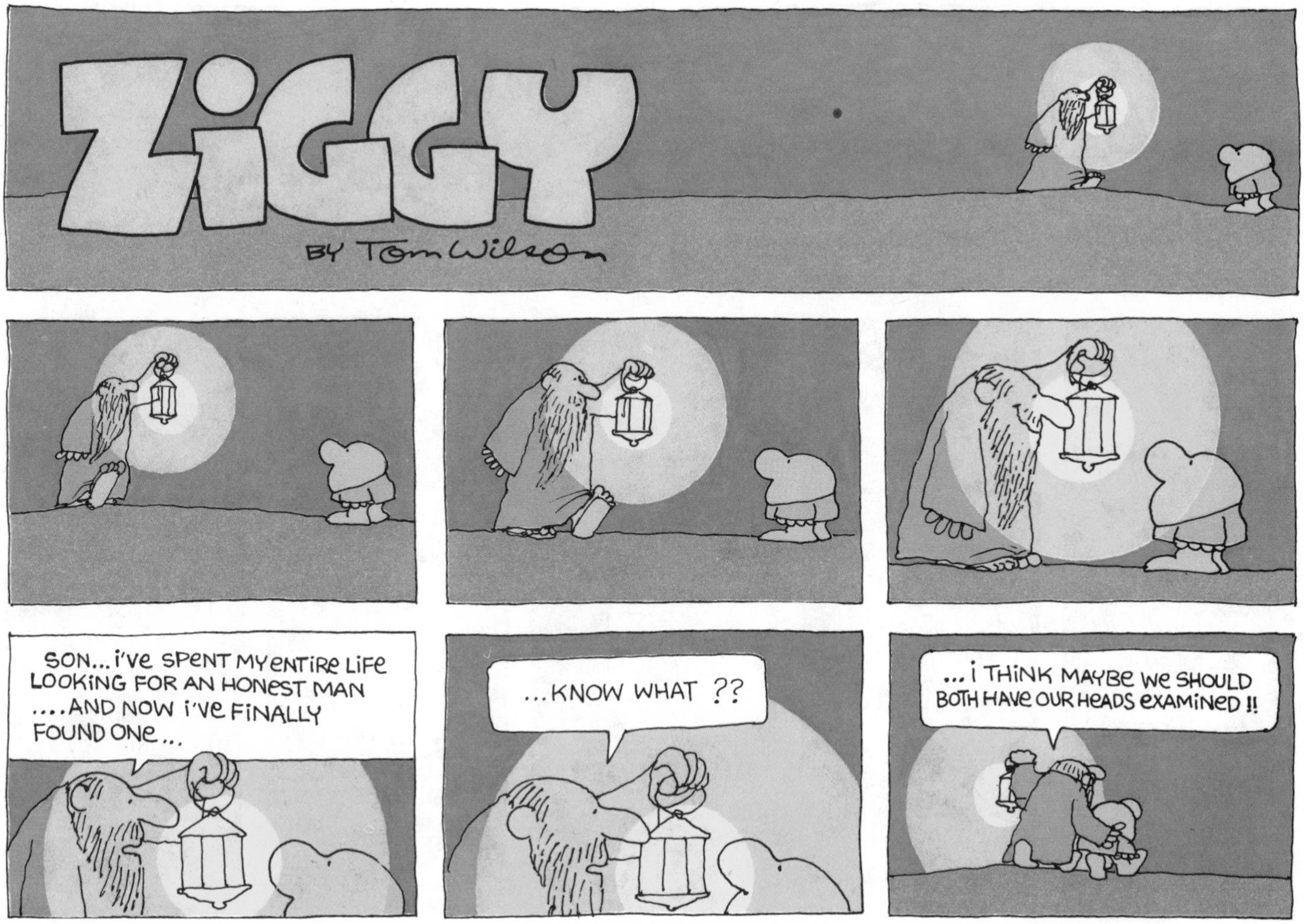
ZiGGY
BY Tom Wilson
SON... i've SPENT MY ENTiRe LiFe LOOKiNG FOR AN HONeST MAN ....AND NOW i've FiNALLY FOUND ONe...
...KNOW WHAT ??
...i THiNK MAYBe We SHOULD BOTH HAVe OUR HeADS eXAMiNeD !!

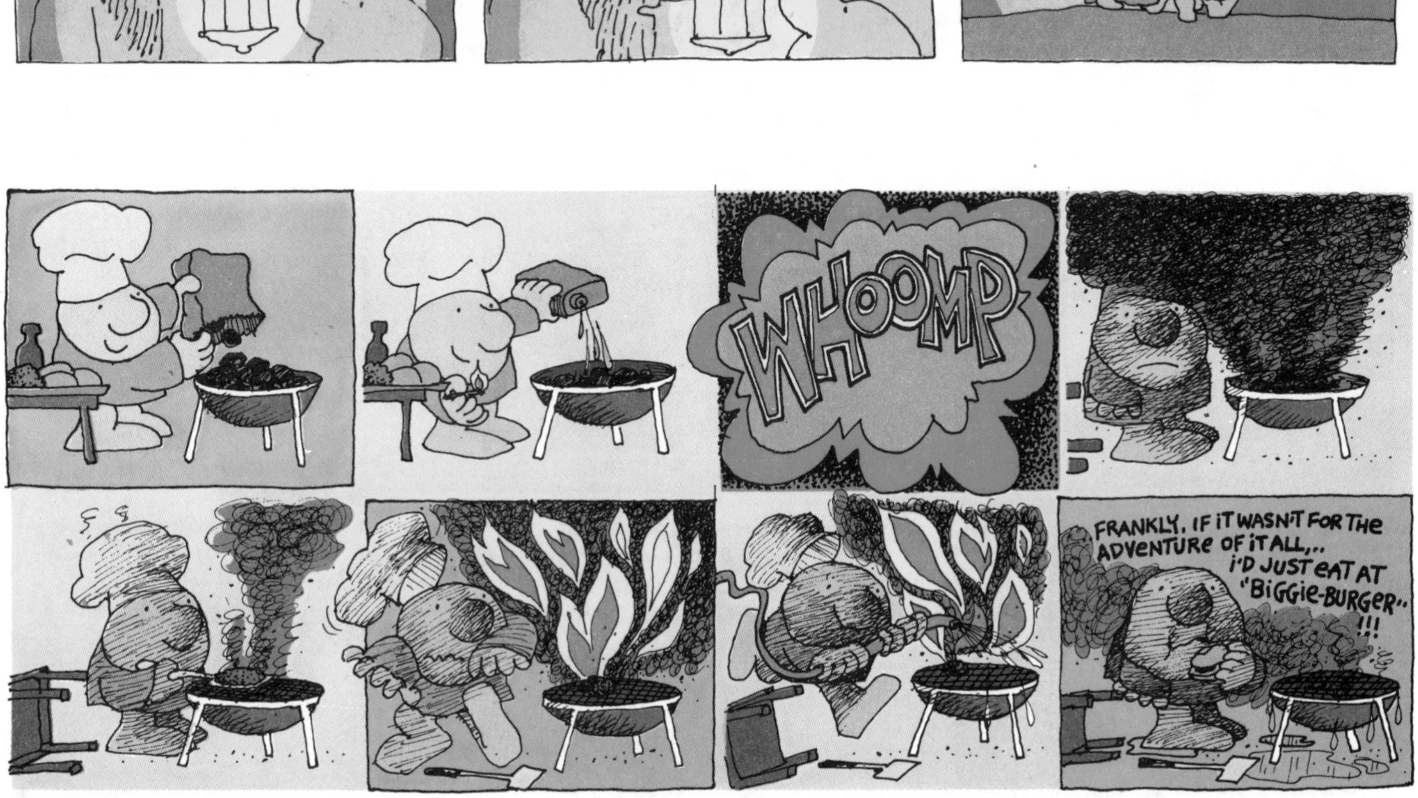
WHOOMP
FRANKLY, IF IT WASN'T FOR THE ADVeNTURe OF iT ALL,.. i'D JUST eAT AT "BiGGie-BURGeR"..!!!

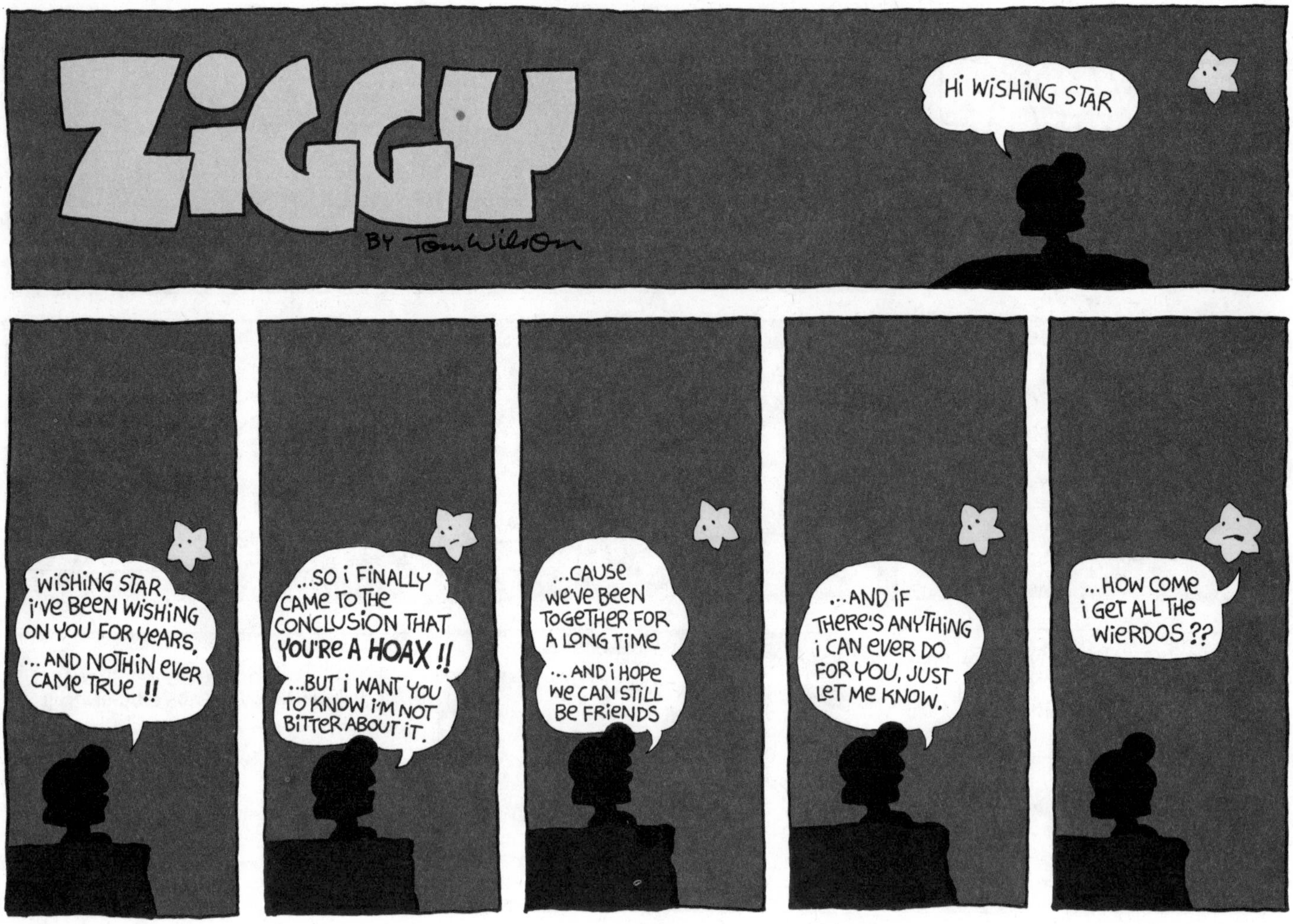
ZIGGY
BY Tom Wilson
HI WISHING STAR
WISHING STAR, i've BEEN WISHING ON YOU FOR YEARS, ...AND NOTHIN ever CAME TRUE !!
...SO i FINALLY CAME TO THE CONCLUSION THAT YOU're A HOAX !! ...BUT i WANT YOU TO KNOW i'M NOT BITTER ABOUT iT.
...CAUSE we've BEEN TOGETHER FOR A LONG TiME ...AND i HOPE WE CAN STiLL BE FRIENDS
...AND iF THERE'S ANYTHING i CAN ever DO FOR YOU, JUST LET ME KNOW.
...HOW COME i GET ALL THE WiERDOS ??

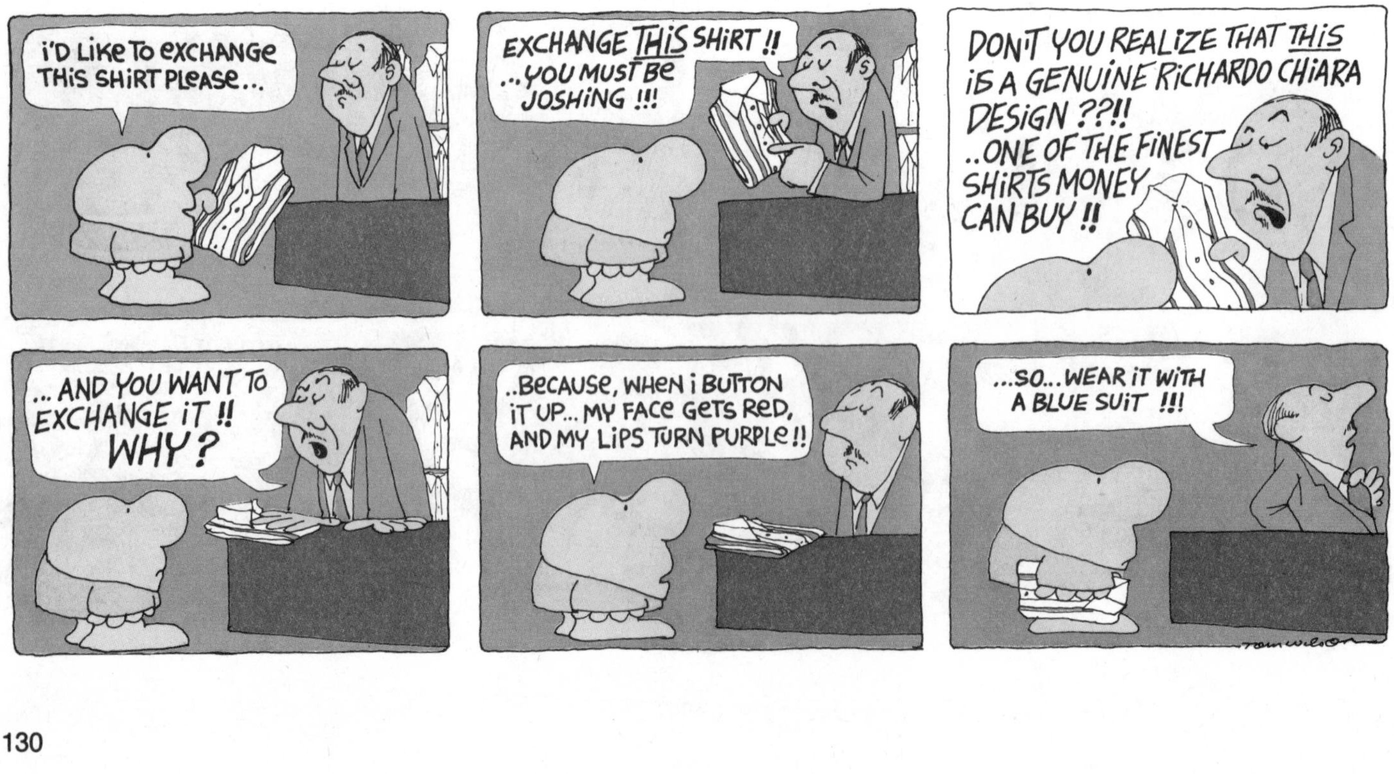
i'D LiKE TO exCHANGE THIS SHiRT PLeASE...
EXCHANGE THIS SHIRT !! ...YOU MUST BE JOSHING !!!
DON'T YOU REALIZE THAT THIS iS A GENUINE RiCHARDO CHiARA DESiGN ??!! ..ONE OF THE FiNEST SHiRTS MONEY CAN BUY !!
... AND YOU WANT TO EXCHANGE iT !! WHY ?
..BeCAUSe, WHEN i BUTTON iT UP... MY FACE GeTS RED, AND MY LiPS TURN PURPLe !!
...SO... WEAR iT WiTH A BLUE SUiT !!!
Tom Wilson

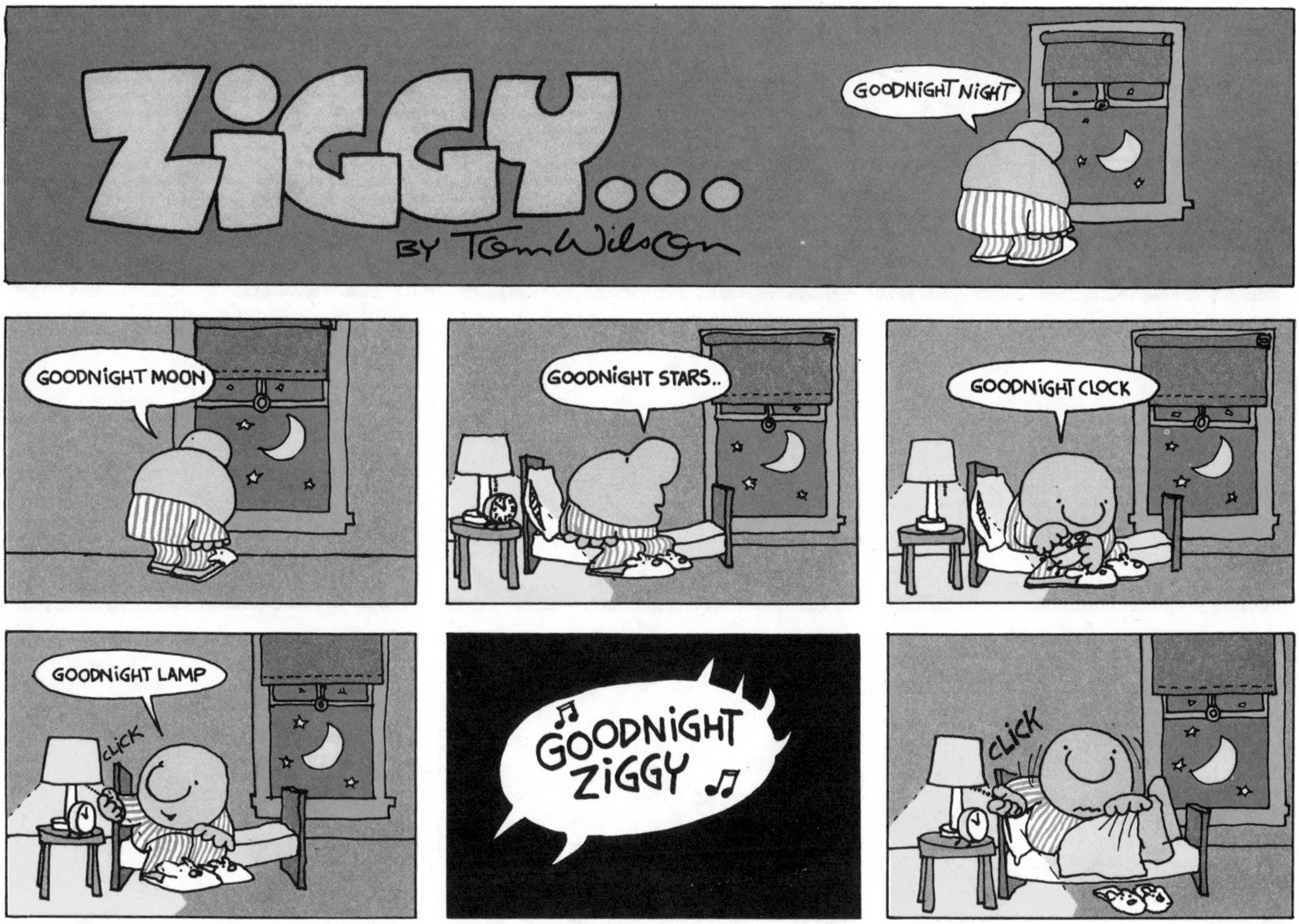
ZIGGY...
BY Tom Wilson
GOODNIGHT NIGHT
GOODNIGHT MOON
GOODNIGHT STARS..
GOODNIGHT CLOCK
GOODNIGHT LAMP
CLICK
GOODNIGHT ZIGGY
CLICK

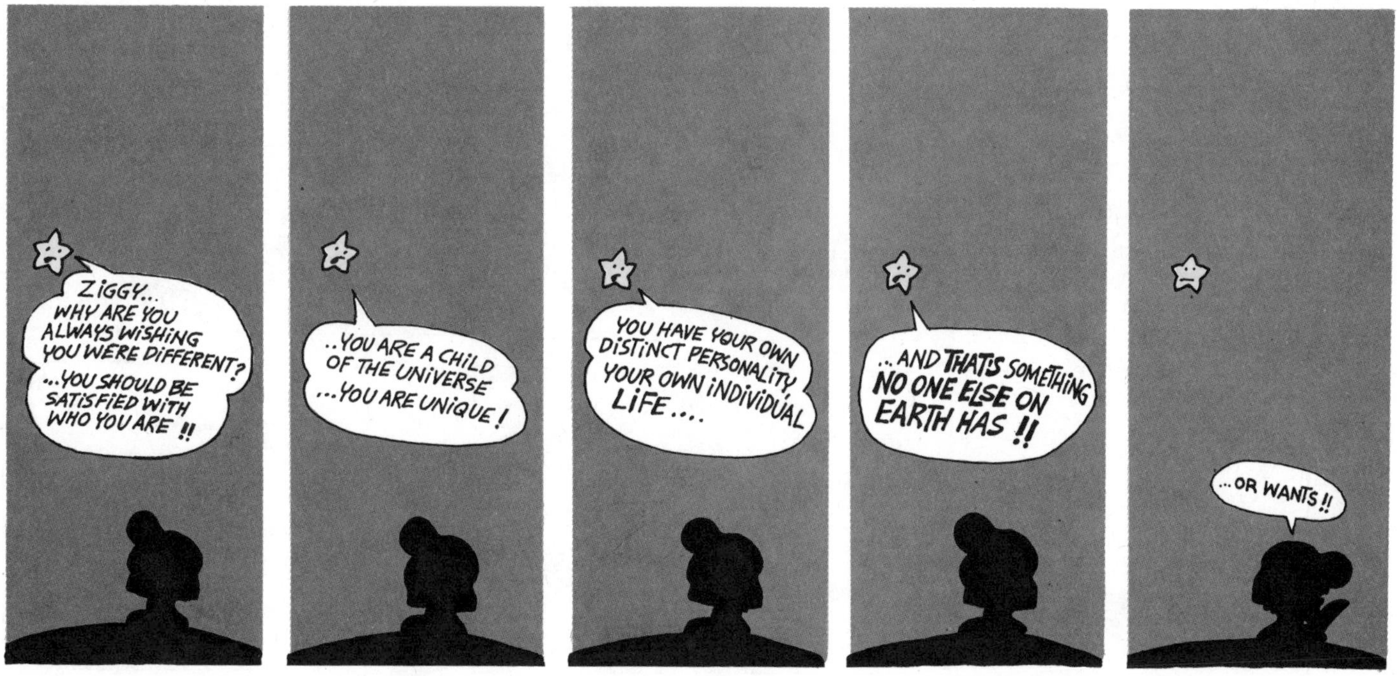
ZIGGY... WHY ARE YOU ALWAYS WISHING YOU WERE DIFFERENT? ...YOU SHOULD BE SATISFIED WITH WHO YOU ARE !!
..YOU ARE A CHILD OF THE UNIVERSE ...YOU ARE UNIQUE!
YOU HAVE YOUR OWN DISTINCT PERSONALITY, YOUR OWN INDIVIDUAL LIFE....
...AND THAT'S SOMETHING NO ONE ELSE ON EARTH HAS !!
...OR WANTS !!

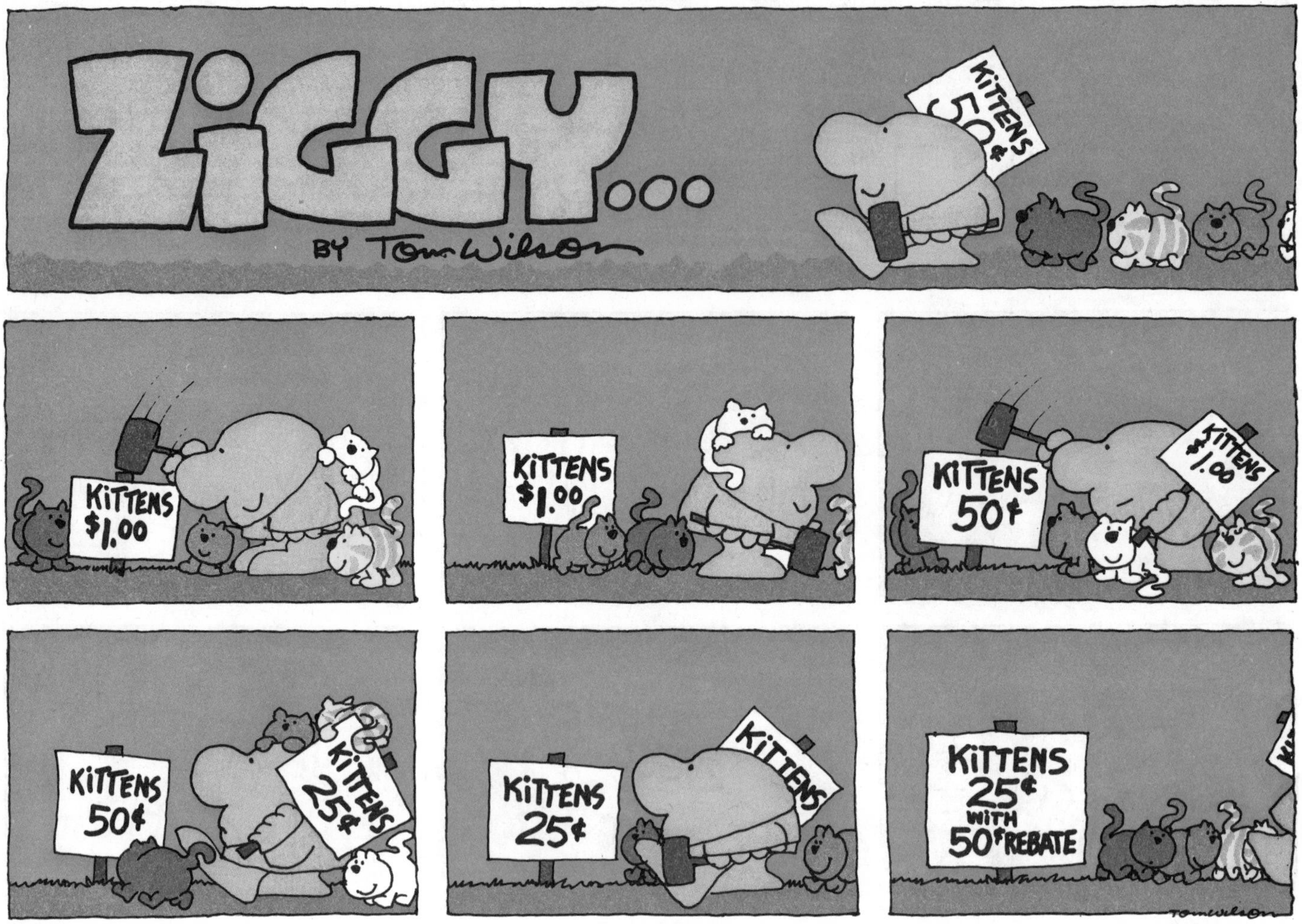
ZiGGY...
BY Tom Wilson
KiTTENS 50¢
KiTTENS $1.00
KiTTENS $1.00
KiTTENS 50¢
KiTTENS $1.00
KiTTENS 50¢
KiTTENS 25¢
KiTTENS 25¢
KiTTENS
KiTTENS 25¢ WITH 50¢ REBATE
Tom Wilson

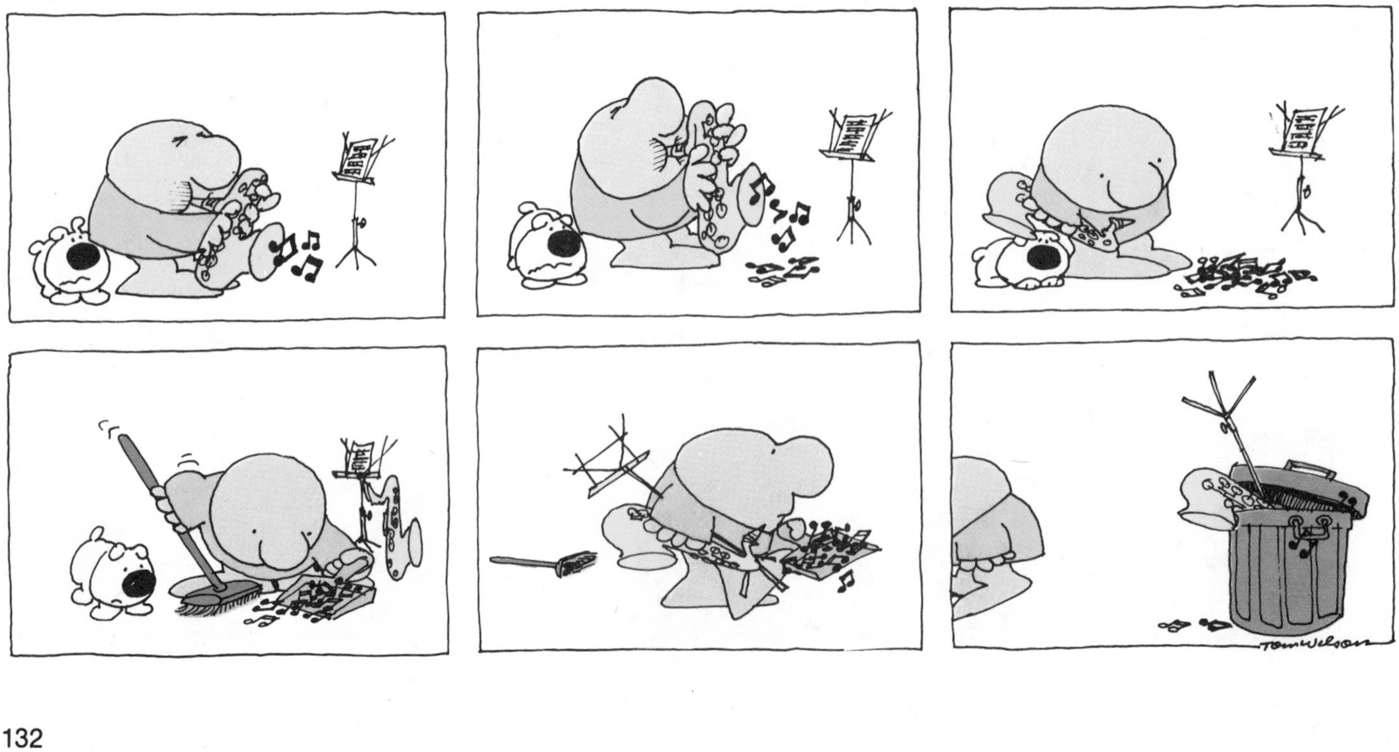
Tom Wilson

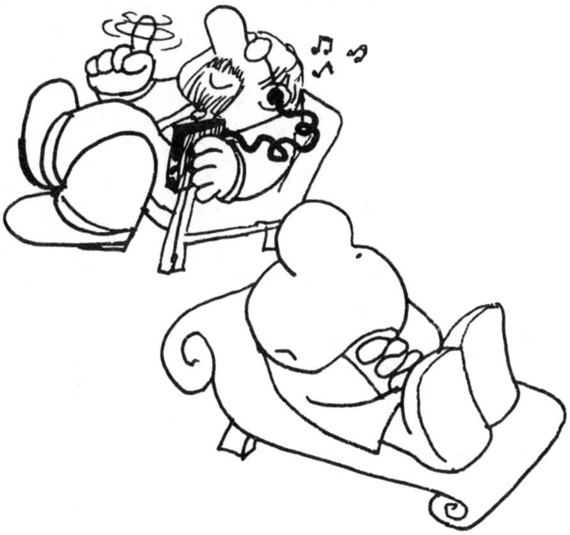

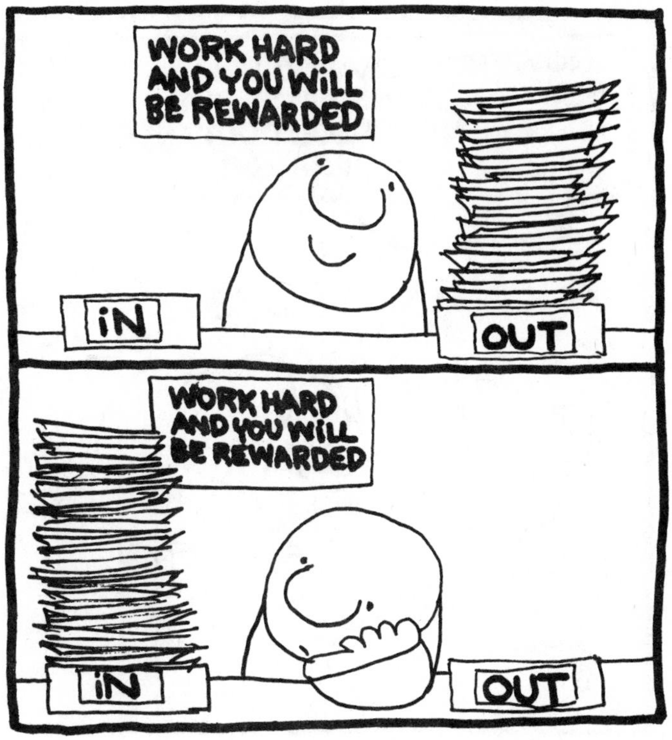
WORK HARD AND YOU WILL BE REWARDED
IN
OUT
WORK HARD AND YOU WILL BE REWARDED
IN
OUT

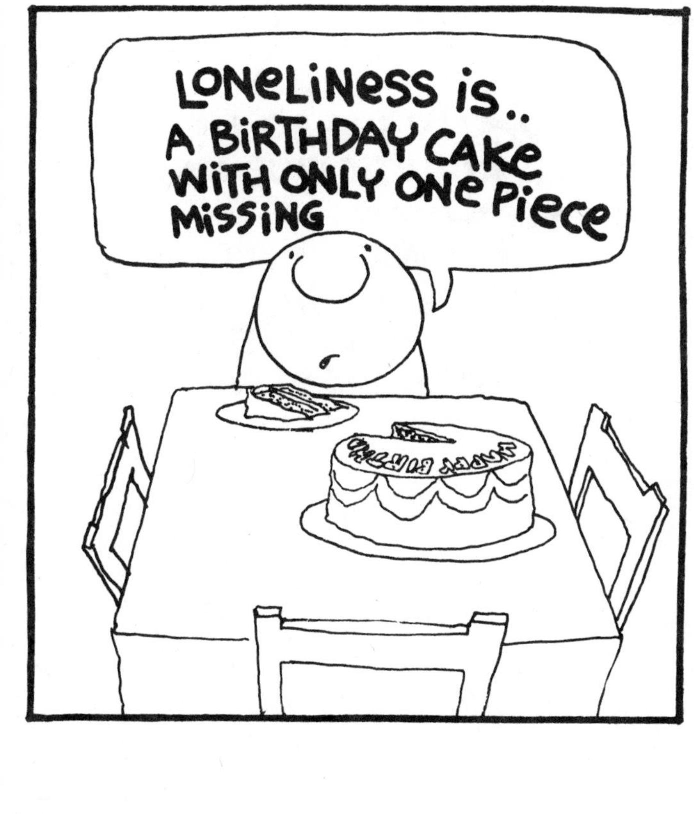
LONELINESS IS..
A BIRTHDAY CAKE WITH ONLY ONE PIECE MISSING

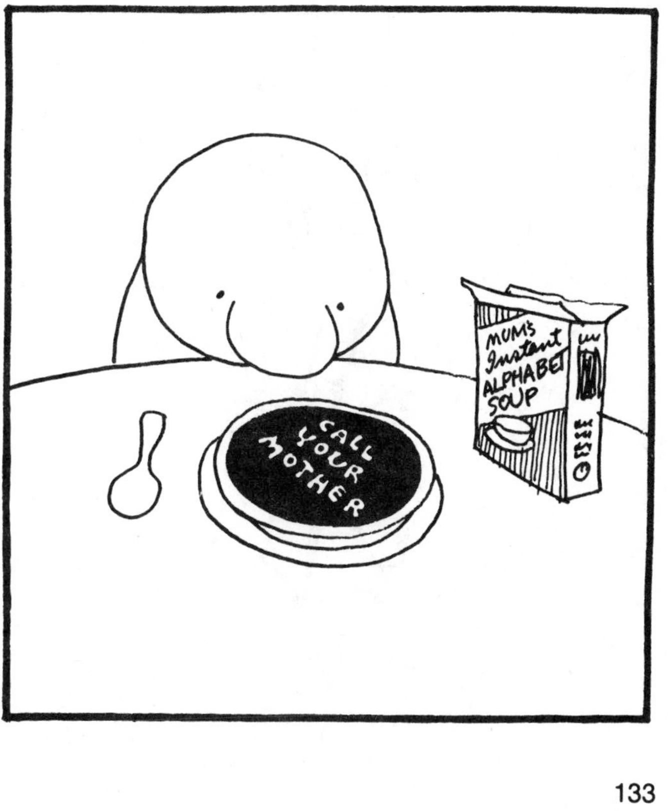
CALL YOUR MOTHER
MUM'S Instant ALPHABET SOUP

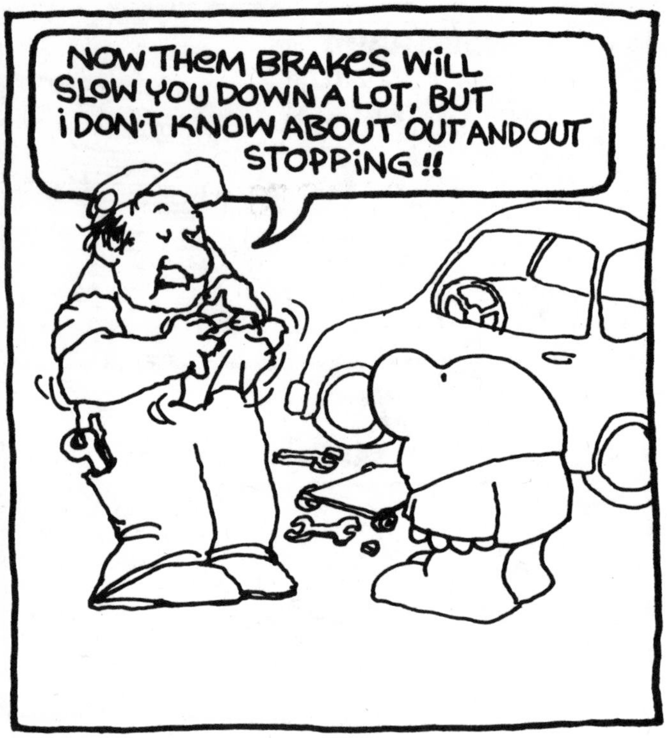
NOW THEM BRAKES WILL SLOW YOU DOWN A LOT, BUT I DON'T KNOW ABOUT OUT AND OUT STOPPING !!

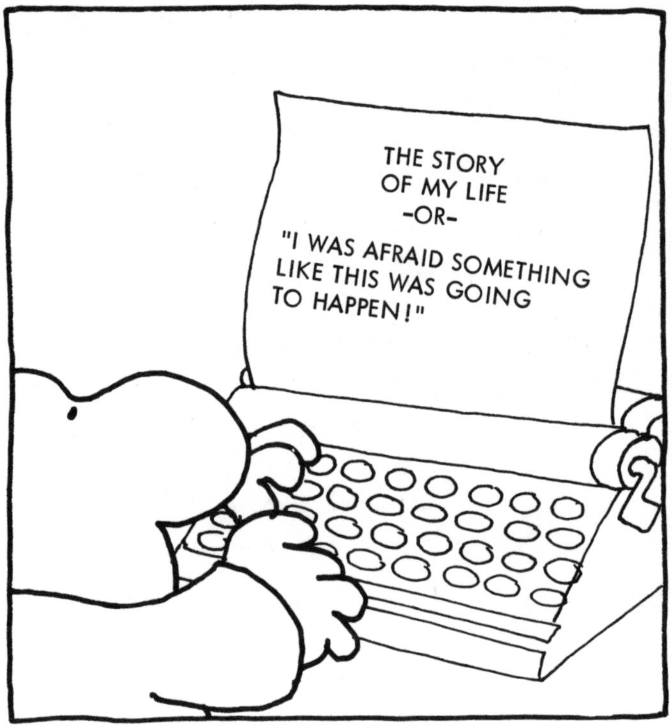
THE STORY
OF MY LIFE
-OR-
"I WAS AFRAID SOMETHING LIKE THIS WAS GOING TO HAPPEN!"

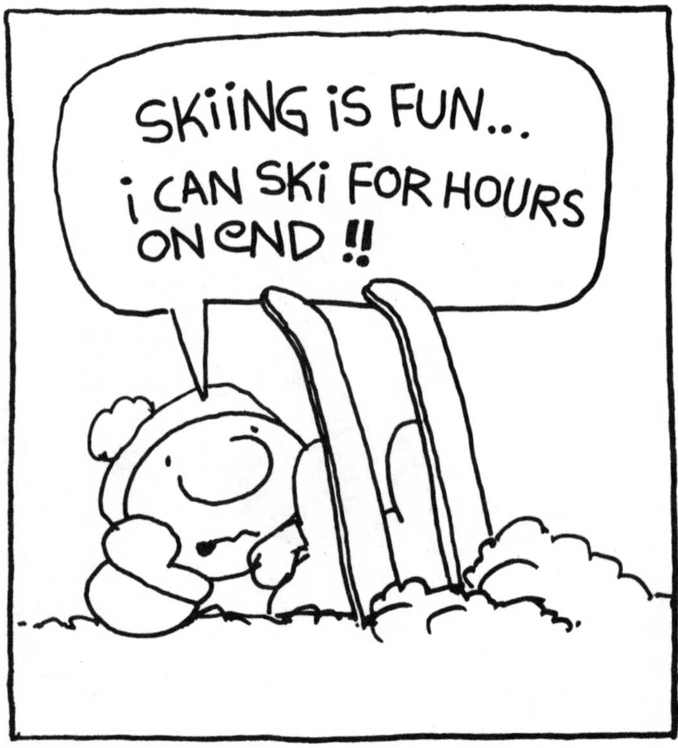
SKIING IS FUN... I CAN SKI FOR HOURS ON END !!

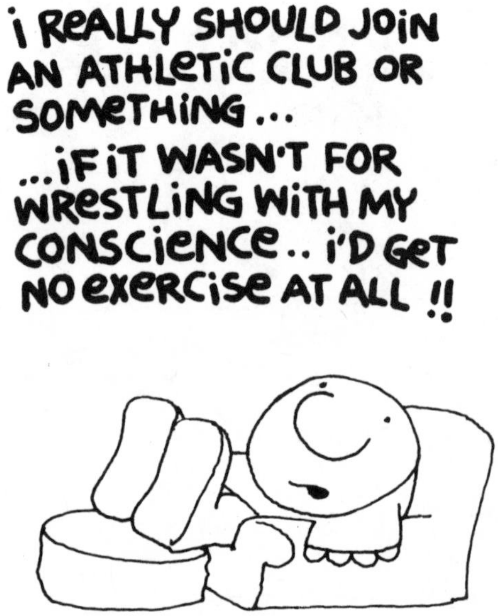
I REALLY SHOULD JOIN AN ATHLETIC CLUB OR SOMETHING...
...IF IT WASN'T FOR WRESTLING WITH MY CONSCIENCE.. I'D GET NO EXERCISE AT ALL !!

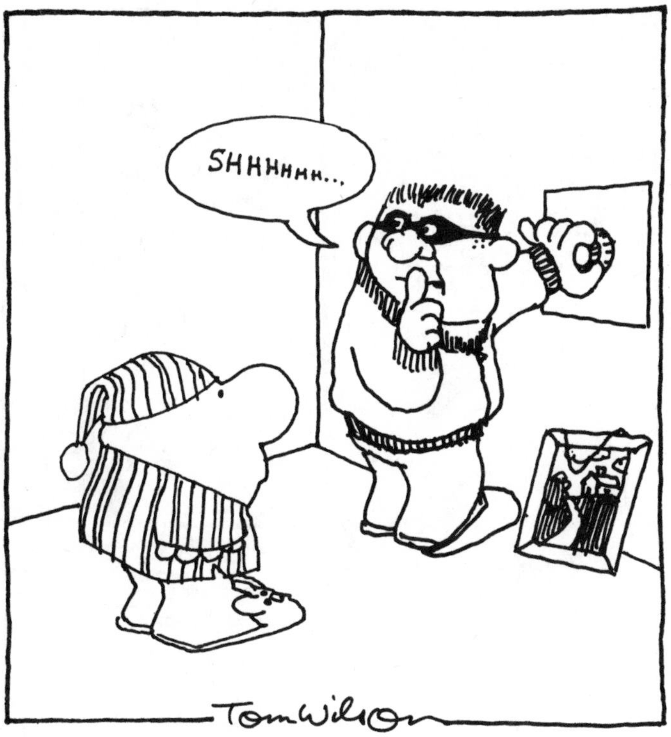
SHHHHHH...
Tom Wilson

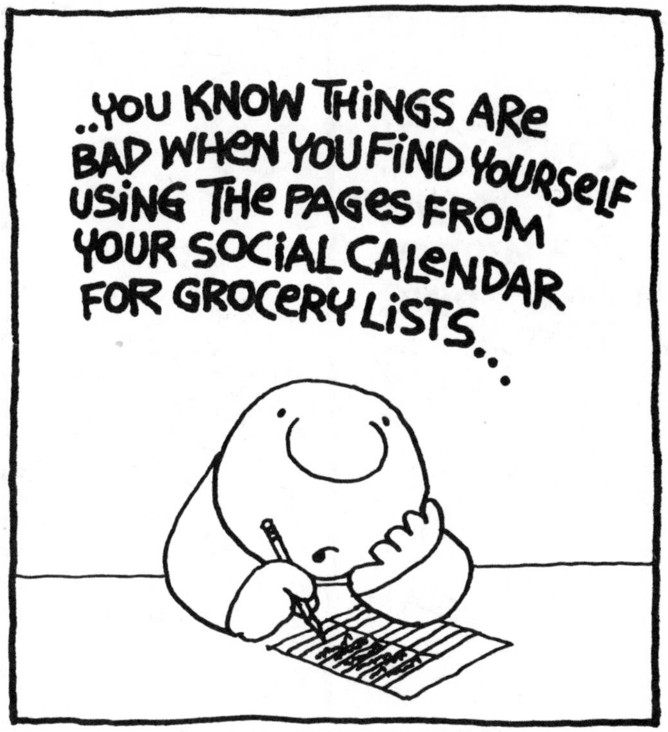
..YOU KNOW THINGS ARE BAD WHEN YOU FIND YOURSELF USING THE PAGES FROM YOUR SOCIAL CALENDAR FOR GROCERY LISTS...

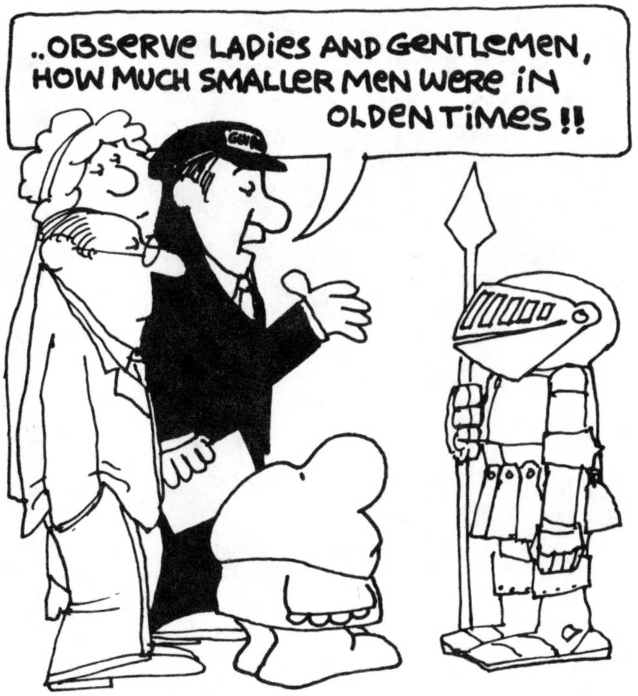
..OBSERVE LADIES AND GENTLEMEN, HOW MUCH SMALLER MEN WERE IN OLDEN TIMES !!

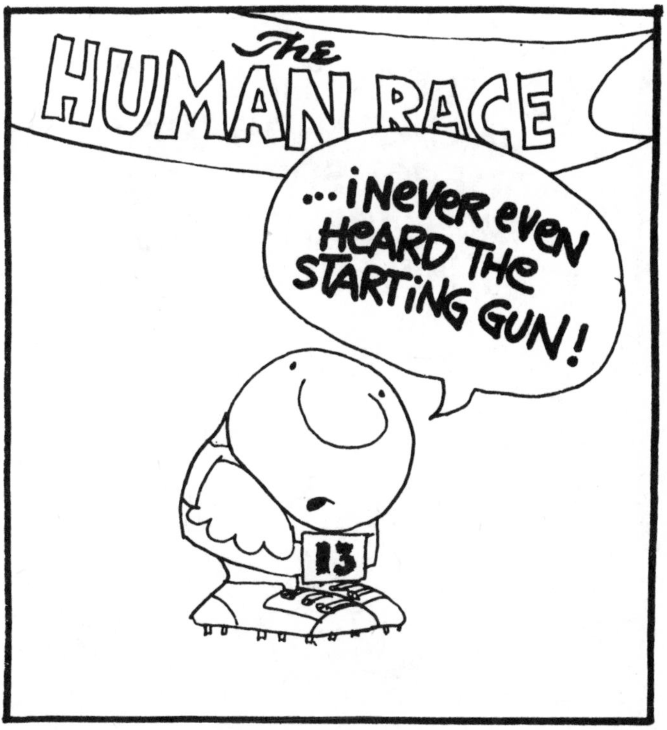
The HUMAN RACE
...I NEVER EVEN HEARD THE STARTING GUN!
13

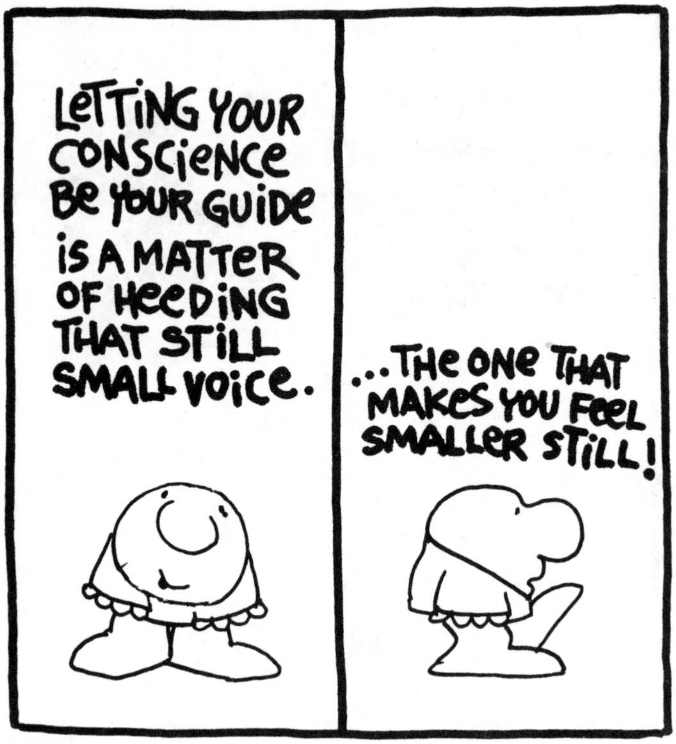
LETTING YOUR CONSCIENCE BE YOUR GUIDE IS A MATTER OF HEEDING THAT STILL SMALL VOICE.
...THE ONE THAT MAKES YOU FEEL SMALLER STILL!

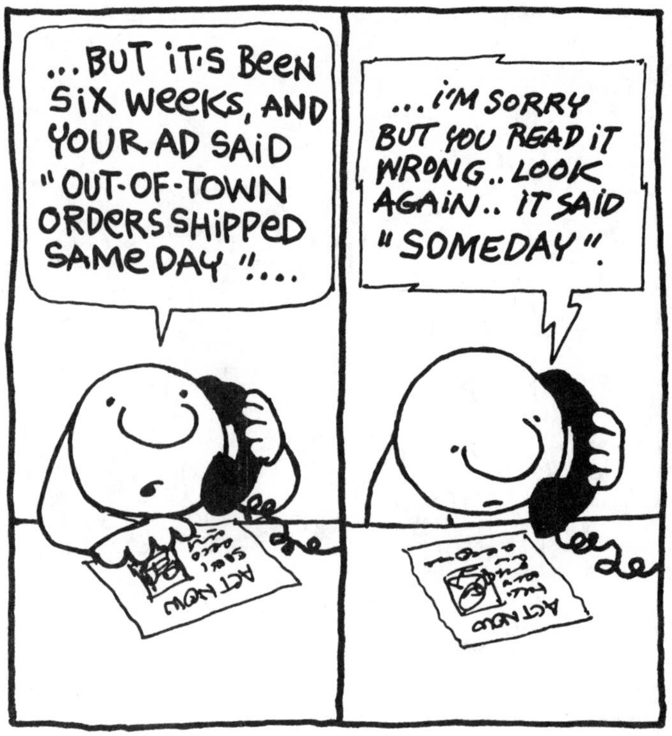
...BUT IT'S BEEN SIX WEEKS, AND YOUR AD SAID "OUT-OF-TOWN ORDERS SHIPPED SAME DAY"!...
ACT NOW
...I'M SORRY BUT YOU READ IT WRONG.. LOOK AGAIN.. IT SAID "SOMEDAY".
ACT NOW

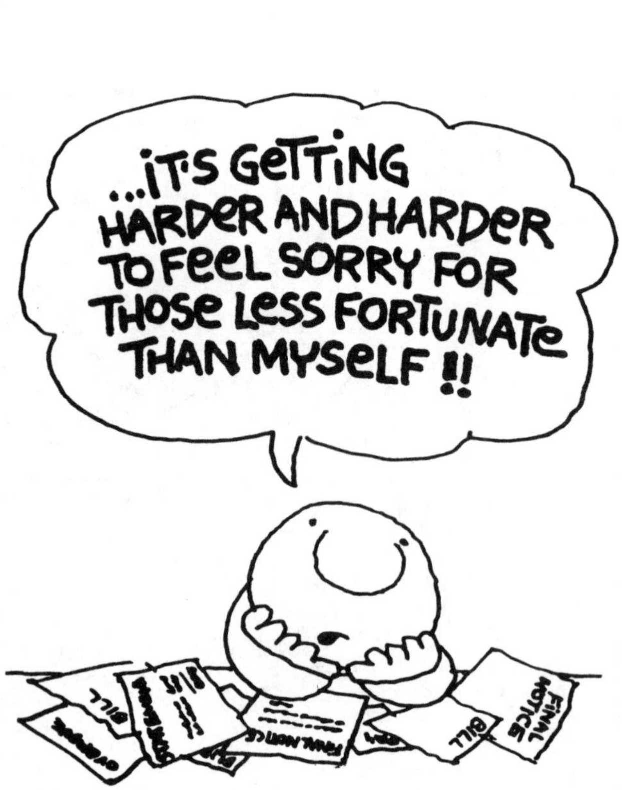
...IT'S GETTING HARDER AND HARDER TO FEEL SORRY FOR THOSE LESS FORTUNATE THAN MYSELF!!
FINAL NOTICE
BILL
FINAL NOTICE

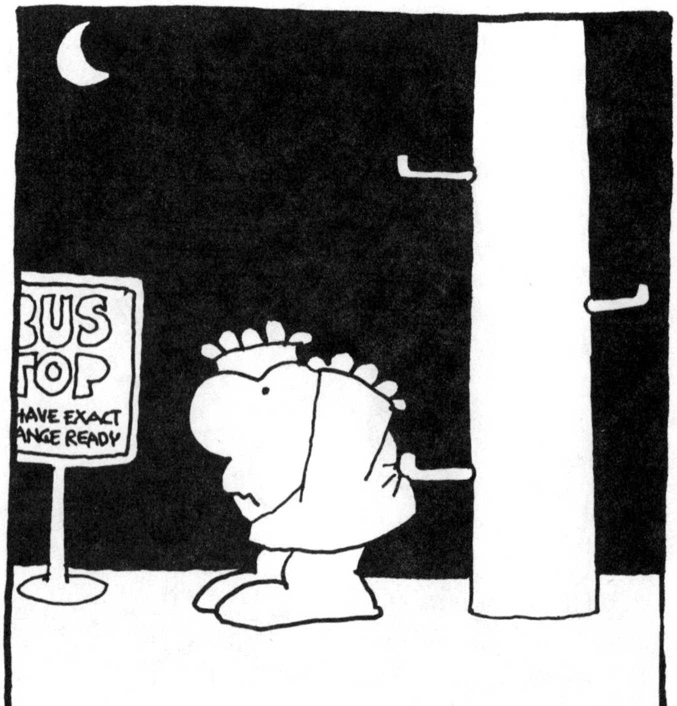
BUS
TOP
HAVE EXACT
ANGE READY

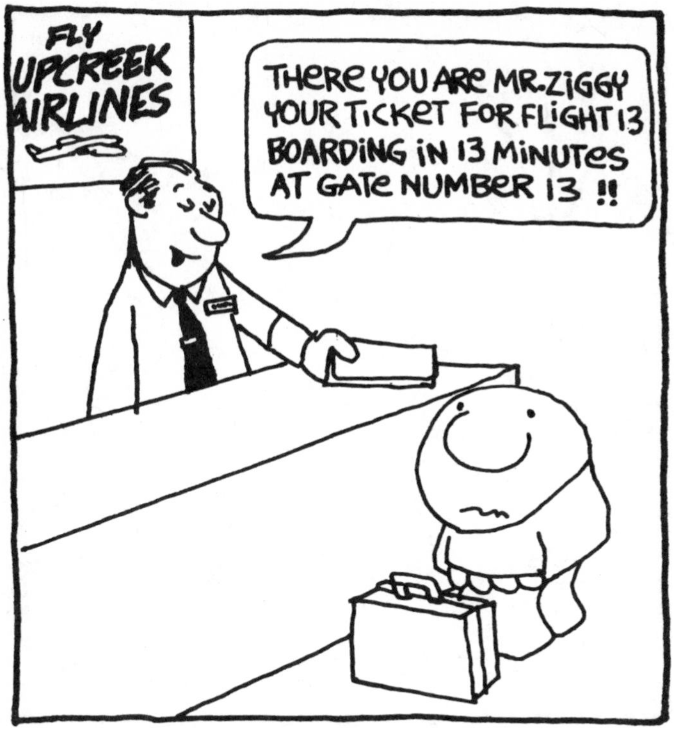
FLY UPCREEK AIRLINES
THERE YOU ARE MR. ZIGGY YOUR TICKET FOR FLIGHT 13 BOARDING IN 13 MINUTES AT GATE NUMBER 13 !!

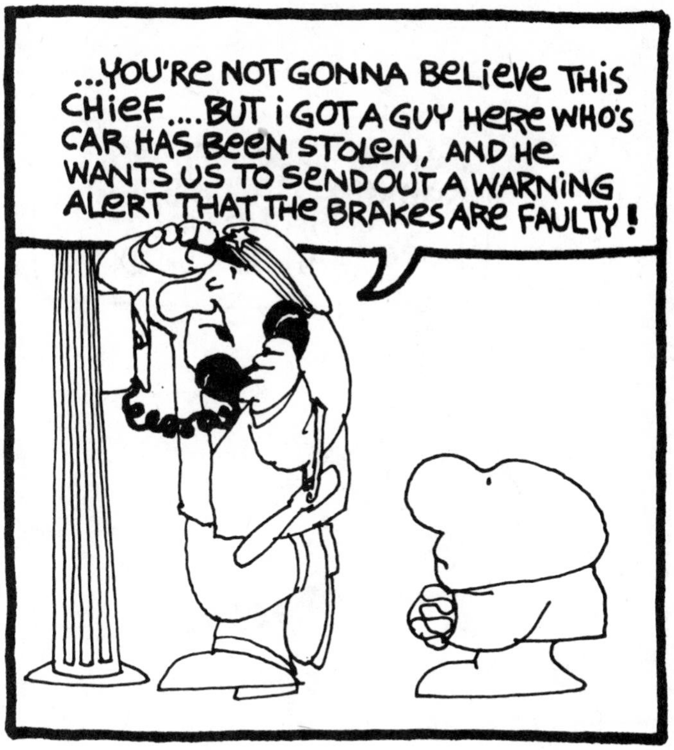
...YOU'RE NOT GONNA BELIEVE THIS CHIEF.... BUT I GOT A GUY HERE WHO'S CAR HAS BEEN STOLEN, AND HE WANTS US TO SEND OUT A WARNING ALERT THAT THE BRAKES ARE FAULTY !

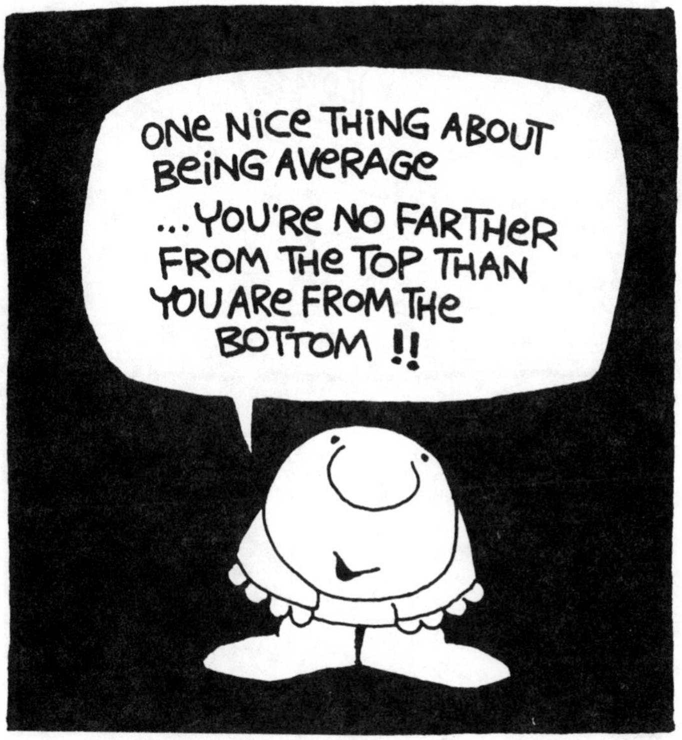
ONE NICE THING ABOUT BEING AVERAGE ...YOU'RE NO FARTHER FROM THE TOP THAN YOU ARE FROM THE BOTTOM !!

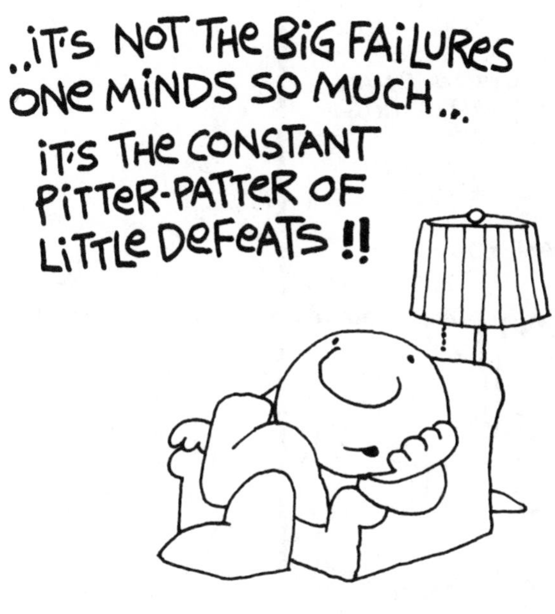
..IT'S NOT THE BIG FAILURES ONE MINDS SO MUCH...
IT'S THE CONSTANT PITTER-PATTER OF LITTLE DEFEATS !!

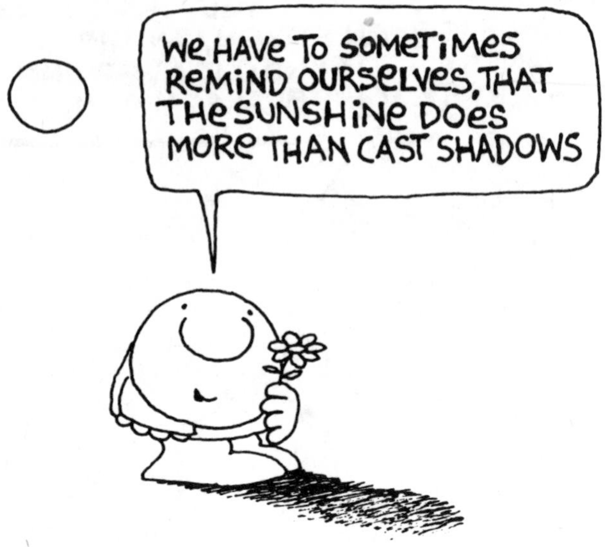
WE HAVE TO SOMETIMES REMIND OURSELVES, THAT THE SUNSHINE DOES MORE THAN CAST SHADOWS

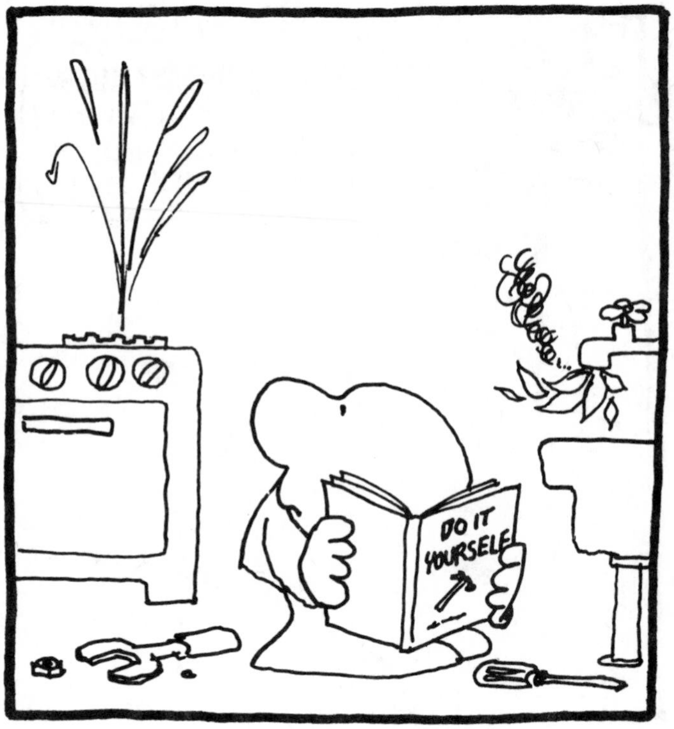
DO IT YOURSELF

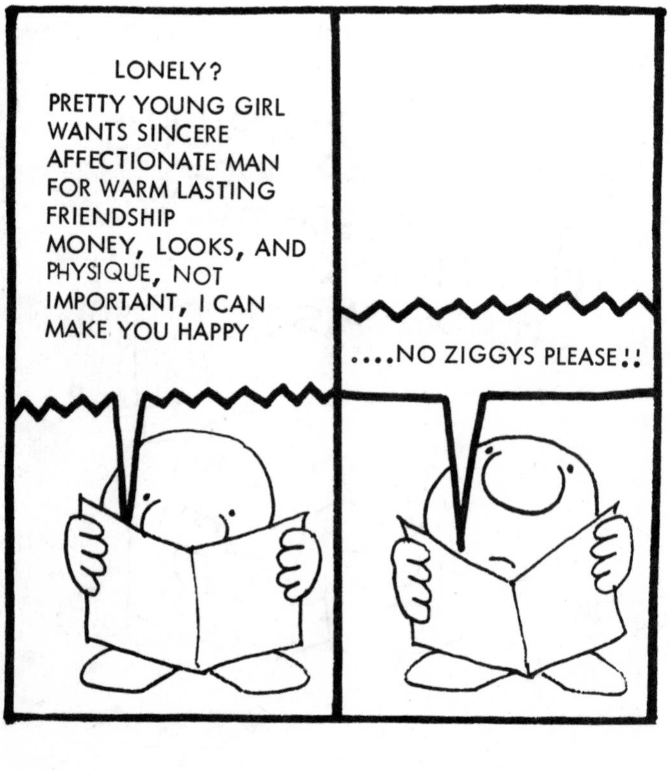
LONELY?
PRETTY YOUNG GIRL WANTS SINCERE AFFECTIONATE MAN FOR WARM LASTING FRIENDSHIP
MONEY, LOOKS, AND PHYSIQUE, NOT IMPORTANT, I CAN MAKE YOU HAPPY
....NO ZIGGYS PLEASE!!

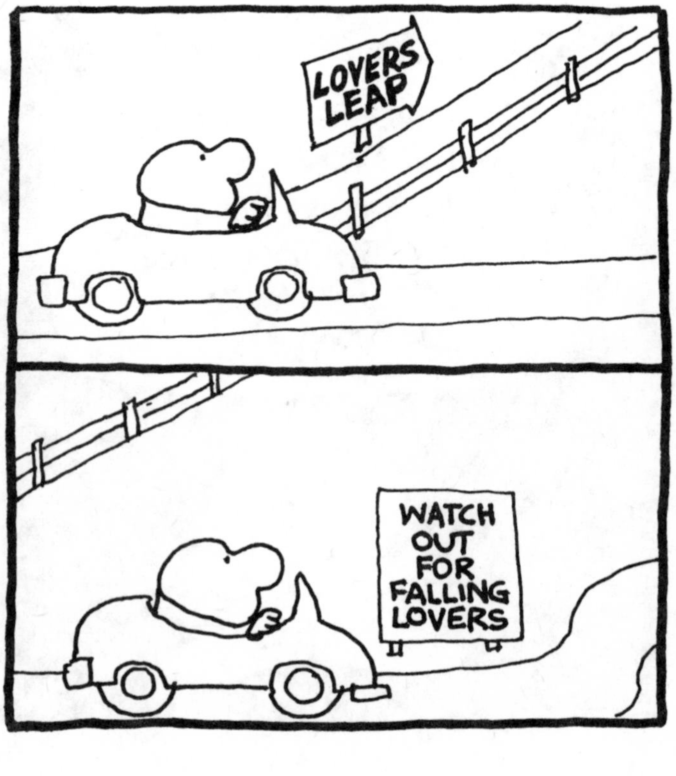
LOVERS LEAP
WATCH OUT FOR FALLING LOVERS

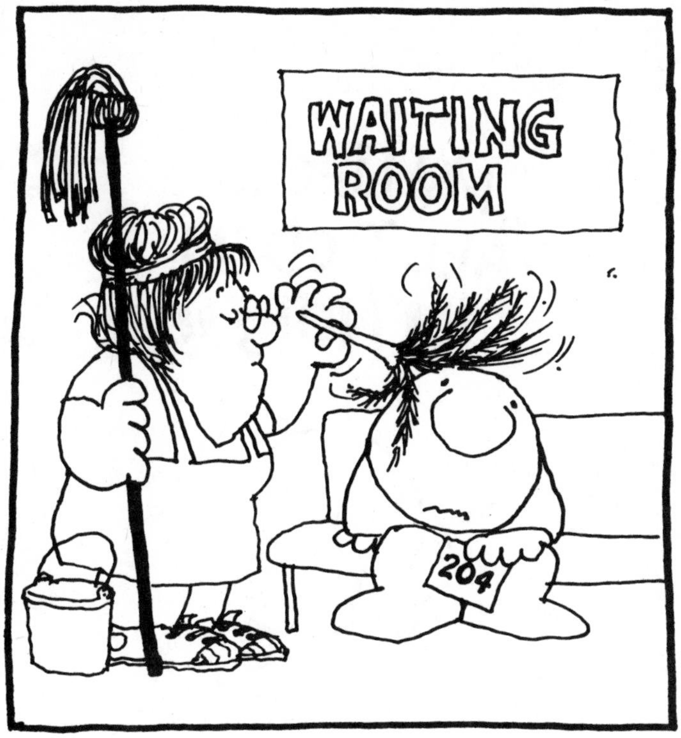
WAITING ROOM
204

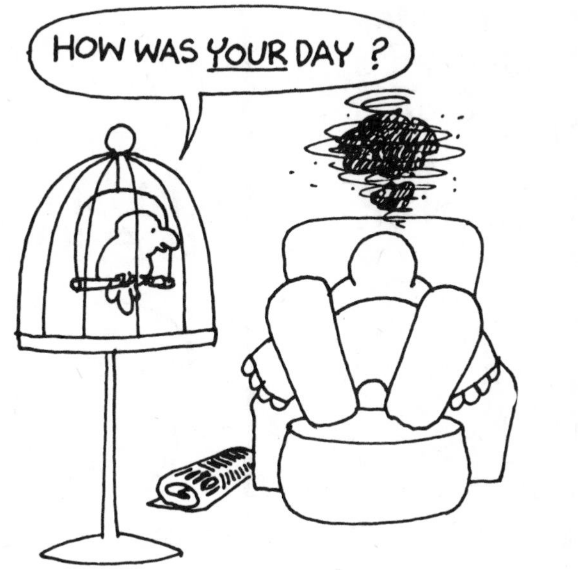
HOW WAS YOUR DAY ?

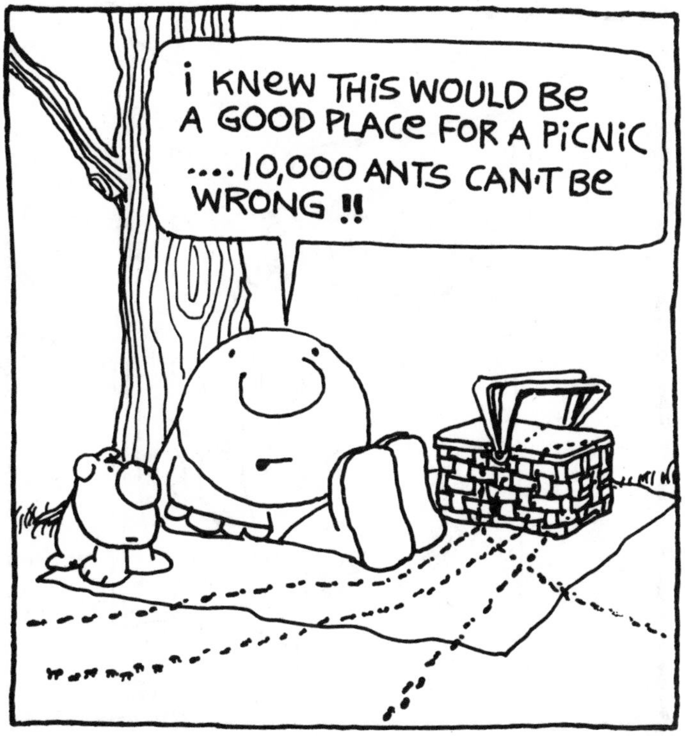
i KNEW THIS WOULD BE A GOOD PLACE FOR A PICNIC ....10,000 ANTS CAN'T BE WRONG !!

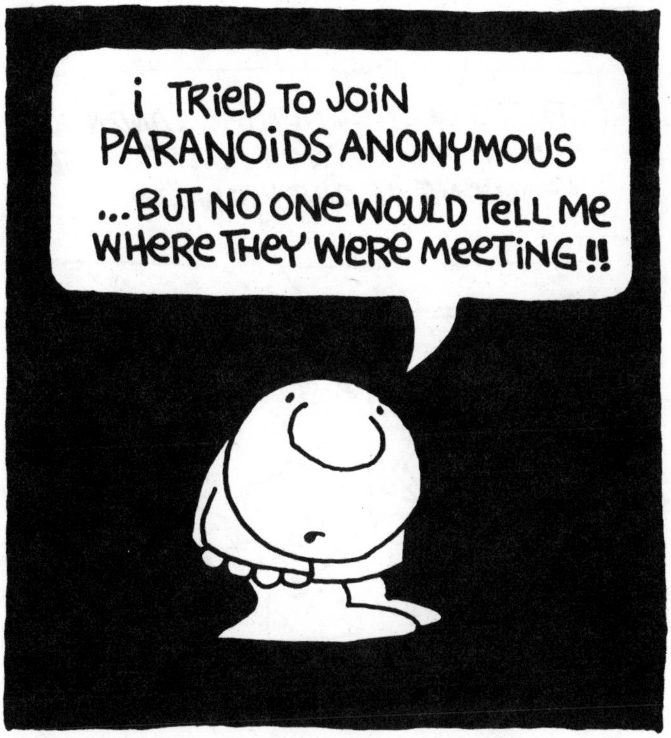
i TRIED TO JOIN PARANOIDS ANONYMOUS ...BUT NO ONE WOULD TELL ME WHERE THEY WERE MEETING !!

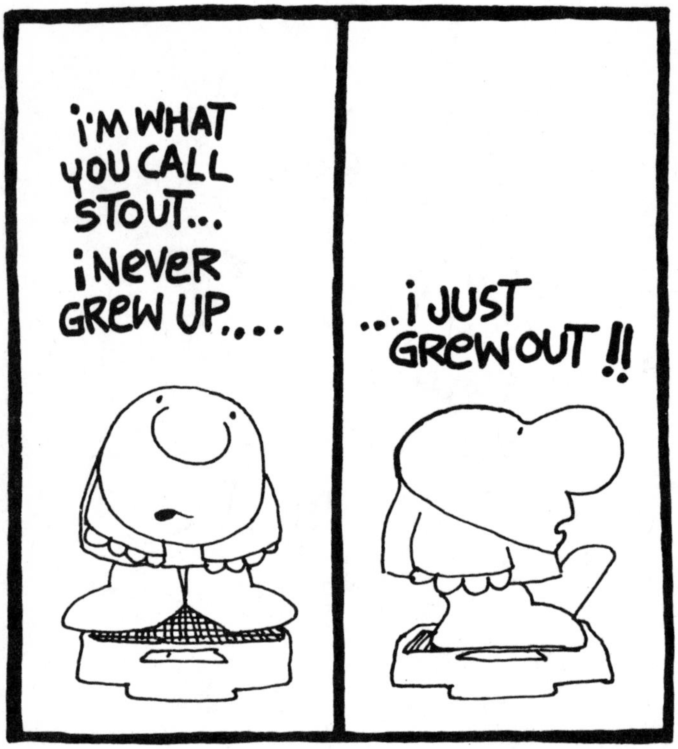
I'M WHAT YOU CALL STOUT... I NEVER GREW UP....
...I JUST GREW OUT !!

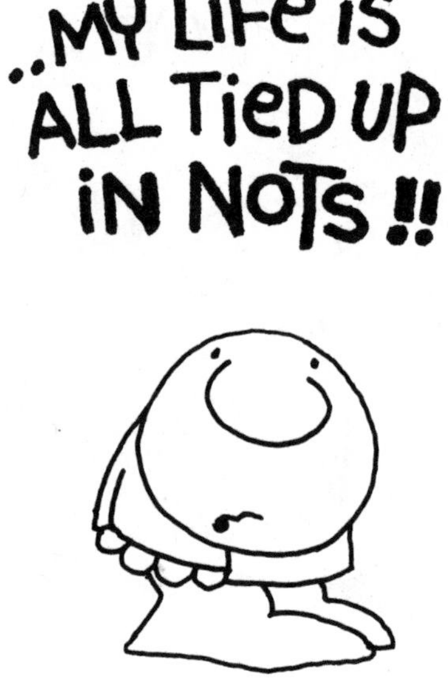
..MY LIFE IS ALL TIED UP IN NOTS !!

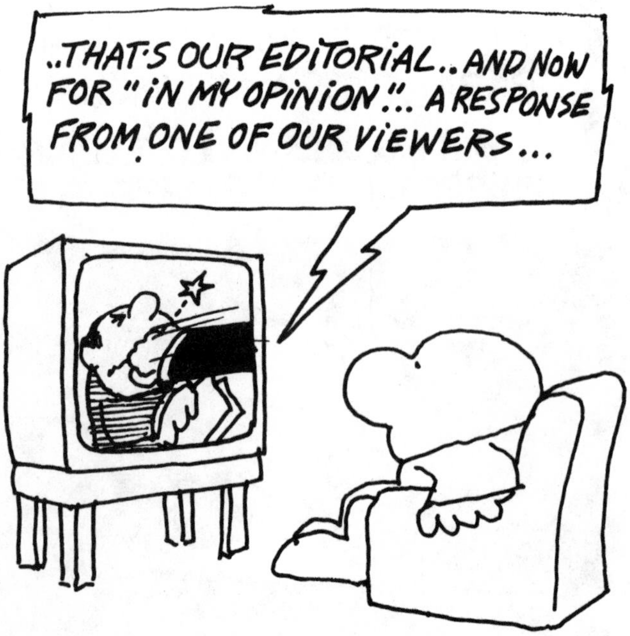
..THAT'S OUR EDITORIAL.. AND NOW FOR "IN MY OPINION".. A RESPONSE FROM ONE OF OUR VIEWERS...

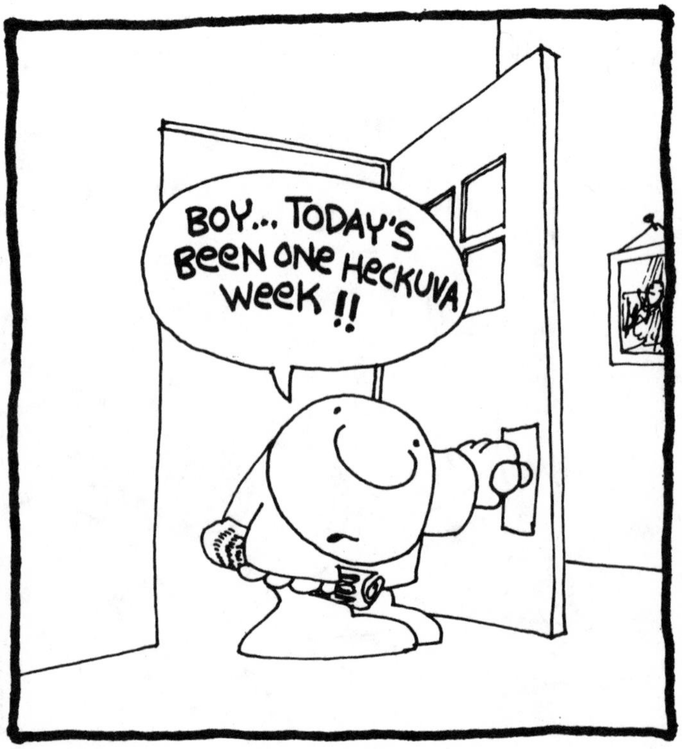
BOY... TODAY'S BEEN ONE HECKUVA WEEK !!

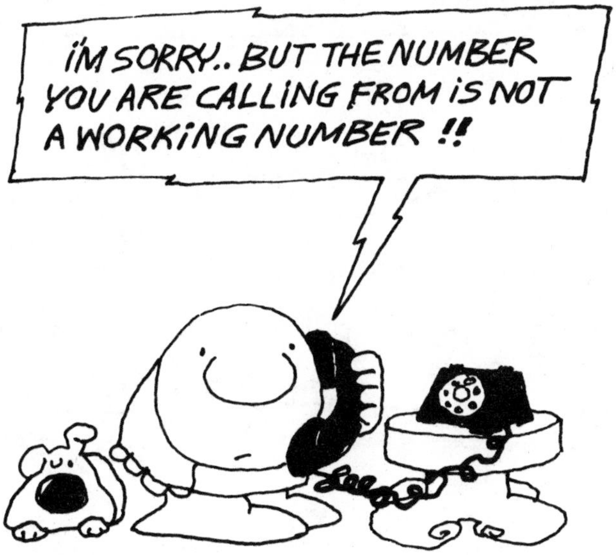

iM SORRY.. BUT THE NUMBER YOU ARE CALLiNG FROM iS NOT A WORKiNG NUMBER !!

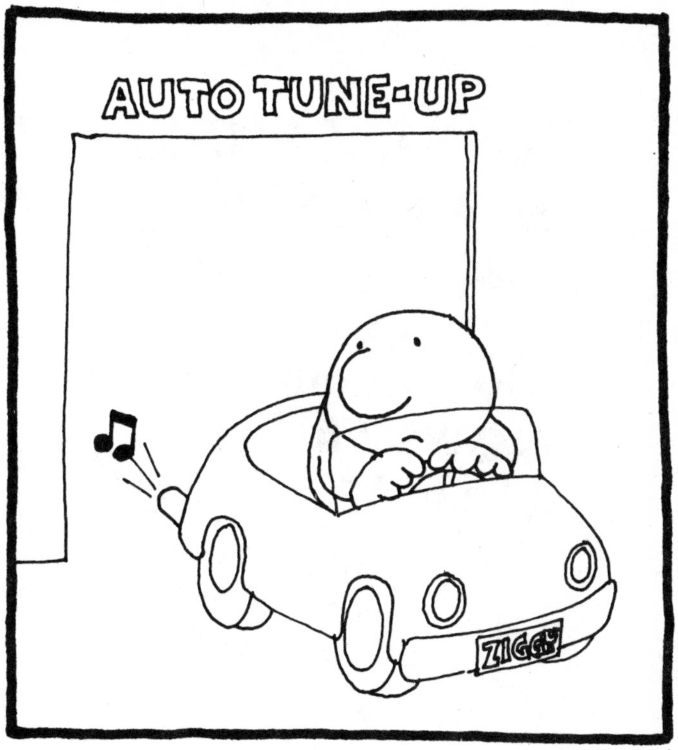

AUTO TUNE-UP
ZIGGY

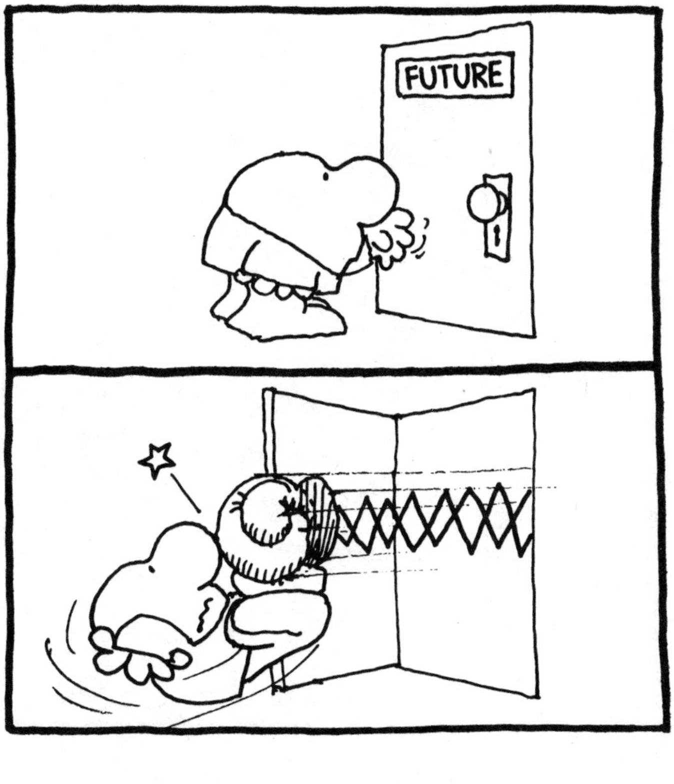

FUTURE

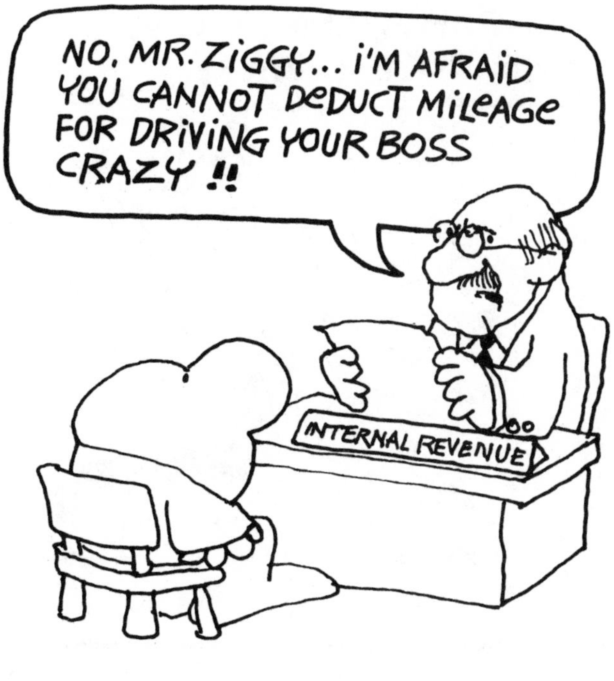

NO. MR. ZIGGY... i'M AFRAID YOU CANNOT DeDUCT MiLeAGe FOR DRiViNG YOUR BOSS CRAZY !!
INTERNAL REVENUE

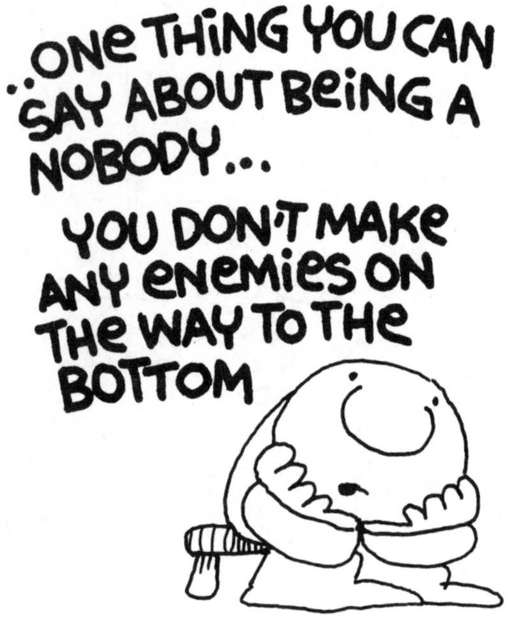
..ONE THING YOU CAN SAY ABOUT BEING A NOBODY...
YOU DON'T MAKE ANY ENEMIES ON THE WAY TO THE BOTTOM

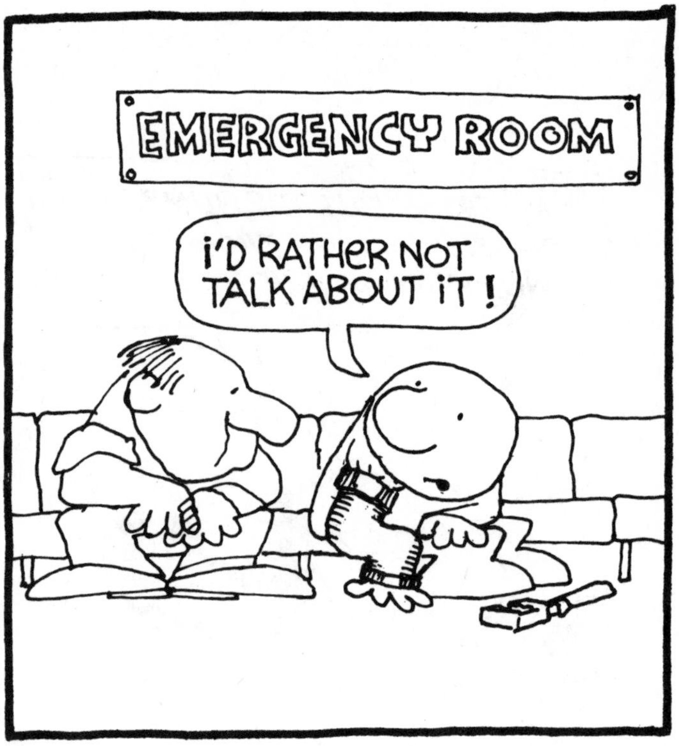
EMERGENCY ROOM
I'D RATHER NOT TALK ABOUT IT!

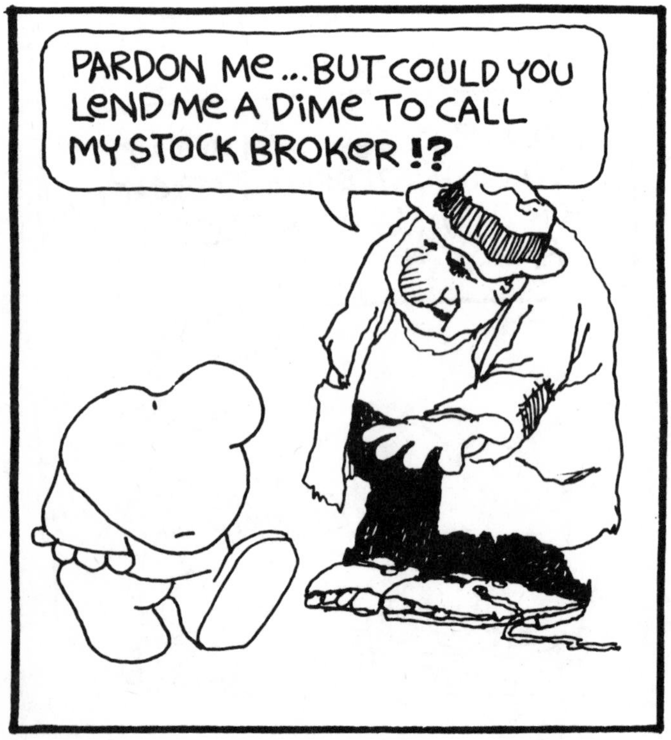
PARDON ME...BUT COULD YOU LEND ME A DIME TO CALL MY STOCK BROKER !?

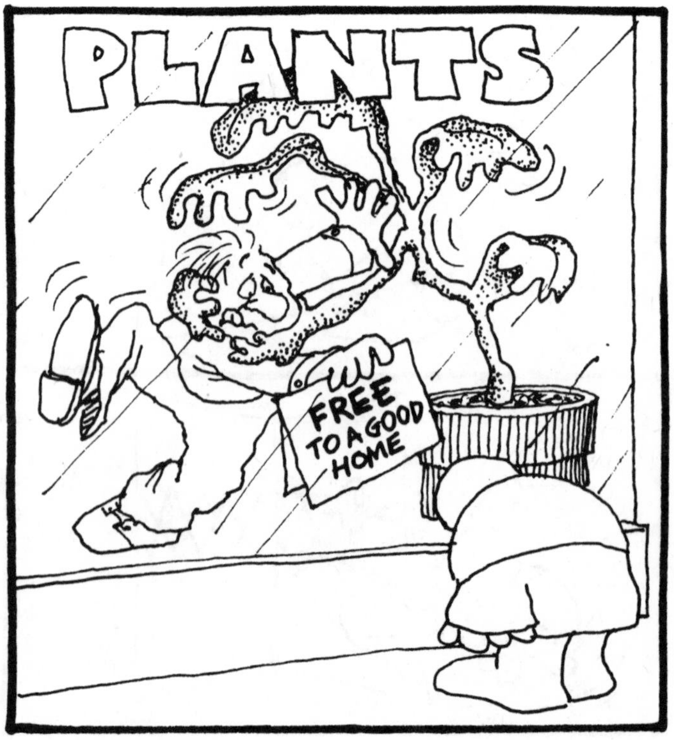
PLANTS
FREE TO A GOOD HOME

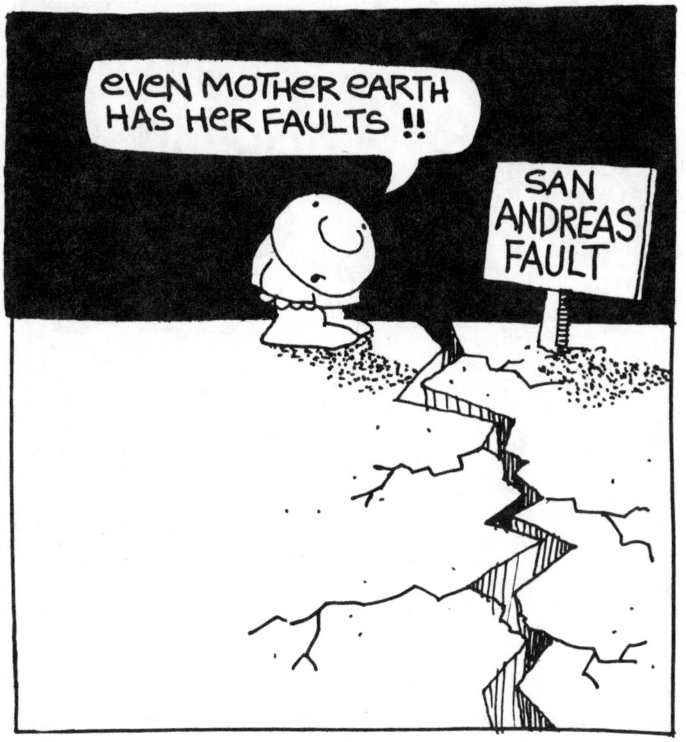
EVEN MOTHER EARTH HAS HER FAULTS !!
SAN ANDREAS FAULT

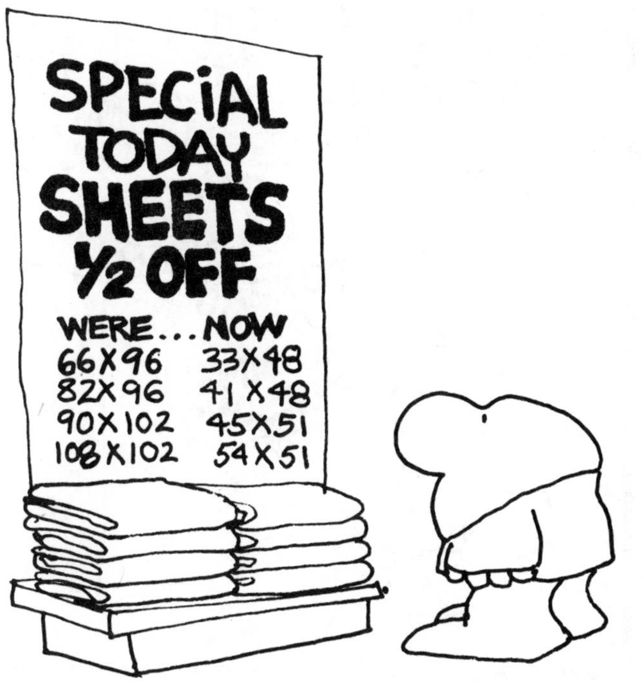
SPECIAL TODAY SHEETS ½ OFF
WERE... NOW
66X96 33X48
82X96 41X48
90X102 45X51
108X102 54X51

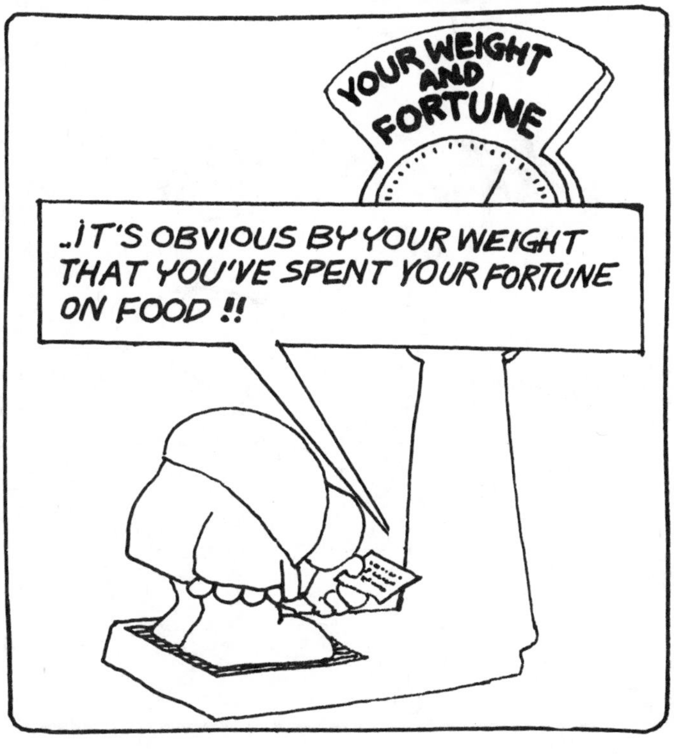
YOUR WEIGHT AND FORTUNE
..IT'S OBVIOUS BY YOUR WEIGHT THAT YOU'VE SPENT YOUR FORTUNE ON FOOD !!

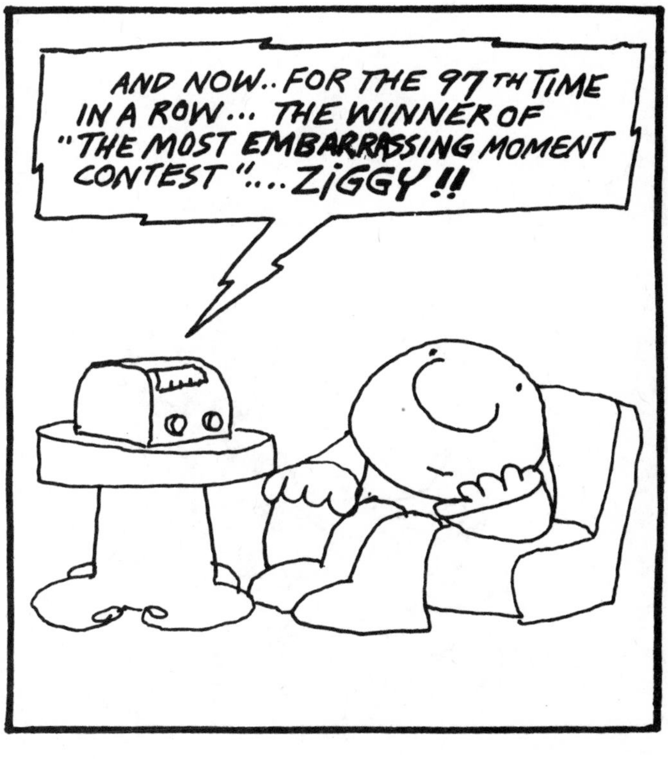
AND NOW.. FOR THE 97TH TIME IN A ROW... THE WINNER OF "THE MOST EMBARRASSING MOMENT CONTEST"... ZIGGY !!

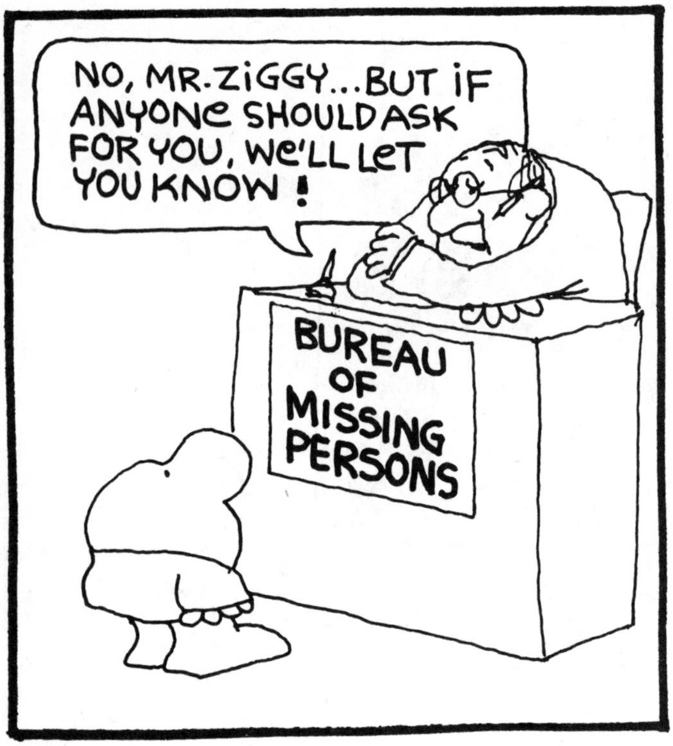
NO, MR. ZIGGY...BUT IF ANYONE SHOULD ASK FOR YOU, WE'LL LET YOU KNOW!
BUREAU OF MISSING PERSONS

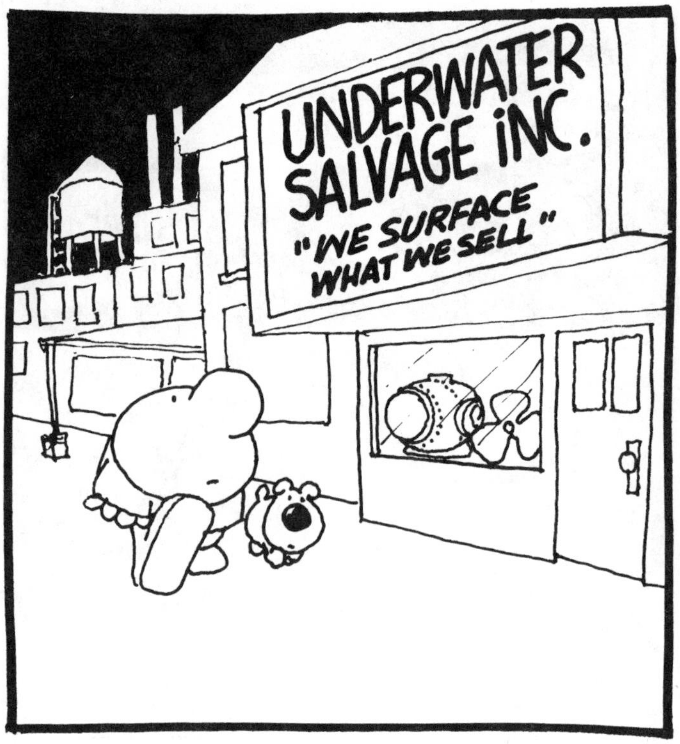
UNDERWATER SALVAGE INC.
"WE SURFACE WHAT WE SELL"

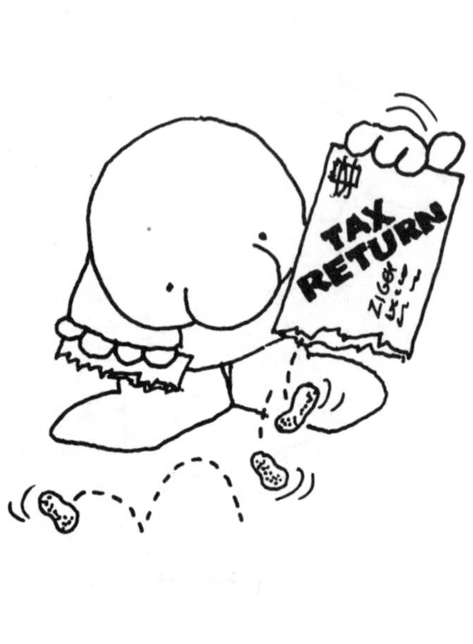
TAX RETURN

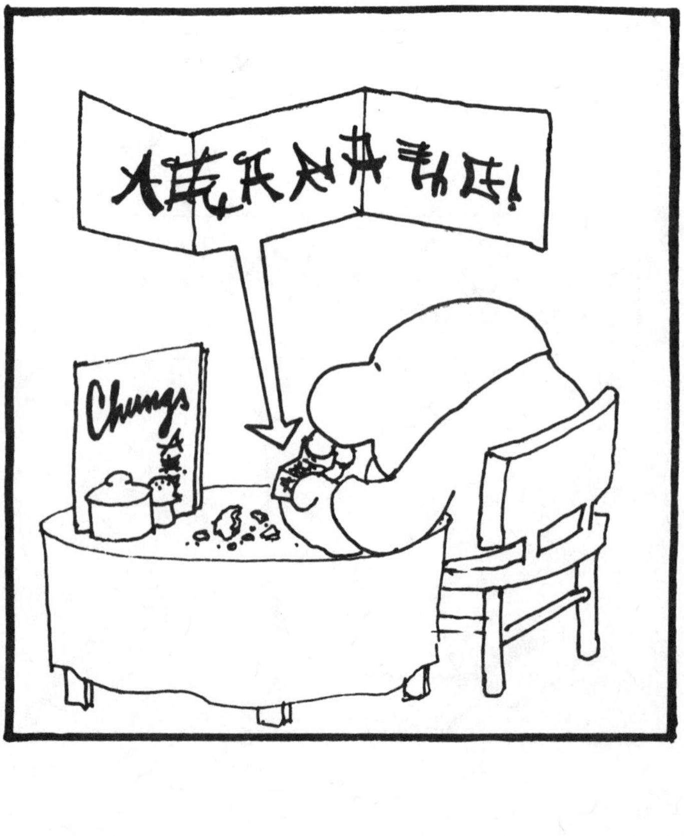
Chungs

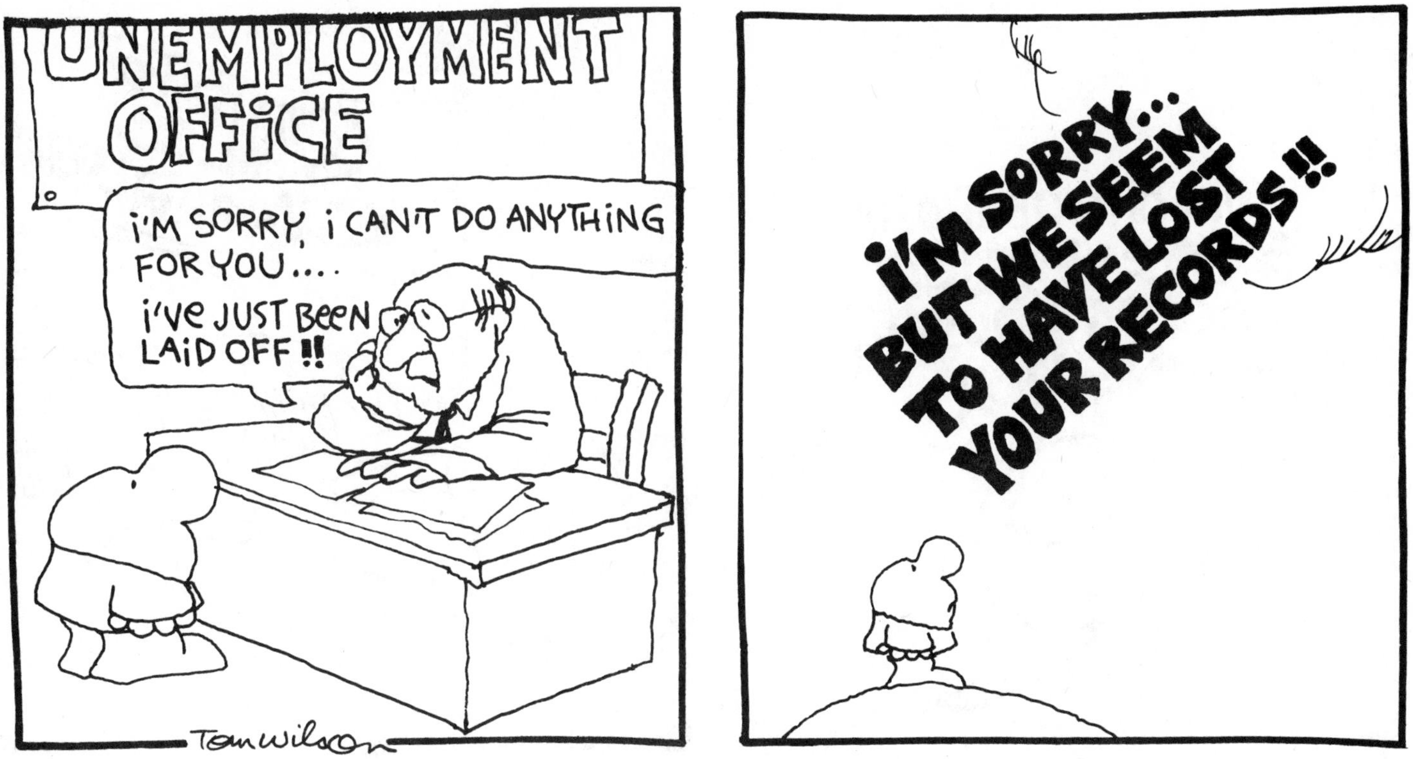
UNEMPLOYMENT OFFICE
I'M SORRY, I CAN'T DO ANYTHING FOR YOU.... I'VE JUST BEEN LAID OFF !!
Tom Wilson
I'M SORRY... BUT WE SEEM TO HAVE LOST YOUR RECORDS !!

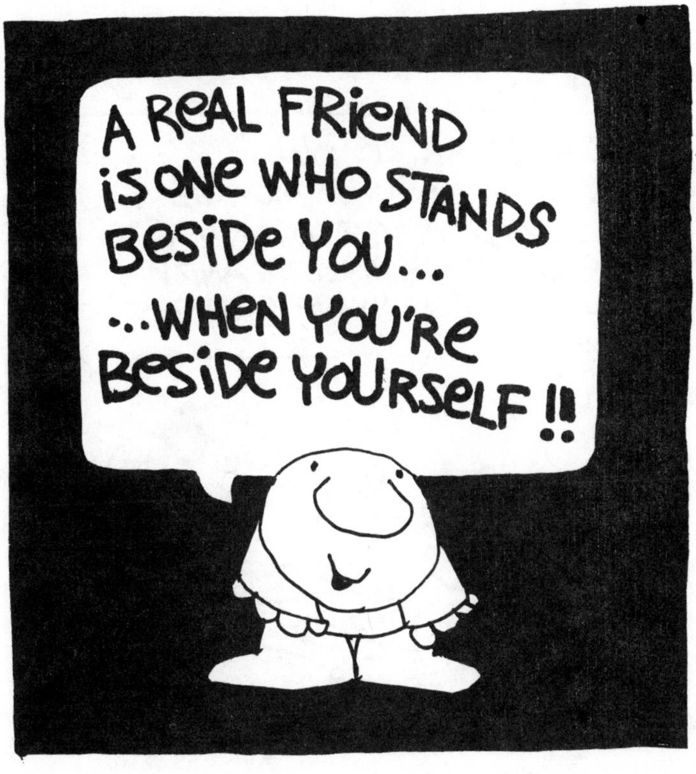
A REAL FRIEND IS ONE WHO STANDS BESIDE YOU... ...WHEN YOU'RE BESIDE YOURSELF !!

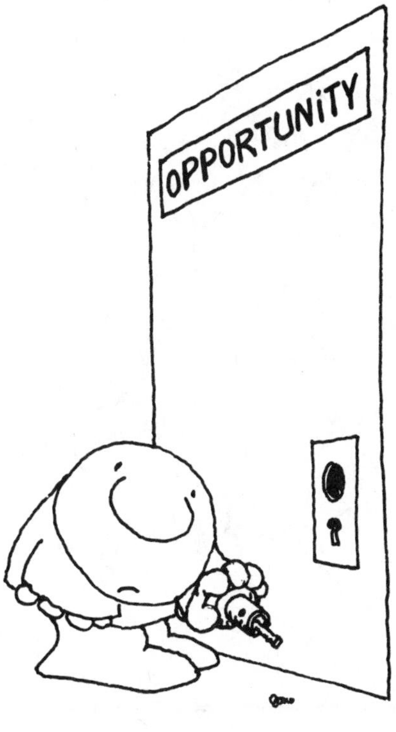
OPPORTUNITY

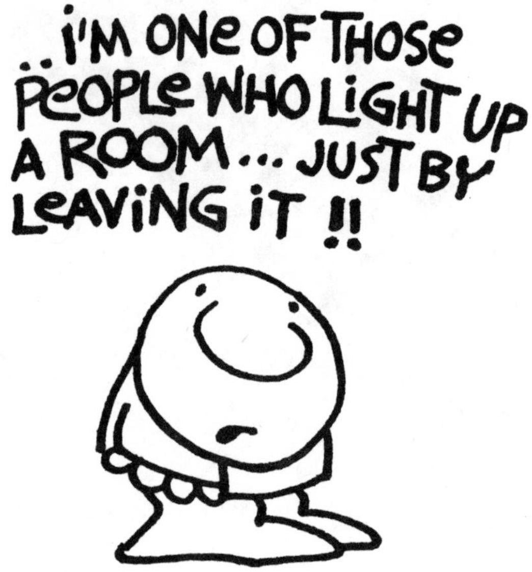
..i'M ONE OF THOSE PEOPLE WHO LIGHT UP A ROOM... JUST BY LEAVING IT !!

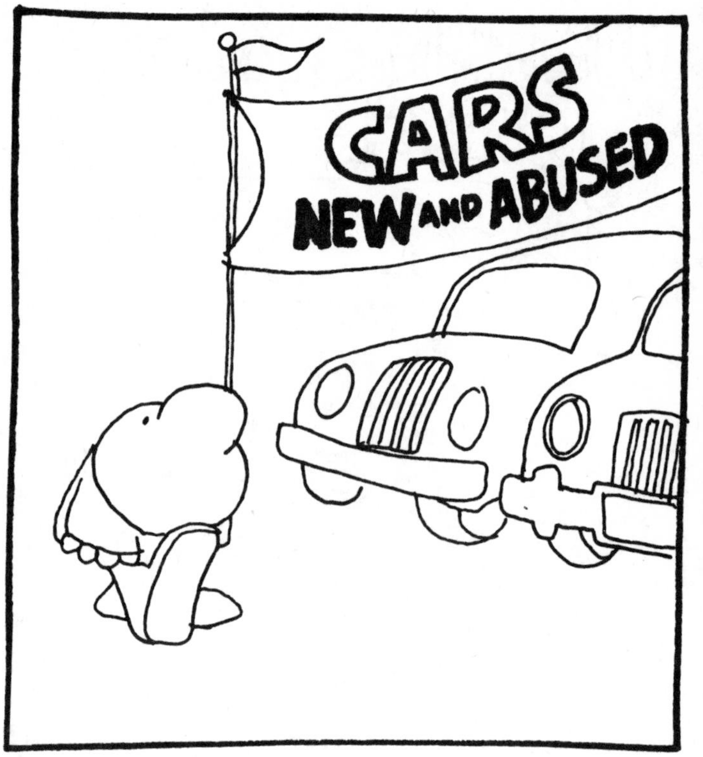
CARS
NEW AND ABUSED

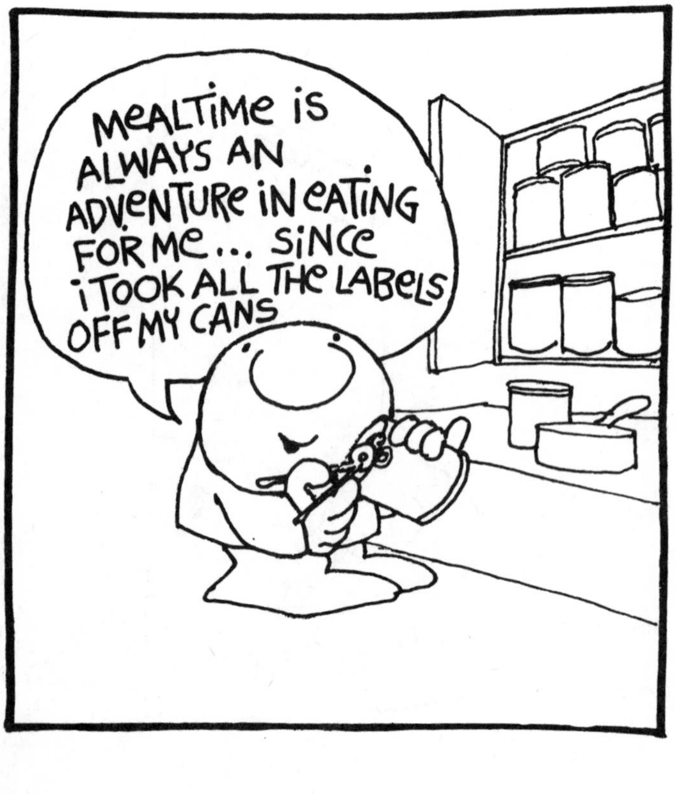
MEALTIME IS ALWAYS AN ADVENTURE IN EATING FOR ME... SINCE i TOOK ALL THE LABELS OFF MY CANS

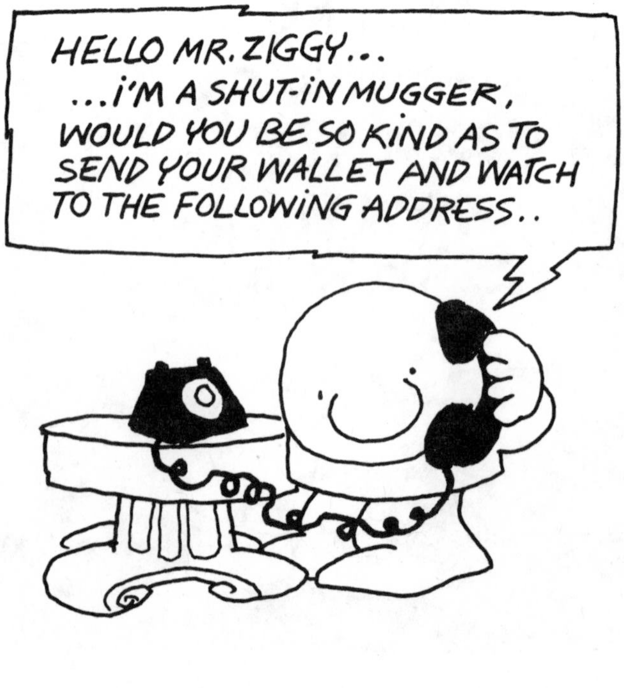
HELLO MR. ZIGGY... ...i'M A SHUT-IN MUGGER, WOULD YOU BE SO KIND AS TO SEND YOUR WALLET AND WATCH TO THE FOLLOWING ADDRESS..

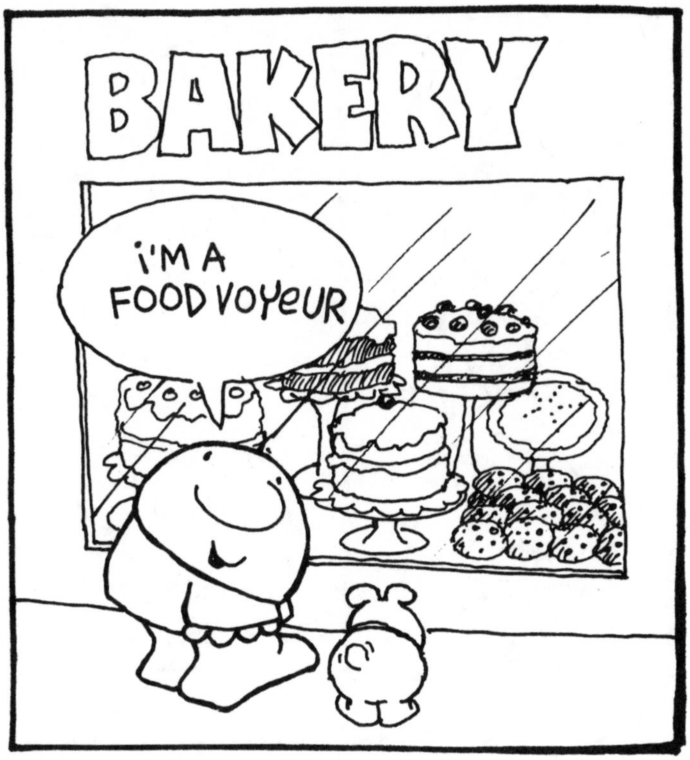
BAKERY
i'M A FOOD VOYeUR

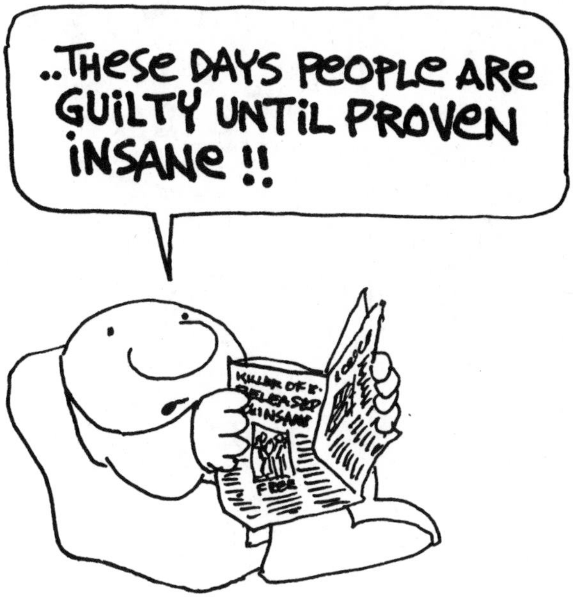
..THeSe DAYS PeOPLe ARe GUiLTY UNTiL PROVeN iNSANe !!

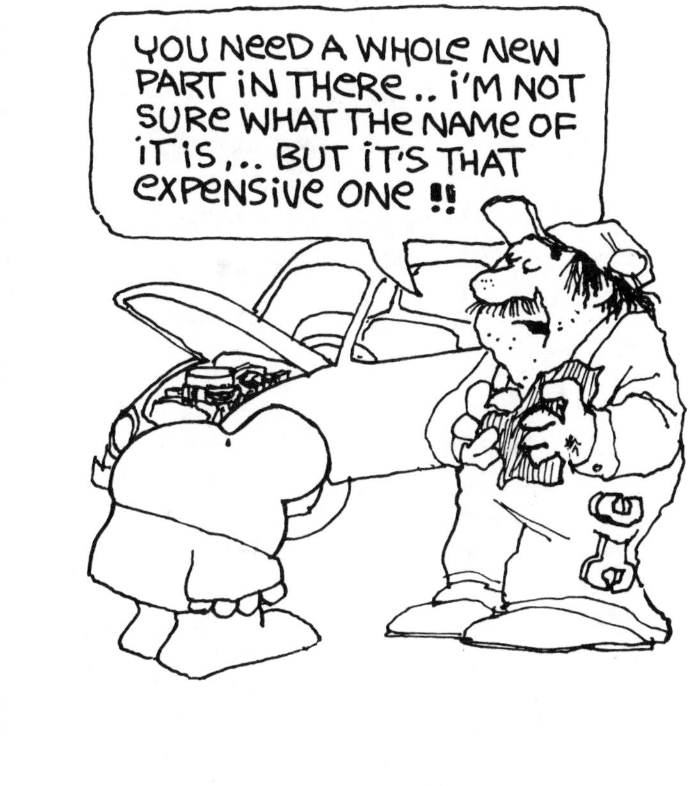
YOU NeeD A WHOLe NeW PART iN THeRe .. i'M NOT SURe WHAT THe NAMe OF iT iS ,.. BUT iT'S THAT eXPeNSiVe ONe !!

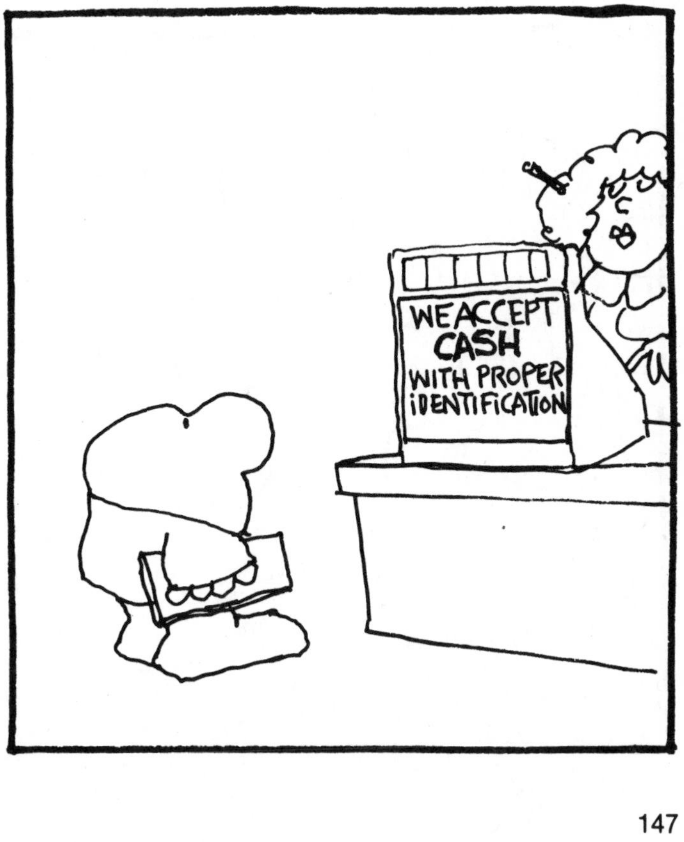
WE ACCEPT CASH WITH PROPER iDENTIFICATION

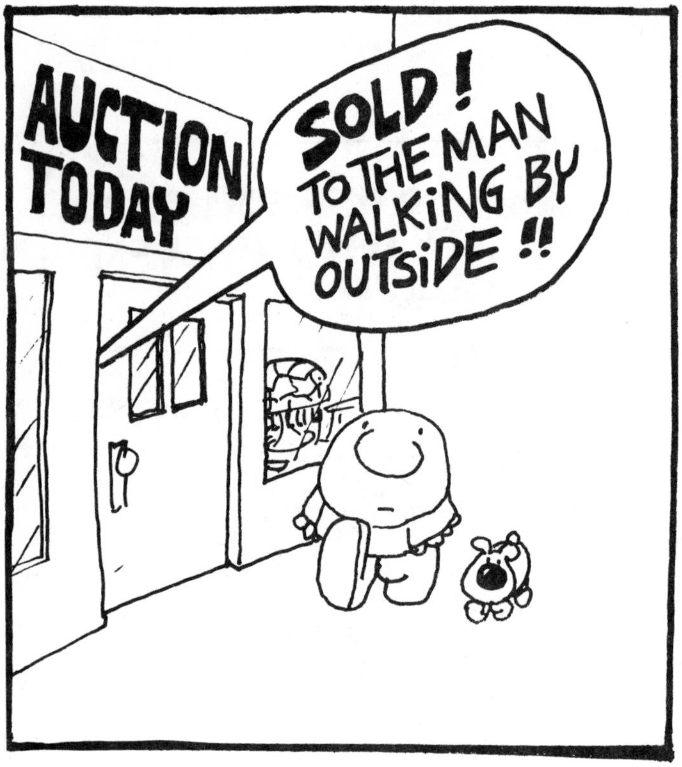
AUCTION TODAY
SOLD ! TO THE MAN WALKING BY OUTSIDE !!

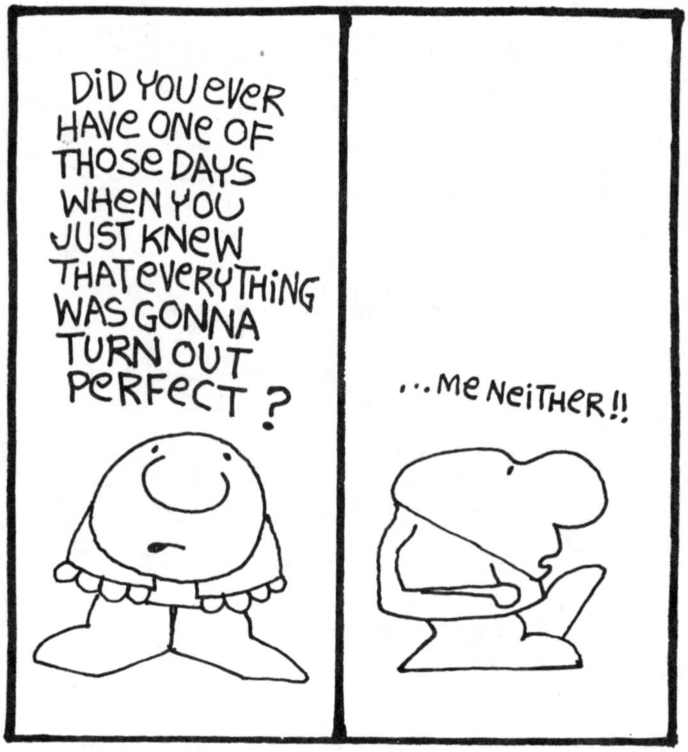
DID YOU EVER HAVE ONE OF THOSE DAYS WHEN YOU JUST KNEW THAT EVERYTHING WAS GONNA TURN OUT PERFECT ?
...ME NEITHER !!

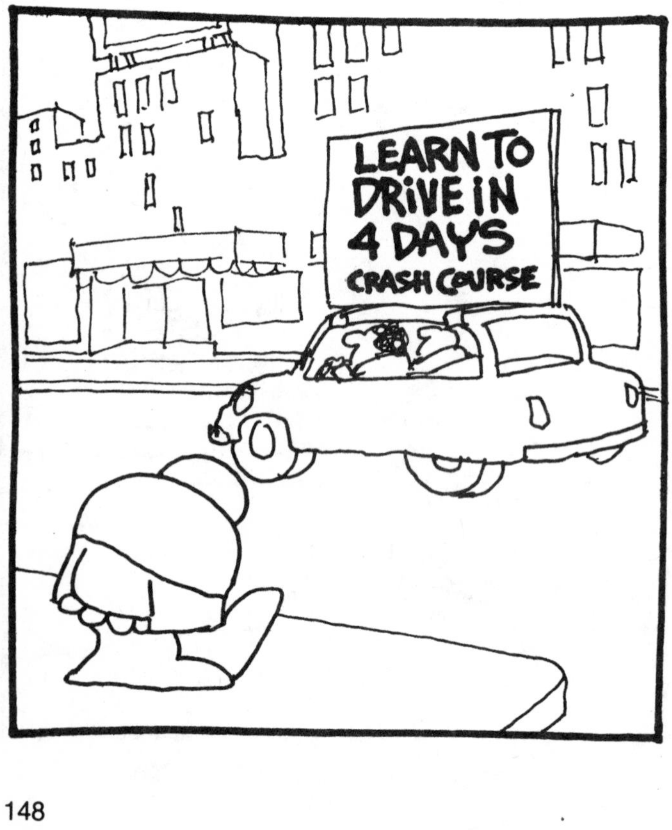
LEARN TO DRIVE IN 4 DAYS
CRASH COURSE

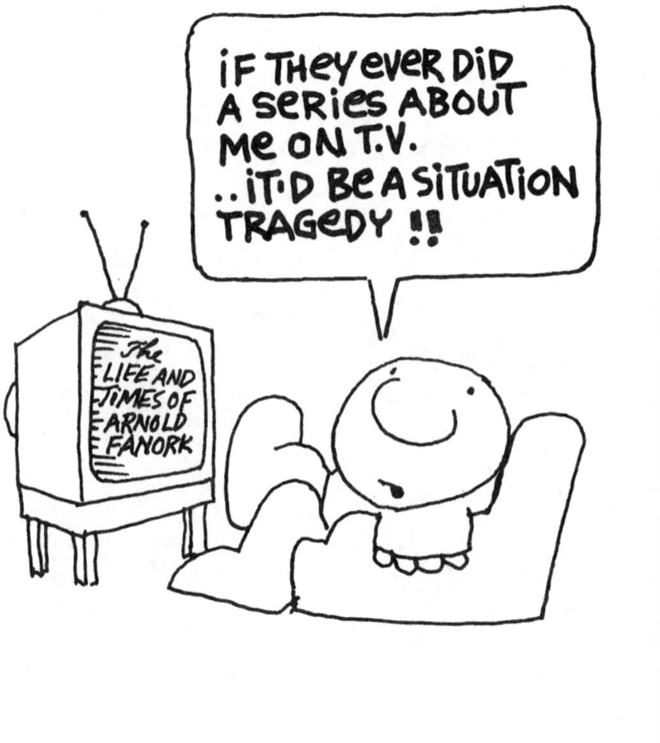
The LIFE AND TIMES OF ARNOLD FANORK
IF THEY EVER DID A SERIES ABOUT ME ON T.V. ..IT'D BE A SITUATION TRAGEDY !!

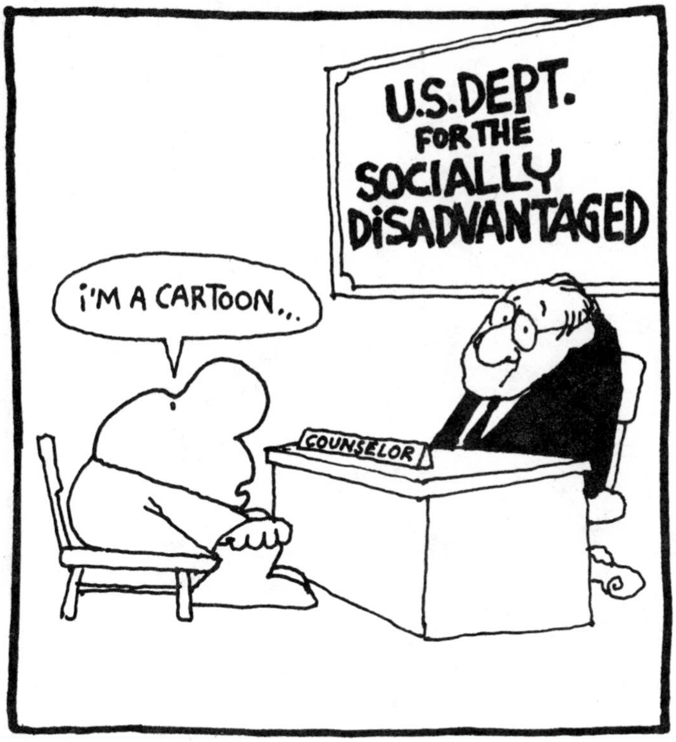
U.S. DEPT. FOR THE SOCIALLY DiSADVANTAGED
i'M A CARTOON...
COUNSELOR

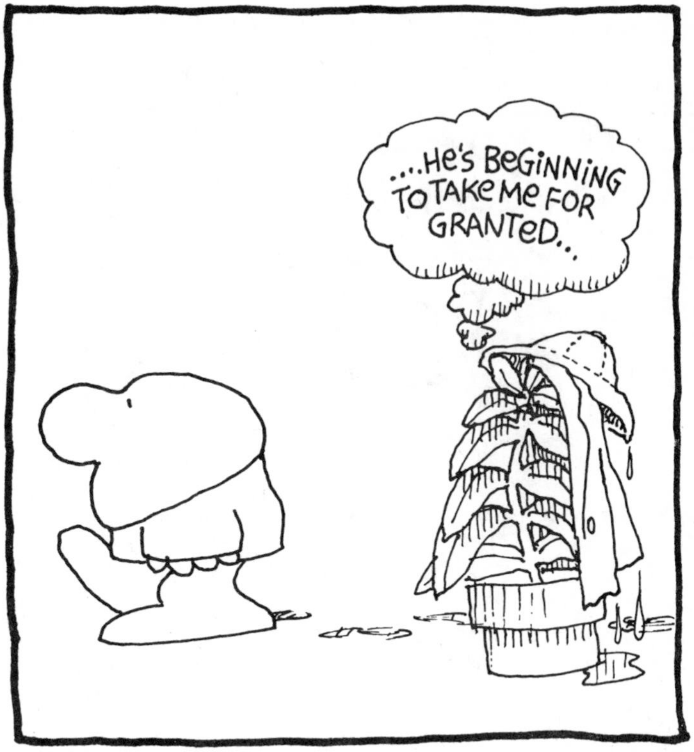
....He's BeGiNNiNG TO TAKE Me FOR GRANTeD...

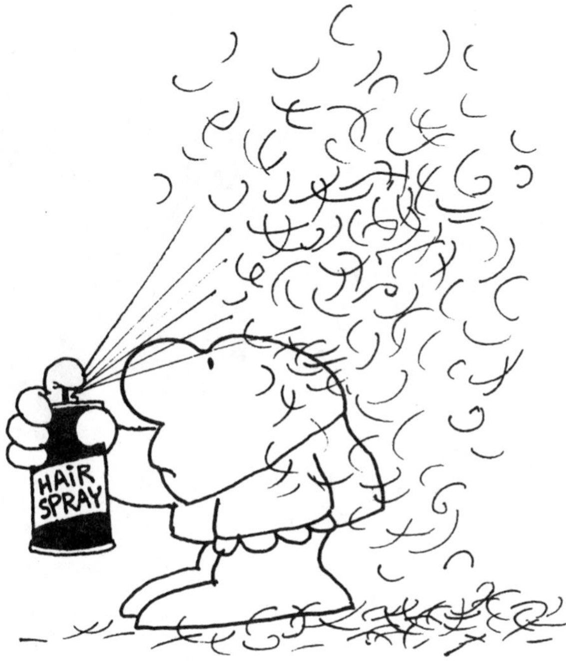
HAIR SPRAY

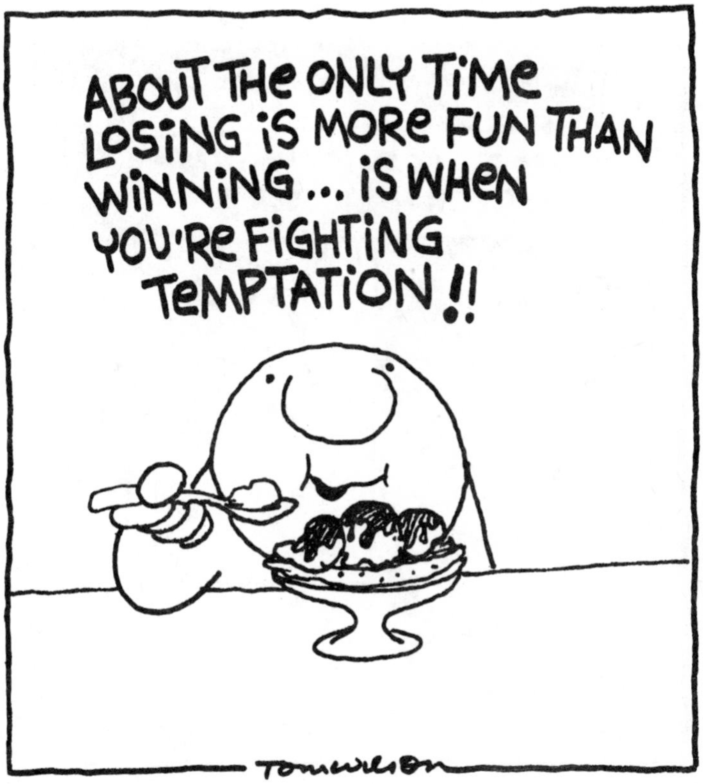
ABOUT THe ONLY TiMe LOSiNG iS MORe FUN THAN WiNNiNG ... iS WHeN YOU'Re FiGHTiNG TeMPTATiON !!
TOM WILSON

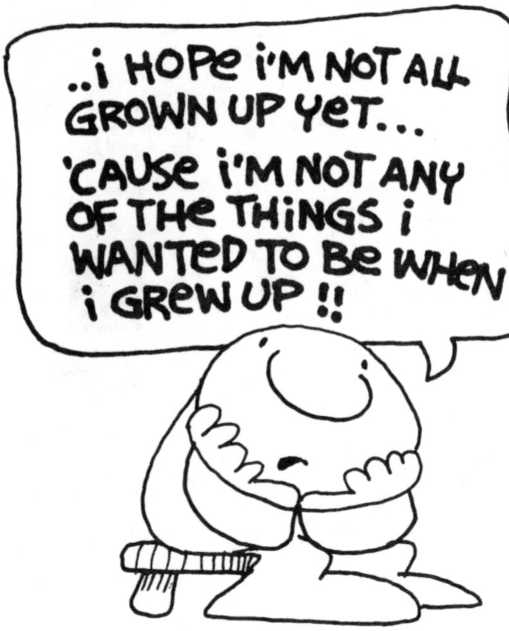
..i HOPe i'M NOT ALL GROWN UP yeT... 'CAUSe i'M NOT ANY OF THe THiNGS i WANTeD TO Be WHeN i GReW UP !!

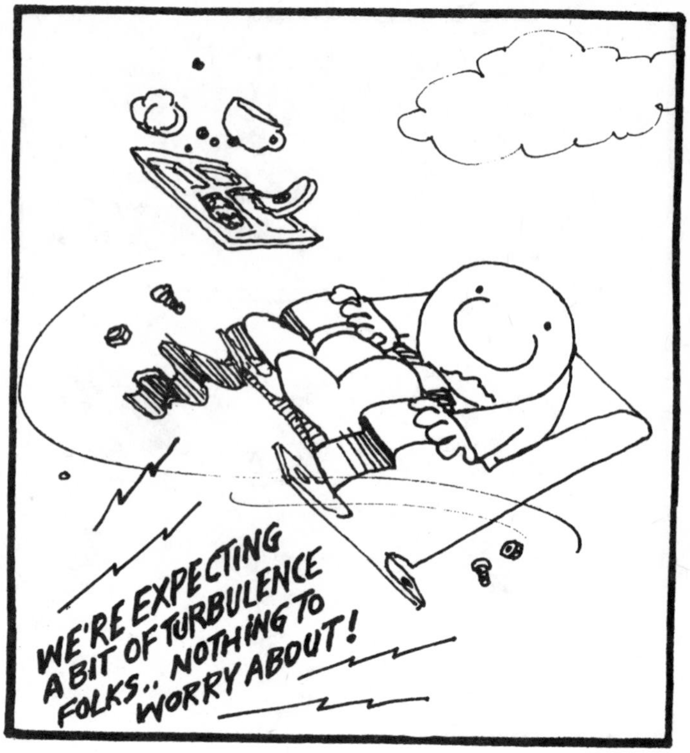
WE'RE EXPECTING A BIT OF TURBULENCE FOLKS.. NOTHING TO WORRY ABOUT!

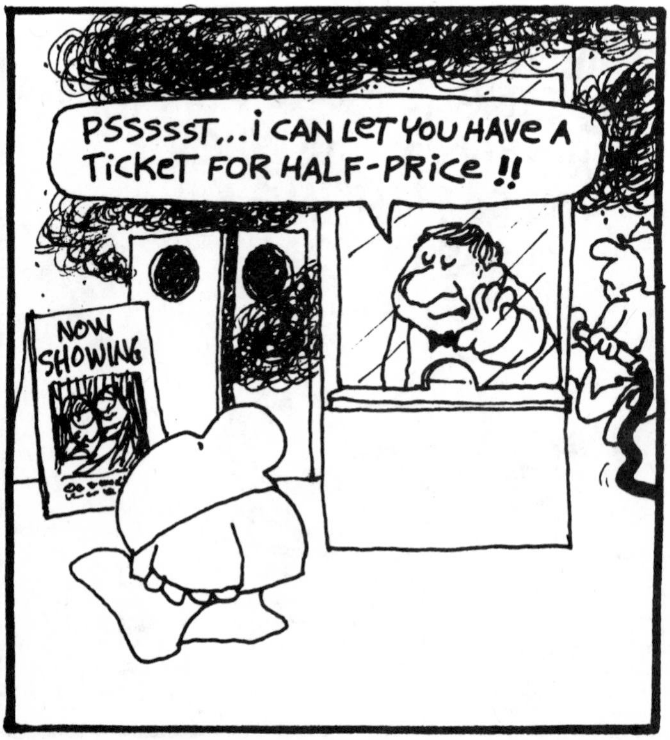
PSSSSST...i CAN LeT YOU HAVe A TiCKeT FOR HALF-PRiCe !!
NOW SHOWING

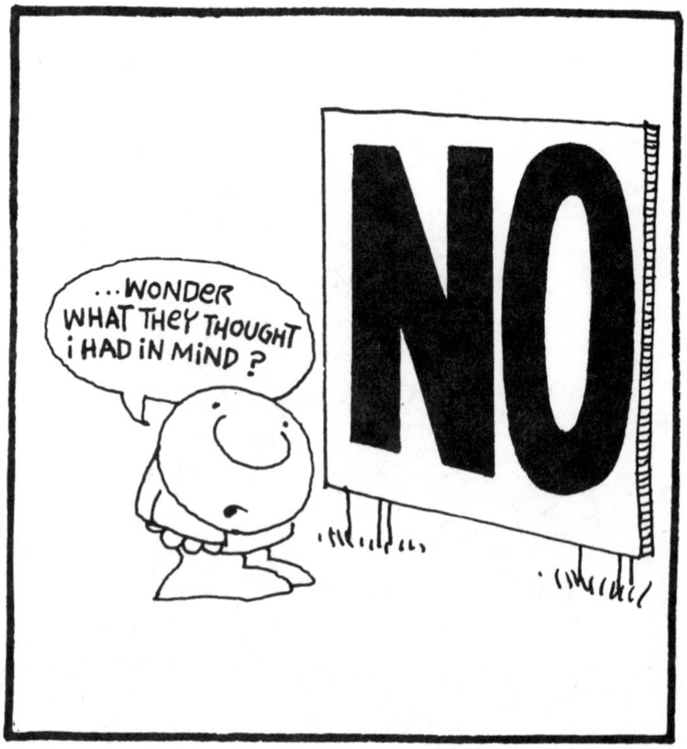
...WONDeR WHAT THeY THOUGHT i HAD iN MiND ?
NO

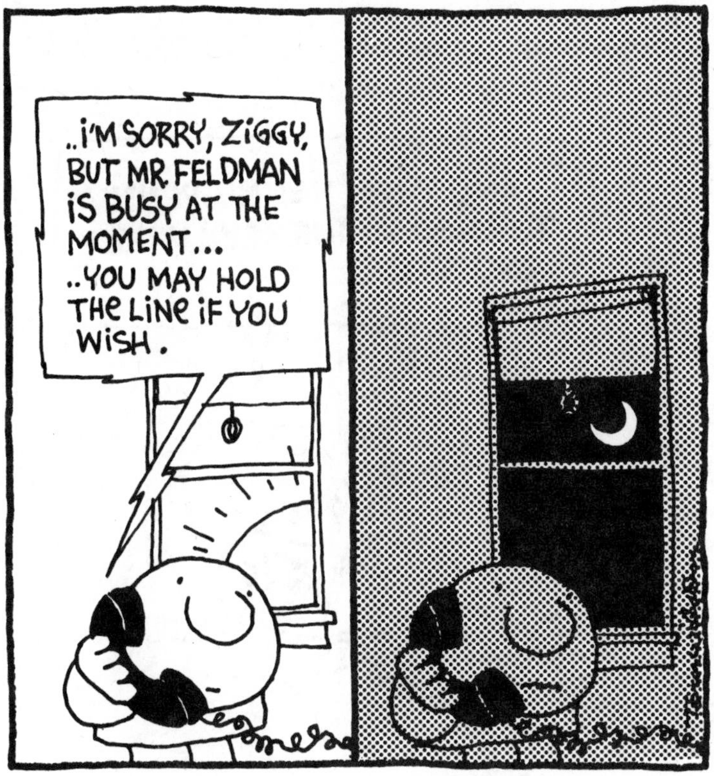
..I'M SORRY, ZIGGY, BUT MR. FELDMAN IS BUSY AT THE MOMENT... ..YOU MAY HOLD THE LINE IF YOU WISH.

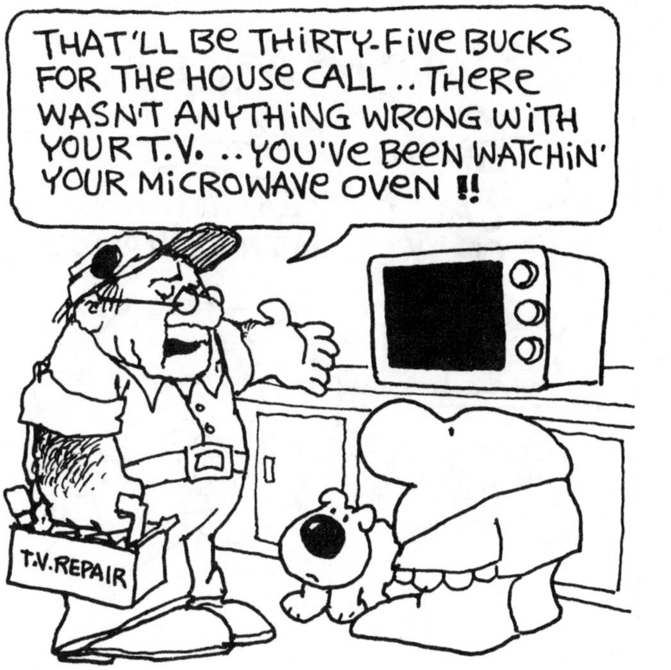
THAT'LL BE THIRTY-FIVE BUCKS FOR THE HOUSE CALL .. THERE WASN'T ANYTHING WRONG WITH YOUR T.V. .. YOU'VE BEEN WATCHIN' YOUR MICROWAVE OVEN !!
T.V. REPAIR

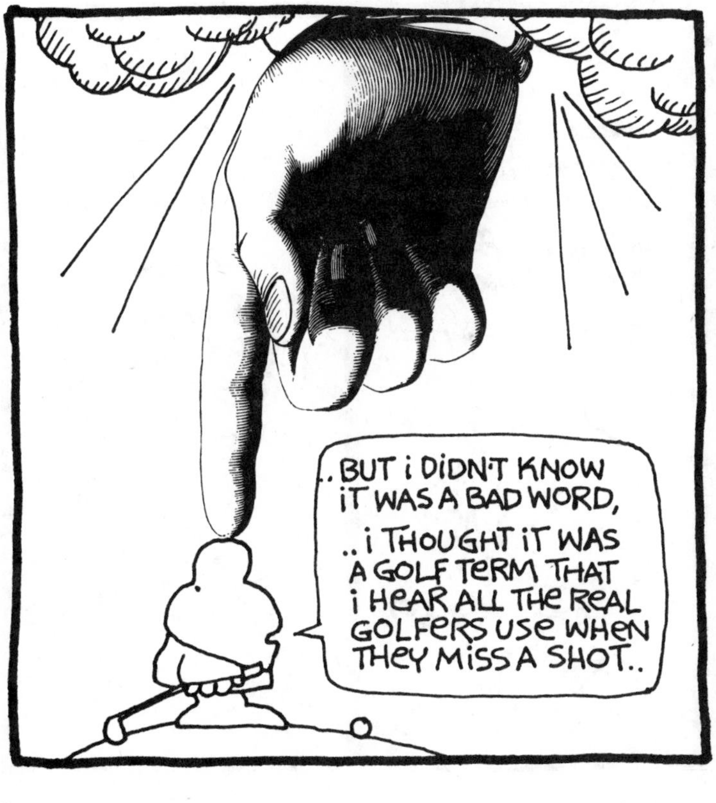
..BUT I DIDN'T KNOW IT WAS A BAD WORD, ..I THOUGHT IT WAS A GOLF TERM THAT I HEAR ALL THE REAL GOLFERS USE WHEN THEY MISS A SHOT..

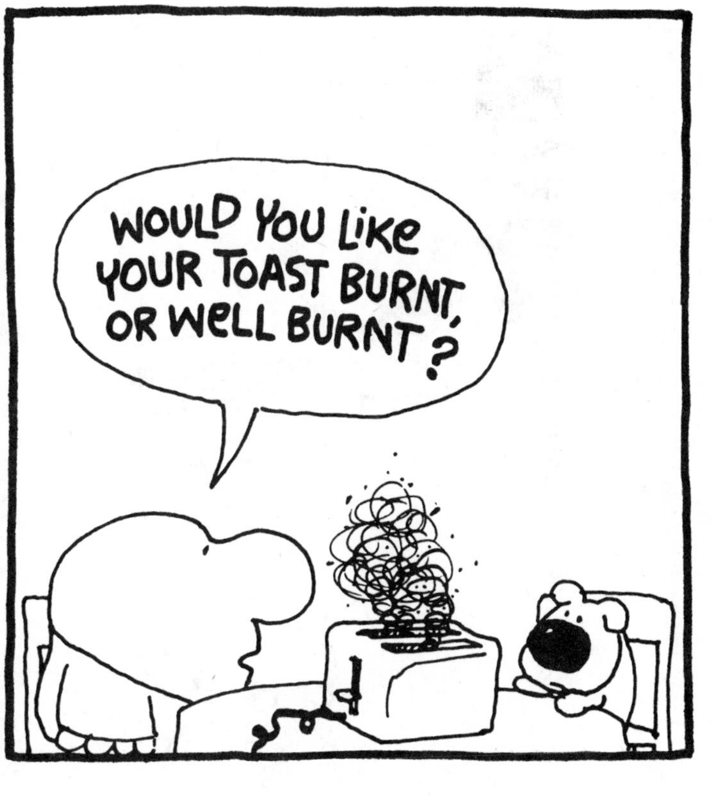
WOULD YOU LIKE YOUR TOAST BURNT, OR WELL BURNT?

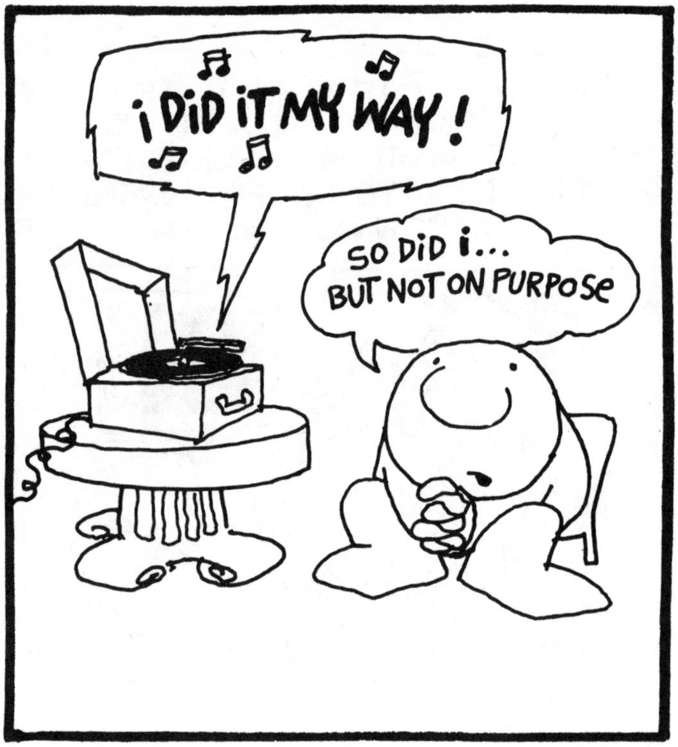
¡ DID IT MY WAY !
SO DID I... BUT NOT ON PURPOSE

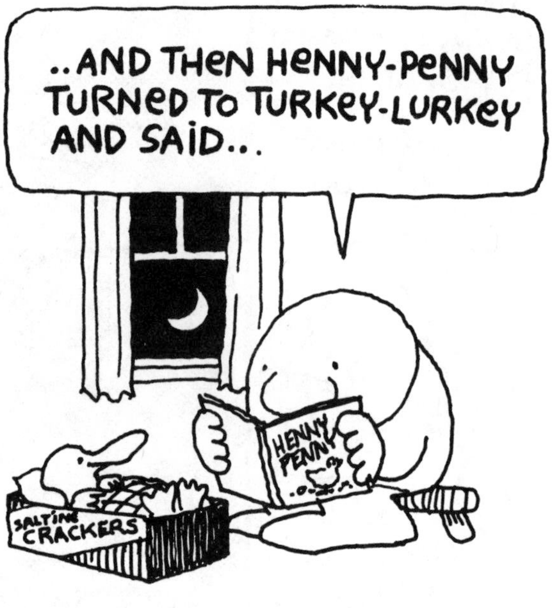
..AND THEN HENNY-PENNY TURNED TO TURKEY-LURKEY AND SAID...
HENNY PENNY
SALTINE CRACKERS

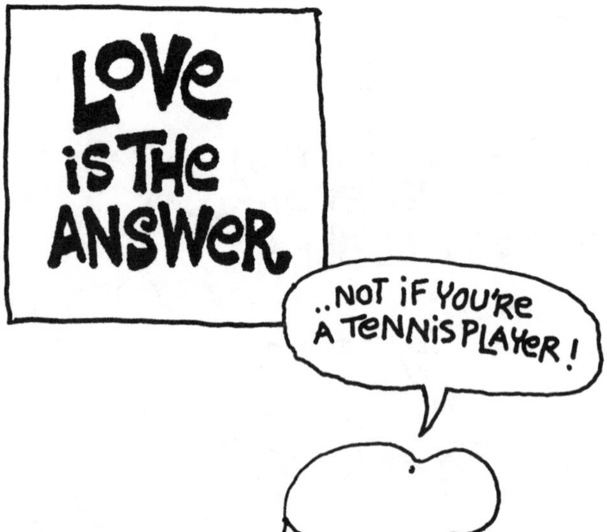
LOVE IS THE ANSWER
..NOT IF YOU'RE A TENNIS PLAYER !

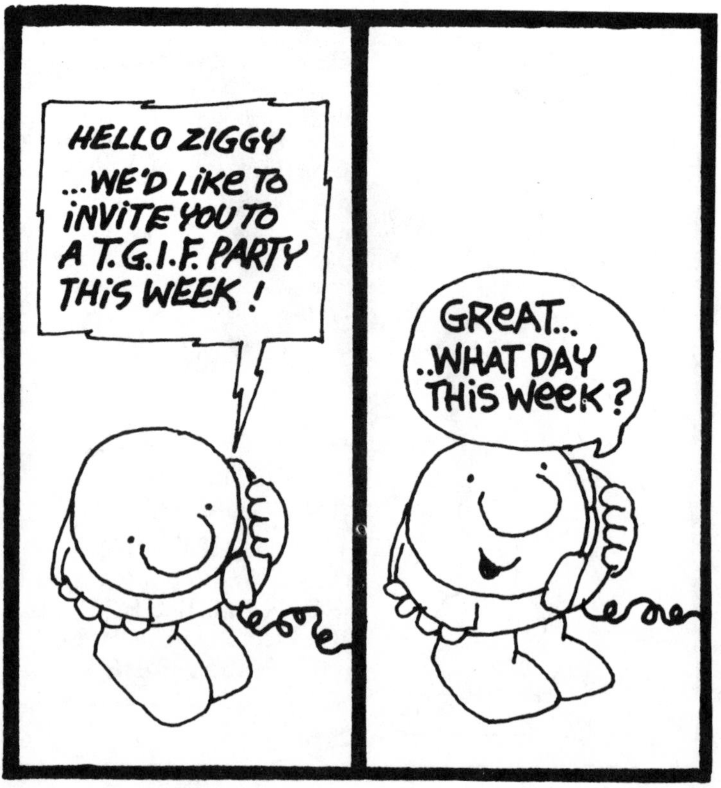
HELLO ZIGGY ...WE'D LIKE TO INVITE YOU TO A T.G.I.F. PARTY THIS WEEK !
GREAT... ..WHAT DAY THIS WEEK ?

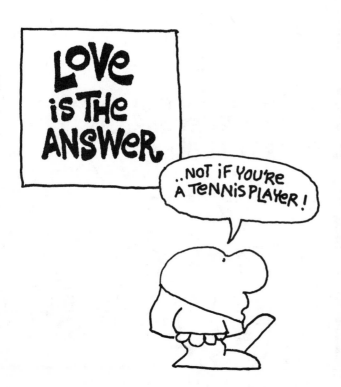

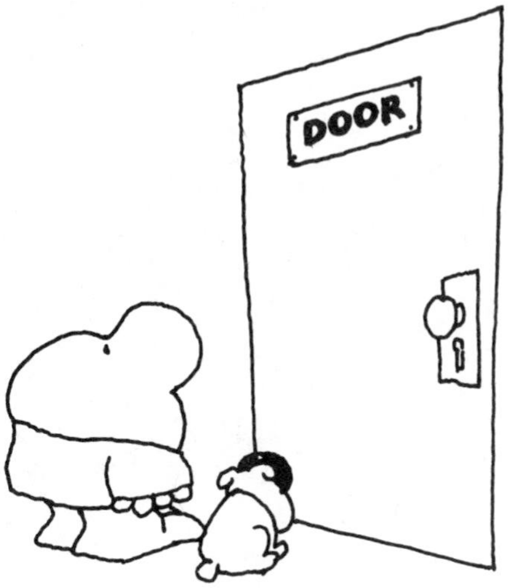
DOOR

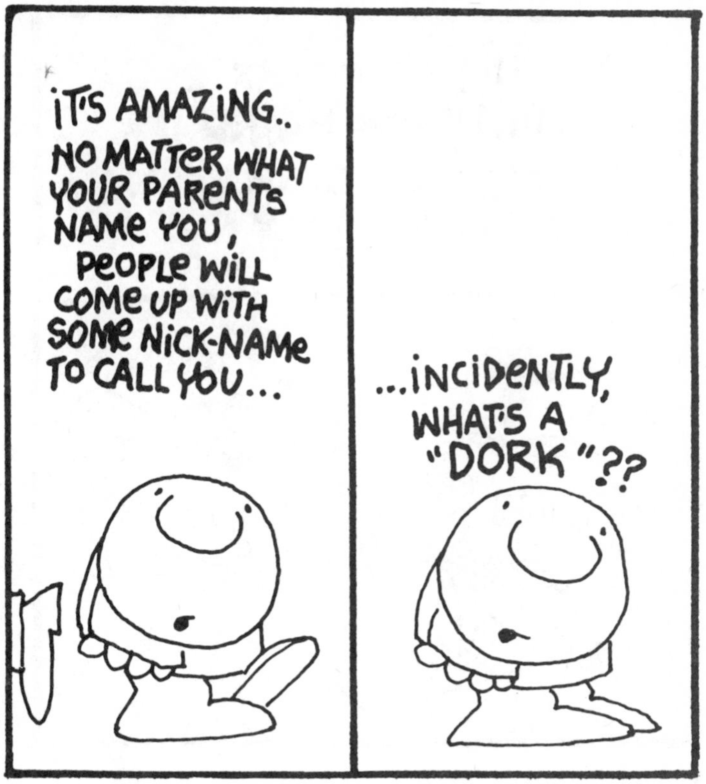
IT'S AMAZING.. NO MATTER WHAT YOUR PARENTS NAME YOU, PEOPLE WILL COME UP WITH SOME NICK-NAME TO CALL YOU...
...INCIDENTLY, WHAT'S A "DORK"??

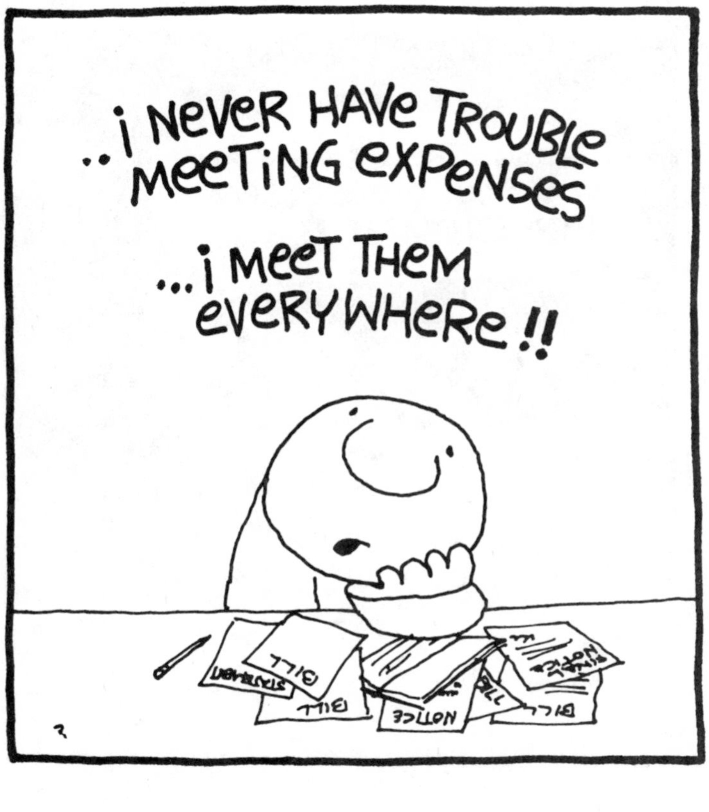
..i NEVER HAVE TROUBLE MEETING EXPENSES
...i MEET THEM EVERYWHERE !!

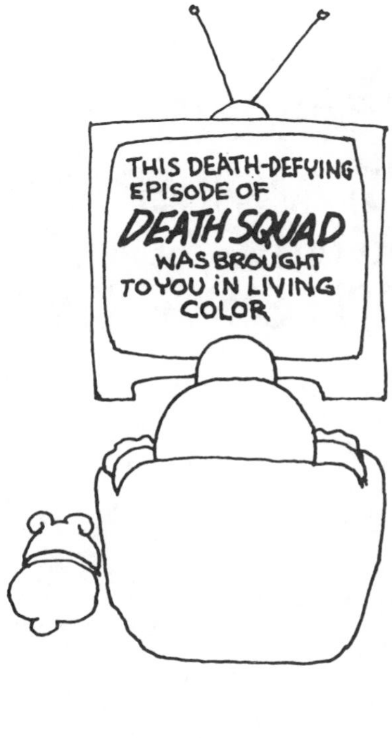
THIS DEATH-DEFYING EPISODE OF DEATH SQUAD WAS BROUGHT TO YOU iN LIVING COLOR

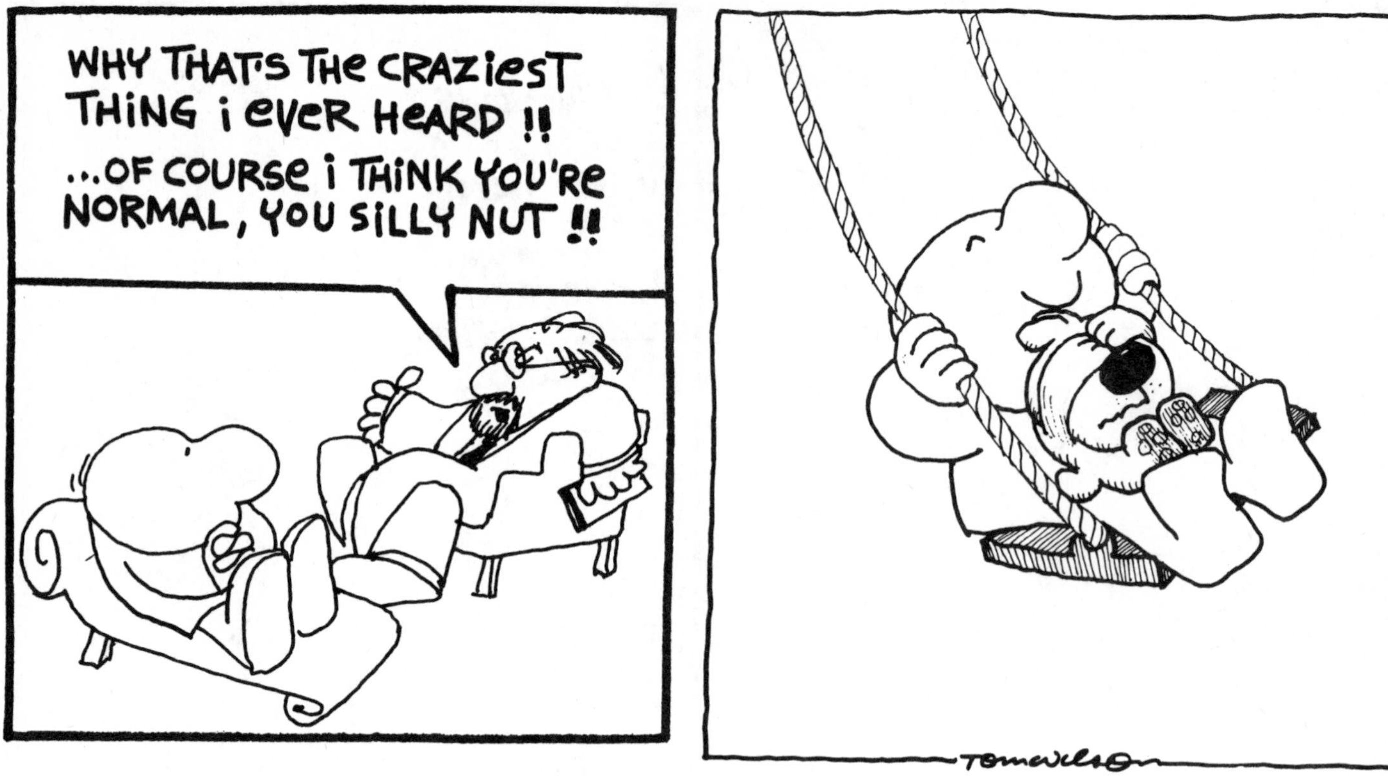
WHY THAT'S THE CRAZIEST THING i EVER HEARD !! ...OF COURSE i THINK YOU'RE NORMAL, YOU SILLY NUT !!

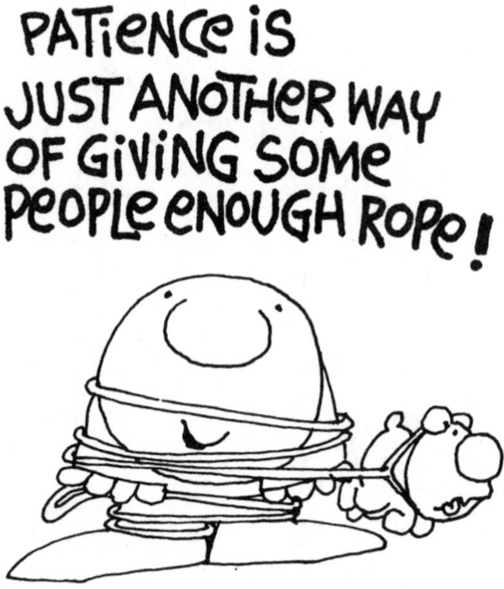
PATiENCE iS JUST ANOTHER WAY OF GiViNG SOME PEOPLE ENOUGH ROPE!

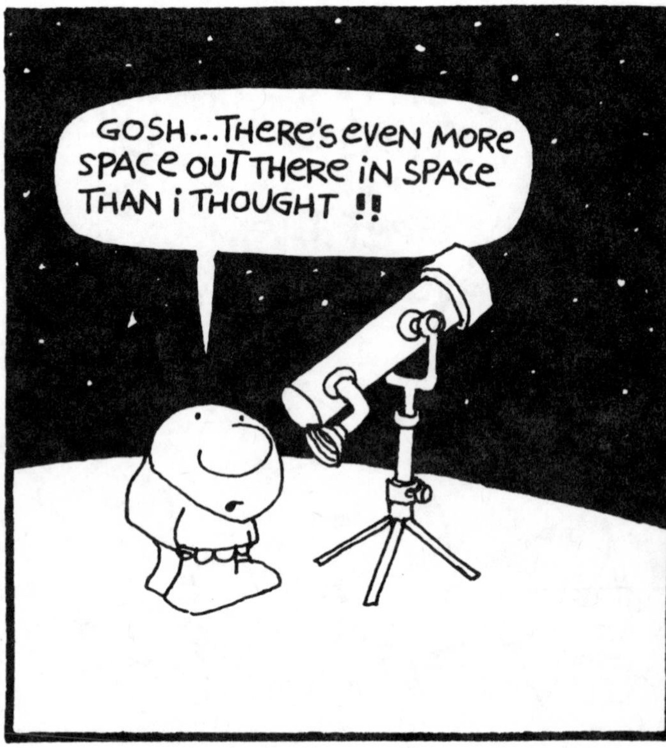
GOSH...THERE'S EVEN MORE SPACE OUT THERE iN SPACE THAN i THOUGHT !!

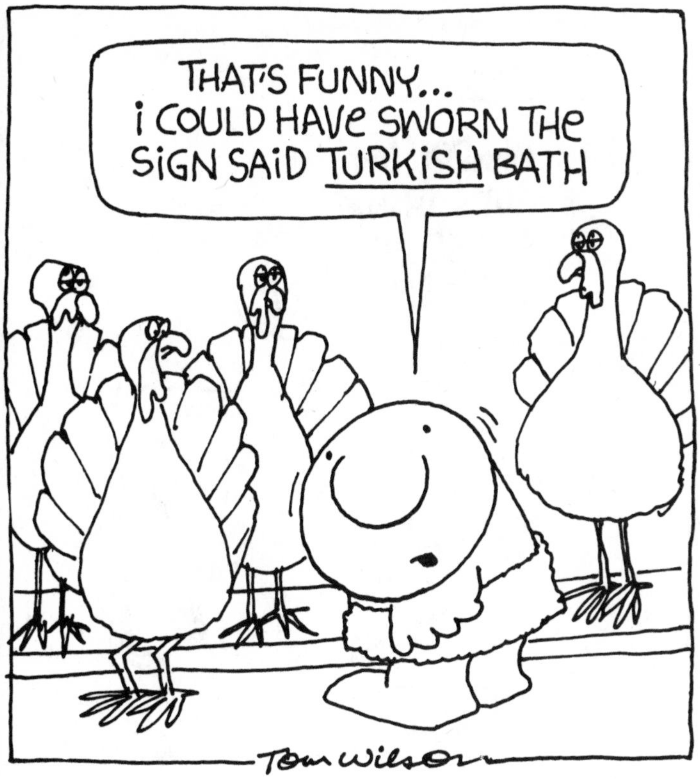
THAT'S FUNNY...
i COULD HAVE SWORN THE SIGN SAID TURKISH BATH
Tom Wilson

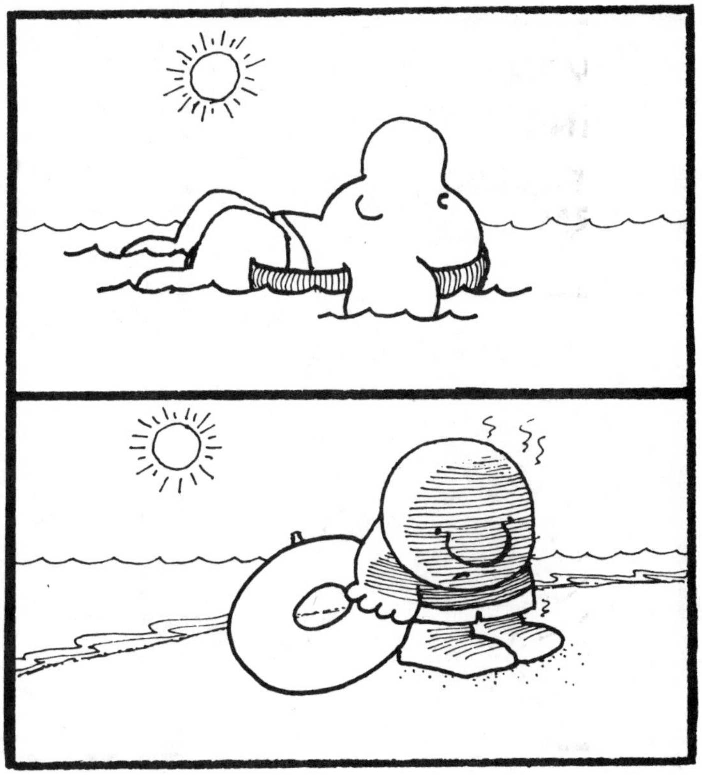

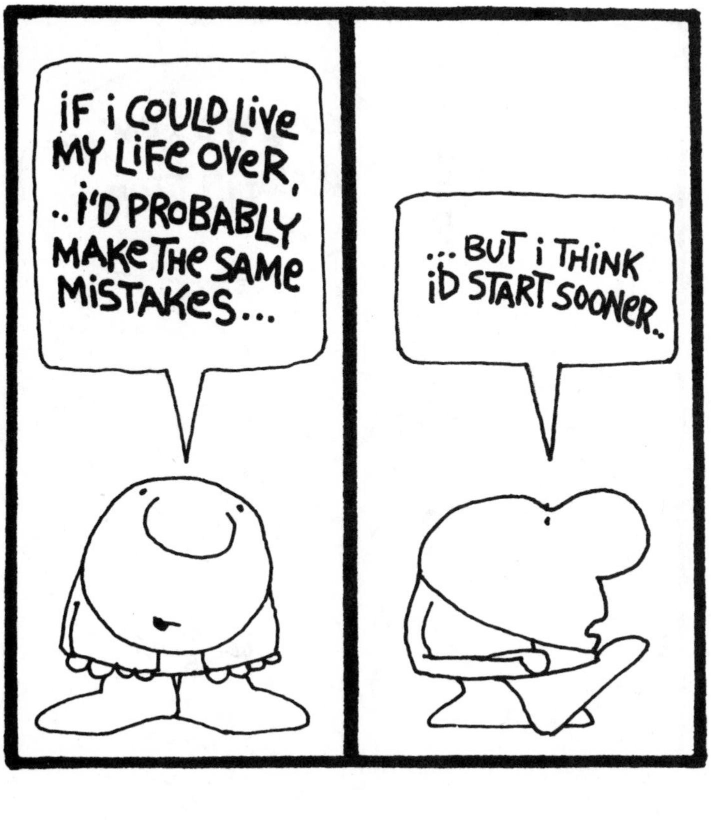
iF i COULD LiVE MY LiFE OVER, ..i'D PROBABLY MAKE THE SAME MiSTAKES...
...BUT i THiNK iD START SOONER..

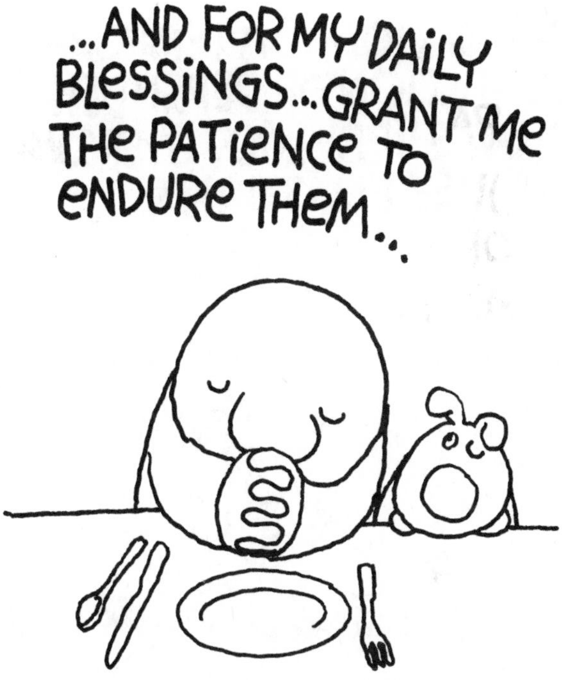
...AND FOR MY DAiLY BLESSiNGS...GRANT ME THE PATiENCE TO ENDURE THEM...

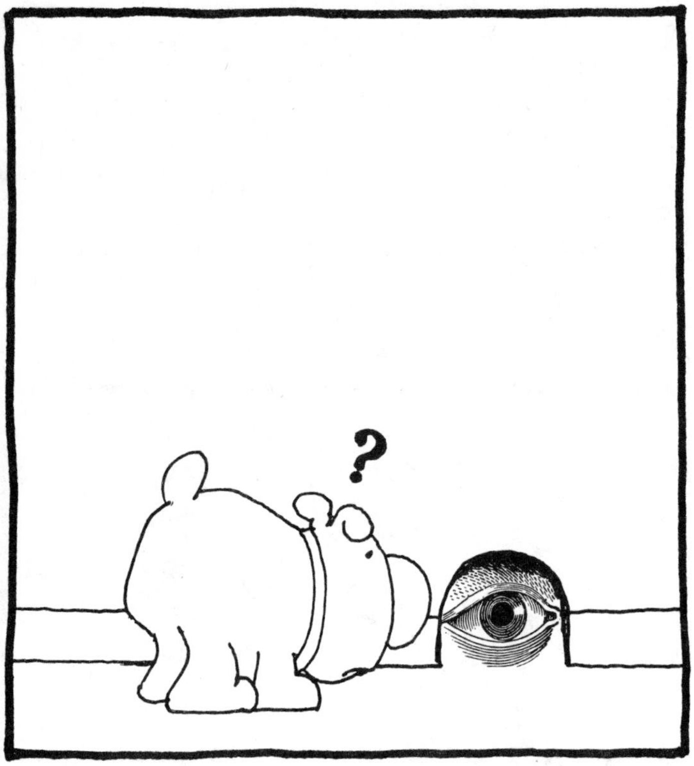
?

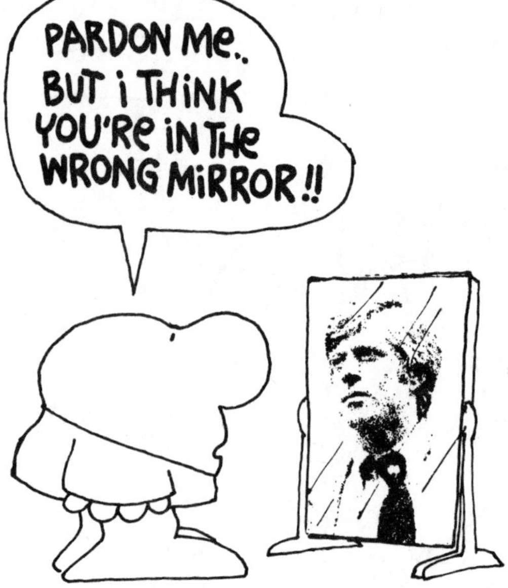
PARDON ME.. BUT I THINK YOU'RE IN THE WRONG MIRROR !!

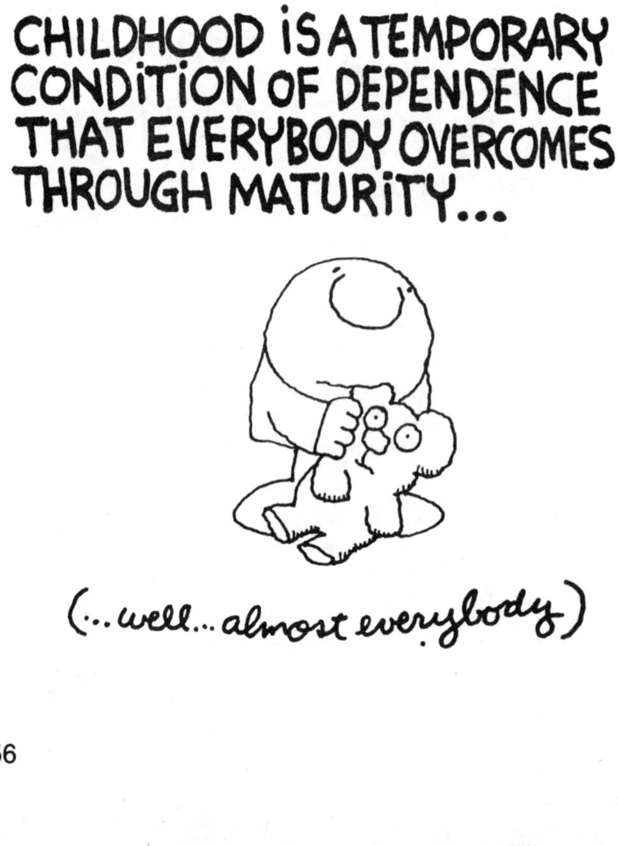
CHILDHOOD IS A TEMPORARY CONDITION OF DEPENDENCE THAT EVERYBODY OVERCOMES THROUGH MATURITY...
(...well...almost everybody)

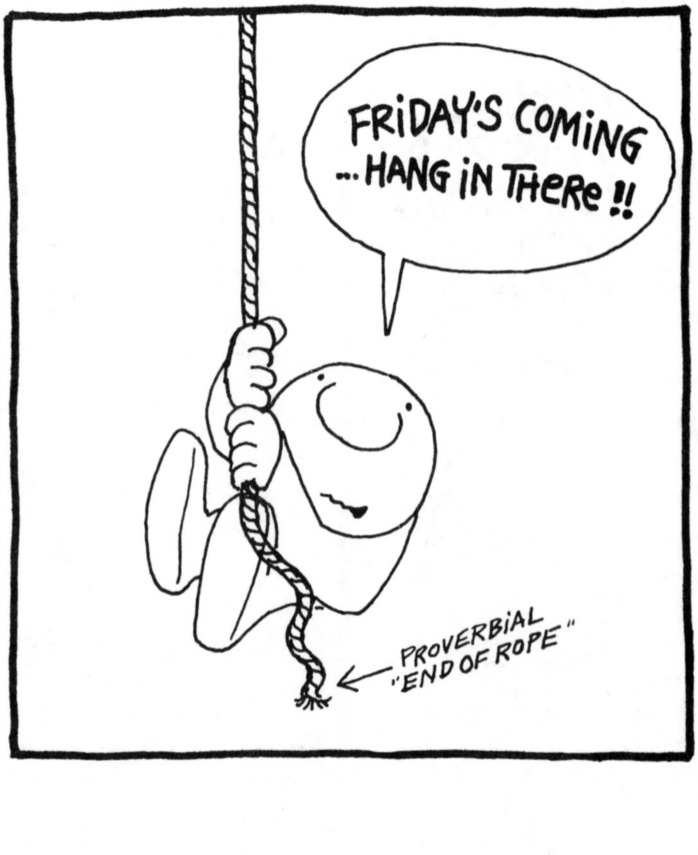
FRIDAY'S COMING ...HANG IN THERE !!
PROVERBIAL "END OF ROPE"

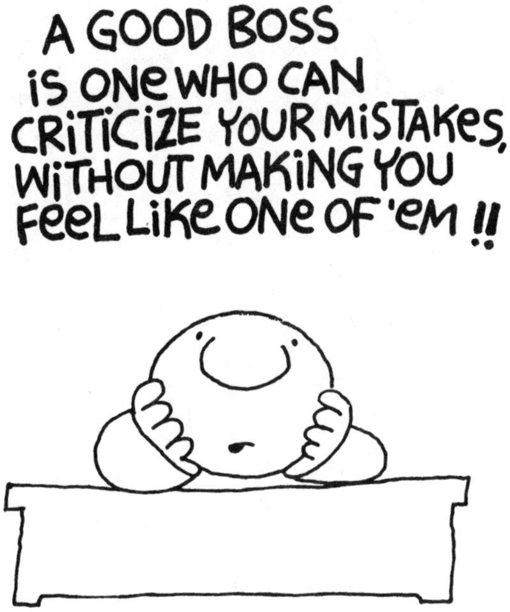
A GOOD BOSS IS ONE WHO CAN CRITICIZE YOUR MISTAKES, WITHOUT MAKING YOU FEEL LIKE ONE OF 'EM !!

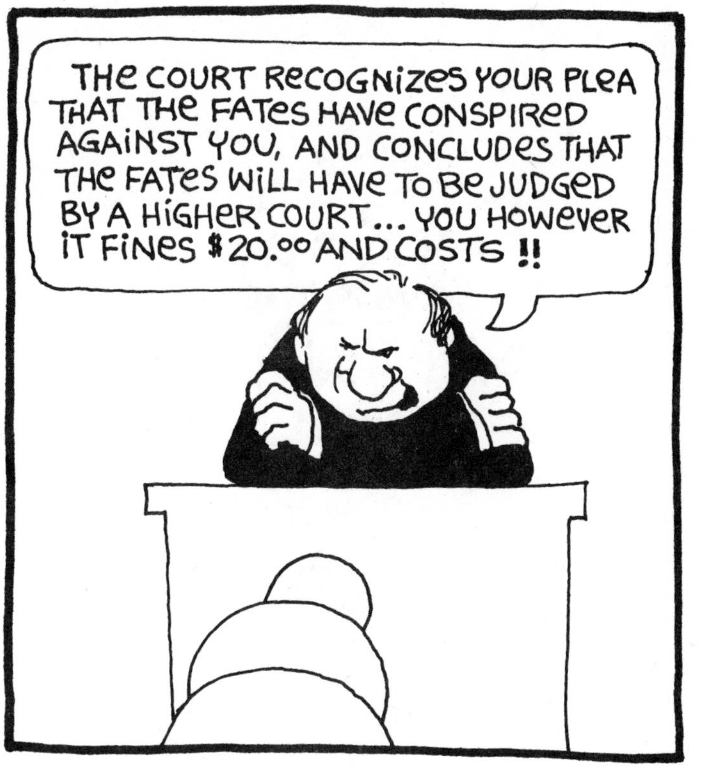
THE COURT RECOGNIZES YOUR PLEA THAT THE FATES HAVE CONSPIRED AGAINST YOU, AND CONCLUDES THAT THE FATES WILL HAVE TO BE JUDGED BY A HIGHER COURT... YOU HOWEVER IT FINES $20.00 AND COSTS !!

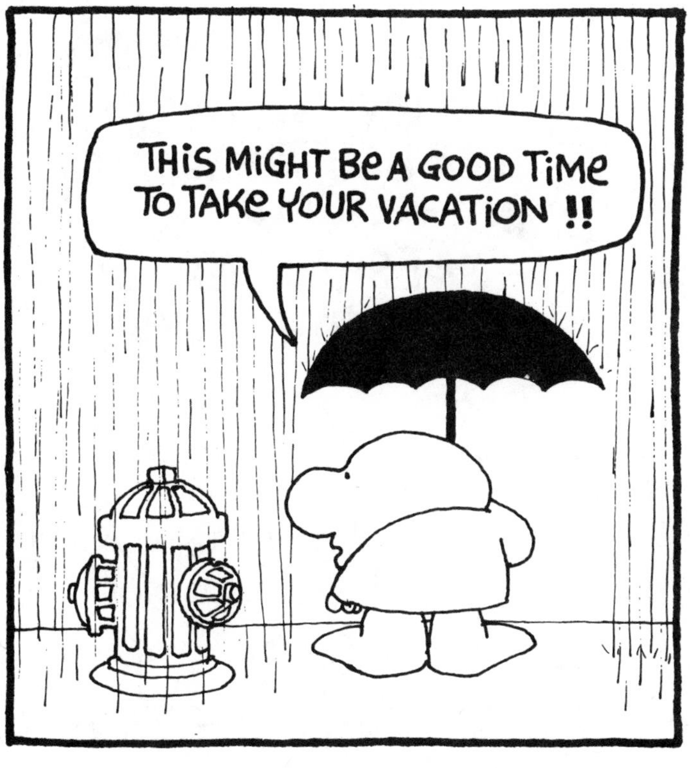
THIS MIGHT BE A GOOD TIME TO TAKE YOUR VACATION !!

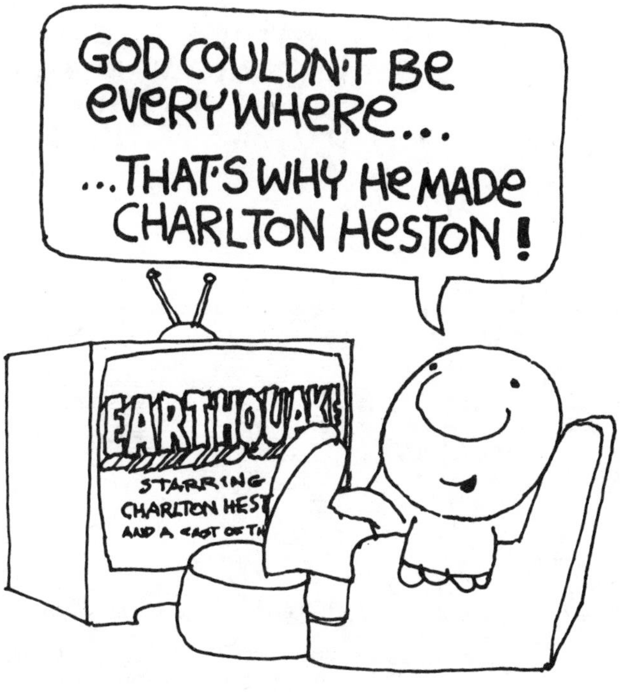
GOD COULDN'T BE EVERYWHERE... ...THAT'S WHY HE MADE CHARLTON HESTON !
STARRING
CHARLTON HEST

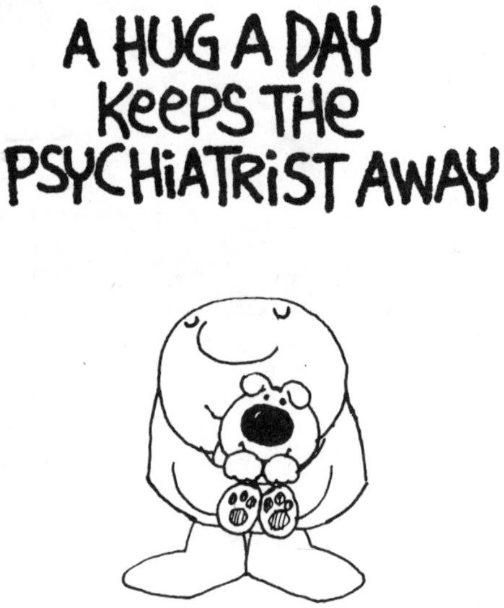
A HUG A DAY KEEPS THE PSYCHIATRIST AWAY

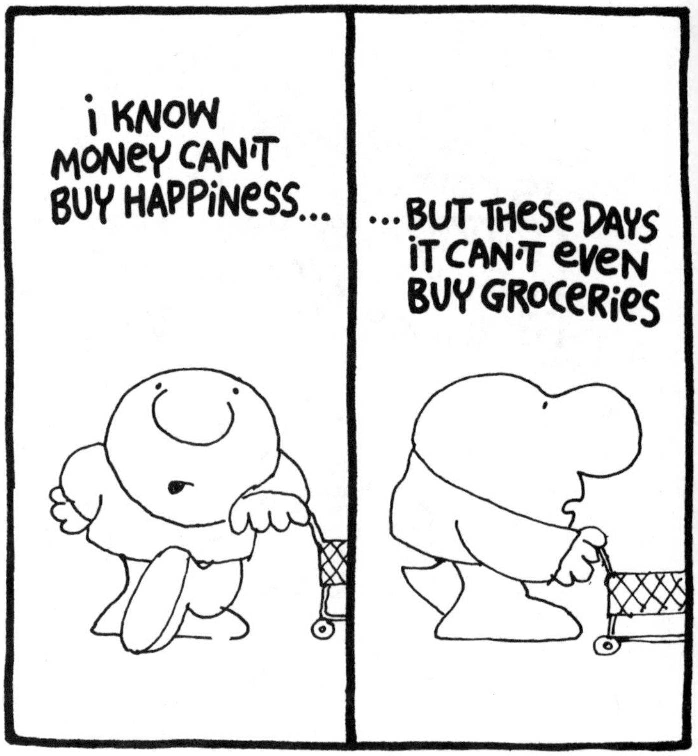
I KNOW MONEY CAN'T BUY HAPPINESS...
...BUT THESE DAYS IT CAN'T EVEN BUY GROCERIES

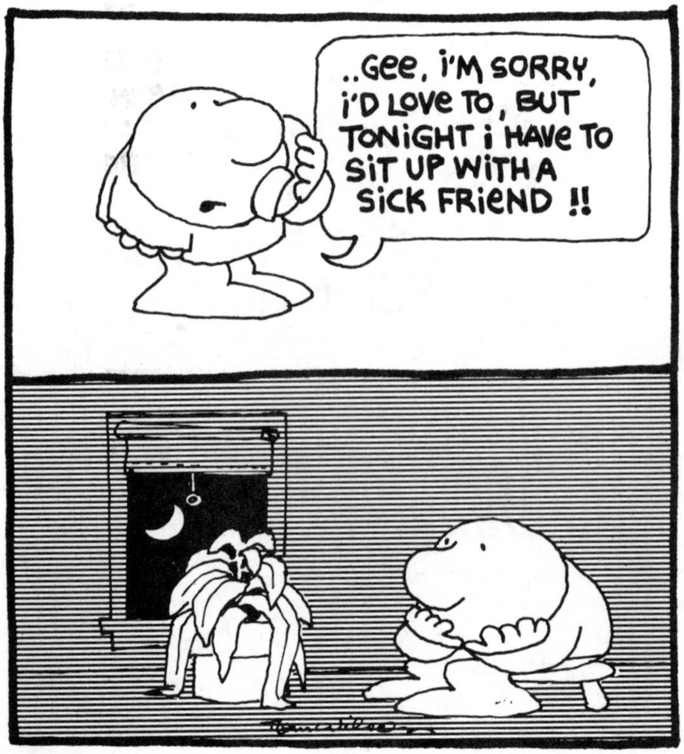
..GEE, I'M SORRY, I'D LOVE TO, BUT TONIGHT I HAVE TO SIT UP WITH A SICK FRIEND !!

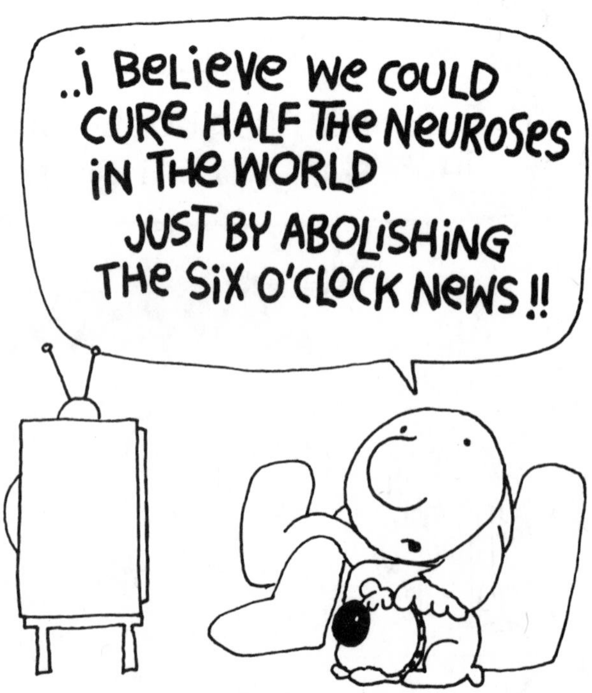
..I BELIEVE WE COULD CURE HALF THE NEUROSES IN THE WORLD JUST BY ABOLISHING THE SIX O'CLOCK NEWS !!

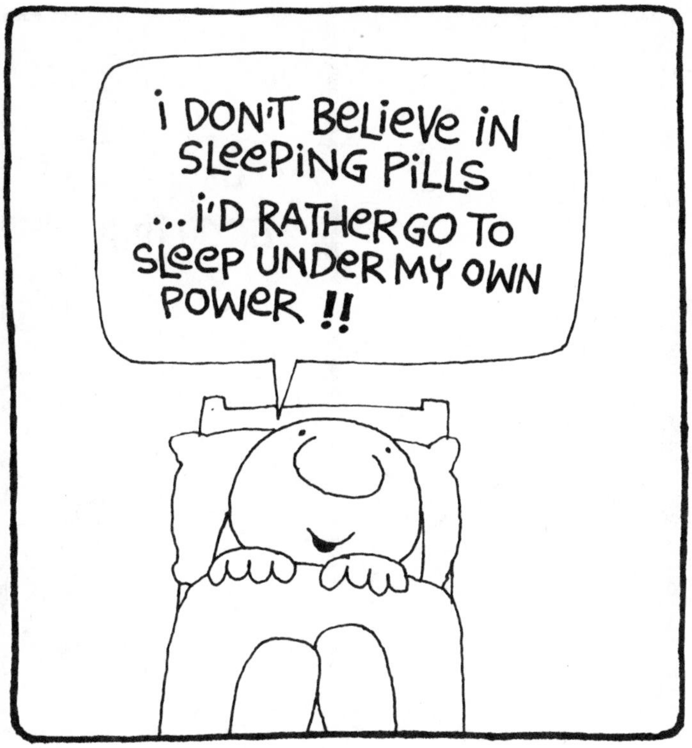
i DON'T BeLieVe iN SLeePiNG PiLLS ...i'D RATHeR GO TO SLeeP UNDeR MY OWN POWeR !!

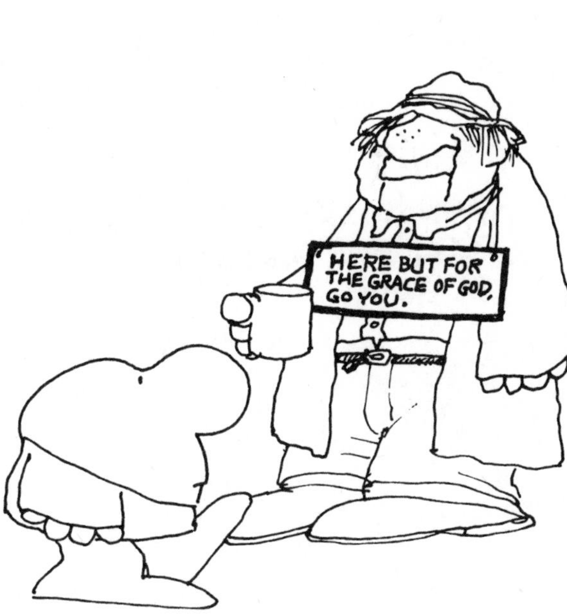
HERE BUT FOR THE GRACE OF GOD, GO YOU.

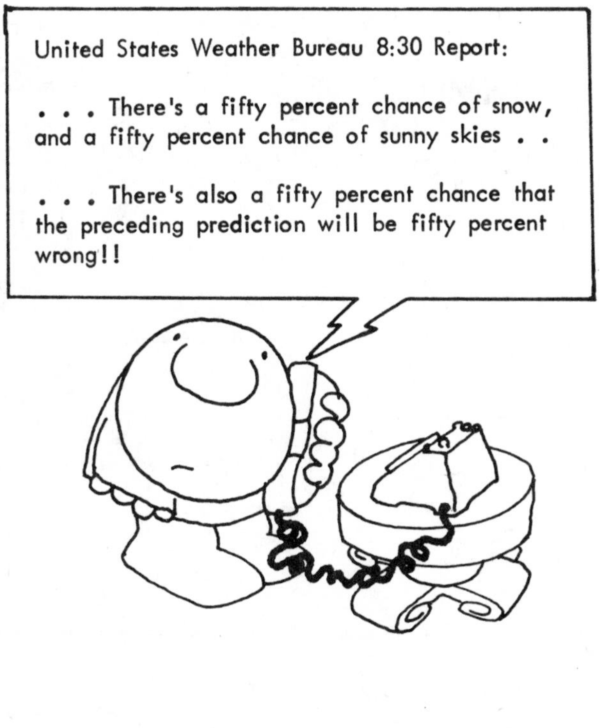
United States Weather Bureau 8:30 Report:
. . . There's a fifty percent chance of snow, and a fifty percent chance of sunny skies . .
. . . There's also a fifty percent chance that the preceding prediction will be fifty percent wrong!!

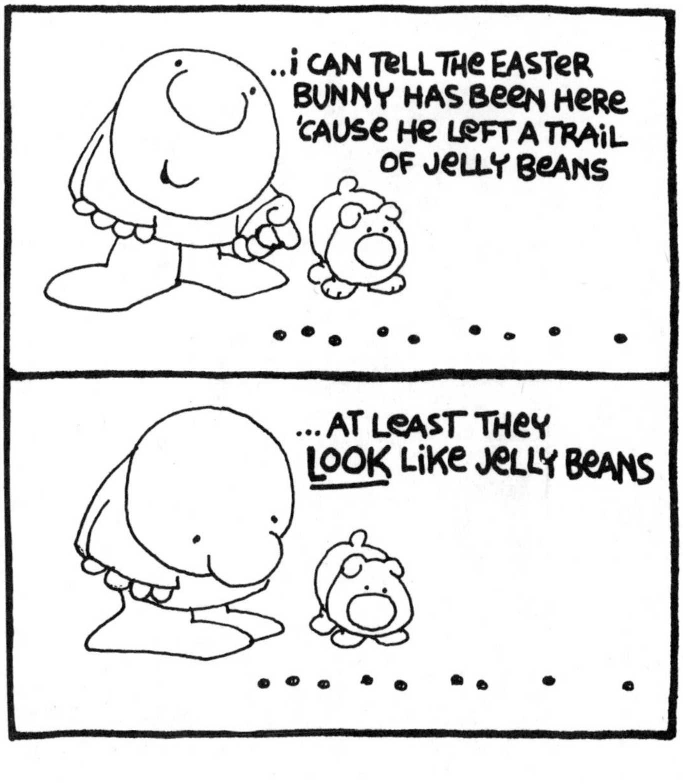
..i CAN TeLL THe EASTeR BUNNY HAS BeeN HeRe 'CAUSe He LeFT A TRAiL OF JeLLY BeANS
...AT LeAST THeY LOOK LiKe JeLLY BeANS

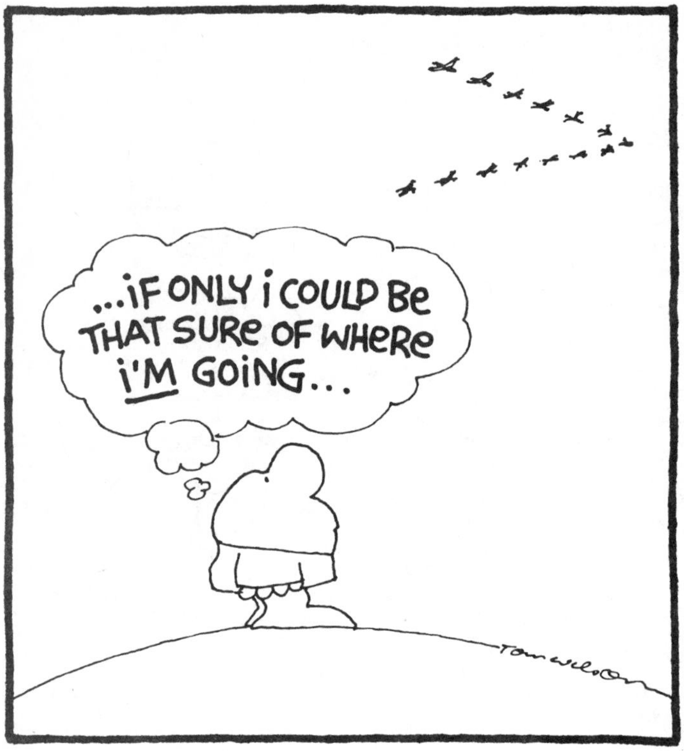
...iF ONLY i COULD Be THAT SURe OF WHeRe i'M GOiNG...

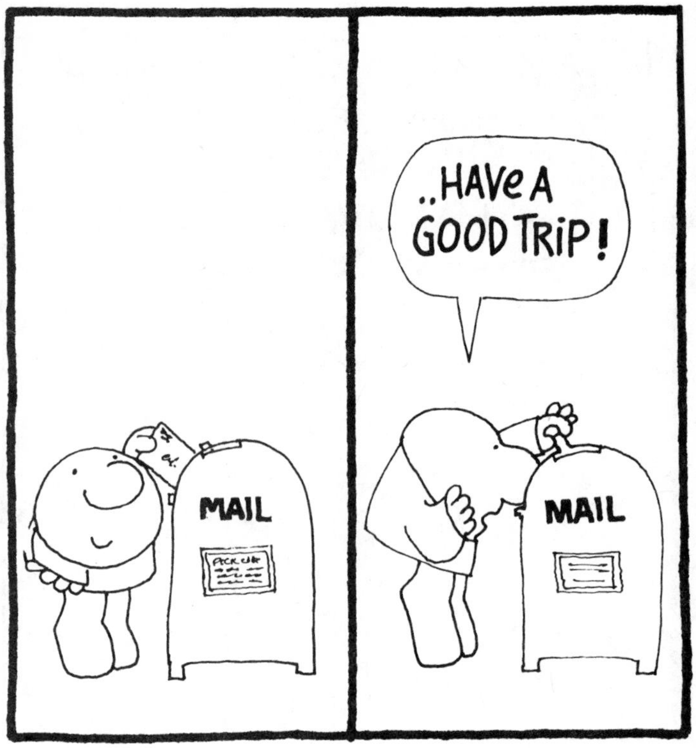
MAIL
MAIL
..HAVe A GOOD TRiP!

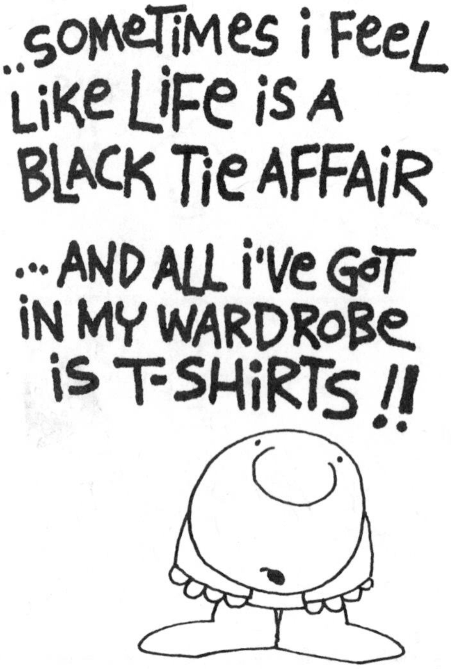
..SOMeTiMeS i FeeL LiKe LiFe iS A BLACK Tie AFFAiR
...AND ALL i'Ve GOT iN MY WARDROBe iS T-SHiRTS !!

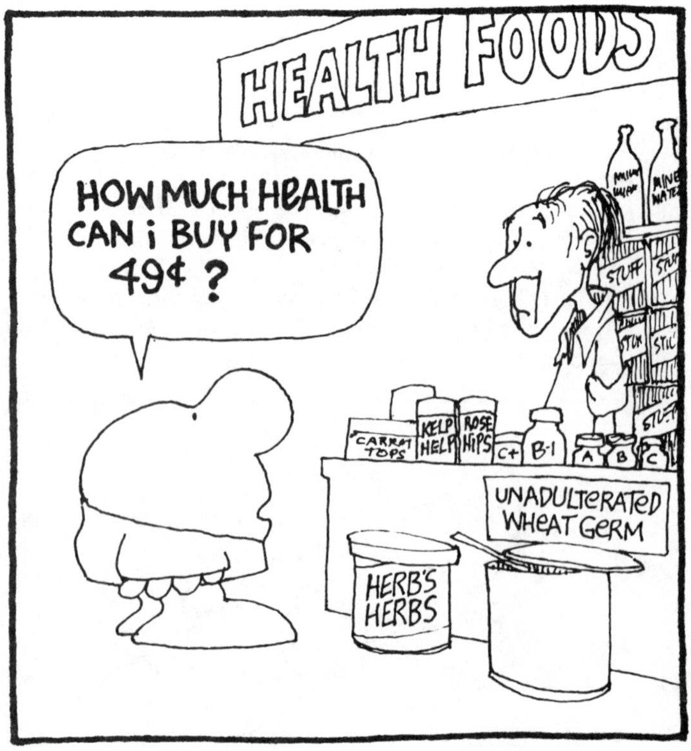
HEALTH FOODS
HOW MUCH HeALTH CAN i BUY FOR 49¢ ?
KELP HELP
ROSE HIPS
CARROT TOPS
C+
B-1
A
B
C
UNADULTeRATeD WHeAT GeRM
HERB'S HERBS

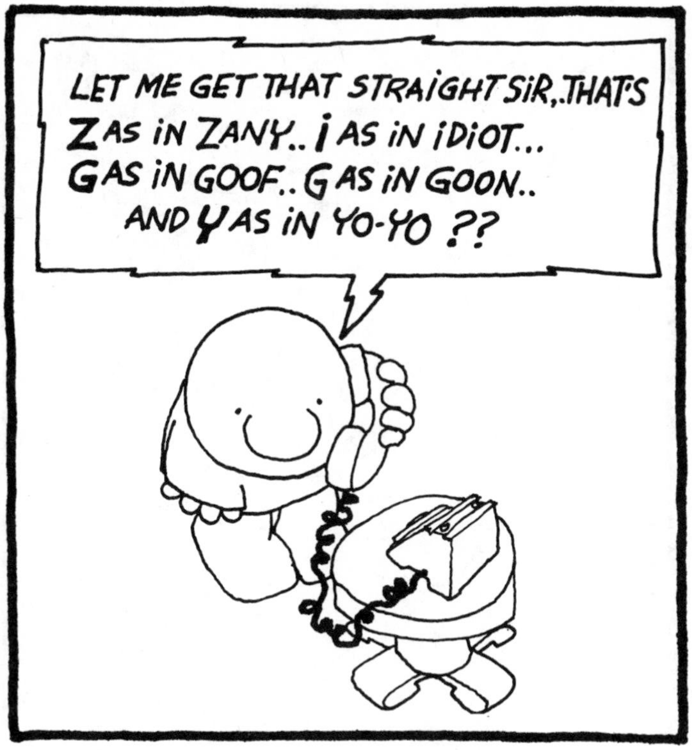
LET ME GET THAT STRAIGHT SIR,.THAT'S Z AS IN ZANY.. I AS IN IDIOT... G AS IN GOOF.. G AS IN GOON.. AND Y AS IN YO-YO ??

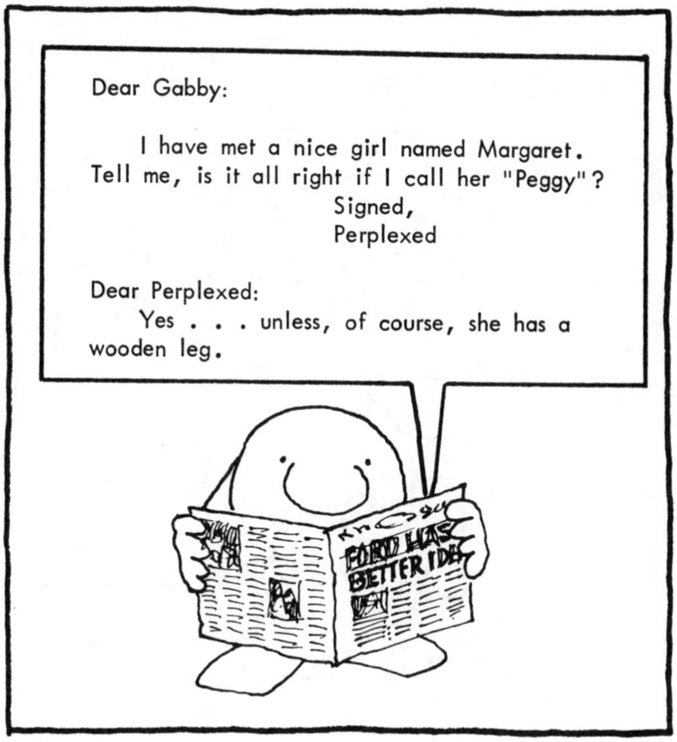
Dear Gabby:
I have met a nice girl named Margaret. Tell me, is it all right if I call her "Peggy"?
Signed,
Perplexed
Dear Perplexed:
Yes . . . unless, of course, she has a wooden leg.
FORD HAS BETTER IDEA

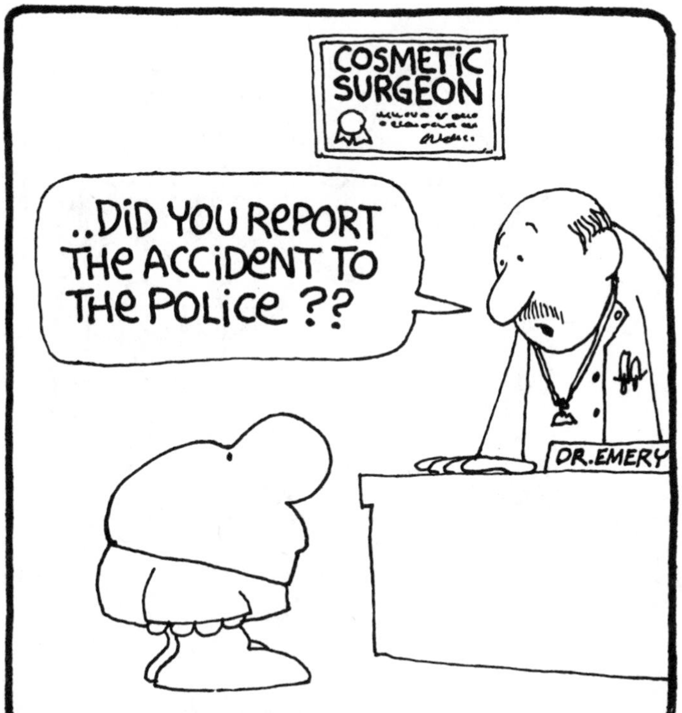
COSMETIC SURGEON
..DID YOU REPORT THE ACCIDENT TO THE POLICE ??
DR. EMERY

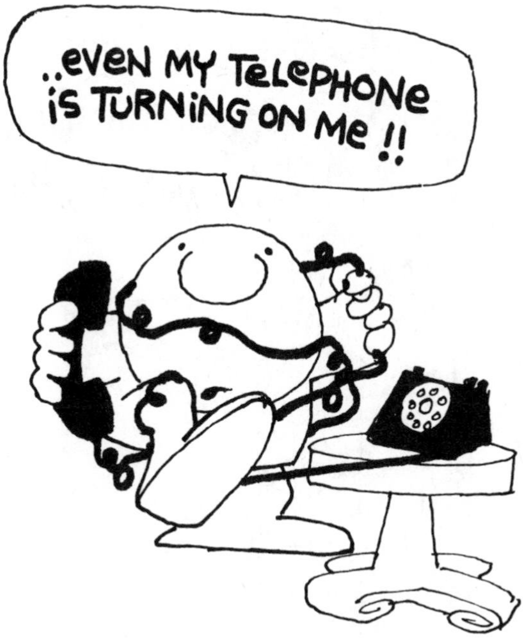
..EVEN MY TELEPHONE IS TURNING ON ME !!

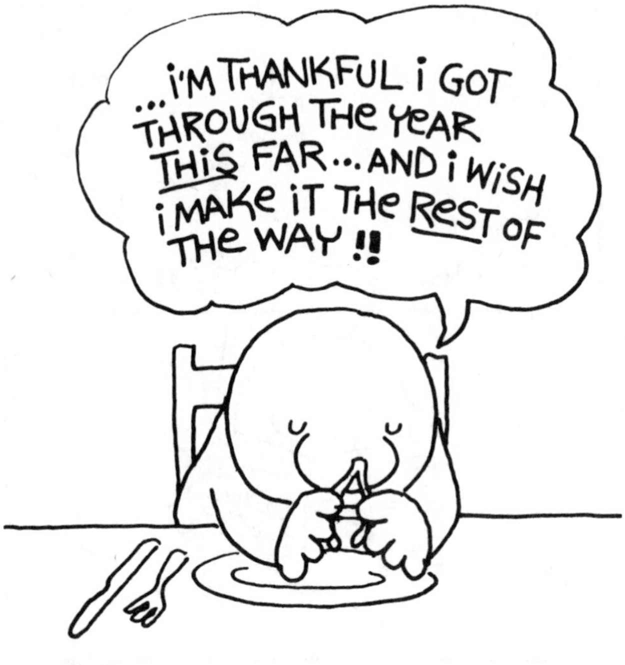
...i'M THANKFUL i GOT THROUGH THE YEAR THIS FAR... AND i WISH i MAKE iT THE REST OF THE WAY !!

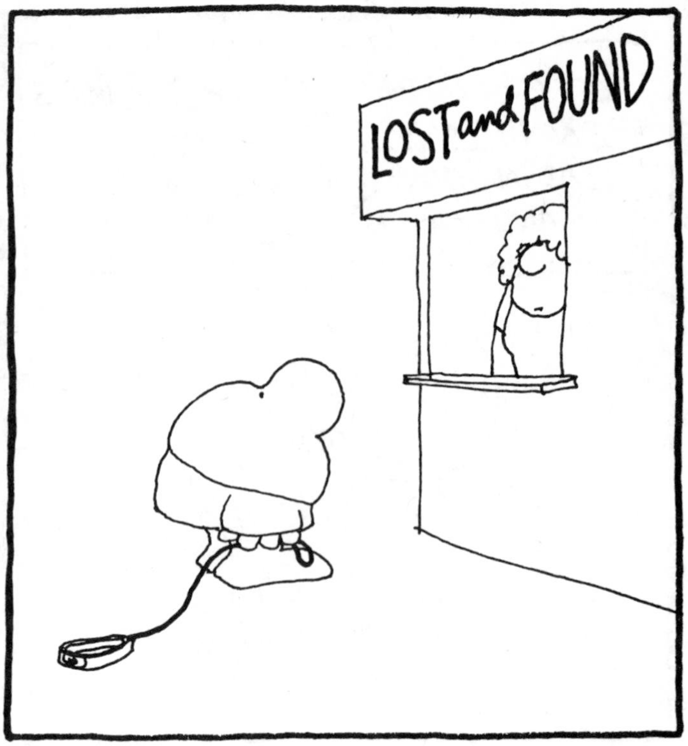
LOST and FOUND

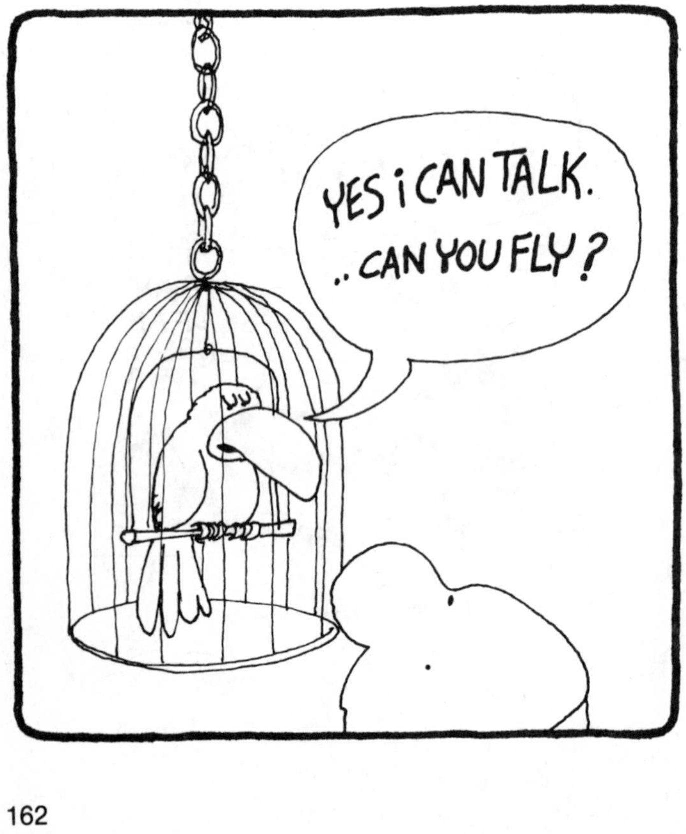
YES i CAN TALK. .. CAN YOU FLY ?

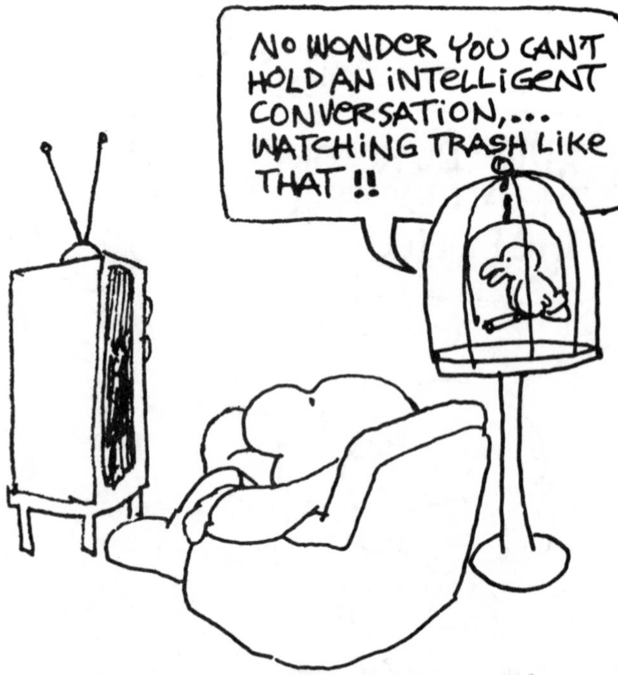
NO WONDER YOU CAN'T HOLD AN iNTELLiGENT CONVERSATION,... WATCHiNG TRASH LIKE THAT !!

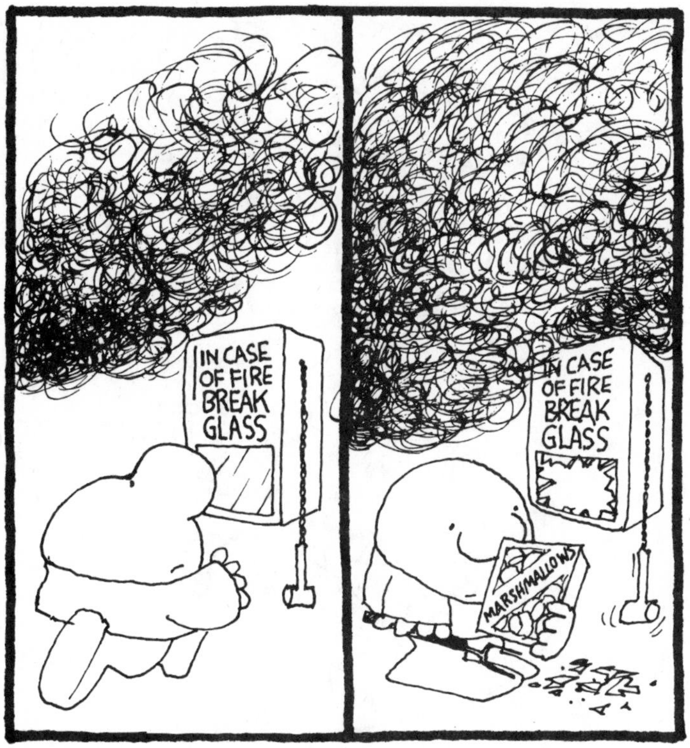
IN CASE OF FIRE BREAK GLASS
IN CASE OF FIRE BREAK GLASS
MARSHMALLOWS

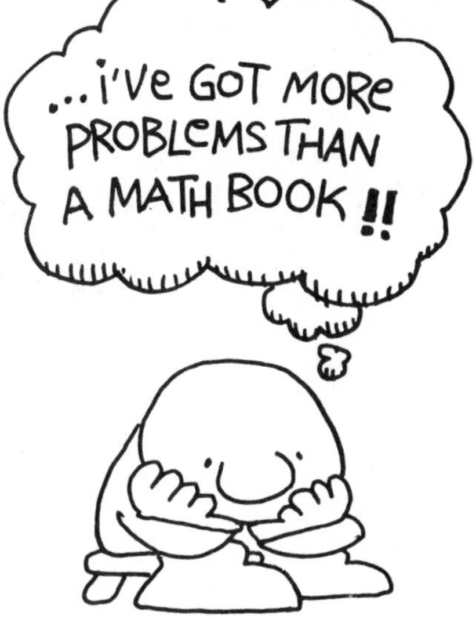
...i've GOT MORE PROBLEMS THAN A MATH BOOK !!

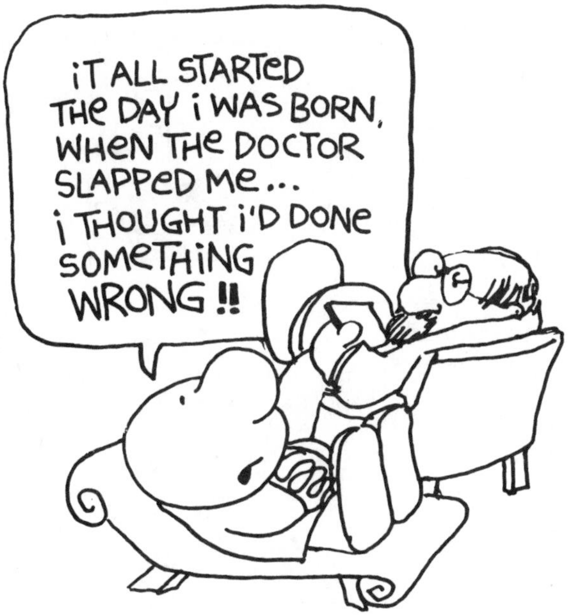
iT ALL STARTED THE DAY i WAS BORN, WHEN THE DOCTOR SLAPPED ME... i THOUGHT i'D DONE SOMETHING WRONG !!

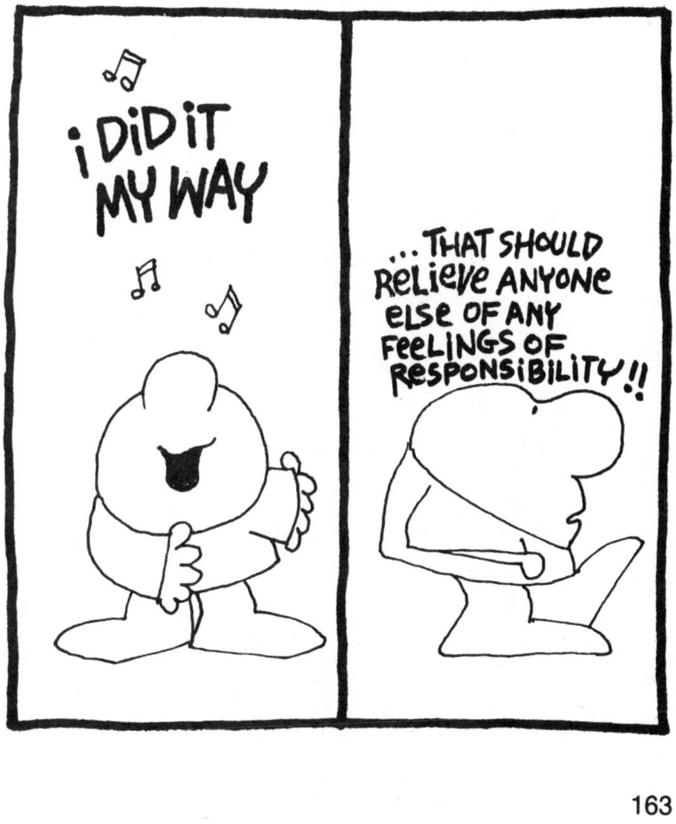
i DID iT MY WAY
...THAT SHOULD RELIEVE ANYONE ELSE OF ANY FEELINGS OF RESPONSIBILITY !!

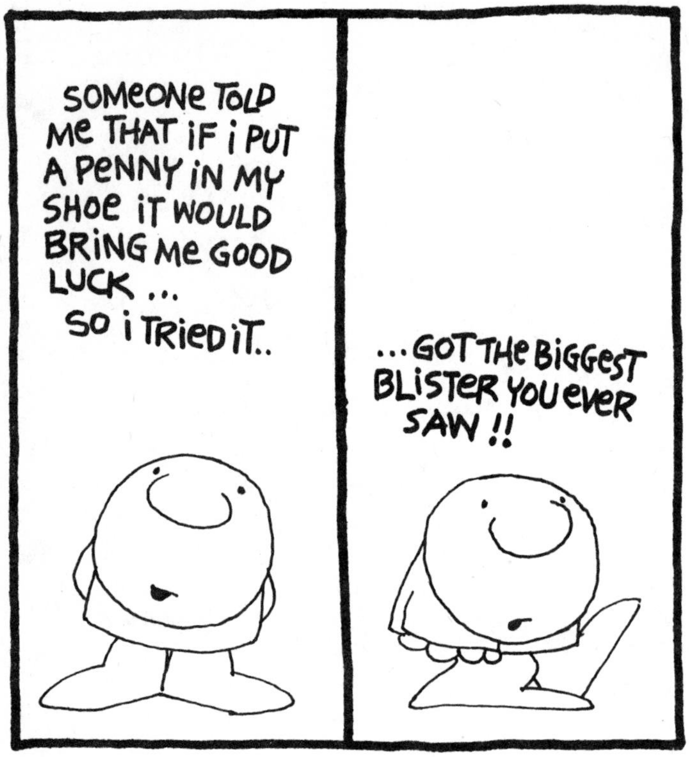
SOMEONE TOLD ME THAT IF i PUT A PENNY IN MY SHOE IT WOULD BRING ME GOOD LUCK ... SO i TRIED IT..
...GOT THE BIGGEST BLISTER YOU EVER SAW !!

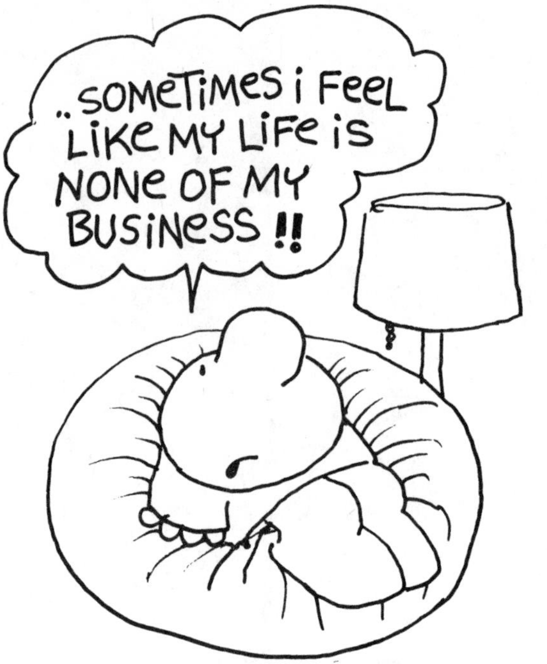
..SOMETIMES i FEEL LIKE MY LIFE IS NONE OF MY BUSINESS !!

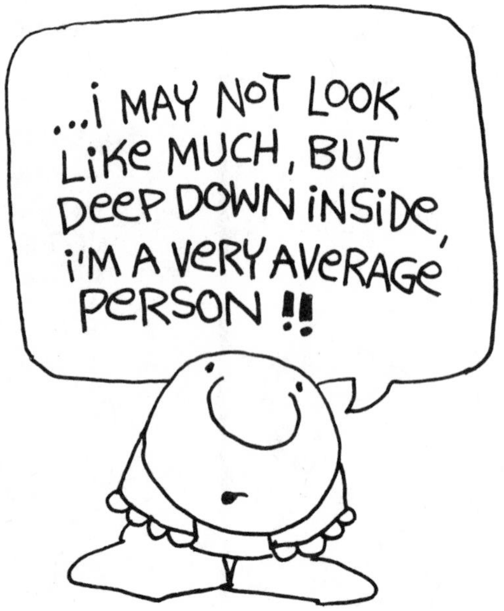
...i MAY NOT LOOK LIKE MUCH, BUT DEEP DOWN INSIDE, i'M A VERY AVERAGE PERSON !!

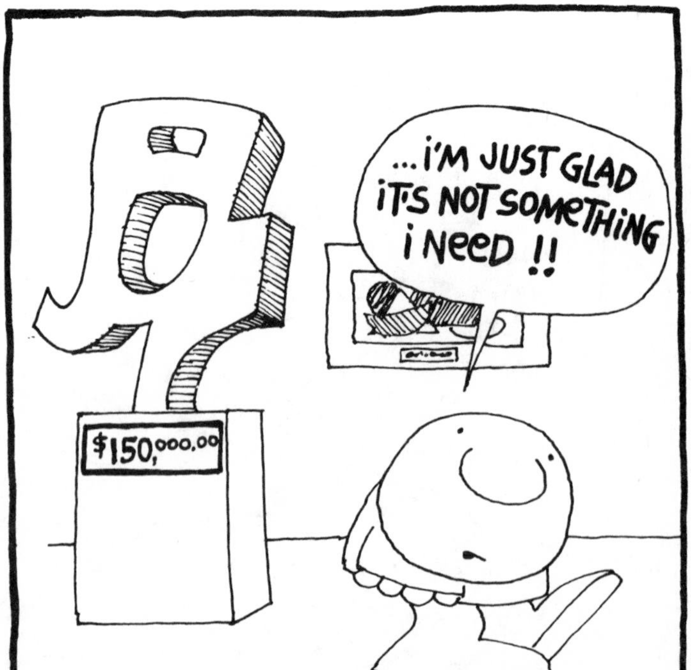
$150,000.00
...i'M JUST GLAD IT'S NOT SOMETHING i NEED !!

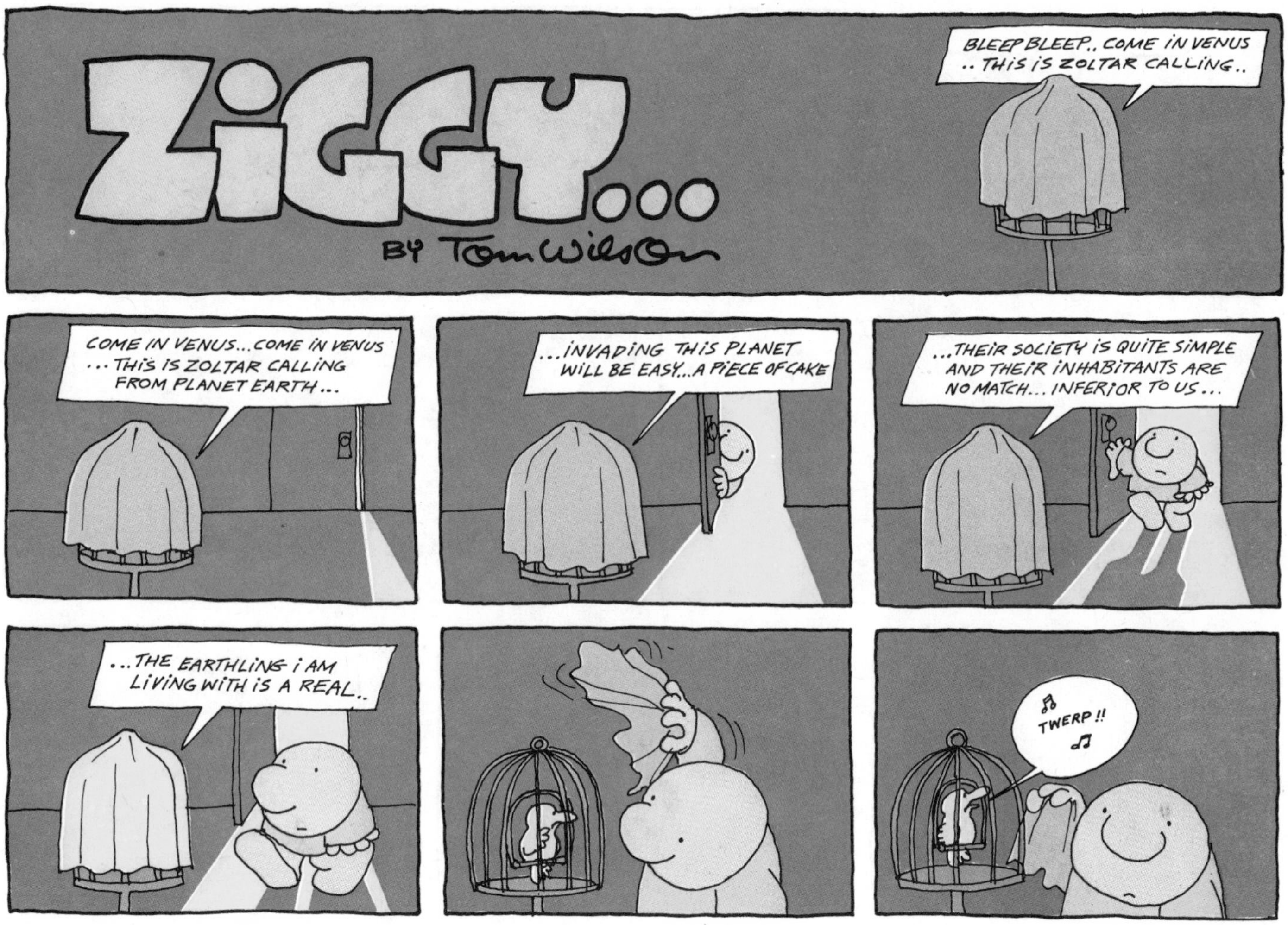
ZIGGY...
BY Tom Wilson
BLEEP BLEEP.. COME IN VENUS .. THIS IS ZOLTAR CALLING..
COME IN VENUS...COME IN VENUS ...THIS IS ZOLTAR CALLING FROM PLANET EARTH...
...INVADING THIS PLANET WILL BE EASY...A PIECE OF CAKE
...THEIR SOCIETY IS QUITE SIMPLE AND THEIR INHABITANTS ARE NO MATCH... INFERIOR TO US...
...THE EARTHLING I AM LIVING WITH IS A REAL..
TWERP !!

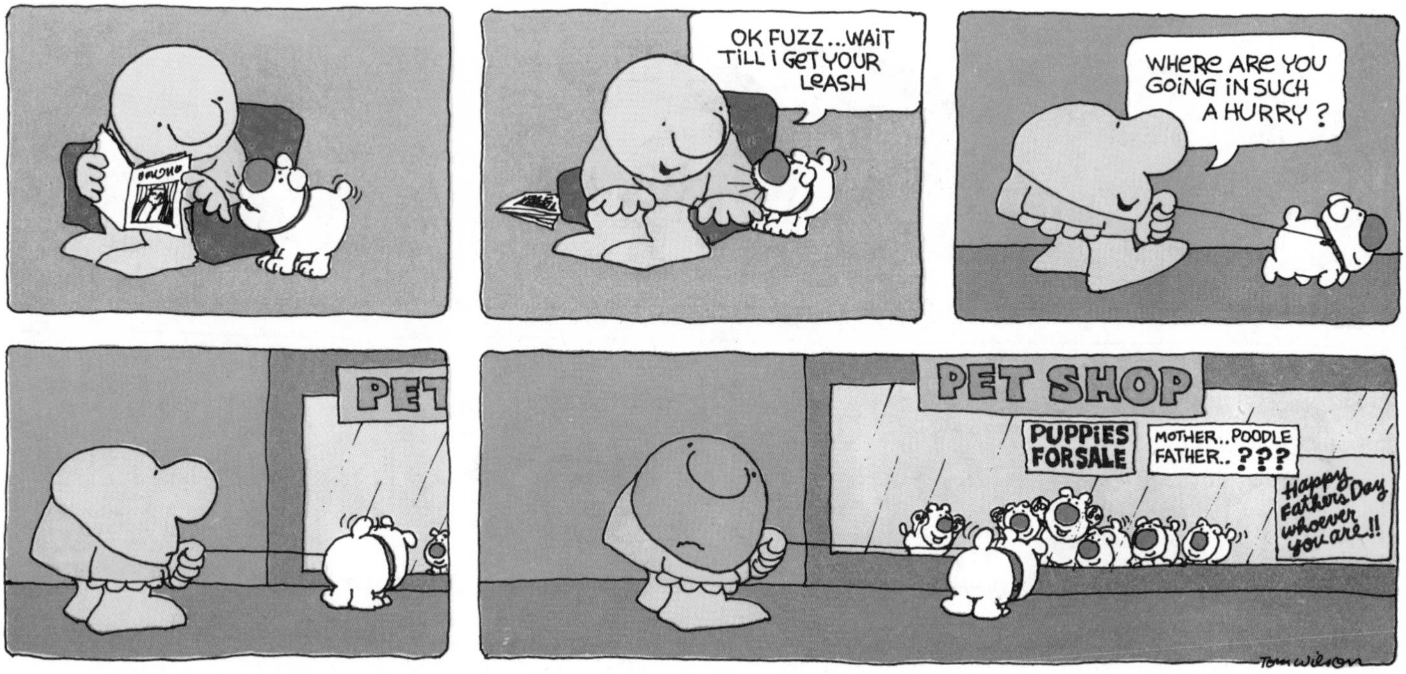
OK FUZZ...WAIT TILL I GET YOUR LEASH
WHERE ARE YOU GOING IN SUCH A HURRY ?
PET
PET SHOP
PUPPIES FOR SALE
MOTHER.. POODLE FATHER.. ???
Happy Fathers Day whoever you are!!
Tom Wilson

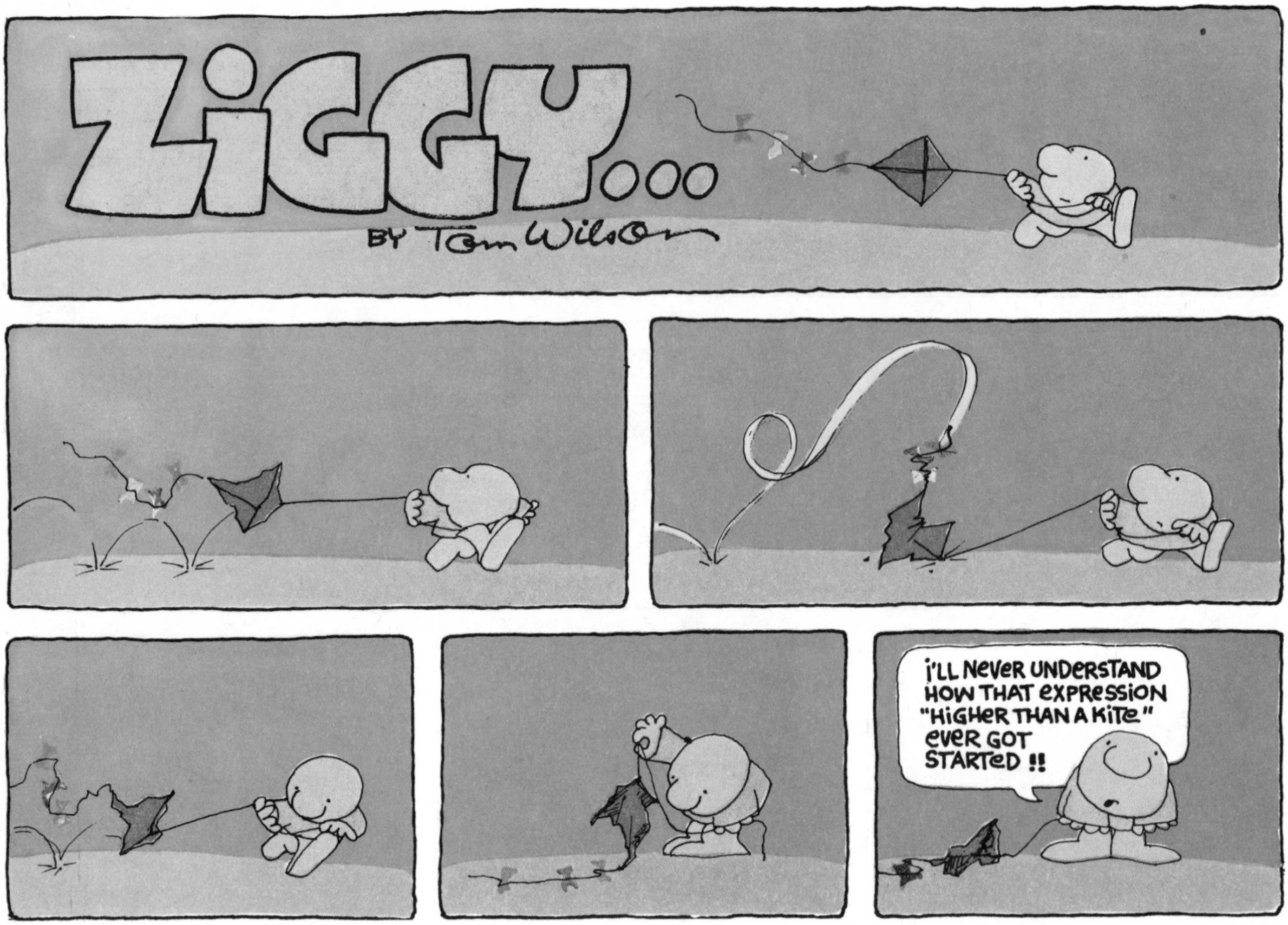
ZiGGY...
BY Tom Wilson
i'LL NEVER UNDERSTAND HOW THAT expression "HiGHER THAN A KiTe" ever GOT STARTeD !!

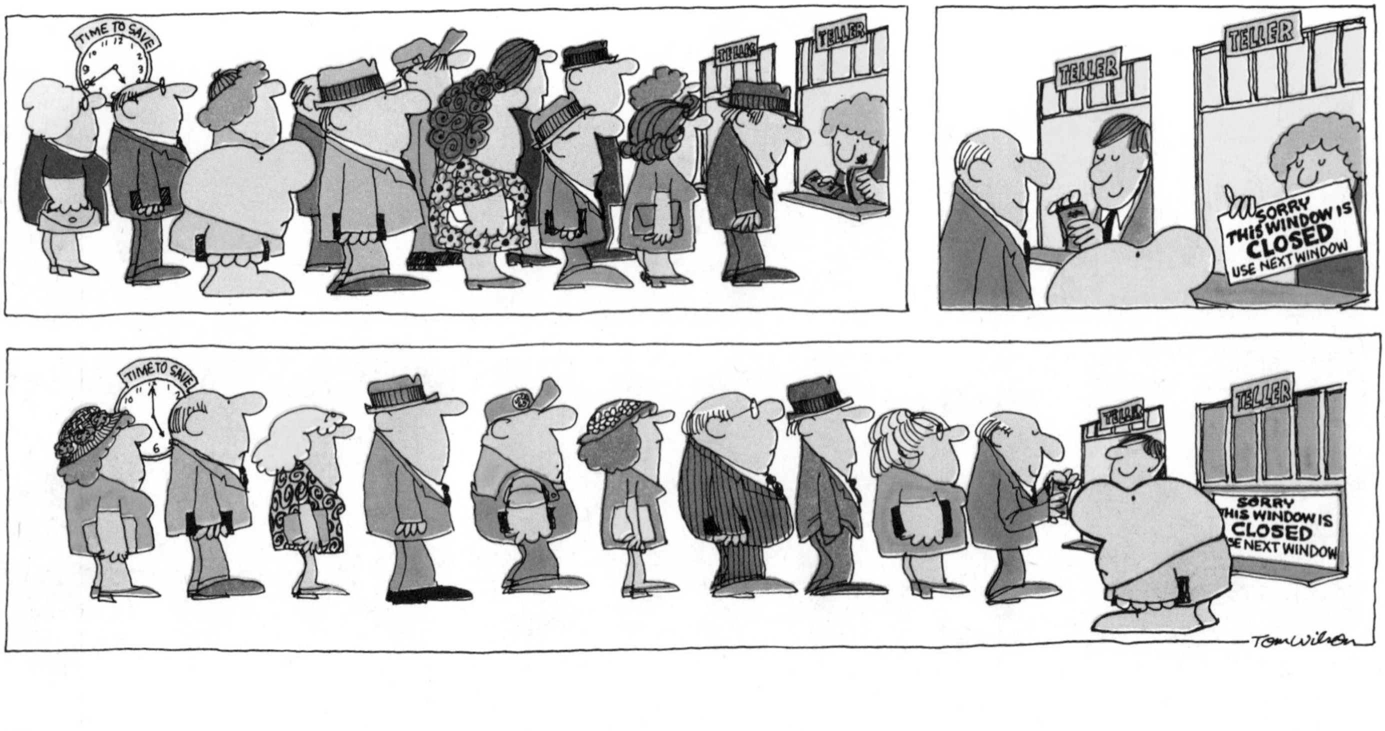
TIME TO SAVE
TELLER
TELLER
SORRY THIS WINDOW IS CLOSED USE NEXT WINDOW
TIME TO SAVE
TELLER
TELLER
SORRY THIS WINDOW IS CLOSED
Tom Wilson

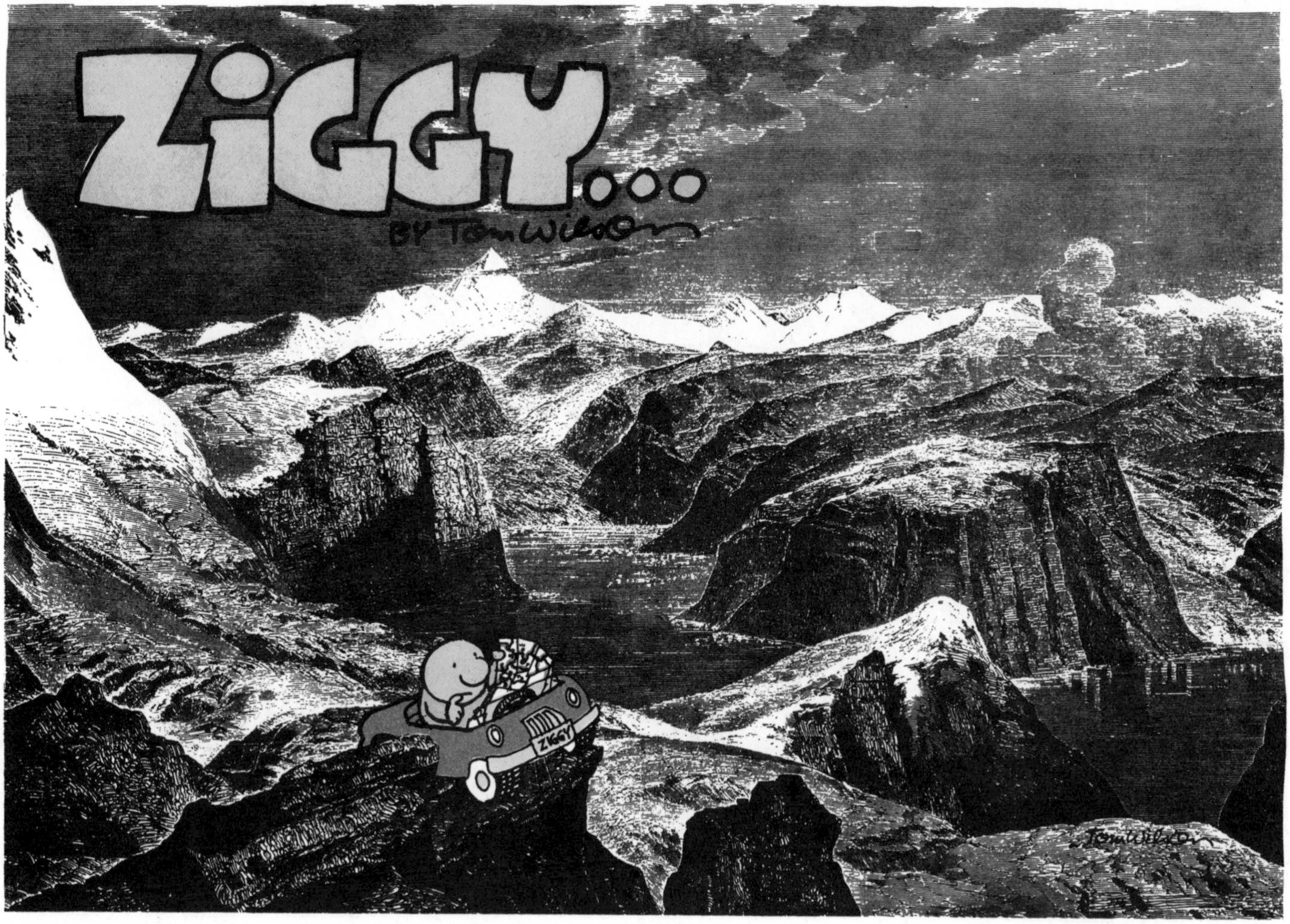
ZIGGY...
BY Tom Wilson
ZIGGY
Tom Wilson

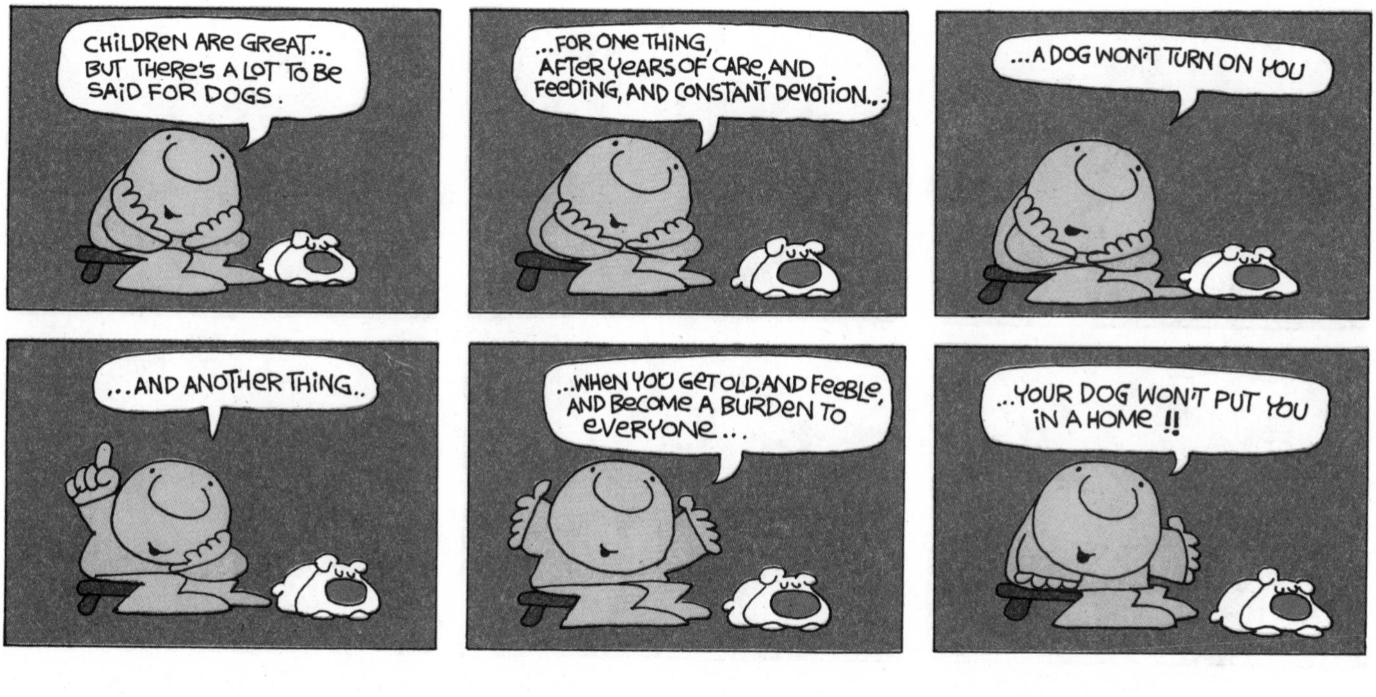
CHILDREN ARE GREAT... BUT THERE'S A LOT TO BE SAID FOR DOGS.
...FOR ONE THING, AFTER YEARS OF CARE, AND FEEDING, AND CONSTANT DEVOTION...
...A DOG WON'T TURN ON YOU
...AND ANOTHER THING..
...WHEN YOU GET OLD, AND FEEBLE, AND BECOME A BURDEN TO EVERYONE...
...YOUR DOG WON'T PUT YOU IN A HOME !!

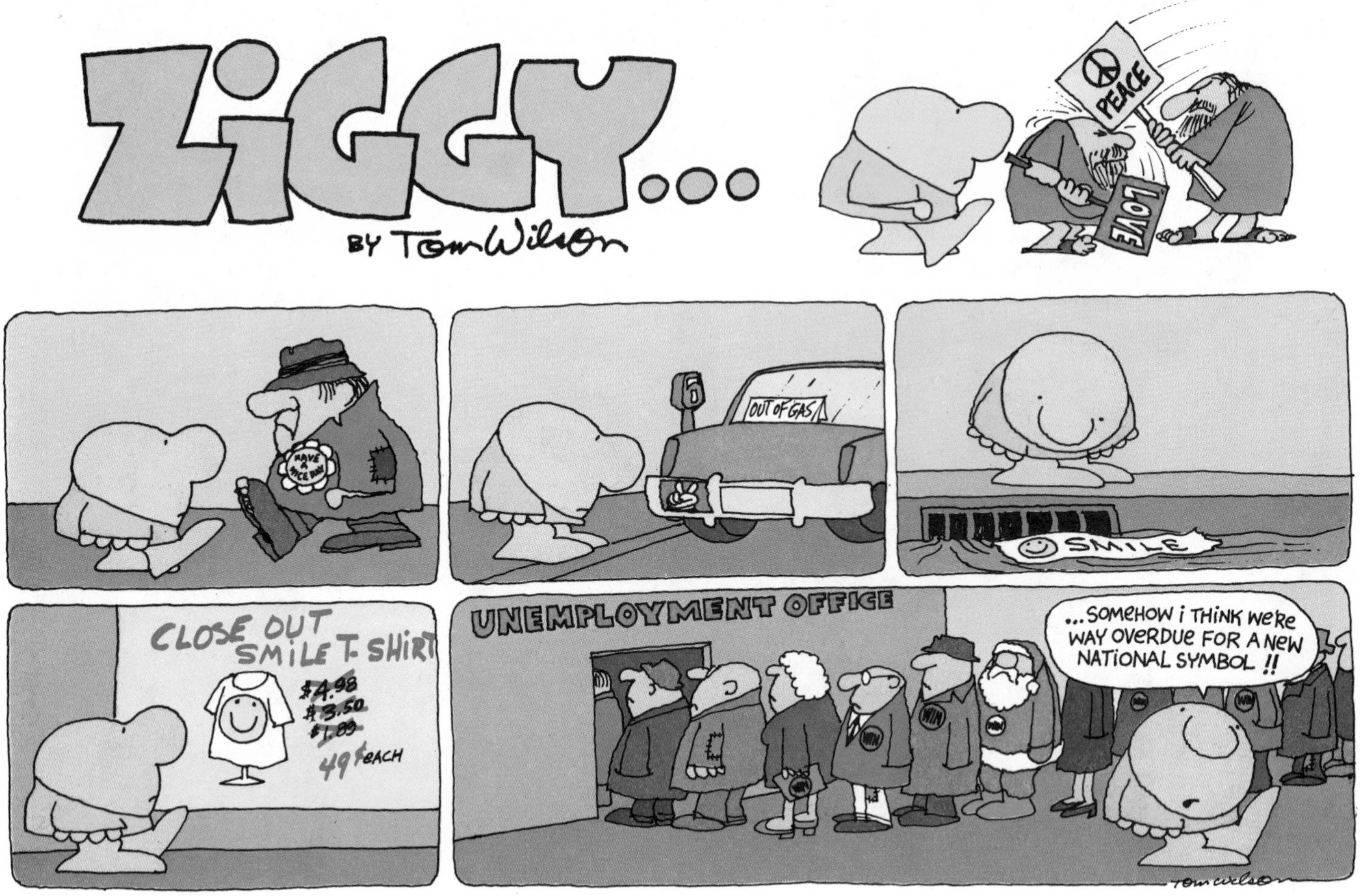
ZIGGY...
BY Tom Wilson
PEACE
LOVE
HAVE A NICE DAY
OUT OF GAS
SMILE
CLOSE OUT SMILE T-SHIRT
$4.98
$3.50
$1.89
49¢ EACH
UNEMPLOYMENT OFFICE
...SOMEHOW i THINK we're WAY OVERDUE FOR A NEW NATIONAL SYMBOL !!
Tom Wilson

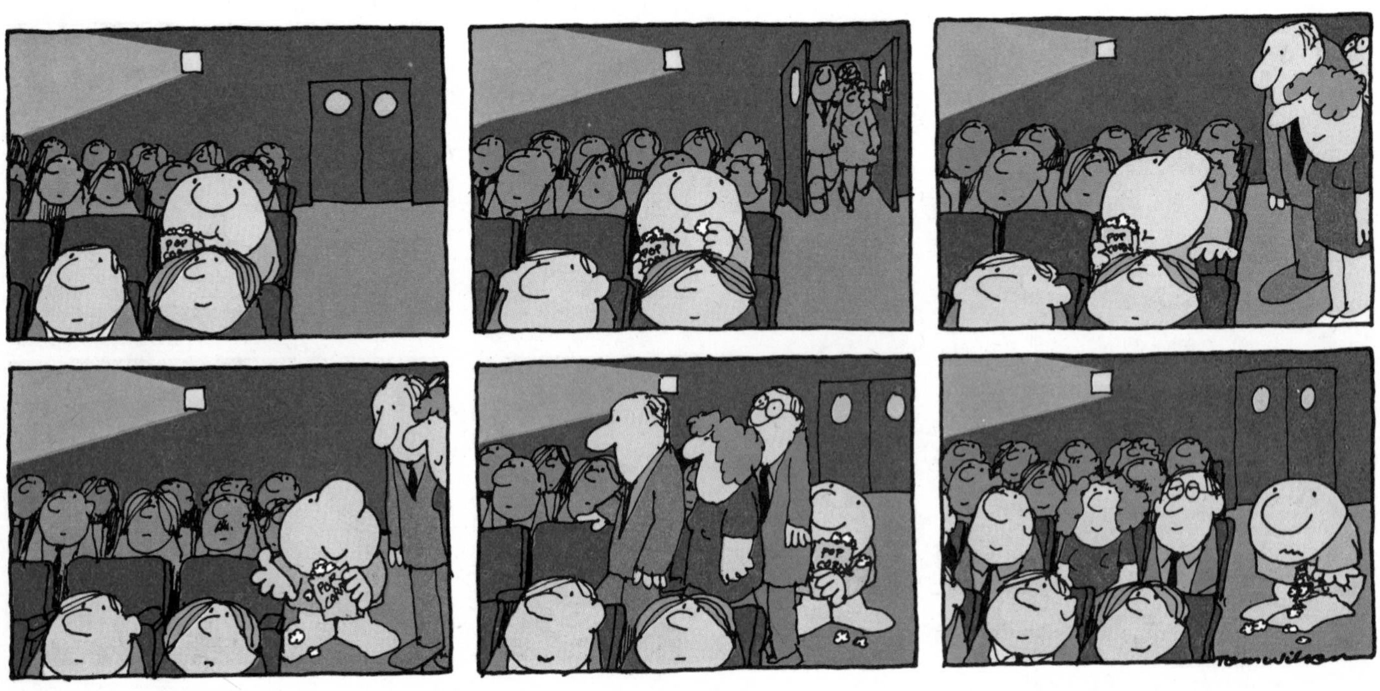
POP CORN
Tom Wilson

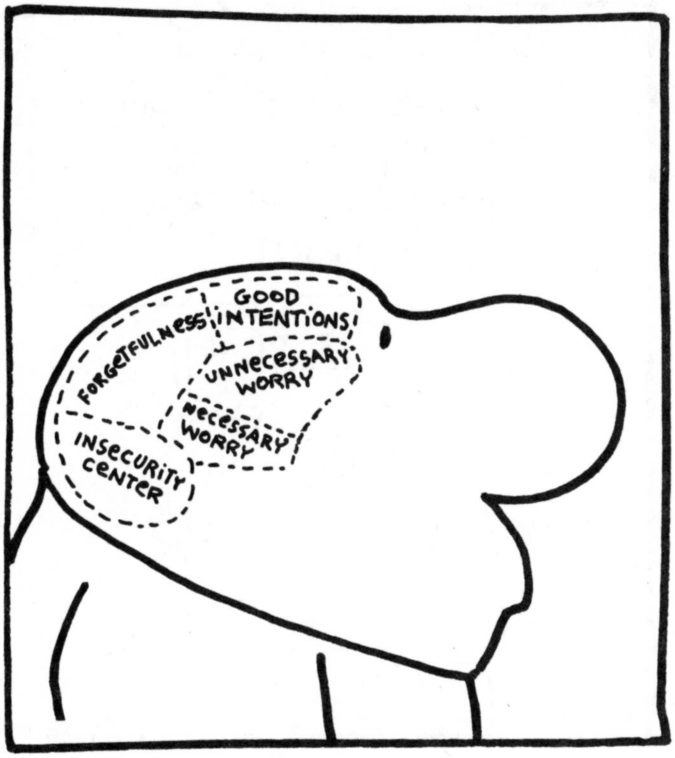
GOOD INTENTIONS
FORGETFULNESS
UNNECESSARY WORRY
NECESSARY WORRY
INSECURITY CENTER

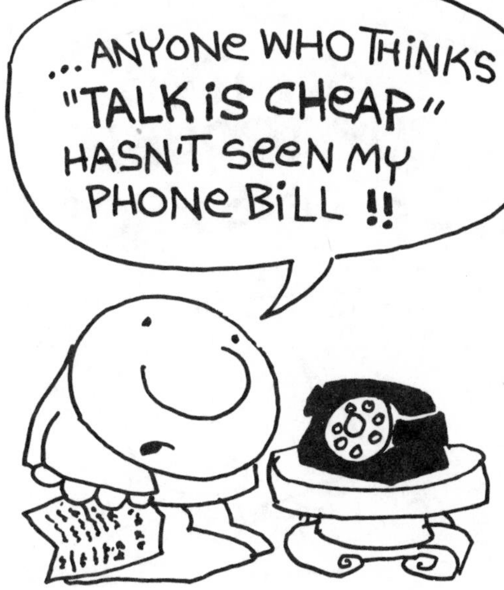
... ANYONE WHO THINKS "TALK IS CHEAP" HASN'T SEEN MY PHONE BILL !!

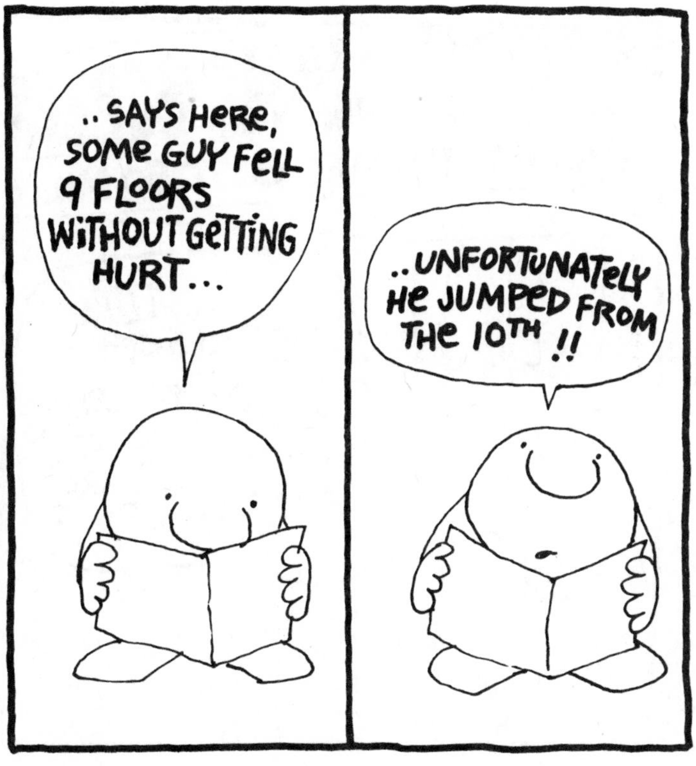
.. SAYS HERE, SOME GUY FELL 9 FLOORS WITHOUT GETTING HURT...
.. UNFORTUNATELY HE JUMPED FROM THE 10TH !!

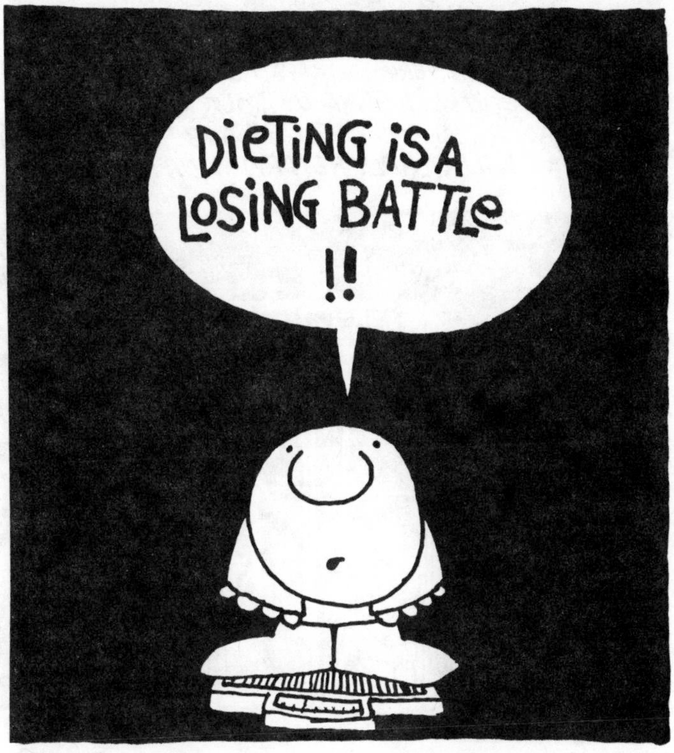
DIETING IS A LOSING BATTLE !!

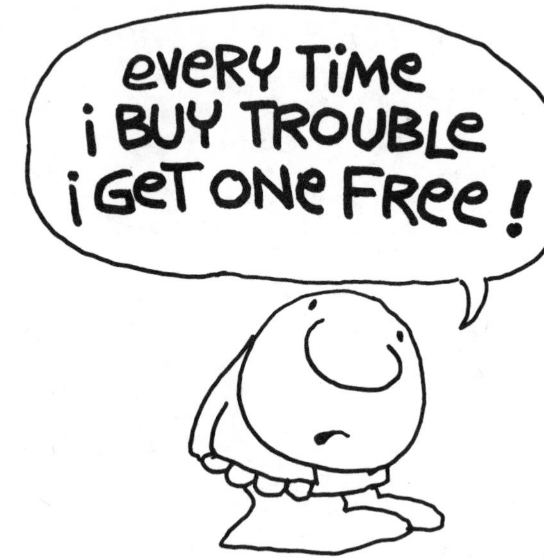
every Time i BUY TROUBLE i GeT ONE Free !

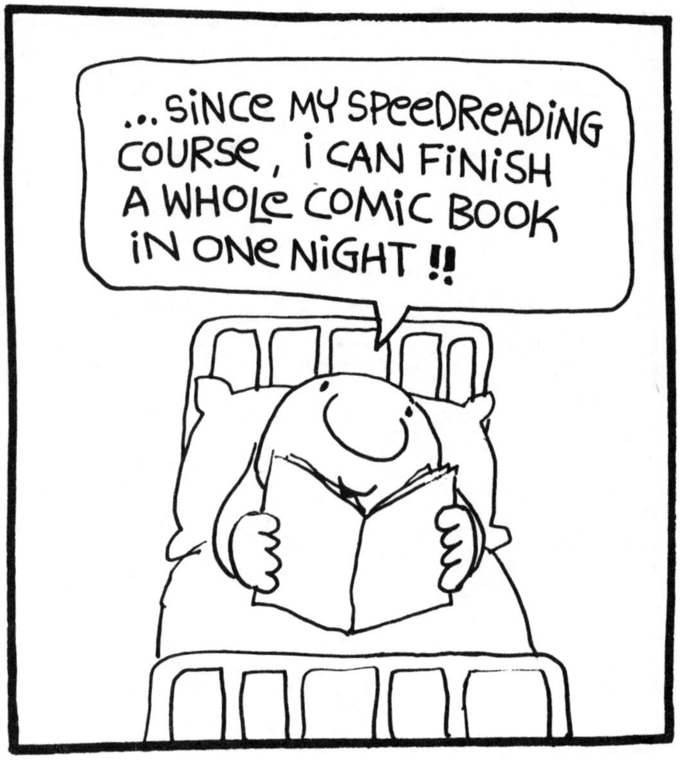
... SiNCE MY SPEEDREADiNG COURSE, i CAN FiNiSH A WHOLE COMiC BOOK iN ONE NiGHT !!

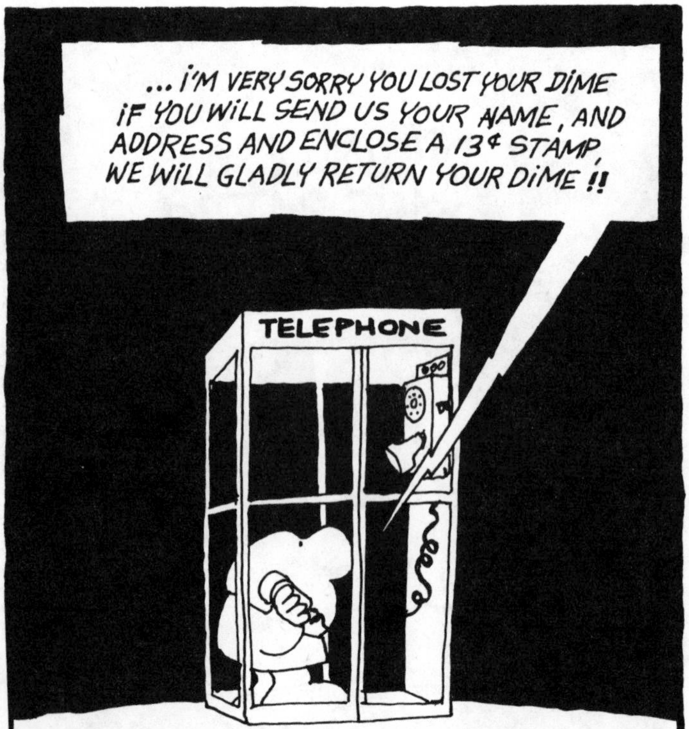
... I'M VERY SORRY YOU LOST YOUR DIME IF YOU WILL SEND US YOUR NAME, AND ADDRESS AND ENCLOSE A 13¢ STAMP, WE WILL GLADLY RETURN YOUR DIME !!
TELEPHONE

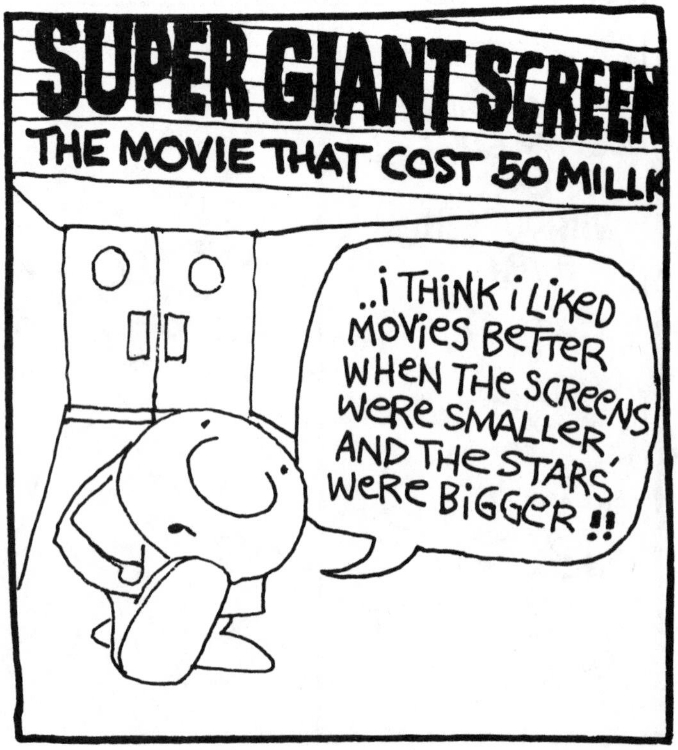
SUPER GIANT SCREEN
THE MOVIE THAT COST 50 MILL
..i THINK i LIKED MOVIES BETTER WHEN THE SCREENS WERE SMALLER, AND THE STARS WERE BIGGER !!

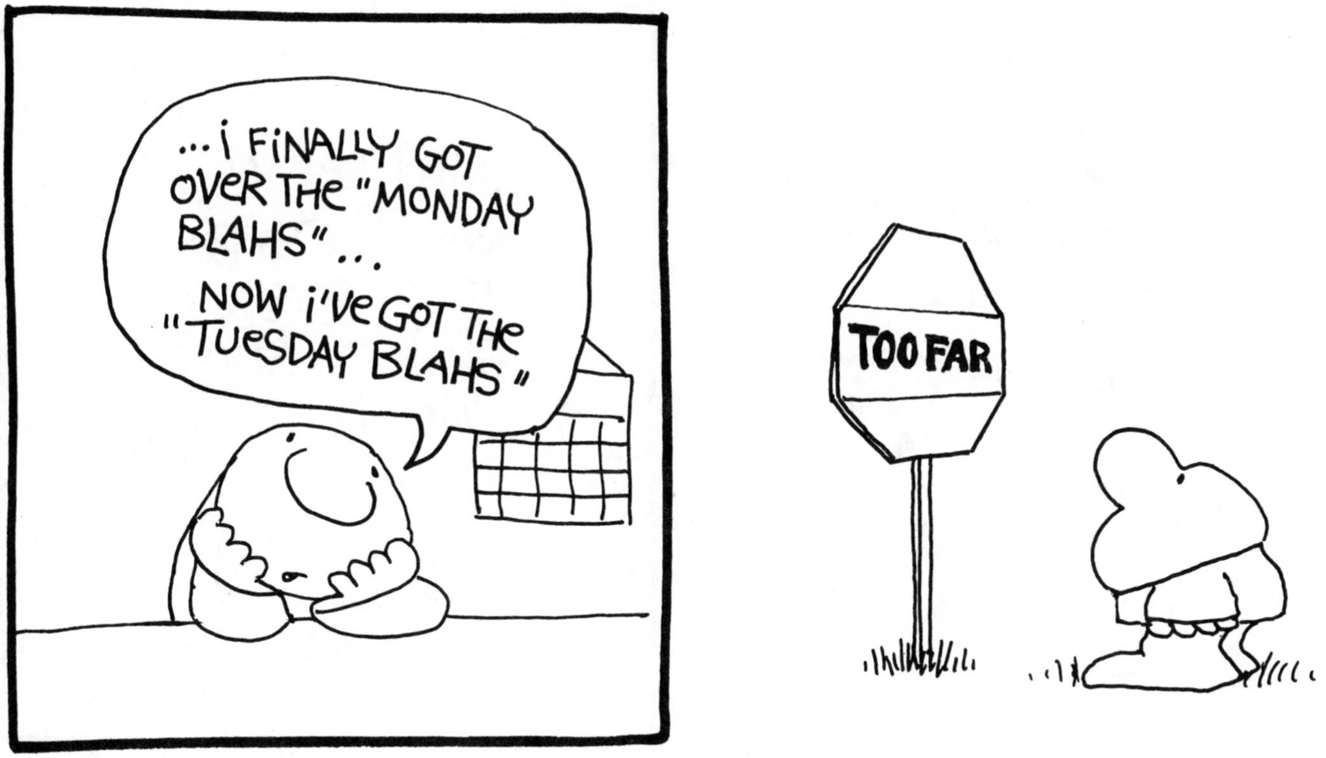
...i FINALLY GOT OVER THE "MONDAY BLAHS"... NOW i'VE GOT THE "TUESDAY BLAHS"
TOO FAR

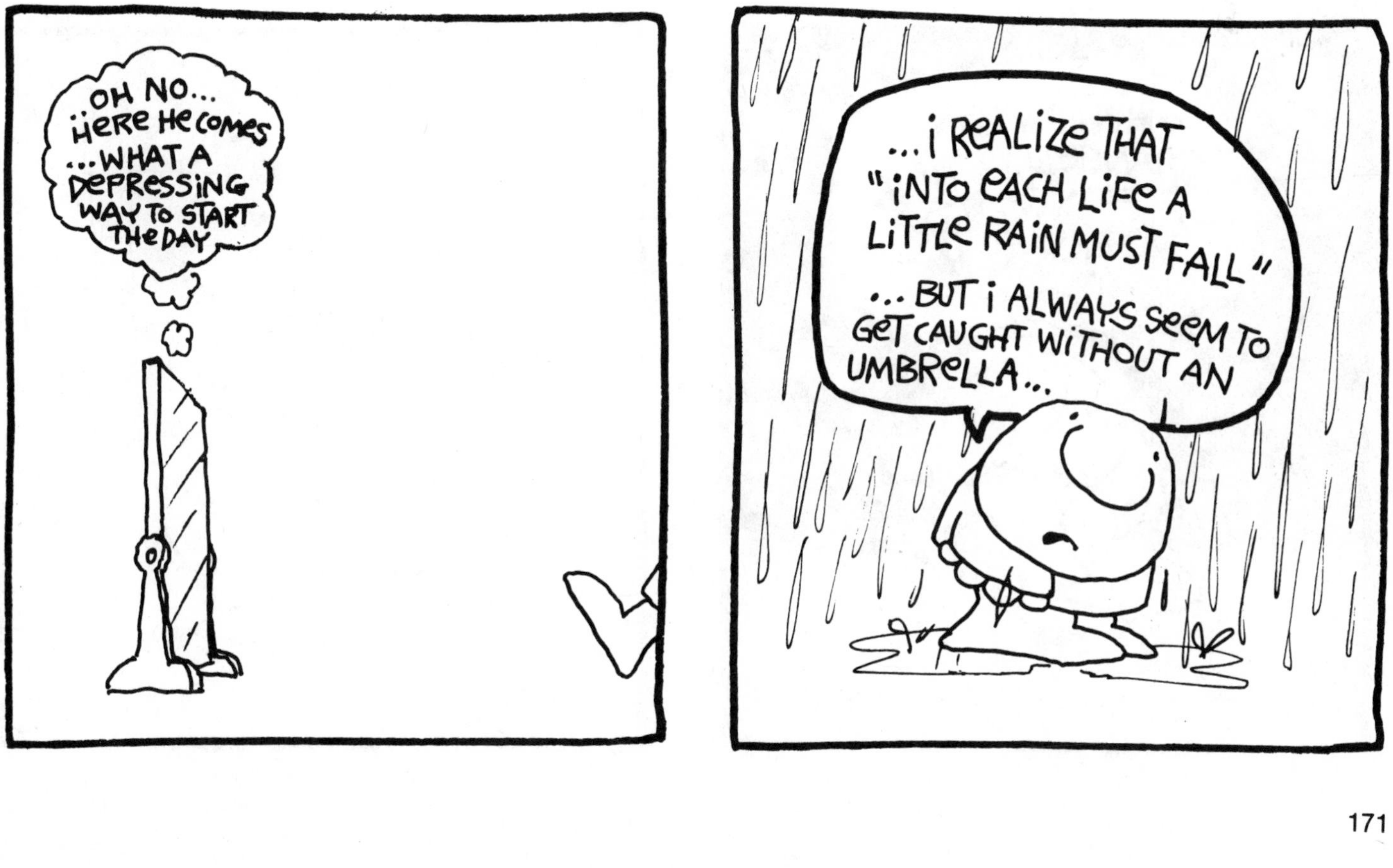
OH NO... HERE HE COMES ...WHAT A DEPRESSING WAY TO START THE DAY
...i REALIZE THAT "iNTO EACH LIFE A LITTLE RAIN MUST FALL" ...BUT i ALWAYS SEEM TO GET CAUGHT WITHOUT AN UMBRELLA...

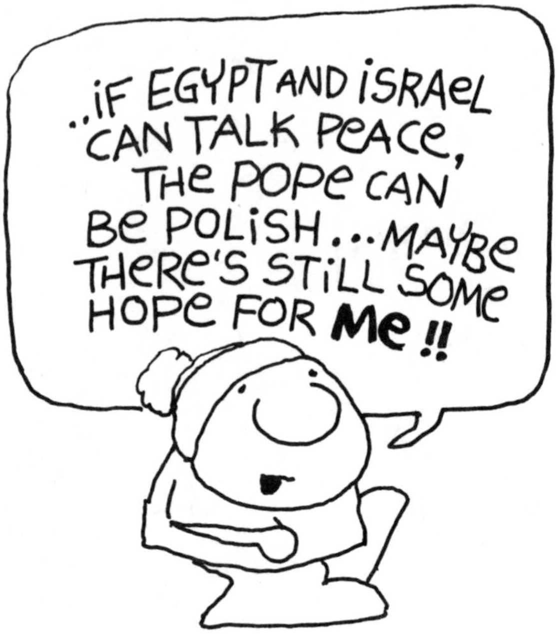
...iF EGYPT AND iSRAeL CAN TALK PeACe, THe POPe CAN Be POLiSH ... MAYBe THeRe'S STiLL SOMe HOPe FOR **Me** !!

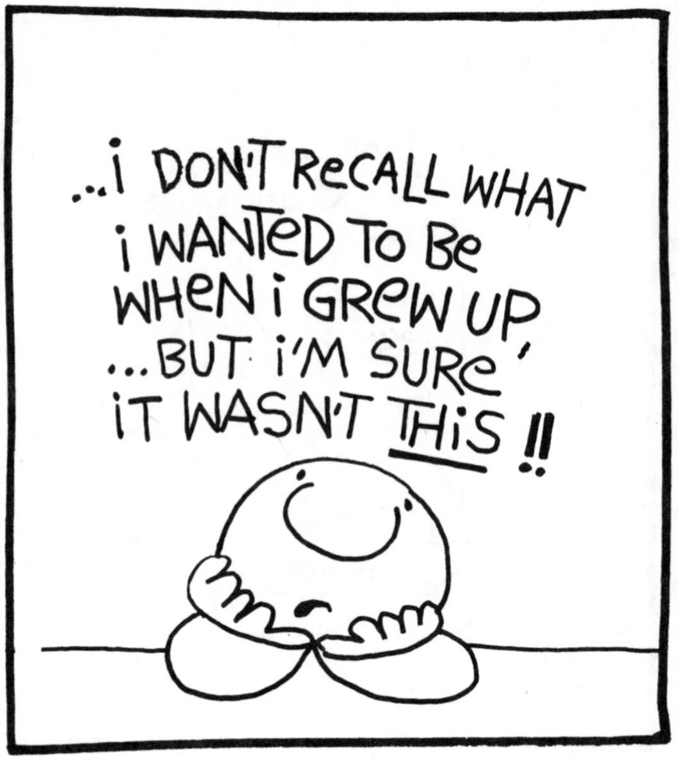
...i DON'T ReCALL WHAT i WANTeD TO Be WHeN i GReW UP, ...BUT i'M SURe iT WASN'T THiS !!

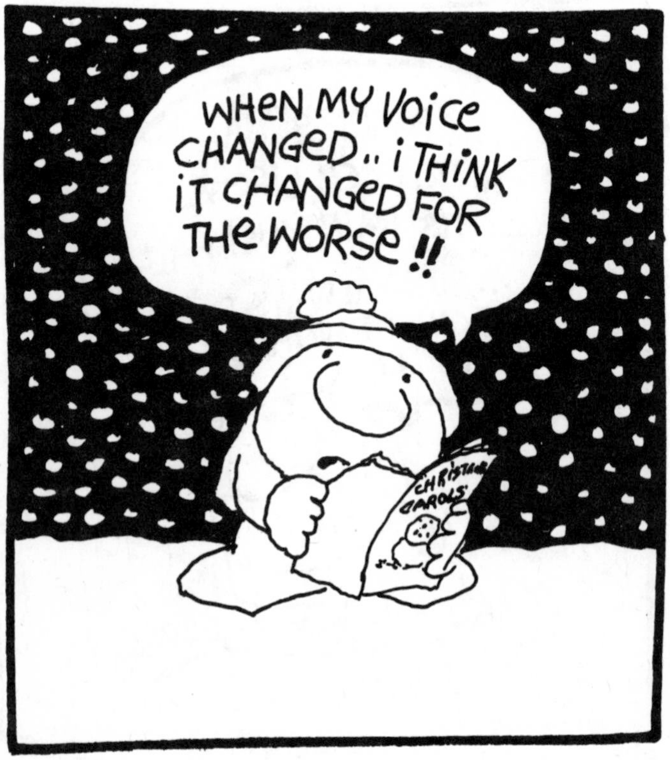
WHeN MY VOiCe CHANGeD.. i THiNK iT CHANGeD FOR THe WORSe !!

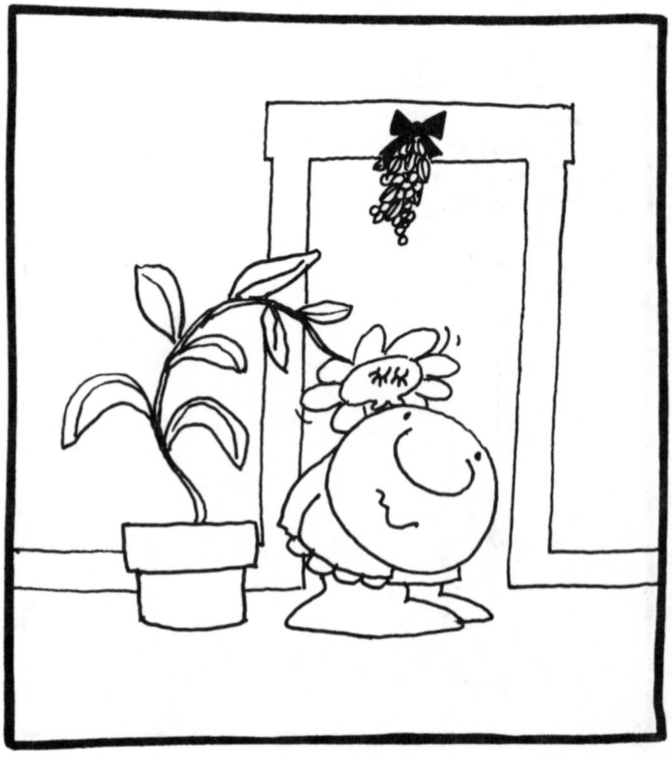

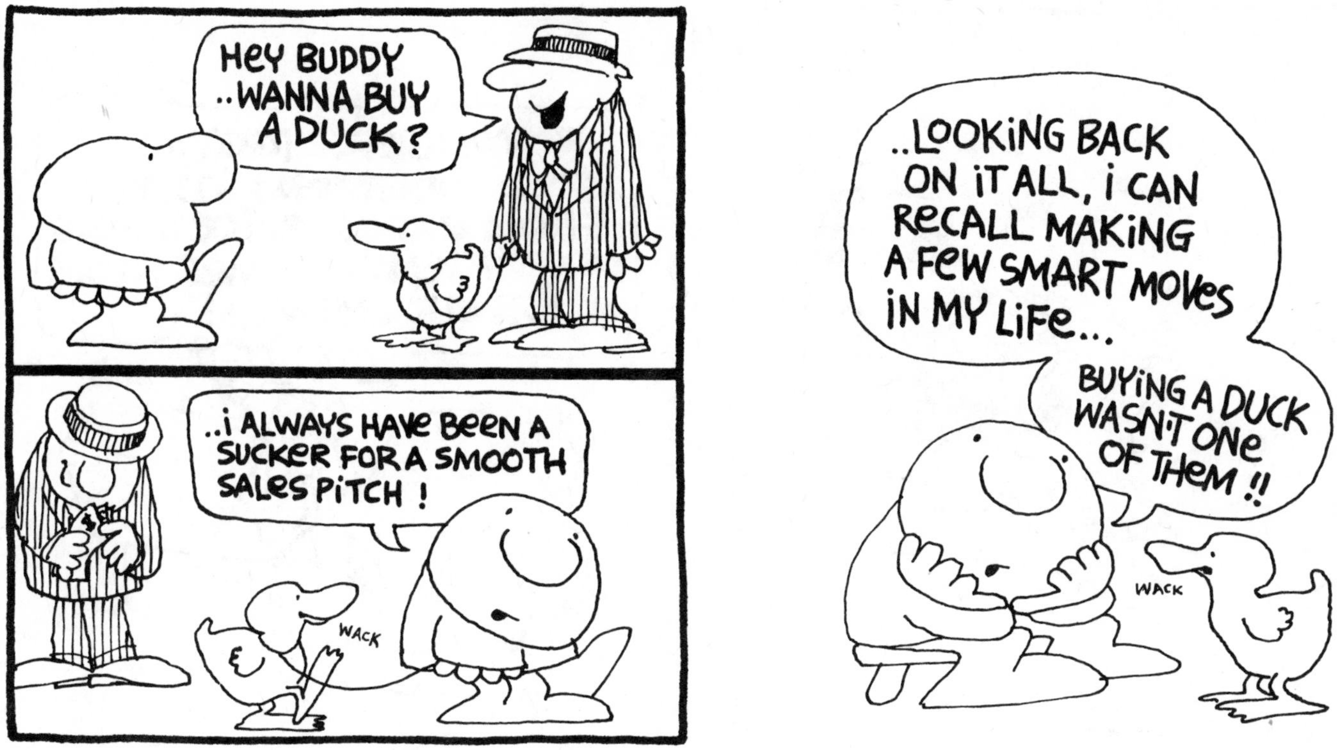
HEY BUDDY ..WANNA BUY A DUCK?
..i ALWAYS HAVE BEEN A SUCKER FOR A SMOOTH SALES PITCH !
WACK
..LOOKING BACK ON iT ALL, i CAN RECALL MAKING A FEW SMART MOVES iN MY LiFE...
BUYiNG A DUCK WASN'T ONE OF THEM !!
WACK

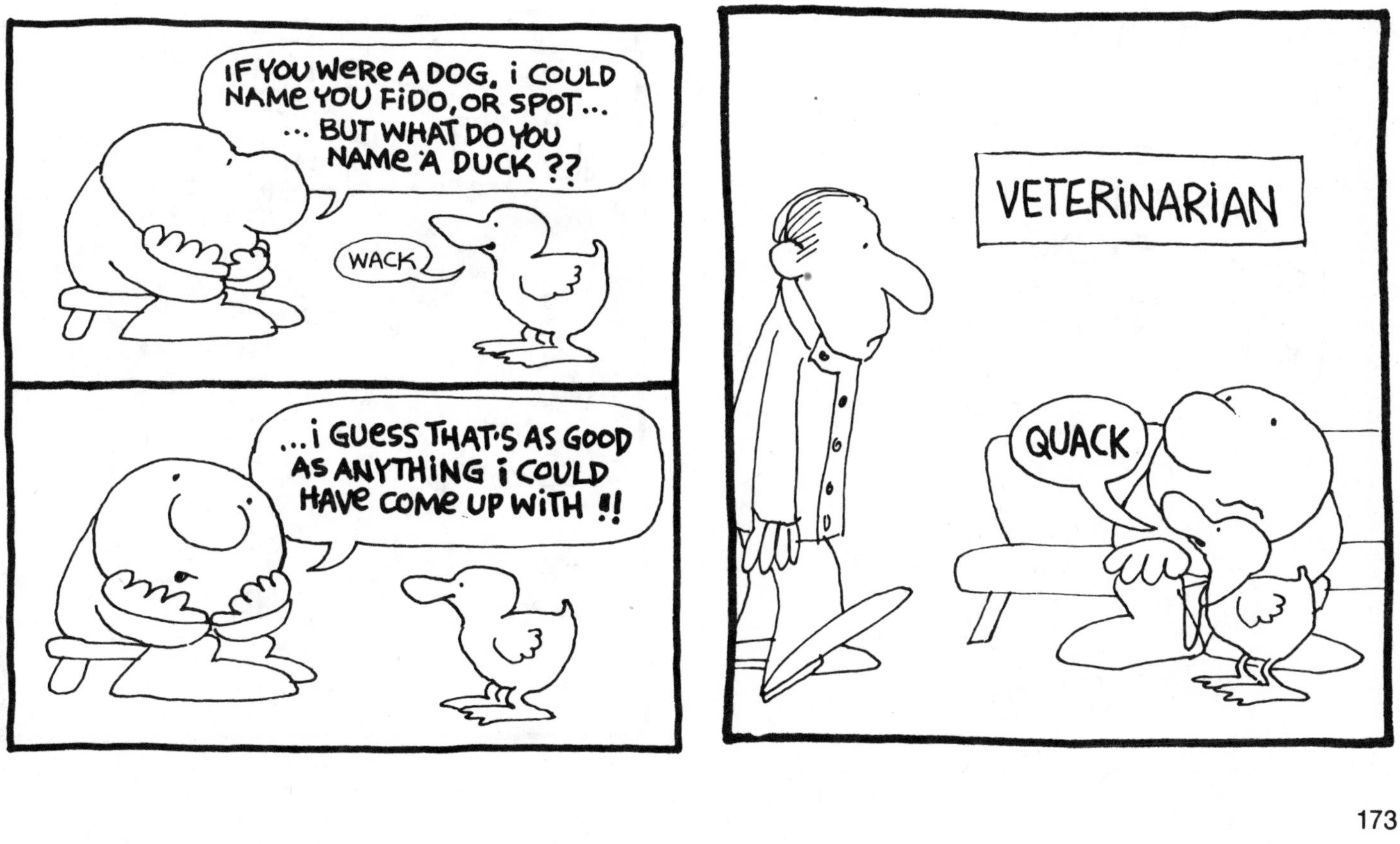
iF YOU WERE A DOG, i COULD NAME YOU FiDO, OR SPOT... ...BUT WHAT DO YOU NAME A DUCK ??
WACK
...i GUESS THAT'S AS GOOD AS ANYTHING i COULD HAVE COME UP WiTH !!
VETERiNARIAN
QUACK

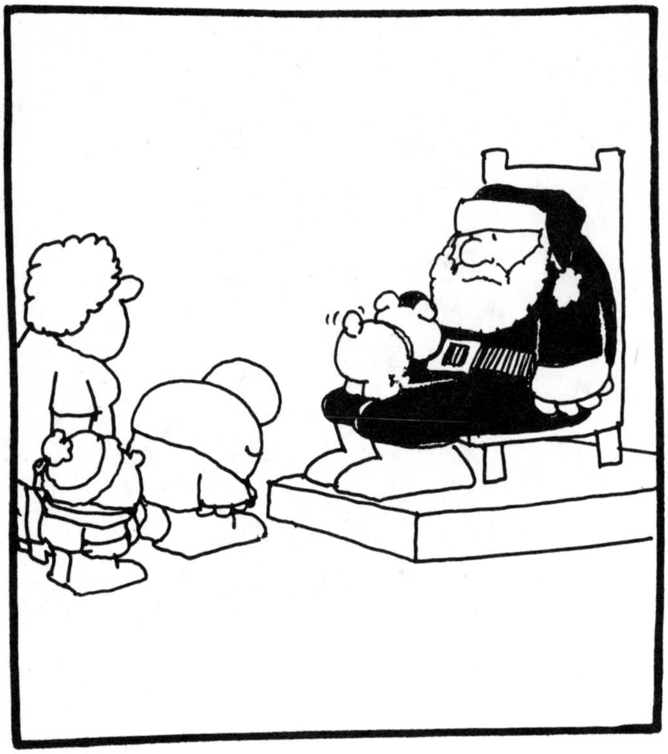

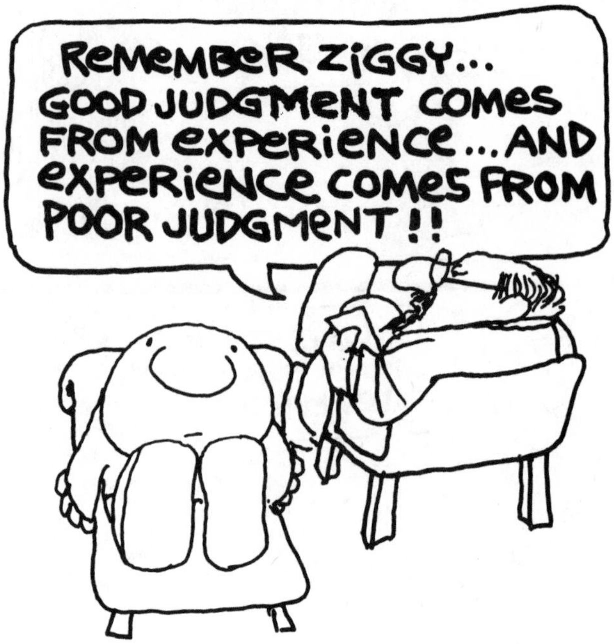
REMEMBER ZIGGY... GOOD JUDGMENT COMES FROM EXPERIENCE... AND EXPERIENCE COMES FROM POOR JUDGMENT!!

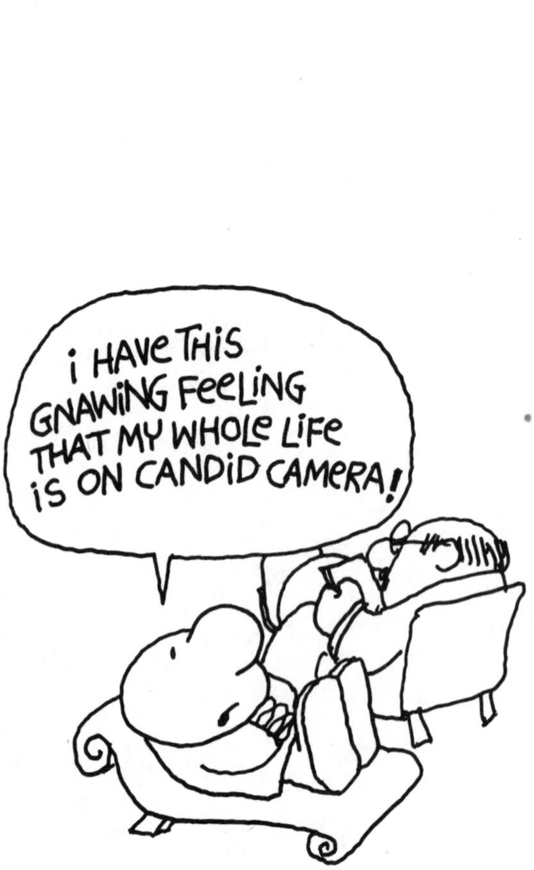
I HAVE THIS GNAWING FEELING THAT MY WHOLE LIFE IS ON CANDID CAMERA!

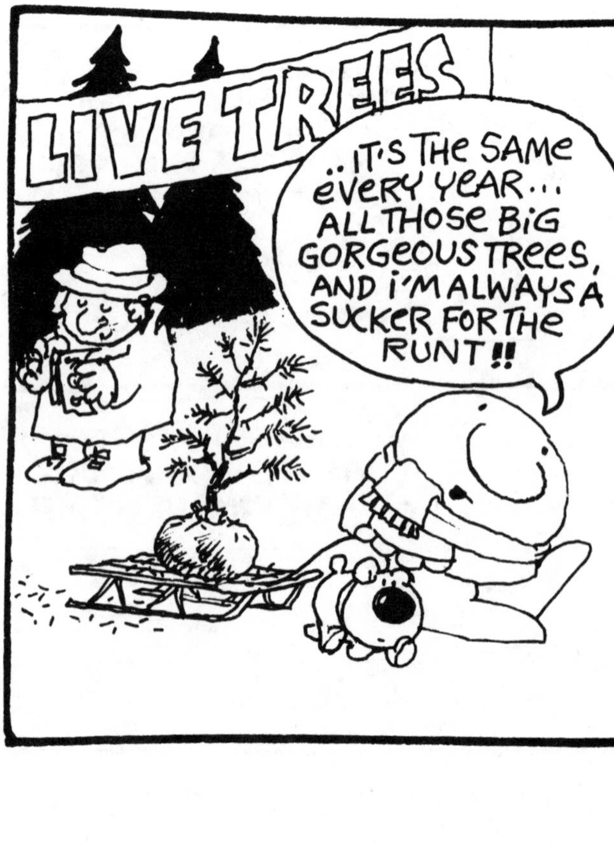
LIVE TREES
..IT'S THE SAME EVERY YEAR... ALL THOSE BIG GORGEOUS TREES, AND I'M ALWAYS A SUCKER FOR THE RUNT!!

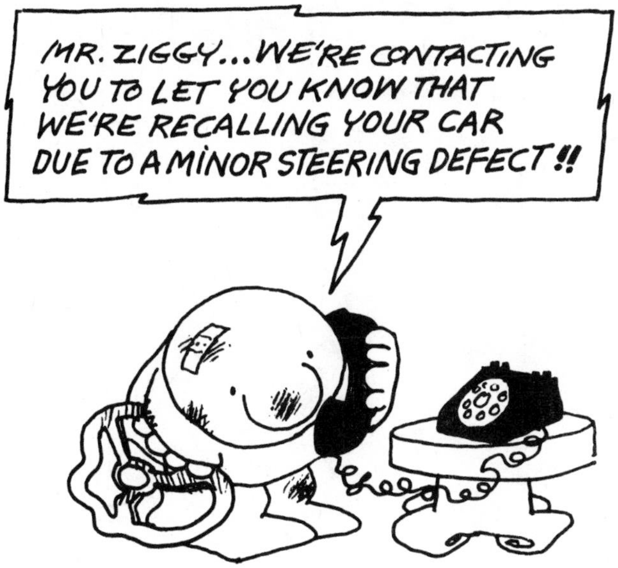
MR. ZIGGY...WE'RE CONTACTING YOU TO LET YOU KNOW THAT WE'RE RECALLING YOUR CAR DUE TO A MINOR STEERING DEFECT !!

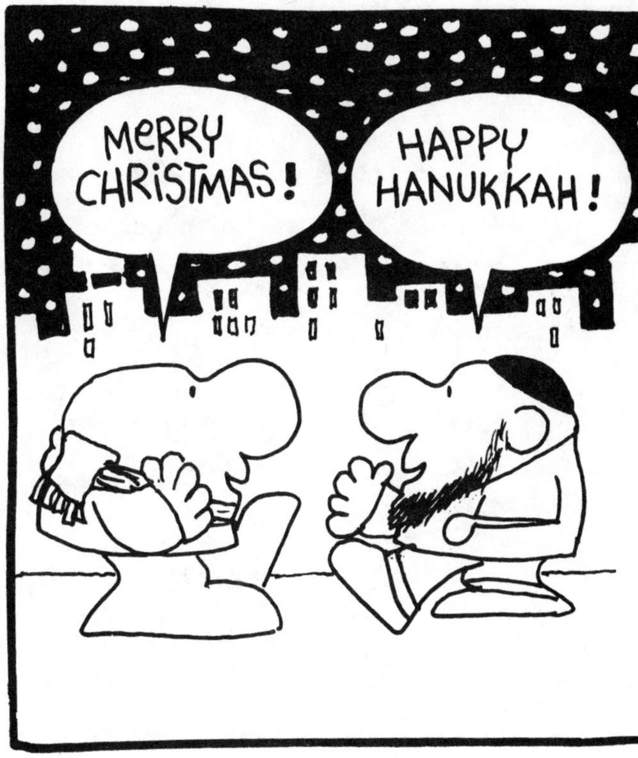
MERRY CHRISTMAS!
HAPPY HANUKKAH!

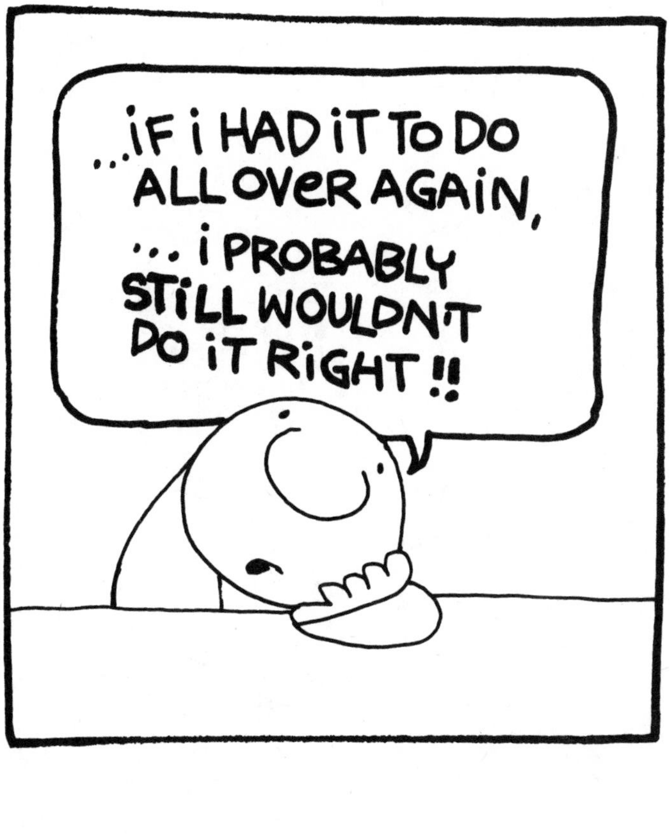
...IF I HAD IT TO DO ALL OVER AGAIN, ... I PROBABLY STILL WOULDN'T DO IT RIGHT !!

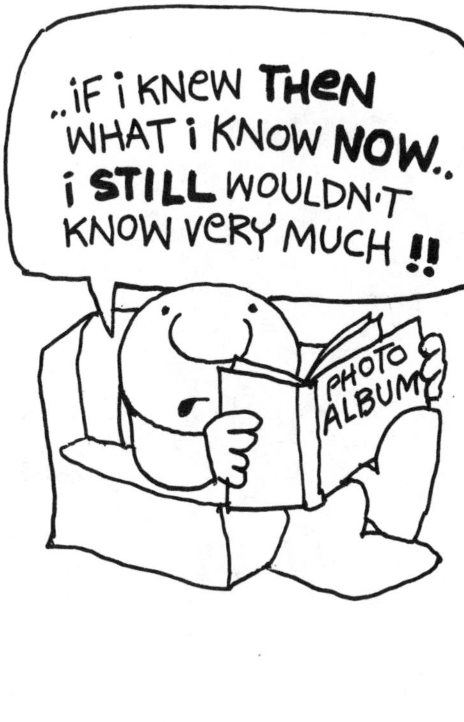
..IF I KNEW THEN WHAT I KNOW NOW.. I STILL WOULDN'T KNOW VERY MUCH !!
PHOTO ALBUM

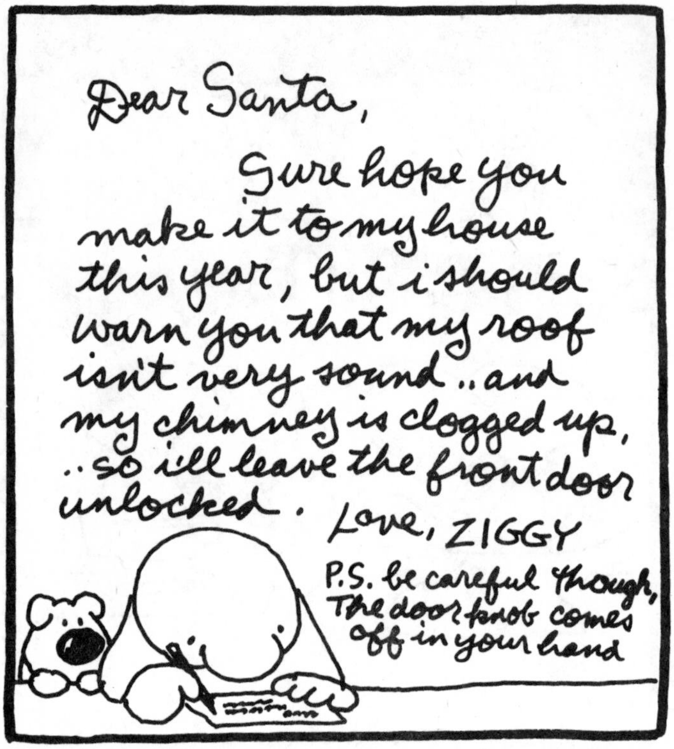
Dear Santa,
Sure hope you make it to my house this year, but i should warn you that my roof isn't very sound.. and my chimney is clogged up, ..so i'll leave the front door unlocked.
Love, ZIGGY
P.S. be careful though, The door knob comes off in your hand

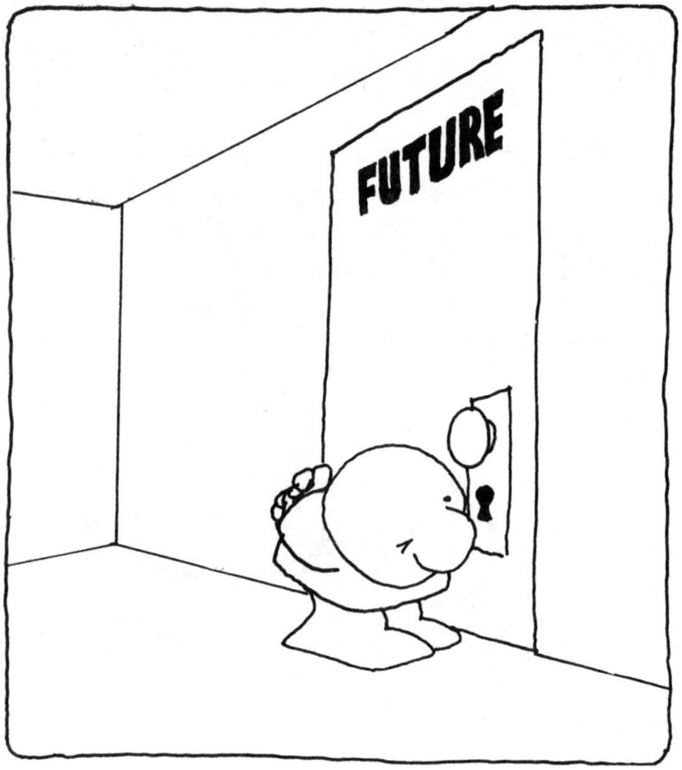
FUTURE

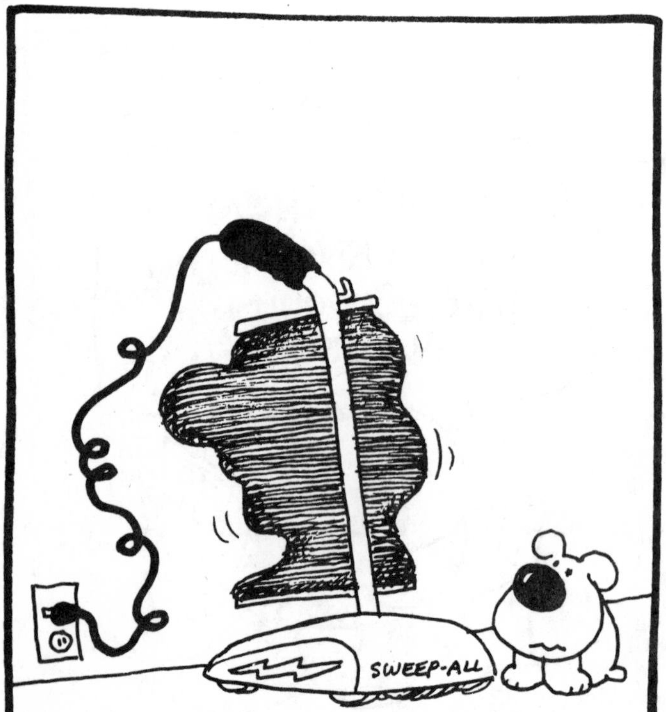
SWEEP-ALL

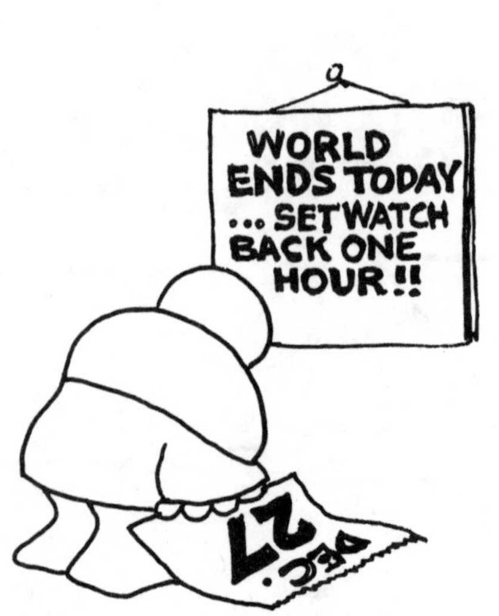
WORLD ENDS TODAY ... SET WATCH BACK ONE HOUR!!
DEC. 27

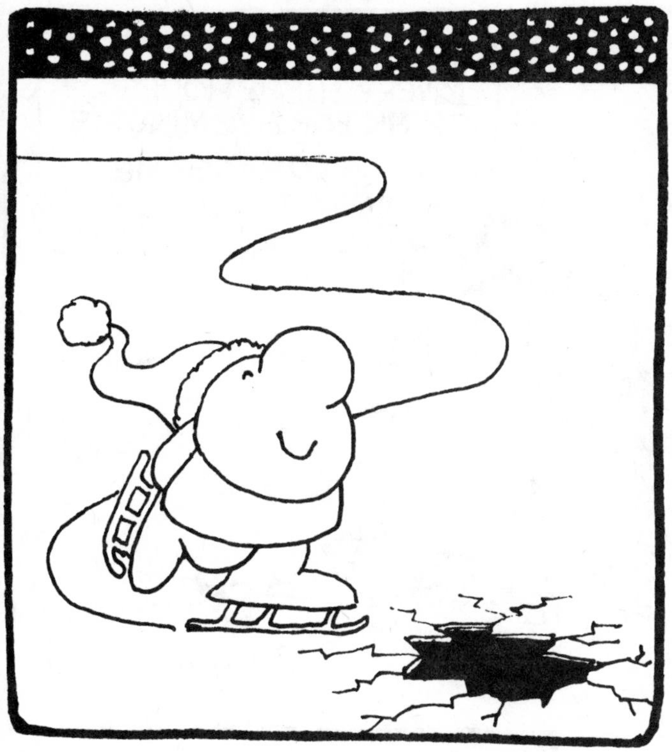

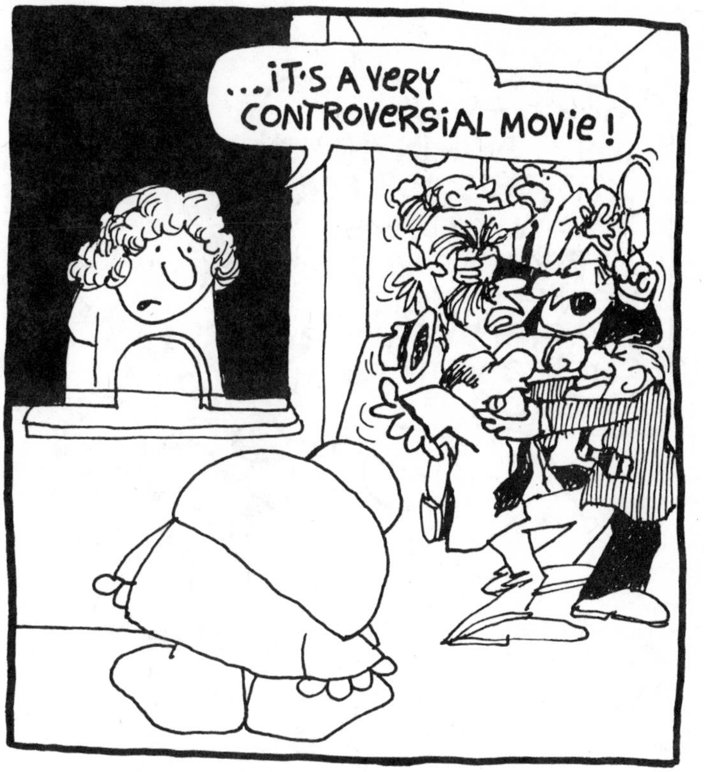
...IT'S A VERY CONTROVERSIAL MOVIE !

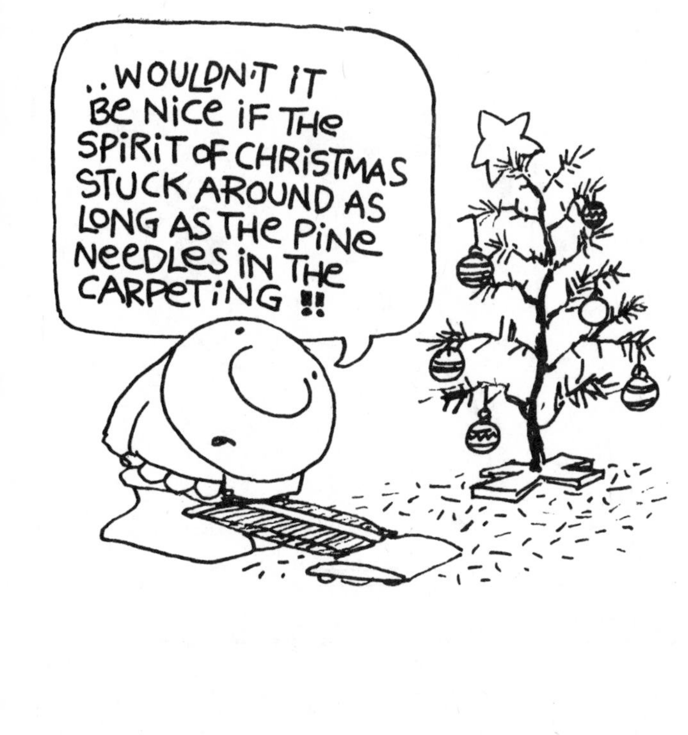
..WOULDN'T IT Be NICE IF THE SPIRIT OF CHRISTMAS STUCK AROUND AS LONG AS THE PINE NEEDLES IN THE CARPETING !!

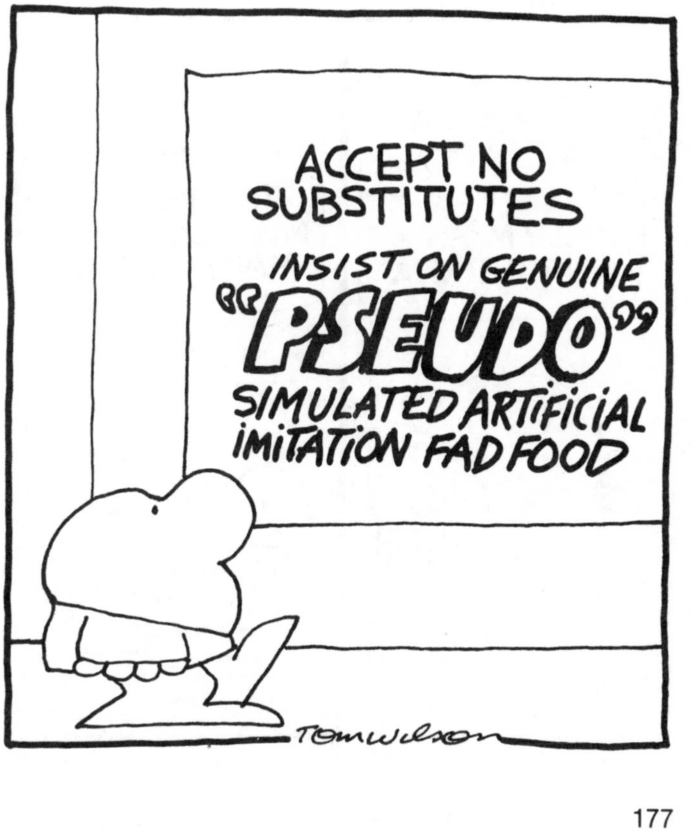
ACCEPT NO SUBSTITUTES
INSIST ON GENUINE
"PSEUDO"
SIMULATED ARTIFICIAL IMITATION FAD FOOD
TOM WILSON

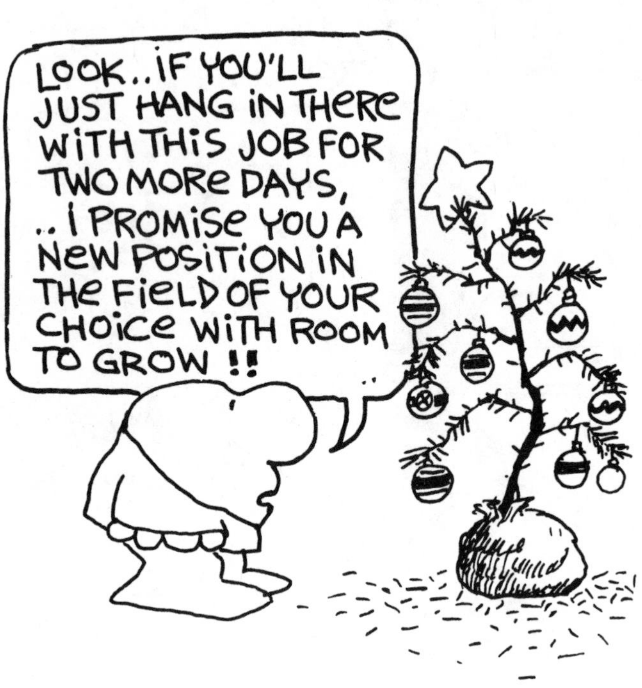
LOOK..IF YOU'LL JUST HANG IN THERE WITH THIS JOB FOR TWO MORE DAYS, ..I PROMISE YOU A NEW POSITION IN THE FIELD OF YOUR CHOICE WITH ROOM TO GROW !!

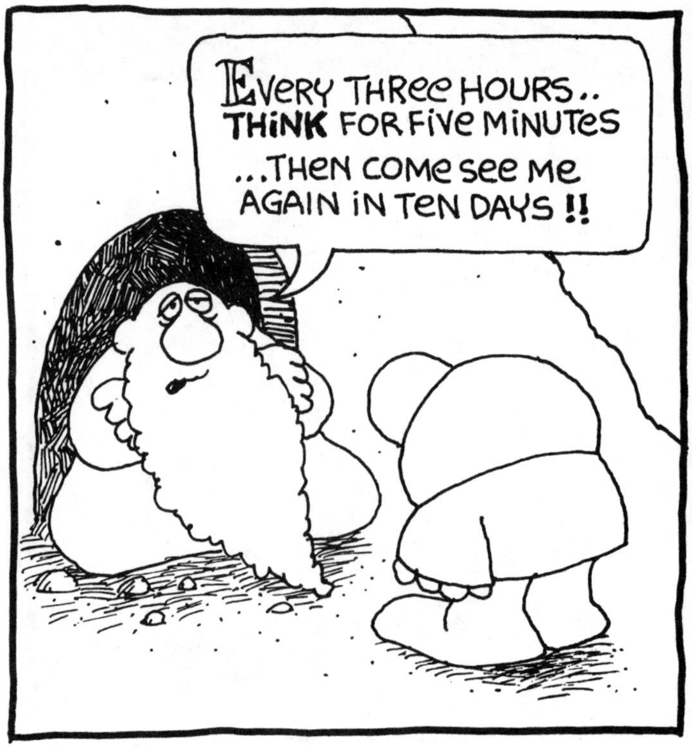
EVERY THREE HOURS.. THINK FOR FIVE MINUTES ...THEN COME SEE ME AGAIN IN TEN DAYS !!

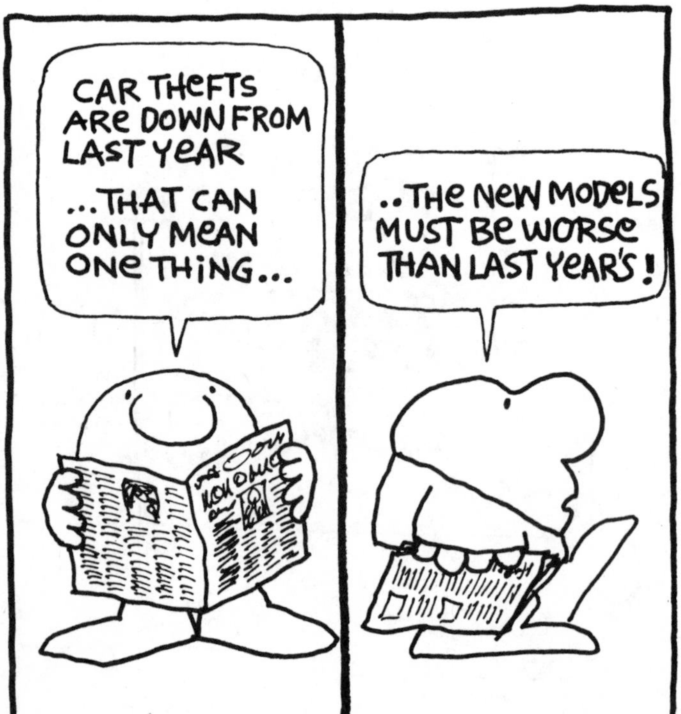
CAR THEFTS ARE DOWN FROM LAST YEAR ...THAT CAN ONLY MEAN ONE THING...
..THE NEW MODELS MUST BE WORSE THAN LAST YEAR'S !

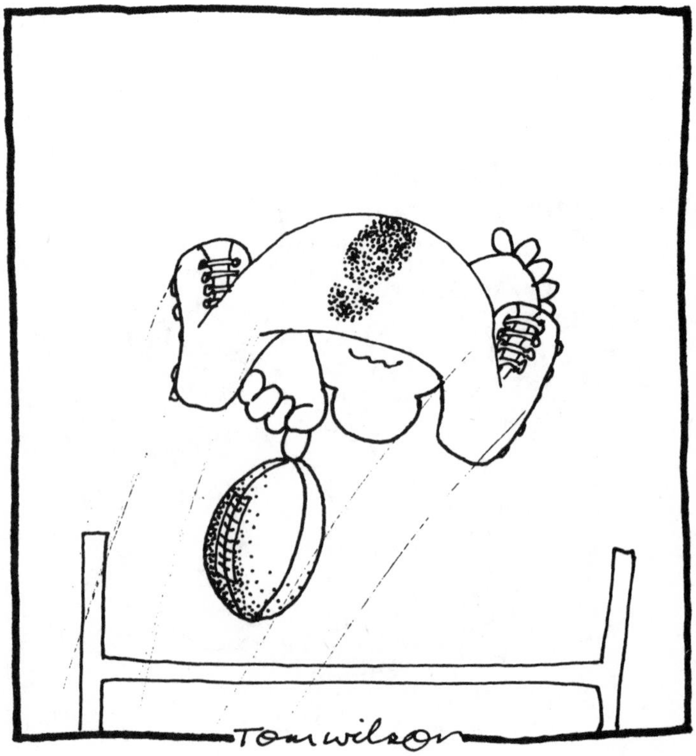
TOM WILSON

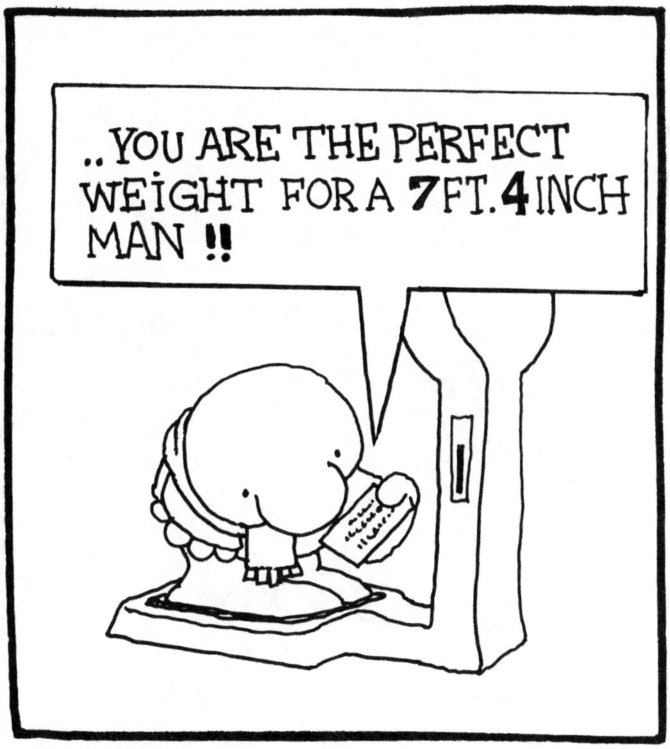
..YOU ARE THE PERFECT WEIGHT FOR A 7FT. 4 INCH MAN !!

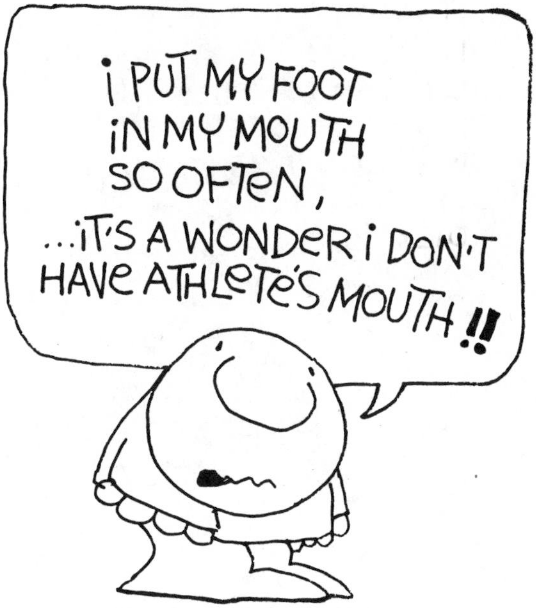
i PUT MY FOOT iN MY MOUTH SO OFTEN, ...iT'S A WONDER i DON'T HAVE ATHLETE'S MOUTH !!

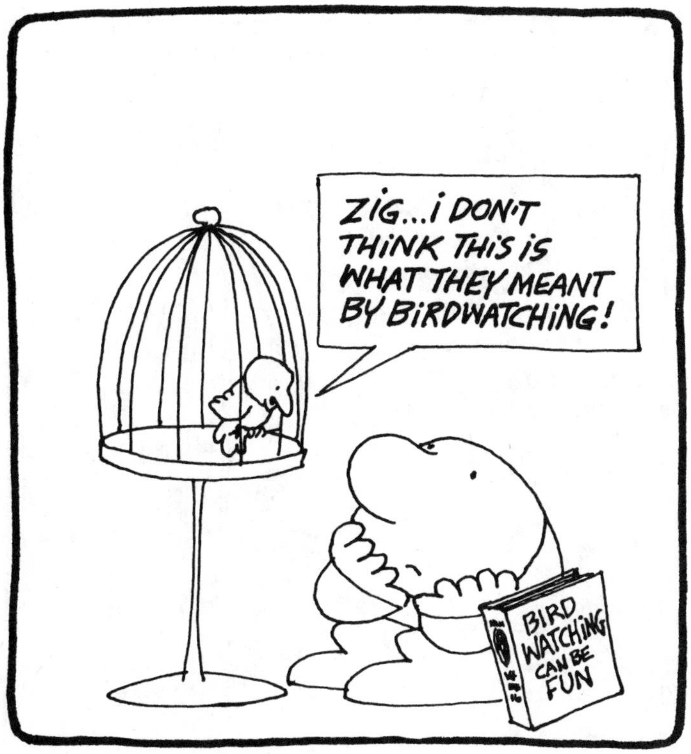
ZIG...i DON'T THINK THIS iS WHAT THEY MEANT BY BiRDWATCHiNG!
BIRD WATCHING CAN BE FUN

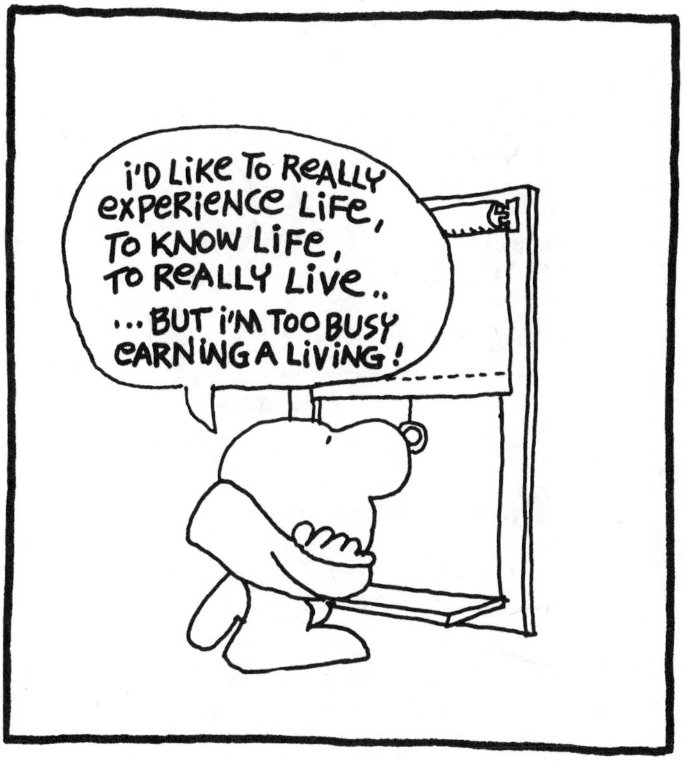
i'D LiKE TO REALLY EXPERiENCE LiFE, TO KNOW LiFE, TO REALLY LiVE.. ...BUT i'M TOO BUSY EARNiNG A LiViNG!

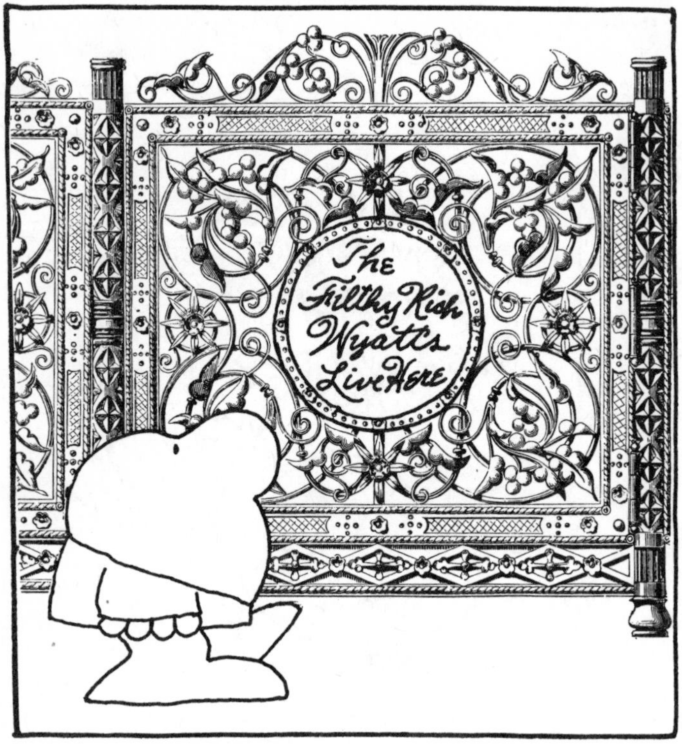
The Filthy Rich Wyatts Live Here

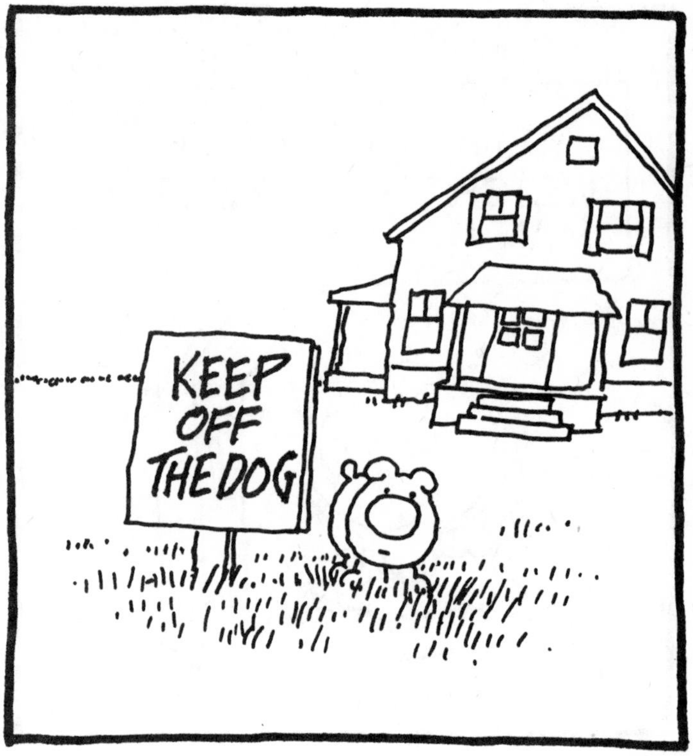
KEEP OFF THE DOG

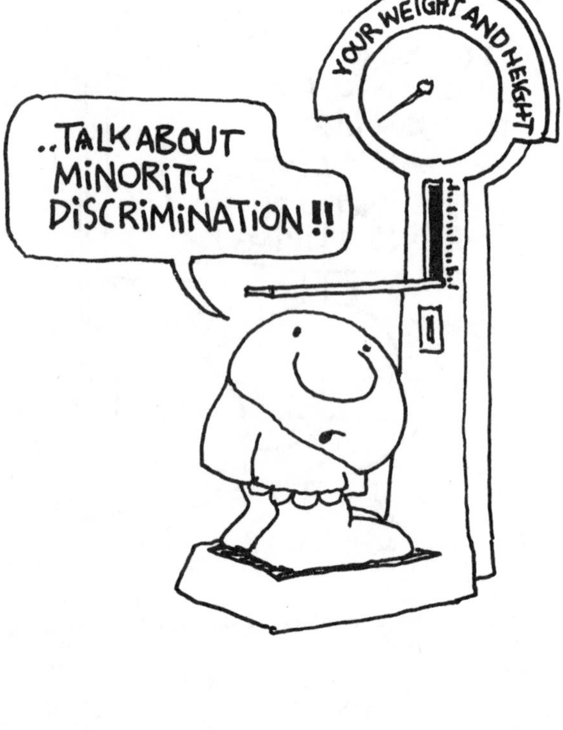
YOUR WEIGHT AND HEIGHT
..TALK ABOUT MINORITY DISCRIMINATION !!

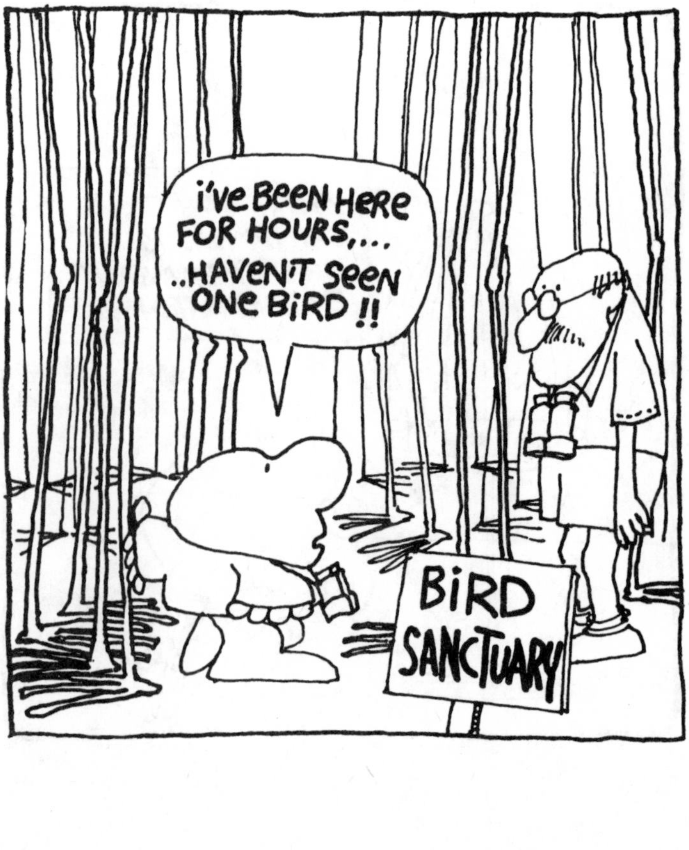
i've BEEN HERE FOR HOURS,... ..HAVEN'T SEEN ONE BIRD !!
BIRD SANCTUARY

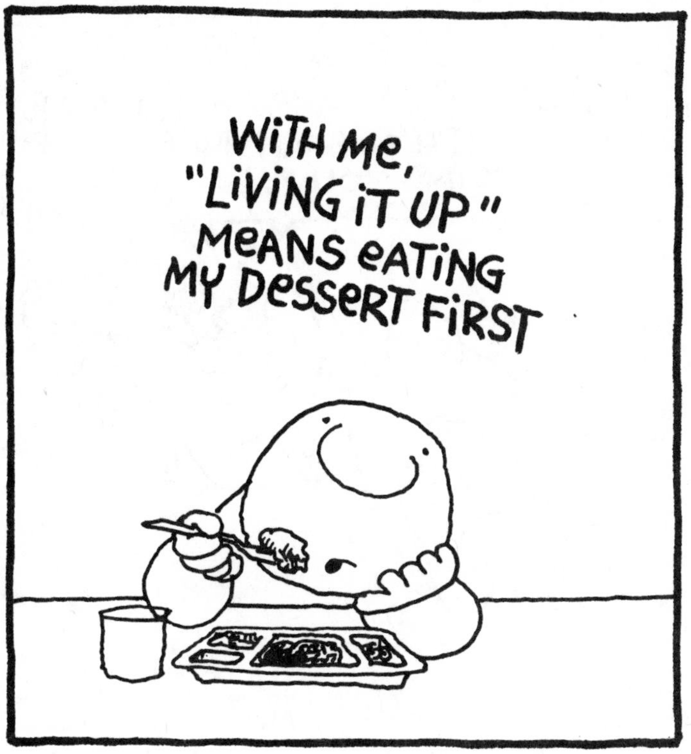
WITH ME, "LIVING IT UP" MEANS EATING MY DESSERT FIRST

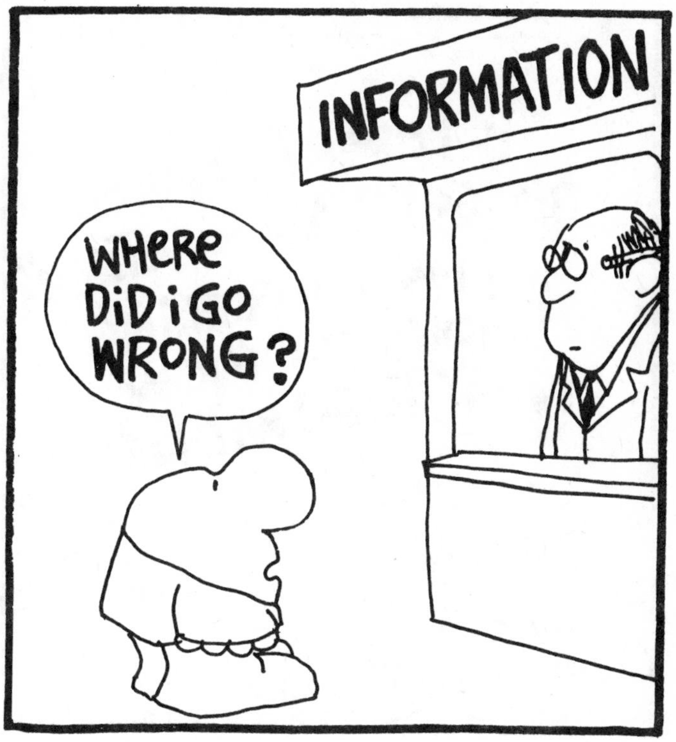
INFORMATION
WHERE DID I GO WRONG?

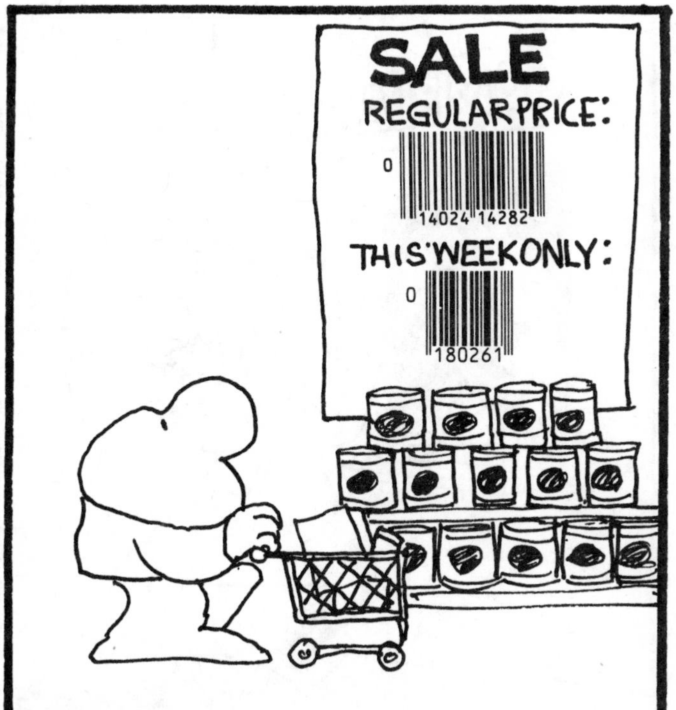
SALE
REGULAR PRICE:
0 14024 14282
THIS WEEK ONLY:
0 180261

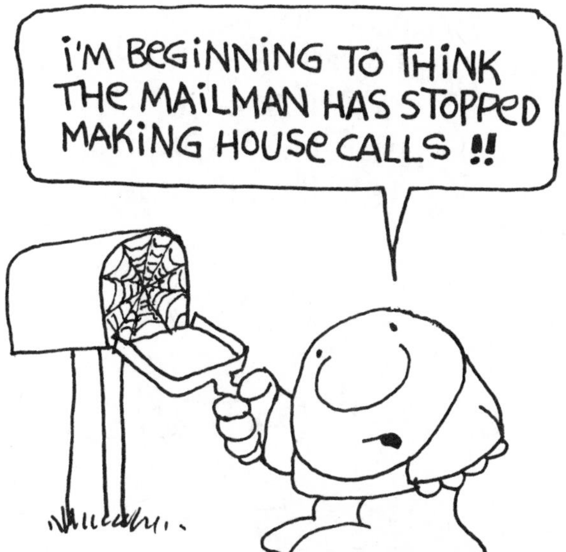
I'M BEGINNING TO THINK THE MAILMAN HAS STOPPED MAKING HOUSE CALLS !!

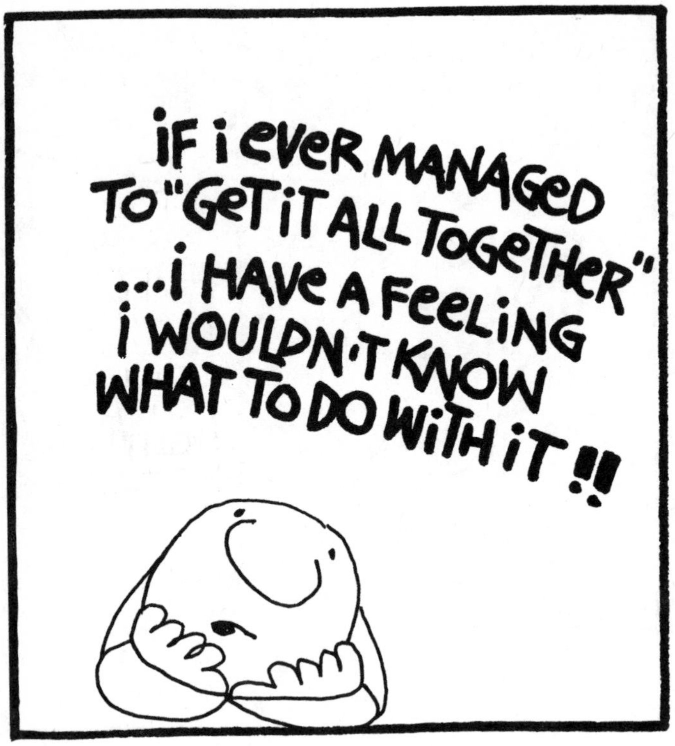
IF I EVER MANAGED TO "GET IT ALL TOGETHER" ...I HAVE A FEELING I WOULDN'T KNOW WHAT TO DO WITH IT !!

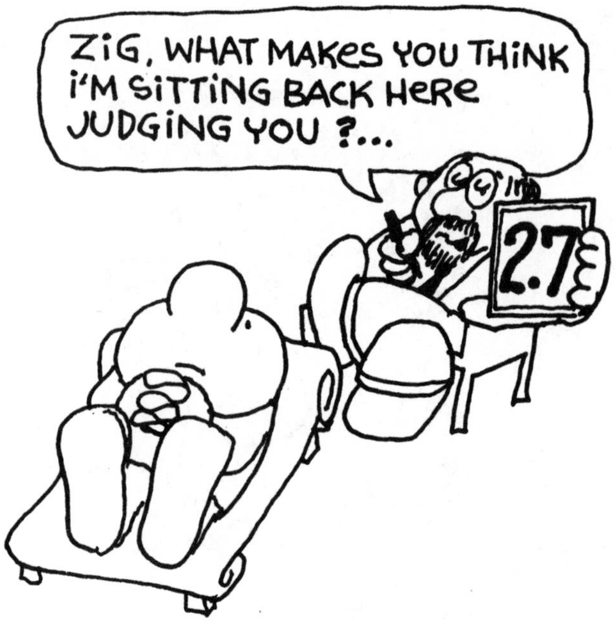
ZIG, WHAT MAKES YOU THINK I'M SITTING BACK HERE JUDGING YOU ?...
2.7

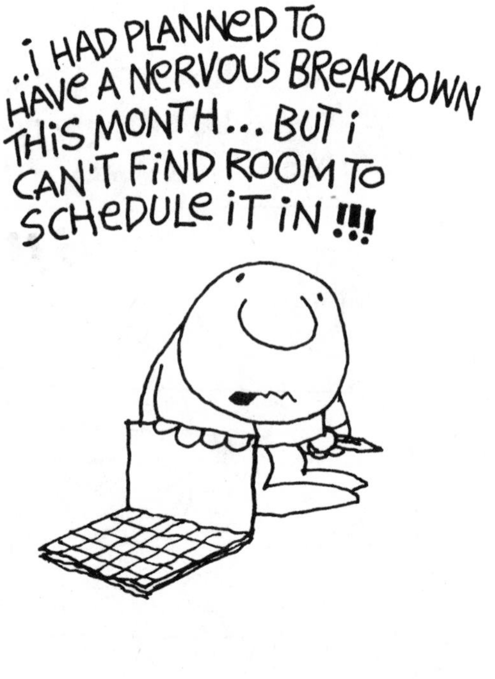
..I HAD PLANNED TO HAVE A NERVOUS BREAKDOWN THIS MONTH... BUT I CAN'T FIND ROOM TO SCHEDULE IT IN !!!

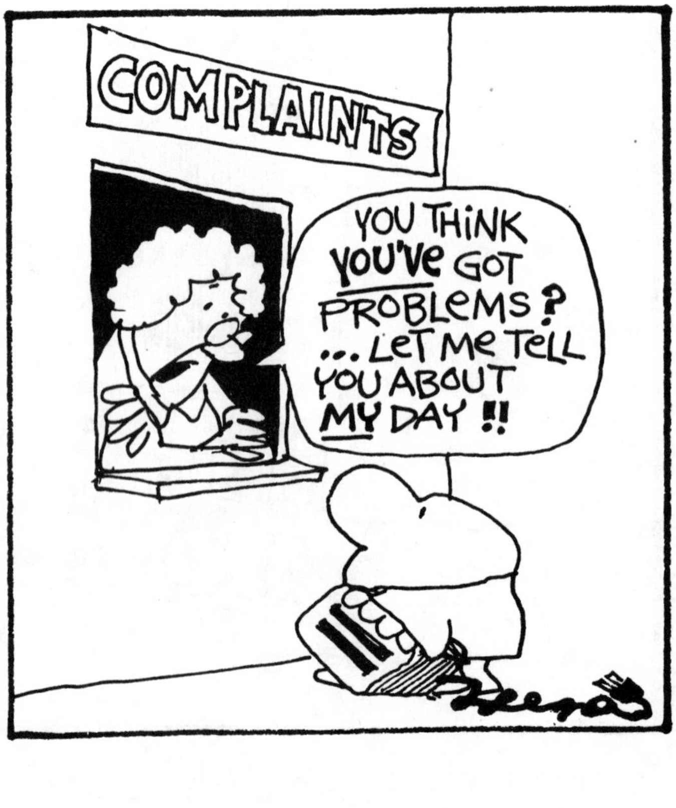
COMPLAINTS
YOU THINK YOU'VE GOT PROBLEMS ? ... LET ME TELL YOU ABOUT MY DAY !!

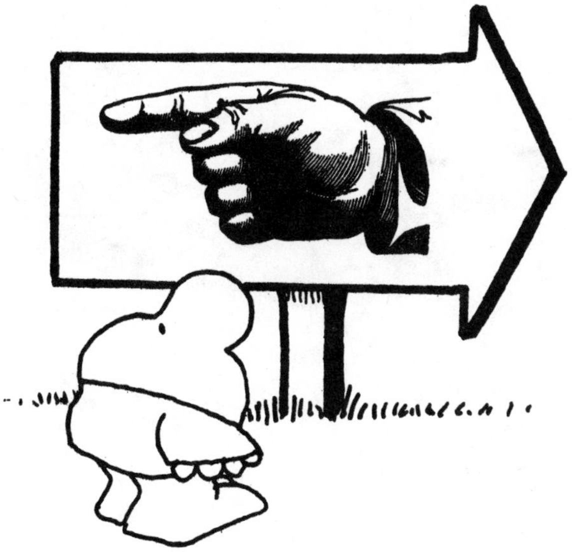

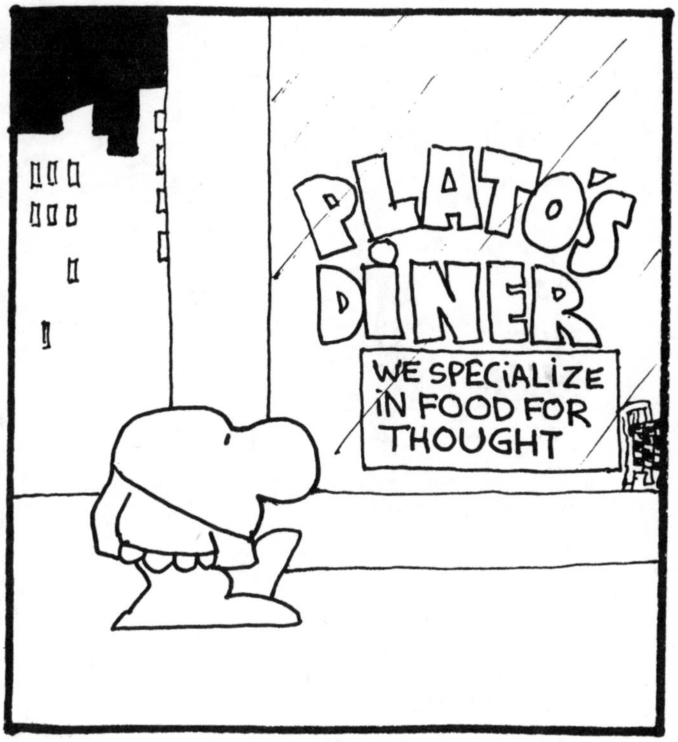
PLATO'S DINER
WE SPECIALIZE IN FOOD FOR THOUGHT

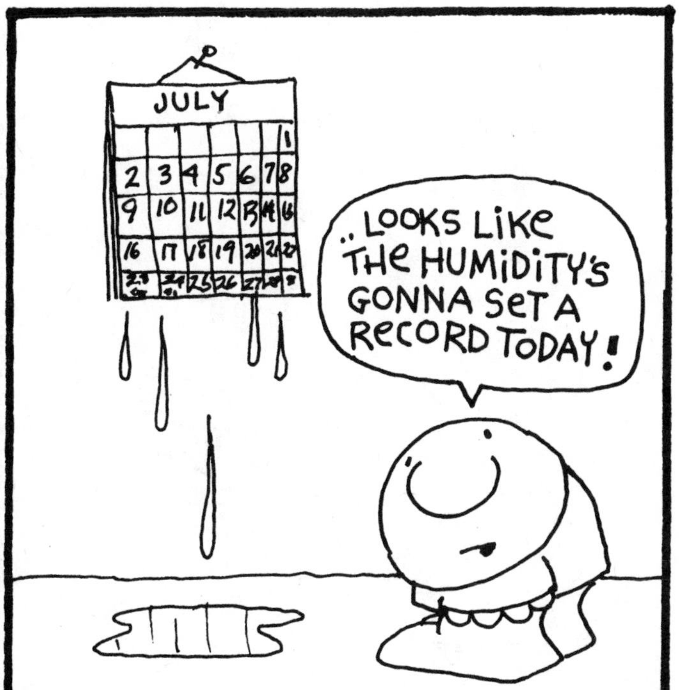
JULY
..LOOKS LIKE THE HUMIDITY'S GONNA SET A RECORD TODAY!

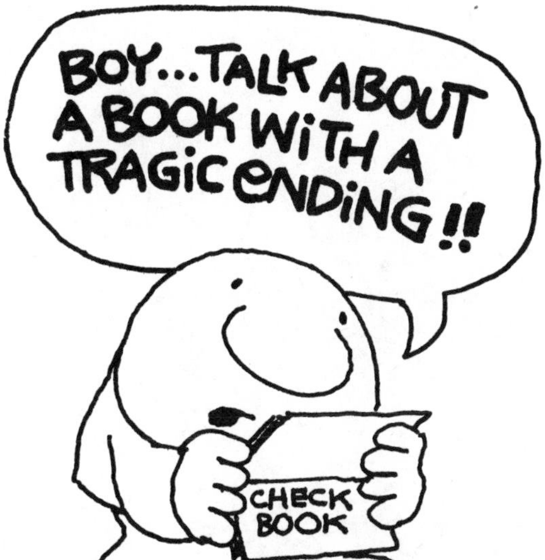
BOY...TALK ABOUT A BOOK WITH A TRAGIC ENDING!!
CHECK BOOK

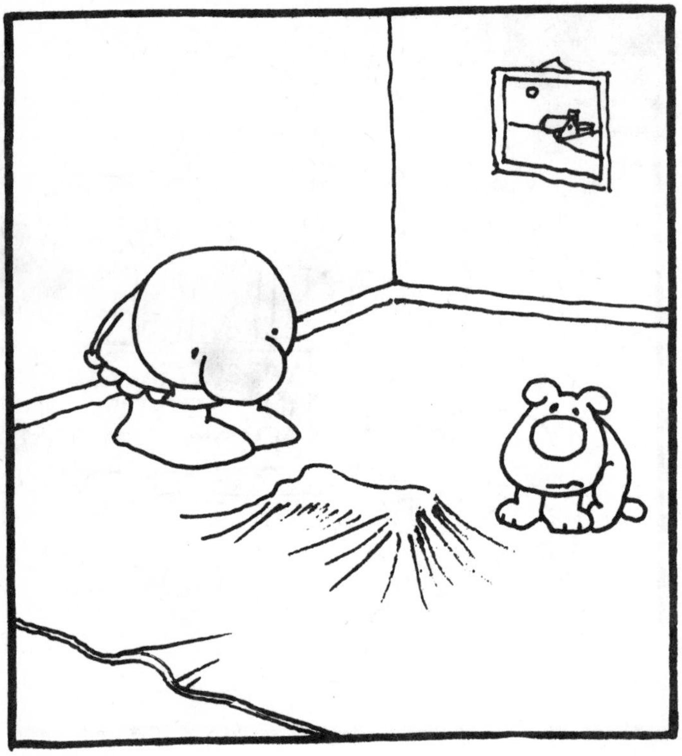

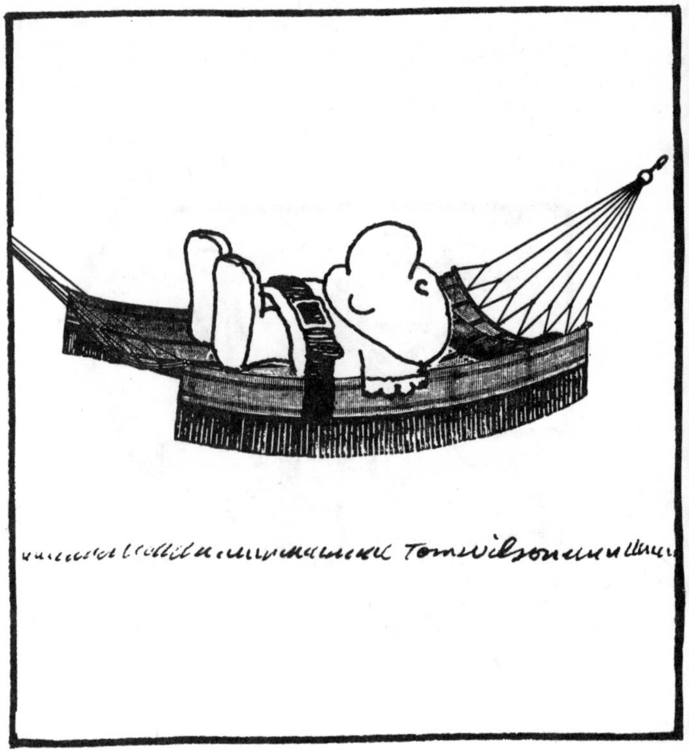
Tom Wilson

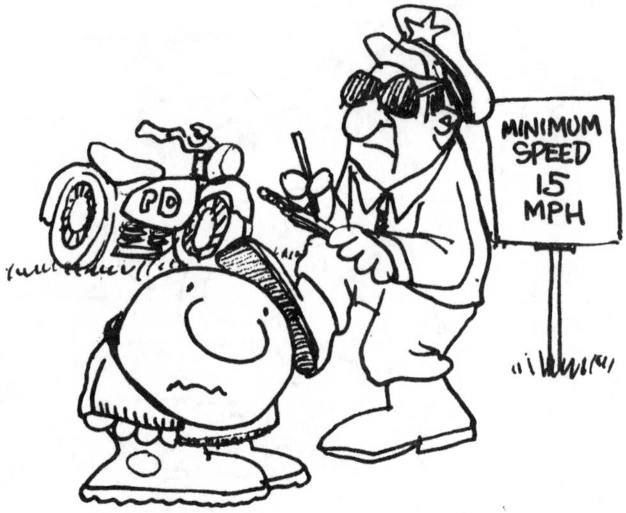
PD
MINIMUM SPEED 15 MPH

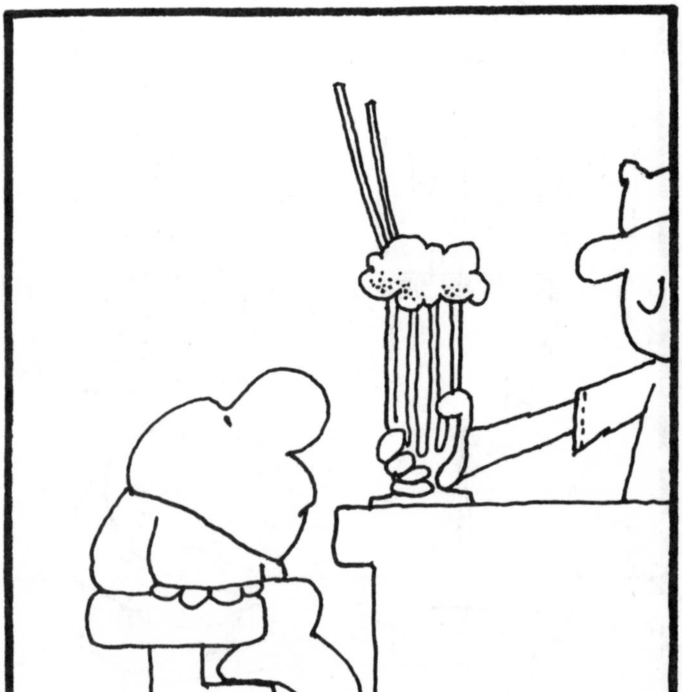

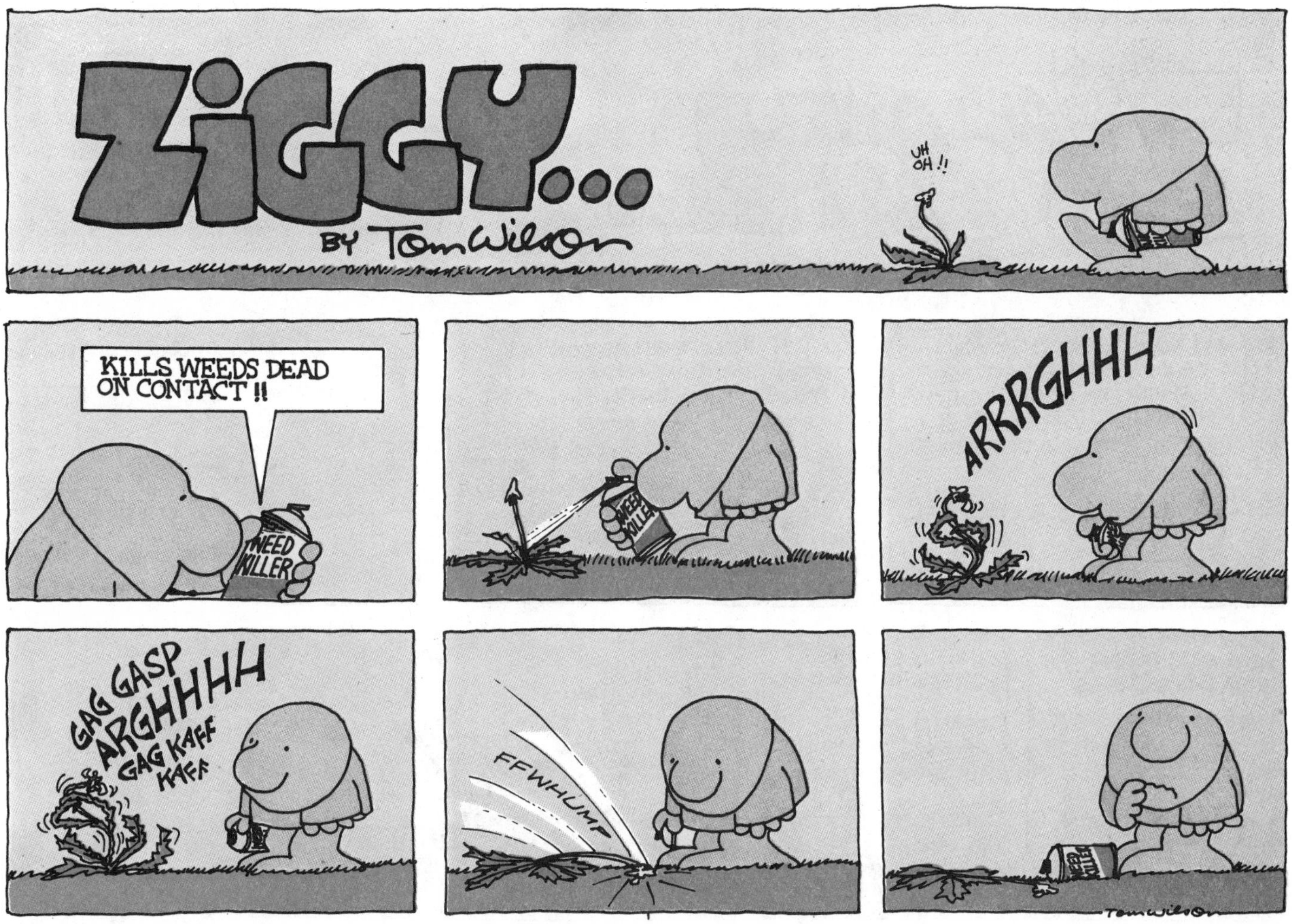
ZiGGY...
BY Tom Wilson
UH OH !!
KILLS WEEDS DEAD ON CONTACT !!
WEED KILLER
ARRRGHHH
GAG GASP ARGHHHH GAG KAFF KAFF
FFWHUMP
Tom Wilson

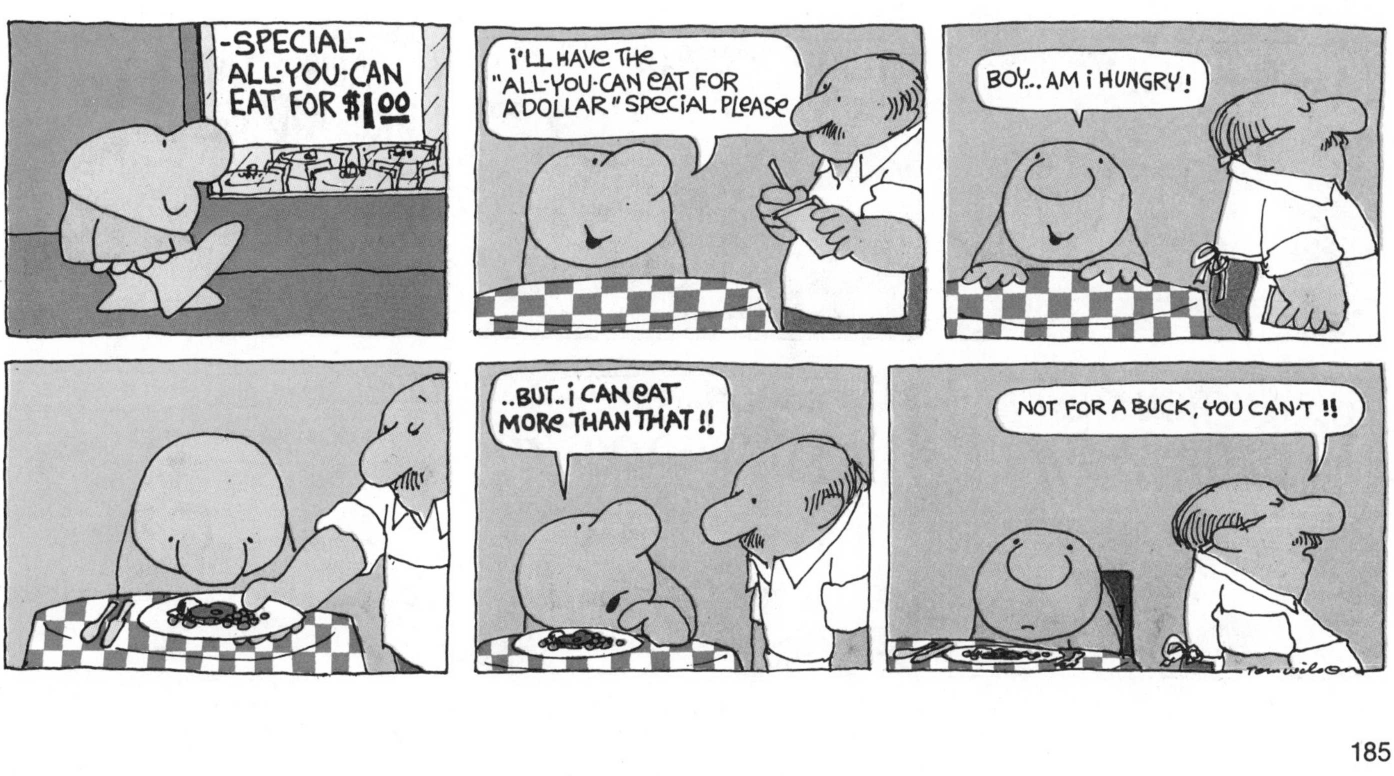
-SPECIAL- ALL-YOU-CAN EAT FOR $1.00
i'LL HAVE THE "ALL-YOU-CAN EAT FOR A DOLLAR" SPECiAL PLEASE
BOY... AM i HUNGRY!
..BUT.. i CAN EAT MORE THAN THAT !!
NOT FOR A BUCK, YOU CAN'T !!
Tom Wilson

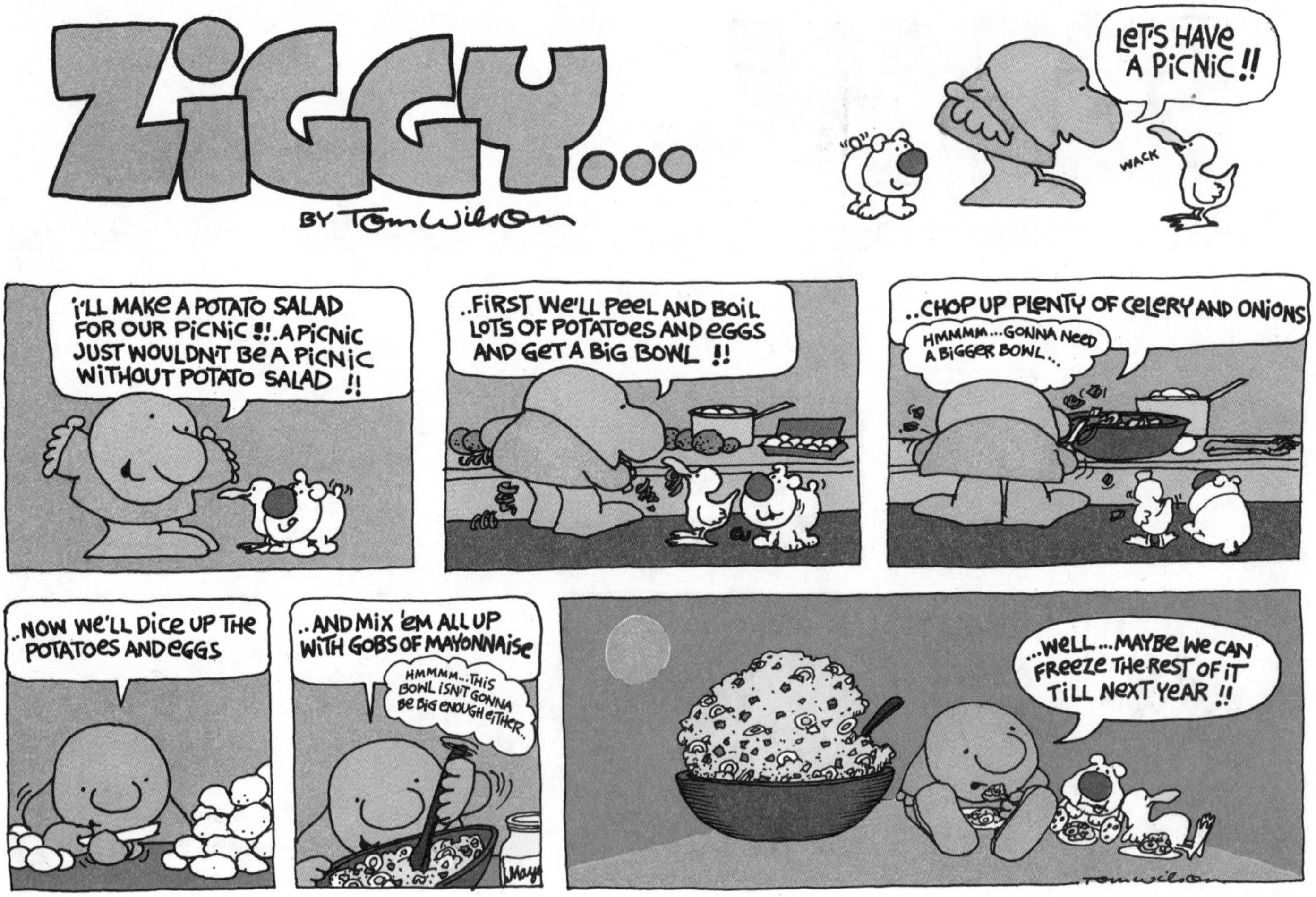
ZIGGY...
BY Tom Wilson
LET'S HAVE A PICNIC !!
"O"
WACK
I'LL MAKE A POTATO SALAD FOR OUR PICNIC !!..A PICNIC JUST WOULDN'T BE A PICNIC WITHOUT POTATO SALAD !!
..FIRST WE'LL PEEL AND BOIL LOTS OF POTATOES AND EGGS AND GET A BIG BOWL !!
..CHOP UP PLENTY OF CELERY AND ONIONS
HMMMM...GONNA NEED A BIGGER BOWL...
..NOW WE'LL DICE UP THE POTATOES AND EGGS
..AND MIX 'EM ALL UP WITH GOBS OF MAYONNAISE
HMMMM...THIS BOWL ISN'T GONNA BE BIG ENOUGH EITHER.
...WELL...MAYBE WE CAN FREEZE THE REST OF IT TILL NEXT YEAR !!
Tom Wilson

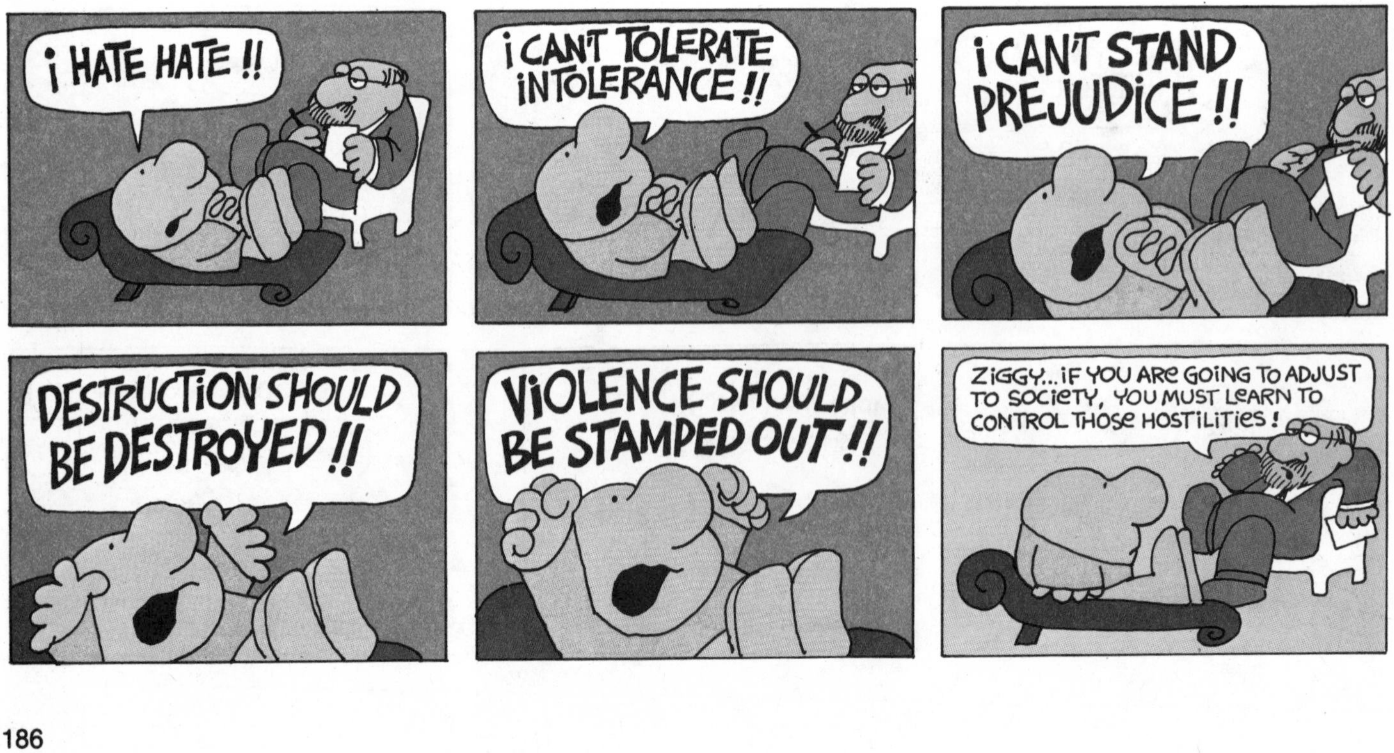
I HATE HATE !!
I CAN'T TOLERATE INTOLERANCE !!
I CAN'T STAND PREJUDICE !!
DESTRUCTION SHOULD BE DESTROYED !!
VIOLENCE SHOULD BE STAMPED OUT !!
ZIGGY...IF YOU ARE GOING TO ADJUST TO SOCIETY, YOU MUST LEARN TO CONTROL THOSE HOSTILITIES !

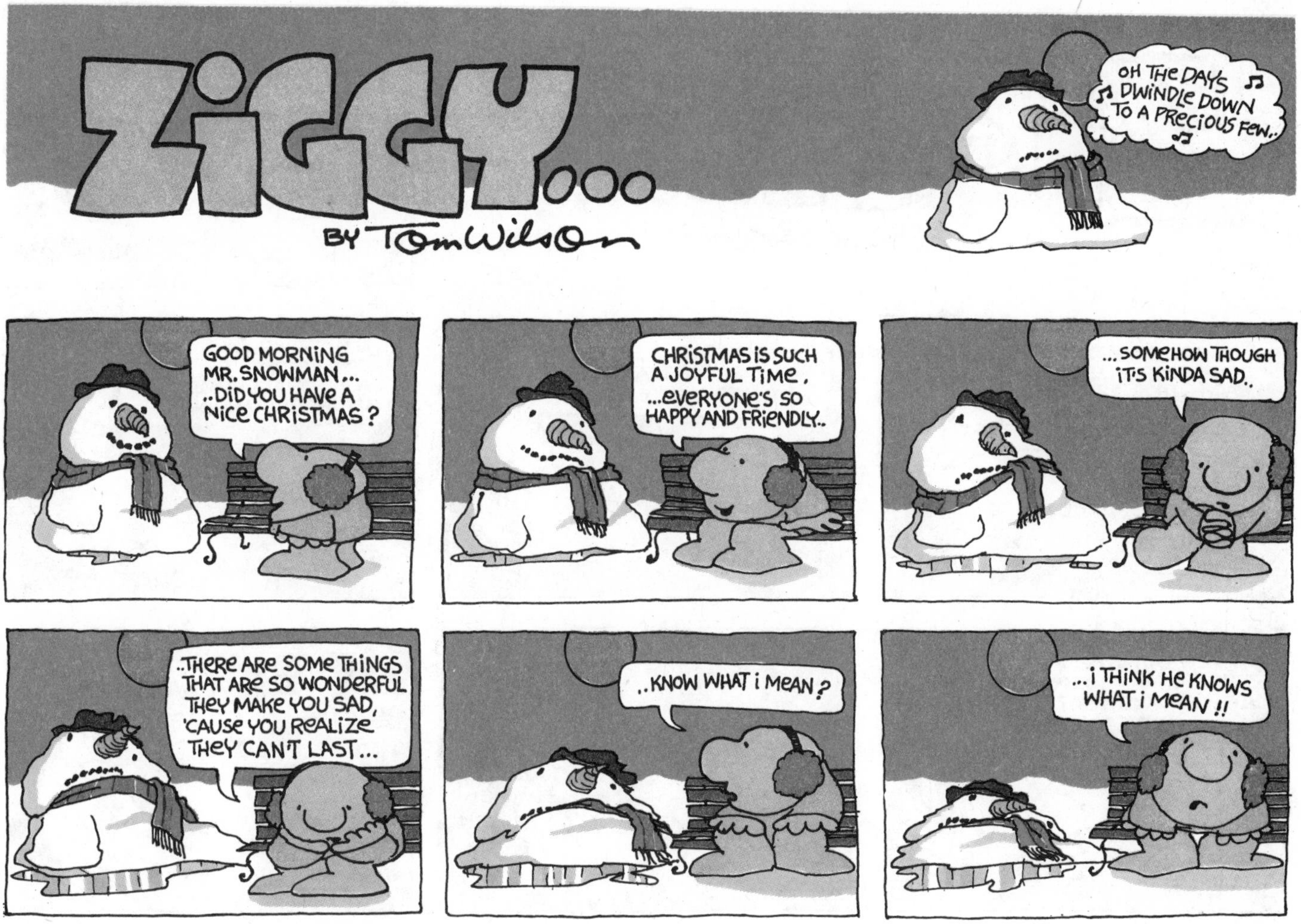
ZIGGY...
BY TOM WILSON
OH THE DAYS DWINDLE DOWN TO A PRECIOUS FEW..
GOOD MORNING MR. SNOWMAN... ..DID YOU HAVE A NICE CHRISTMAS?
CHRISTMAS IS SUCH A JOYFUL TIME, ...EVERYONE'S SO HAPPY AND FRIENDLY..
...SOMEHOW THOUGH IT'S KINDA SAD..
..THERE ARE SOME THINGS THAT ARE SO WONDERFUL THEY MAKE YOU SAD, 'CAUSE YOU REALIZE THEY CAN'T LAST...
..KNOW WHAT I MEAN?
...I THINK HE KNOWS WHAT I MEAN!!

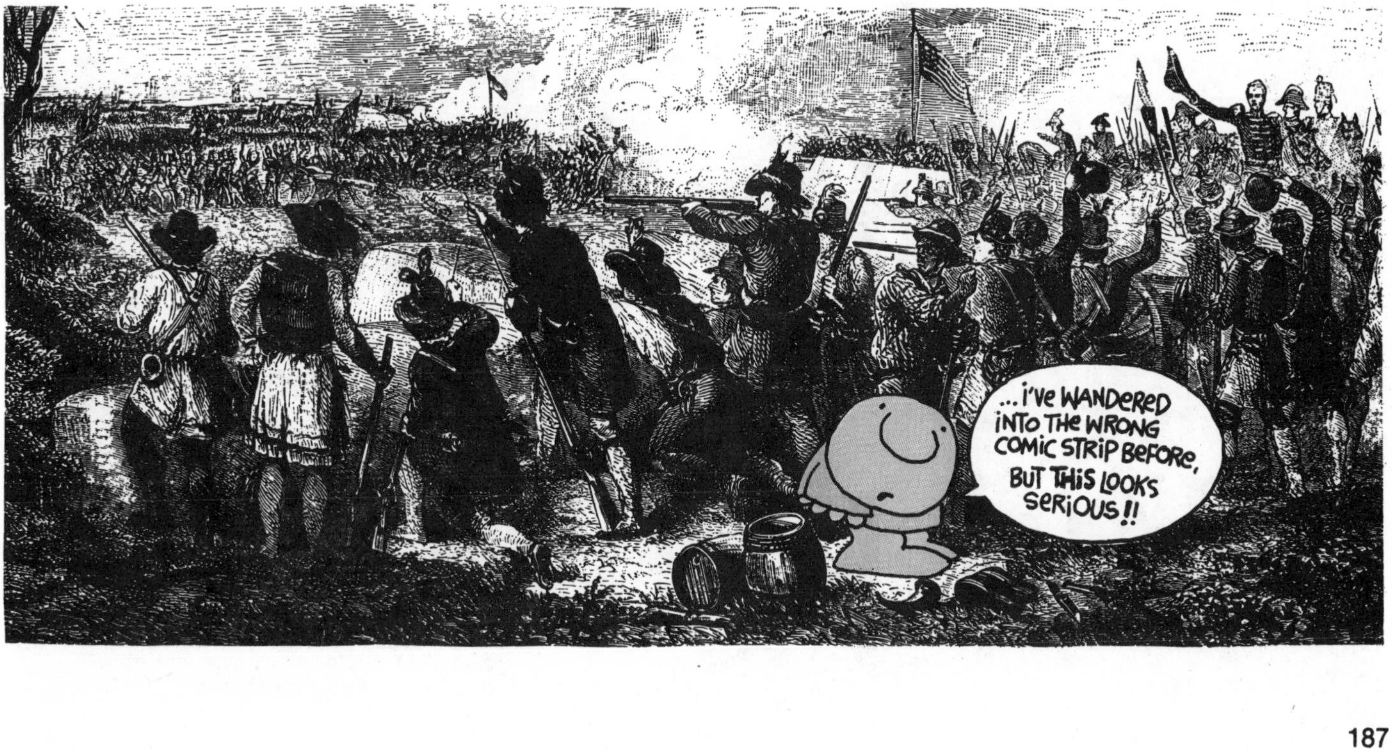
...I'VE WANDERED INTO THE WRONG COMIC STRIP BEFORE, BUT THIS LOOKS SERIOUS!!

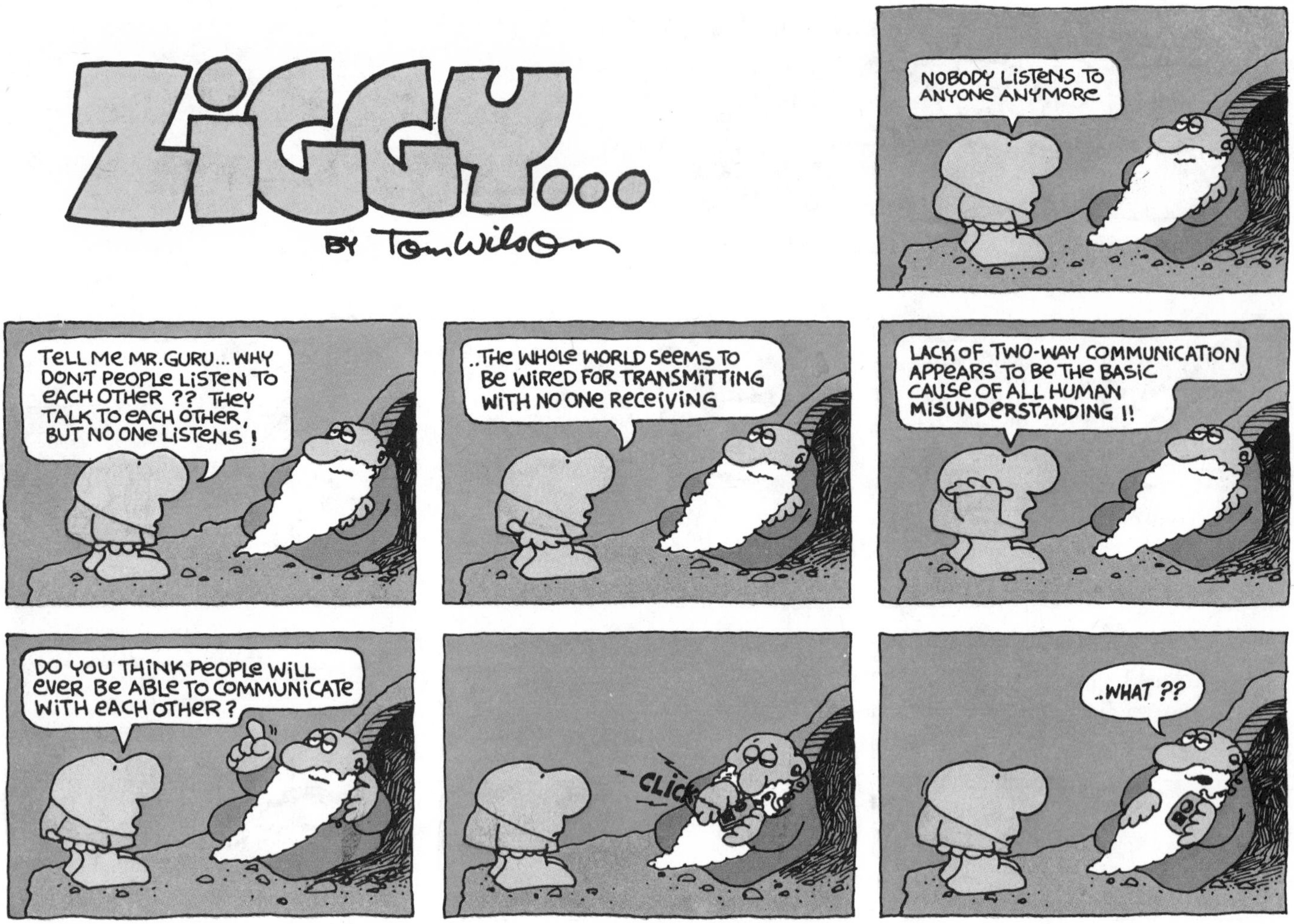
ZIGGY...ooo
BY Tom Wilson
NOBODY LISTENS TO ANYONE ANYMORE
TELL ME MR. GURU... WHY DON'T PEOPLE LISTEN TO EACH OTHER ?? THEY TALK TO EACH OTHER, BUT NO ONE LISTENS!
..THE WHOLE WORLD SEEMS TO BE WIRED FOR TRANSMITTING WITH NO ONE RECEIVING
LACK OF TWO-WAY COMMUNICATION APPEARS TO BE THE BASIC CAUSE OF ALL HUMAN MISUNDERSTANDING !!
DO YOU THINK PEOPLE WILL EVER BE ABLE TO COMMUNICATE WITH EACH OTHER ?
CLICK
..WHAT ??

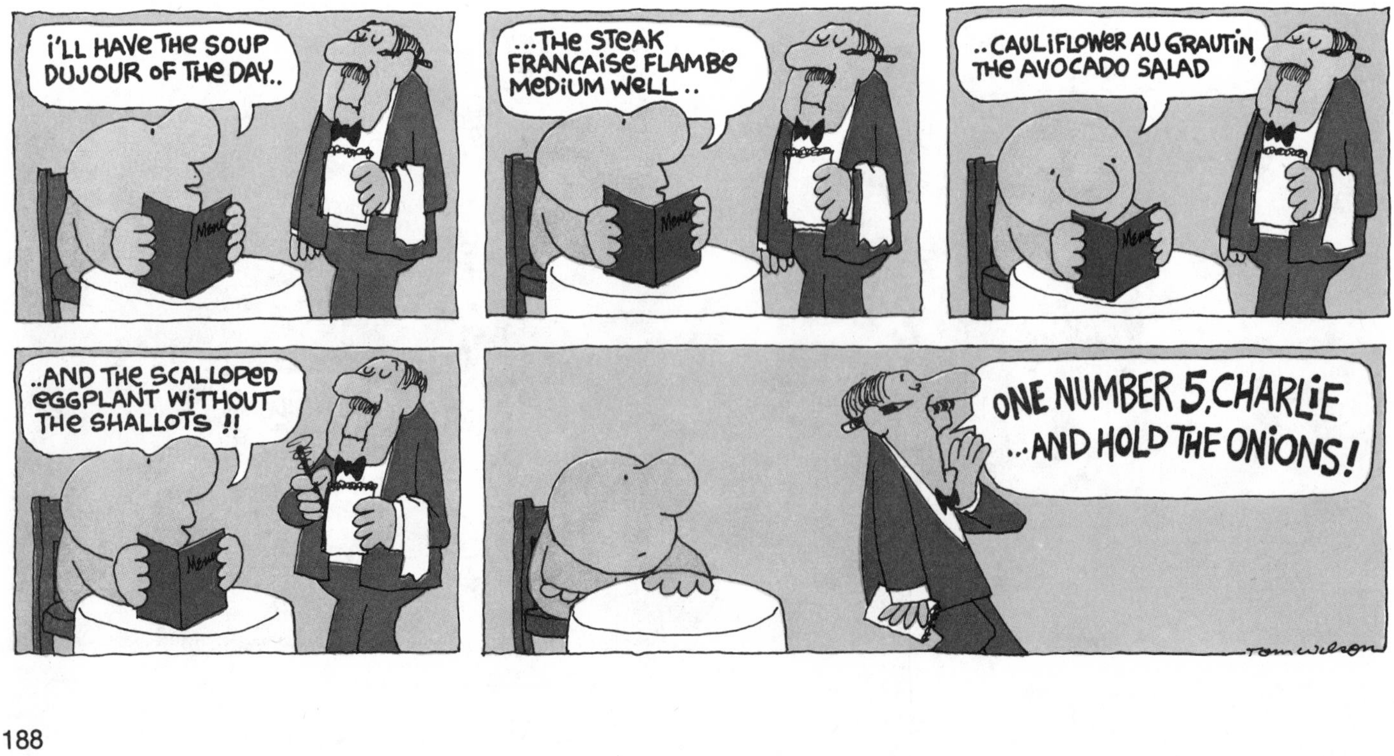
I'LL HAVE THE SOUP DUJOUR OF THE DAY..
...THE STEAK FRANCAISE FLAMBE MEDIUM WELL..
..CAULIFLOWER AU GRAUTIN, THE AVOCADO SALAD
..AND THE SCALLOPED EGGPLANT WITHOUT THE SHALLOTS !!
ONE NUMBER 5, CHARLIE ...AND HOLD THE ONIONS!
Tom Wilson

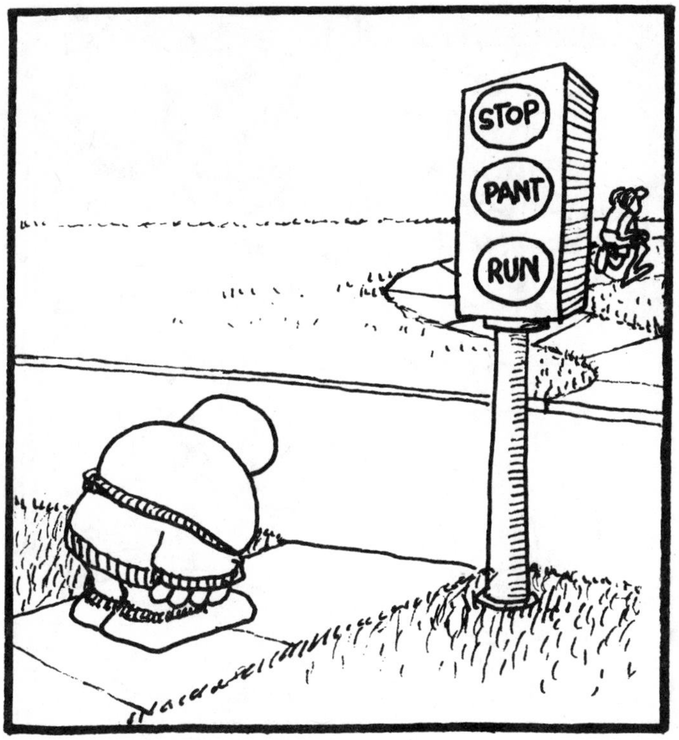
STOP
PANT
RUN

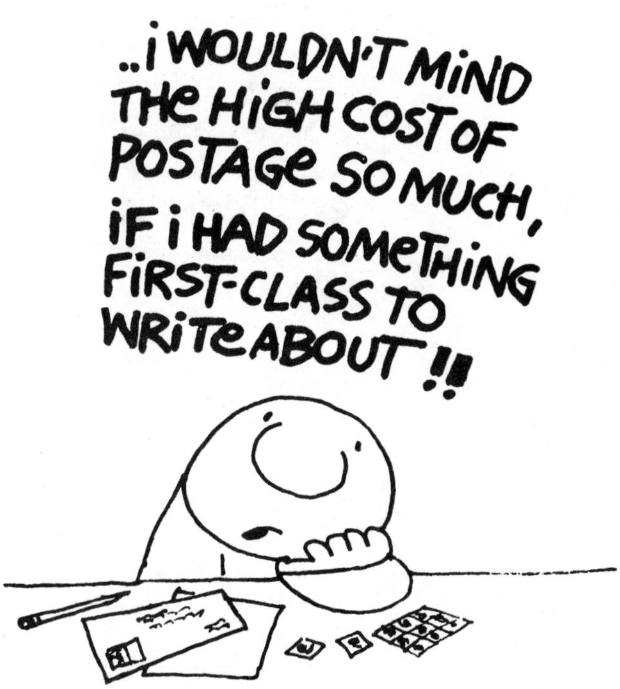
..i WOULDN'T MiND THE HiGH COST OF POSTAGE SO MUCH, iF i HAD SOMETHiNG FiRST-CLASS TO WRiTE ABOUT !!

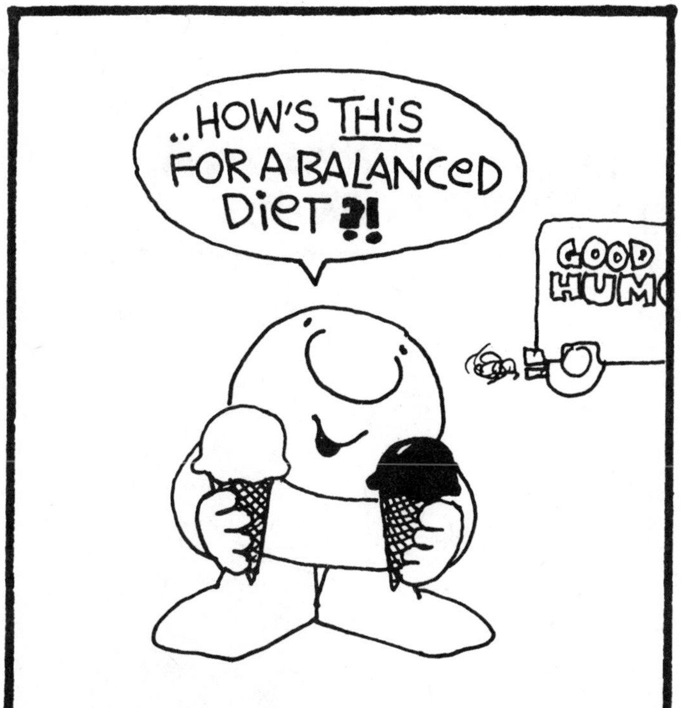
..HOW'S THiS FOR A BALANCED DiET ?!
GOOD
HUM

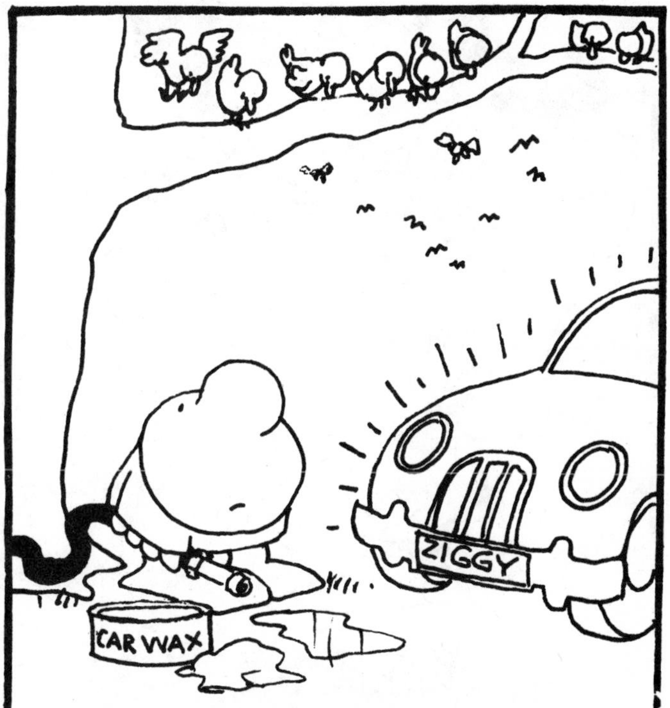
ZIGGY
CAR WAX

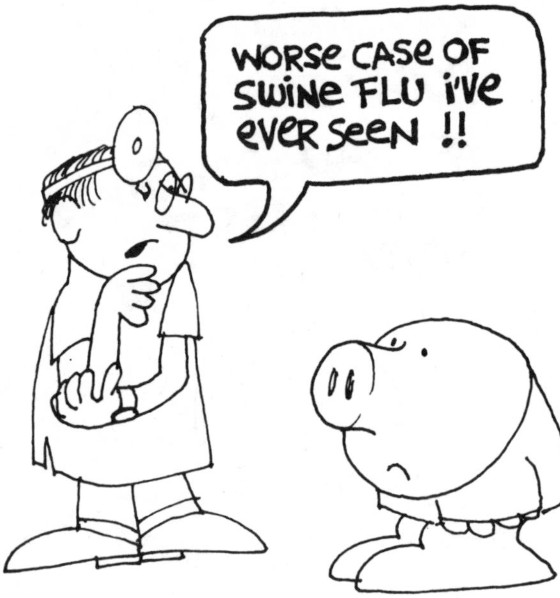
WORSE CASE OF SWINE FLU i've ever SEEN !!

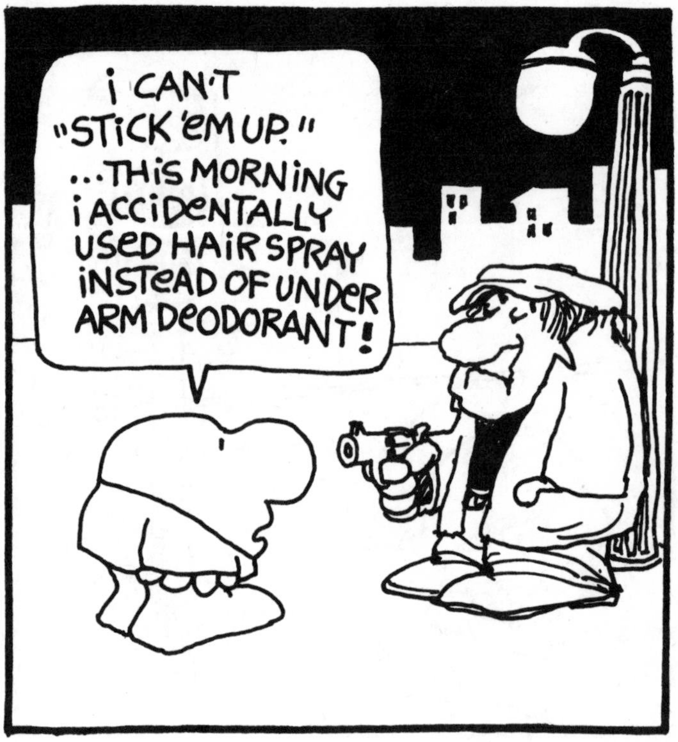
i CAN'T "STiCK 'EM UP." ...THIS MORNiNG i ACCiDENTALLY USED HAiR SPRAY iNSTEAD OF UNDER ARM DEODORANT!

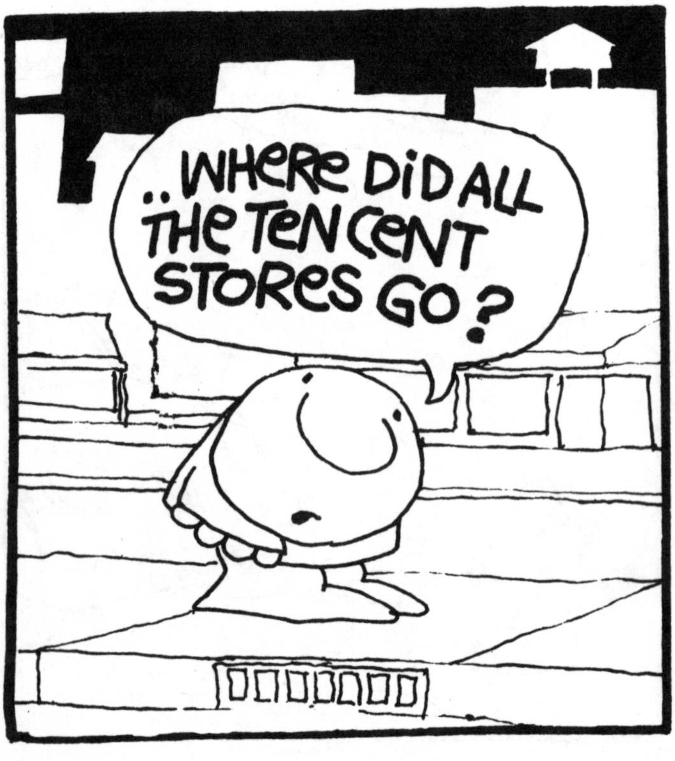
..WHERE DiD ALL THE TEN CENT STORES GO?

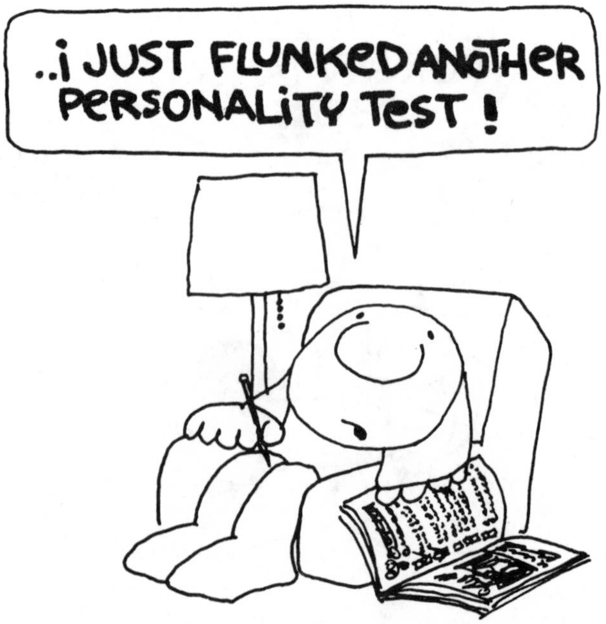
..i JUST FLUNKED ANOTHER PERSONALiTY TEST!

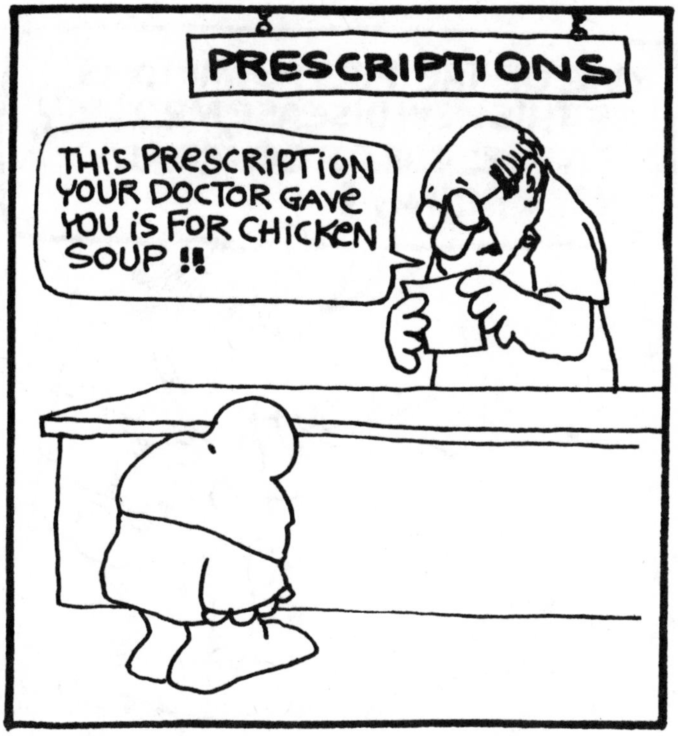
PRESCRIPTIONS
THIS PRESCRIPTION YOUR DOCTOR GAVE YOU IS FOR CHICKEN SOUP !!

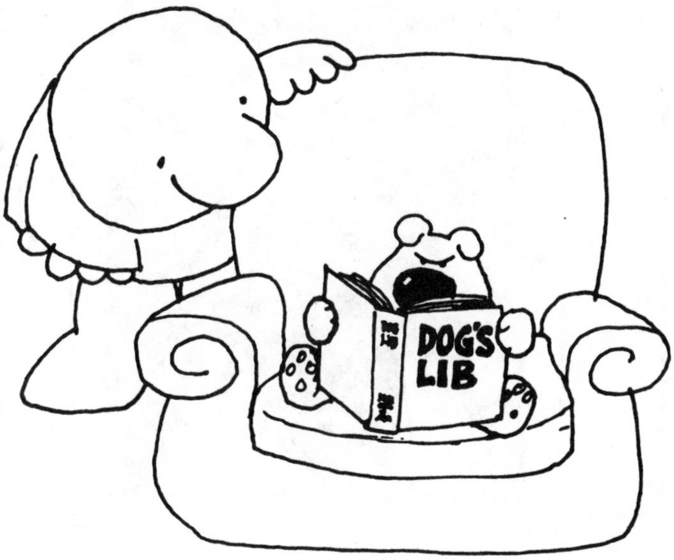
DOG'S LIB

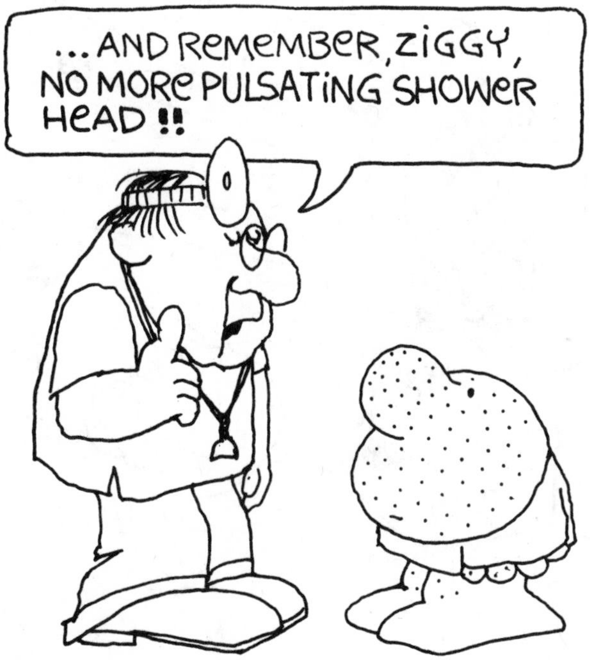
...AND REMEMBER, ZIGGY, NO MORE PULSATING SHOWER HEAD !!

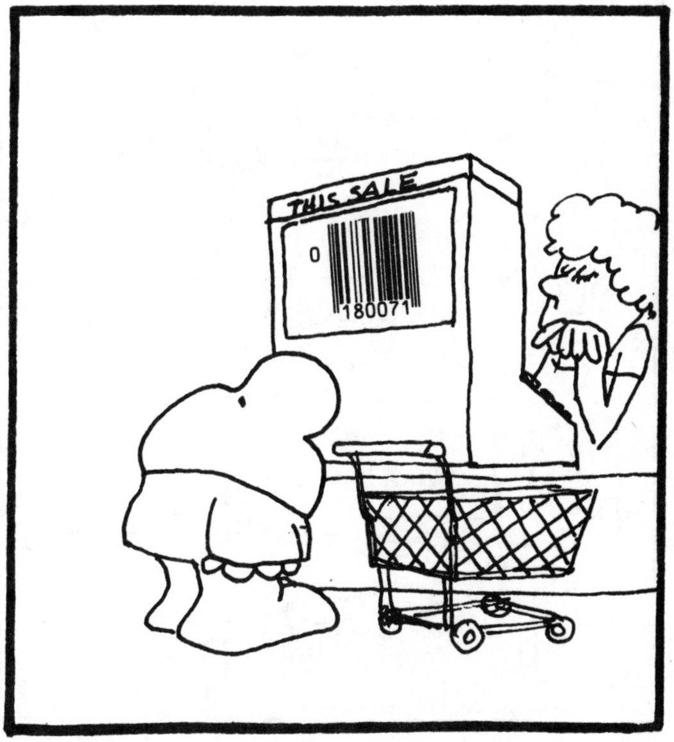
THIS SALE

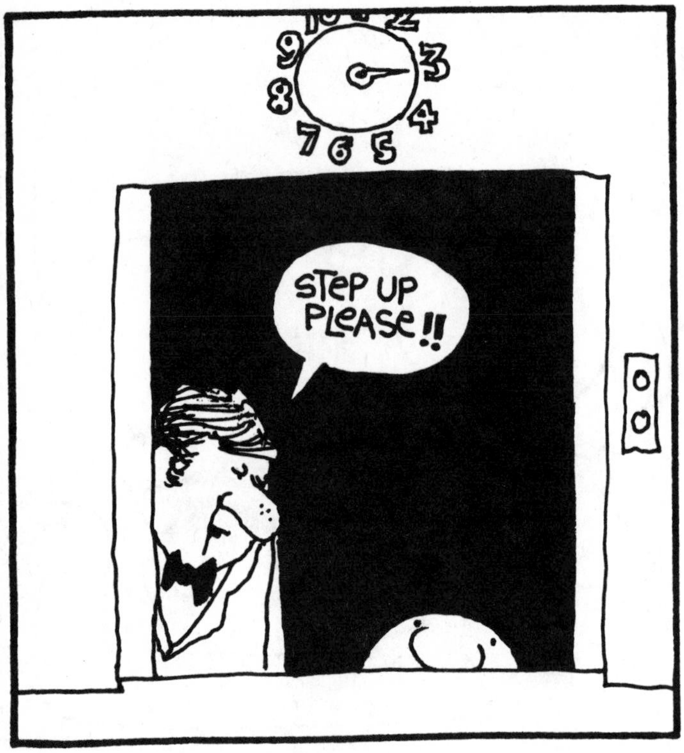
STEP UP PLEASE!!

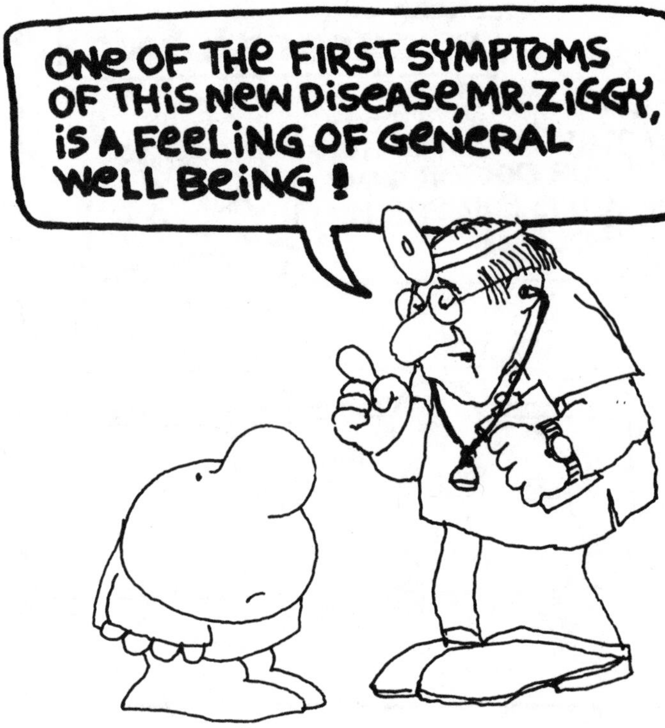
ONE OF THE FIRST SYMPTOMS OF THIS NEW DISEASE, MR. ZIGGY, IS A FEELING OF GENERAL WELL BEING!

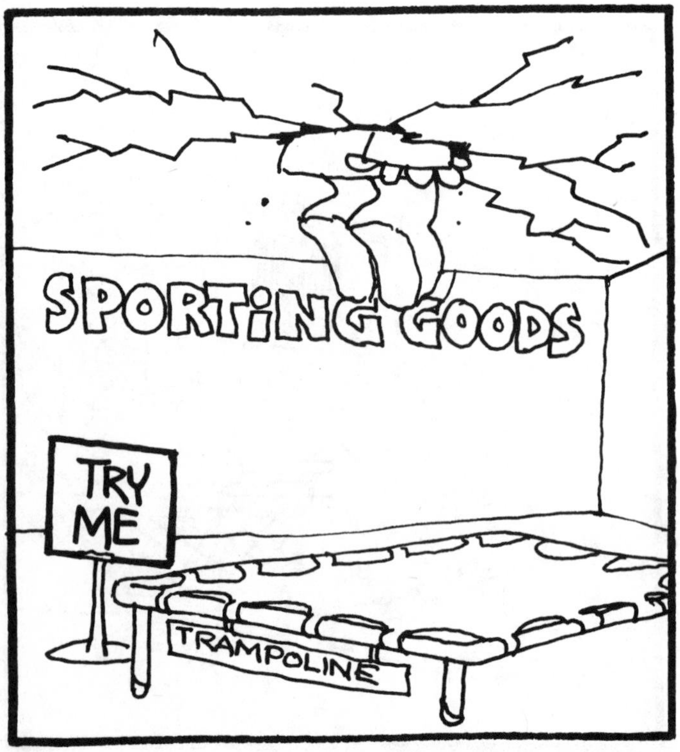
SPORTING GOODS
TRY ME
TRAMPOLINE

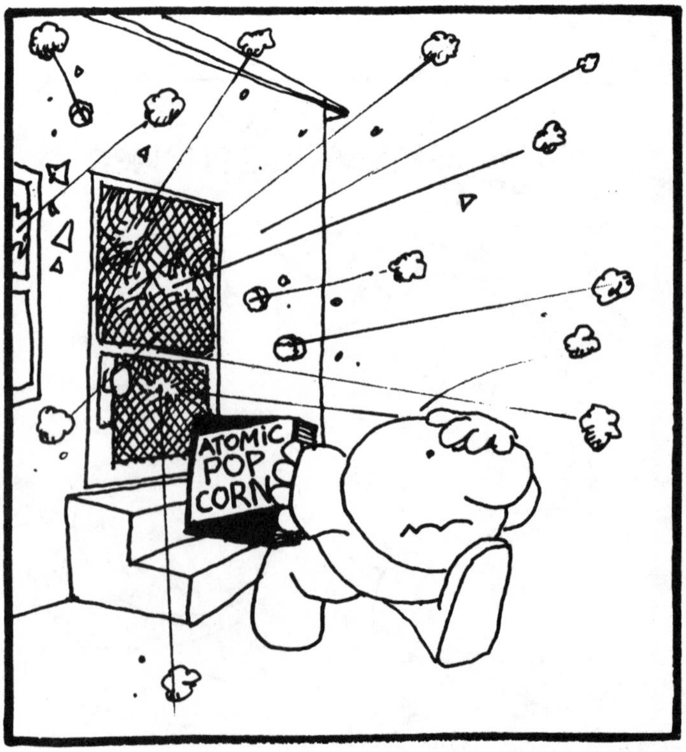
ATOMIC POP CORN

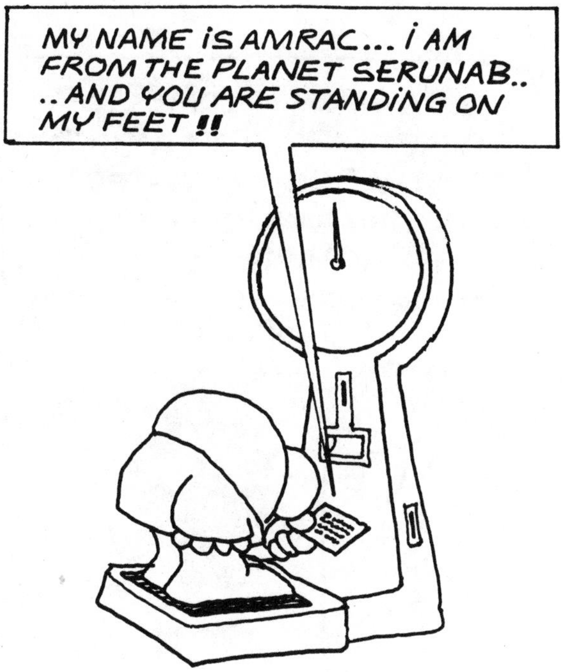
MY NAME IS AMRAC... I AM FROM THE PLANET SERUNAB.. ..AND YOU ARE STANDING ON MY FEET !!

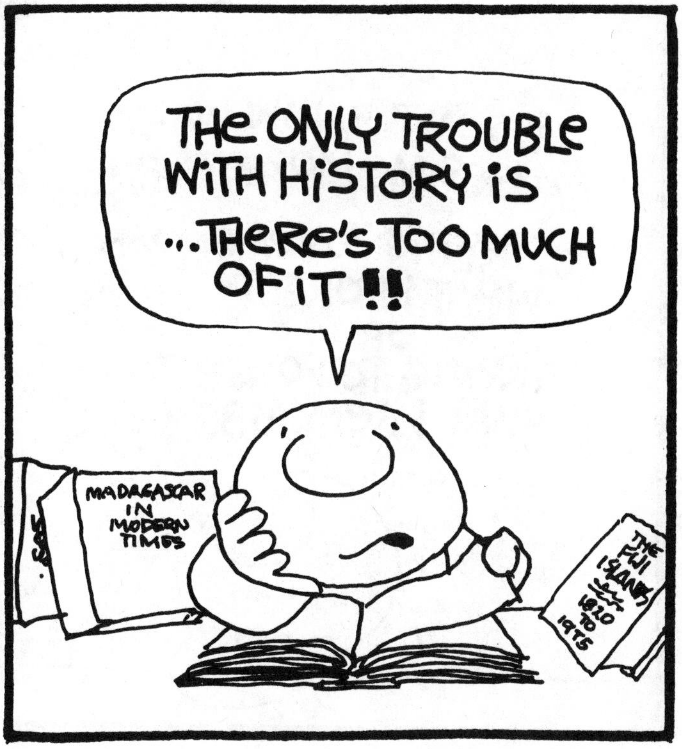
THE ONLY TROUBLE WITH HISTORY IS ..THERE'S TOO MUCH OF IT !!
MADAGASCAR IN MODERN TIMES
THE FIJI ISLANDS 1820 TO 1975

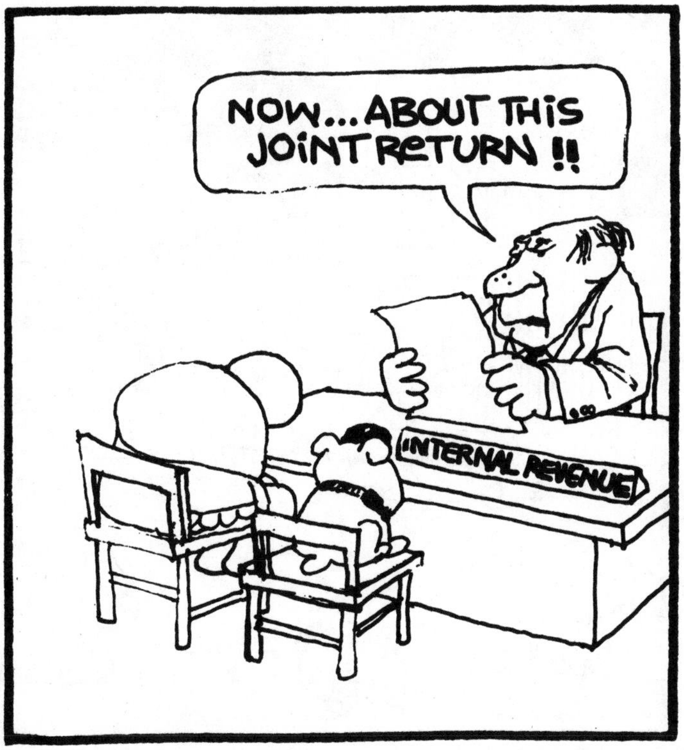
NOW... ABOUT THIS JOINT RETURN !!
INTERNAL REVENUE

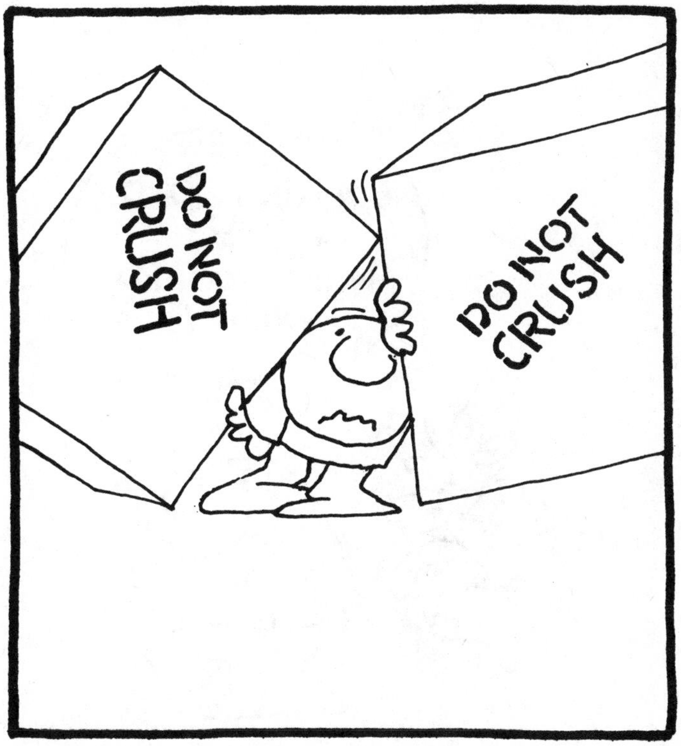
DO NOT CRUSH
DO NOT CRUSH

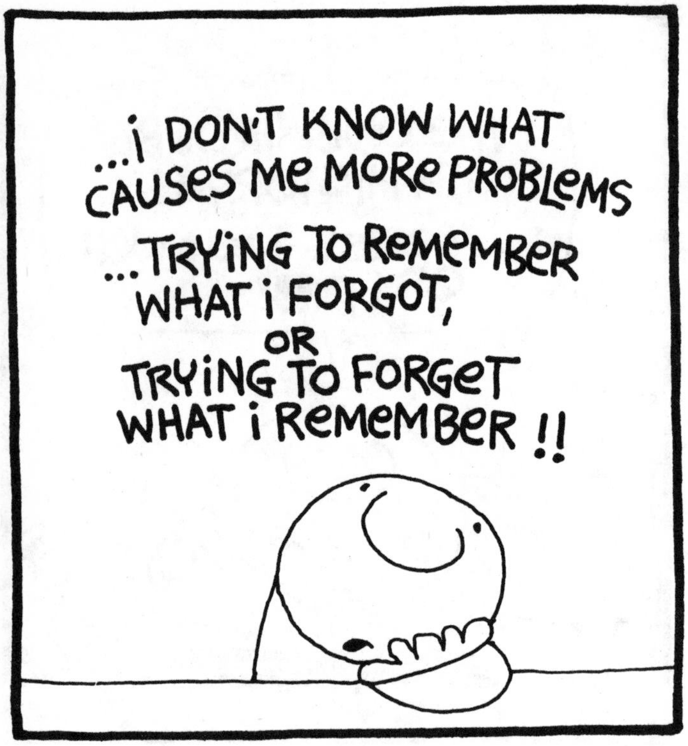
...i DON'T KNOW WHAT CAUSES ME MORE PROBLEMS ...TRYING TO REMEMBER WHAT i FORGOT, OR TRYING TO FORGET WHAT i REMEMBER !!

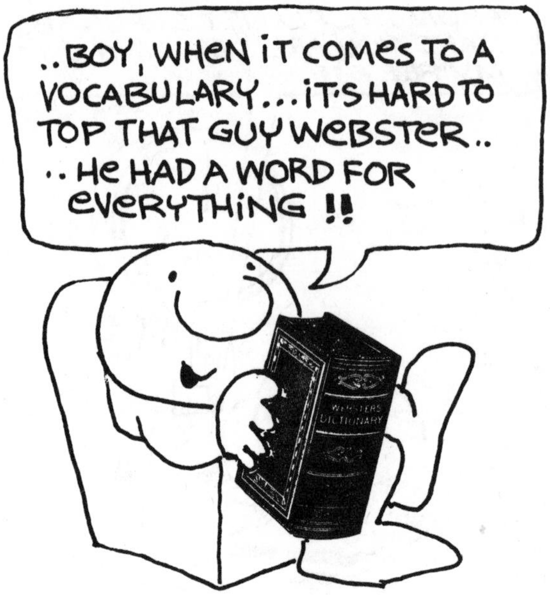
..BOY, WHEN iT COMES TO A VOCABULARY... iT'S HARD TO TOP THAT GUY WEBSTER.. ..HE HAD A WORD FOR EVERYTHING !!

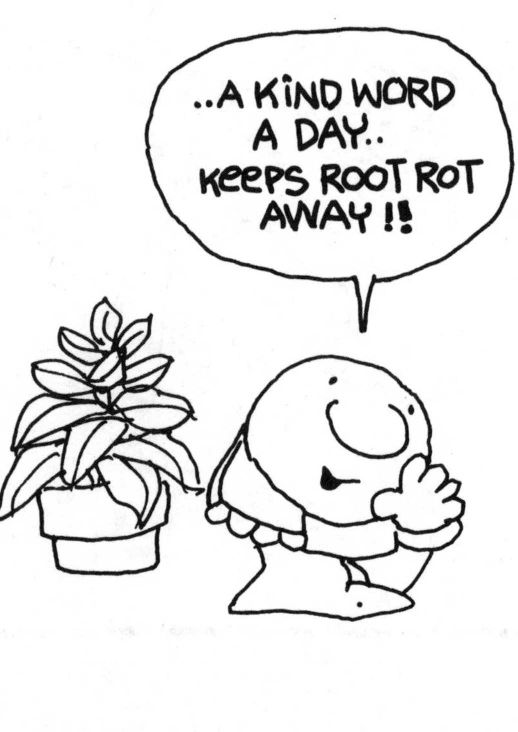
..A KiND WORD A DAY.. KEEPS ROOT ROT AWAY !!

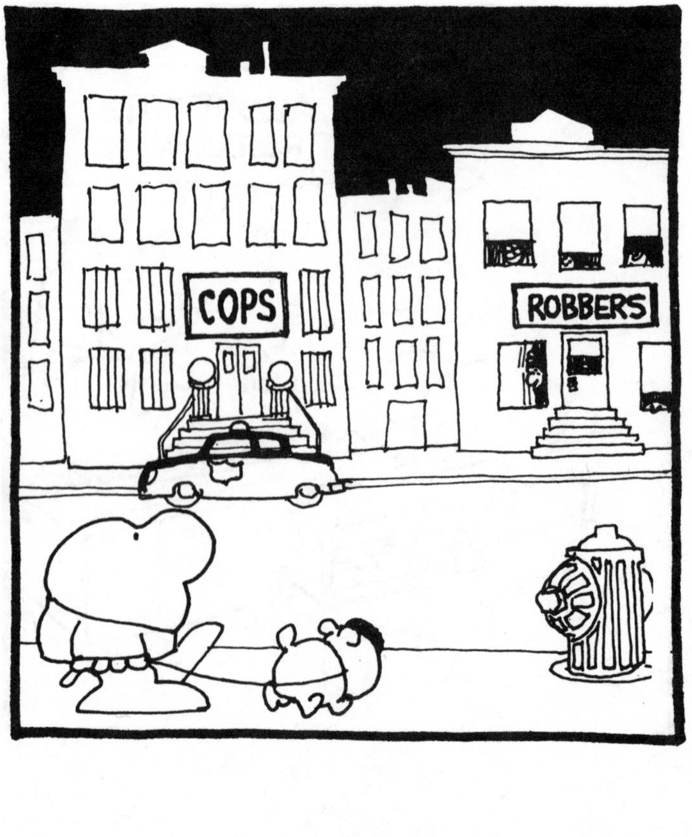
COPS
ROBBERS

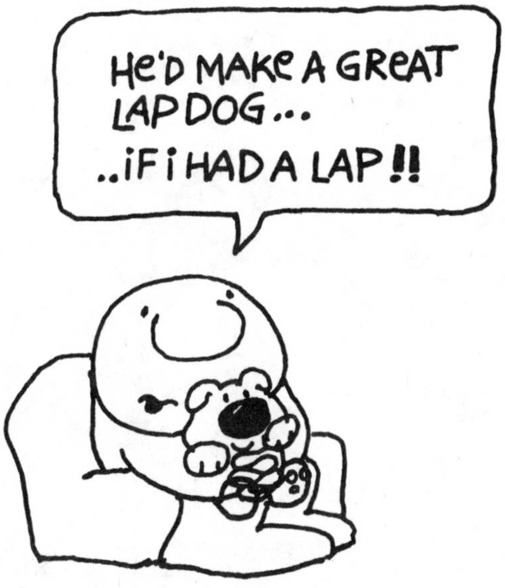
HE'D MAKE A GREAT LAP DOG... ..iF i HAD A LAP!!

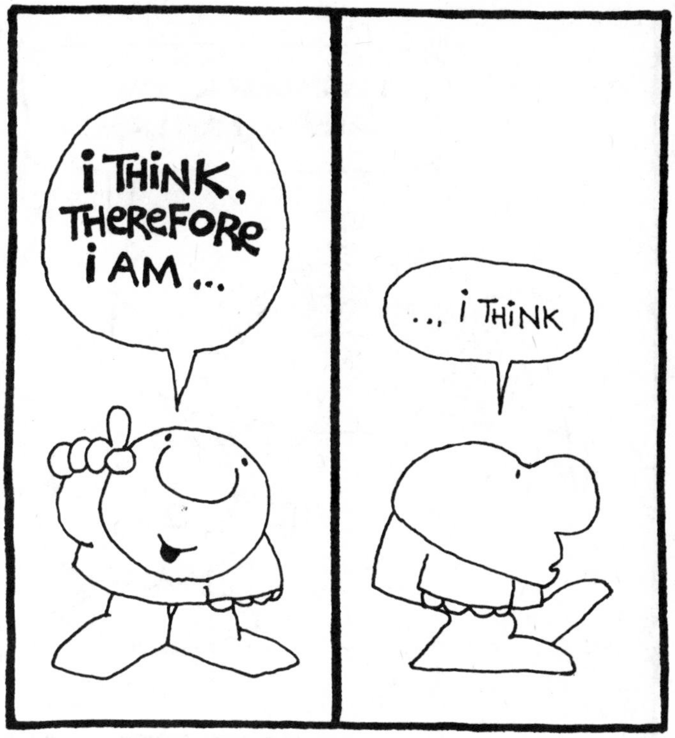
i THINK, THEREFORE i AM...
..., i THINK

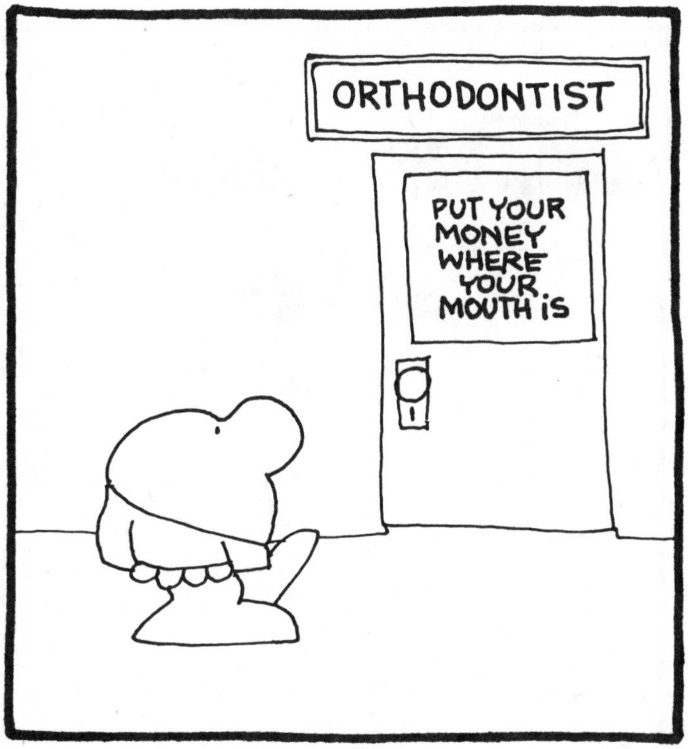
ORTHODONTIST
PUT YOUR MONEY WHERE YOUR MOUTH IS

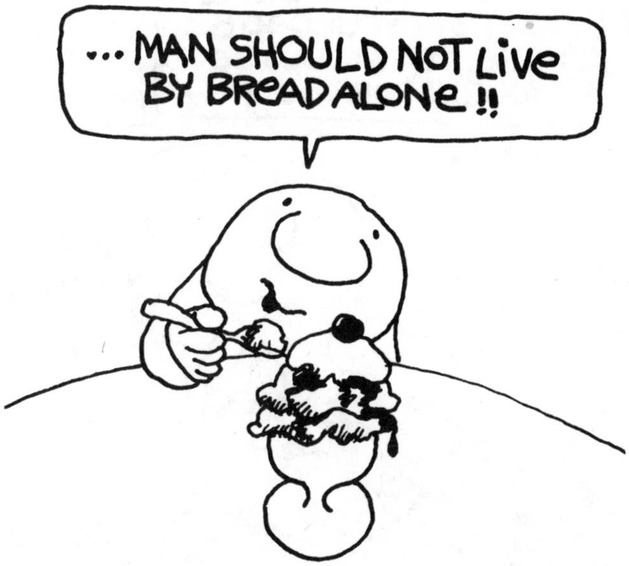
...MAN SHOULD NOT LIVE BY BREAD ALONE!!

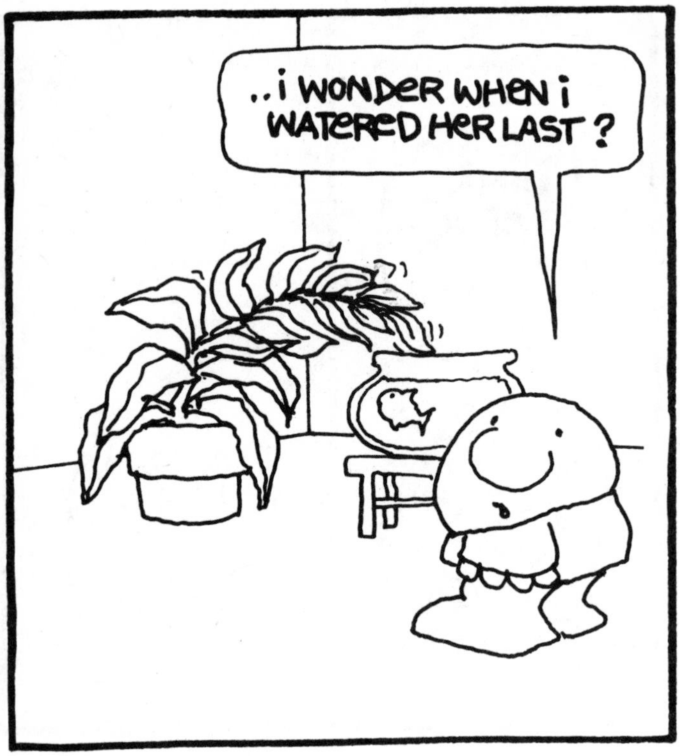
..i WONDER WHEN i WATERED HER LAST ?

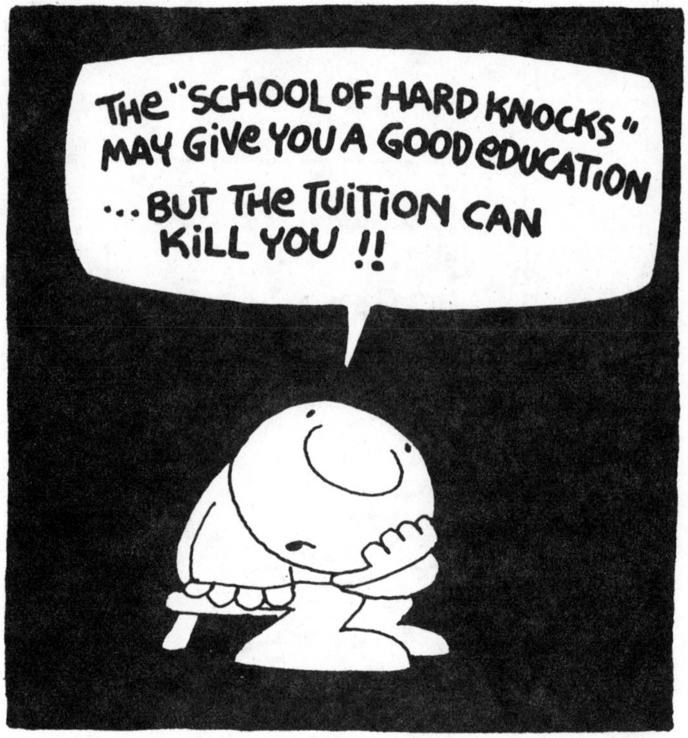
THE "SCHOOL OF HARD KNOCKS" MAY GIVE YOU A GOOD EDUCATION ...BUT THE TUITION CAN KILL YOU !!

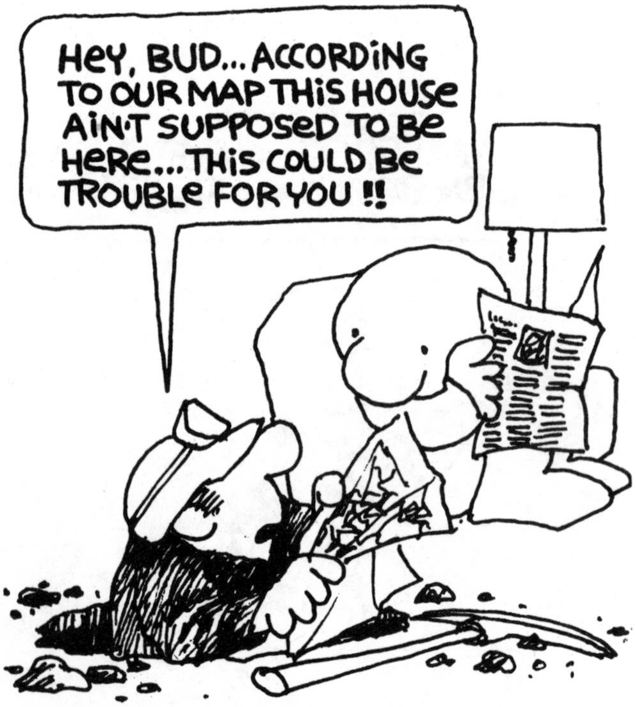
HEY, BUD...ACCORDING TO OUR MAP THIS HOUSE AIN'T SUPPOSED TO BE HERE...THIS COULD BE TROUBLE FOR YOU !!

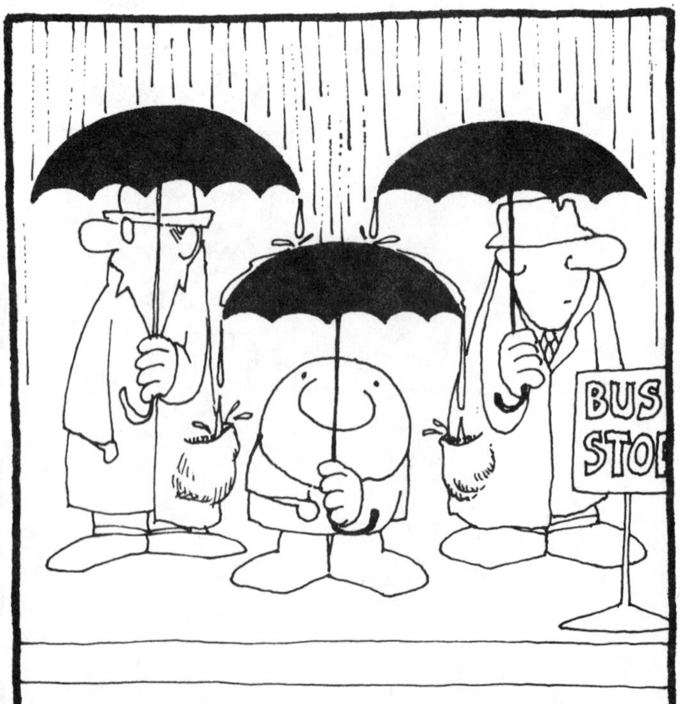
BUS

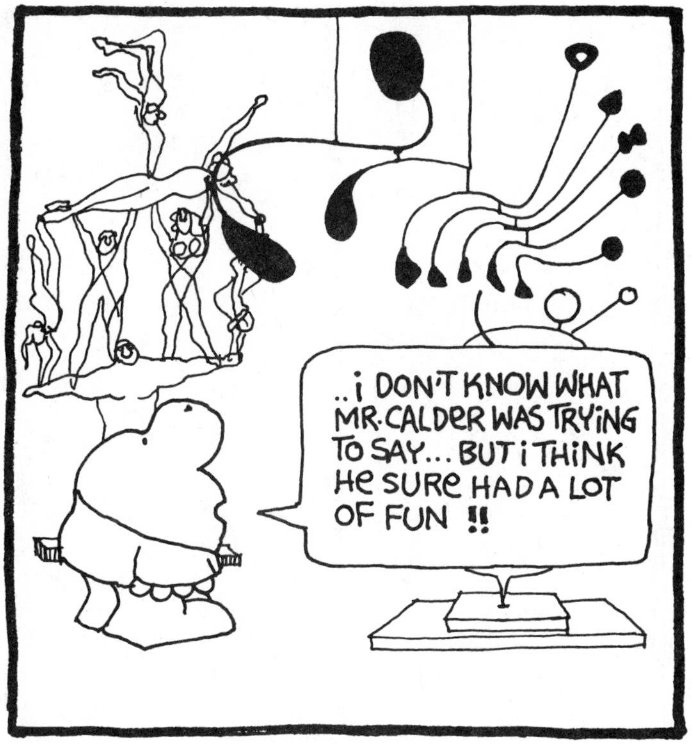
..i DON'T KNOW WHAT MR. CALDER WAS TRYING TO SAY... BUT i THINK He SURE HAD A LOT OF FUN !!

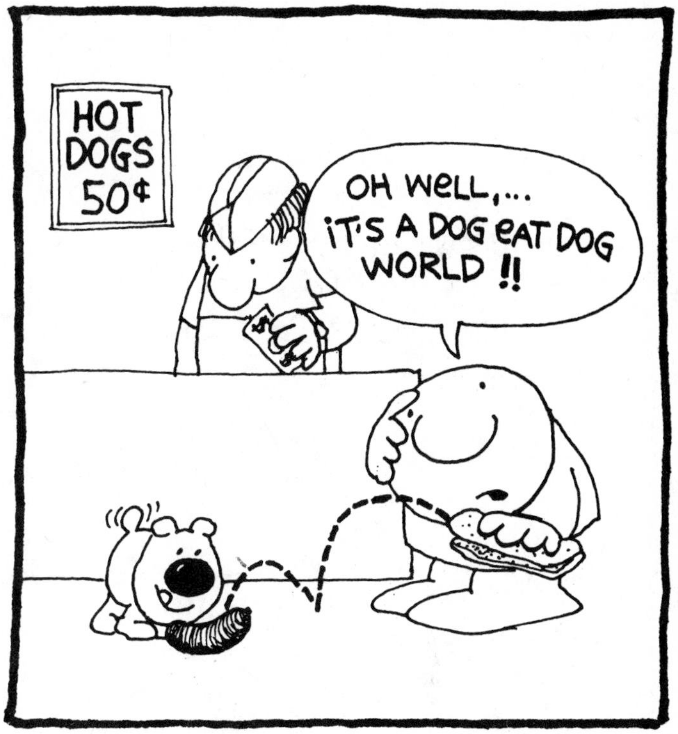
HOT DOGS 50¢
OH WELL,... iT'S A DOG eAT DOG WORLD !!

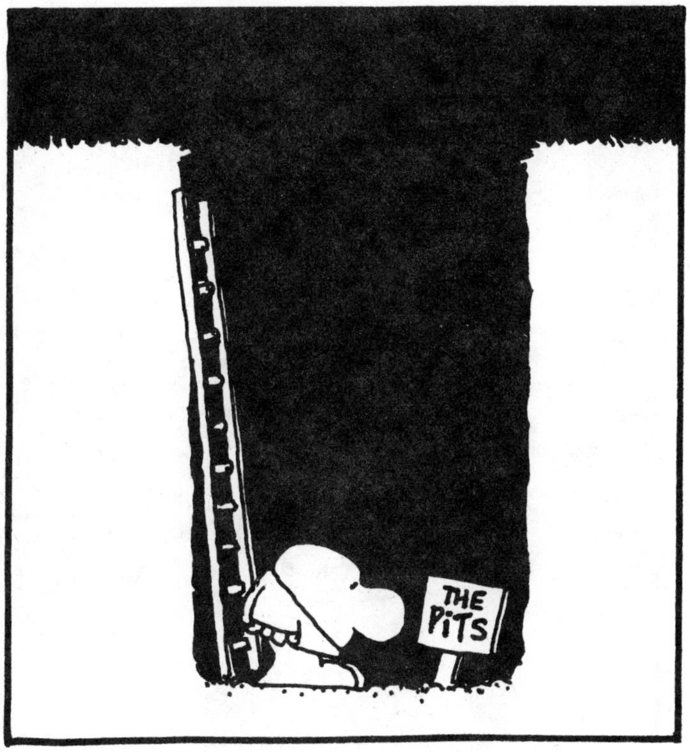
THE PITS

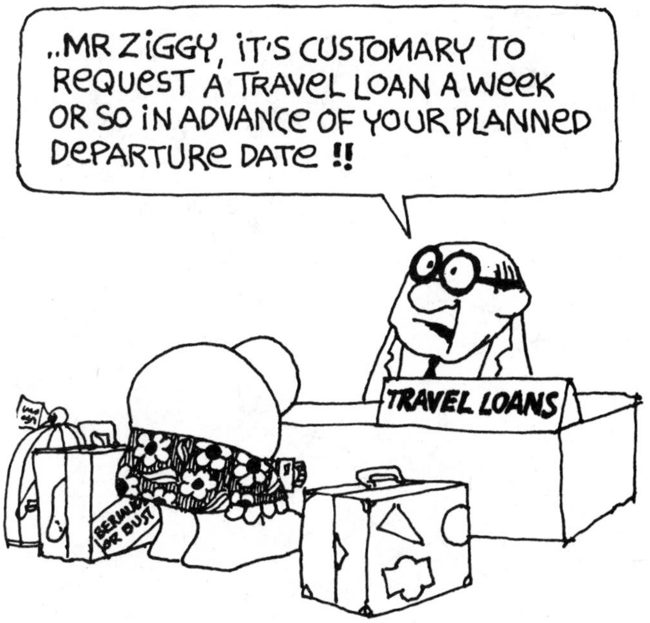
..MR ZiGGY, iT'S CUSTOMARY TO ReQUEST A TRAVEL LOAN A WeeK OR SO iN ADVANCe OF YOUR PLANNeD DePARTURe DATe !!
TRAVEL LOANS

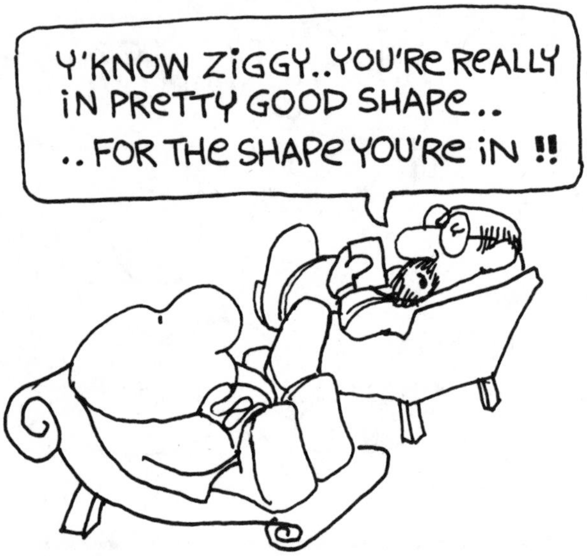
Y'KNOW ZIGGY..YOU'RE REALLY IN PRETTY GOOD SHAPE..
..FOR THE SHAPE YOU'RE IN !!

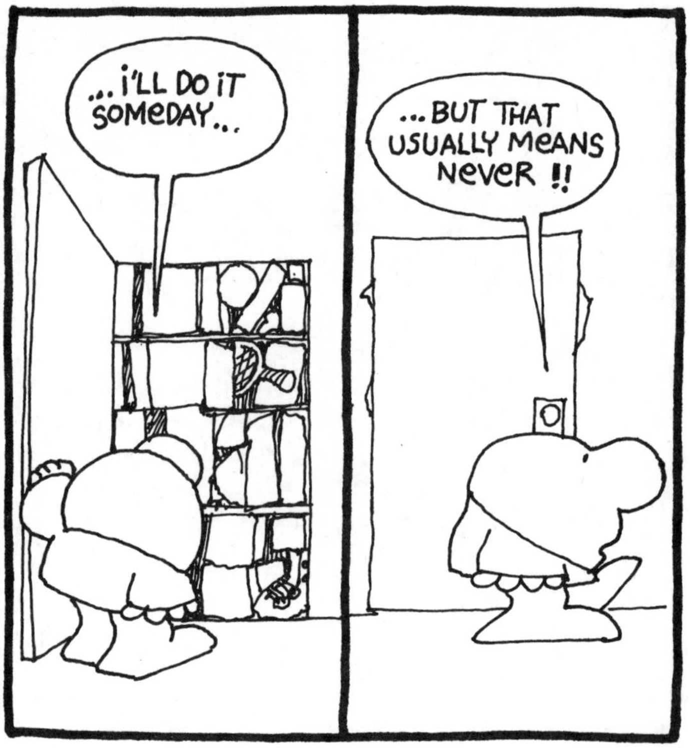
...I'LL DO IT SOMEDAY...
...BUT THAT USUALLY MEANS NEVER !!

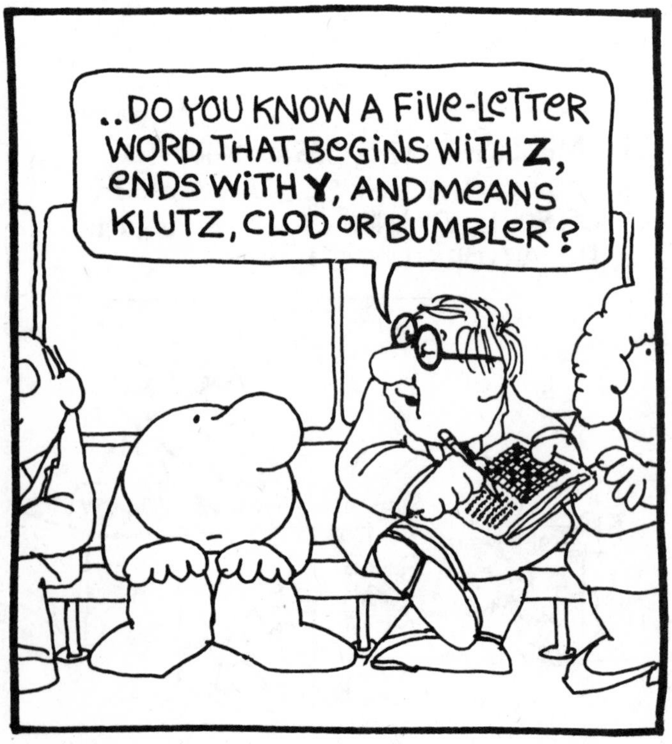
..DO YOU KNOW A FIVE-LETTER WORD THAT BEGINS WITH Z, ENDS WITH Y, AND MEANS KLUTZ, CLOD OR BUMBLER?

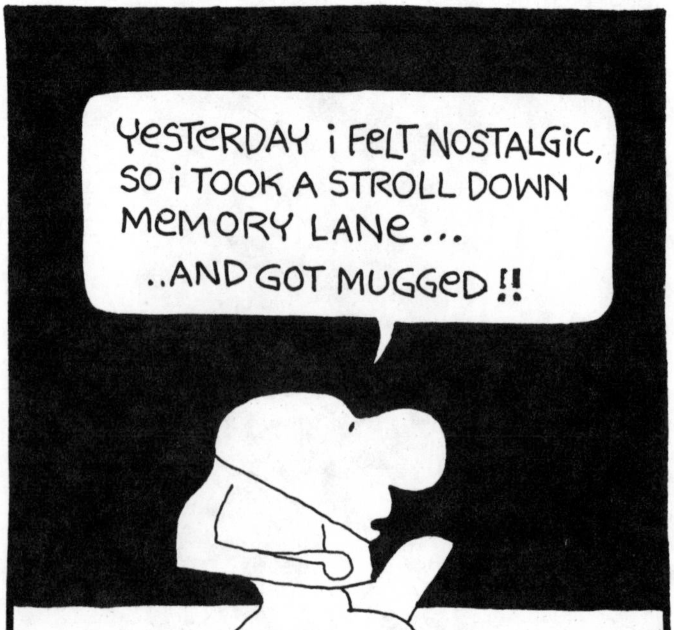
YESTERDAY I FELT NOSTALGIC, SO I TOOK A STROLL DOWN MEMORY LANE...
..AND GOT MUGGED !!

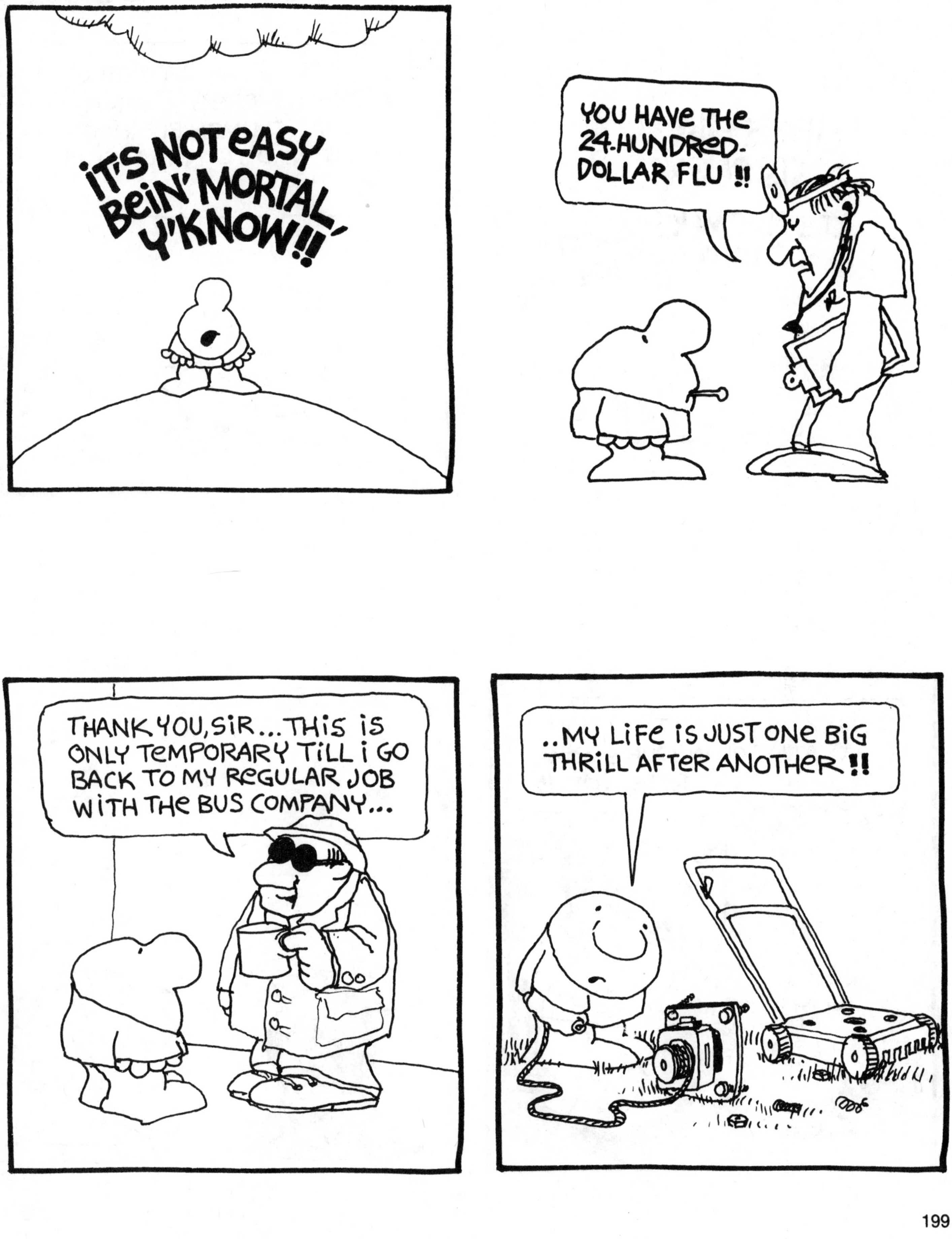
IT'S NOT EASY BEIN' MORTAL Y'KNOW!!
YOU HAVE THE 24-HUNDRED-DOLLAR FLU !!
THANK YOU, SIR... THIS IS ONLY TEMPORARY TILL I GO BACK TO MY REGULAR JOB WITH THE BUS COMPANY...
..MY LIFE IS JUST ONE BIG THRILL AFTER ANOTHER !!

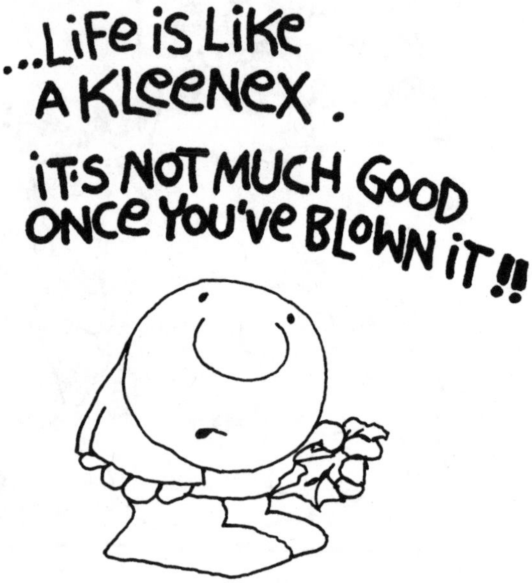
...LIFE IS LIKE A KLEENEX.
IT'S NOT MUCH GOOD ONCE YOU'VE BLOWN IT!!

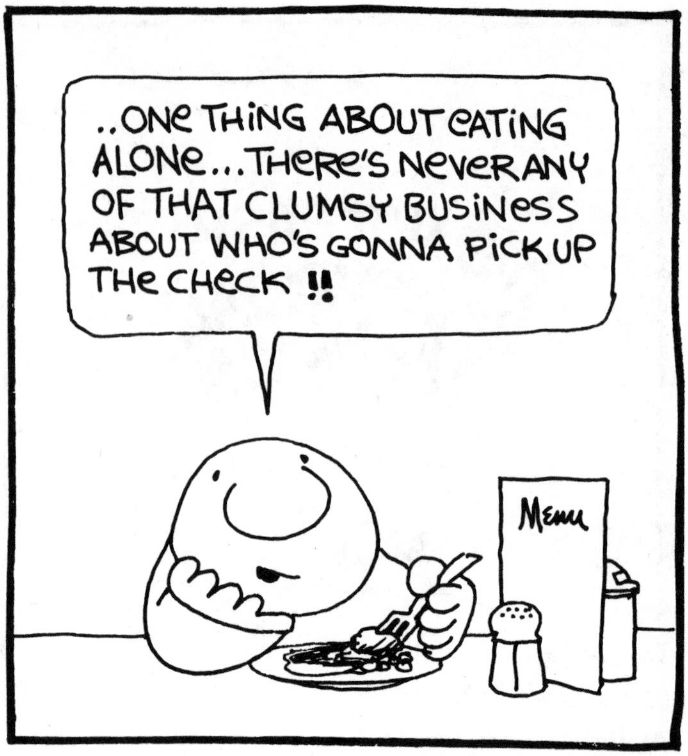
..ONE THING ABOUT EATING ALONE...THERE'S NEVER ANY OF THAT CLUMSY BUSINESS ABOUT WHO'S GONNA PICK UP THE CHECK !!
Menu

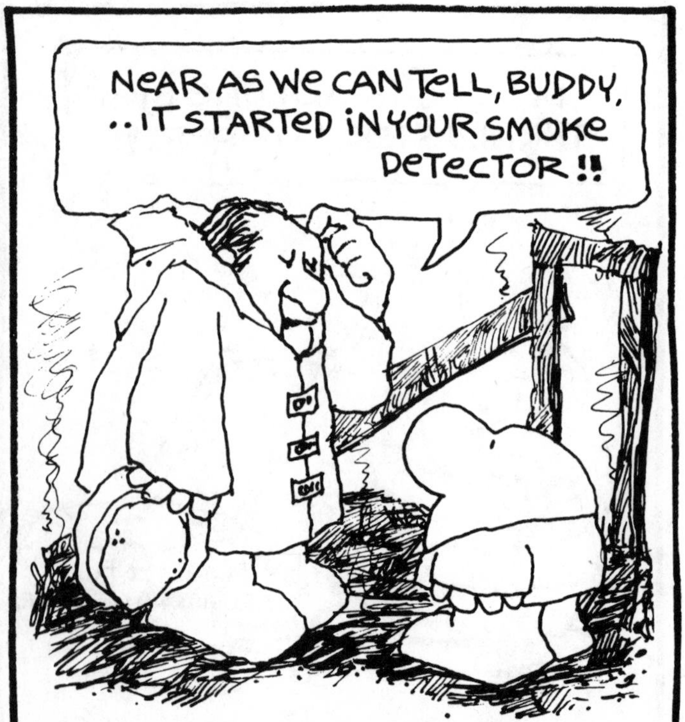
NEAR AS WE CAN TELL, BUDDY, ..IT STARTED IN YOUR SMOKE DETECTOR !!

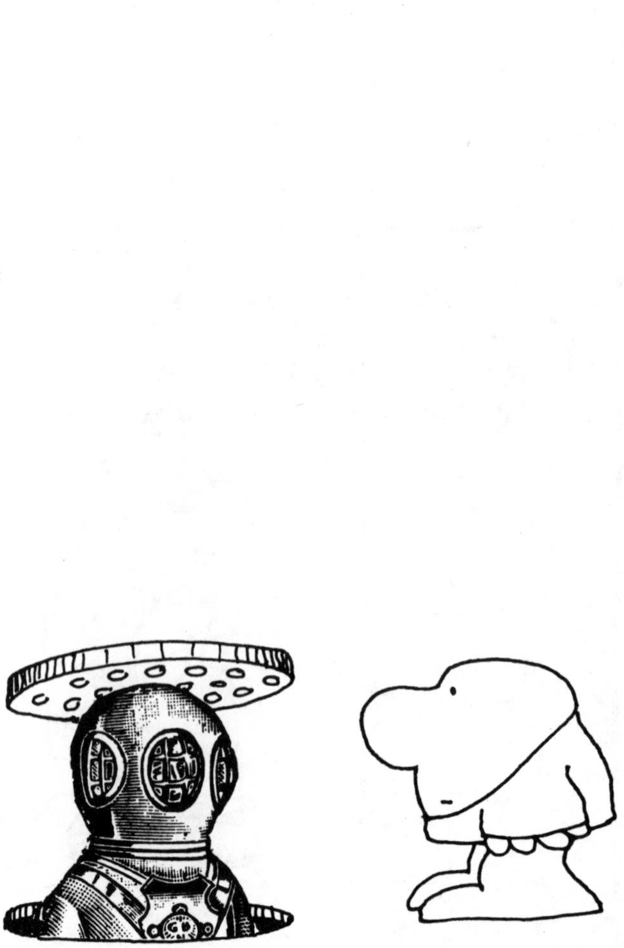

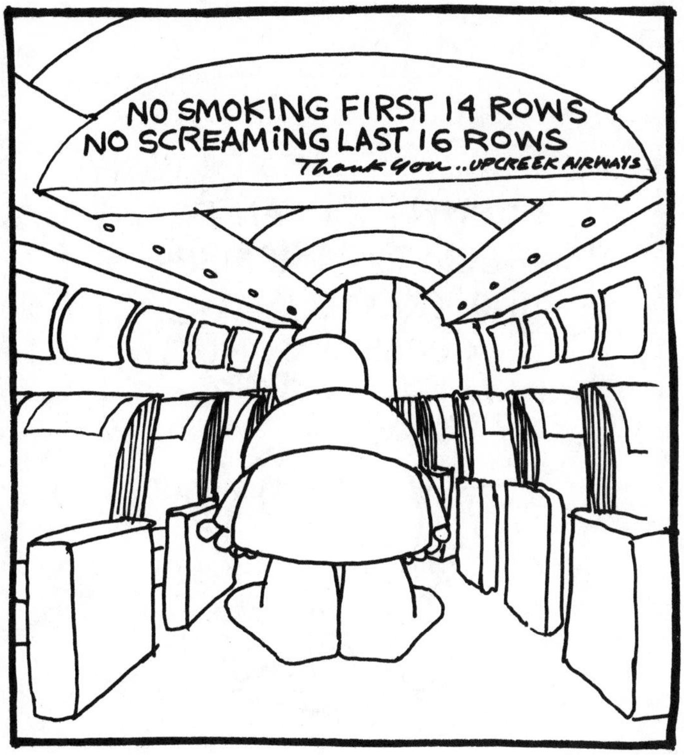
NO SMOKING FIRST 14 ROWS
NO SCREAMING LAST 16 ROWS
Thank You ...UPCREEK AIRWAYS

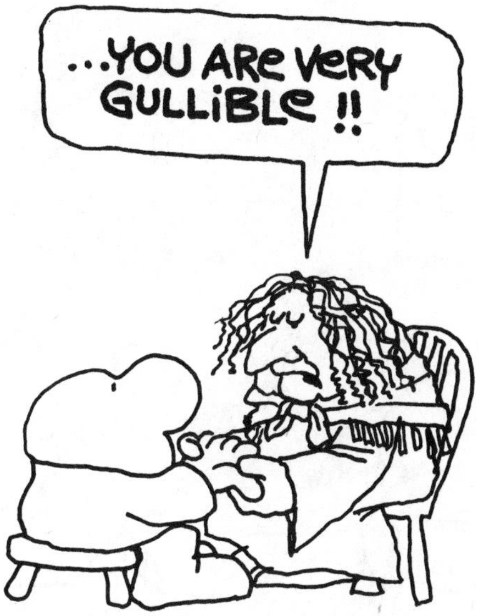
...YOU ARE VERY GULLIBLE !!

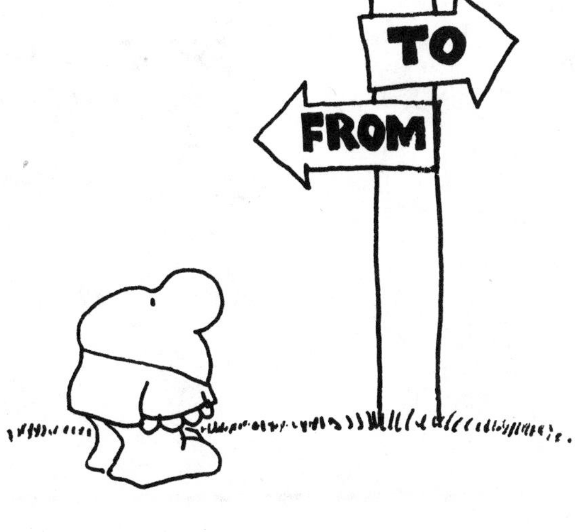
TO
FROM

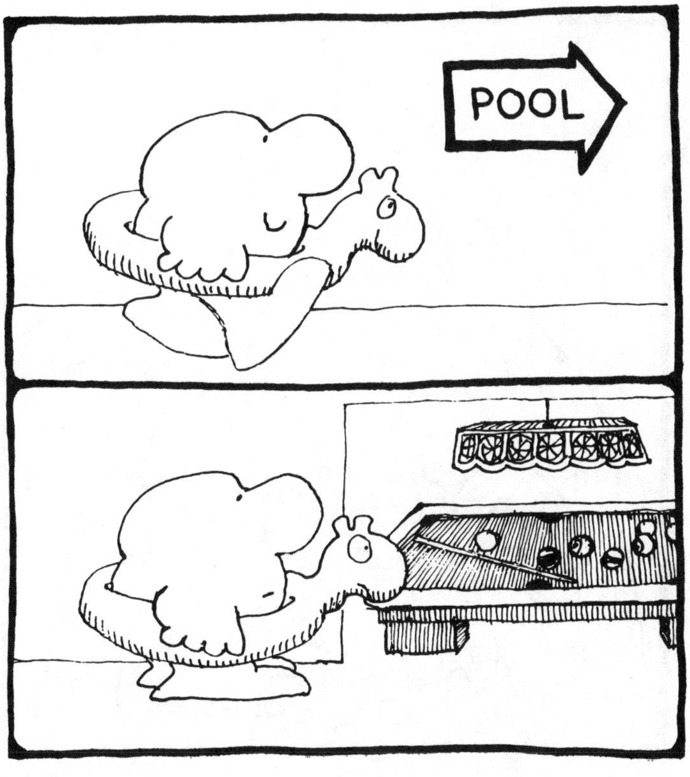
POOL

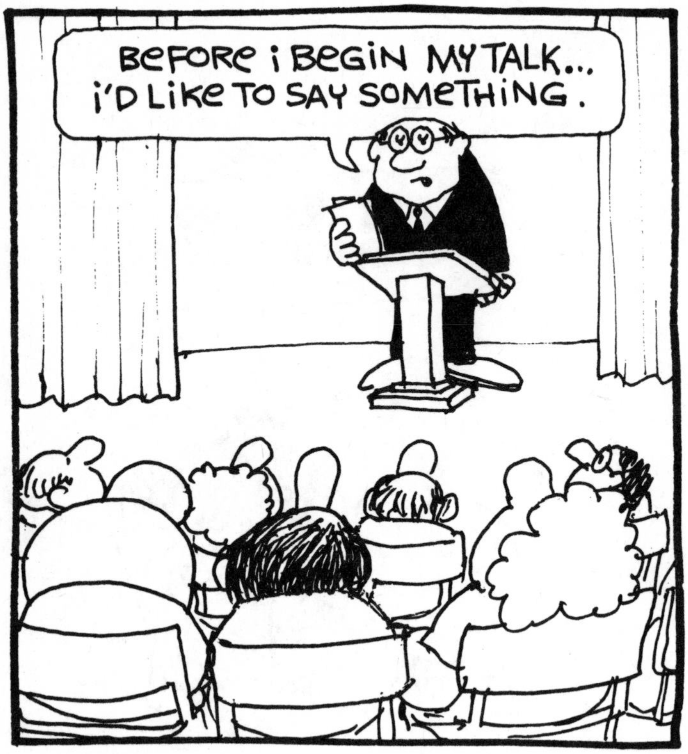
BEFORE i BEGIN MY TALK...
i'D LIKE TO SAY SOMETHING.

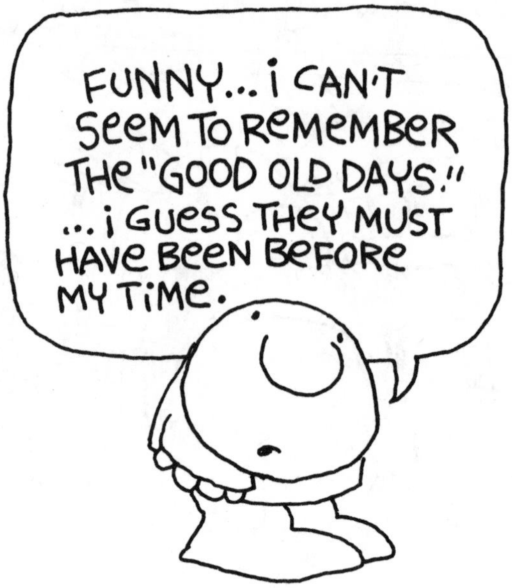
FUNNY... i CAN'T SEEM TO REMEMBER THE "GOOD OLD DAYS." ...i GUESS THEY MUST HAVE BEEN BEFORE MY TIME.

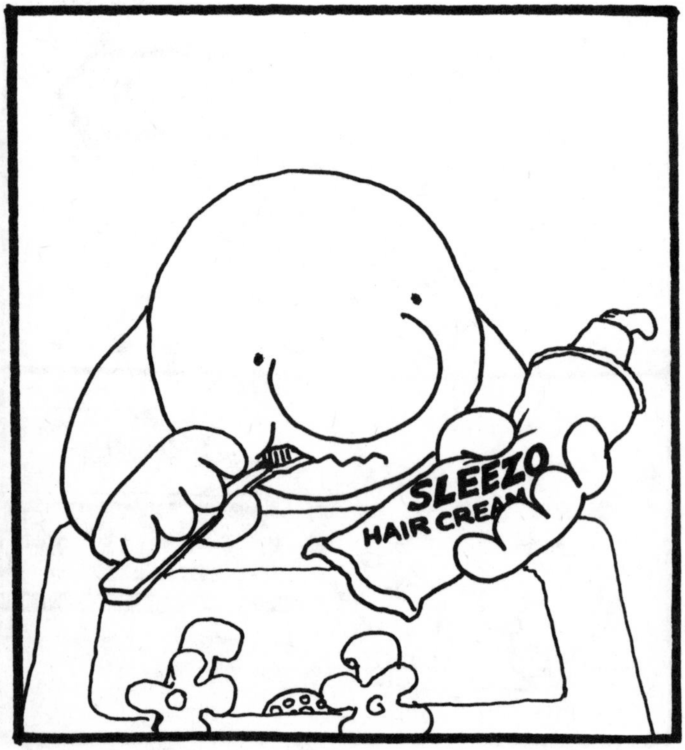
SLEEZO
HAIR CREAM

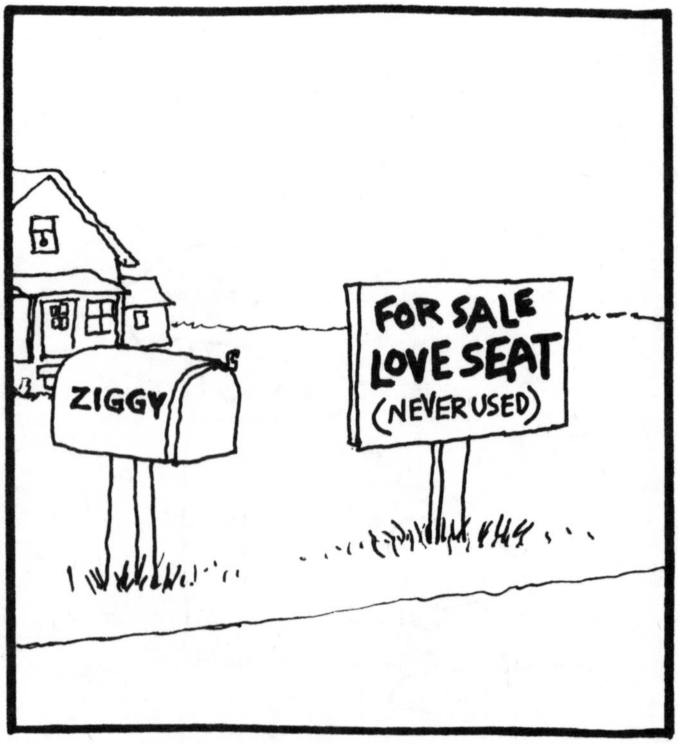
ZIGGY
FOR SALE
LOVE SEAT
(NEVER USED)

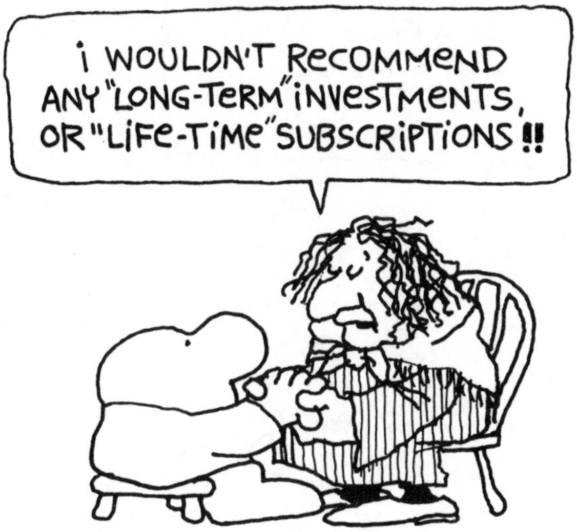
I WOULDN'T RECOMMEND ANY "LONG-TERM" INVESTMENTS, OR "LIFE-TIME" SUBSCRIPTIONS !!

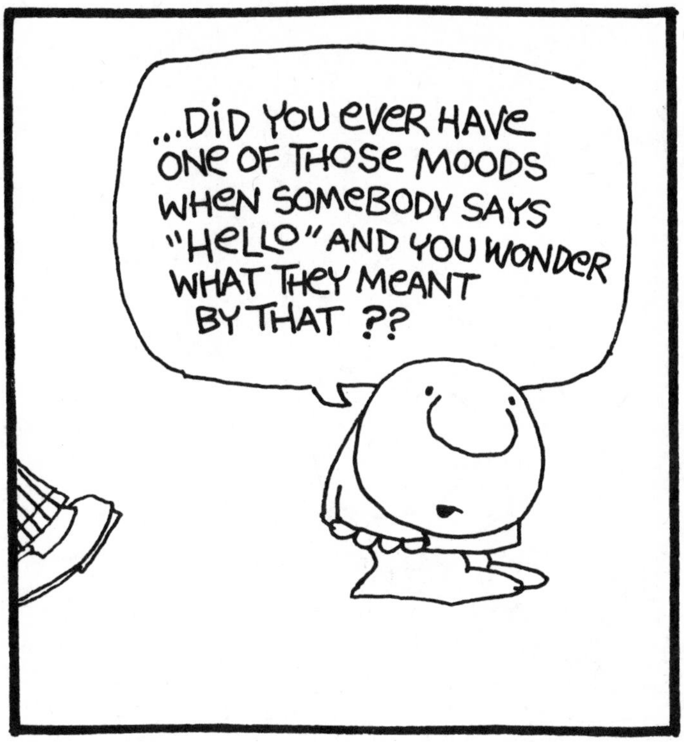
...DID YOU EVER HAVE ONE OF THOSE MOODS WHEN SOMEBODY SAYS "HELLO" AND YOU WONDER WHAT THEY MEANT BY THAT ??

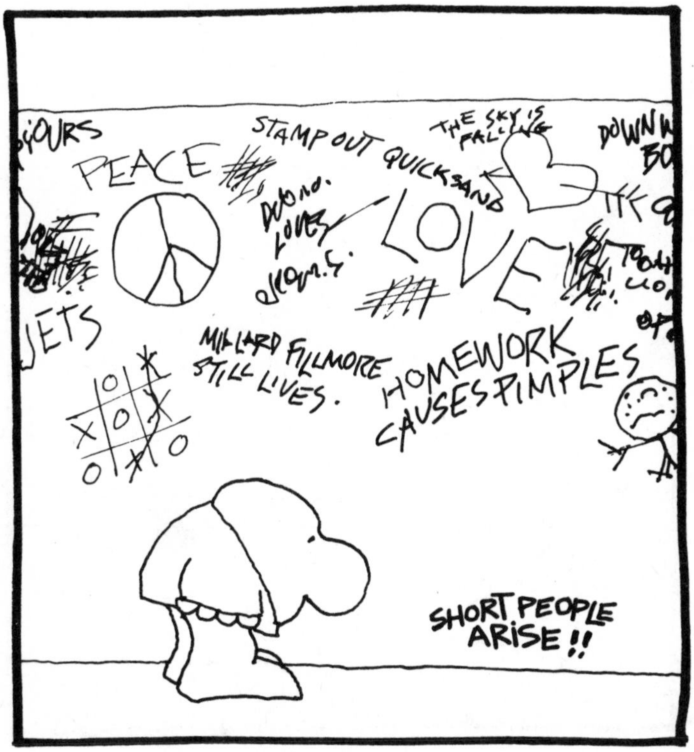
STAMP OUT QUICKSAND
THE SKY IS FALLING
PEACE
LOVE
JETS
MILLARD FILLMORE STILL LIVES.
HOMEWORK CAUSES PIMPLES
SHORT PEOPLE ARISE !!

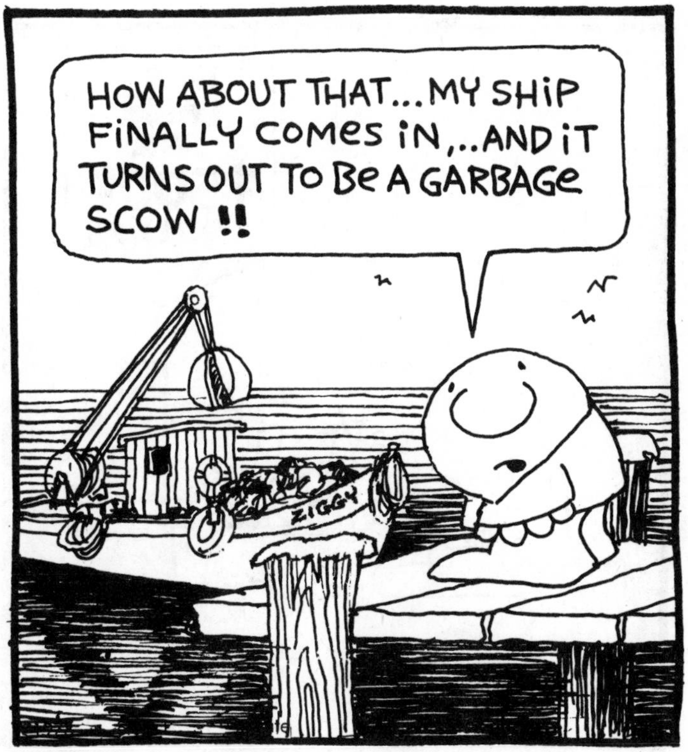
HOW ABOUT THAT... MY SHIP FINALLY COMES IN,..AND IT TURNS OUT TO BE A GARBAGE SCOW !!
ZIGGY

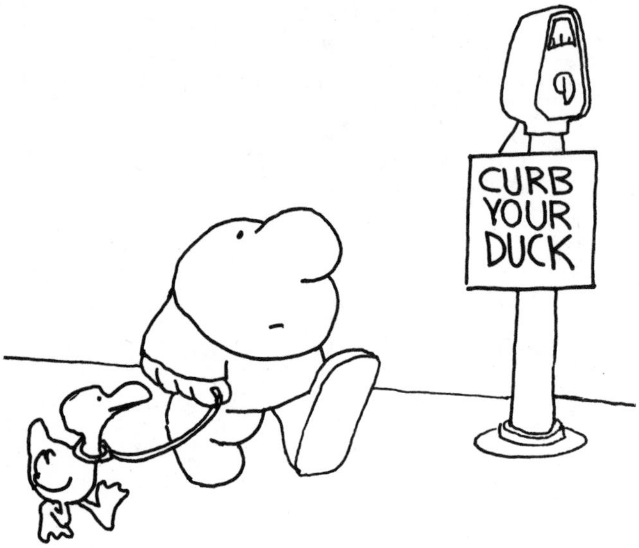
CURB YOUR DUCK

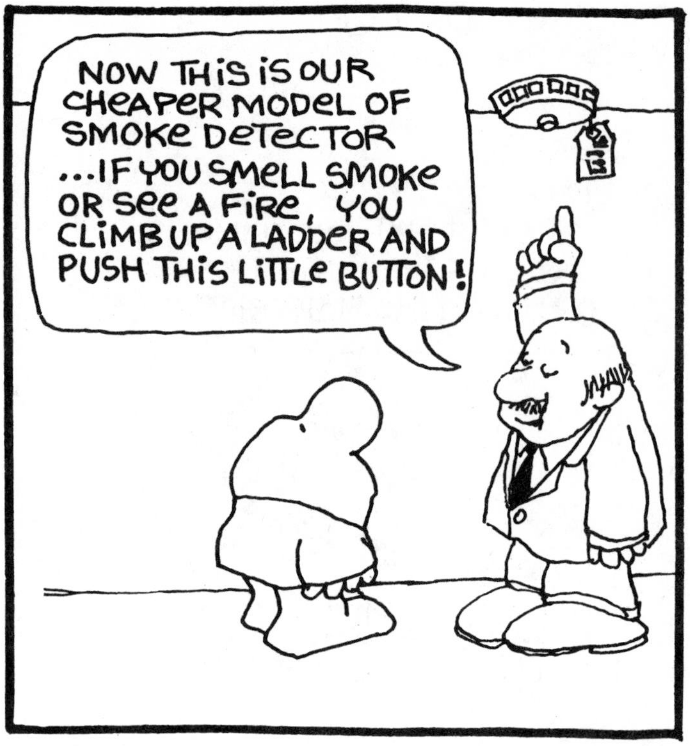
NOW THIS IS OUR CHEAPER MODEL OF SMOKE DETECTOR ...IF YOU SMELL SMOKE OR SEE A FIRE, YOU CLIMB UP A LADDER AND PUSH THIS LITTLE BUTTON!

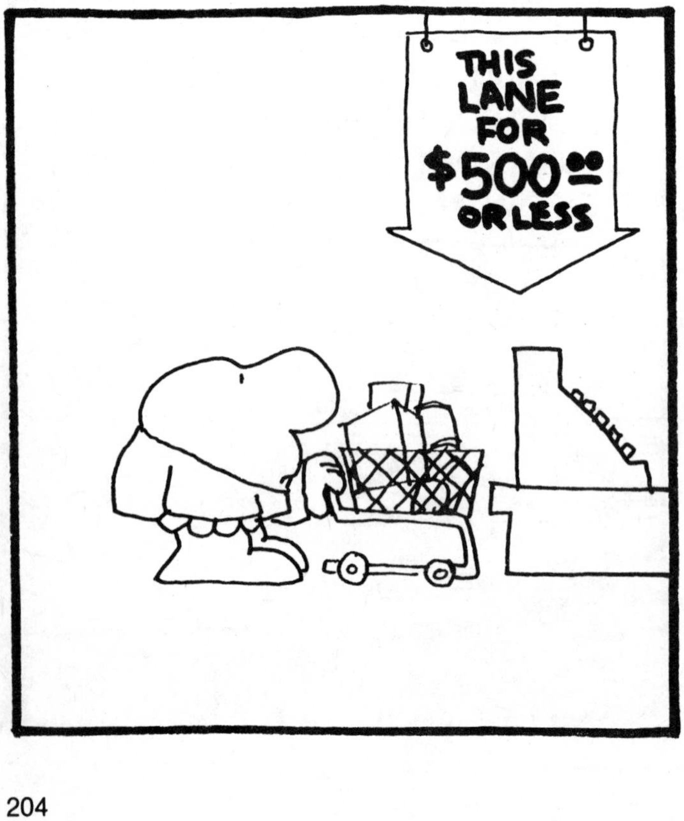
THIS LANE FOR $500.00 OR LESS

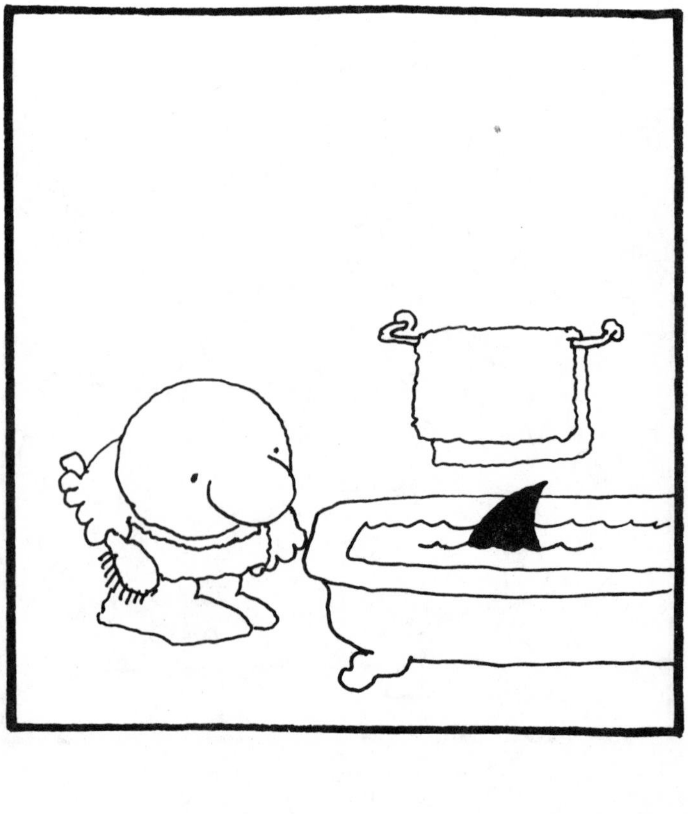

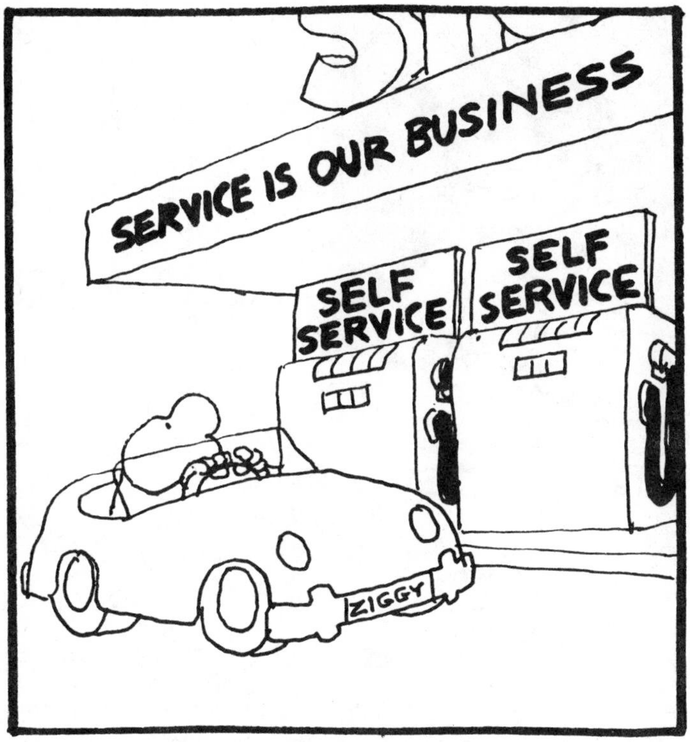
SERVICE IS OUR BUSINESS
SELF SERVICE
SELF SERVICE
ZIGGY

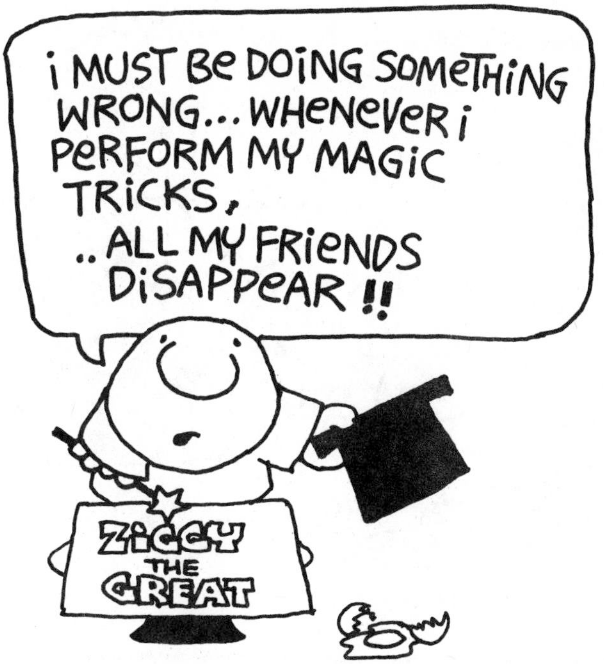
i MUST Be DOiNG SOMeTHiNG WRONG... WHeNeVeR i PeRFORM MY MAGIC TRICKS, ..ALL MY FRieNDS DiSAPPeAR !!
ZIGGY THE GREAT

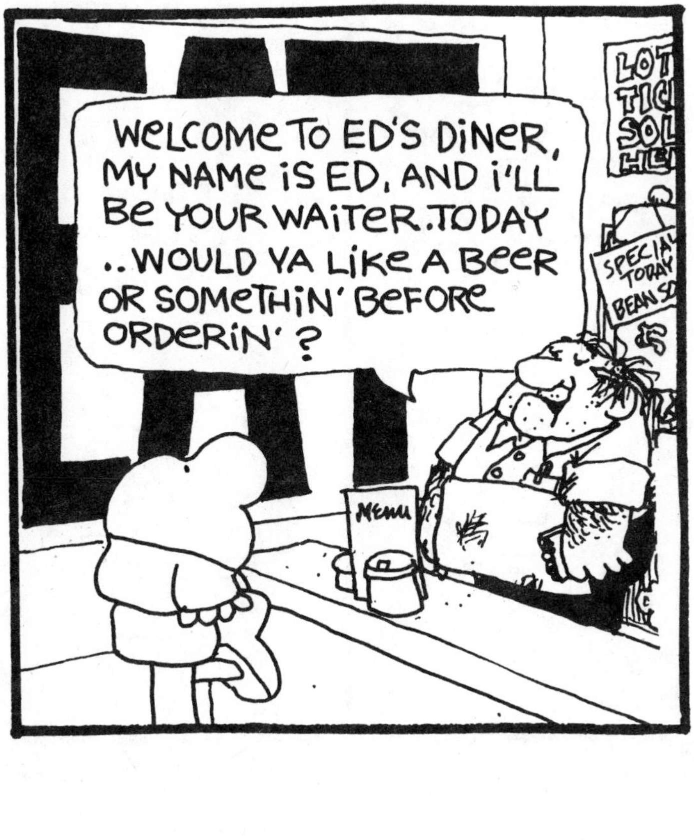
WeLCOMe TO ED'S DiNeR, MY NAMe iS ED, AND i'LL Be YOUR WAiTeR TODAY ..WOULD YA LiKe A BeeR OR SOMeTHiN' BeFORe ORDeRiN' ?
MENU

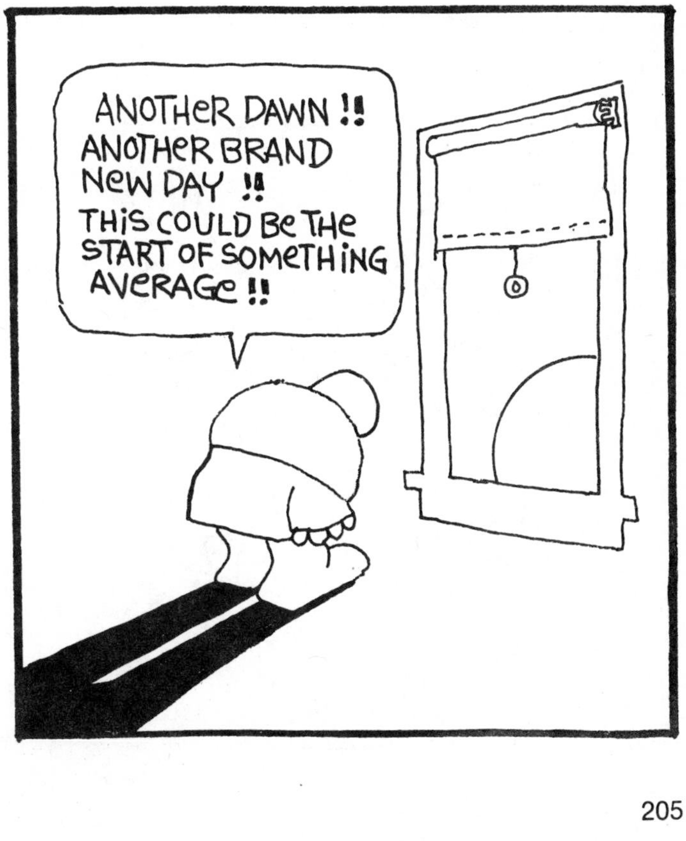
ANOTHeR DAWN !! ANOTHeR BRAND NeW DAY !! THiS COULD Be THe START OF SOMeTHiNG AVERAGe !!

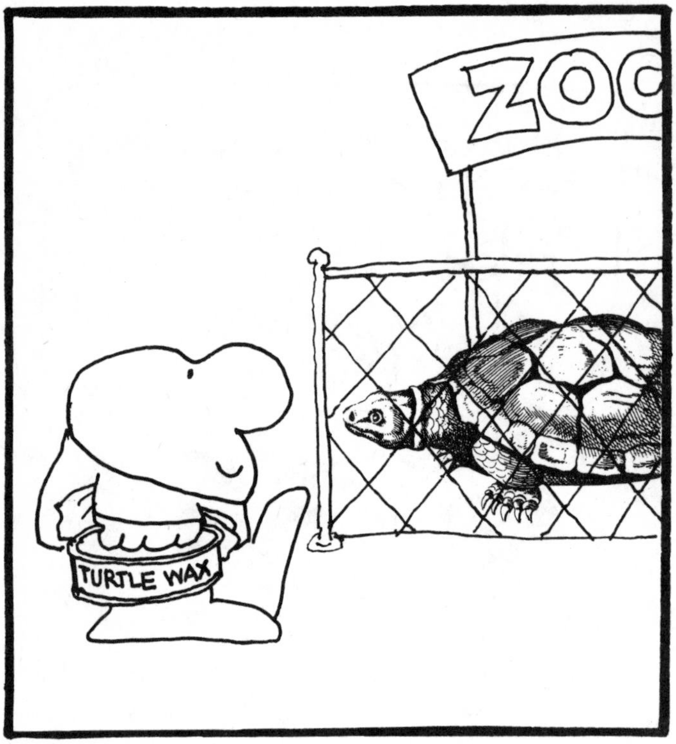
ZOO
TURTLE WAX

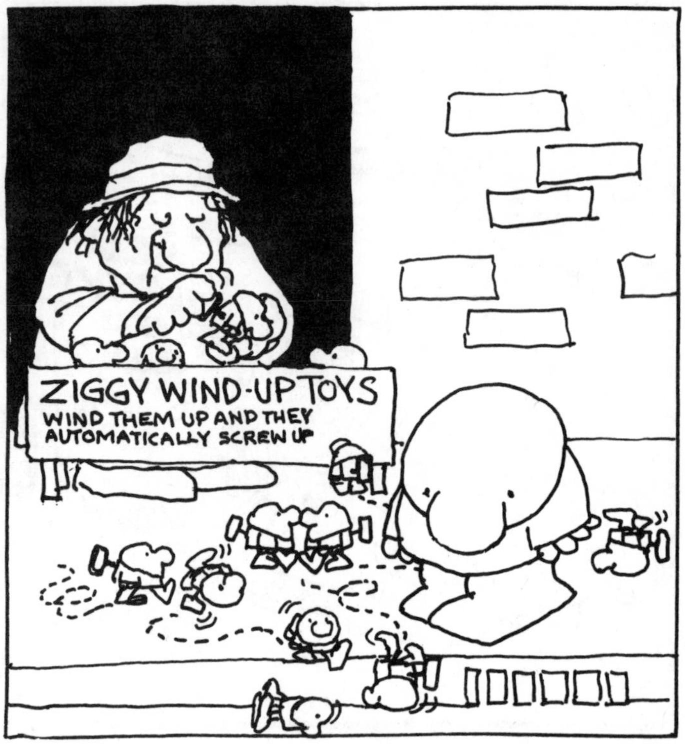
ZIGGY WIND-UP TOYS
WIND THEM UP AND THEY AUTOMATICALLY SCREW UP

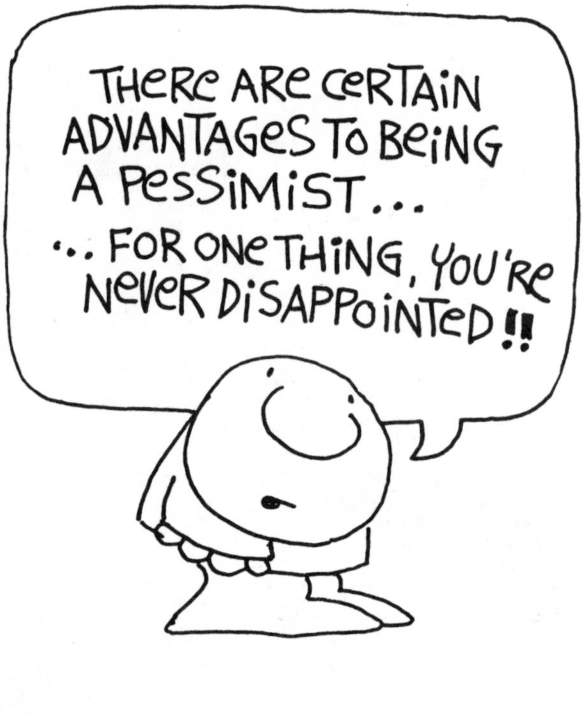
THERE ARE CERTAIN ADVANTAGES TO BEING A PESSIMIST...
... FOR ONE THING, YOU'RE NEVER DISAPPOINTED !!

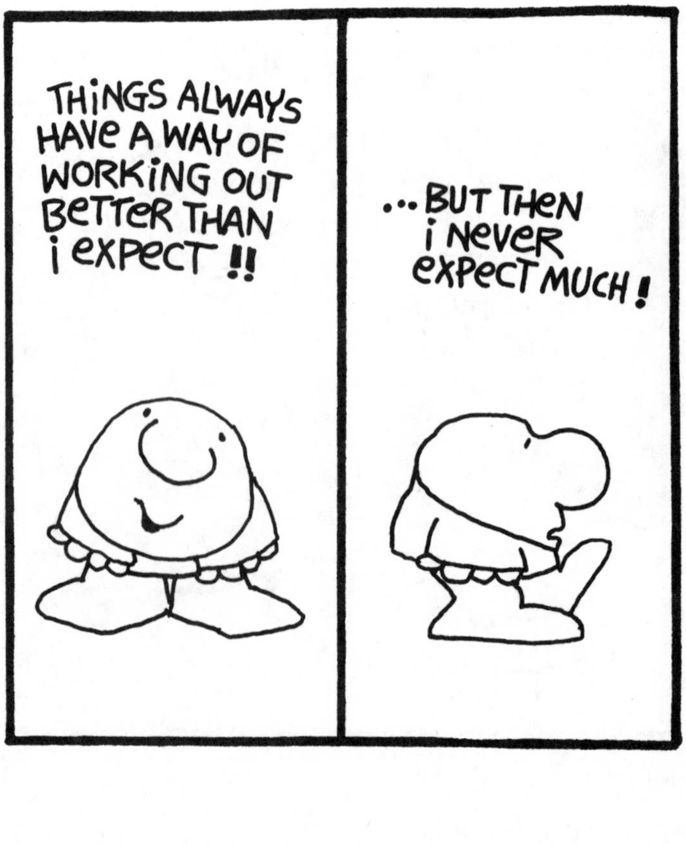
THINGS ALWAYS HAVE A WAY OF WORKING OUT BETTER THAN I EXPECT !!
... BUT THEN I NEVER EXPECT MUCH !

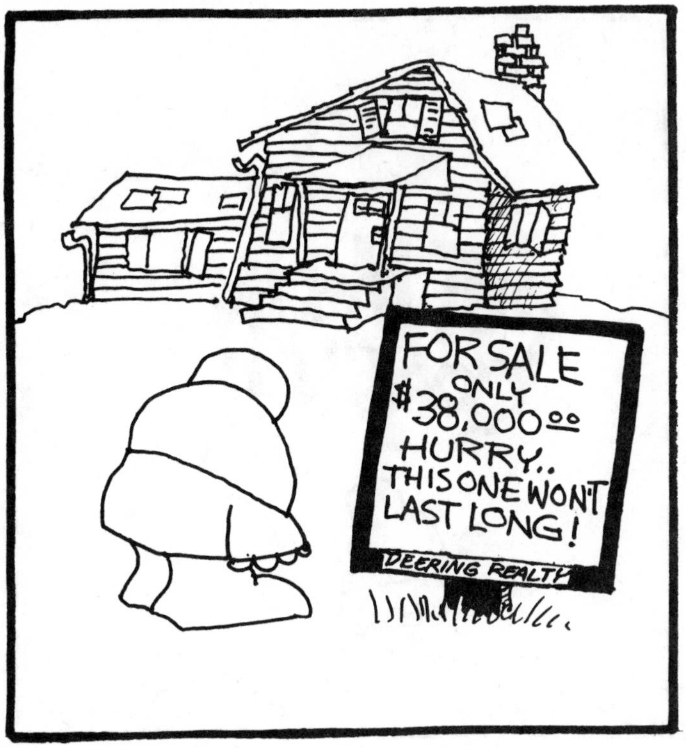
FOR SALE
ONLY
$38,000.00
HURRY..
THIS ONE WON'T
LAST LONG!
DEERING REALTY

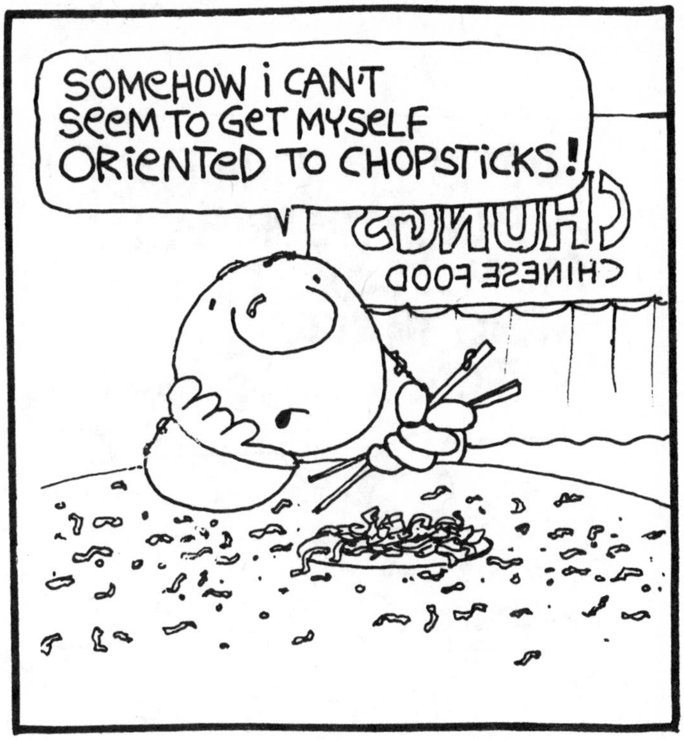
SOMEHOW I CAN'T SEEM TO GET MYSELF ORIENTED TO CHOPSTICKS!
CHUNGS
CHINESE FOOD

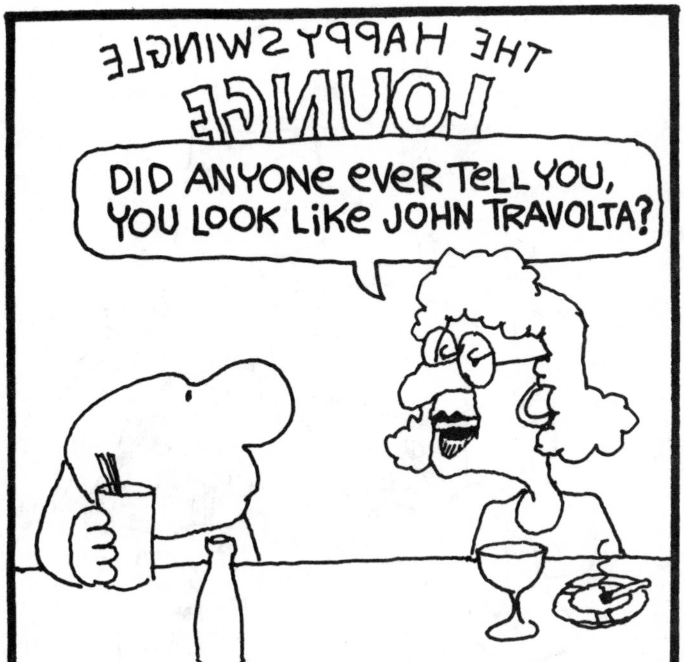
THE HAPPY SWINGLE
LOUNGE
DID ANYONE EVER TELL YOU, YOU LOOK LIKE JOHN TRAVOLTA?

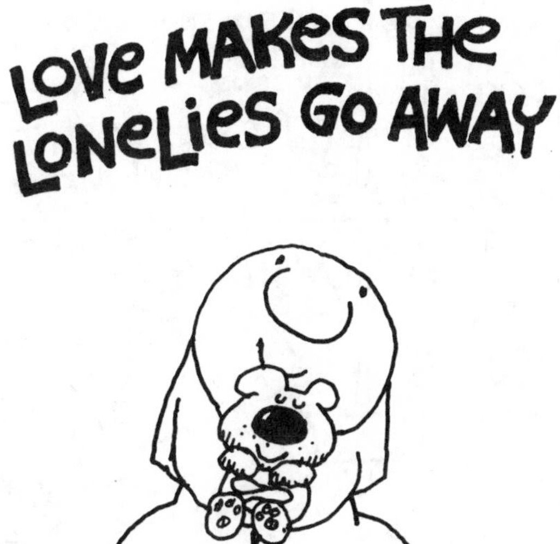
LOVE MAKES THE
LONELIES GO AWAY

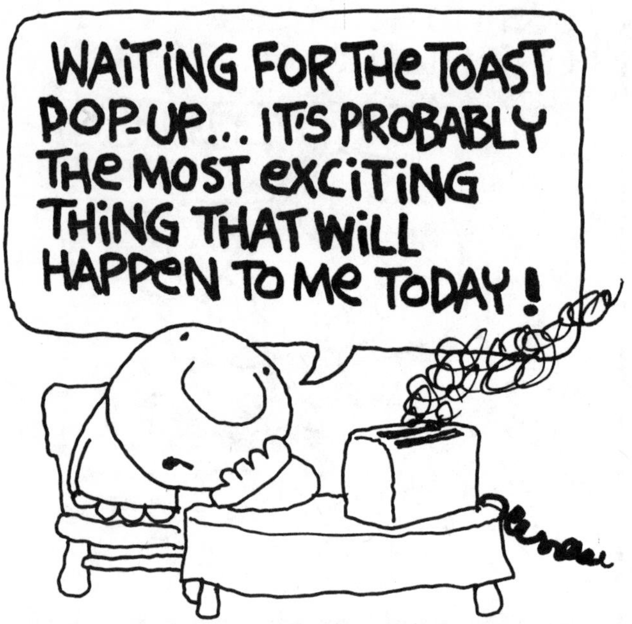
WAITING FOR THE TOAST POP-UP... IT'S PROBABLY THE MOST EXCITING THING THAT WILL HAPPEN TO ME TODAY!

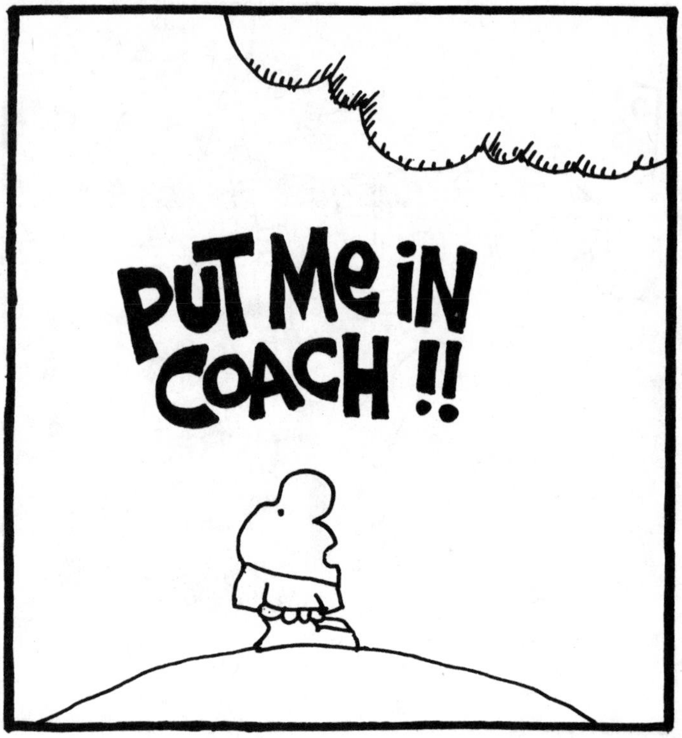
PUT ME IN COACH!!

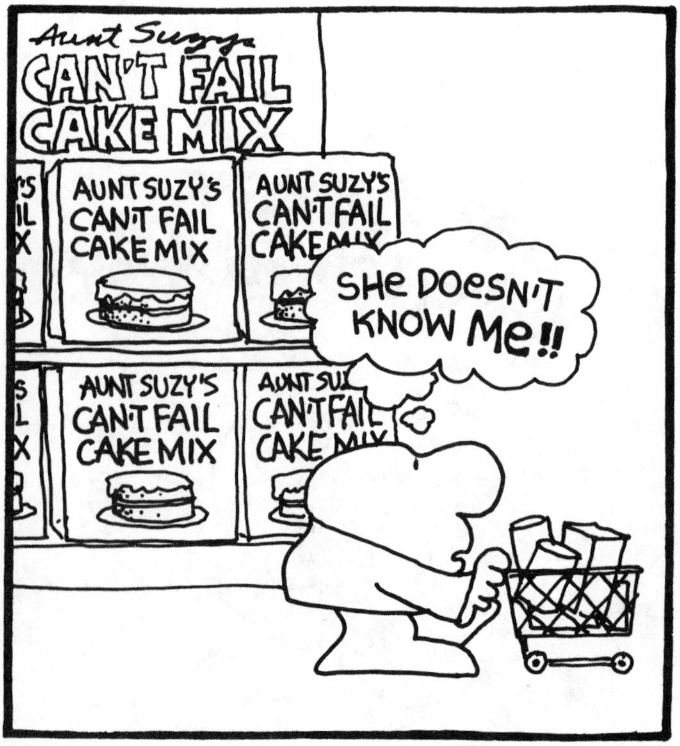
Aunt Suzy's
CAN'T FAIL
CAKE MIX
AUNT SUZY'S CAN'T FAIL CAKE MIX
SHE DOESN'T KNOW ME!!

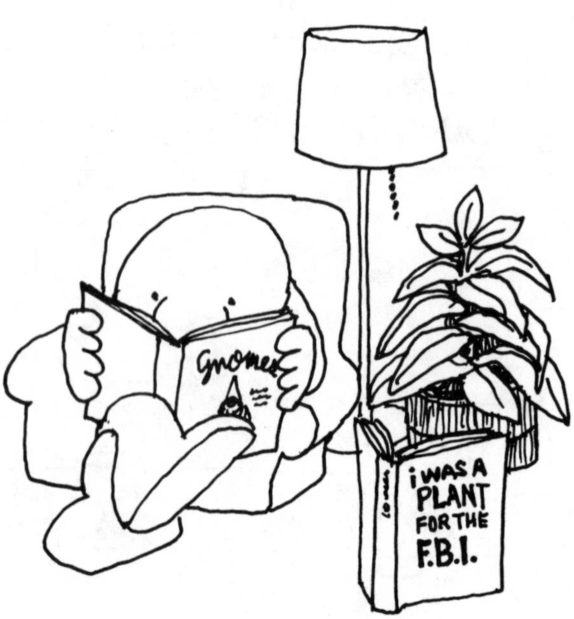
Gnomes
I WAS A PLANT FOR THE F.B.I.

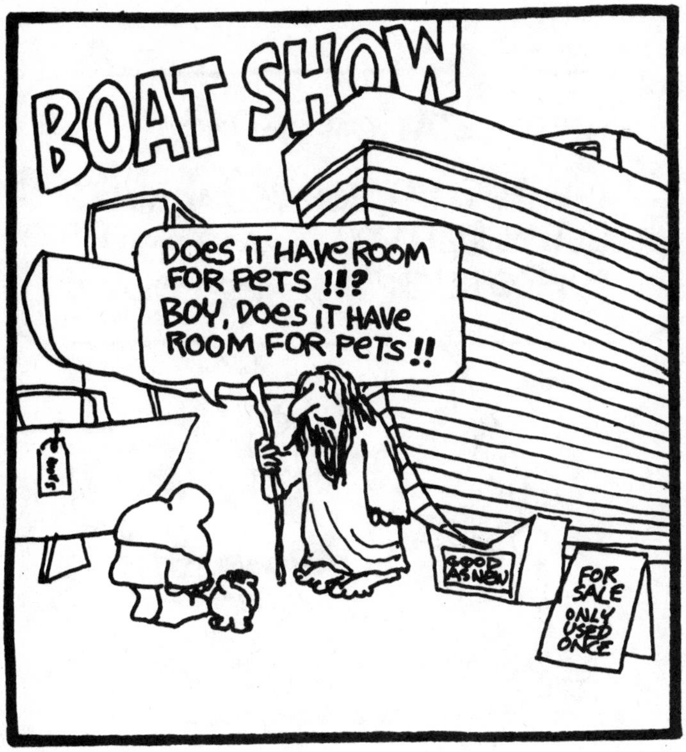
BOAT SHOW
DOES IT HAVE ROOM FOR PETS !!?
BOY, DOES IT HAVE ROOM FOR PETS !!
GOOD AS NEW
FOR SALE ONLY USED ONCE

YOGURT DOESN'T TASTE QUITE AS GOOD AS IT LOOKS ... BUT IT TASTES A LOT BETTER THAN IT SOUNDS !!

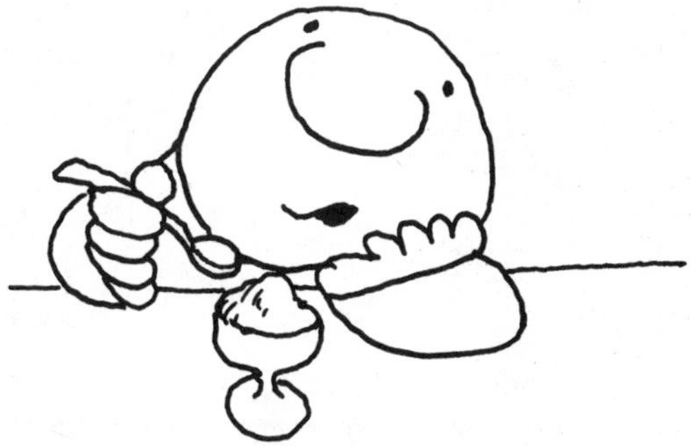

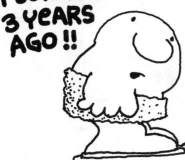

DIETING IS A LOSING BATTLE ... IN FACT I SURRENDERED 3 YEARS AGO !!

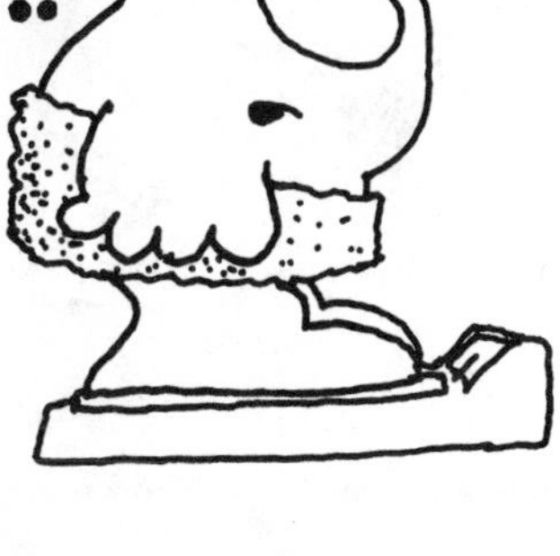

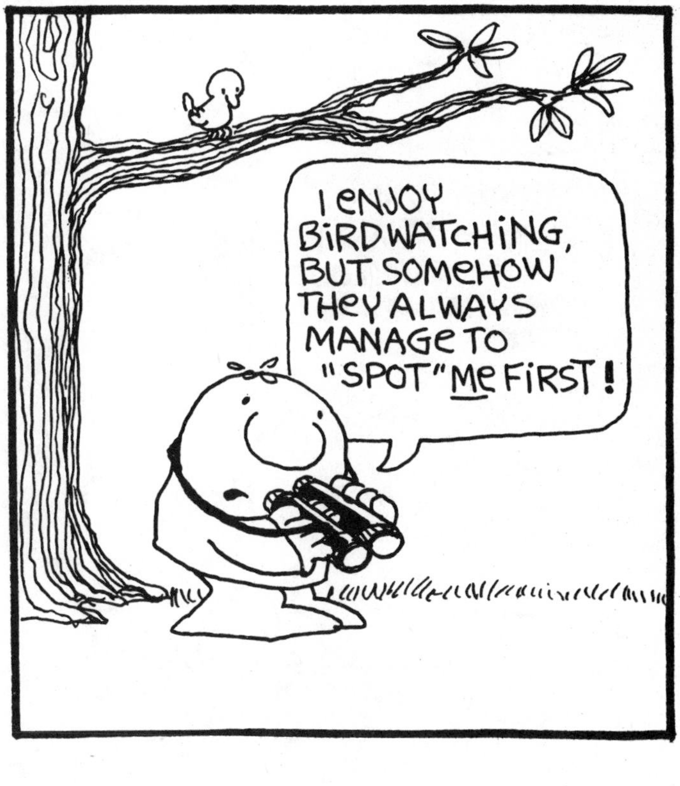
I ENJOY BIRDWATCHING, BUT SOMEHOW THEY ALWAYS MANAGE TO "SPOT" ME FIRST !

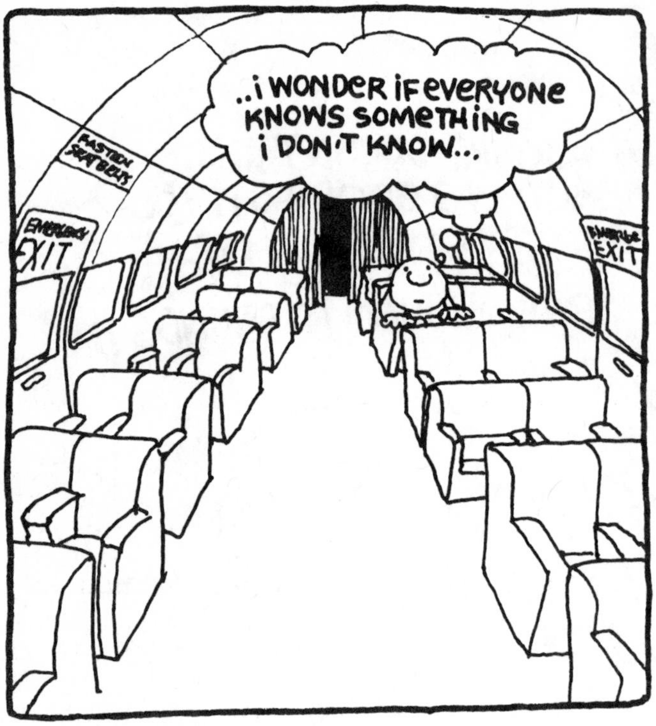
..i WONDER iF EVERYONE KNOWS SOMETHING i DON'T KNOW...
EXIT
EXIT

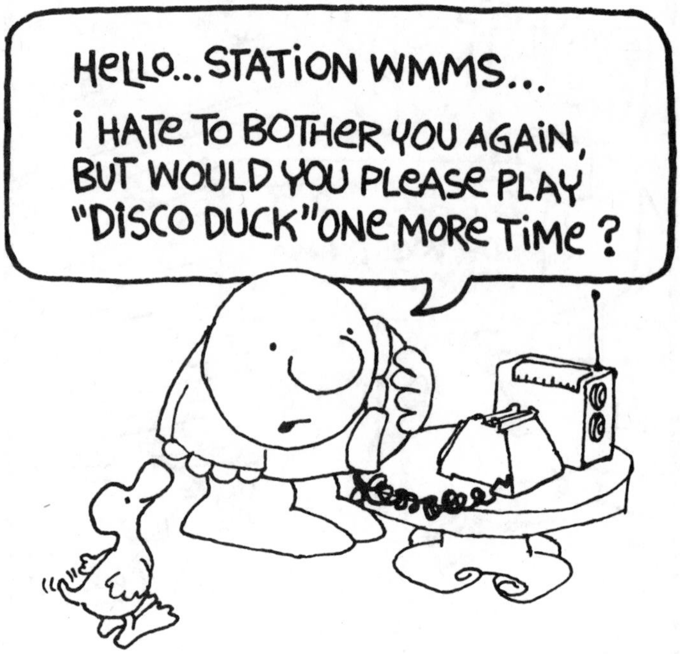
HELLO...STATION WMMS...
i HATE TO BOTHER YOU AGAIN, BUT WOULD YOU PLEASE PLAY "DISCO DUCK" ONE MORE TIME ?

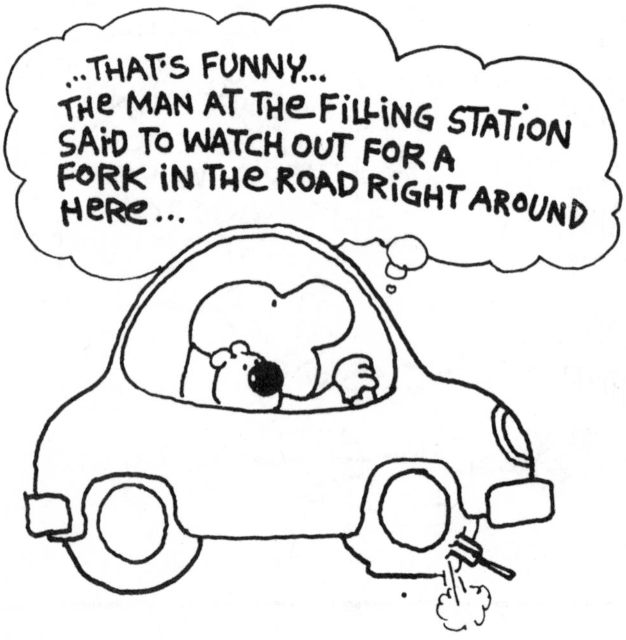
...THAT'S FUNNY... THE MAN AT THE FILLING STATION SAID TO WATCH OUT FOR A FORK IN THE ROAD RIGHT AROUND HERE...

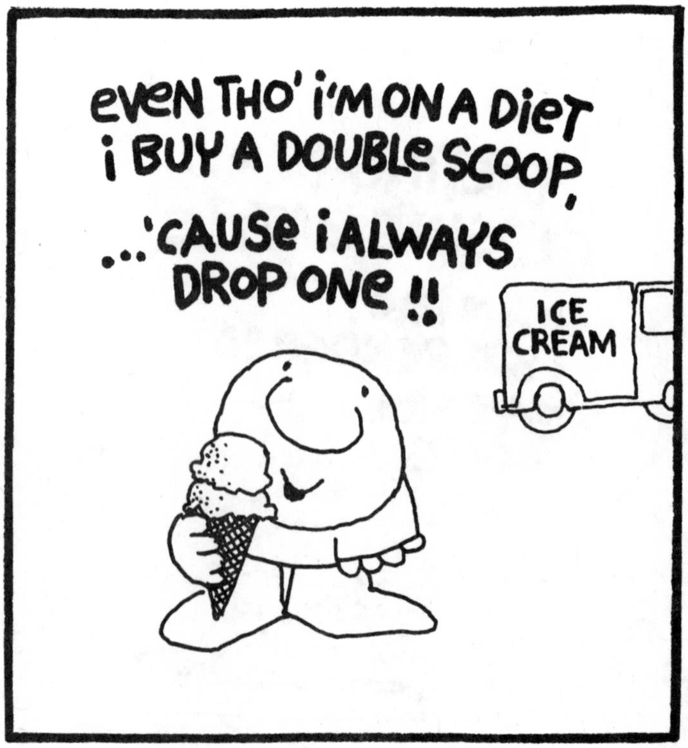
EVEN THO' i'M ON A DIET i BUY A DOUBLE SCOOP,
...'CAUSE i ALWAYS DROP ONE !!
ICE CREAM

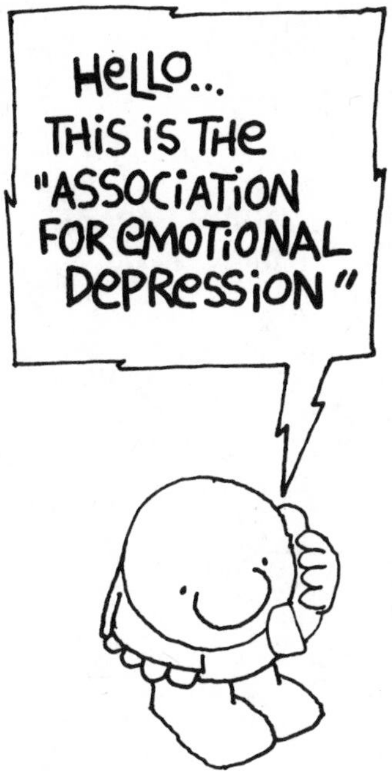
HELLO...
THIS IS THE "ASSOCIATION FOR EMOTIONAL DEPRESSION"
..NO THANKS.. I DON'T NEED ANY !!

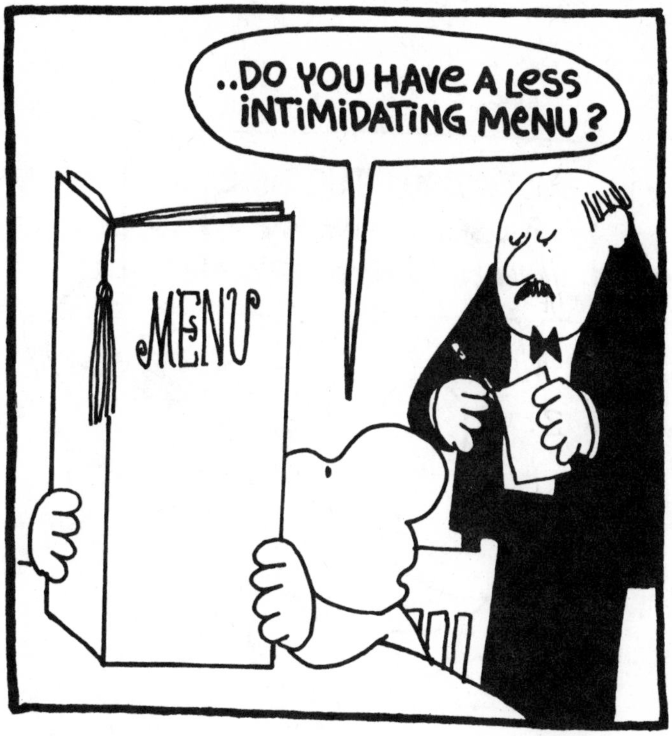
..DO YOU HAVE A LESS INTIMIDATING MENU ?
MENU

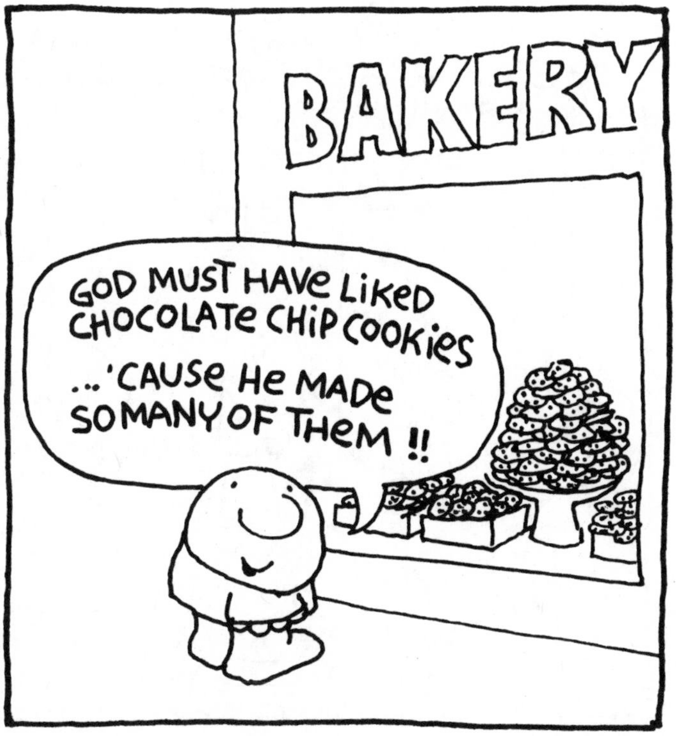
BAKERY
GOD MUST HAVE LIKED CHOCOLATE CHIP COOKIES
...'CAUSE HE MADE SO MANY OF THEM !!

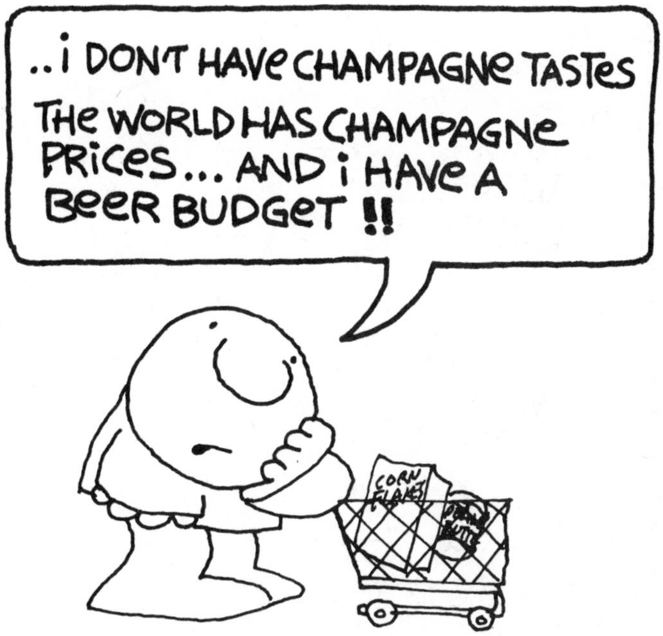
..I DON'T HAVE CHAMPAGNE TASTES
THE WORLD HAS CHAMPAGNE PRICES... AND I HAVE A BEER BUDGET !!

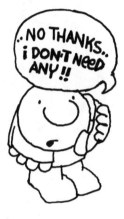

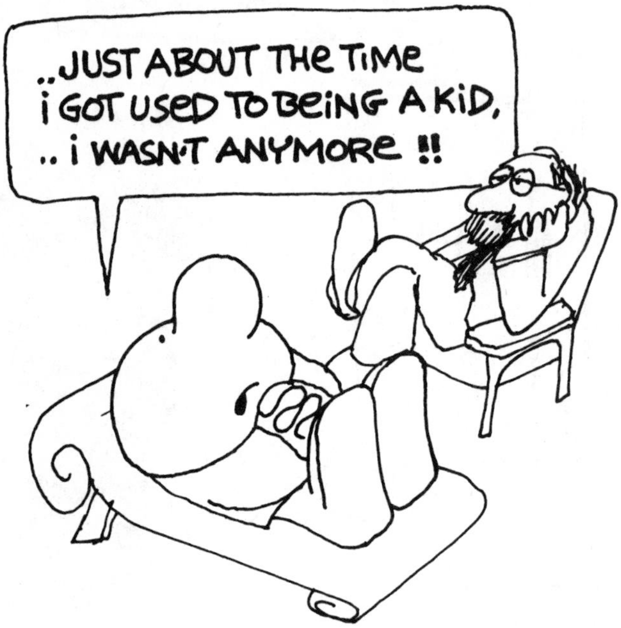
..JUST ABOUT THE TIME i GOT USED TO BEING A KID, .. i WASN'T ANYMORE !!

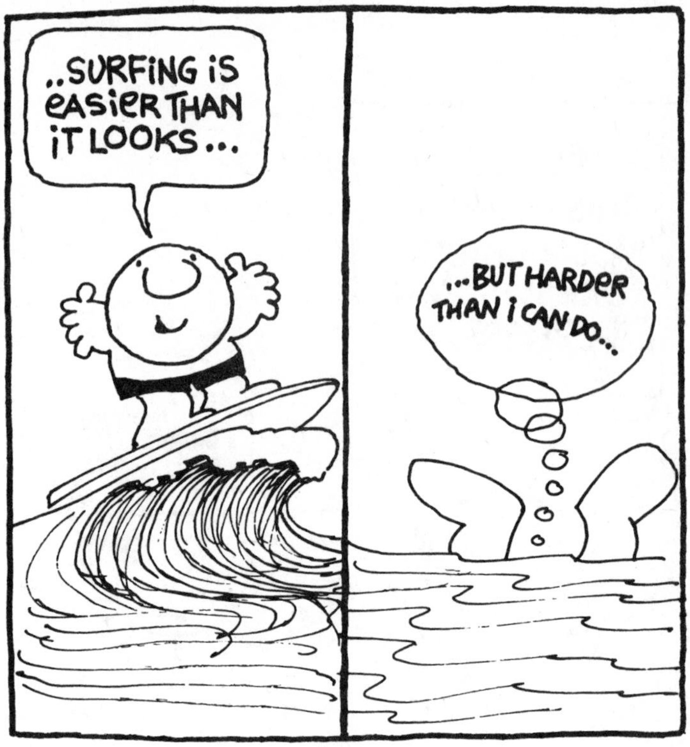
..SURFING IS EASIER THAN IT LOOKS...
...BUT HARDER THAN I CAN DO...

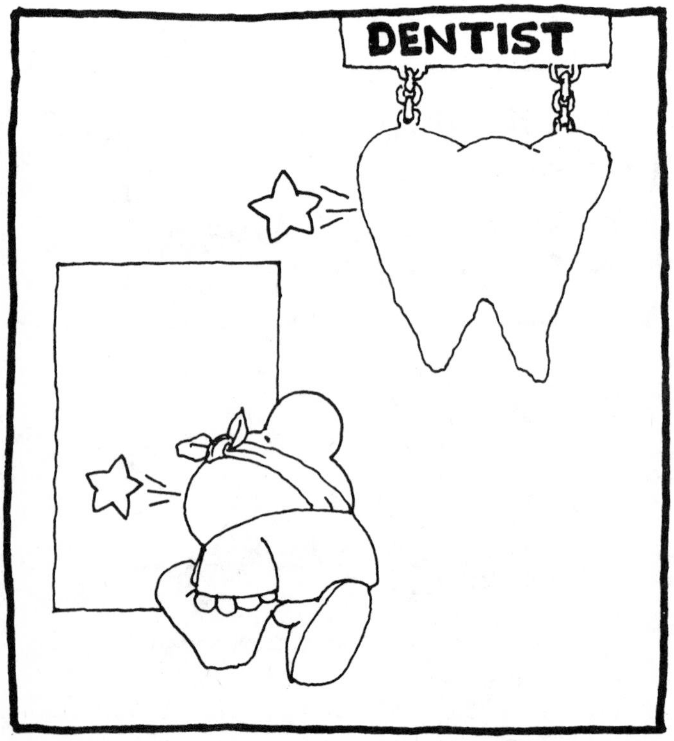
DENTIST

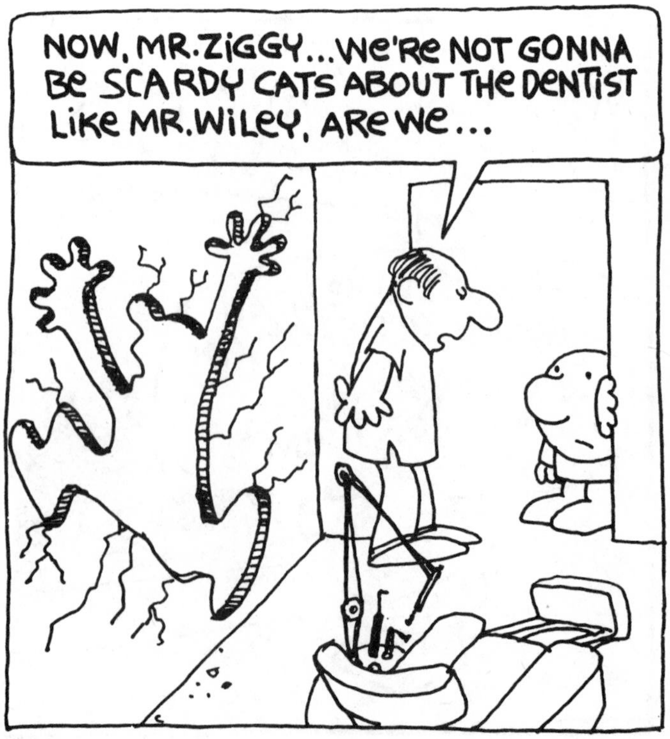
NOW, MR. ZIGGY... WE'RE NOT GONNA BE SCARDY CATS ABOUT THE DENTIST LIKE MR. WILEY, ARE WE...

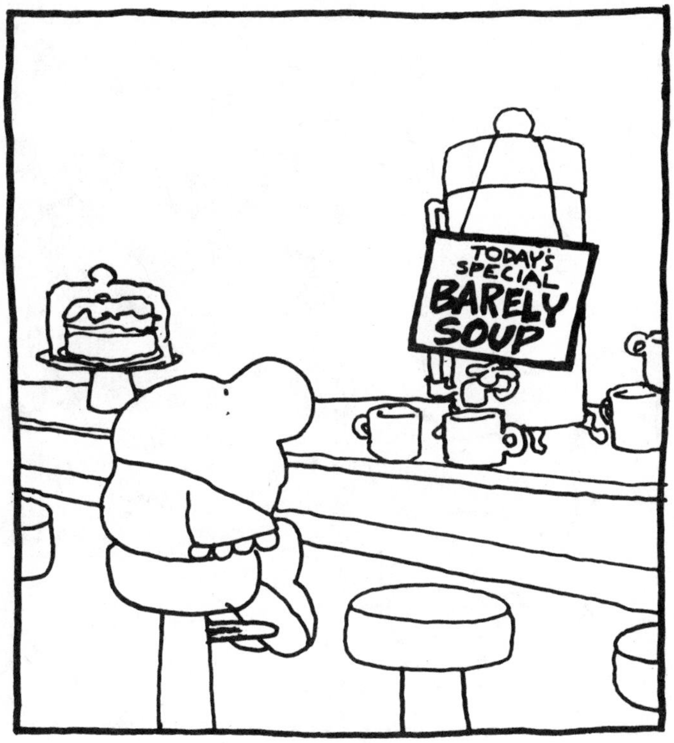
TODAY'S SPECIAL
BARELY SOUP

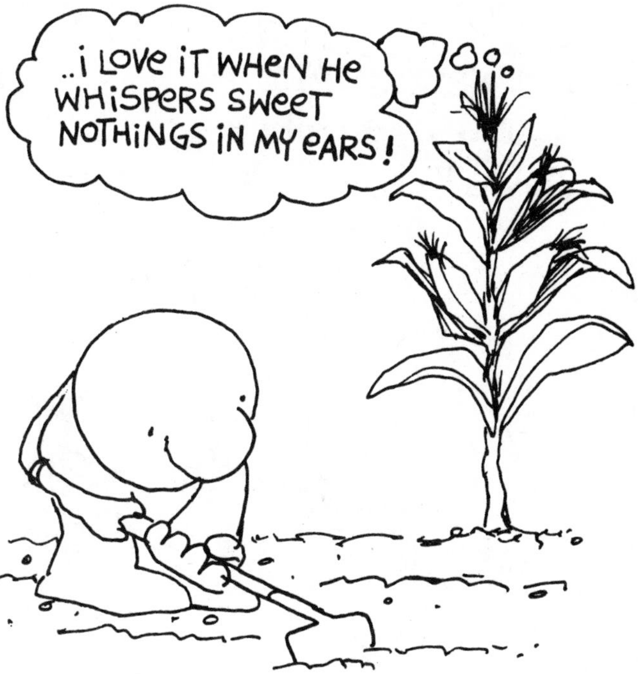
..i LOVE iT WHEN HE WHiSPERS SWEET NOTHiNGS iN MY EARS!

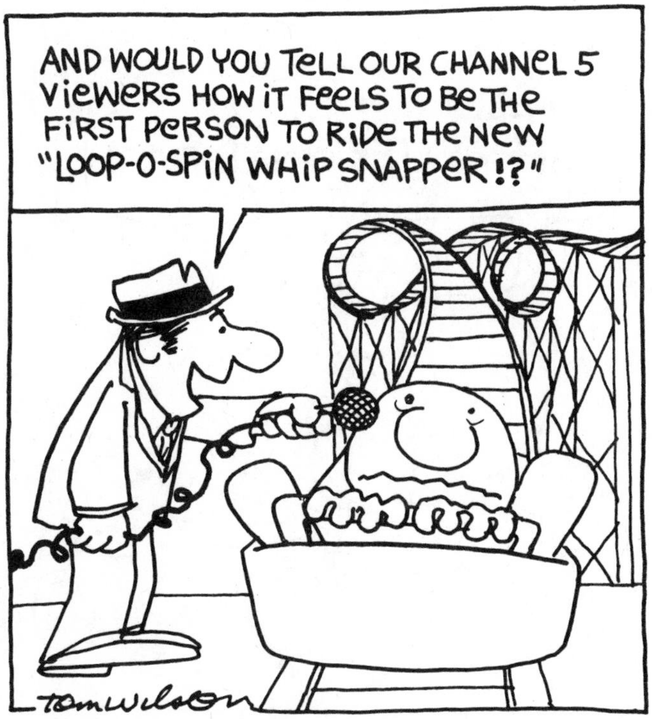
AND WOULD YOU TELL OUR CHANNEL 5 VIEWERS HOW iT FEELS TO BE THE FIRST PERSON TO RIDE THE NEW "LOOP-O-SPIN WHIP SNAPPER!?"
TOM WILSON

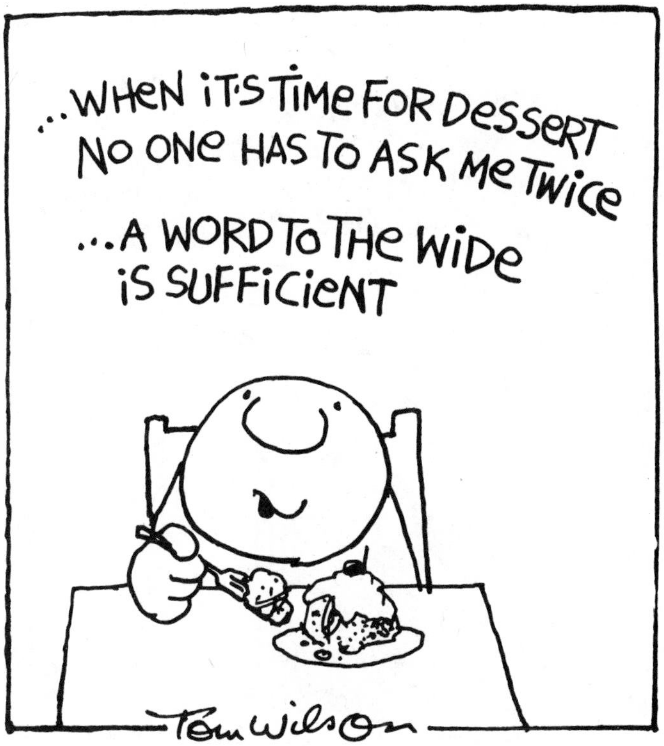
...WHEN iT'S TIME FOR DESSERT NO ONE HAS TO ASK ME TWICE
...A WORD TO THE WIDE iS SUFFICIENT
TOM WILSON

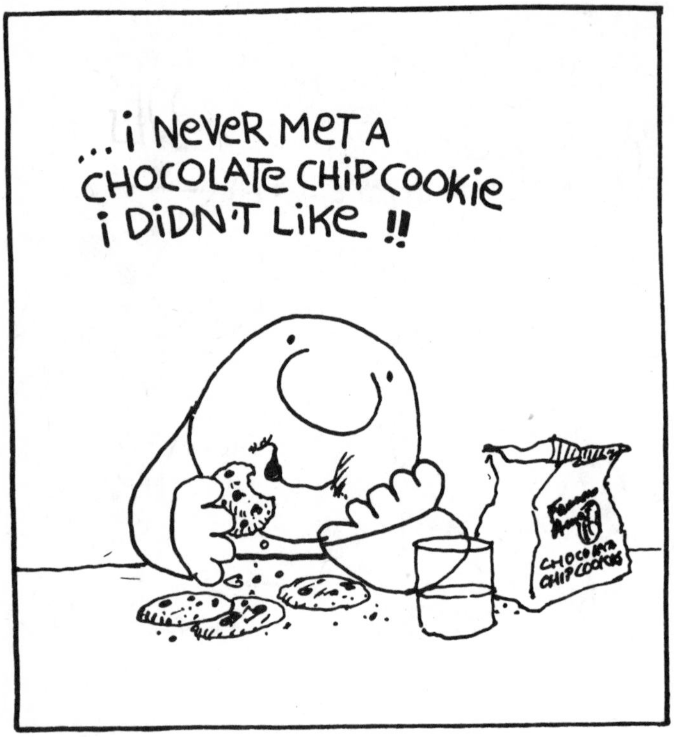
...i NEVER MET A CHOCOLATE CHIP COOKIE i DIDN'T LIKE !!

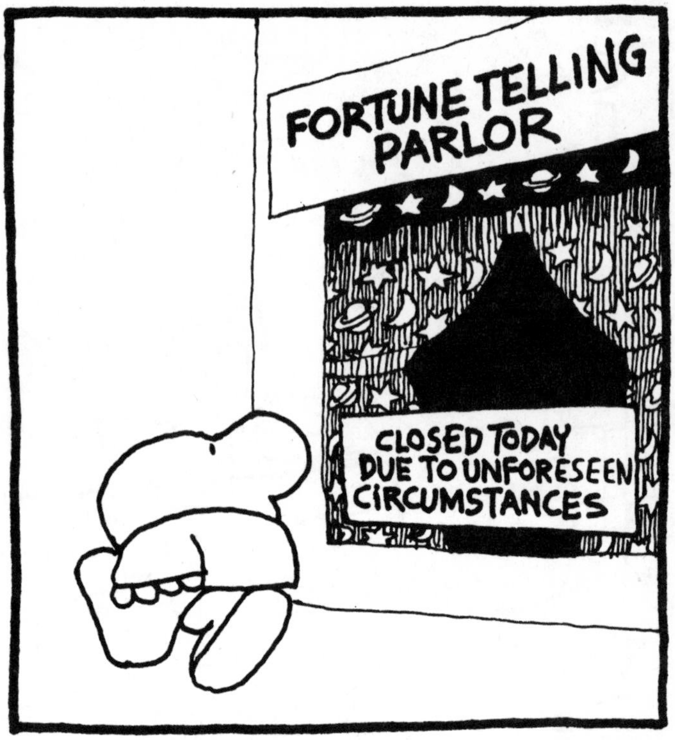
FORTUNE TELLING PARLOR
CLOSED TODAY DUE TO UNFORESEEN CIRCUMSTANCES

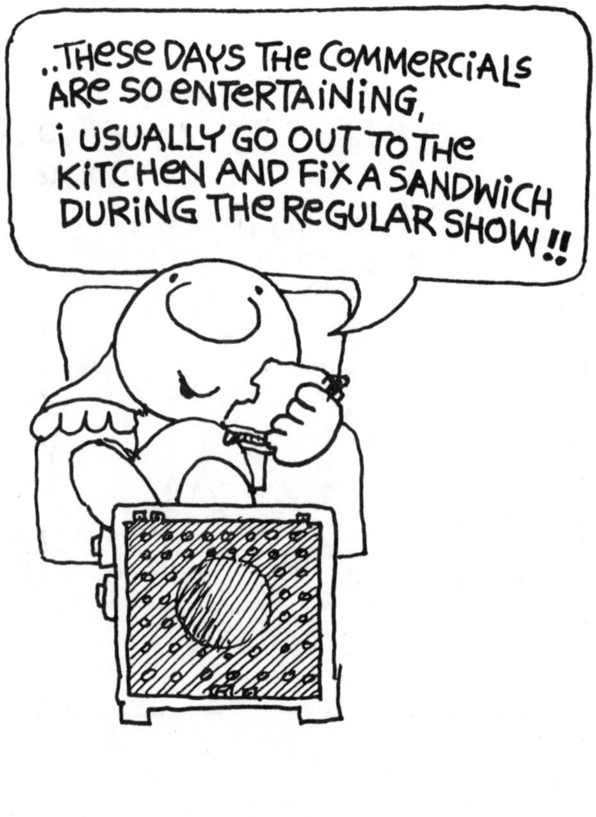
..THESE DAYS THE COMMERCIALS ARE SO ENTERTAINING, i USUALLY GO OUT TO THE KITCHEN AND FIX A SANDWICH DURING THE REGULAR SHOW !!

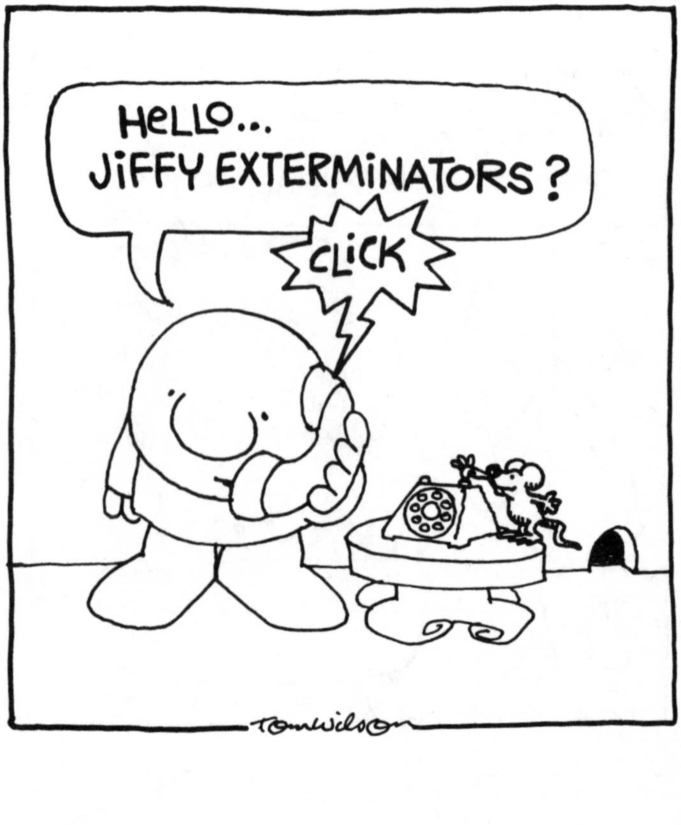
HELLO... JIFFY EXTERMINATORS ?
CLICK

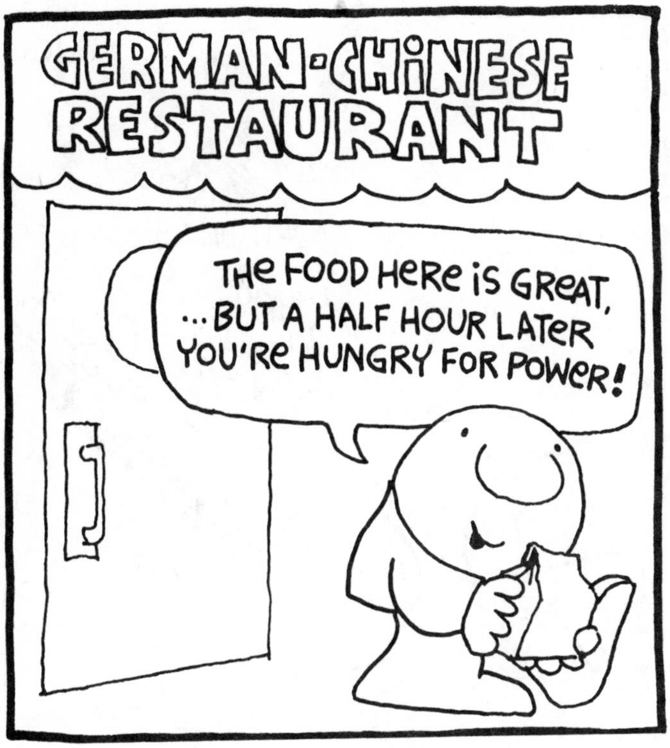
GERMAN-CHINESE RESTAURANT
THE FOOD HERE IS GREAT, ...BUT A HALF HOUR LATER YOU'RE HUNGRY FOR POWER!

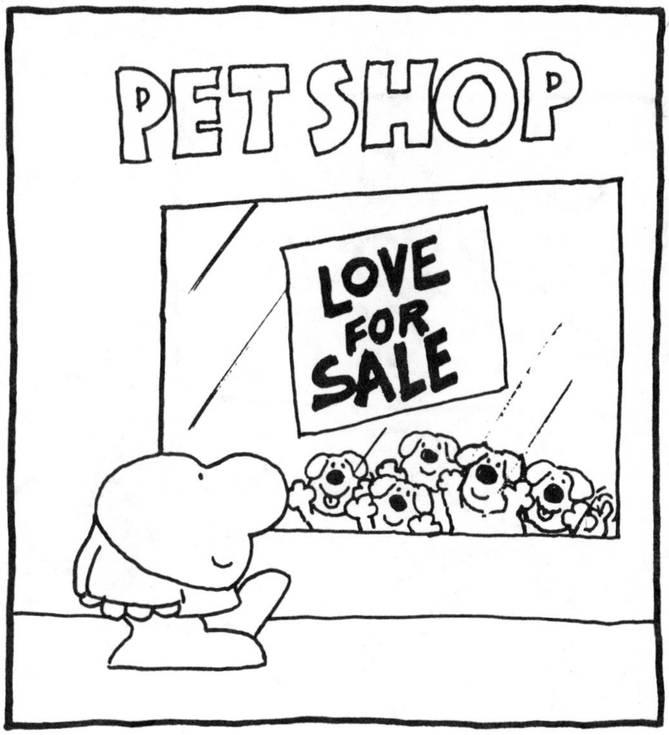
PET SHOP
LOVE FOR SALE

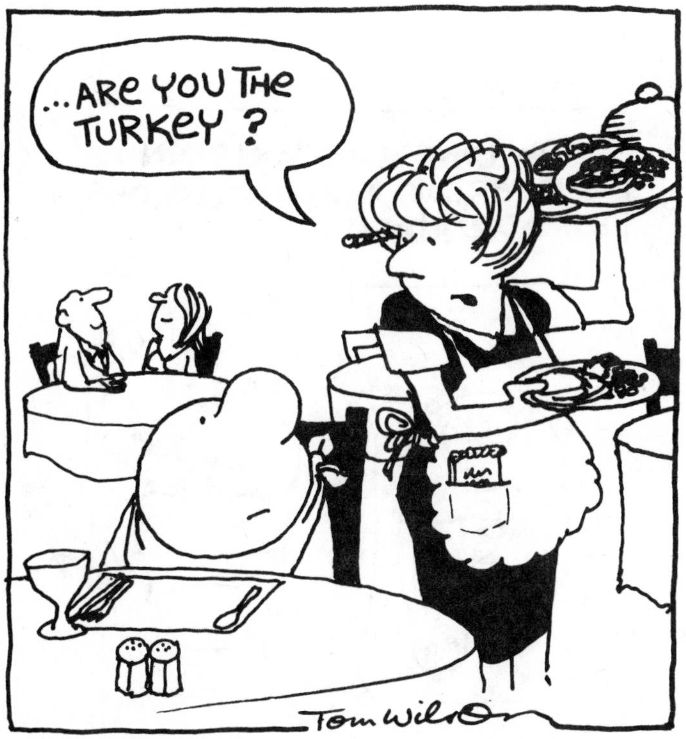
...ARE YOU THE TURKEY ?

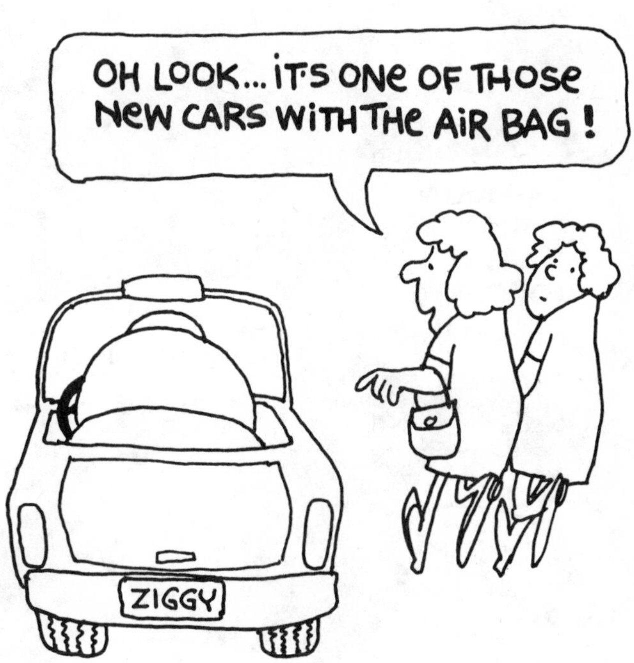
OH LOOK... IT'S ONE OF THOSE NEW CARS WITH THE AIR BAG !
ZIGGY

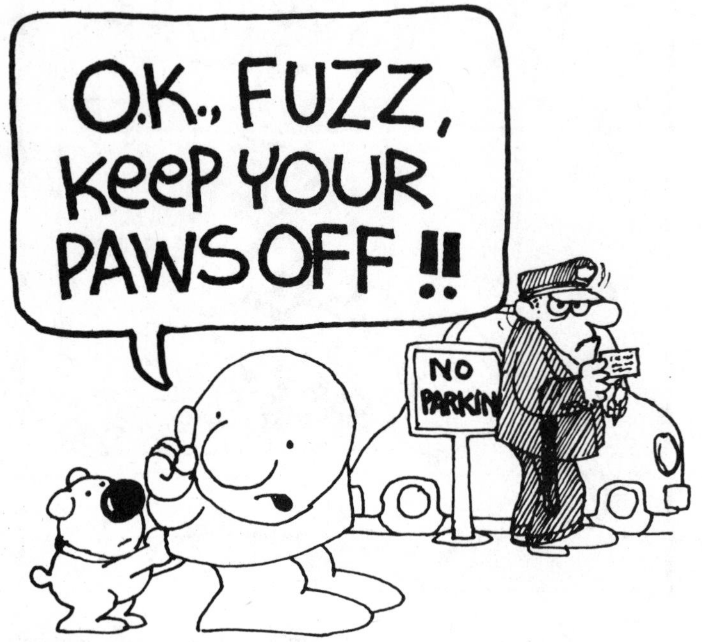
O.K., FUZZ, KEEP YOUR PAWS OFF !!
NO PARKIN

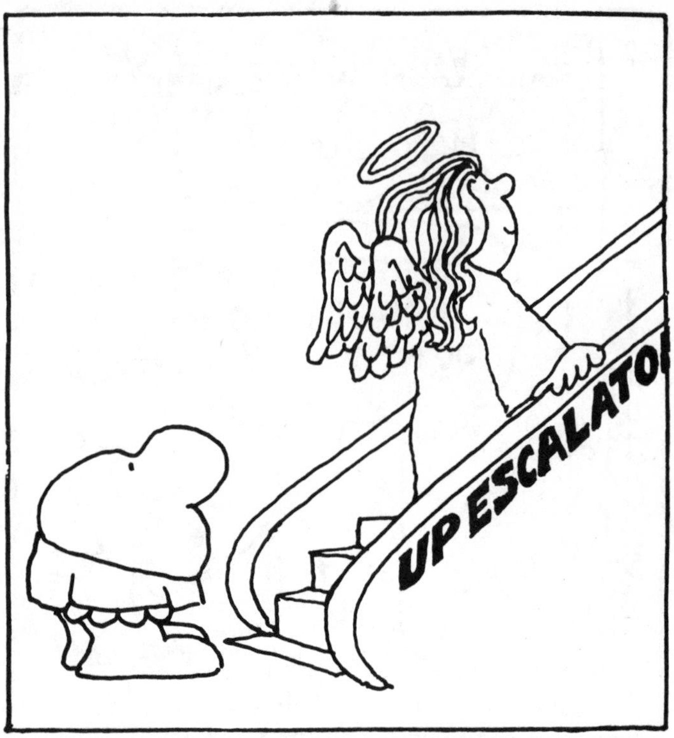
UP ESCALATO

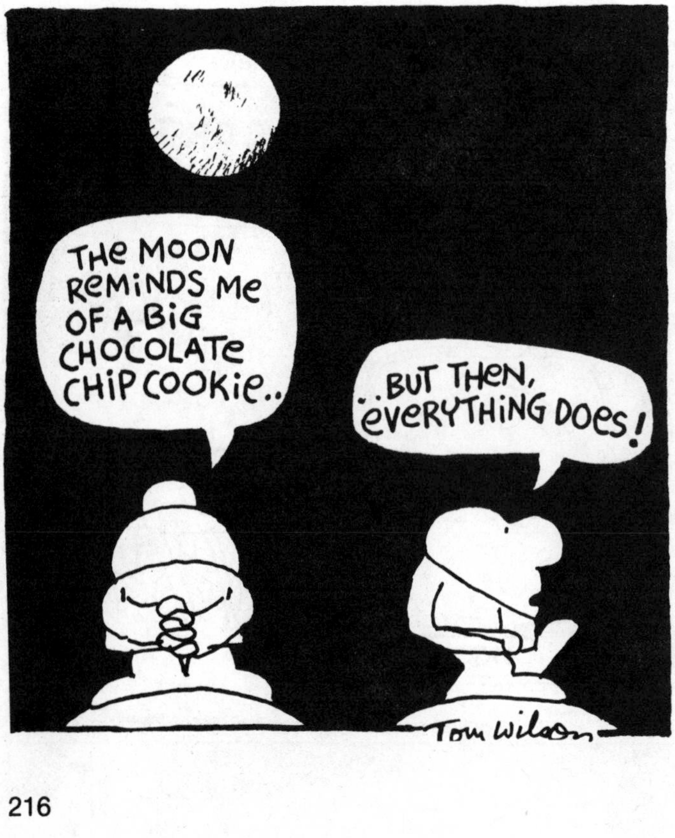
THE MOON REMINDS ME OF A BIG CHOCOLATE CHIP COOKIE..
..BUT THEN, EVERYTHING DOES!
Tom Wilson

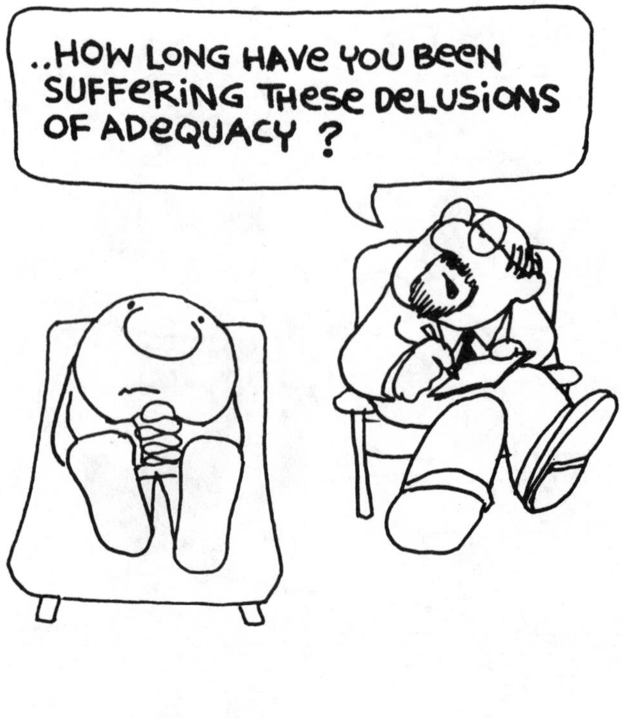
..HOW LONG HAVE YOU BEEN SUFFERING THESE DELUSIONS OF ADEQUACY ?

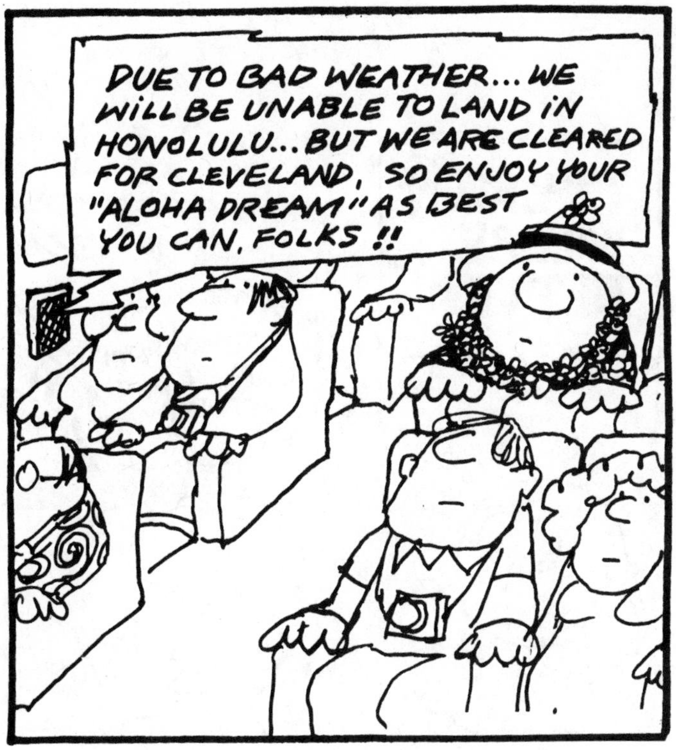
DUE TO BAD WEATHER... WE WILL BE UNABLE TO LAND IN HONOLULU... BUT WE ARE CLEARED FOR CLEVELAND, SO ENJOY YOUR "ALOHA DREAM" AS BEST YOU CAN, FOLKS !!

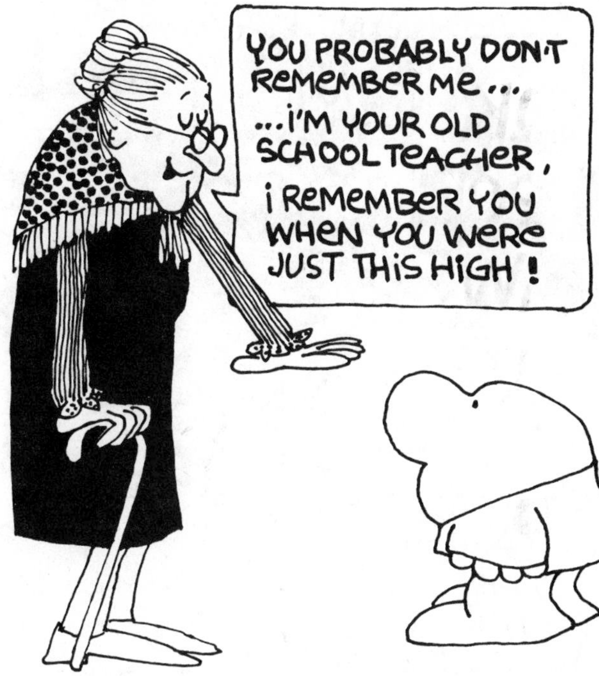
YOU PROBABLY DON'T REMEMBER ME...
...I'M YOUR OLD SCHOOL TEACHER, I REMEMBER YOU WHEN YOU WERE JUST THIS HIGH !

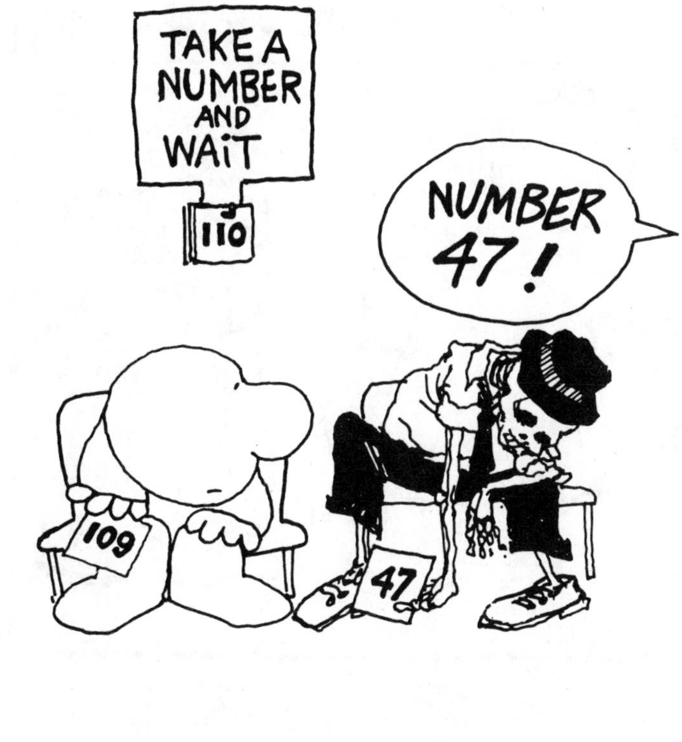
TAKE A NUMBER AND WAIT
110
NUMBER 47 !
109
47

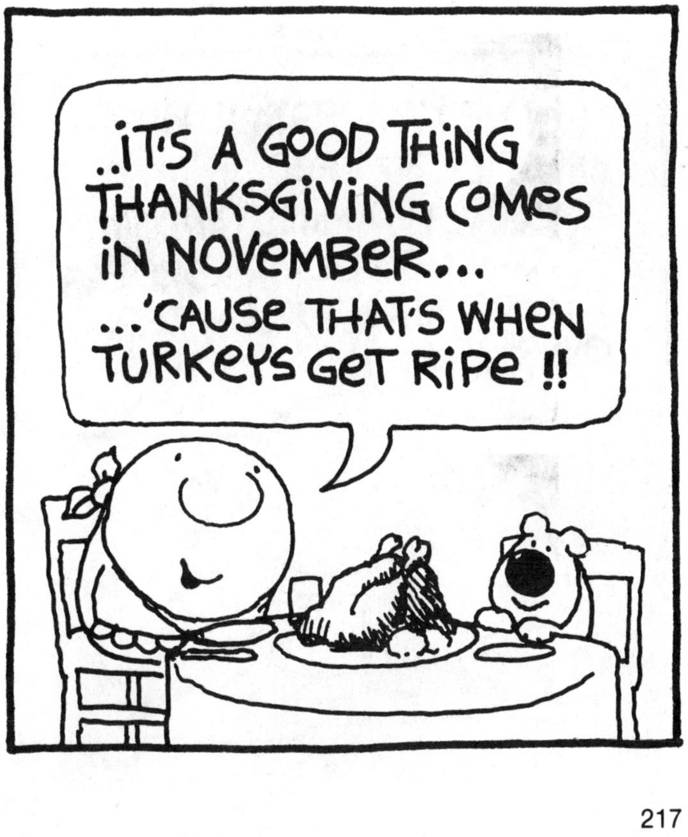
..IT'S A GOOD THING THANKSGIVING COMES IN NOVEMBER...
...'CAUSE THAT'S WHEN TURKEYS GET RIPE !!

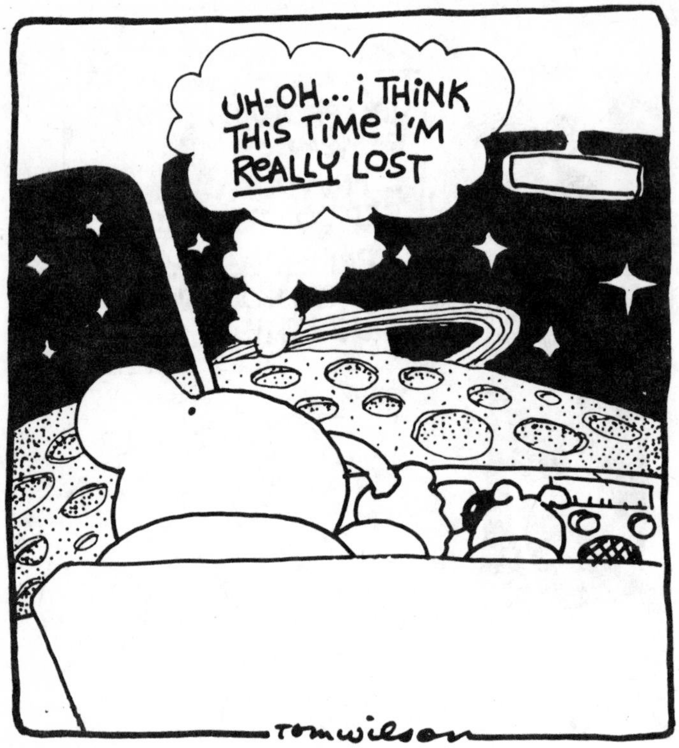
UH-OH... i THINK THIS TIME i'M REALLY LOST
tomwilson

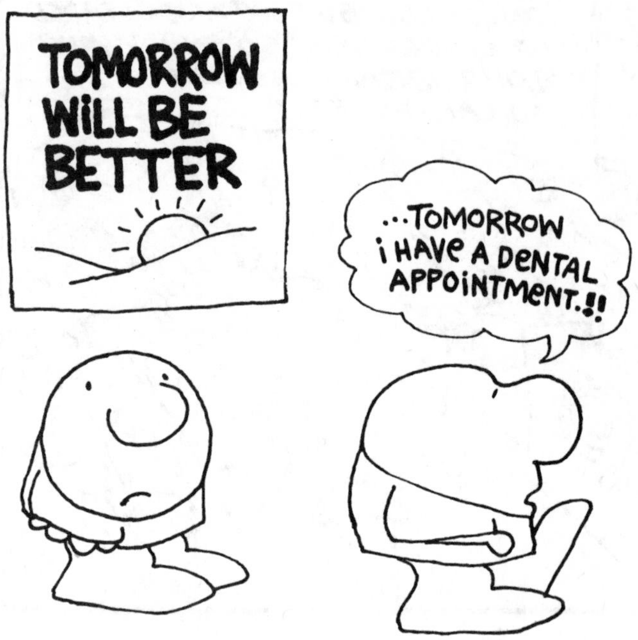
TOMORROW WILL BE BETTER
...TOMORROW i HAVE A DENTAL APPOINTMENT.!!

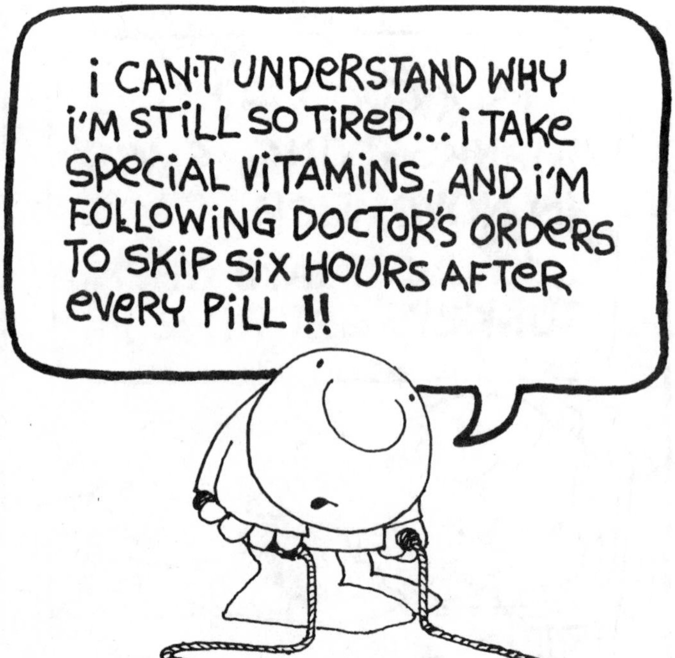
i CAN'T UNDERSTAND WHY i'M STILL SO TIRED... i TAKE SPECIAL VITAMINS, AND i'M FOLLOWING DOCTOR'S ORDERS TO SKIP SIX HOURS AFTER EVERY PILL !!

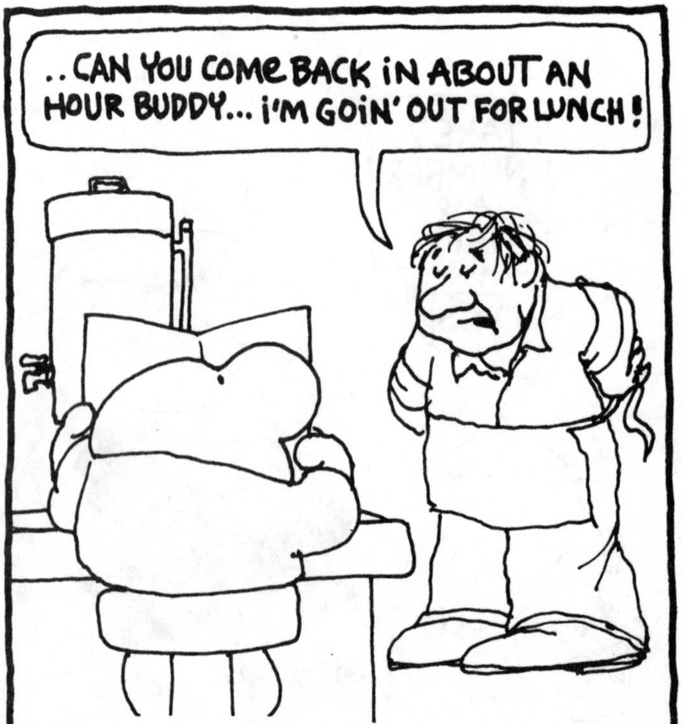
..CAN YOU COME BACK iN ABOUT AN HOUR BUDDY... i'M GOIN' OUT FOR LUNCH!

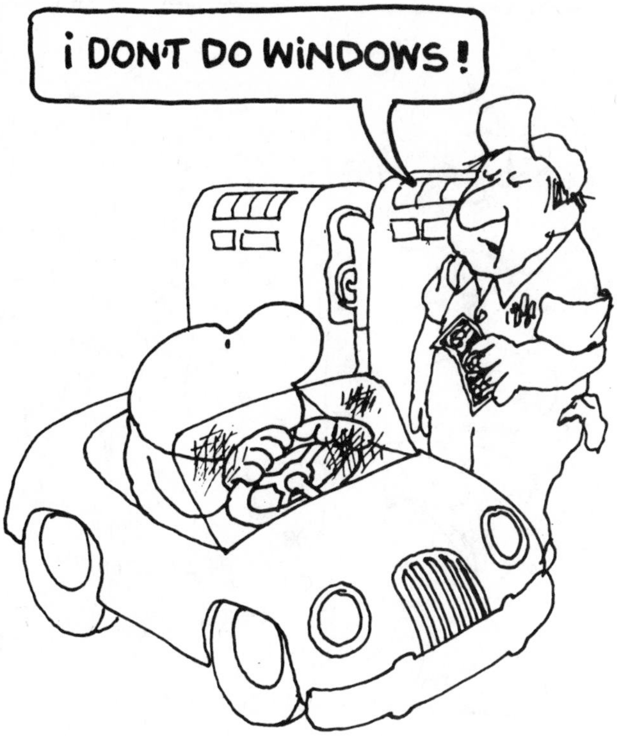
i DON'T DO WiNDOWS!

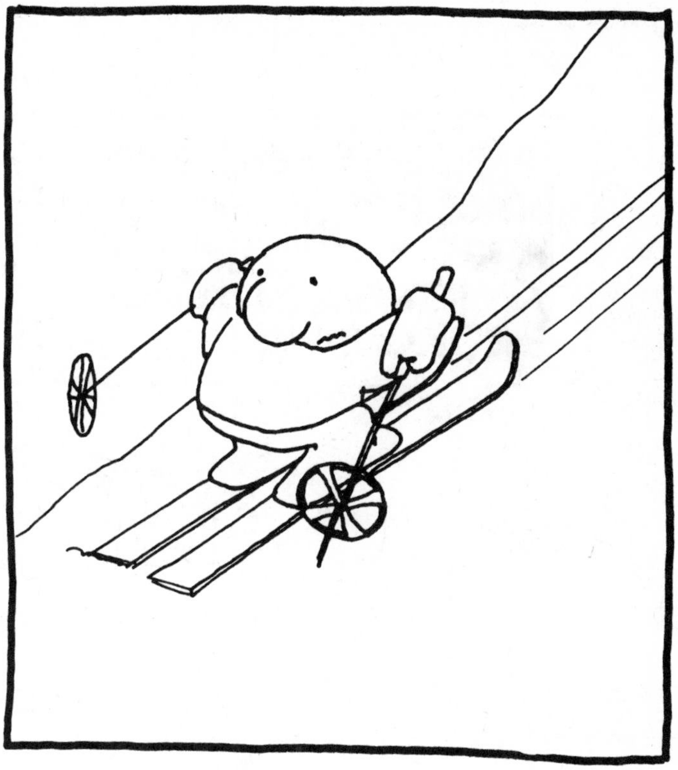

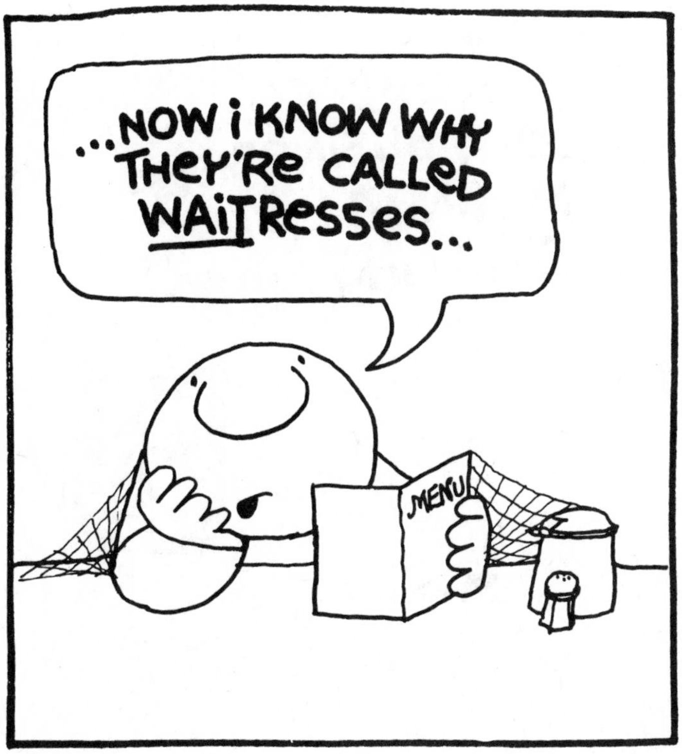
...NOW i KNOW WHY THEY'RE CALLED WAITRESSES...
MENU

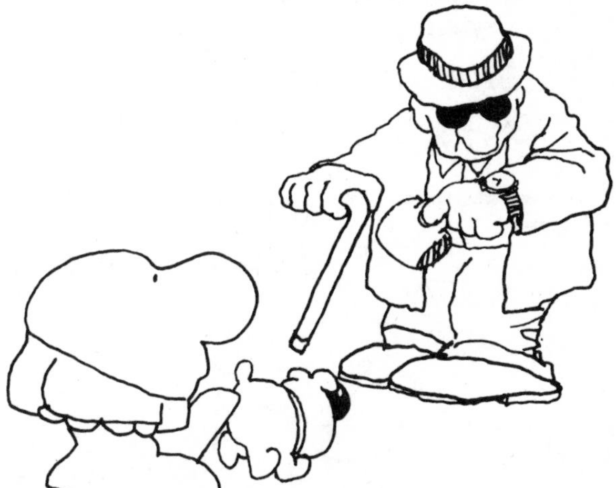

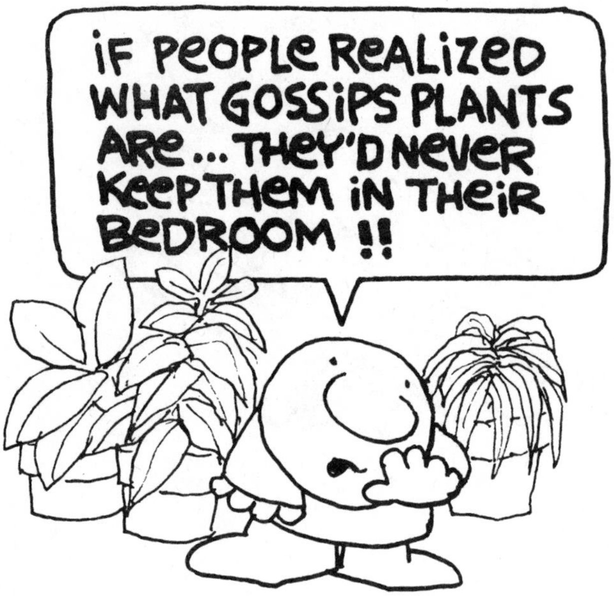
IF PEOPLE REALIZED WHAT GOSSIPS PLANTS ARE... THEY'D NEVER KEEP THEM IN THEIR BEDROOM !!

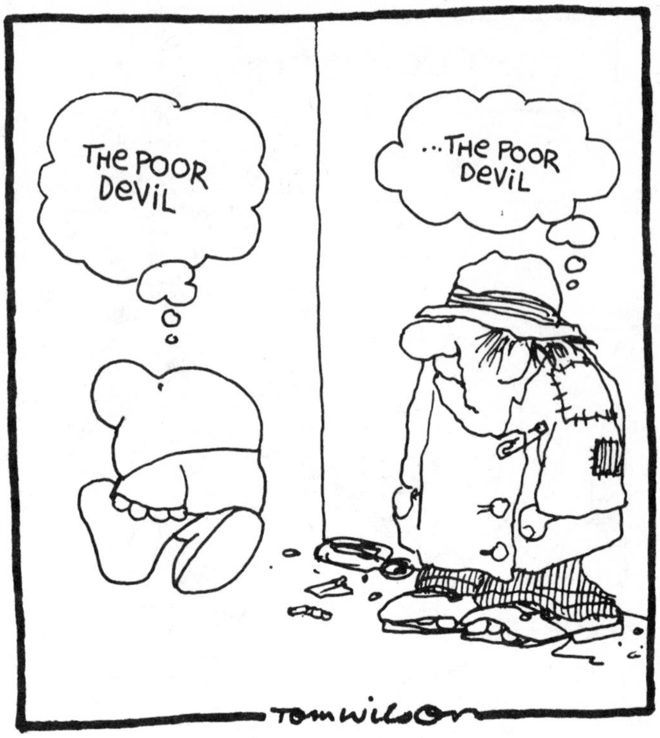
THE POOR DEVIL
...THE POOR DEVIL
TOM WILSON

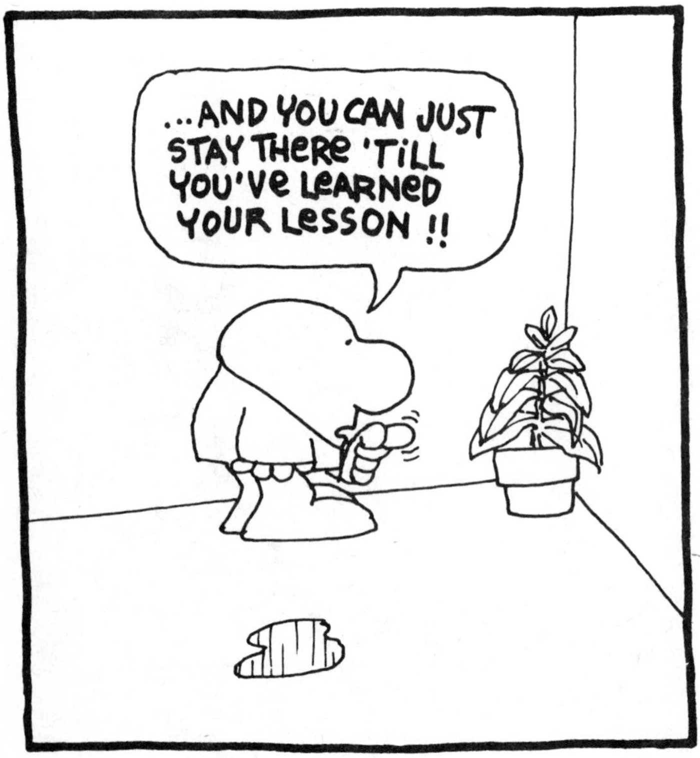
...AND YOU CAN JUST STAY THERE 'TILL YOU'VE LEARNED YOUR LESSON !!

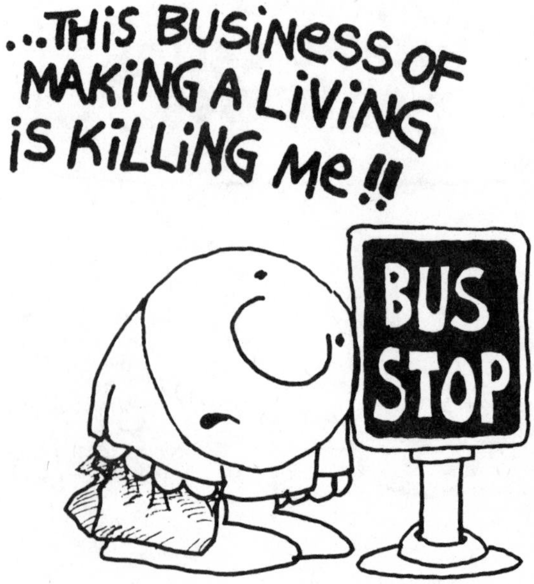
...THIS BUSINESS OF MAKING A LIVING IS KILLING ME !!
BUS STOP

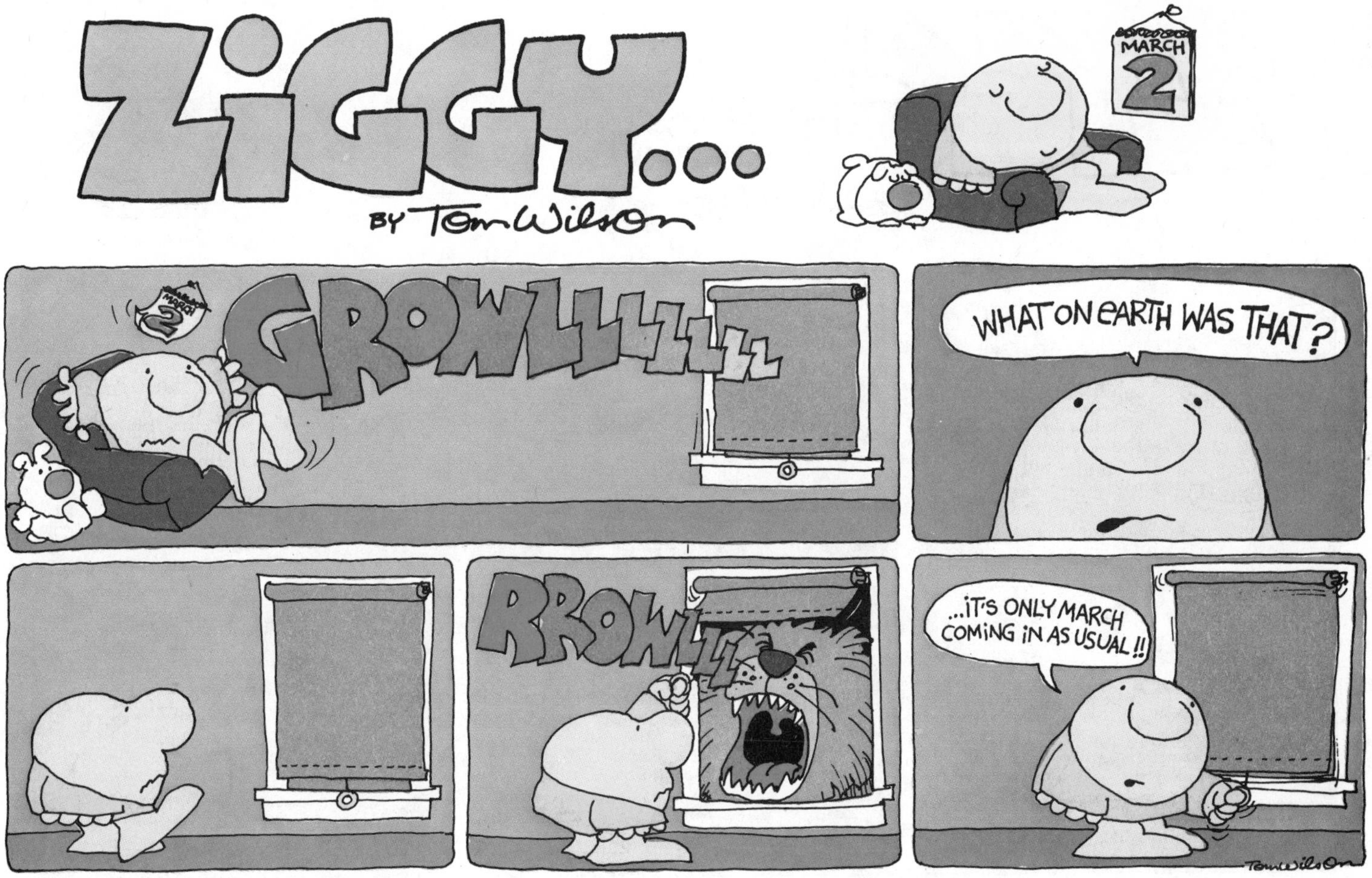
ZIGGY...
BY Tom Wilson
MARCH 2
GROWLLLLLLL
WHAT ON EARTH WAS THAT?
RROWLLL
...IT'S ONLY MARCH COMING IN AS USUAL!!
Tom Wilson

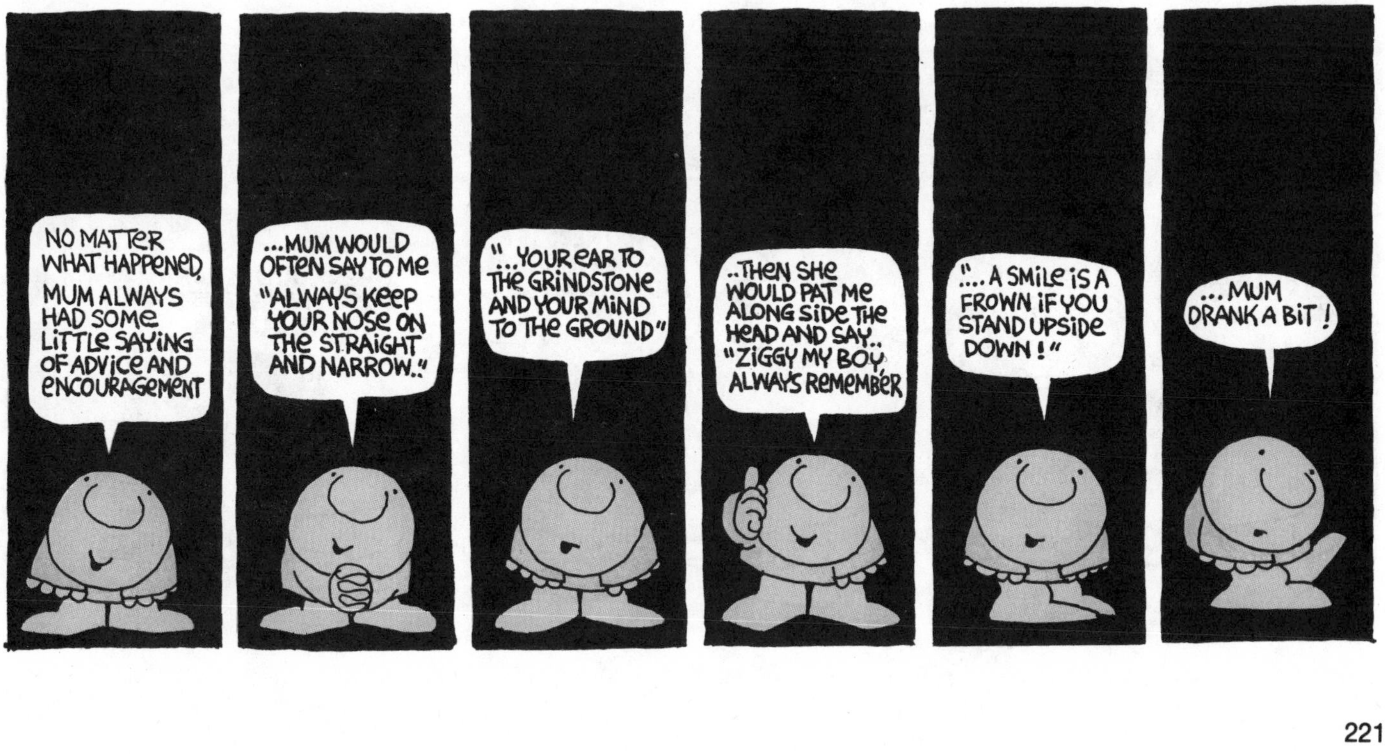
NO MATTER WHAT HAPPENED, MUM ALWAYS HAD SOME LITTLE SAYING OF ADVICE AND ENCOURAGEMENT
...MUM WOULD OFTEN SAY TO ME "ALWAYS KEEP YOUR NOSE ON THE STRAIGHT AND NARROW.."
"...YOUR EAR TO THE GRINDSTONE AND YOUR MIND TO THE GROUND"
..THEN SHE WOULD PAT ME ALONG SIDE THE HEAD AND SAY.. "ZIGGY MY BOY, ALWAYS REMEMBER
"...A SMILE IS A FROWN IF YOU STAND UPSIDE DOWN!"
...MUM DRANK A BIT!

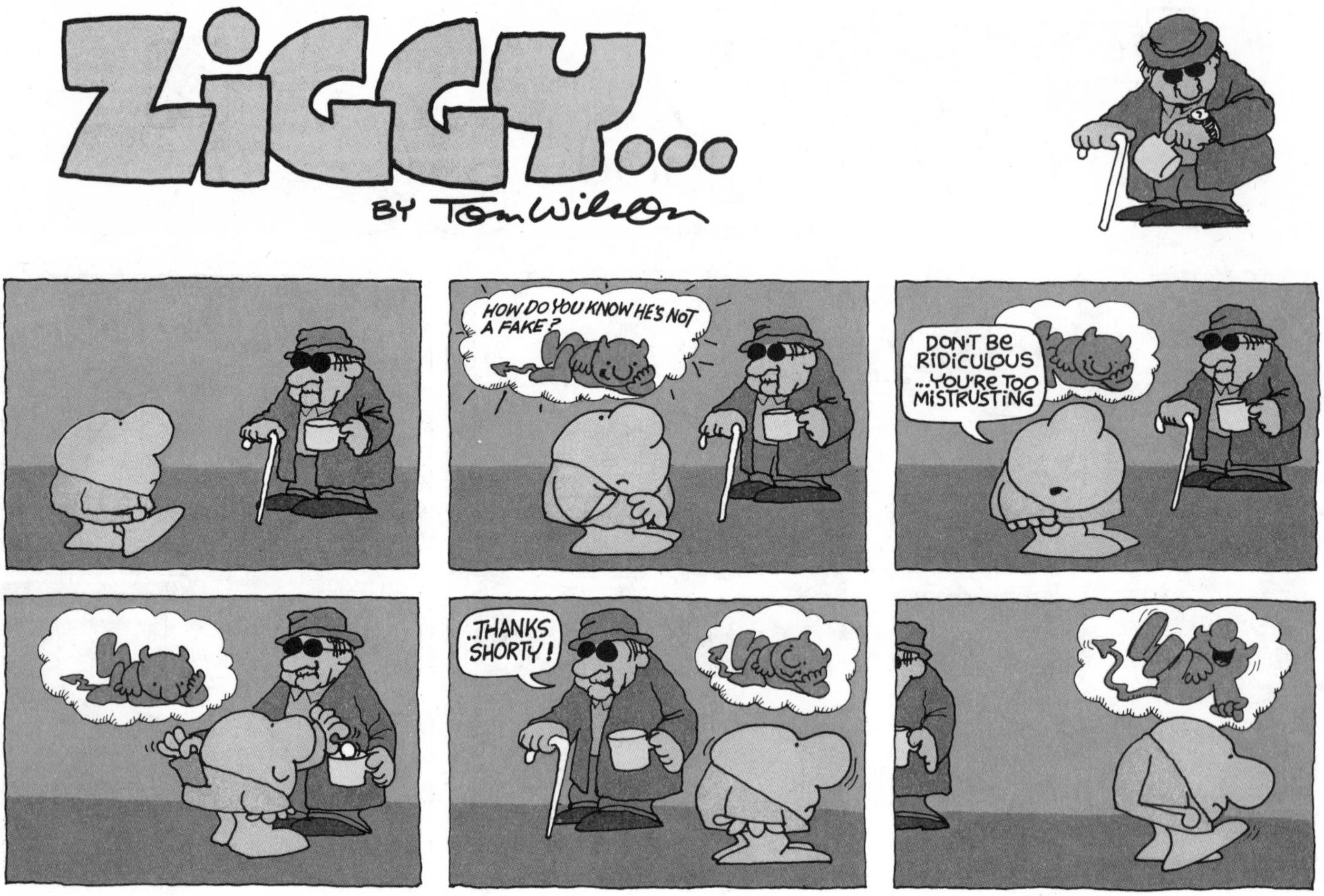
ZIGGY...
BY Tom Wilson
HOW DO YOU KNOW HE'S NOT A FAKE?
DON'T BE RIDICULOUS ...YOU'RE TOO MISTRUSTING
..THANKS SHORTY!

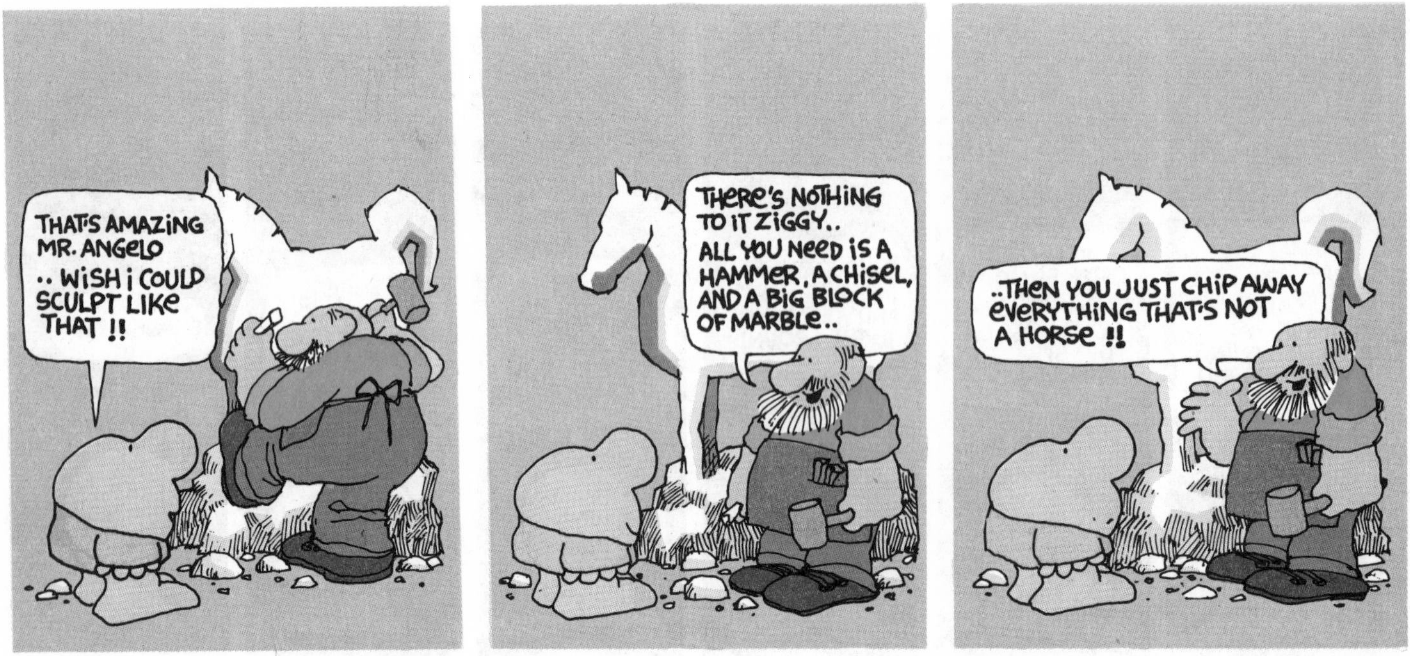
THAT'S AMAZING MR. ANGELO .. WISH I COULD SCULPT LIKE THAT !!
THERE'S NOTHING TO IT ZIGGY.. ALL YOU NEED IS A HAMMER, A CHISEL, AND A BIG BLOCK OF MARBLE..
..THEN YOU JUST CHIP AWAY EVERYTHING THAT'S NOT A HORSE !!

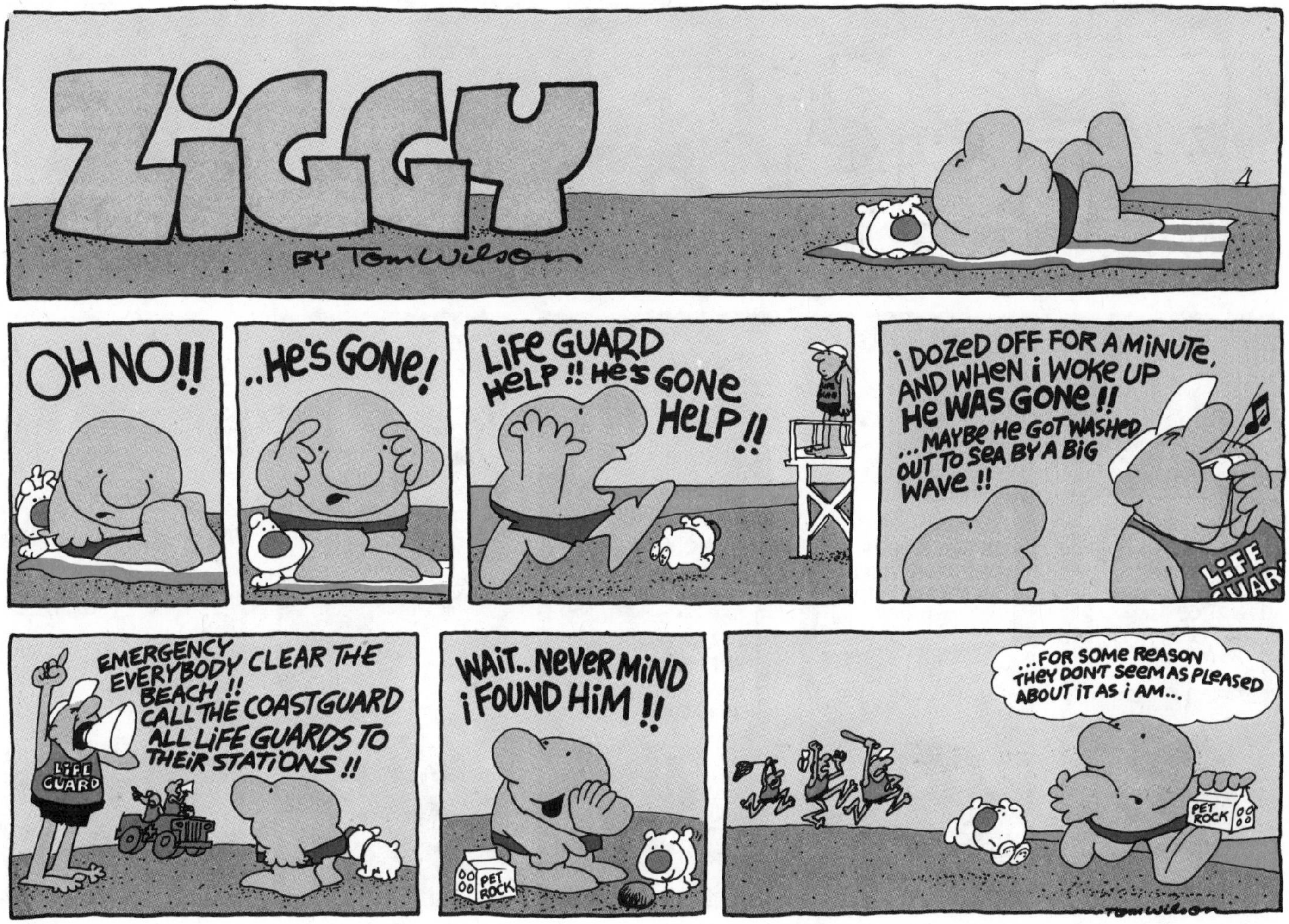
ZIGGY
BY Tom Wilson
OH NO!!
..He's GONE!
LIFE GUARD HELP!! He's GONE HELP!!
i DOZED OFF FOR A MINUTE, AND WHEN i WOKE UP He WAS GONE!! ...MAYBE He GOT WASHED OUT TO SEA BY A BIG WAVE!!
LIFE GUARD
EMERGENCY EVERYBODY CLEAR THE BEACH!! CALL THE COASTGUARD ALL LIFE GUARDS TO THEIR STATIONS!!
LIFE GUARD
WAIT.. NEVER MIND i FOUND HIM!!
PET ROCK
...FOR SOME REASON THEY DON'T SEEM AS PLEASED ABOUT IT AS i AM...
PET ROCK
Tom Wilson

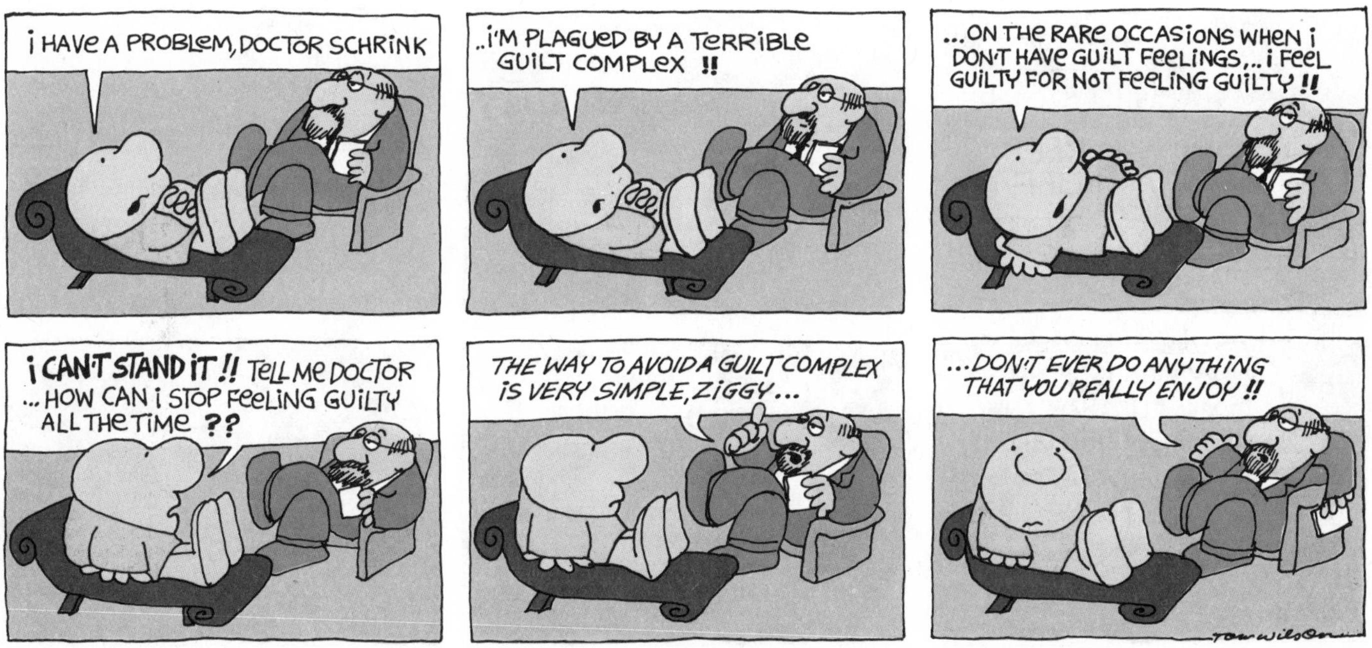
i HAVE A PROBLEM, DOCTOR SCHRINK
..i'M PLAGUED BY A TERRIBLE GUILT COMPLEX!!
...ON THE RARE OCCASIONS WHEN i DON'T HAVE GUILT FEELINGS,...i FEEL GUILTY FOR NOT FEELING GUILTY!!
i CAN'T STAND IT!! TELL ME DOCTOR ...HOW CAN i STOP FEELING GUILTY ALL THE TIME??
THE WAY TO AVOID A GUILT COMPLEX IS VERY SIMPLE, ZIGGY...
...DON'T EVER DO ANYTHING THAT YOU REALLY ENJOY!!
Tom Wilson

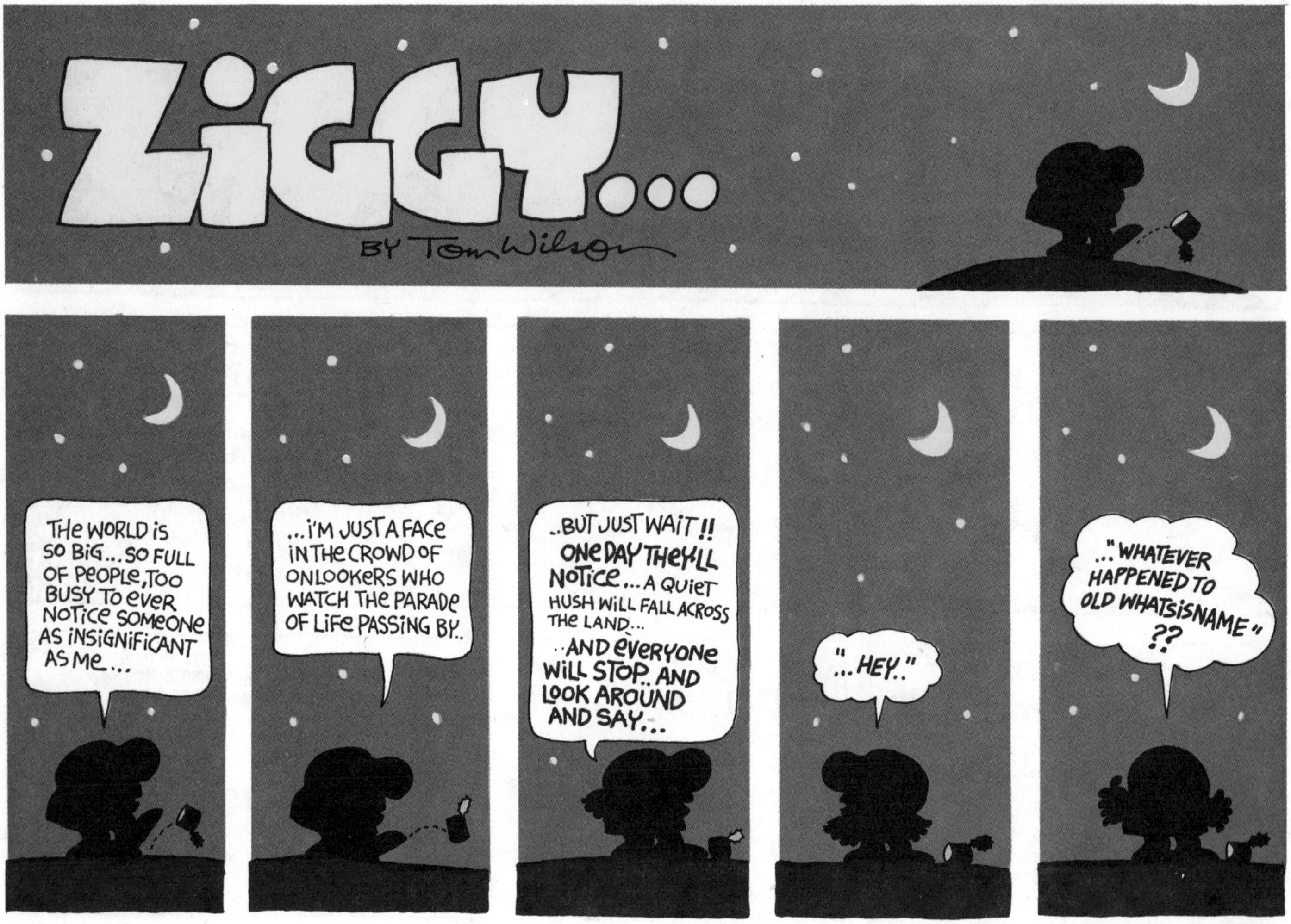
ZIGGY...
BY Tom Wilson
THE WORLD IS SO BIG... SO FULL OF PEOPLE, TOO BUSY TO EVER NOTICE SOMEONE AS INSIGNIFICANT AS ME...
...I'M JUST A FACE IN THE CROWD OF ONLOOKERS WHO WATCH THE PARADE OF LIFE PASSING BY..
..BUT JUST WAIT!! ONE DAY THEY'LL NOTICE... A QUIET HUSH WILL FALL ACROSS THE LAND... ..AND EVERYONE WILL STOP.. AND LOOK AROUND AND SAY...
"...HEY.."
..."WHATEVER HAPPENED TO OLD WHATSISNAME"??

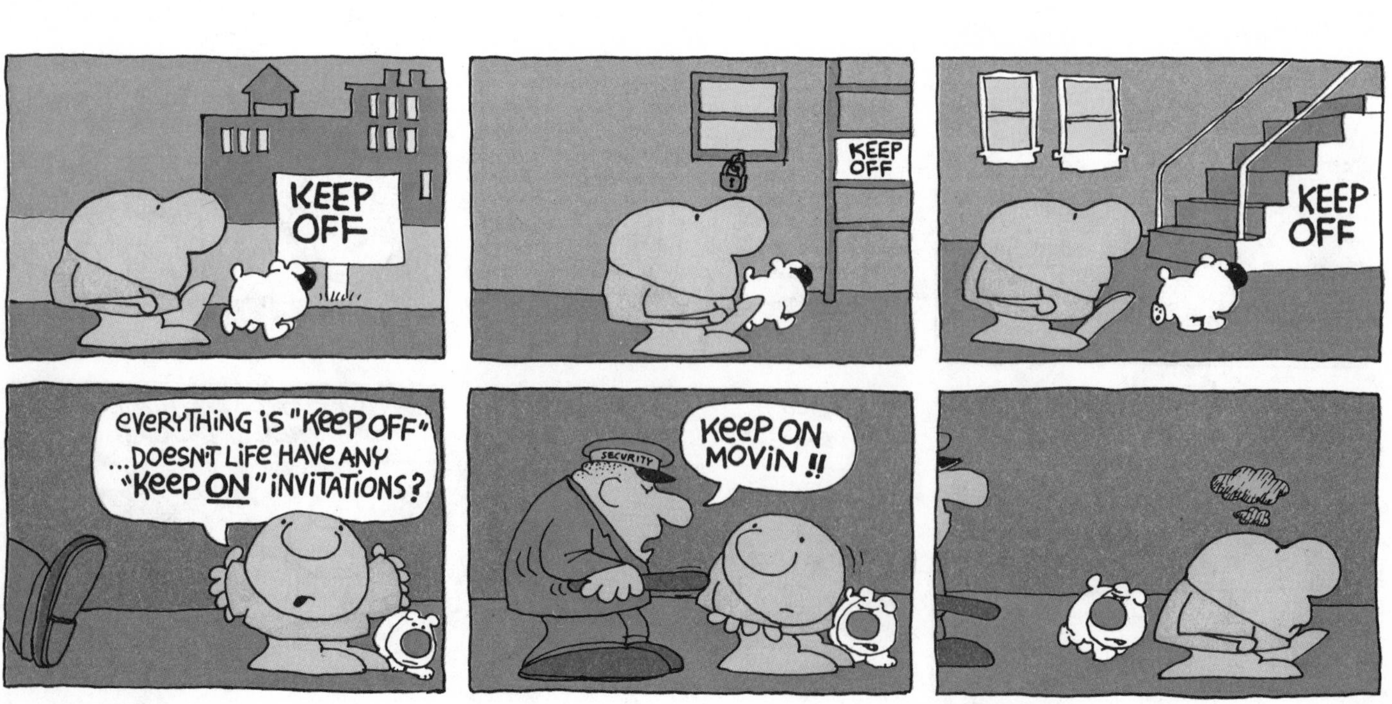
KEEP OFF
KEEP OFF
KEEP OFF
EVERYTHING IS "KEEP OFF" ...DOESN'T LIFE HAVE ANY "KEEP ON" INVITATIONS?
SECURITY
KEEP ON MOVIN!!